DICKINSON COLLEGE

John Dickinson, Copy, by Horace T. Carpenter, of life portrait by Charles Willson Peale, 1770.

DICKINSON COLLEGE

A HISTORY

BY

Charles Coleman Sellers

MIDDLETOWN *Wesleyan University Press* CONNECTICUT

Library of Congress Cataloging in Publication Data

Sellers, Charles Coleman, 1903–
  Dickinson College; a history

  Includes bibliographical references.
  1. Dickinson College, Carlisle, Pa. — History.
LD1663.S4   378.748'73   72-5117
ISBN 0-8195-4057-9

Published in cooperation with Dickinson College

378.748
Se4d
89237
June 1974

Manufactured in the United States of America

First edition

To

BARBARA SELLERS

Amor coronat opus

CONTENTS

ILLUSTRATIONS

Unless otherwise specified, all illustrations are reproduced by courtesy of Dickinson College.

FOREWORD

THE Bicentennial History project, authorized by the Board of Trustees on January 28, 1967, has had a dual purpose: first, the book in your hands; and second, a systematic further development of the College Archives, so that all aspects of Dickinson College history may be available to scholars in a range beyond the scope of any single volume. Since the History staff has had oversight of all the manuscript collections, the source materials in general history have been involved as well, with the preparation of a printed *Guide* to the whole.

The staff has been smaller than was at first anticipated. Mrs. Martha C. Slotten has been with the operation from the first, with a coordinating hand on its routine work and its many special services. Mrs. Myrna M. Allshouse initiated the work on the History's statistical appendices and pursued various lines of research before departing in 1970 to assume the more glamorous duties of a college president's wife. Mrs. Madeleine H. Warlow carried on for her. Completion on schedule was aided by the Library staff as a whole, particularly Mrs. Dorothy J. Bowers, presiding over Reference and Interlibrary Loan. All owe a debt of gratitude to Mrs. Laura de la Torre Bueno for her final editing of the manuscript, winnowing out small errors and suggesting changes which have added clarity and grace.

The President of the Board of Trustees and the President of the College not only watched all this activity with a heartening confidence in its ultimate fruition, but made their files fully

available, adding much that was no longer of immediate con-
temporary interest to the Morris Room collections. George
Shuman, Jr., whose administrative records go back to President
Corson's day and beyond, has been always kind and thoughtful.
Older faculty members such as Herbert Wing, Jr., and J. Clair
McCullough, those to whose lives and labors this history is in
part a monument, have been at pains to supply us with data.
Department heads and many other faculty and administration
colleagues have volunteered generously and responded to every
call for help.

Equally so the alumni, and none more earnestly and effectively than the late Boyd Lee Spahr, '00, the papers of whose
long trusteeship were added at last to the thousands of others of
broad or specialized historical importance which he had
donated through the years, and who read and criticized the
earlier chapters of this work as they were written. No less warmly devoted to Dickinson's past and future, a triumvirate of
alumni has been a constant presence with counsel, encouragement and material aid: Roscoe O. Bonisteel, '12; Whitfield J.
Bell, Jr., '35; and Walter E. Beach, '56.

Fellow librarians and archivists have all responded sympa-
thetically to our endeavor, and to those who have wrestled with
our problems we owe particular thanks: Miss Dorothy J. Walsh
of Allegheny College; Edwin Schell of the Baltimore Conference
Methodist Historical Society; W. B. McDaniel, 2nd, of the Col-
lege of Physicians of Philadelphia; G. William Stuart, Jr., of
Cornell University; D. Wilson Thompson and Mrs. John F.
Brougher of the Cumberland County Historical Society; Ken-
neth E. Rowe of Drew University; David E. Estes of Emory
University; Howard R. Emler of Girard College; Dr. Sarah Dow-
lin Jones of Goucher College; Nicholas B. Wainwright and Peter
J. Parker of the Historical Society of Pennsylvania; Miss Eugenia
Calvert Holland of the Maryland Historical Society; William A.
Hunter of the Pennsylvania Historical and Museum Commission;
Frederick E. Maser of the Philadelphia Conference Methodist
Historical Society; William B. Miller and Gerald W. Gillette of
the Presbyterian Historical Society; John H. Ness, Jr., of the
Commission on Archives and History, United Methodist
Church; Mrs. Harold Hayes of the University of Maryland; and
John W. Spaeth, Jr., of Wesleyan University.

To the following individuals we owe a multifarious debt of gratitude for their interest and always generous support: Mrs. Francis J. Ahern; George Allen; Mrs. William H. Allen; Milton B. Asbell; James L. Axtell; John F. Bacon; Charles Gilbert Beetem; Tom H. Bietsch; James Kelvey Bindley; William S. Bowers; Kenneth R. Bowling; Arthur H. Brown; Miss Dorothy Bryan; Lyman H. Butterfield; William J. Byers; Mrs. Dean C. Chamberlain; George Clark; Mrs. G. Dawson Coleman; Robert Grant Crist; Marwood Darlington; Richard Beale Davis; Hon. Edward S. Delaplaine; Donald J. D'Elia; Mrs. Roy A. DeLong; Mr. and Mrs. James O'Hara Denny, 3rd; Francis P. Derick; L. C. Dieter; Trudeau Early; Mrs. Ruth E. Engelken; Allen B. L. Fisher; Perry S. Flegal; Mrs. C. Guiles Flower; Milton E. Flower; Mrs. Kenneth S. Gapp; Clarke W. Garrett; Wilbur J. Gobrecht; Ronald Goldberg; Miss Lydia M. Gooding; Mrs. Charles Goodyear; John Harley; Miss Helen Harris; Mrs. Helen Scott Harris; Mrs. Katherine Conway Haymes; Elmer C. Herber; Spencer R. Hurst; A. Witt Hutchison; Mrs. Paul L. Hutchison; Charles W. Karnes; Miss Alta M. Kimmel; Rudolf and Clara Marburg Kirk; Miss Amy R. Knox; Burton R. Laub; Henry Logan; Mrs. Jean Longacre; E. Miles Ludwig; Miss Marjorie McIntire; Mrs. Andrew Duncan McIntosh; Mrs. Kathleen Briner Meals; Mrs. Marion D. Neece; Frederic W. Ness; Mr. and Mrs. Meyer P. Potamkin; Mrs. Lydia Bond Powel; J. Stuart Prentice; Lambert Prettyman; George E. Reed; Henry A. Riddle; Miss Eleanor Conway Sawyer; Joseph H. Schiffman; Robert D. Schwarz; Mrs. Rippey Shearer; Mrs. Howard Shepler; Miss Rebecca Hart Shriver; Mrs. Ernest Sipple; Mrs. Harry S. Sisk; A. Russell Slagle; Douglas Sloan; Albert V. and Gurney Poulson Sloan; Mrs. J. Ohrum Small; Miss Jane V. N. Smead; Alan C. Smith; Mrs. Margaret Kellogg Smith; James H. Smylie; Mrs. Fred W. Sonn; Boyd Lee Spahr, Jr.; Roger F. Stanton; Laurence C. Staples; Mrs. John Clothier Stokes; C. R. Walter Thomas; Roger K. Todd; Mrs. Elmer Trego; Mrs. Alice P. Trippe; Mrs. Robert P. Turner; Mrs. Ann Regan Weinert; R. Wallace White; and Bell Irvin Wiley.

DICKINSON COLLEGE

There is a river, the streams whereof make glad the city of God.

Psalm 46, 4

I

PLOT AND CAST

IT moves past us like a ritual procession of priests and dancers. Education is the life of a civilization, always religious at heart, linking present truth to far or farthest ideals, its traditions cherished and guarded, innovations held back by elemental fears. Here in Carlisle there is no sharp beginning to the tale. It had come upon that steady current of learning and love of learning, powerful, intolerant, eager, disputatious, subtly and sapiently devout, swept by contradictions and mystical longing, flowing out from Scotland to Ireland and America. Here was Christian doctrine speaking in the language and sophistry of the ancient pagan world, as it had done in the universities of Paris and Bologna centuries before. It belonged with the Continent, this Scottish erudition, far more than with Britain's Oxford and Cambridge which, in those early years, it greatly surpassed in efficiency and vigor. [1]

Even before county and town, Cumberland and Carlisle, had been set apart in 1751, classical learning was there with the Presbyterian congregations. Its story in this frontier village was much the same as elsewhere, then and later—first, a learned pastor taking pupils, then a grammar school regularly organized under pastoral auspices and applying, in time, for the presbytery's supervision and support and the blessing of the annual synod. Here boys from ten into their teens would learn the Latin and Greek languages, the basis of all formal education. They might study also other branches of learning, mathematics, geography, surveying or navigation, and perhaps have some instruction in logic, criticism, philosophy and, surely, "moral philosophy," the application of sound doctrine to right living. Philosophy was on the level of higher education, and the boy who had taken it might enter college with advanced standing, perhaps win his degree in a year. A school with such a curriculum was only a step away from degree-granting status. The grammar school, in what became an almost universal American pattern, would remain as an adjunct of the college. It made possible the acceptance of boys who might wander in, as they did, from distant parts and at any time of the year. If badly prepared in the languages they need only be assigned to the school until ready. The American college term ranged from two to four years—three on an average—but with their preliminary school work most boys would be on campus for a longer period.

The school at Carlisle, at the time of its first acquisition of land, March 3, 1773, had been open and organized, complete with master, board of trustees and board of visitors, certainly since 1769—and for ten years before that had been in existence as the usual educational function of every established Presbyterian congregation. When Dickinson College received its charter, September 9, 1783, that combined operation of school and college came into being—to continue, with ups and downs, until 1917. The new College took over school and schoolhouse and absorbed the school's trustees into its own enlarged board. This was a forward step combining a glow of religious fervor with all the stars and light of patriotism. It had the force of a prophetic personal expression in the voice of Benjamin Rush, physician, teacher, politician. The long war was ending then and Americans, free and victorious, were turning with a surge of triumph to the future. Dr. Rush had signed the Declaration, marched with the army, and now stood determined that the Revolution must go on toward a greater, a wholly American, consummation. [2] His new college, far to the west "over Susquehanna," would be a first foundation stone, and he gathered about him like-minded trustees, men of God, soldiers, men of business and the law, to carry forward the plan.

Regard now the trustee, promoter and patron of education.

In Europe, schools consisted of teachers and students. Educated gentlemen might hold positions of concern, might be invited to appear at examinations (always oral) to make sure that the sophistication of the coming generation equalled their own. But in crossing the wide Atlantic the campus had acquired this third element, more prestigious and powerful than the other two. Here the trustee was far more than a prototype for the young. These gentlemen raised the funds and managed them. They not only had oversight of the educational program, but planned and managed it, curriculum included, hiring and dismissing teachers, regulating student behavior to the last detail if they so chose. Much has been written of "trustee interference" in American colleges of the eighteenth and early nineteenth centuries, with Dickinson, Princeton and the University of Pennsylvania cited as outstanding examples of the evil. [3] Distrust of the teacher was implicit in their role. Distrust of the student was expressed in restrictive regulations covering every moment of his time. These trustees held an authority conferred upon them by law, and acted with a sense of duty akin to religious faith. The charge of "interference" would have surprised them very much.

The charter of Dickinson College admitted no member of the faculty to the deliberations of the Board. Gradually, however, in the first half century of its history we see the Board seeking faculty advice (though never accepting it without amendment), sparingly beginning to delegate some few powers, and then even calling in the faculty for consultation. Meetings were small in these early years—often with only nine members, a bare quorum. Clergymen formed the most learned part. The others who came to meetings were town and county aristocracy with a provincial elegance and sophistication akin to the neighboring culture of the South. These families were patrons of the theater and encouraged the boys to perform, though faculty and clerical trustees frowned upon it. Play-acting and much else in the open field of life and learning would be stifled by that wave of fundamentalist revivalism which swept America, at its height from 1790 to 1830, a reaction against the eighteenth-century Enlightenment which profoundly affected the colleges.

Religious influences, active in one way or another in them all, have given Dickinson elements of dichotomy and disturbance from the first. Dr. Rush, taking over a Presbyterian school, counted his College as a Presbyterian institution. He needed an established organization from which to draw students, political support, money. Yet he saw public financing as essential and soon learned that the College must be non-denominational to get that. Dickinson's equivocation of being "non-sectarian" under sectarian "auspices" has a long history. More—Presbyterianism had been split by George Whitefield's revivals of the 1740's into "Old Side" and "New Side," a rancorous division present at Carlisle throughout.

That division was a major factor in the transfer of the College to Methodist control in 1833. The old Board resigned, a new Board took over. No nonsense of it-is-and-it-isn't now—this was to be a Methodist college. And yet—though upon a quite different register of heat and light—the Methodists were also of two minds. The new Board and the faculty it appointed belonged to a new and young minority with intellectual ideals. The Church as a whole, massive in size and growing ever larger on a wide wave of emotion, distrusted intellectual "coldness," held classical learning in very low regard and would have no truck whatever with any notion of an educational standard for its ministry. Here, obviously, is the reason why the new trustees of Dickinson kept the independence which the charter gave them, making one change only, that the President of the College should also be President of the Board.

That arrangement lasted until 1912, when an amendment put through by the Board's youngest and most progressive member, Boyd Lee Spahr, restored the office John Dickinson had held. By then the alert and partisan intellectualism of the first Methodist faculty was a thing of the past. The Methodist conferences were deploring their slender hold upon the College under its charter. Alumni were deploring the College's failure to keep pace with its contemporaries. Boyd Lee Spahr envisioned a Dickinson rivalling the best small colleges of the East, and there can be no doubt that he regarded his action as a first step in an escape from a built-in parochialism. In 1931 he himself was elected President of the Board, where he would continue, annually reelected, for thirty-one years.

It has a unique quality of drama, this career. An intense affection and pride runs through it all—intelligent, humorous, carried along by a fullness of knowledge of the campus, its history, almost every aspect of its life. By his knowledge and his large giving he dominated the Board, working with representative committees but controlling almost every decision. He was the first to bring to his colleagues' startled attention the new concept of trusteeship as imposing a duty of personal generosity. Too long had they thought of themselves only as guardians of the temple. Some continued to do so, but the coming of Spahr to the presidency brought fresh vigor to Board and campus. He pressed for advances, yet with caution and compromise. He was a conservative of the protective, constructive sort. Inevitably, in time, he became more remote from educators and educational trends at Dickinson or elsewhere, more defensive, more legalistic in control. Voices were raised in protest, just as his own had been against ministerial dominance. When the ultimate crisis came his leadership was unimpeachable under the charter of 1783 but clashed sharply with widely approved practices of 1956. A new President—as usual, a Spahr choice—inherited the conflict of Dickinson College administration against American Association of University Professors, and was enabled by it, at long last, to accomplish that liberation which Spahr himself had set out, so long before, to achieve.

Benjamin Rush had publicly excoriated the reverend Provost of the University of Pennsylvania as a drunkard and sower of vice. The Doctor judged with severity those who did not accept his own opinions. The Presidents of Dickinson must be—and were—subject to control. Exclusion from trustee meetings tied their hands effectively. In the little American colleges of that day the president was only the most eminent of a small group of teachers, presiding at commencement, doing all the routine administrative work, meeting the Seniors in their classes in Moral Philosophy. Without a voice in policy, and subject to abrupt orders from on high, the position had little to commend it.

All this changed dramatically under the Methodist regime. The President of the College as President of the Board could dominate its affairs. Some did so. Yet only too soon church politics entered in. Methodism was compounded of strong emotion on the one hand, tight organization on the other. The College became involved in the system. Pressures to seal it in were sustained through the years by emotion. Charles Francis Himes, devoted alumnus of 1855, brilliant and beloved professor, could win only belated, half-hearted support in planning a modern curriculum, and his brief career as Acting President was quickly terminated in favor of a clergyman. He resigned from the faculty seven years later, frustrated and embittered. Boyd Lee Spahr may well have had Himes, a fraternity brother, in mind in his search for an escape from this baleful influence. Certainly—though not always with success—he sought presidents who would be acceptable to the church group and yet above church politics. He and his fellow trustees faced these and other problems with scarcely a thought of faculty acceptance, and never dreaming that faculty might ultimately play a decisive role.

Trustees sit enthroned. They wear the crown of altruism. They are sceptred and successful men. Teachers have been altruistic largely in their willingness to work for little pay and that, as the world sees it, is not a sign of success. "Those who can, do. Those who can't, teach." Theirs is a profession still often invaded as well as dominated by outsiders, yet out of the trustee-faculty relationship, out of great purposes shared together in a sort of connubial unease, has come the teaching profession as it stands today in our country. The theologue turned pedagogue is a familiar spectacle in history, feckless at times, at times superlative. At his worst in those early years he had a fear and distrust of learning. "The very cultivation of the mind has frequently a tendency to impair the moral sensibilities, to induce that pride of conscious ability and variety of attainments which . . . are . . . affectations offensive to God." Or, more succinctly, "Without religion a college is a curse to society." [4] Devout laity readily accepted the view which Noah Webster put before them at the laying of the first cornerstone at Amherst, that the primary aim and hope of education is "to reclaim and evangelize the miserable children of Adam." [5] It all sustained the ritualistic character of the curriculum of those years. From desk, as from pulpit, reverent acceptance must come. Learning must substan-

tiate faith and loyalty. The textbook appears, a gospel, reflecting like the moon a pale light of divine authority.

Yet the Protestant ministry is inherently a teaching profession, concerned with learning and with human values. As the
teacher developed a professional status of his own these concerns remained, and educational theory and practice took shape
with the profession. It begins with that appalling emphasis on
discipline, accompanied by the elimination of every corrupting
amusement. Discipline was the key to everything, and "mental
discipline" its inner core. "Mental discipline" developed and
exercised what were thought to be the twelve separately constituted "faculties of the mind." [6] Success, then as now, depended
more on the character of the individual teacher than on the
theory, his wisdom and independence more strongly reflected
than the abstract principle. Theory will change while practice
stands. The educator of today may talk of the primacy of
"learning to learn" in a world of rapidly advancing knowledge,
and decry packing the mind with facts of transient importance.
Yet we find virtually the same idea put forward again and again
a century and more ago, as, for instance, by such an experienced and sensitive professional as Dickinson's Alexander Mc-
Clelland, Professor of Rhetoric, Metaphysics and Ethics, 1822
to 1829:

> He aimed to impart to his students his own enthusiasm. He gave
> young men the secrets of mental discipline, imparted to them a mas-
> tery over their own minds; and instead of storing them with their own
> acquisitions, sought rather to train them to habits of patient and
> persevering investigation for themselves; and thus put them in the way
> of making continued acquisitions while life should last. [7]

McClelland was at Dickinson at the time of the famous
"Yale Report," President Jeremiah Day's declaration in defense
of the established pattern of classical study and moral orthodoxy, Christ and the pagan authors in a traditional, and interesting, conjunction. Dickinson's President Mason had already affirmed it: "Experience has shown that with the study or neglect
of the Greek and Latin languages, sound learning flourishes or
declines. It is now too late for ignorance, indolence, eccentricity
or infidelity to dispute what has been ratified by the seal of

ages."[8] The Yale Report would set a standard of inert respectability for American colleges everywhere.

Yet this was also the Jacksonian era of rough, practical democracy. Publicly-supported education on the lower levels would come in the 1830's, with Pennsylvania a leader and the little community of Carlisle in a front position too. John Price Durbin's young Methodist faculty was opening professional careers to the boys of what had been a working-class denomination. These young men took moral philosophy away from the Scottish philosophers to Paley and Butler, but that core purpose of the Scottish tradition, to give the student specific knowledge and the ability to apply it, was kept intact. They also were influenced by Yale, but were too intelligent to accept any pattern out of hand. They were looking for what the eighteenth-century Philadelphia educators had sought, what Thomas Jefferson had called a "useful American education"—classics, to be sure, but also modern languages, mathematics, history, ethics, natural history and a "natural philosophy" which would include chemistry and agriculture.[9] Dickinson had a standard of science teaching set by Thomas Cooper in 1811. This new faculty had Spencer Fullerton Baird, with his immense knowledge and verve, his innovation of field trips as a part of his course, and it had Charles Francis Himes.

Himes had a background of study in Germany. Dickinson faculty and students had long been aware of the lure of the German universities, the new emphasis on research, the new ideal of pure scholarship. Dickinson had been one of the first to introduce elective studies, breaking away from the concept of a fixed, perfected, immutable "course of study" for all comers. Dickinson's trustees, of course, were less open to suggestion, and some professors went about their affairs with an answering quietude. There were those to whom the occasional religious revival gave an ample, if illusory, sense of progress. With the last years of the nineteenth century we can begin to measure faculty competence in advanced degrees, though this, too, can be illusory. So many of the best of the old-timers had their bachelor's only, and President Charles Nisbet, for all his years at the University of Edinburgh, had not even bothered to take that. The Ph.D. first appears as an honorary with Himes and Morgan, and then, with the rise of the American universities, becomes the mark of the professional—though there were still mavericks like Mulford Stough to bring in the freshness and independence of the amateur.

Throughout this long chronicle, too, one can measure competence in terms of faculty-student rapport. All Dickinson history is sprinkled with bizarre disciplinary cases, but in the years of an intellectually alert faculty the relationship is, on the whole, warm and close. In an era of intellectual stagnation faculty and students are at odds, even virtually at war. But the students were more than a reflection. This necessary but rarely respected element of the College community had been a power from the first, and aware of it.

Students of the eighteenth century, quite as well as those of the twentieth, knew when their tuition fees made the difference between solvency and disaster. They had brought the haughty Board of Trustees to heel in the spring of 1794, and again in the strike of November 7, 1798. In this history we see student pressures in two aspects. In one mood, the mood of that strike, they are out to make the road to the degree as short and easy as possible. In the other, an opposite and reasonable view, they demand an education tailored to the careers they have in prospect. But to the historian, any strong pressures from this third estate may always be taken as a sign of weakness in the other two—lacklustre classes, dead-pan social regulations, an unstable treasury.

Charles Nisbet, heading the first Dickinson College faculty, found American students very different from those he had known in Scotland. There he had seen them crowding the universities to earn by hard work and privation a place in the professional class. These young Americans from indulgent families were sure of their future livelihoods and unenthusiastic about drudgery for a degree which was by no means necessary to success. In their growing nation class distinctions meant little to anyone. They had small reverence for constituted authority, in College or elsewhere—and must have been drawn to Nisbet on that score as well as by his learning and wit. "The public men here," the Doctor would observe, "are a set of mean rogues generally." [10] To his trustees Nisbet was a perennial calamity, but, measured by the success of his students in afterlife, his performance as a teacher was superb, his presence at the College its one sure title to fame.

On the whole, however, though these students were teenagers at the unruly stage of adolescence, they reflected the safe opinions of their parents and teachers. They were addressed by their professors as "Gentlemen," or "Mr. So-and-so," and yet, after the establishment of dormitory life about 1810, faced a harsher "parental" rule than most of them had ever known before. The activities of every hour were scheduled. American college regulations might have been made for prisoners, or soldiers in barracks. Dr. Benjamin Rush, a warm humanitarian on every count and firmly opposed to the dormitory system, even considered a sort of uniform, varying with each class, not to encourage an esprit de corps, but so that delinquents might be easily recognized.

Many of the boys coming to Carlisle were from the South, a large enough proportion to influence all the others. They were impatient of restraint, with pervading romantic dreams and a sharply defined sense of honor. Moving from preparatory school to college, the boys had outgrown physical restraints, and the trustees had ready for their government a system of trials imposing fines and other forms of retribution, with the faculty expected to act as detective, constabulary and prosecutor, but themselves remaining as an ultimate, often merciful, court of appeal. The faculty on their part knew the greater effectiveness of gentle rebuke and appeal to reason, and eventually succeeded in having these written into the laws as a first recourse. Nisbet, a notoriously mild disciplinarian, had also applied with marked effect that stinging sarcastic wit which trustees themselves had learned to fear.

The most significant feature of student life in Nisbet's day and for more than a century after was the literary society. Belles Lettres was founded in 1786, and Union Philosophical three years later. They had American antecedents, Princeton's Cliosophic and Whig of 1769 and 1770, William and Mary's Phi Beta Kappa of 1776 and others. Like the University of Edinburgh's Speculative Society, founded in 1764, they were an excellent training ground for lawyers and other public men. Other new colleges adopted the idea, and these student groups became the most vital and stimulating thing in the American educational process, evoking more loyalty, effort and enthusiasm than anything else. Here was a link to the world around the students not to be found in their studies. In the society halls the members were their own masters, imposed their own rules and penalties, debated the issues of the day from the broadest down even to so touchy a commonplace as the competence of one of their teachers. Here, within the walls, was a measure of effective student government which might well have been encouraged and extended.

Here, too, was a link to the public eagerly sought and much enjoyed. Their "exhibitions" drew appreciative crowds of old and young. It was all part of that emphasis upon oratory which pervaded every level of American education from Colonial times on through the early years of the republic. The culture of the whole age was vocal, its authors writing to be read aloud, its poets to be declaimed. A sermon, a political debate, a lecture, would always draw an audience of connoisseurs in the niceties of platform eloquence. Even examinations, always oral, fitted the pattern, and the final proof of the earned degree was each student's commencement oration.

The eventual decline of the literary societies is one of the sad notes in this lively chronicle. Trustees and faculty, watchful and suspicious, increasingly asserted their authority over them, as over every other aspect of student life. Any assertion of power invites the rise of countervailing forces. Since about the time of the Yale Report, a new student movement had been rooted and spreading—the social fraternities. They reached Carlisle in their insidious growth just at mid-century, greeted here as elsewhere by official alarm and condemnation. Unlike the clubs of the eighteenth century or the literary societies of the nineteenth, they had no intellectual purpose. With their vows of secrecy and arcane rituals, they defied for many years the efforts of faculty to give them one. Their Greek-letter symbols mocked the classicism imposed by academic authority. These were now the Greeks among the barbarians, the charmed and mystic inner circles of brotherhood.

The fraternities brought a happy solidarity to student life. War with the faculty from these unassailable bastions became a joyous thing, and in Dickinson's archives the student damage accounts alone give impressive evidence of its lively character. Dickinson's official ban on fraternities has never been repealed. Tacit and then open recognition came as fraternity men moved into the alumni and then the faculty. By the turn of the century they were an established, and then a necessary, element in institutional functioning—and made subject as the old societies had been to faculty regulation.

The fraternities had changed the whole tempo of college life. Students were coming to Carlisle as elsewhere with the good times in view, the games, pranks, music, fights and fanfare. Formerly the liberal arts colleges had languished in comparison to the professional schools, whose student rosters were regularly filled. Now these pleasures had added a new value to the college degree—the fraternity pin, the close continuance of college friendships. Faculty might feel qualms as they watched the burgeoning extracurriculum, but college administrators soon sensed what it could do for the school. They became tolerant of the pranks, the damage, and they rejoiced in the hilarity of returning, and contributing, alumni.

The American college of the first half of the twentieth century, with its euphoria of brotherhood, love, gaiety, athletic prowess, class rivalries, violent repression of the neophyte, is a far cry from the ideal of those who had founded and tried to shape the system. All this had come from the students themselves, and much of the substantial development of the curriculum as well. The scholarly student, with a blatant anti-intellectualism all around him, had exerted effective pressures of his own. Intrinsic change, the decline of the fraternities, the fusion of the whole into a coherent community with a new unity of ideals—these have come from student initiatives after years of educators' futile effort.

The new academic scene, welcomed by professors, accepted by alumni and trustees, remains one part of all that had gone before. Here is only a widening and deepening of currents as ancient as the rivers, flowing through all history, joining earth and Eden in unfolding truth. The voices of the past are in its air. Strongholds of quiet exploration, of impartial searching and informed controversy cannot be built in a day. Our founders are with us still. Dr. Rush had set up, in a lonely village by a ruined fort, a new bastion where learning was to stand inviolate. *"Tuta libertas,"* John Dickinson had called it then—"a bulwark of liberty." [11] Yet the Doctor, with his strange compound of augury, anger and tough observation, would have been looking forward to more than a fortress—to aggressive thought and action, to a community of scholars where learning is both imparted and created, a living progression, free and imperishable.

Cupola of West College.

The faithfull minister must fight Christ's batles wt Courage & intrepidity & not as one unconcerned about what he stands by, but must boldly contend for the honour of his Lord & Earnestly strive for the faith of the Gospel.

John Steel, sermon, August 21, 1753

2

CURTAIN RAISER

WITH all else in order, there was still the question about a girl in Londonderry. It would seem that the candidate had already answered this to his own satisfaction by marrying another, not long after his arrival in America. Synod, however, before admitting any man to the sacred calling, must have full assurance upon every point of worthiness. In knowledge of Scripture, in doctrine, in adherence to the Westminster Confession of Faith, John Steel had shown himself beyond challenge or demur. He could preach cogently from a given text. He could write and speak Latin and had an adequate command of Greek. It was agreed that the Presbytery of New Castle might accept him as a licentiate upon trial, while a letter went out, and an answer was awaited, to clear up that rumor of a previous promise of marriage. This was at Philadelphia, at the annual meeting of Synod, May, 1742. The reply, when it came, must have shown that, if promise there had been, the lady was now ready to renounce it, a reasonable view. Synod, on May 24, 1744, received from the New Castle brethren their report of Mr. Steel's ordination.[1]

So began a ministry of preaching and teaching which, as if drawn by some inner force toward the storm centers of danger and disputation, would end in the remote frontier village of Carlisle thirty-five years later. Even before his ordination, John Steel had supplied churches out along the western fringe of settlements. For the Presbytery of Donegal he had gone to Rockfish and Roanoke in the spring of 1743, and in the fall was at Great Conewago, near what is now Hunterstown, not far from Gettysburg.[2]

From these events and those which followed one can draw a picture of the man—aged about twenty-eight, bearing himself with the firmness and assurance of one of God's elect, speaking plainly and with decision, a man made for leadership. Friends could rely upon him, and he would not relent toward an enemy. He would face danger readily, and hold all the loyalty and admiration that comes to the resolute and brave man. He would acquire, in time, a good measure of worldly wealth, another sign of predestined favor from above.

The minutes of the Presbytery of Donegal, September 7, 1743, record Great Conewago's call to "Mr. Steel, Probationer of the Presbytery of New Castle," and with this there is a notation on a unanimous agreement regarding a school, the papers on which (alas) had been mislaid.[3] Among ministers such as these, whose sermons were, in effect, lectures on theology rather than mere appeals to faith and kindiness, education was a primary concern. Teacher's desk and pulpit stood together, schoolroom form and pew. Great Conewago must have promised a congenial field for him, but it was a teacher's desk that would keep John Steel in New Castle Presbytery for the next eight years.

This school was quite new, and beyond the usual thing in parish education. It would be both classical and philosophical, a practical step toward the foundation of a college. It was opened in that autumn of 1743, in a room in the home of the Rev. Francis Alison on Thunder Hill, near New London Crossroads in Chester County, Pennsylvania, and not far from the Delaware line.[4] Five years before, the Synod of Philadelphia had taken up the problem of maintaining an educated ministry so far from the universities. In 1739 it had approved a plan, but then the outbreak of war with Spain, the mustering of men and resources for the Caribbean expeditions, had delayed it. War and the threat of war with France remained, but now also an open conflict within the church had brought a countervailing urgency, and the school was opened with full Synod support.

From 1735 to 1742, classics and theology had been taught at Gilbert Tennent's "Log College" at Neshaminy, north of Philadelphia. New London followed as a prompt, but not a spiritual, successor. Between them lay the Old Side–New Side, Old Light –New Light division of the Presbyterian Church. "Hell-fire Tennent," as William Smith had dubbed him, was a New Side man, and the Log College was being extolled by Whitefield as having brought "New Light" to the wilderness.[5] New Light men cherished the ideal of a learned ministry, but were evangelists as well, lighters of the fires of revival, following inspiration from within as often as synodical direction, ·calling upon the people to accept God's love, promising heavenly grace. It was a new sort of religion, a new escape from sin, a new choice between eternal weal or woe.

To Old Side men all this was Methodism, or worse. It was the error of Pelagianism, of "self-righteousness," as if one could by a mere act of one's own will change the will of Omniscience. They stood with the stern traditional doctrines, with church government, with settled lines of authority and no man preaching unbidden to another's flock. Both sides still subscribed devoutly to the Westminster standards of 1646 and all the essential structure of Calvinism, but differed in implied doctrine and on many points of practice.[6] Disputes on the qualification of a candidate for licensure and ordination (piety and visionary experience weighed against close-knit theology) and the qualifications of elders aroused intense excitement and had an inevitable tendency to political maneuvering. On these issues the organization had split in 1741—a New Side synod based at New Brunswick, an Old Side synod in Philadelphia, but the schism present and rankling everywhere. The rival synods would come together again in 1758, but the rankling and rivalry would go on, and would have their profound effect, years later, on the history of Dickinson College.

The Log College had been little more than a theological school with general training of grammar school quality, but on the whole, in classroom as in the field, New Side had all the initiative and verve.[7] New Side founded its College of New Jersey in 1746. The New Side spirit made for a broader curriculum, and to this may be credited the fact that natural science and other studies of a practical sort were being taught in most schools and colleges by mid-century.[8] New London, meanwhile, continued as Old Side's chief educational establishment, a room in a farmhouse only, committed to traditional procedures, and yet—as is ever the way in education—winning a deserved success and lasting reputation by the personal quality of its teachers, Francis Alison, Headmaster, John Steel, his usher, and others as time went on. Synod's prime objective was training for the ministry, but a majority of the boys were gentlemen's sons getting a gentleman's education and, as the masters earned much of their income by boarding and lodging pupils, this was an important part of the operation. The masters, it should be added, still served the local pulpits also. One of John Steel's sermons has survived from these days: "For the 4th Sabbath of Novr 1748. *Deo Sit Gloria.*"[9]

We know nothing of John Steel as teacher, but much of Francis Alison under whom he worked. Alison was a native of Donegal, north Ireland, a graduate of the University of Glasgow who had crossed the Atlantic in 1735, at the age of thirty. His first occupation was as tutor in the Maryland home of Samuel Dickinson. Samuel Dickinson's young son, John, was only eight years old when the family moved south to Dover, Delaware in 1740. It is a reasonable conjecture, though not supported by any contemporary evidence, that he was one of the boys of prominent local families who continued their education at the New London School.[10] Certainly George Read, one of John Dickinson's close friends and associates of early days, was a pupil there. Another pupil, later a teacher, has left us a description of its course of study.

Matthew Wilson remembered the school as "a *seat of learning* . . . of great and deserved renown . . . on the most generous and broad bottom, for all denominations of christians equally; which was *visited, examined* and *encouraged by the Synod of Philadelphia.*" Alison had carried it beyond Tennent's range of classics and theology. "As *knowledge* and *composition* or *writing* and *speaking,* are the *greatest ends* of a *liberal education,* we received the greatest advantage from his *critical examination every morning* of our *themes* in English and Latin, *epistles* English and Latin, *descriptions* in verse, and especially our *abstracts* or abridgements of a paper from the *Spectators* or *Guardians* (the best standards of our language) *substantially contracted into one of our exercises.*" He carried his boys on into "a *course of philosophy, instrumental, natural* and *moral*"—a version of the Moral Philosophy course offered to college seniors in these and many later years. Francis Alison, as Matthew Wilson looked back upon his youth, was "like Prometheus, Cadmus, or even Apollo of old," remembered not only for great learning but for wit, "*facetious* among chosen friends," and for a "*fancy* vigourous and lively." [11]

Alison, with a reputation as the best classical scholar in America, left New London for the Philadelphia Academy in 1752. In 1756, the Academy became a college under that dedicated, hard-driving Scotsman, William Smith. There Alison, who had been honored with Yale's M.A. the year before, and Glasgow's D.D. in 1758, became Smith's Vice Provost. Though the College had no church connection, Alison continued to be active in Presbyterian affairs. When he had left New London, so also had John Steel, but for a field more to his liking and more strictly within the fold of Old Side orthodoxy. As for the academy they had begun together and carried forward so successfully, it was taken over by the Rev. Alexander McDowell, who moved it to Elkton, Maryland, and then, in 1767, to Newark, Delaware. Chartered and endowed, its history touches that of Dickinson College in later years, and stands in the background of the present University of Delaware.

John Steel, whose first call had been to the wilderness churches, had now returned to that field, just as a storm of flame and terror was about to break over the mountains of the Pennsylvania frontier. The records of the Presbytery of Donegal, 1750 to 1759, are lost, but we have glimpses of him, here and there, from other sources. In 1752, he had charge of the churches of East and West Conococheague, now Greencastle and Mercersburg. His "old white church" in the western parish was surrounded by a stockade when the Indian raids began after Braddock's defeat in the summer of 1755. It was garrisoned by its own military company, commanded by the pastor. [12] The "Reverend Captain" becomes a legend of the embattled wilderness. After his fort on Church Hill was burned by the enemy, he was commissioned a captain in the provincial service. [13] That was on March 25, 1756, with orders "To take post at McDowell's mill, upon the road to the Ohio, which you are to make your Head Quarters, and to detach Patroling partys from time to time to scoiur the woods, in such manner as you shall Judge most consistent with the safety of the Inhabitants." [14] He sent back information from the front, received and distributed supplies, enlisted recruits. [15] His men guarded farmers at their work, and dashed in pursuit of the raiding braves, but everywhere the outer settlements were being abandoned. People were in flight even from Carlisle. Steel was at Carlisle in the fall and winter of 1756. Here the wagon roads ended and the pack horse trails began. Here the town's foremost citizen, Colonel John Armstrong, was strengthening the defenses of the place—he who, that August, had revenged Braddock by his fiery assault on the Indian town Kitanning, far to the west. Provost William Smith was there in that autumn, on a tour "to settle free schools," a dubious errand with panic everywhere and refugees on the move. [16]

By 1758, things were looking up. Then the royal and provincial forces mustered at Carlisle for their advance upon Fort Pitt, moving out at last in three long columns, "with drums tapping at the head of each," to keep them within distance of one another in the forest shadows. [17] The days of terror and despair had passed. Auspiciously also—though events would prove it an impermanent solution—the two rival Presbyterian synods reunited. It was time, now, for the Reverend Captain to think first of his sacred calling. His family, Margaret Steel and their brood of six daughters and three sons, must have found a refuge somewhere during those years of Steel's Fort and the ravaged land, perhaps at Carlisle, perhaps at York, since we hear of him in both places. But it is Carlisle that he has in mind for a settled living.

Just west of the town by a mile and a half, on a hill above Conodoguinet Creek, stood the old log church of Meeting House Springs. For ten years it had been without a settled pastor, though we may feel sure that Captain Steel had filled its pulpit from time to time. Carlisle was now a boom town of the west, expected to grow quickly in size and prosperity. The Episcopalians would soon be building a church at its heart on the public square, and the Presbyterians, overwhelmingly the larger denomination, should have their meetinghouse there as well. This was the parish for John Steel, and he would take the congregation in from Meeting House Springs to the town. Unfortunately, however, another shared the thought. Like so many, the congregation had been an uneasy mixture of Old Side, New Side, and New Side had a candidate of its own. As a result, with the union, there would be two congregations instead of one, and more sharply divided than ever. Old Side Donegal Presbytery had been a comfortable coterie of Captain the Rev. John Steel, Captain the Rev. John Elder, and four other stalwarts of like persuasion. The union had now added to their number one of their own ilk and four New Siders. One of the four was coming in upon his own nomination, and this was the one who had also chosen Carlisle as the vineyard he would till in the Lord's service.

George Duffield of the thin, sensitive, ascetic face was a man of twenty-seven, as against John Steel's ripe age of forty-four. He had graduated from the College of New Jersey in 1752, had been a tutor on its faculty, 1754 to 1756, and had then won success as a travelling revivalist. He had been in Carlisle at the time of the death of his first wife, September, 1757. And his remarriage, at Carlisle, March 5, 1759, had brought him into the family circle of Colonel Armstrong, that man of perspicacity and power—bringing him also a full expectation of taking charge of this substantial pastorate. [18] In April, however, at his first meeting with the presbytery, he was staggered to hear John Steel called to the church at Carlisle, a call followed by Steel's hurried installation a few days later. One can imagine Mr. Duffield's dismay. He reveals it himself in the following letter to the Rev. John Blair, whose congregations near Shippensburg had been broken up by the Indian raids of 1756, and who had gone back to succeed his brother, Samuel, as pastor of the church and principal of the classical school at Fagg's Manor. Unfortunately the letter did not reach Mr. Blair, at least not by any direct route. It came first into the hands of Mr. Steel, who read:

Carlisle, Ap. 20th. 1759.

Revd. Dear Uncle,

Our affairs here look with an aspect as gloomy both in Church &

state as when our Indian Enemys infested our Borders, if not more so.

Mr. Steel, since his being over here, has assiduously labour'd for a party, and after having appointed two week day Meetings upon it, and people Not attending so as was desir'd, they finishd their subscriptions on Sab. before Presbytery.

Very few in the Town have yet subscribd, and whether they will I don't know. The affair was carried on with as much Privacy as the Nature of the thing wou'd admit, and very few of the principal Men consulted in it. At the opening of the Presbytery, I joind them according to my Intention. The first affair brought before them was a Call for Mr. Steel from this and the lower Congn. It was without Deliberation presented to him, he immediately accepted it and the Instalment was appointed the following tuesday. Accordingly he was install'd last Tuesday, to be two thirds of his Time here, and the other below. This has revived a party spirit, and very generally disgusted our People up this way against the Plan of Union. There was the highest Probability of a very comfortable Union in this Congregation, which was the very Reason of the Matter being so precipitately hurried on.

Many are enraged and say, if the Synod allow of Such proceedings they cant see what they mean by uniting, and yet suffer their Members to act directly contrary to the Plan of Union, not the least Regard being had to it thro' the whole of this affair, More than it never had been. 'Twill not do for me to move it at Synod, but I can't help thinking the Synod ought to consider Such proceedings as directly oppose their Designs, and disregard their Authority.

Mr. Steel's and the Design of his stiff Adherents was to root me out of this, expecting either that I cou'dn't get a Subsistance, or that the Presbytery wou'dn't Install two of their Members in the same Place. In the first they'l find a grand Mistake; and for the last, if the pby. refuse, when applied for, I shall apply to Synod. I shall live peaceably if I can safely, but if they are for overbearing, Welcome Contention.— I am more pleased with the Union, & more sensible of the Duty of regulating Presbyterys, since I join'd here: I choose this Presbytery, tho' I hardly expect much Comfort in it for a while.

> I am, &c.
> George Duffield.

Little comfort would he have. Steel laid the offensive letter before the Presbytery, October 20, 1760. Duffield responded, April 29, 1761, with direct complaint: "Mr. Steel even before his settlement here, appear'd disposed to keep at an unbrotherly distance from Mr. Duffield." Mr. Steel had refused to baptize an ailing child of Duffield's flock, unless the family would join his congregation, and had kept others from joining Duffield, though Duffield had encouraged some to join with Steel. More, and worse, was told: Mr. Steel had openly expressed his opinion that "he had rather his Meeting house were burn'd, than that such a Fellow as Mr. Duffd. shou'd preach in it, or words of that Import." To top it all, the letter, which he believed to be a plain statement of fact, had been intercepted, kept several months in spite of a promise to return it, and a "low underhand" use made of it, accompanied by implications that Mr. Duffield was a liar. [19]

Mr. Duffield may surely be pardoned for regarding such conduct with severity. Mr. Steel's view, on the other hand, is well enough explained in his sermon of August 21, 1753, where (speaking in general terms only) he warns us that "it is common for Seducers to put on a good appearance as it is sometimes Expedient for the Devil, in order to do his work the more effectually, to transform himself into [an] angel of Light & by so disguising their designs by smooth words and a pretended Zeal they gain the Esteem of such who have more of good affection than a setled judgment. It is therefore no small part of ye faithfull Shepherd to guard ye flock agt such wolves who approach ye folds in Sheep's clothing that they may do the more hurt." In such wise the feud went on, these two and their partisans, and would be echoing still, seventy years later, with a later George Duffield as target—old grudges flowering afresh among the trustees to Dickinson College.

Duffield, gentle and persuasive, had also some of the passion and intensity of his Huguenot ancestors. More, he had Colonel John Armstrong. The Colonel wrote to Thomas Penn, then in England, asking for a site for a church on the northwest corner of the square, opposite the grant to the Episcopalians. [20] This received a favorable reply, as he could be sure it would. But such a transaction took time, and time was lacking, with Steel's people already building nearby, at the northeast corner of Hanover and Louther Streets. [21] Duffield, duly called and installed in September, 1759, must meet the challenge at once, and so his meetinghouse was going up the while on precisely the opposite side of the square and equally near to the market and the fort: "a wooden building, south of the stockade," on the southwest corner of Pomfret and Hanover Streets. [22] The re-united Synod, learning of two rival meetinghouses in Carlisle, had at once expressed its grief "that there should be a spirit of animosity still subsisting amongst the people . . . and do warmly recommend to the people of both congregations to fall upon healing measures, and lay a plan for the erection of one house only, and enjoin it upon Messrs. Steel and Duffield to unite their counsel and use their influence to bring about a cordial agreement." [23]

Small chance now of that. Mr. Steel has it in mind to unite the congregations, but under his own leadership only. He is emerging now as a man of property. His home is on the other side of Hanover Street from his church. His wide tract of land toward Bedford in the west is rising in value and he is a substantial investor in Carlisle town lots. [24] We find him (along with Francis Alison, Alexander McDowell and other staunch characters) subscribing £6 per annum to the fund for the relief of poor ministers, a sum which may be contrasted to his starting salary at the New London school, £15 a year, a mere tenth of his present stipend. [25] On the back cover of one of his manuscript sermons, "For ye 2nd Sab. of Jany. 1769 for ye Evening," there is written out a schedule of interest accretions for a ten-year period, supporting other evidence of his having become, by that time, banker for his congregation, lending money for its projects. [26]

But what of education? In the midst of all this turmoil it was still the pastoral duty of each combatant to promote it. Boys could study Greek and Latin, learn their catechism as well, and never come near those fine-spun canons of belief and disputation. One tantalizing source is an appended "Chronological Table of Important Events" in Josiah Rhinehart Sypher's *School History of Pennsylvania,* published in Philadelphia, 1868. It lists, for 1760, "Classical school established in Cumberland Valley." [27] This must surely have been at Carlisle, as Conway Phelps Wing and others have assumed. [28] Inclusion under "Important Events" implies positive information, though no source is given. The date corresponds with the coming of the competitive Steel-Duffield ministries to Carlisle.

Yet with such strong evidence of bad feeling, *ex anima*, total and irrevocable, it is not easy to conceive of the two pastors joining in any mutual effort. New Side parents might have put their boys under Mr. Steel's tutelage, or Old Siders sent theirs to Duffield, but the two gentlemen would hardly have conducted an institution together. Duffield had come fresh from his experience as a tutor at college. We have one record of a boy "sent to a grammar school under the tuition of the Rev. George Duffield," about 1763, and another of a young Irishman prepared in theology partly under George Duffield, "then of Carlisle."[29] Steel, a teacher for nine years with Dr. Alison, was the superior in experience, yet the thin and scattered evidence leaves it to conjecture when, or whether, he was teaching at Carlisle. We only know for a certainty that a grammar or Latin school, described in the *Pennsylvania Gazette* of January 11, 1770, had been functioning there "for several years past." It belonged then with John Steel's congregation, and one can enlarge the picture somewhat by following Mr. Steel's rising importance in the little town.

Both Duffield and Steel had other pastoral charges outside Carlisle, but Steel's were the larger. If Duffield had a prime advantage in Colonel (later General) John Armstrong, New Side stalwart, as kinsman and ally, the other had his own devoted and determined elders, among whom the name of Captain John Montgomery should be noted. Armstrong was virtually the founder and father of Carlisle, a man of sophistication and power. But Montgomery, storekeeper, soldier, farmer, judge and politician, would rise steadily in repute, becoming at the last a Member of Congress and the most active trustee of Dickinson College. His early dispatches as commander of a company of provincial troops in the French and Indian War have obviously been written for him, even to the signature. He was then, as the urbane Armstrong noted in 1758, somewhat wanting in "horn, hair & hoof."[30] When at last we find him with pen in hand, composition and spelling show him as less expert with it than with the sword. Yet Montgomery, lacking education admired it in others and stood with school and college as a warm promoter—a rock of conservatism in religion and politics, and a successful man.

After the Peace of Paris, February, 1763, Carlisle would grow in population and prosperity, but first another tribulation must be borne. On the cover of one of those sermons of Steel's, all written in that fine, cramped script and bound in booklets small enough to lie in the palm of the hand, you will find the catchwords of his text from Isaiah, 9: 12, 13: "For all this his anger is not turned"; and under that, "June 4th, when the first Acct. Came of indians doing damage—1763." As the prophet of old had seen the Syrians before him and the Philistines behind, so John Steel saw an unregenerate people between French and Indians: "We wt ye nation we belong to are concerned in a long war wt but little Success, & it is not yet come to a conclusion, & tho' both Civil & religious Liberty in a great measure depend on ye issue of ye war, yet alas, we Continue impenitent, & wickedness yet is on ye prevailing hand among us, & tho by means of this war we are much impoverished & feel ye effects of it, yet we lay it not to heart, & therefore we have much ground to fear yt God will bring ye Calamities of ye war yet nearer to us, nay unto our very bowels as he did lately in Scotland." [31]

This was Pontiac's Conspiracy, which set the whole frontier aflame again, with troops marching through Carlisle once more and the brutal murder of the peaceful Conestoga Indians by "Paxton Boys" from old John Elder's congregation. The furious political campaign of 1764 saw the Presbyterians solidly united against Ben Franklin's party. That had been in October. Peace came at the year's end, with the long pack trains assembling at Carlisle. Then came the chance discovery among the pack train loads of scalping knives and arms for the Indian trade, the news spreading like wildfire through the woods and bringing out the "Black Boys" to raid the trains and seize the contraband. War and the threat of war lingered through these years. In January, 1768, frontier ruffian Frederick Stump and his servant, Hans Eisenhauer, murdered ten Indians, men, women and children, in a drunken frolic—ample provocation to the tribes for war. The two were jailed at Carlisle and then, when ordered brought to Philadelphia, set free by a mob. John Steel followed the pack two miles from town, "but laboured with them in vain," as it was reported to Governor Penn. [32] It was, like the Paxton riot, an ugly business, with much expostulation, recrimination and self-defense, and no effective action. Some tried to fix the blame on Duffield's people because Colonel Armstrong, as justice, had detained the prisoners after the order had come to send them to Philadelphia for questioning, and so had given the mob its chance. [33] In February, at the request of Lieutenant Governor John Penn, Steel headed a group sent west to evict, if possible, settlers who were taking up Indian lands before the completion of a treaty. [34]

So much for politics. On the ecclesiastical side, matters of greater import to the school had been taking shape. In April, 1764, Mr. Steel agreed to give equal time to the congregations of Carlisle and Silver Spring, at a combined salary of £150 a year. [35] He, John Elder and four others had announced their dissatisfaction with the "new modelling of Presbyteries" that had taken place after the union of 1758, and set up their own Presbytery of Donegal for a number of years. [36] This cut them off from the Synod, but Steel and his elder, Montgomery, sometimes appeared at its annual meeting. In 1767 the Synod refused them any recognition, and then, in the next year made a regrouping of presbyteries without geographical reference, an expedient to preserve some sort of harmony for a time at least. [37]

Meanwhile, on a higher level, powerful Old Side forces were moving in upon a New Side stronghold. Dr. Samuel Finley, President of the College of New Jersey, had died in 1766. The united church had been supporting this college and now—as Francis Alison and other conservative leaders saw it—there had come an opportunity to put an institution heretofore "unfit to make scholars . . . on a better foundation." [38] A satisfactory president must be chosen, together with some new faculty and trustees, and this would be combined with a strong financial inducement. The Princeton trustees, needing the support of the united church, nevertheless sensed an Old Side scheme to take over the whole, and there can be little doubt that this is what Alison and his coadjutors had in mind. It was now notorious that the Irish ministry was becoming increasingly New Light— embracing a view "inconsistent with the doctrine of Original Sin." [39] All the while that the Ulster presbyteries had been reaffirming their sturdy faith in strict Calvinist doctrine, their young men had been returning from the University of Glasgow with more liberal ideas, and so effecting a quiet revolution. [40] Unless checked, Princeton might do the same.

Alison, as of December 4, 1766, had in mind himself as President, teaching "Moral Philosophy, the institutes of the law of nature & metaphysicks," and John Ewing of his Philadelphia faculty in the chair of Mathematics and Natural Philosophy. [41] Alexander McDowell and Matthew Wilson, then conducting the school at Newark, might be an alternate choice which would give "our gentlemen satisfaction." It is significant that for lesser faculty he tossed in the name of Duffield as teacher of languages. This would show his willingness to promote some New Side men as well. It also shows that Duffield was considered a capable teacher of languages. But most of all, it suggests an eagerness to alter the situation at Carlisle. Yet even as a delegation was on its way from Philadelphia to put forward an irresistible proposition, the Princeton trustees adopted a course designed both to defeat the Old Side maneuver and add new lustre to their institution. They elected as President an eminent and liberal-minded Scottish clergyman, John Witherspoon.

Still the issue hung precariously in balance. Would Witherspoon accept? The invitation, warmly urging him to do so, was followed by other letters from America warning him against it. In April, 1767, he at last declined, the balance tipped by Mrs. Witherspoon's unwillingness to part from home and friends forever. But Princeton had on the ground an ardent young alumnus pleading its cause and refusing to accept rejection. Benjamin Rush of the Class of 1760 was a medical student at the University of Edinburgh, 1766 to 1768, and he now continued to pursue the matter with an almost poetic fervor. In giving his refusal, Dr. Witherspoon had strongly recommended his close friend and protégé, Charles Nisbet, the young minister at Montrose. He had written to Nisbet and to Rush, and fully expected an accomodation to be reached. It was here that Rush first learned of Nisbet's reputation for great learning and a scintillating wit. Yet the young doctor was not a man for second choices. He was with the Witherspoons at Paisley in August, 1767, turning all his persuasive charm upon the lady, and it worked. The Witherspoons would sail from Greenock in the spring of 1768.

Back at Princeton, meanwhile, Alison's forces had renewed their pressure for participation and the trustees seemed ready to yield, at least in part. In October, 1767, they elected a compromise candidate to the presidency, Samuel Blair, aged twenty-six, who would step aside should Witherspoon come after all. He was a nephew of John Blair, to whom Duffield's famous letter had been addressed, and who, as a man acceptable to both parties, had been appointed Professor of Divinity. [42] Then came the news of Rush's success—signalling victory for New Side and the collapse of Old Side ambitions.

There was thus still no bastion of higher education dominated by the conservative party. The College of Philadelphia had no sectarian tie, and Alison's superior, Provost Smith, was an Episcopalian. Defeated at Princeton, Old Side would strengthen its defenses elsewhere. A charter was secured for Newark Academy to place it on a more permanent footing, and it became an object of special interest and attention from Vice Provost Alison, John Ewing, the sharp young mathematician on Philadelphia's faculty, and others. [43] This mood of umbrage and rededication was reflected also at Carlisle.

Carlisle was showing signs of high promise as a prosperous market town and, perhaps, a future metropolis of the west. Handsome stone houses were clustering near the square. The old log courthouse had been replaced by a spacious brick one in 1766, and, by deed dated in September of that year, Thomas and Richard Penn had finally conveyed the land on the square's northwest corner, not to Duffield's group, but to John Steel, John Montgomery and other "trustees appointed by the Presbyterian congregation of Carlisle." [44] As for Mr. Duffield, he had been named by the Synod to accompany the venerable Charles Beatty on a tour through the western settlements in that fall of 1766, stirring up religious zeal among the lonely farms and even a hope of awakening the Indians to God's love [45] —this last an aspiration which had probably never warmed to enthusiasm in the breast of John Steel. The congregation of the Second Presbyterian Church of Philadelphia, New Side, had sent Mr. Duffield a call in 1763, again in 1766 and again in 1771. He went at last in September, 1772, and was formally installed in the following year. [46] His Carlisle flock sought vainly to lure him back in that year, but would continue to see him from time to time as a visitor.

Duffield's departure had been presaged in the acquisition by Steel's congregation of their church site on the Carlisle public square. Here would be built a larger and grander edifice than the older two, and one in which all could come together. The first contract was signed on February 16, 1769; a second on April 26, 1771. [47] Robert Smith, of the Carpenters' Company of Philadelphia, had drawn the plans. [48] Another memo scribbled on the cover of a John Steel sermon reads, "Feb. ye 4th Sab. 1771. When it appears we are on ye Brink of a Spanish & french war"—an apprehension then sweeping the colonies, but happily dispelled. [49] By 1772, the new church was at last roofed over. Though it would not be entirely finished for another twenty years, it could now be used for worship, and—we may surmise—for the school. [50]

Since sometime in 1769, the school had had a master to give full time to it, a young minister from Ireland. The hand of Alison may be seen here, as well as John Steel's. To any experienced educator it would have been obvious that the American Presbyterian Church needed but one college. But if Alison's party could not control Princeton from within, it could still set up a secondary system on an equally secure foundation. These schools would adhere to the old standards, and the life of the college would depend upon them. As a beginning, there would be two, Newark in the East and in the West, Carlisle. That announcement in the *Pennsylvania Gazette* of January 11, 1770, is unsigned but explicit:

> *Carlisle, January* 1770.
>
> WHEREAS a LATIN SCHOOL has for several Years past, been erected in this Town, and is now kept by Mr. HENRY MAKINLY, who professes to teach the Latin and Greek Languages in the most concise and perfect Manner.   In order therefore that the School might be settled upon a regular Footing, Trustees are chosen to take Care of it, and a certain Number of Gentlemen, of good Repute in the literary World, have engaged to visit and examine the Scholars, as often as it may be convenient.
>
> From these Considerations, we flatter ourselves that this School will continue for many Years, and be productive of the most important Advantages, as it is constituted under these Regulations, and

continued in a Town both pleasant and healthy, where Lodgings may be had in, or convenient to Town, at the Rate of Nine Pounds a Year, a Thing scarcely to be got in the Neighbourhood of any other Seminary in the Province. These Advantages, duly considered, we hope will be a sufficient Inducement for Gentlemen to send their Children to said School. [51]

With Mr. Duffield's departure, the Synod had left it to the two congregations to unite under Mr. Steel, hopeful that when his pastorate should come to its close they might be able to agree amicably upon a successor. Thus it is that the grant of land made by Thomas and John Penn, March 3, 1773, for the purpose of building a schoolhouse names three New Side men among the nine patentees. They were Colonel John Armstrong, Stephen Duncan and William Lyon, prominent citizens all. The others also were community leaders: Steel's old stalwart, John Montgomery, William Irvine, Robert Magaw, Robert Miller, George Stevenson and James Wilson. Of the nine, all but Miller and Stevenson would serve later as trustees of the College.

On December 13, 1773, the church "now under the pastoral care of the Rev. Mr. John Steel," having found itself "under great inconveniences for want of being a body politic in law," was granted a charter by the Penns. [52] Twelve trustees were named, again with New Side representatives among a majority of Old Side men. All was now fixed upon a safe foundation. Steel and Alison could feel confident of the school's growing with the town, sheltered in the Church, firm in doctrinal and classical probity.

Yet this was the year also of the destruction of the cargoes of tea, to be followed in the next by the punitive acts of Parliament and the meeting of the first Continental Congress on September 5, 1774. Thirteen years earlier, American papers had featured news of two men who claimed to walk the earth "by the order of Heaven. They say that the World will infallibly be at an end in 1773. . . ." [53] It was not to be quite as final as that, yet the year we mark as the beginning of Dickinson College history had little about it of a bright dawning. Eight more years would pass before a schoolhouse would be built upon the newly granted lot, and there would be at least two years with no school held at all. War, an enemy alike of religion and the intellectual life, would be darkening hopes and sweeping plans aside.

O GLORIOUS change! O happy day! that now be-
holds the Sciences planted where barbarity was before!

Rev. Dr. William Smith, commencement sermon,
Philadelphia, 1757

3

THE LATIN SCHOOL

AT CARLISLE

HENRY MAKINLY (he spelled his name consistently so, though others, including his children, used the more accepted form, "McKinley") must have arrived in Carlisle in the summer of 1769, and probably in response to an appeal for a teacher from Steel or Alison. On November 20, 1770, he purchased (at sheriff's sale) a house on the southeast corner of Hanover Street and Locust Alley, and that event is the best clue we have to the date of his marriage to John Steel's daughter, Elizabeth.[1] Lydia, the oldest girl, was probably already married to Robert Semple. John Steel, Jr., nineteen at this time, had the law in view as a career, and it is interesting to note that George Duffield, Jr., would also choose that more worldly area of persuasion and contention. The other Steels were Margaret (named for her mother), Mary, Sarah, Robert, Andrew (aged six) and Jean. We know that the father, now a man of fifty-five, owned two fowling pieces, and so can picture him out with his sons for sport and game, a man of action ever. His bold life and his success were such as his son-in-law would now seek also.

Henry Makinly, like young John Steel, was a minister launching his American career from the springboard of an educational establishment. In Ireland, he had been ordained, March 4, 1766, as pastor of the congregation at Moville in Derry Presbytery, County Donegal—romantic names: Moville, "the plain of the ancient tree," and Donegal, even more aptly, "the fortress of the foreigners."[2] Before Makinly, impoverished Moville had had only four settled ministers since 1715, all for short terms, and he had no successor there until 1784.[3] Once in America, however, he figures as a teacher, soldier and farmer, his clerical call, apparently, quite left behind. The Carlisle tax lists show him as owner of two cows in 1773; two cows, two horses in 1775. The years bring children to his knee, Henry, John, Daniel, James; Martha and Margaret.[4] Daniel would have a son, Daniel, who will in time appear in the Dickinson College arena, playing a small part opposite George Duffield, grandson of the Duffield of these early days.

Makinly's work was fundamentally college preparation, although all the American schools—again, following the Scottish trend—varied their fundamental grounding in the classics with courses useful to those who would go directly into business or a profession. Many of his pupils went to Princeton; some, particularly those with medicine in mind, to the College of Philadelphia. Best known of them all was John Armstrong, Jr., the old Indian fighter's brilliant, sardonic son, who left Princeton in 1775 for a military career, earned some distinction as a staff officer and Washington's resentment as author of the "Newburgh Letters" of 1783, was Congressman, Senator, Jefferson's minister to France and Secretary of War in Madison's war cabinet. George Stevenson, aged eleven, was put to school with Makinly in 1770, to be launched six years later upon his memorable career as Revolutionary soldier, physician, trustee of Dickinson College and a founder and first President of the Board of Trustees of the University of Pittsburgh.[5]

Another boy, Elisha Macurdy, whose schooling must have begun about 1772, remembered a second teacher. "One of his instructors," Macurdy's careful and devout biographer informs us, "was the late Judge Creigh . . . who is recollected by many yet living, as a prominent Elder in the Presbyterian Church of Carlisle. Another, was a gentleman, who was son-in-law of the Rev. John Steel, of Carlisle, but whose name has been forgotten. Under his direction he commenced the study of the Latin language, but had not advanced far, when his studies were interrupted and the school dispersed, by the breaking out of the war of the Revolution."[6]

John Creigh had arrived upon this scene in 1761, bearing his certificate of membership in the church at Carmony, near Belfast, where his father and grandfather had been ruling elders.[7] A survey of the streets and town lots of Carlisle was drawn by him three years later: "This Plan made Octr. 25th. A.D. MDCCLXIV by Jno. Creigh."[8] It shows one of his own lots next door to "Steel's meeting house," and he would continue to invest in others. How long he continued as a teacher is not known. On May 4, 1770, he began filling the pages of his "Precedent Book" with copies of legal forms written out in his almost copperplate schoolmaster's hand.[9] Here, obviously, he is looking forward to the career he was to follow in public office and legal affairs. One section, however, consists of tables of "Simple Interest," pointing to his work at the school as well as to the future. He would become, like his forebears, an elder of his church, a practical man active in community and private affairs, a trustee of the College and the sire of later College figures.

From this and other fragmentary evidence, we have a picture of the grammar school at Carlisle, Ranged on the benches in one or two rooms, we have a "Latin school," a "mathematical school" and an "English school," with Henry Makinly hearing the recitations in Latin and Greek and John Creigh leading others from simple to higher mathematics and topping these off with surveying and navigation, vital subjects for all young Americans. Handwriting, English composition and declamation also must be learned. There are probably twenty to thirty boys in all. John Steel is certainly a presence, and one much in evidence at the periodic examinations, when the Board of Visitors, those "Gentlemen of good Repute in the literary World," would foregather to taste and test the progress of learning. For many years to come, in school or college, all examinations would be oral, with questions posed not only by teachers but by official visitors and the invited public as well. As classical learning was the mark of the gentleman, so it must meet the rigors of this regular confrontation, the whole affair a town holiday and even the hoi-polloi who could not read or write alert to it. Scotland's famous pedagogue, Thomas Ruddiman (even in far-away America, Ruddiman's *Rudiments* had long been the most widely favored Latin grammar), always appeared for these occasions in his grizzle wig, lightly powdered, orange-colored suit with broad gold lace on the scarlet waistcoat, and full-ruffled shirt. [10] Carlisle's gentlemen of literary repute did quite as well we may be sure—long faces and careful questions, chirping answers from the scholars, then their Latin declamations; while the ladies, so beautifully dressed, so handsomely overawed, were ready with their ripples of applause.

That grant of land for a schoolhouse, March 3, 1773, stands as a point of climax in both Colonial and school affairs. Later in the year, Dr. John Ewing, once a pupil of Alison and Steel and now Professor of Mathematics with Alison at Philadelphia, went to Britain to solicit funds for their erstwhile New London Academy, now at Newark. [11]

"Many difficulties arise in ye course of our business," he wrote home from London, February 20, 1774. "The destruction of ye Tea at Boston and ye sending it back from Phil'a greatly retards our progress. We are almost accounted Rebels here and many say that they will not give money to those who refuse to submit to ye Parliament of Great Britain.

"Dr. Witherspoon has also wrote against, alleging that our Academy will hurt the Jersey College and that it is intended to teach other doctrines in Divinity than what are taught in his College. Although this will hurt us, yet it will not defeat our mission." [12]

Before he had sailed from Philadelphia, Ewing's good friend, Benjamin Rush, a loyal Princeton man but oblivious to Witherspoon's fear that a competing college might arise at Newark and unaware also of the existence of the school at Carlisle, had wished him all success, adding that he would be glad to see another academy like Newark "on or near the Susquehannah." [13] Responding to his friend's enthusiasm, Ewing had written to Rush from London, hopefully, of a Presbyterian college or academy in western Pennsylvania, another in North Carolina. [14]

While Dr. Ewing, having found London cool to his appeals, was preparing to carry them to Scotland, the news of Parliament's Boston Port Bill had spread through America, stirring indignation everywhere. John Montgomery was chairman of the meeting at Carlisle, July 12, 1774, which condemned the measure and endorsed the call for a Continental Congress. A year later, with Washington's provincial army besieging Boston, all Cumberland was in a fervor of martial preparation, with John Steel the captain of a company once more and Montgomery on the Committee of Safety. John Creigh would be Lieutenant-Colonel of militia, no less, as of April 9, 1776, and a member of the convention which met at Carpenter's Hall, Philadelphia, in June, and voted unanimously to commit Pennsylvania to the issue of independence from Britain. Cumberland's delegation had itself taken that stand at a stormy meeting in the Carlisle town square—stormy because lawyer James Wilson had dared to brave the overwhelming majority and argue for delay. Wilson was fearful lest immediate separation might destroy the dominance of the ruling political class (as indeed it did). He was decried and rebuked for his audacity—most loudly of all by schoolmaster Henry Makinly, and Makinly was rebuked in turn by John Montgomery's Committee of Safety for the slur on Wilson's patriotism. [15] On that July 4th of the Declaration, John Steel was at Lancaster, where militia delegates, officers and privates, elected their brigadiers.

The army, in this summer, was disastrously defeated around New York, with the surrender of Fort Washington by Colonel Robert Magaw of Carlisle the heaviest blow of all. All New Jersey was lost, and then, in the winter campaign of Trenton and Princeton, as suddenly regained. New regiments were being thrown together to make good the regular army's terrible losses. One of these was the Twelfth of the Pennsylvania Line, Continental Army, men mostly from the forests of the upper Susquehanna, but with one company from Carlisle, its captain Henry Makinly.

In the State Archives at Harrisburg there is a list of applicants for commissions in the Twelfth, with some names crossed off and others checked as "good," or "good man," and one of these last is Makinly's. The recruiting of a company was up to its captain, and Makinly had done well. His commission is dated October 1, 1776, and between that date and early December he had enlisted a force of full regulation strength, seventy-two in all, with First Lieutenant William Sayers, Second Lieutenant John Hay, four sergeants, four corporals, a fifer and a drummer. [16] Young Robert Steel was among his privates. Andrew Maclean, who had been a private with Captain John Steel, Jr., was now a sergeant with Makinly. [17] Young Dr. Francis Alison, son of the Vice Provost at Philadelphia, had been appointed Surgeon of the regiment. [18] On December 18, the northern contingent left Sunbury, coming down the river in boats. They may have been joined by Makinly's men at Harris's Ferry for the long cross-country march and the arrival at camp to throbbing drum and screaming fife, flags crackling in the winter wind.

Among the few things of value in Henry Makinly's estate were a watch (£4.10) and a pair of silver spurs (£2.5). Somehow, watch and spurs, time and compulsion, might symbolize the teacher and yield a concept of the soldier as well—an ambitious, adventurous, decisive man. In January, the Twelfth Pennsylvania is with Washington in northern New Jersey, facing the British lines defending New York. On February 19, Makinly is in Philadelphia with an order from his Colonel, William Cooke of Northumberland, for $3,000 cash "to be apply'd in recruiting my Battalion." [19] Even so early, the ranks of the Twelfth were thinning faster than they could be refilled. A number of its best men were detached for service in the Northern Department with Daniel Morgan's famous regiment of riflemen. These backwoodsmen, crack shots every one, were the elite of the army. With such a force, Robert Magaw had swept up from Carlisle to Cambridge in the summer of 1775, and jubilantly had written home, "The hunting shirt is here like a full suit at St. James'. A Rifle man in his Dress may pass Centinels & Go about where he pleases." [20] Colonel Cooke's riflemen, posted between Quibbletown and Amboy, fought at Bound Brook, Piscataway, Short Hills, Bonhamtown and in other skirmishes, with men killed and wounded and one sizeable group taken prisoner when other detachments failed to support them. The men of the Twelfth were used as shock troops at Brandywine, where John Carothers of Carlisle, lieutenant in another company, was killed; and they again met heavy losses in the debacle at Germantown.

When the army crept into camp at Valley Forge, the ranks of this and other regiments had been sadly depleted. Here our schoolmaster is briefly glimpsed again in the orderly book of General Edward Hand, January 14, 1778: "Was stolen out of

Capt. McKinley's tent on the evening of the 9th instant, a silver hilted small sword, the guard stamped D. S. the gripe twisted and plain wire—the scabbard black leather." [21] In January also, Makinly was at Carlisle, where he drew rations from the commissary at the ordnance works. [22] The little town was wholly given over to the preparing of materiel of war, the courthouse an arsenal where cartridges were being made, the barracks outside a manufactory and repair shop of artillery. [23] Perhaps this reunion with Elizabeth, and probably also the state of affairs in his regiment, determined Makinly to give up his command. Of the formal resignation of his commission, as of his departure from his pastorate at Moville, no formal record remains, a fact into which one might, perhaps, read something of his character. On March 4, 1778, the Twelfth suffered a final indignity—its Colonel was cashiered. [24] When the army broke camp on June 18, Captain Makinly was reported as having "Left the Regt. . . . determined to resign," and that stands as the date of his resignation. [25] In July, all that remained of the Twelfth was combined with the Third Pennsylvania in a general "arrangement" of the regiments which brought companies up to strength but sent many officers into a "supernumerary" limbo. On the military side, a mood of optimism prevailed. "The general opinion here of both Whig and Tory," George Duffield wrote from Philadelphia to Captain Postlethwaite in Carlisle, "is that the English will before long evacuate N York, or leave at most only a garrison . . . ." [26]

So much for the classicist gone to war. John Creigh fared more comfortably. He held a commission as a militia officer as early as April 29, 1776, had oversight of military prisoners (among them André and Despard) and on July 31, 1777, became captain of a company in Colonel John Davis's Second Battalion, Cumberland County militia. [27] He is said to have been in action at Germantown in the fall of that year. On April 7, 1777, he had been appointed clerk of the Orphans' Court of Cumberland County, Register of Wills and Recorder of Deeds, offices which he resigned on February 9, 1779. [28] More, in June he had been named an associate justice for the County under the new left-wing government of the state, of which he was an earnest supporter. [29] Finally, at about this time he had become an elder of the Church, an honor and responsibility he would retain until his death in 1813 at the ripe age of seventy-two. [30]

While Creigh in these years had laid the foundation for a full life as a substantial citizen, Makinly had come to a brief flowering and fast decline. From Colonel John Davis he bought a plantation of four hundred acres on Conodoguinet Creek. Here he had houses, lands (in diminishing acreage, by the tax lists), horses and cattle, and "a Negroe Wench" to help Elizabeth with chores and children. Here his first season was a bad one, due to the great flood of August, 1779—the worst "ever known by the oldest Liver on the Creek," as Captain Samuel Postlethwaite wrote to General William Irvine. It had destroyed the pasture for the Continental horses and reached up even to Colonel Blaine's garden. "Capn. Makinley lost all his corn & potatoes." [31]

In that August of the flood, too, the Reverend Captain, "John Steel, V. D. M.," as he was wont to sign the roster—*Verbi Dei Minister*—passes forever from this scene. Margaret Steel had died in February, and her husband had written his will in May, "being apprehensive that my present disorder will issue in death." He left a large estate, with bequests to all the coming generation, to Elizabeth Makinly £200, and £400 to her children.

Francis Alison died on November 28. By an act passed on the 27th, the liberal party controlling the Pennsylvania legislature had annulled the charter of the old College of Philadelphia, creating in its place the new University of the State of Pennsylvania, supported by an endowment of confiscated lands. Dr. William Smith, Anglican and suspected Tory, was replaced as Provost by Alison's pupil, friend and colleague, John Ewing. It was a victory for Presbyterian influence in education, as well as for the radical Constitutionalist Party, which had strong Presbyterian support.

In March, 1780, George Duffield wrote to a friend in Carlisle, inveighing against rising prices and popular indifference, "Our people are asleep, or mad, or worse—everything from abroad promises Great Britain being reduced to an absolute necessity of coming to reasonable terms in the course of the present campaign." [32] Duffield, as one of the two Chaplains of

Congress, had his own record of Revolutionary service, in official circles and with the troops. He was in Carlisle from time to time in these and later years, a landowner with a circle of family and friends, a man of influence in the village still.

Carlisle must now endeavor to reestablish its grammar school. John Steel had set a standard from his years of teaching with Alison, and this too must be brought back. But the events of the war had taught John Montgomery and the other trustees a lesson. They had seen Makinly become a planter, Creigh a public official. To each, the schoolroom had been only a step to something better. Judge Creigh was now a patron of education of a rather homely sort. Makinly, who might have done better as teacher than farmer, gave his life to the struggle by the creek. He died between 1784 and 1786, and the settlement of his estate, a long-term affair administered by John Steel, Jr., left Elizabeth and the children in poverty. [33] The trustees now saw the need for a teacher to whom the work was neither a sideline nor a stepping-stone. They must find a real professional with whom to start anew; and in this they succeeded admirably, acting, probably, on George Duffield's recommendation. In 1780, they brought James Ross from Philadelphia to Carlisle.

In trusteeship and administration there are ample links between Carlisle Grammar School and Dickinson College. In faculty there is this one only, yet for the purpose we could not wish a better. On September 12, 1780, Ross purchased a home in South Hanover Street—himself described in the deed as "James Ross of town of Carlisle and teacher of the Greek and Latin Languages." [34] In the tax lists of 1781 and after he appears as "Schoolmaster," or "Latin Master," and then, after 1784, "Professor." He was a grave, tall man, a full six feet in height, with sandy hair and florid face, stern and dignified. He dressed formally, with glistening buckles at the knee and on his shoes, his hair long and tied with velvet ribbon in a queue. On the street he wore a military style cocked hat and carried a cane. His boys would scamper round a corner rather than meet him there, since he would have been sure to greet them in Latin and expect a response in kind. In the schoolroom, where almost all conversation was in the learned tongue, the rules of grammar and decorum alike were meticulously enforced. As in public he demanded the respect due to a professional man, so at home he ate from silver plate and maintained every mark of that social status belonging—though so rarely accorded—to a teacher. His wife, Rosanna, may be found characterized upon her tombstone in the Old Graveyard at Carlisle, as "an amiable pious woman, an affectionate wife, a sincere friend." They had no children. [35]

James Ross had been born in Oxford Township, Chester County, May 18, 1744, the son of William Ross, an immigrant from Ireland. He had been educated under John Blair at the Fagg's Manor school, where he excelled in languages, though his comprehension of mathematics, along with metaphysics and moral philosophy was, in the recollection of a fellow pupil, "but slender." [36] This concentration upon the one area continued through life. He knew that in a complete command of the ancient tongues he held a position of unassailable importance in the learned world. He saw, as time went on, how rare so thorough a knowledge as his own was becoming. Though its value had already been challenged, he had no reason to expect retreat from a standard so firmly fixed. His were still, and long would be, the foundation studies in American higher education. When Dickinson College employed a Professor of Mathematics who was as poor a classicist as Ross was a mathematician, an observer noted that "each regarded the other as a very ignorant man." [37]

An academic specialist in this day was seen as an oddity, and James Ross was regarded by the public around him as a creature of childlike, but endearing, simplicity. By the same token, this may explain his occasional displays of professional impatience and his failure to identify himself firmly with any of the smaller communities in which he lived. He was keenly aware not only of the respect, but of the remuneration, due him. Indeed, our first professor had not only a full sense of professional standing, but an immediate concern for what we now term "the economic status of the profession." We may be sure that he had come to the Carlisle school with a clear understanding as to his control over tuition fees up to a stipulated sum. At the College, he watched these matters and was not backward in bringing them to the attention of the Board of Trustees:

Gentlemen,

Permit me briefly to observe, that it affords me much satisfaction to find, that the money arising from tuition, & entrance since last meeting of your board, is fully adequate to the salary then voted me. That, if my past, & present services merit your approbation, I humbly entreat you will be pleased to grant such addition of salary as the present accession of students may easily admit, & your own good judgment may direct. Suffer me to observe, that a consciousness of services well-rewarded engages even the best of men to execute the trust reposed in them with alacrity, & unremitting punctuality.

James Ross. [38]

He gained his point, but when his salary began to run into arrears under financial pressures, he crisply resigned the post he had held so long. That was in 1792, and later changes of base show his insistence that his own evaluation of his services must be met. This attitude on the part of a teacher was not always well received. He was teaching in Harrisburg in 1795, where the *Oracle of Dauphin* announced his impending departure in a sourly contemptuous little item: "being offered two pistareens and a five-penny bit more in Franklin county." [39]

Such inflexibility is natural to a man constantly expounding and enforcing immutable rules of grammar and constantly sharing thought and word of the noblest sages of ancient times. It is said that Ross, listening to the arguments of counsel at a trial and hearing one of them state that there is no rule without an exception, was startled into denying the assertion in an audible tone, stating that, "Nouns of the second declension in *um*, are *always* of the neuter gender." [40] Here was an orderly life, but not a restricted one. He knew vast reaches of Latin poetry by heart and delighted in giving voice to them. A friend and fellow spirit of the poet Philip Freneau, he celebrated events of his own day in the stately ancient speech and rhythms. Like Freneau, he took a liberal view of national affairs. Under trustees dominated by conservative opinion here stood an admirer of Jefferson, a man to whom Andrew Jackson would shine as a Marcus Horatius or Scipio. Though the College's first president, Dr. Nisbet, was politically all to the right, his relationship with Ross was cordial. The two could talk freely together in the learned tongue and, happily, shared the same canons of Latin pronunciation. Nisbet is twice honored in Latin poems by Ross, and there is evidence that he first persuaded Ross to publish under his own name.[41] The Latin master brought out a dozen texts, beginning with his *Selectae e Profanis Scriptoribus Historiae.* His Latin Grammar of 1802 was in print as late as 1845. In addition, there were the poems in pamphlet and broadside, newspaper and magazine.

Ross had been a teacher since the 1760's, when he was apparently at the College of Philadelphia or its grammar school.[42] The master's degree awarded him by the College in 1775 was his first academic honor, to be followed by Princeton's M.A. in 1818.[43] In 1823 he received the LL.D. of Allegheny College, where he had been a member of the Board of Trustees since its founding. From 1801 to 1809 he had been at Lancaster, a conspicuous figure on the faculty of Franklin College. The other years were all spent in grammar schools or academies, the last as a private teacher of Latin and Greek in Philadelphia. There he was a faithful attendant at the First Presbyterian Church where he kept, in his pew in the gallery, a little reference shelf of the sacred writings in the two ancient tongues he loved, his own immediate link to an approaching immortality.[44]

He had come to Carlisle in 1780 to take charge of an established institution soon to advance in importance. Its trustees were now determined to put up a building on the lot they had acquired March 3, 1773, and indeed he may well have exacted a promise from them to do so. More, they would seek a broader church support than just the one congregation; and, following the example of Newark, they would petition to be permanently incorporated under a state charter. These matters, however, waited more than a year upon the rigors and uncertainties of war. In October, 1781, the Presbytery of Donegal met at Carlisle. To the south, Washington and Rochambeau held Yorktown in siege and exciting news was expected from day to day. On October 18 the trustees, headed by Colonel John Montgomery, declared their intention of incorporating the school, asked for a committee of visitors "to examine the same at least twice a year" and for six new trustees, ministers from Gettysburg, Mercersburg, Sherman's Valley, Rocky Spring—the whole wide boundaries of Donegal.[45] One can sense enthusiasm riding high in the proposal's prompt and hearty endorsement. Even as it was being voted, men were at work at the foundations of the "latin Schoolhouse," this part of the endeavor going forward under the management of John Creigh, himself a liberal subscriber to its cost.[46]

By November 26, Judge Creigh's accounts itemize "2 Quarts whiskey," evidence that the work was going briskly forward into the first spate of sharp cold weather. Come spring, a like entry (April 3, 1782), "5 Quarts & 1 pint Whisky a Raising Rafter," tells us that the roof was up, or nearly so. It was a two-storey building of the native brick, about twenty feet square, fronting on Liberty Alley.[47] The lot was 60 feet in width and 240 back to Pomfret Street. This gave plenty of room, and relieved the Pomfret Street neighbors of the hazards and annoyances of a schoolhouse close to their windows and kitchen gardens. There it stood, and the next step would be to secure it by charter to posterity forever. This was entrusted to Colonel Montgomery, now a member of the state legislature, by which the act of incorporation must be passed.

John Montgomery had stood upon the forefront of resistance to Britain but was in no sense a radical. Temperate and steady, he stood with James Wilson, John Dickinson and their like. As Whitfield Bell has characterized him, "Subversion of the American ruling class was no part of his program, and his unvarying attitudes toward levelling demands were contempt and anger."[48] Even through his execrably labored letters one can still discern what his friend Sharp Delaney called Montgomery's "passionate honesty."[49] He was a conservative in an age when conservatism still had its forward-looking affirmations, and one of these, close to church and community in his thinking, was the Latin school at Carlisle. Elected to the Assembly in this October of 1781, the Colonel was at odds with the party defending the state's radical constitution, and at odds also with most of his fellow Presbyterians, its ardent supporters. A swing to the right had brought him in, and a swing to the left would take him out a year later.

In the meantime, he was in Philadelphia ready to present his bill; and ready also, it must be inferred, to interest well-to-do gentlemen in the new foundation as a cause deserving their financial support. This school had a building of two rooms, and space for more. Carlisle was to have an academy with a full curriculum—"on a broad bottom," in the pleasant phrase then current. So it was that he brought the subject forward one summer day in 1782 at a gathering on the porch of William Bingham, reputedly the richest man in America. It was another of the gentlemen there, however, who responded instantly and warmly to his theme, and the conversation went on for a long time, intimately between the two.

The Colonel was well acquainted with Dr. Benjamin Rush, in whose office his son, William, had served his medical apprenticeship a few years before. The Doctor was one of those men who, giving his attention to a topic, at once endow it with importance—a straight and slender, energetic figure, high forehead, aquiline nose, a long sharp chin and firm small mouth with the outjutting lower lip of a man who speaks much and with vehemence. He rarely smiled, but his large blue eyes had a captivating intensity, and sometimes an urgent benevolence, as he listened or spoke. He was a man of dignity and force, a friend to such good causes as the Colonel had in hand, an enemy of the political innovators of his time but, in his own way, an innovator himself of rare and intuitive daring. These two talked together at length there on Bingham's porch, the Doctor vigorously and relentlessly reshaping the other's simple vision of a school, invoking his religion, his patriotism, his "passionate honesty" to prove that the plea to the legislature, to the public, should not be for an academy of any sort, but for a college.

The Colonel, a reasonable man, was slow to accept this proposition. He had lived with the school for a long time. He knew its past proponents and the community it served. Perhaps also he sensed what travail would lie ahead for him in maintaining a college. To the Doctor there was no thought of that. He overturned every doubt. The community would have a greater fullness of growth and fame. Patrons of education would give more generously, investors in frontier lands as well, sure that the seeds they cast would bring a harvest of every sort of gain. But above all he was moved by the sense of victory in the air around them, of the long war won, of an emerging nation, a republic such as the world had not seen before, of the hazards of its future for which a continuing leadership must arise, informed and ready, an intellectual aristocracy.

All this, in the Doctor's mind, burned like an inner fire. For this he had said his say in Congress and signed the Declaration, marched with the army, served the sick in camp and hospital, labored with the human wreckage after battle. For this he had been denouncing that state constitution of the "Furious Whigs," and for this in time he would take a leading part in the formation of new constitutions, state and national. To Dr. Rush the seven long years of war were only the brief beginning of the American Revolution. The great deeds lay ahead. In the modest proposal of this pious, simple backwoods soldier he had found one element of that future, at hand, alive, needing only to be transformed to meet the larger view.

Now, as ever, his mind leapt forward toward vast fulfillments. They must be achieved "by natural means," by men steadily working out the will of God. Education would be their instrument. "Civilization, human knowledge and liberty must first pervade the globe," he wrote. "They are the heralds of religion. . . . Christians should endeavor to cultivate the peaceful dispositions which the millenium is to introduce into the mind, and daily repeat in their prayers, 'Thy kingdom come.' " [50]

In this spirit, on Bingham's porch, plans for the school were abandoned, and plans for the college begun. It would be stormy from the start. Educators and clergymen would oppose, the Doctor defend, protest, attack. Tempers would rise to fever heat and peaceful dispositions disappear in the swirl of benevolence and bitterness. So also within the institution itself high and harsh emotions would live on in counteraction—the sweetness of benign John Dickinson counterpoised by the startling acerbity of Nisbet, his close friend, and the contention between faculty and trustees echoing on beyond their time. Yet to Dr. Rush, after twenty years of travail and concern, the thought of that first long talk together would still bring its renewal of tenderness and faith, turning again to Montgomery with reminder and reassurance:

> Bingham's porch may wear away, but the ideas conceived on it by two of the trustees will have their full accomplishment, and Dickinson College will one day be a source of light and knowledge to the western parts of the United States. [51]

C'est dans le gouvernement républicain que l'on a besoin de toute la puissance de l'éducation.

Montesquieu, *De l'Esprit des Lois,* 1748

The country which their wisdom and valour had rescued from external domination was now to be improved in its internal resources .... Among these thousand objects of attention and deliberation, the education of youth claimed and was admitted to a distinguished plane.

"A Sketch of the Rise, Progress and Present State of Dickinson College," *Port Folio,* 1811

4

THE CHARTER

THE full-length portraits of Dr. Rush in poses chosen by him-self—Peale's of 1783, Sully's of 1812—show him as a philos-opher at ease among his books. The earlier gives the titles of many: not only basic medical works such as Sydenham, on which the Doctor's practice was based, but a Bible (in French), Butler's *Analogy of Religion, Natural and Revealed, to the Con-stitution and Course of Nature,* Pascal's *Pensées,* Thomas Reid's *Inquiry into the Human Mind,* James Beattie's *Essay on Truth,*[1] Algernon Sidney on *Government* and Sir William Temple's wide-ranging works. There they are, within easy reach, while the Doctor himself is composing a lecture, his pen poised over the words, "Sec. 29. We come now, Gentlemen, to investigate the cause of earthquakes." This is Rush as he wished to be remem-bered, but the small portrait by Edward Savage gives us a better characterization, a face of smouldering vigor, with contentious mouth and implacable eyes, while the profiles in Sharples' pastel and the medal by Moritz Furst bring out the revelation of forehead, nose and chin.[2] In the medal, particularly, the beak-like nose is mercilessly revealed. Its reverse returns to the Doc-tor's posture toward posterity. It shows us a river winding from a great distance toward the sea. The name of his country home, "Sydenham," appears, and below it, on a rock, the words, "READ. THINK. OBSERVE."

Here was a philosopher who had come into this broad view out of the narrow, if warmly beating, heart of American New

Side Presbyterianism. He had been born and bred in it, graduating from Princeton in 1760 while still in his fourteenth year, a medical student after that, then a traveller and student abroad, taking his M.D. at the University of Edinburgh, elected Professor of Chemistry at the College of Philadelphia at the age of twenty-three, and now America's best-known physician and most successful teacher of medical science. His thinking had far outgrown any dogmatic partisanship, but the foundation laid in childhood remained—that intimate awareness of the love of God and that passionate impulse to reach the heart of its mystery. The evangelism absorbed in childhood had enlarged his study of medicine into a search for the elemental unity of God and Nature. He was to find it in Bishop Butler's *Analogy* and, even more appealingly presented, in the *Observations on Man* of David Hartley, a physician like himself, a devout churchman also, pastoral in his concern for others.[3]

The unifying doctrine which Dr. Rush drew from these sources and extended in his own writings and lectures enlarged his sense of personal mission. He acknowledged no segments or boundaries to Christian duty—medicine, politics, social reform, education, all were one. He had never an instant of self-doubt. It was all part of his success as a physician and of his power in persuasion everywhere. Later, in the terrible yellow fever epidemics which he fought with such selfless, noble courage, he remained oblivious to the fact that public acceptance of his simple formula of bleeding and purging was being reflected dramatically in a rising death rate.[4] In this way, often with simplified, readily acceptable theory, he did battle with evil on all fronts, a hard-riding champion of all humanity, opening the first free dispensary in America, heading movements for the abolition of slavery, for penal reform, temperance, for a more enlightened, more effective political leadership, and here, at the very heart of it all, for education.

He saw education as a preparation for life, not the mere polish of gentility. That was American thinking, and William Smith had established it in his curriculum of balanced culture and utilitarianism at the College of Philadelphia in 1756.[5] There on Bingham's porch, impelled as were others by the urgency of an imminent new era, Rush was afire to head the coming educational advance. To him, the Revolution had only just begun. The war was only "the first act of the great drama." [6] Stability and progress must be secured for all time—schools in every county, colleges and a national university for the elite. To his political enemies American democracy meant equal vote and influence for every man. To Rush it meant rule by an elite drawn from the whole. This was as much God's way as he himself was God's instrument. To Montgomery he writes, with the inspiration of Bingham's Porch fresh upon them both, "Let us be active, my friend, in rescuing the state from the hands of tyrants, fools and traitors. Heaven has committed a great and important trust to our care." [7] And, after the founding of the College, more coolly to John Jay, "This College is at present wholly in the hands of gentlemen of liberal minds—men who have been uniformly friendly to the Union of the States & the power of Congress, and opposed to those romantic ideas of government which are equally destructive of liberty & republicanism." [8] Prophet and seer, he foresaw the millenium—a Christian world of wisdom and holiness.[9] "Our school of the prophets," he would call his college at Carlisle, dedicating it to "the extension of the Kingdom of Christ and the empire of reason and science in our country." [10]

To snatch up John Montgomery's plans for a school and transform it into a college instead was typical of this versatile and volatile mind. He created a hopeful framework, sure that God and the saints would join with him to fill it in—an administrative procedure not unique in academic history. [11] Dr. William Smith was then in Maryland, changing a school into a college, winning strong financial and political support, projecting a broad educational system. Smith, the heavy-set, heavy-drinking cleric and career educator, was a very different man from the lean, temperate, intense Rush, latent tuberculosis in his body, his brain fired by a faith in its divine motivation. Contrast to these the years of planning and effort in which their fellow educational reformer, Thomas Jefferson, built his University of Virginia.

Rush, inspired opportunist, had seized upon that grammar school, an essential adjunct of almost every American college, a foundation stone. It was a Presbyterian school, and his first thought was to keep it firmly so. On September 3, 1782, soon after Bingham's Porch, he composed his "Hints for Establishing a College at Carlisle," to be circulated within his own denomination. [12] The faculty, he wrote, would be solidly Presbyterian, operating upon an income from the state. He would soon learn that to gain the second provision he must abandon the first—or at least cast over it a veil of equivocation. He brought forward the "nearly central" situation of Carlisle, the low cost of living there (a major plea for the school in 1770), and a statement, later to be disputed, that "the village of Carlisle is one of the most healthy spots in the state." It would help to bring Pennsylvania's German population into the national culture, a cause which was to involve him in the founding of Franklin College at Lancaster a few years later.

The Doctor's "Hints," intended as a sound and high appeal, drew stormy opposition. The Presbyterians, he had written, had won too large a place in government for their own good. Let them turn instead to building a greater promise for the future in education. The new college in the west would promote "one common center of union." Princeton balked at this. Old Side, New Side jealousies grew warm again. Was the Doctor with one party or the other, or creating a nursery for his own roving theology, said to be tainted with the heresy of universal salvation? His "Hints" gave a harder jolt to the Philadelphia school. "As an act of Justice," let the Presbyterians withdraw from the University of the State of Pennsylvania, from which Dr. Smith and its Episcopalian founders had been ejected in 1779, and let its old charter be restored.

October elections came. Presbyterian votes, strongly in support of the radical state constitution of 1776, defeated Montgomery for Assembly, where he was to have introduced a bill for the college charter and endowment. It was all another sad failure, in the Doctor's view, to be "wise for posterity." To Montgomery he wrote, "I fear our scheme for a college over Susquehannah will be retarded by its wanting your support in the house." However, Mr. Dickinson, who was being urged for President of the Supreme Executive Council, that is, governor of the state, was their friend both in politics and in the college plan. He had promised liberal gifts to endowment. "I intended to have proposed to you to call the college after him and his worthy lady, JOHN AND MARY'S College." [13] By November 5 Dickinson's election seemed certain, while Montgomery's friends "will push you hard for a seat in Congress . . . . Don't forget the child of our affections, 'John and Mary's College.' Adieu." [14]

"John and Mary's College," with its implication of a royal status equal to that of William and Mary, was too much for the gentle and retiring "Pennsylvania Farmer," but he agreed to the use of his name; and now Montgomery, attending Congress in Philadelphia, is reporting back to Colonel Magaw at Carlisle on the forward sweep of affairs:

> . . . we are making great Progress in taking subscriptions for a college at Carlisle. I believe that we will be able to raise near 5000 £ in this city our Presdt has subscribed 600 £ in Land. Mr. Wilson gives 300 £ pattaned Land above subury, Mr. Bingham 400 £ specie, Blair Mc-Clanaghan will give us 300 d pattaned Land, many others will give Largely I think that it is time to pettion the Assembly for a Charter. I wish you woud Endeavor to promote one at Carlisle. We shall meet with opposition but I am perswaded that we will be able to carrie it into Effect . . . .[15]

Opposition there was indeed. To look first at the broad view—education as the educators saw it—the state of the existing colleges was desperate. They needed support, not competition. The war had been a disastrous interruption and now they must virtually be founded anew. In New York, King's College was preparing to reopen as Columbia after eight years' abeyance. The trustees at Princeton were looking for funds with which to repair their hall and reestablish normal classes, and some years would go by before they could do it. Rush was aware of John Witherspoon's fears, but hoped they would be "restrained by the feelings of ancient friendship," as, in a good Christian spirit, they were. [16] In Philadelphia, the University's life had been precarious, for all its endowment from the state. Here, without denominational support, there was more reason than at Princeton for alarm. Bleak years were ahead, with competition from the new colleges, Dickinson and Franklin, prolonging the slow recovery. [17]

A closer view shows the heart of the opposition. The Presbyterian Church had long been a formidable political power, and Dr. Rush was upsetting a delicate balance within an organization long torn by dissension and still living with hair-triggered tempers and doctrines. Nassau Hall had been the New Side college to which Old Side and New Side schools were sending students in a spirit of newly and narrowly adjusted accomodation. Now this doctor was admonishing the society as a whole to forget politics and concentrate upon education, while at the same time transforming a Church-sponsored school into a new and rival college, apparently dedicated to his own uncontrolled and uncontrollable thinking.

The tall and handsome mathematician, John Ewing, Provost of the University of the State of Pennsylvania, ridiculed Dr. Rush's proposal as "the moon-shine project." Right beside him stood George Bryan, political leader of the Presbyterian faction: "Believe me, sir, it is a scheme of dividing the Presbyterian interest, and preparatory to transferring back the University to the narrow foundation which it formerly stood on . . . ." [18] Judge Bryan had been a member of Gilbert Tennent's Second Presbyterian Church, but at Tennent's death in 1764 had changed to the First Church, Old Side headquarters. He was an alert, well-read Irishman, a liberal, practical man, who had headed the left-wing Constitutionalist Party throughout the war. John Ewing was his pastor. He had taken a leading part in the act of 1779 creating the University, with Ewing at its head. Throughout all this, Rush had been his vigorous opponent. To strike at the heart of this new scheme, Ewing and Bryan wrote to General Armstrong and to others at Carlisle, with cogent arguments as to why there should be no change in the status of the school. Thus we find old John Armstrong, Carlisle's leading citizen, responding to Rush with a measured and realistic view in favor of "moderate academies with not less than two professors" for the back country until community development gave proof of need and support for something better; in short, arguing for the school as it had been under Makinly and Creigh. [19] To this he added the fear of splitting the Presbyterians once more by setting up a rival to the College of New Jersey. Strong voices among the clergy of Cumberland, led by Robert Cooper and John Craighead of the churches at Middle

Spring and Rocky Spring, also spoke out against the plan. These New Siders had long regarded John Steel's congregation and school as a source of trouble and were not of a mind to see more.

Rush countered with friendly urgency and veiled threat for some, with outright fury for others. To have accused him of "a scheme of dividing the Presbyterian interest" was as impolitic as it was untrue. The Doctor was a partisan of ideas, not factions. He retaliated with charges of coarse political maneuvering in the establishment of the University four years before. He had since become so far resigned to the new order as to accept a professorship on the medical faculty, and from this intramural position was now denouncing rascality and demanding a change. It was in this way that the founding of Dickinson College became an act of retribution for what had happened at the University. "God," as Benjamin Rush would declare when his charter was at last enacted into law, "has frowned upon the impious act." [20]

Dr. Ewing was deriding the "moon-shine project" as early as April, 1783. [21] In June, he received at his house a man strongly recommended by mutual friends in Europe, one who was to stand briefly in that pale lunar glow. The Rev. William Hazlitt, a graduate of the University of Glasgow, was a person of great erudition and charm, a Presbyterian minister who had gone far beyond the catechism in his thinking and is remembered now as one of the founders of New England Unitarianism. He was resolute yet never obtrusive in his independence. Accompanied by his wife and two small children (one of whom, then aged five, was to figure in literature as essayist and critic), he had thrown himself, almost penniless, into the arms of America, land of liberty. Americans responded warmly, among them both Ewing and Rush. Rush offered to find him pupils for a school, promised him "great things" beyond this, and saw in him one well fitted "to cultivate a rational mode of thinking, and to disperse that darkness which overspread the land." [22] Ewing went farther. He dated Hazlitt for a sermon at New London in July, and, finding him well received in that center of Old Side orthodoxy, sent him on in August to Carlisle, with the hope that the vacant pulpit there might receive him, and with the suggestion that he might also become head of the projected college—it being anticipated that church and college would share talent and expense in this way.

Thus Ewing would help a learned and worthy colleague, of whom Rush approved, and gain an influence of his own over the college, should college there be. He would also save Rush's rumored Scottish candidate the long journey into a hazardous milieu. Later, he would be obliged to declare his ignorance of Hazlitt's unorthodoxy. Of that danger, however, one other Philadelphia clergyman had been instantly aware. This was, in Hazlitt's accurate phrase, "the zealous Dr. Duffield" of the Second Presbyterian Church.[23] George Duffield had dashed off a warning letter to his erstwhile flock, setting General Armstrong and other stalwarts firmly against the candidate. Hazlitt retreated from the scene in September, at about the time of the enactment of the college charter. Had he remained a fortnight more with the friends he had made at Carlisle (or so Ewing assured him) he "would have been accepted on his own terms" by both church and college.[24]

The "moon-shine project" became a legal reality on September 9, 1783. Lawyer James Wilson had drafted the charter, though all its essential provisions must be attributed to the Doctor.[25] Passage had been assured by substituting a statement on financial resources already in hand for the still-cherished idea of a state endowment, and by a declaration of independence from sectarian control. Forty charter trustees were named, men carefully chosen by Rush to represent all power groups and regions of the Commonwealth. A majority, however, were Presbyterians, insuring the continuing predominance of that affiliation.[26] In this way, the College became the first church-related institution of higher education in Pennsylvania, setting a pattern of mingled freedom and alliance for itself and others.[27]

Of the forty trustees, only nine were needed for a quorum, thus assuring control by those living near the institution. Twelve were from the Carlisle area, among them almost all the trustees of the old Grammar School, including General Armstrong and the Rev. Dr. Cooper, both of whom had been won over to the college plan. Armstrong's approval had been almost a condition of success and Rush had worked vigorously for it, topping his

Benjamin Rush. Pastel by James Sharples.

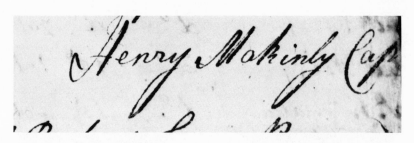

Autograph of Henry Makinly, as Captain, Twelfth Regiment, Pennsylvania Line.

THE TRUSTEE OATH, 1783

We, the trustees of Dickinson College in the state of Pennsylvania, having severally sworn or affirmed, "that we will be true and faithfull to the Commonwealth of Pennsylvania; and that we will not directly or indirectly do any act or thing prejudicial or injurious to the Constitution or Government thereof as established by the Convention" and "that the state of Pennsylvania is, and of right ought to be a free, sovereign and independent state—and that we do forever renounce and refuse all allegiance, subjugation and obedience to the King or Crown of Great Britain—and that we never have since the Declaration of Independence directly or indirectly assisted, abetted or in any wise countenanced the King of Great Britain, his generals, fleets or armies or their adherents in their claims upon these United States, and that we have ever since the Declaration of Independence thereof demeaned ourselves as faithful citizens and subjects of this or some one of the United States—and that we will at all times maintain and support the freedom and sovereignty and independence thereof" do agreeably to the Direction of the Act of the General Assembly of the Commonwealth of Pennsylvania entitled "An Act for the Establishment of a College at the Borough of Carlisle, in the County of Cumberland, in the State of Pennsylvania" hereunto respectively subscribe our names—

argument with what a college could do for land values, and the need for new centers of population, rivaling Philadelphia. [28] It was a factor few could overlook. Educational ideals and land speculation were to be partners in the American mania for college founding. It came out in legislative debate on the charter, as assemblyman the Rev. Joseph Montgomery, cleric and judge from Dauphin County, pled hard in committee and very nearly succeeded in changing the site from Carlisle to what Rush, his brother-in-law, was pleased to call "the sickly banks of the Susquehannah." The proposals of John Harris for laying out the city of Harrisburg were waiting for action later in that session, and there was a feeling already in the air that this town-to-be by the broad river should become the capital of the state—perhaps also of the nation. [29] Joseph Montgomery's name had been on the list of charter trustees, but was hurriedly stricken from it in reprisal for these "insidious maneuvers." [30]

So far so good. On Monday, September 15, fifteen of the forty met at Mr. Dickinson's home, took the prescribed oath of office as laid down in the charter, and addressed themselves to the tasks of finance and organization. On Thursday they met again at Dr. Rush's, with a final meeting on Friday at Independence Hall, to lend conspicuous dignity to the final session. Colonel Montgomery was not with them, Congress having adjourned to Princeton after the mutiny of the Pennsylvania Line. Mr. Dickinson had been elected President of the Board, and chaired its deliberations with that gentle urbanity and pleasant, soft-voiced modulation of tone which his friends would always remember with affection. [31] In the business in hand, centering as can be imagined upon money, he, as the largest donor, could turn to the others with ease and authority. His own gifts, however, were by no means sufficient to carry the whole operation, and in the face of this they voted to seek funds from individuals and from private groups, and to petition the state for a continuing endowment such as the University enjoyed. The hope was to raise at least £10,000 in gifts, topped by a state grant of £500 a year. One can discern the presence of wishful thinking, so often a weakness of inexperienced development officers. Faculty was also discussed in optimistic terms. It must be headed by a man of such eminence that his name alone would guarantee a respectable student body. A new building must also be in prospect, and the absent John Montgomery was commissioned to inquire into the purchase of land and the erection of an edifice. Having discussed this and other necessary business, they adjourned to meet at Carlisle on the 6th of April following.

Far to the west, at York, on that same September 15, the Rev. John Black, charter trustee, scratched out a letter to Dr. Rush, giving him his first word of the presence of Mr. Hazlitt at Carlisle. Mr. Black was a lively young man who found relaxation from the duties of a large pastorate in playing popular airs on the flute, and he handled his subject with humor.

"We were amused here of late," he wrote, "with a curious maneuvre of Dr. Ewings. He was so very thoughtful as to provide a Principal for our College, upon the supposition that the *unreasonable* scheme (as he was pleased to call it) should take place. By letters to three of the principal inhabitants of Carlisle, he strongly recommended a certain Mr. Haslet, as a minister of the gospel, &c. Unhappily for the doctor, he thereby disgusted some of his warmest political friends, particularly General Armstrong. The most discerning people there look upon Mr. Haslet as a thorough-paced Socinian." [32]

Had Ewing's ruse succeeded, it would indeed have taken Dickinson College upon a wider orbit that its founders planned. However, as an English friend observed of Hazlitt, "he would have been a wretched schoolmaster . . . for by teaching his students invariably to tell the truth and align their actions and beliefs he would have disqualified them from making their way in the world." [33] Hazlitt retreated to Boston before returning to England. Duffield brought charges against Ewing in presbytery—promoting a heretic. They were not sustained, but it was a warning to Rush to be wary in looking overseas for a college head.

Others were looking overseas. Mr. Bingham, on whose porch all this had begun, was off to England, where he had agreed to solicit funds. John Witherspoon and General Reed were also going soon on behalf of the College of New Jersey; and others for Columbia, Dartmouth, Brown. It seems rather touchingly naive that, at war's end, Americans should turn again to the mother country for sustenance. They were to be uniformly unsuccessful. Rush was urgently canvassing his British friends, but only his pleas for books, in which he stressed that even the "sweepings" of their libraries would be acceptable in "this nursery of humanity," brought a response. [34] Now, however, while hopes were running high, Nassau Hall held a glitteringly auspicious commencement to mark its revival after the war. This was on September 24, 1783, with George Washington in the audience, along with the Marquis de la Luzerne and an array of the gentlemen of the Congress. His Excellency suffered noticable embarrassment when young Ashbel Green, the valedictorian, turned to pronounce a eulogy upon him as "the man whose gallant sword taught the tyrants of the earth to fear oppression and opened an asylum for the virtuous and free," but afterward responded with a gift of fifty guineas. [35] There Colonel Montgomery heard a degree of Doctor of Divinity awarded in absentia to Charles Nisbet, minister of the congregation of Montrose in Scotland, as a cleric of great learning who had dared to support the American cause.

On Bingham's porch, at his very first concept of the idea now coming to fruition, Dr. Rush had recollected the name and fame of Nisbet, whom Witherspoon, fifteen years before, had so warmly urged in lieu of himself to head the college at Princeton. [36] Witherspoon had been a solid tower of success in college, church and state, boldly and heartily American from his first landing on our shore. Here was a man who might do as well or better, a name and a light of learning to transform Colonel Montgomery's grammar school into a collegiate institution of the first order. Here was a man who had spoken out for America and suffered for it, a man who possessed such a wealth of erudition that he was known as "the walking library," a man who spiced wisdom with wit, was esteemed for sound piety and who, as an adopted son of the new republic, would spread his brilliance everywhere. He was well known to old Dr. John Erskine of Edinburgh, long a correspondent of Rush. His friendship with Witherspoon would quiet that gentleman's fears of the new college and insure a cooperation between the two institutions, of which Witherspoon's willingness to grant the D.D. was auspicious evidence.

Its charter provided for a "Principal" of Dickinson College, not a "President," the title in general use in American colleges, a divergence in which one can see again the persuasiveness of Rush at work, his eye on Nisbet. The head of the University of Edinburgh had always been its "Principal." Charles Nisbet, son of a poor Scottish schoolmaster, had entered the University in 1752, studied there for two years, and then for six years more at its Divinity Hall, completing the course with his license to preach in 1760 at the age of twenty-four—a stocky, vigorous young man known for wide learning and sharp wit. He had entirely supported himself throughout, by frugality, private tutoring, and by writing anonymous articles for the popular press. He seemed to read everything he could find, and remember everything he read. He was "skilled in Hebrew, including the Chaldee, Greek, Latin, French, Italian, Spanish, German, and probably Erse." [37] He could repeat most of Homer by heart, and in English most of Cowper, of whose poems he was particularly fond. As a student he had bought books and parts of them in sheets, shipped up from London as wrapping paper, which may be one reason for the diversity of his abstruse knowledge. His friends could not mention an author with whom he was unfamiliar. The people of Montrose, a well-to-do and highly desirable charge, found him the kindliest of pastors, but one who, after a time, was inclined to take a caustic view of their community as a whole, being overheard to remark, for instance, that if the wall around the insane hospital must be extended it might as well circle the entire town. [38] His position was sustained by some highly-placed friends, notably the Earls of Buchan and of Leven, both of whom were sympathetic to the American cause and friends of Benjamin Rush. Lady Leven, who had been Wilhelmina Nisbet, was a close friend of the pious Selina, Countess of Huntingdon, and both of these ladies were friends of the minister of Montrose.

At those first meetings of the Dickinson College trustees, there had been general approval of Nisbet's nomination, could he be persuaded to come, and on December 5, 1783, Dr. Rush wrote to Montrose to sound out the candidate upon his probable unanimous election at the meeting in the spring. Here he painted a glowing picture of American life, its prosperity and future: "destined by heaven to exhibit to the world the perfection which the mind of man is capable of receiving from the combined operation of liberty, learning, and the gospel upon it." And of the trustees, "I have taken great pains to direct their attention and votes to you. From the situation and other advantages of that College, it must soon be the first in America. It is the key to our western world." [39]

Success or failure now hung, as all believed, upon whether a famous man of learning such as Nisbet would cross the Atlantic to head the work. [40] Nisbet was at first all eagerness. [41] But even before the trustees had received his reply, others had moved to dampen his ardor. "Insidious maneuvers" are seen once more. Sometime in March, 1784, at the Harp and Crown tavern in Philadelphia, we find Dr. John Ewing in private conversation with Mr. James Tod, a Scottish schoolmaster who had been only a few months in America, had an acquaintance with Dr. Nisbet and was at this time teaching school in a room provided for him by Ewing. Mr. Tod agreed to write a warning letter to Montrose, setting forth the objections to the new college and the manifold hazards surrounding it. [42]

Soon after this, on what Rush called "the great and solemn 6th of April," the trustees met for the first time at Carlisle, fifteen of them. Both Rush and Dickinson were there, along with two former opponents of the venture, The Rev. Robert Cooper, with his pleasant, sympathetic air, and old General Armstrong, stern and proud, his approval confirmed by a $1,000 subscription. Three colonels of the late war were present, Hartley, Magaw and Montgomery. A Carlisle lawyer and a Carlisle physician, Stephen Duncan and Samuel A. McCoskry, both would be long associated with the College. Six more Presbyterian clergymen completed the group: smiling John Black; Alexander Dobbin; John King; the two Linns, John and William; and Samuel Waugh. Dobbin, the Scot who had been teaching a school at Gettysburg since 1773, could be counted upon to send students across South Mountain to the College. King of Mercersburg, out where John Steel had labored and fought, had been a teacher too, as full of solid logic as Steel had been, and driving it home in a slow, hoarse voice. At high noon they all marched in procession to the Episcopal church on the square to

hear, with ladies and gentlemen of the village, Mr. Black's sermon on "The Utility of Seminaries of Learning," his text from
Saint Paul, "For knowledge puffeth up, but charity edifieth." [43]
This done, the fifteen sat down with other guests at John Montgomery's table. Serious business began at five at the courthouse,
Mr. Dickinson opening the session with a reaffirmation of purpose and a promise to support by every means in his power this
new effort to improve "the character of the man, the citizen
and the Christian." [44]

That evening and the following day were alive with plans
and business. Dr. Nisbet was elected Principal, and James Ross
Professor of Languages. So far, Mr. Ross had been collecting
tuitions and, in effect, running the school entirely as an operation of his own. Dr. Rush brought forward the name of the Rev.
Robert Davidson of the University of Pennsylvania to teach
history and geography if, as anticipated, he should be acceptable also as pastor of the Presbyterian church. He suggested that
William Linn might be assistant pastor and a professor. Beyond
that, Rush averred, recruiting should be from other denominations, to avoid the charge of sectarianism. [45] He had Erasmus
Middleton, an Anglican minister, in mind for moral philosophy, logic and metaphysics, with the idea that he might fill
the Episcopal pulpit at Carlisle on the same half-salary terms.
Against this John Montgomery stood out stoutly. The Colonel
wanted no more foreigners. Americans were good enough for
him, and besides, there was a shadow of doubt on Middleton's
orthodoxy as there had been on Hazlitt's: "He may be a very
proper person but I woud not wish to have any that is in the
least tincktured with methoditizem." [46]

This discussion reflects the state of the College funds,
which was low. At this meeting, £257/15/0 was reported in
cash, £1,382/17/6 in certificates, and land to the value of
£1,200; and Mr. Bingham's letter on the "present circumstances
and disposition of the people" in England closed that door. [47]
All their efforts had brought in far less than would be needed,
far less than William Smith had raised so readily for Washington
College, but Dr. Rush had no thought of letting money take
precedence over action. On the morning of the 7th the group
toured "Washingtonburg," or, more popularly, "The Works,"

the old army ordnance post just outside the village. Here was a chance to get a campus ready-made, by gift or easy purchase from the federal government. It was agreed that the buildings, with almost no alteration, would serve admirably, and to make application for them. [48]

Rush and Dickinson, as a committee, submitted their design for a seal, a matter which, as the ultimate symbol of corporate existence, appealed strongly to the Doctor. This was the last meeting of the Board which Dickinson would attend, and Rush would be present at only one more. These two were, in fact, turning over the immediate management of their creation to local trustees and the community. The community, appropriately, topped off the whole affair with a banquet at James Pollack's tavern. Pollack, a prosperous landlord, told Rush how thirty years before he had cut logs for the first house built in Carlisle. Carlisle was moving forward, and fully appreciative of the new distinction thrust upon it by the President of the State of Pennsylvania and the patriotic Philadelphia doctor. [49]

A fortnight later, President of the Board Dickinson sent Dr. Nisbet formal notice of his election as the Principal of Dickinson College. Rush, knowing in what level terms this missive would be couched, followed at once with a summons of his own, all eloquence, and "rising," as Lyman Butterfield has described it, "to one of those O! altitudo's that he employed with remarkable success in obtaining presidents for colleges." [50] He pictured a newborn infant, cradled at Carlisle:

> To *you*, sir, it lifts up its feeble hands. To *you*, to *you* alone (under God), it looks for support and nourishment. Your name is now in everybody's mouth. The Germans attempt to pronounce it in broken English. The natives of Ireland and the descendants of Irishmen have carried it to the western counties. The Juniata and Ohio rivers have borne it on their streams through every township of the state that lies beyond Carlisle. Our saints pray for you as the future apostle of the Church in this part of the world. Our patriots long to thank you for defending the cause of America at a time when and in a place where she had few friends. And our statesmen wish to see our youth formed by you for the various duties they owe to the republic. I beg leave to inform you that the trustees of the College do not expect that £ 50-0 0 sterling [already sent as an advance] will defray the expenses of the passage of your family to America. It was upon this account

that they voted that your salary should commence on the day of your embarkation. [51]

A generous salary had been voted, but Rush, all unaware of the machinations of Ewing and Tod, must needs add his loftier persuasion as well, and, it must be affirmed, in words which came straight from his own burning idealism. This was truly his child. He had been told that Nisbet had a fear of the sea and he sought to calm it, taking his text from Matthew, 14:27: "It is I; be not afraid."

> Remember the words of the Saviour—"*It is I*"—"I, who govern both winds and waves. I, who have qualified you with so many gifts and graces for the station to which you are called. I, who by my Providence have made your name known and dear to the people of America. I, who have many people in that country to be enlightened and instructed, directly or indirectly, by you. I, who preside over the whole vineyard of my Church and, therefore, know best in what part of it to place the most skillful workmen. It is I, who call you to quit your native country and to spend the remainder of your days in that new world in which the triumphs of the Gospel shall ere long be no less remarkable than the triumphs of liberty. I have now done with ministers of my Providence. Washington and the Adamses have finished their work. Hereafter I shall operate on the American States chiefly by the ministers of my grace." [52]

At Montrose, therefore, with both warning and allure before him, Dr. Nisbet was in an anguish of indecision. He had been in touch with Witherspoon who was guardedly discouraging. Lady Leven thought Ewing and Tod might be in the right. The Earl of Buchan frankly opposed his going. [53] From Princeton, Witherspoon's son-in-law, Samuel Stanhope Smith, was answering his harassed appeal for information on American educational ways and prospects in a straightforward way. [54] If Rush had been overpersuasive, Nisbet could never complain that Smith had misinformed him. On his own part, over the lure of high salary and high social eminence, he worried lest a trustee board of forty, of different sects, might never agree, and that it seemed "but an *indigested* scheme." [55] Finally, he sent Rush the gist of Tod's letter and demanded an explanation.

Here, since Tod had mentioned Ewing's name, Dr. Rush

saw their full perfidy exposed. For the man who endeavors first to create the appearance of success and then to endow it with reality, an attempt to burst the bubble at the outset is just so much more ruthless an injury and affront. On September 29, 1784, a long letter, apparently drafted by Rush and signed by Dickinson, full of reassurance and deploring those who had given "an unfavorable and invidious account of our undertaking," went back to Montrose. [56]

Then, a month later, another and more terrible blow fell. John Dickinson, consulting only his own conscience, wrote the newly-elected Principal "to request that you will not think of coming to America . . . untill I can assure you that the prospect is much more favorable." Their plans were being "exceedingly discouraged and impeded." The charter might even be repealed. He sent a copy to Rush with the hope that, "Considering all Circumstances, you will approve . . . . Upon the whole, I have obeyed the authoritative Dictates, according to my judgment, of Honor and Justice." [57]

Thus the Doctor, moving to meet Ewing's attack, encountered "treachery" at the very heart of his inner circle. He responded with cold fury. Honor and justice, to his mind, were with the College only, and only madness or villainy elsewhere. Dickinson had just made a handsome gift to Princeton. Worse, as governor, he was ex officio a trustee of Ewing's University—a foothold in the camp of the enemy. Rush, who had so extolled Dickinson's character, now hinted that he had gotten his high office by bribery. [58] It was his way of striking back. Threatened by thunderbolts, assailed by protest and plea, Dickinson agreed to write a second letter as antidote to the first, to be reinforced by one from the trustees as a body.

This left the Doctor's anger free to play once more on Ewing, whose career, as his eye surveyed it now, amounted only to a succession of acts of infamy. The transformation of the College of Philadelphia into the University of the State of Pennsylvania, 1779, had been but the first step in Ewing's conspiracy to make himself master of the entire educational system. Every shred of gossip was accepted and magnified. Of such a man the worst must be true. Rush had drawn the picture succinctly for Dr. Nisbet in a letter of August 27, 1784:

I will give you his portrait in a few words. In the vices of the heart he
has few equals. Revenge, envy, malice and falsehood rankle forever in
his bosom. But this is not all. He is deficient in outward morality. His
servant was fined a few weeks ago for driving his wagon on the Sabbath day, if not by his order, *certainly* by his permission. He has been
seen reeling in our streets. Don't be uneasy at reading these things. He
has brought no reproach by this conduct on our holy religion, for no
man at any one time of his life ever believed him to be a religious
man. [59]

Woe betide that moment when such emotions move from
private incubation into the cooler air of public attention. For
Dickinson College the experience came first on September 8,
1784, with an anonymous communication to the *Pennsylvania
Journal,* filling the whole of one page. The legislature at this
time was considering petitions protesting the act of November
27, 1779, "for altering or rather abolishing the COLLEGE
CHARTERS of this city," and the writer presented the history
of the founding of the University as a coup d'etat in which
Presbyterians had effected the removal of William Smith in an
attempt to gain control of the entire educational structure. At
the end he took note of the effort to dissuade Nisbet from
coming to Dickinson College, and quoted one key sentence
from Mr. Tod's letter: "Some time ago Dr. Smith and all the
Episcopal people were turned out of the College of Philadelphia
and the direction and management of it put into the hands of
the Presbyterians." Dr. Rush was making plain his belief that
the letter to Nisbet was Ewing's, signed by Tod. He put Ewing
in the position of confessing his own iniquity. One cannot imagine the Provost making such a statement but, with other parts
of the letter more surely ascribed to him, he would have trouble
denying it.

To drive the point solidly home, the *Journal* of September
11 contained another anonymous blast, nearly as long as the
first, reiterating the charges and adding others, such as the mis-
appropriation of charitable funds. Here Rush quoted at greater
length from the Tod letter and repeated the plaintive query in
which Dr. Nisbet had summarized his own predicament, "Who
can tell how soon the Episcopals may turn out the Presbyterians
at Carlisle." Having brought the matter to this climax, the article then concludes virtuously:

There may be *some mystery* in Dr. Ewing's not signing the letter in question, but of this I cannot judge. It does not seem credible to me that Dr. R____ is a person that would condescend to be the tool of any party, or that gentlemen of probity and reputation, should join in inviting a man who had never injured them, to a place that should prove ruinous to his family.

At the same time, the Doctor was writing to Montrose with personal warmth and opalescent urgency. A room in his house "goes by the name of 'Dr. Nisbet's room.' My little folks often mention your name, especially my *boys,* who have been taught to consider you their future master. Possibly this will be the last letter you will receive from me on the other side of the Atlantic. To the direction and protection of Heaven I commit you, till I take you by the hand on the peaceful shores of Pennsylvania. Adieu! Adieu!" [60] And to John Montgomery, "Go on with your collections. Get money—get it honestly if you can. But get money for our College."[61] His own appeals flowed out to friends at home and overseas. And again to Montgomery, who had begun once more to lose heart: "*Give over our College!* God forbid! . . . We *must* succeed . . . . We have overcome Mr. Dickinson's treachery." [62]

So they had. Nisbet would sail in the spring. But Ewing remained to be crushed and, with the turn of the year, cudgels were rattling yet again. "A Traveller," in the *Freeman's Journal,* February 9, 1785, assailed the character of Rush: "mischievous and implacable enemy . . . . A LIE is generally his instrument." Under his own name and in the more sedate *Pennsylvania Packet* of the same day, Ewing addressed his fellow citizens. He had been in the west on official business, surveying the boundaries of the state with David Rittenhouse. He now deplored the attacks made upon him in his absence and dealt as best he could with the matter of the Tod letter, specifically denying ever having stated that the Presbyterians had ejected the Episcopalians from the University.

Parry and counterblow came in the *Packet* of February 17, with Rush, over his own name, stating his case "TO THE CITIZENS OF PENNSYLVANIA." He pleaded the cause of his college, and gave his reasons for founding it in detail. It was "absolutely necessary to preserve liberty," and, situated so near the center of the state, would be "the best bulwark of the blessings obtained by the revolution." Largely Presbyterian it might be, but it had become so "without fraud or violence." From this oblique thrust he then struck directly at Ewing, a man of "such malignity of heart, and such an ingenuity in vice, as would make a man of feeling wish that he belonged to another species of beings."

Ewing's riposte was in the *Packet* of the next day. Rush struck back in the issue of March 2, calling upon all to witness "that you have been the AGGRESSOR in the controversy between us." The historian must be grateful for facts and insights gained from this ridiculous skirmishing, but it was the brilliant little lawyer and litterateur, Francis Hopkinson, who brought the whole down to earth in the gust of laughter it deserved. Phrases on the broad or narrrow bottom of an educational establishment had appealed irresistibly to his sense of humor, and his adroit summary of the whole affair silenced the combatants:

> The learned divine *hoists* the university, and exposing its naked skin, exclaims with admiration—"Oh charming! behold and see what a broad bottom is here!" Whereupon the physician immediately *hoists* *Dickenson college*, and with equal eloquence descants upon its narrow *bottom.*—"Look, says the divine, on this capacious disk—on the one side sits the *pope;* on the other side sits *Luther;* and see how snug *Calvin* lies between them both." [63]

The scene ends with Ewing flogging the "narrow bottom of poor *Carlisle,*" and Rush "the broad bottom of the university." From first to last it had been an affair such as any college president or public relations director of today would regard as totally calamitous. Coming at the very outset, with all hopes dependent upon both public and private aid, it was a disaster. Nor was there any restorative in sight, save only the high repute of the great scholar due to arrive from Scotland.

The Nisbets sailed from Greenock on April 23, 1785. At about the same time, responding to that thrifty plan for pastor-professorships, the church at Carlisle called Robert Davidson to be its shepherd. This, at least, held balm. He would succeed, mirabile dictu, in uniting the long-warring factions of this congregation; and while his career as an educator was not a distinguished one, he would also soften the divisive forces, potentially rancorous and explosive, within the College. He would serve the institution for twenty-four years, five of them (though he was denied the title) as its Principal. On his tomb in the Old Graveyard at Carlisle one reads, "A blessed peacemaker . . . winning and affectionate . . . . " It was true, and it had not been easy.

Unobtrusively also, Davidson was John Ewing's man at Dickinson College, tolerated but never respected by Rush. Since 1774, he had been Ewing's assistant pastor at the First Church, and at the College and University his Professor of History (Dickinson had a separate standing for this discipline some fifty years before its general appearance). [64] Ewing had proposed him for membership in the American Philosophical Society in 1781. Failing of election then, he had succeeded in 1783; and now, in 1784, the University had given him a D.D. as its parting blessing. He would hold first place in the Carlisle church, and Nisbet, when he came, would figure only as his assistant. At the College he would often be first in fact if not in name. He not only held a direct and useful tie to the Philadelphia institution, but had access to all points of influence in the Presbyterian structure, as Nisbet did not. The greater power was his through all those years of his tenure, though his sparkle of little talents was far outshone by the other's bitter genius, deep humanity and learning.

At Carlisle, Davidson would begin as "Professor of History, Geography, Chronology, Rhetoric and Belles Lettres." [65] He would later add the natural philosophy course to this repertoire, Ewing's influence having made him a dabbler in science, with a particular zest for astronomy. One Carlisle boy remembered him long afterward as "a middle sized man of general information," and this puts it rather well. [66] He was an amateur also of sacred music and had composed a few pieces. He made pictures, too, copying engravings in pen and ink. One of them would win praise from an artist, Mr. Neagle, a memory long treasured. Like James Ross, he loved poetry, and as a poet himself would now shine in conjunction with Isabella Oliver, sweet singer of the Conodoguinet. Of his own published works, the first and best known appeared on the eve of his departure for Carlisle. His

Geography Epitomized, a rhymed description of the world, won him the frank contempt of every Dickinson student through all those years, for he used it as a text, requiring them to buy it and to memorize the insipid verses. Besides published sermons, his other works include a *New Metrical Version of the Whole Book of Psalms* and *The Christian's A,B,C, or, Golden Alphabet for the Use of Children.* Here was a busy, pious and above all willing man of thirty-four, married but still childless. His first wife was a very plain woman, much his elder. Early in his ministry, she had nursed him through an illness. Learning that her attentions had ripened into love, he married her, revealing a spirit of accomodation which helps to explain his character and the attitude of others toward him.

Benjamin Rush, waiting in Philadelphia for Nisbet's arrival, sent an agenda for the June trustee meeting at Carlisle. [67] A house must be found for the Principal. Curriculum and other regulations must await his arrival for final consideration. Davidson must be elected. Provision must be made for a teacher of German. In a state whose population was nearly one-third German, the Doctor felt this to be essential. Dr. Nisbet must be authorized to tour Pennsylvania, Maryland and Delaware, raising funds and recruiting students. Witherspoon had done so on his arrival in America. This, as they all knew, was the prime essential. John Dickinson and others had established an endowment which, with a good enrollment, might suffice—but only narrowly and without a building program.

On Wednesday, June 8, the Nisbet ship was on the Delaware River and Dr. Rush excitedly making ready for their meeting on the next day, dashing off a letter to Montgomery on preparations for receiving the new Principal at Carlisle. He must be met and escorted into town by the trustees, the courthouse bell must be rung at his approach and, as he crossed the schoolhouse threshold, an address of welcome must be spoken. Davidson would attend to that. "The news of these things will make a clever paragraph in our Philadelphia papers and help to allure scholars to our College . . . . I shall do everything in my power to show the Doctor to advantage to our citizens. Adieu. O! Virtue—Virtue! Who would not follow thee blindfold!" [68] All

these last weeks his heart had been high. Now the consummation was at hand—the banners of science and religion at full
staff:

> Delightful task! to accompany the progress of population and govern-
> ment with the standards of science and religion! Happy County of
> Cumberland and highly favored village of Carlisle! your hills (once
> responsive only to the yells of savages and beasts of prey) shall ere
> long awaken our young philosophers from their slumbers to trace the
> planets in their courses. And thou, Canedoginet, whose streams have
> flowed so long unnoticed and unsung, on thy banks shall our youth
> first feel the raptures of poetic fire! [69]

The time of attendance, after leaving the grammar school, may be four years: the first for the critical study of the Latin and Greek, geography, and the first six books of Euclid: the second for algebra and the higher parts of the mathematics: the third for logic, criticism, ancient and modern history: the fourth for natural and moral philosophy, with the elements of natural jurisprudence.

Charles Nisbet, *Hints on Education*, "written soon after his arrival in America"

I anticipate a revolution in our state, big with human happiness, when the farmer and the scholar shall be blended together and when the same men who have been competitors for fame at our colleges shall be competitors for honor in the councils of the state.

Benjamin Rush, "To the Citizens of Pennsylvania of German Birth and Extraction," August 31, 1785

5

NISBET IN HIS PRIME

CARLISLE, eagerly watching in the sunlight and bells of that
early Independence Day, saw a stoutly built man in ministerial
black, sharp nose, bright eyes, under a full white powdered wig.
Such a wig, almost unique in America, set him apart as the sage
from afar he was. Yet the sage had an observant eye, missing
nothing, and, for all his fleshiness, a light, strong step. They
would find him as agile in body as mind, a good horseman and a
man who, on foot, could keep pace with any ordinary rider.[1]
With him—all somewhat overawed by the alien wildness of this
holiday scene—they saw his wife, his nineteen-year-old son who
had just been graduated with distinction Master of Arts of the
University of Edinburgh, the two little girls and his youngest, a
boy of eight.[2] They all spoke, of course, with a broad Scots
brogue, but this mattered little in a country where every other
schoolmaster seemed to be a Scot. When Robert Heterick left
the old academy at York and was succeeded by "a Quaker
gentleman," the boys laughed contemptuously at the newcomer's speech, which had none of the thick burr of a learned
man.[3] Carlisle people gave the Nisbets all the warmth of a frontier welcome, hushed by the respect due to the vast erudition of
"a walking library." Later, they would find their own high spirit
matched and overmatched in this man's needling ironic wit.

As for the Nisbets, through the dust cloud of their mounted
escort into town, they saw a village of about fifteen hundred
souls, untidy log houses along unpaved streets and then, as they

neared the square, find mansions elegantly built of the native gray stone clustering about the courthouse and churches.[4] New college and sage from afar had brought a faster beat to that frontier sense of future. John Steel's fine meetinghouse was being renovated to make room for Duffield's Pomfret Street congregation—Old Side, New Side, united under the smile of Dr. Davidson, blessed peacemaker. Sure sign of expected growth in commerce as well as learning, a newspaper, *The Carlisle Gazette and the Western Repository of Knowledge,* was nearly ready to begin its run, with a bit of Latin, no less, on its bannerhead: *"MULTAS IT FAMA PER ORAS."*[5] Its first number would appear on August 10, 1785, with a congratulatory address elegantly composed by a student "on the rising grandeur and encreasing reputation of Dickinson College . . . already are her courts crowded with a train of ardent votaries."[6]

Now to those courts the sage must come, face-to-face with reality at last. After the glowing letters from Dr. Rush, after the praise and promises—after that reception at Philadelphia where John Dickinson and so many others had crowded in to take his hand and hear his voice, where George Duffield had pledged a sermon and collection for the College (inspiring Rush's "blessed times and changes! The lamb & the lyon will soon lie down together!")[7]—after all this he found a small brick schoolhouse in a narrow lane, one room below and one above. Here James Ross, now standing deferentially at his elbow, had been teaching a roomful of ten-to-teen-age boys their Latin and Greek. That was the old Grammar School, essence of college preparation, but there must also be "English school" for other preparatory subjects, and where to put the college classes remained a question indeed. At the Works, perhaps. The trustees, were hopeful, confident, intolerant of doubts, and in Philadelphia Nisbet had been assured of absolute control.[8] The College had some apparatus, too: a telescope and globes. The library was surely an unusual one to find in the midst of a forest. Back in March, 1783, John Dickinson had promised five hundred volumes from the famous collection of his father-in-law, Isaac Norris, but had since sent out more than three times as many. With the gifts still coming in from friends of Dr. Rush, with Nisbet's personal library of about fourteen hundred titles, here were

book resources any college in America might envy.[9] Shelves
were being set up for Nisbet's books in the house which the
trustees had rented for him at the Works, the hoped-for campus
of the future.

The trustees were pledged to this expense, to all the costs of
the voyage from Scotland and to a salary for the Principal
which could also have been the envy of other college presidents.[10] They expected, to be sure, that the Doctor would earn
it not only by organizing the curriculum and teaching the senior
classes, but by touring the states and raising money as John
Witherspoon had done, and was still doing, for Nassau Hall.
Development was a president's business, then as now. Yet Dr.
Nisbet had now to face inadequacies within himself. He had
always been an outsider, had always figured as a learned, caustic
critic of the men and times around him—coming out in print
against the King's ministries again and again and almost arrested
for treason during the American war, taking issue with the great
William Robertson in the General Assembly of the Scottish
Kirk, lashing the town council of Montrose.[11] Here in free
America virtually the whole population was the establishment.
In Philadelphia he had been thrilled by the respectful attention
of "the republicans here," who "never deign to bestow these
where they are not in earnest, as they have nothing to ask of
any man living."[12] Well enough for the moment; but very soon,
seeing a society without class distinctions, a government dependent on a fickle and ignorant majority, a clergy with no
public support, and nowhere any fixed orders of social and
political leadership, he felt himself one of a nation plunging to
disaster. Emotionally, he needed those elements of security. He
could not handle groups with authority, commanding respect.
He could criticize but not persuade. His punishing wit often
brought laughter but never love. One close friend put his finger
on it:

> "He never seemed happy in his situation. In Scotland he was a repub-
> lican. As far as I can judge from letters I had from him, after going to
> America, he was nearly monarchical. During his residence at Mon-
> trose, he was still shooting the arrows of satyre at the Magistrates.
> This threw a sort of shade over his character, and made him pass for
> what he was not, an ill-natured man. But he had such an irresistible

desire of saying smart things, that he seldom let any opportunity of doing so pass, at whatever expense. Often he pained his friends, by using the language of scripture, rather in a jesting mode of application." [13]

From the first, there was repining in the little house at the Works. Morning and evening mists from the millpond nearby brought a fear of fever and ague to the little family. Shut indoors with the oppressive American heat around them, they thought of home. On their mantel the big bracket clock made by William Robb of Montrose watched them steadily. You could set it either to chime the hour or to play any one of three Scots tunes, "Twee Side," "Corn Riggs" or "Bonny Brook." [14]

Dr. Rush received a letter from the Principal, dated July 18, 1785, which instantly aroused his alarm, displeasure and contempt. Anne Tweedie Nisbet, it seemed, was just as craven as Mrs. Witherspoon had been when she had resisted the idea of the move to America. But Mrs. Nisbet, having come, wished now to return, and the children had joined her in pleading with their father, not only in dread of the ague but suffering from "the desiderium patriae or maladie de pais so fatal to the Swis." [15] In a letter of five days later, however, these fears and doubts were barely discernible. The trustees would meet in August, and Nisbet gave his view of what was needed. A master must be found for the Grammar School. With pupils entering in all stages of preparation it was "impossible that Mr. Ross should at once teach them the Principles of Grammar, & discharge his office of humanist to the higher Classes." Both Ross and Robert Johnston, teacher of mathematics, had too many in their classes. The appointment of Robert Davidson for history, chronology and geography (delayed, perhaps, for Nisbet's approval) must go through, but this should not "supercede the Election of a Professor of Natural Philosophy." Nisbet, obviously, had become aware of Davidson's dabbling in science and his incompetence to teach it on college level. He expressed urgent hopes that Congress would grant the buildings and that Rush would "continue your Activity with Regard to the funds." [16]

To others, the Principal was less reticent in implying that he had been lured into this barren land under false pretenses. He would never be able to take the advice that old John Erskine of Edinburgh sent with a gift of book, "Remember that you have two ears and but one tongue." [17] Erskine knew that Nisbet's complaints would soon be appearing in the Scottish press.

When Dr. and Mrs. Rush arrived in Carlisle for the trustees' meeting on August 9, fever and ague had at last taken hold at the Works. Newcomers, especially when weakened by a transatlantic voyage, were subject to it. Natives regarded it lightly. So also Dr. Rush. He did not call. When on the next day he opened a plaintive, incoherent note, beginning, "And is this thy Kindness to thy Friend?" his eye stopped at the dating by the signature, "Tomb of Dickinson College, Augt. 10th 1785." [18] He would answer rebuke with rebuke. He did not go.

By charter, the Principal of the College had no place on its Board of Trustees. Had Nisbet been a Witherspoon he might have remedied this, at least by establishing a pattern of consultation. At this meeting the curriculum was to be determined, the organization of the whole completed. The trustees, fourteen of them with old John Armstrong sitting as President pro tem, went ahead with their business, contemptuous of Nisbet's plight and feeling no need whatever for his counsel—setting a precedent which would long endure. These gentlemen understood the duties and dignity of college trustees and would not demean the institution by any wavering. It was theirs to administer the whole, the faculty's to submit to their direction.

The eight clergymen, a majority, were all Presbyterians except Henry Ernest Muhlenberg and William Hendel. General Armstrong, Colonel Hartley, Colonel Montgomery and Stephen Duncan were lawyers. Two medical men, Samuel A. McCoskry and Rush, made up the company, and of them all only Rush had given thought to the whole range of educational policy. His concepts were original and bold—at the same time owing much to the directions set by William Smith at the College of Philadelphia. He foresaw a national system of public schools and colleges with a single "federal university" at its summit. [19] The culminating study would not be Moral Philosophy (so long to be the final fare of American college seniors), but history and government, the principles and practice of agriculture, commerce and manufacturing, with chemistry and natural history to the fore. The modern languages would take precedence over the ancient. Let Greek and Latin be studied for content, not for grammar. Athletics would be cultivated, an unheard-of thing. Schools for women had a place in his system, with emphasis on "the principles of liberty and government." [20]

Rush knew better than to advance the whole of this program at a meeting where the majority would be certain to oppose—to say nothing of that uncompromising classicist abed at the Works. At a later date he would refer openly to Greek and Latin as "offal learning" which "brutalized" the intellect, and declare the American Indian languages a more useful study. [21] The *Plan of Education for Dickinson College* which his committee brought in on August 11 is in his hand—a tentative first draft, a step forward rather than a manifesto. [22] One must look beyond it for the full intention of this man of inspired eagerness and ready anger. It goes back to his childhood and that one principle from which, as he saw it, all else must flow—love. In one of his essays he has written:

> The world was created in love. It is sustained by love. Nations and families that are happy, are made so only by love. Let us extend this divine principle to those little communities which we call schools. Children are capable of loving in a high degree. They may therefore be governed by love. [23]

"Mothers and school-masters," he went on, not governments or clergy, "plant the seeds of nearly all the good and evil which exist in our world." Now, in his *Plan,* "as the fear of The LORD is the beginning of all wisdom, and should be the end and Object of all education," Rush gave religious instruction first place. It is interesting, however, that he specified not mere chapel attendance, but discussions and compositions on theology, and that his colleagues voted that provision out. "Moral Discipline" came next, enforced by a scale of punishments from admonition to expulsion. This emphasis was highly orthodox, and would be for years in American educational theory, where we find it stated over and over that learning without morality and discipline is evil.

Rush's curriculum began with a division of four classes above the grammar school, Freshman, Sophomore, Junior and Senior.

This was allowed to stand, though it would be many years before a four-year course would be achieved. One can see this feature as the measure of an institution's strength, and not many colleges had yet reached it. [24] Latin and Greek headed the list of studies. The Doctor might not approve, but it could not be otherwise and be called a college. He added Hebrew for good measure, another learned tongue for which, with faculties recruited so largely from the clergy, it would not be too hard to find a teacher. Then came French and German, his real interests. The recent French alliance had given our colleges and college students a new awareness of French literature, of French commercial ties. On German, the Doctor had long held strong convictions: a subject vital for Pennsylvania. He had sought at once a cooperative program with the German Reformed Church, where, however, his motives had been suspected:

> The English, who are here, are now establishing a second school in Carlisle, for which purpose they, at our last coetus, desired our assistance, and also some Reformed teachers. Since we had reasons to fear that this might tend to suppress the German language, and even our nationality, and might be to the disadvantage of our religion since they might accept a Reformed teacher only as a matter of form, we excused ourselves on the ground of disability. [25]

Philology, rhetoric, criticism and logic were in the *Plan,* with exercises in composition and public speaking, all necessary preparation for citizenship in a republic. So also were history, chronology and geography, with the myths and antiquities of the ancient world. To these last he had added the antiquities of Egypt, a surprising new point of emphasis so long before Bonaparte and Champollion. Moral philosophy was there, but Rush had specified that it was to include "government & the law of nature & nations"—and so it would in Nisbet's lectures. Finally, there was to be a full course of mathematics and as full a one as possible of general science, or "natural philosophy." Chemistry had been entered, later to be crossed out, perhaps for lack of a teacher, perhaps in the clerical fear (shared by Nisbet) that too much concentration of the material weakened one's awareness of the divine.

Examinations (always oral in this day) were to be held regularly. A thesis upon a subject chosen by the student would be required for graduation and must be defended in public at commencement. [26] This was a long advance over the carefully coached commencement orations which in practice would prevail. Regulations for the Library were laid down, as also for the governance of the Grammar School and its more plebeian adjunct, the "English school." Rush had a fixed aversion to dormitories. The boys must lodge with village families. As things stood, of course, it could not be otherwise. He also presented his case for "swimming, skating and such other exercises as are innocent, conductive to health and external elegance." This section of the manuscript is marked, in another hand, "Expunged." Also expunged was his provision that students wear coats with a distinguishing badge for each class. Here the deletion was wise, for specified dress, always intended chiefly as an aid in detecting malfeasance, had no success at Hampden-Sidney, Princeton, Harvard or wherever tried. The Rush view of dormitories would become moot later, but be overriden by trustees and faculty. We hear no more of the graduating theses, each of which, as he had wisely ordered, was to be bound and preserved in the Library. Nothing of that sort was done until a hundred years had passed.

It is hardly conceivable that any alteration in that first draft of the *Plan* occurred while Rush was there to defend it. The minutes of August 11 tell us that it "was debated by Paragraphs & adopted by the Board." It would be reviewed by a committee appointed on October 19, when Rush was no longer present. A year later, he was scolding the Board by letter because the *Plan* had not been formally adopted by the faculty also. [27] It was then once more "debated by paragraphs & after several alterations adopted." [28]

A report of the doings of August, 1785, is spread out in the second issue of the new *Carlisle Gazette.* The adoption of the *Plan* was announced with a touch of public relations fanfare: "very extensive and includes several branches of literature not hitherto taught in any of the American colleges." Here also we read of the election of Dr. Davidson as "Professor of HISTORY, and the BELLES LETTRES, to teach also CHRONOLOGY and GEOGRAPHY." [29] Some of those new "branches of literature" were no doubt expected to appear within the fold of Belles

Lettres as presented by Davidson, versatile soul. We read too of the "English school," now to give a full range to the preparatory department. Robert Tait, an experienced Scottish pedagogue who had made the voyage with Nisbet, was in charge. Tait's advertisement, headed, "EDUCATION," is printed directly below the news. "Just arrived from Edinburgh," he solicited pupils for his school "under the direction of the Trustees of Dickinson College," in the schoolhouse in the alley—"where he proposes to teach the English and French Languages Grammatically. Also, Writing, Cyphering, and Bookkeeping."

The English school began operations immediately, making, after a fashion, the beginning of that modern language program desired by Rush, not to mention bookkeeping, a practical aspect of mathematics he approved. So also would he approve, and had perhaps suggested, that final clause in Mr. Tait's invitation: "Young Ladies who chuse to study any of these branches, and have not already acquired them, may, (if they please) have separate hours for themselves." The English school was soon in trouble, however, and would be an irregular operation at best. By December, Montgomery was complaining to Rush of Tait's behavior, and in May the trustees dismissed him. [30]

That issue of the *Gazette* sought also to gladden the community with news that the Rev. Charles Nisbet was "perfectly recovered from his late indisposition." From this we can infer that Nisbet was present at the public exercises of the College also covered in the paper. These had been held on Monday, August 15, and must have been planned originally as the inauguration of the new but now reluctant Principal. There had been an oration "in praise of Mathematics," spoken by young John Montgomery, and then a "Dialogue" between John and another trustee's lad, Robert Duncan. Montgomery as Philemon, and Duncan as Eugenius, they went at it in "a spirited and graceful manner," and with many a flattering allusion to their elders:

> How can we but admire, & love, & praise,
> The generous few, who toil, and watch, & plan,
> That learning may diffuse'her cheering light
> On us, and all mankind?
> > We thank you all,
> For every wish express'd, & plan design'd

The infant sons of *Dickinson* to bless.
  And you, dear sir, safe from your native land
Arriv'd, we welcome to these calm retreats.
By your kind aid we hope ere long to reap
Those honours that reward the student toils. [31]

Yet he unto whom these last lines are addressed, on the very day the *Gazette* appeared, was writing to the Presbytery of Brechin begging for assurance that he could be taken back into his living at Montrose. His erstwhile colleagues would receive this plea with a coolness akin to that of Dr. Rush, wishing him "prosperity & success in your present usefull & honourable station." [32]

From the varying accounts of Nisbet's illness it is clear that the fever and ague had been only a mild affliction, and that his trouble was a nervous prostration in the face of the difficulties with which he was now expected to contend, resentment at unsubstantiated promises, frustration in being wholly subject to trustees who could dictate but not sustain. He lost all energy, his mind wandered childishly, and on into the winter pain and trembling of the under jaw still afflicted him. [33] In the meantime, October 16, he had sent his resignation to the trustees. They agreed to finance his return, and appointed Davidson Acting Principal. The Nisbets were waiting for a Scottish ship that could carry them safely home, but winter came before the vessel and cooler weather—and that cool reply from Brechin—brought second thoughts. By the turn of the year he was an eager candidate for reelection.

Even before Nisbet's resignation, Rush had been looking for a successor—this time an eminent American. He had in mind Jonathan Edwards, Jr., Professor of Languages at Princeton. Yet to old Colonel Montgomery a Down East Yankee was no better than any other foreigner. "I see you are fond of the great sages in the eastern countries," he wrote. "Well, then, let us send to China and get one." Montgomery was for Davidson. He added a P.S. to the letter, " . . . this between ourselves you know that we obtained the Charter and Endowments not by the aide of the new lights but Even in opposition to them but now when they see us going on they wish to push themselves into the best places." And then, significantly, for he had declared himself sick of Old Side, New Side politics, "Dr. Davidson stands high here and is no party man or as little so as any clergyman . . . . "[34]

Rush, too, had had enough of clerical conniving. It rankled him that John Ewing still had influence in the affairs of his college. It made the crisis with Nisbet doubly humiliating. Learning that Montgomery had been in correspondence with Ewing, he nearly broke entirely with his old friend. Also, before Nisbet's resignation, the Colonel had sent the trustees a strong statement in favor of Davidson, thickly urgent in his soldierly way but also with a certain academic cogency that might well have come from the Provost.[35] In his fury and frustration, Rush broke with the beloved church of his fathers and became, for a time, an Episcopalian. "You wonder," he explained to Montgomery, "at my leaving the Old Side church. It was because I detected the father of the Old Side party, Dr. Ewing, in lying, drunkenness, and profane conversation, and afterwards found him supported by *Old Side* Presbyterians and New Side Skunks in every part of the state."[36]

So now the issue was between Nisbet and Davidson. Davidson might have had it, but for Rush on the one hand and, on the other, John Dickinson's sympathy with Nisbet's plight. Take him back, Rush urged, cutting his salary from £400 to £300 until the College recover from the damage he has done. "If the Doctor will do his duty and give over whining and complaining, I shall love and serve him as much as if nothing had happened."[37] That, however, was unlikely to occur. Nisbet had been directly consulted at least once in that fall or winter— "but when I presented a few hints to the meeting of the Trustees, not the smallest attention was paid to them, though I knew that many of them approved them in their heart. Everything was ordered according to the old *mumpsimus.*" This went to the Earl of Buchan in a long letter of December 15, 1785, full of disillusionment with ignorant and foolish trustees holding an absolute power without appeal, the teachers "mere day-labourers for seven hours a day, summer and winter," with only the two one-month vacations; the students acquiring, many of them, only "a decided aversion for books and learning."[38]

Nisbet complained no less to Benjamin Rush who, at least, could never rightly be called an old mumpsimus. He flatly refused to cease his criticism of American ways, and sneeringly reminded the Doctor of how he had been summoned from Scotland "to make War on Ignorance . . . ":

> I cannot agree with you that a Person at the Head of this College could have the Influence you mention, especially if he is to be restrained to simple Panegyric on the Manners of the times, & to teach, along with three other Persons, in a Room not twenty feet square . . . . The Hubbub & Confusion of such a Place would confound St. John himself, & St. Job too, if he were concerned with it, tho' sanctioned by the Example of the admired University of Philadelphia. But as your Regulations are professedly changeable, it is to be hoped that this Absurdity will soon be removed. Perhaps you designed to awaken my Ambition by mentioning that you hoped that Providence had such a Person in View for this College as might prove at St. John in Religion & Lycurgus in Politics. Though these are Hyperbolical & big Words you know that I once had a Desire to approach as near as possible to the Purport of them, if not deprived of promised Support, or fettered by Regulations that would render success impossible. In every European Seminary the Teachers are allowed to exercise their Judgment as to the Mode of teaching, & the Division of the time of their Pupils betwixt public Lectures & private Study . . . .[39]

Again, he taunted Rush on the absence of all the most prominent trustees, leaving the institution at the mercy of

> mean local Prejudice. To erect a College in the Corner of a Grammar School is a Scheme that was never thought of in any other Age or Place of the World, & to call a Person to teach, without allowing him a Place for that Purpose, seems pretty strange & can only have the effect to make the Boys lose their Time & Money & the Teachers their Labour & Reputation. They talk indeed of building another Apartment, of the same Size with the present, & that they will begin in the Spring, but this gives no Relief at present, & will even, if carried into Execution, only hinder the College from increasing.

To this he added allusions to the mud of the Carlisle streets in every winter thaw and to the morass around him at the Works, "which by the summer heats may be rendered an Avernian

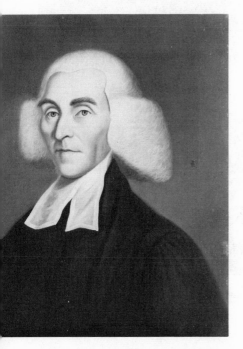

Left: George Duffield (1732–1790). By Charles Peale Polk, 1790. Right: Charles Nisbet. By an unidentified Scottish painter, *c.* 1780.

Carlisle, *c.* 1797. The spire marks the Courthouse. Buildings at the left are "the Works." By Edouard Charles Victurnien Colbert, Comte de Maulevrier, from Colbert's *Voyage dans l'Interieur des Etats-unis* (Baltimore, 1935).

Literary Society Halls, in West College, 1804–1896.

In Denny Hall, 1903.

Lake, that may choke the Birds of the Air as well as the Inhabitants of the Earth." [40] The *Gazette's* item of February 8, 1786, that the trustees were now unanimously in Nisbet's favor, probably came from Rush, to whom John Black was writing, a week later, that "Genl. Armstrong and his party, it is said, are now fixed on Dr. Nisbet, whilst Coll. Montgomery &c. are determined for Dr. Davidson." [41] James Ross broke into the *Gazette* with a fervent poem in Latin celebrating Nisbet's recovery from illness, a touching gesture in behalf of a fellow classicist from one who, democrat and patriot ever, had little in common with him otherwise. [42]

Then early that spring, the democrats and patriots, the hopefuls, had their first bright ray of justification. On April 7, 1786, the Pennsylvania Legislature granted £500 and ten thousand acres of land to Dickinson College. The prophet in Philadelphia was jubilant. "We have passed the Red Sea and the wilderness. A few of us it is true have been bitten by fiery serpents in the way, but the consciousness of pure intentions has soon healed our wounds. We have now nothing but the shallow waters of Jordan before us." There must be publications, "a short history of the rise and progress of our College, a copy of our charter and our plan of education, a list of the contributors to our College, and an account of our professors, Library, &c." [43] The addition to the schoolhouse was begun, and building was well advanced when the trustees met on the 10th of May.

At that meeting, Charles Nisbet was reinstated as Principal of Dickinson College at a reduced salary, with Colonel Montgomery's party amiably concurring. In August the Board had authorized the Principal to go "on a mission" into the neighboring states, accompanied by a trustee. This authorization was now renewed. Let him prove that he deserved a better wage. Dr. Davidson had recently returned from such a foray, and had had more success than Nisbet, alas, would experience in wider travels. On the next day, the Board met in the church to hear the new Principal deliver a sermon on *The Usefulness and Importance of Human Learning.* It was ordered to be printed. There followed *An Address to the Students of Dickinson College,* also published. [44] The *Address* appeared soon after with an Edinburgh imprint, evidence that the Doctor himself thought it the better piece, and certainly it was with this audience that his sympathies lay.

Dr. Davidson's report on his term as Acting Principal was received. It showed a school and college body of eighty. He had made a division into four classes with the Grammar School as one, but admitted that students had not been "regularly formed" into them. With such a motley assembly in terms of preparation and only two college professors, himself and Ross, to deal with it, he could hardly have done better. Tait had been replaced by Robert Johnston, teacher of mathematics, who was preparing himself in astronomy and hoping for appointment to a professorship at this meeting. He got it. As Professor of Mathematics he would be allowed to try his hand at natural philosophy as well. Johnston had been a tutor at the College of Philadelphia for three years after his graduation there in 1763, had gone into medicine and had marched off to war, January 16, 1776, as surgeon of William Irvine's regiment. As a teacher of science, however, he proved a total failure. He was hurriedly divested of that duty, and resigned from the faculty in something of a huff. Two years later, he was back as a trustee, elected at the same time as General Irvine. Johnston was a popular figure, a friend of Washington. He taught for a while in Delaware, then voyaged to China, returning at last to the life of a country squire in Franklin County. He bequeathed £50 to the College.[45]

So it would eventually devolve upon Davidson to teach the science course, along with so much else. In the meantime, and very possibly in response to his new dignity as Professor of Belles Lettres, the Belles Lettres Society of Dickinson College had been organized, May 20, 1786, with eleven students adopting and signing its constitution. Belles Lettres, so long to hold high prominence on the Dickinson College scene, began as an independent student group much like the original Phi Beta Kappa and others of the sort. It was exclusive in character, being limited at the outset to sixteen members. Like Phi Beta Kappa, it was dedicated to self-improvement and pledged to secrecy. [46] One member of the faculty only, on request, might be admitted to a meeting, and the early minutes show no sign of faculty intervention. The impulse for its founding may have come from the students themselves, or it may have been that Davidson, or a trustee with memories of Whig or Cliosophic at Princeton, saw this as a way of regularizing entirely independent student enterprise. On December 29, 1785, some of the boys had much diverted the town with a theatrical entertainment, "The Fatal Discovery," accompanied by a farce, "High Life Below Stairs." Trustees and professors both had looked askance at this; while the *Gazette*, speaking for the town, had opined that "a well regulated theatre is capable of being rendered a great school of virtue," and had advised the addition to the faculty of "a master in the art of speaking." [47]

The art of speaking (an emphasis Dr. Nisbet deplored) became a major concern of Belles Lettres. Fortnightly meetings were held at first, the members either appearing with a composition or debating a prescribed issue; and, as may be imagined, the debates were the more popular activity. Three years later, August 31, 1789, ten students founded a second society, the Union Philosophical. [48] This completed the pattern of two rival, ardent loyalties, vying for "literary" distinction, the pattern to be present in almost every American college for many years to come, bringing a freshness and vitality to the curriculum as nothing else could possibly have done. The societies, meeting weekly as membership grew to the point where every student belonged to one or the other, were to the humanities what the laboratory would be to the sciences, and more. They would have the best libraries on campus (though each largely duplicated the other), bring in the most stimulating speakers, discuss vital contemporary topics and maintain, at first on the platform and later in print, an invaluable rapport between campus and town.

The subjects they debated reveal the students' character, along with professorial and home influences and, occasionally, the mood of rebellion. Anticipation of love and marriage is seen repeatedly—"Whether the love of Liberty or the love of Women is the strongest passion?" Women won, 5–4. [49] "Do the Clergy or women have the greater influence on the Morals of Mankind?" The clergy took this, hands down, March 2, 1793. Novel reading was condemned in Belles Lettres debates, August 8,

1789, and again on June 21, 1806, which is rather surprising since the Society's library, in contrast to that of the College, was fairly well stocked with fiction. [50] Slavery was condemned "by a Majority," August 12, 1786; and a warm debate, March 16, 1793, on "Whether is the War now carrying on against the Indians just or not?" was followed by a vote (suggestive as to where the strongest reasoning lay) that no vote be taken. Young Roger Brooke Taney had supported that tactful omission.

Taney, on June 22 of that year, was one of those supporting the negative view of the question, "Whether are Dr. Davidson's Lectures on Natural Philosophy an eligible way of acquiring a knowledge of that science?" They carried their point. Taney thought his college perhaps unique in allowing the students themselves to determine who should hold the places of honor at commencement, salutatorian and valedictorian. [51] Since each society sought to capture both, the issue was often decided by non-members, and in time faculty intervention was inevitable. Taney himself was valedictorian in 1795. He always remembered Belles Lettres as an important factor in his training for the law, rejoicing, he tells us, "to meet in the business of life gentlemen who have been trained and disciplined in its exercises and whose conduct and acquirements reflect credit upon it." [52]

Taney and seven others lodged and boarded with James McCormick, the most popular of the professors, always friendly and concerned, teaching mathematics and, later, natural philosophy, 1788 to 1814. McCormick was also one of the first to publish in his field, supplying the astronomical calculations for Carlisle's *Western Almanac*. [53] It was rarely given to the drillmasters in the foundation subjects, Latin and Greek, to be popular, although the young alumni who often did a stint as head of the Grammar School and helped occasionally with college classes might be so. Taney and others were much attached to Charles Huston, who later became a justice of the Pennsylvania Supreme Court. Huston was succeeded by Henry Lyon Davis who at age nineteen was carrying the full load of Professor of Languages with the hearty approval of Dr. Nisbet and the student body generally. This youth, who later became President of St. John's College, appealed grandiloquently to the students when, by "blackest artifice," he found himself suddenly out of a job. At a student gathering he had, it seems, suggested a few lines from Pope as appropriate for the title page of the new edition of *Geography Epitomiz'd* being printed at Carlisle in 1794:

> Here embryo thoughts in wild disorder lye,
> Here newborn nonsense first is taught to cry.
> Maggots half formed in Rhyme exactly meet
> And learn to crawl upon Poetic feet. [54]

The proposal reached Davidson and must surely have influenced his prompt action, though the new professor, William Thomson of the Newark Academy, was an experienced and agreeable man, who gave good service for the next ten years.

Modern languages would not have a professor until Claudius Berard came in 1814. English grammar was being taught by Davidson in 1788, though Taney, in his day, found it left to the students' reading, nourished also by Nisbet in his lectures and his work with the commencement orations. [55] Once installed as Principal, Dr. Nisbet would not miss a single day of classes until death took him from the scene—a fidelity to his students which is matched by an equally consistent contempt for his trustees. [56] In his *Address to the Students*, he had made clear his intention:

> In order to discover the genius and capacity of students, and to suggest useful hints for conducting their studies and regulating their conduct, I am convinced that private acquaintance and conversation are of great use. It will therefore be agreeable to me to receive visits from all of the students, as often as their studies and mine will permit, and to suggest to them what may be useful, as well as to resolve their doubts and difficulties, being determined to act as the private preceptor, as well as the public instructor of every student, without exception or respect of persons, who comes to this seminary in quest of useful knowledge. [57]

As for what constituted "useful knowledge," his position was equally clear:

> The classics are useful, not from their being writ in dead languages, or because it costs a great deal of pains to read them: but they are valuable as models of just thinking, examples of true taste, and monu-

ments of the wisdom and capacity of ancient nations, and have been the delight and wonder of many successive generations. [58]

Nor must it, resting on this foundation, be remote from the present:

> The book of nature is continually open before us, and if we are only attentive, we will be daily gaining new information, both with regard to the natural and moral world. Solon boasted that even in his old age he was always learning something. In the course of our lectures we have endeavored to illustrate the doctrines we have taught you by solid arguments and instances drawn from history and real life, and have uniformly condemned the futility of those who compose theories of human nature from mere imagination, instead of drawing from real life. [59]

The idea of training in practical skills as a useful preparation for life would be in the minds of forward-looking American educators for many years to come. Dr. Nisbet had little patience with it. He wrote to his friend, Alexander Addison:

> The Methodists have a College at Abingdon in Maryland, in which the Scholars are allowed no Play, but are obliged to spend the Intervals of their Lessons in the Operations of Agriculture & Gardening, as they have a Farm & Garden for the Purpose. It is probable that these last Branches of Science are the only ones that are taught with Success in this College, which Dr. Rush has held up in the Columbian Magazine as a model for others. The Conceit of it was borrowed from Rousseau's Emiline. [60]

In the same letter he described his own teaching and his method:

> My occupation is to read Lectures on Logic, Metaphysics & Moral Philosophy, to which I premise a short Account of the Greek & Latin Classics, a Course of Lectures on the History of Philosophy, & another of Criticism, & sometimes explain a Classic critically in the Beginning before my Class is fully assembled. I oblige my Students to write out all the Lessons ad longuam, at least I enjoin them to do so, that as they have not time to read, they may at least acquire a few Ideas, & Dr. Davidson has lately conformed to this Custom. [61]

This was "prelection." "So far as I can learn," he added,

"it is not the Custom in any of the American Colleges to teach by Prelection, but merely by way of Exercise & Examination, tho' a Lecture was sometimes read to the students, on entering a new Branch of Science." [62] He read each lecture so slowly that the class could write down the whole, using quarto sheets which they would later have bound in solid calf. At a place and time when text books were rare indeed, each student who performed the whole emerged with a book, and some of the books were later read by the young men to classes of their own. Each was obliged also to compile a shorter volume of "Questions and Answers" on the subject in hand. Upon this they would be drilled in catechistic fashion, no doubt a dismal business under Davidson, but with Nisbet continually enlivened as he made each point an occasion for discussion and enlargement. [63]

Roger Taney, like others, had been sent to Carlisle because of Nisbet's reputation. He and others dwell upon the warmth and affection with which the Doctor was regarded by his students, their debt to his great learning and kindness. The College was a college in its founding years by virtue of Nisbet alone. Of course they were shaken by his acid contempt for the American government and social structure, which he believed dedicated to roguery and headed for disaster. They were ardent patriots, sharing Rush's view of America as the hope of the world. They were Jeffersonian democrats, many of them, too, and Carlisle itself was strongly of that complexion. Throughout the country at the turn of the century, a left-wing wave in politics and religion was at crest, and college students were feeling its force. Nisbet's students, amazingly tolerant of his "monstrous heresies," simply rested their pens when a lecture took that turn. [64] One of his duties as Principal was to examine newcomers, and some of his popularity must have been that which comes to the friendly and understanding admissions officer. Taney's classmate, Edwin Atlee, tells in verse how he rode to Carlisle, a mounted servant jogging deferentially behind, and went at last

with trepidation,
To stand the usual Examination.
At the appointed hour, and wonted place,
Master and Candidate met, face to face:

Somewhat abash'd and aukward was the latter,
Who well perceived it was no trifling matter.
Enquiry made—where he'd left off at School?
He answered: and pursuant to the Rule,
Was told to construe where he last had read.
This, with apparent boldness, he essay'd:
But, whether by fatality or no,
He open'd on a Speech of Cicero.
Just at the Threshold stood S. P. Q. R.
A host of Capitals which made him stare,
As much, as if what those Initials stood for
Had met his view.—"Why what's the ninny gude for!
"Canna ye mak' the meaning oot at a'?
"Hoot mon! ye canna fin' it on the Wa!"
Thus spake the Principal, whose keen black eye,
O'erhung by pond'rous brow, could well espy
The lad's confusion; but he soon reliev'd him
From the sad puzzler which had so much griev'd him,
Then humbly thanking the facetious Scot
For kindly solving this quadruple knot,
Eugenius caught the thread, and follow'd on,
Till o'er th'appointed portion he had gone.
Thro' various other Exercises led,
Reviving what lay dormant in his head,
With honour he the tedious trial pass'd,
And by just Sentence, with his Peers was class'd. [65]

The functions of advisor and disciplinarian do not well combine. Only rarely did Dr. Nisbet turn his crushing sarcasm upon a student—only when richly deserved, and then with telling effect. [66] In general, in an age when strict government of the young was given such primary attention, colleagues and trustees thought him far too easy-going. [67] His comment when he found James Ross caning a grammar school boy became famous: *"Hoot!* Ye're puttin' it in at the wrong end!" [68]

In Nisbet the students saw a professor solidly at war with the overlords of their small world, and he had their admiration as one who dared defy authority. It was a position which the Doctor made equally clear to students and trustees. In 1791 he stated in his regular report to those gentlemen:

The Trustees will be pleased to reflect that Students are not to be considered merely as Animals, that need only Food, & a Hole to sleep in, but that they ought to be considered as rational Creatures, who need Retirement, Quiet & Conveniency for exercising & improving their faculties by Study, in order to attain that Knowledge which is necessary to enable them to discharge the Duties of Life with Propriety, & to be useful to themselves & to their Country, in the various stations to which they may be called.

He carries the point forward at excessive length, and yet a little more may be worth quoting as so applicable to mid-twentieth century practice:

That Students in the Situation of those in the present Boarding Houses cannot prosecute their Studies to Advantage will be evident to every rational Person who will take the Trouble of visiting all, or even a few of them, as they will find that they are extremely straitened, & that too many are lodged together, so that they have little or no Opportunity for Study, & prove Interruptions instead of Helps to each other.

And altho' some young Men, on Account of their having contracted a vehement Thirst after Knowledge, or from Strength of Genius, & superior Activity of Mind, may prosecute their Studies with Success amidst manifold Inconveniencies, yet it would be as irrational to expect that the Generality of young Men should be able to do the like as it would be to expect that all Men might become Giants, because some Men have grown to the Stature of Eight Feet & upwards.

The Trustees ought to consider, that a Number of young Boys, when crowded into a narrow Lodging, must necessarily contrive to spend their time in some Way or other, and when they find it impracticable to pursue their Studies, they will either go out to seek such company as they can find, or be engaged in such trifling Conversation & Amusements as Youth are too much disposed to pursue in the Absence of their Parents & Teachers.

The Trustees ought not to wonder, if this Seminary produces but few good Scholars, nor that many young Men take a Disgust at their Studies, & leave the College before the Course of public Lessons is finished, when they reflect on the Situation of most Students in this Place, where so many are crowded together, without Conveniency for Study, that if the Trustees were to order their Teacher of Mathematics to measure their Apartments, & to report the Square Contents of their Lodgings, it is probable they would find that the Space allowed to each, at an Average, would not be much greater than that which, according to the Calculations of Mathematicians, was allowed to each Individual of the lesser Kinds of Cattle in Noah's Ark, when the mere Preservation of Life was the only thing intended. [69]

Vice-Principal Davidson, earnest, prim and satisfied, Ewing's man, was the active administrator through these years. But Rush, Ewing, the trustees, were all set at nought by Nisbet. It was the portly, bitter Scot who brought to these young men, as every college should, their contact with intellectual greatness, with the human spirit undefiled by mendacity, compromise or surrender. Nisbet, in that first interim of shock and dismay, had been appalled by the contrast between these young Americans and the lads of North Britain who, as he himself had done, would toil for learning in frugal desperation—that spirit which was peopling this western world with teachers. But through the years from 1786 to the end it was nonetheless with his students that he held firm and frank rapport. To young Samuel Miller, his future biographer, the personal contact with Nisbet was the truly memorable part of his life at Carlisle. Miller had come to join the graduate course in theology which the Doctor taught from 1788 to 1791. [70] Through one winter he spent every evening at the Nisbet house, enjoying with the others a new world "of rich amusement and information, . . . an extraordinary knowledge of men, and books, and opinions, such an amazing fund of rare and racy anecdotes, all poured out with so much unstudied simplicity, with such constant flashes of wit and humour, and with such a peculiar mixture of satire and good nature as kept everybody whether young or old hanging upon his lips." [71]

Take any day through all these early years, under sun or cloud, there in Liberty Alley where, as John Penn saw it in 1788, the "college or school-house" stood, "a small patched-up building of about sixty by fifteen feet." [72] From inside, if he had paused there, he might have heard Davidson's class in geography reciting some of the hated rhymes—

> Round the globe now to rove, and its surface survey,
> Oh, youth of America, hasten away;
> Bid adieu for a while to the toys you desire . . . [73]

this, from the introduction to the book, an acrostic on its author's name—until released and pouring out with their hockey
sticks to a game of bandy-ball up and down the long and narrow
college yard. After which, refreshed, let them come back to a
less fretful, more fruitful, hour with Dr. Nisbet.

Hundreds of his lectures survive in student transcripts. To
the college educator of today they may be worth a sampling, if
only to glimpse the teaching method of this "walking library"
unwillingly stranded at a far and desolate outpost of the sophistication of his time. The sneering anger of his letters is muted
here. The boys are his hope, his future and his friends. Take, for
instance, the opening of a prelection in the Moral Philosophy
course on the subject of sincerity and (doubly tender now in
the professor's mind) the honoring of promises. The boys have
their paper and ink before them, their quills in hand, and he
begins:

> Sincerity or the love of truth is the companion of innocence,
> dignity and true greatness of mind. Simulation and dissimulation,
> however calculated for the purposes of knavery and concealment, and
> commended by crooked and shallow politicians, are the arts of cow-
> ardice and the cloak of villainy. We hope you will remember that
> simulation is pretending to a disposition which we have not, and
> dissimulation is concealing the character, or a disposition which we
> have.

> Quod non est simulo, dissimuloque quod est. Vulg.

> Prudence will indeed direct that we should not express all our
> thoughts, or communicate them to every body; but sincerity will by
> no means permit that we should tell what is not true, or even that we
> should conceal the truth to the injury of another. There may be a
> lying in silence or gesture as well as in words; but sincerity will lead us
> to condemn as a lie every artifice that has a tendency to deceive
> another. Lyars and politicians may value themselves as much as they
> please for indirect dealing, but it is the part of cowards and fools,
> because they cannot remain long unknown. Most men will set a mark
> on those whom they have once detected in lying and dissimulation,
> and will make it a rule never to believe them. Hence liars meet with
> no credit even whilst they speak the truth. When their mean arts are
> once discerned we always read their speeches backwards, and under-
> stand them as well by the application of the rule of contraries, as if
> they spoke truth. The only chance a lyar has of cheating is to speak

truth, which by being disbelieved, will answer his purpose as well as lying. The strict performance of a promise or contract belongs to truth as well as justice, as it is only on presumption of their speaking truth that we make any contracts with men or trust their promises in any instance. Those who break their promises and contracts, or make engagements without intending to keep them, ought to be excommunicated from civil society. Vicious habits commonly begin in little matters. Want of punctuality and delay of performance of promises degenerate by degrees into downright perfidy and knavery. To violate a promise in a small matter is a step to violating it in a greater. The man who is perpetually pleading excuses, and making explications of his promises in order to elude performance, is already corrupted and destitute of integrity. Truth is the only bond of human society, and when it is violated, society is no longer tenable. Impudence and perjury are the natural attendants of lying and insincerity. A callousness of mind takes place after giving in to a habit of this kind, whereby the mind becomes hardened and prepared for the most infamous practices. If a character of this kind is once fixed on a nation or people, though by the villainy of a few, it will require ages of honesty and sincerity to convince the world that it is a calumny. Sincerity alone qualifies men for friendship, as none will ever chuse for friends those whose words they cannot trust, and whose promises are deisgned only to deceive and insnare. Falsehood is naturally so hateful that even knaves abhor one another, when they find they have been cheated, and falsehood can never be amiable, even to those who practice it. We may say of falsehood, perfidy and treachery what Virgil said of Alecto, one of the furies,

> Odit et ipse pater Pluton, odere sorores
> Tartareae monstrum . . . Aeneid vii. 327.

Truth and sincerity are the inseparable companions of justice; so we often call both of them by the complex name of honesty.

The last quality which constitutes virtue or moral perfection, is fortitude or strength of mind. This is the consequence of, and depends entirely upon, the other habits of which we have been speaking, and is totally inseperable from them as well as unattainable without them. The person who is benevolent, just, wise and sincere is and ought to be firm in his purposes, and need not and ought not to be diverted from them, because by these habits he is ever supposed to be good, and fortitude is only a firm adherence to the right. Wicked men may have a desperate and imprudent boldness, which may be mistaken by some for true courage. Ignorance may sometimes be bold merely because it is blind, and at other times, for the same reason, it is

fearful from a consciousness of guilt, and the prevalence of imagination, which multiplies the objects of terror. But a person who is
conscious that he is destitute of virtuous qualities cannot possess
rational and true courage. Malice and anger may on some occasions
counterfeit its appearance; but their strength being exhausted, cow-
ardice, the natural companion of guilt and falsehood, immediately
takes its place. Courage or strength of mind is absolutely necessary to
keep us close to the path of virtue and to enable us to persevere in the
pursuit of moral excellence. Without this, innocence might give way
to temptations, and we might be carried quite contrary to our judgments by the example of the multitude. Some young men whose
minds inwardly approve of virtue, yet for want of courage are carried
against their conscious and inward persuasions. A wise man ought to
be steady in his resolutions, because he may expect to meet with
many things that will tend to divert him from them. The firmness of
mind that belongs to virtue is founded on reason, and connected with
the possession of every other excellence.

> Justum et tenacem proposite virum,
> Non civicum ardor prava jubentium,
> Mente quatit solida . . . Hor. [74]

Samuel Miller tells us of Nisbet's "electrifying the whole
class" at the close of a lecture, but one finds that it is never
quite like that at the end. He recaptures their attention by
laughter in mid-course. He will brighten a long discourse on the
use and misuse of words by bringing in a few examples of
misuse that have been blessed by custom—how "the
Spaniards . . . commend the bravery of a person who runs great
risques in their bull-baitings by calling him a 'Son of a Whore,'
and the English Bucks applaud a friend by calling him 'A
damn'd clever Fellow.' " [75] A culminating story, built up in rich
detail, such as that of how Omai, the Tahitian chief, having
learned from Johnson's Dictionary that "to pickle" meant "to
preserve," took his final leave of Lord Sandwich by praying
"that God Almighty might pickle his Lordship to all eternity"—
this would not end the hour, but serve to hold them for one
final application of his central theme. [76]

So it goes, confronting the boys with ideas, with authors
from ancient to modern times, Pliny's fabulous natural history,
much of Pascal, much of La Bruyère, and on to Sir Thomas

Browne (and Dr. Fell), to Robert Boyle ("a person of great probity and worth"), or Samuel Werenfels of Zurich and his *De Logomachus Eruditorum* of 1702 ("which may be read with pleasure and instruction"). Others must be cited with warning or distaste, the great Voltaire, sentimental Rousseau, or, even more dangerous, Scotland's own David Hume. Hear him open another lecture on the morning of Tuesday, January 24, 1788, with winter in the windows and small comfort from the fire against the wall. The course in Philosophy. Quills are dipped once more, ideas in melee again. The theme is that resounding impact of Scottish common sense upon the armored logic of the great John Locke:

> Simple Ideas comprehend all those which we receive from our senses, which are necessarily divided into five classes, according to the organs by which they are perceived. Thus, Colours are simple ideas, as the mind cannot divide them into parts. The same thing may be affirmed of the ideas received by our other senses. Compound ideas must be resolved into such a number of simple ideas as they comprehend, before the mind can distinctly perceive them. In perceiving sensible ideas, the mind seems to be entirely passive. On the contrary, it seems to be active also with regard to those of Reflexion and Abstraction. Indeed it may be said to be active in a considerable degree even with regard to those ideas that are received by means of the senses, at least attention and a willingness to perceive appear to be necessary for receiving ideas in that manner, as for want of this many things are often said within our hearing, which notwithstanding we do not hear; and many objects are exposed to our sight, which however, we do not see.
>
> When the mind has perceived any idea, it necessarily pronounces some judgment concerning it, and first of all it infers or concludes the existence of those objects without itself from which it receives these ideas or impressions. It is by means of our ideas alone that we infer the existence of sensible objects around us, and discover their several properties and qualities. Yet some philosophers would have us believe that the ideas we receive of external objects do not necessarily infer the existence, or give us any knowledge of the objects from which we receive them. Mr. Locke has detailed to the world as a capital discovery, that Colour, Figure, Taste, Heat and Cold, and the other secondary qualities of Matter do not exist in bodies themselves, but solely in the mind which perceives them, and is at great pains to prove that nobody ever questioned, viz. that inanimate bodies are not per-

cipient beings, nor in the least conscious of the impressions which they make on beings endowed with the power of Perception. To say that there is no heat in the fire, meaning that there is no such sensation as we feel when we are actually exposed to it, is a mere childish quibble, and unworthy to be mentioned among Philosophers, as no man was ever so ignorant as to imagine any thing of this kind. Yet the generality of philosophers, since Mr. Locke's time, have followed his notions, and by secluding from the consideration of the mind every thing except its own ideas, without considering these as the true representations of originals actually existent, have rendered the existence of external objects extremely problematical, and given great advantage to the Sceptics, which they have carefully improved.

Father Mallebrance [77] and the Cartesians, who first set on foot the notion of our seeing all things in God, imagines that it is the Deity who excites in our minds the ideas of external objects, and the objects themselves are only the occasion, but not the cause of exciting ideas in our minds, and in delivering the doctrine concerning the origin of our ideas, they lay it down as a caution, that we ought not to believe that any thing in the external objects is the cause of those ideas that we receive from them. The Cartesians attributed all the effects in nature to the immediate agency of the Deity, and allow external objects to be only the occasions of the ideas excited and the effects produced by them. A love of subtlety and the affectation of singularity, together with a desire of avoiding those difficulties that pressed upon the other hypothesis, seem to have led these philosophers to so strange conclusions. The obscurity of the subject led those on both sides of the question to advance sundry things not easily conceivable. Mr. Locke and his followers, by affirming rashly that the mind perceives nothing except its own ideas, have laid a foundation for general scepticism, or doubting of the existence of external objects, which Mr. Hume has improved into a regular system without departing in the least from those principles which Mr. Locke had laid down in his celebrated Essay on the human Understanding. And it is truly a scandal to the philosophic reputation of the present age that the ingenious Dr. Reid was obliged to write [an] octavo volume, full of laborious reasoning, merely to prove the existence of external objects, which is rendered quite uncertain by Mr. Locke's hypothesis, and to bring us back to the level of children and savages, who have no doubts concerning the existence of objects that are perceivable by their senses. [78] Dr. Priestley has endeavored, though feebly, to defend Mr. Locke's doctrine on this head, [79] but it is to be hoped that the increasing light of Reason and common Sense will quickly destroy the credit of these fanciful and mischievous theories, which tend to subvert the foundation of human knowledge, and to destroy all distinctions between truth and falsehood, virtue and vice. [80]

Deftly, an appreciation of literature is brought in. He recites poetry, passages often from Horace, Thomson and Pope. He dwells on the necessity for rational thinking and the accurate use of words, telling them, in that recurrent subjective note, how to be a teacher stimulates one to greater precision in thought and word. The use of repetitive, slightly variant words and phrases as a means of clarifying an idea is explained, while all the time he is using the device itself—moving forward to a eulogy upon plain terms and clean sense, illustrated, again, by an anecdote:

> The late Dean Swift was remarkable for studying plainness in his sermons in order to prevent misconceptions in the minds of his hearers, and having accidentally used the phrase, "an avaricious man," in composing a sermon, he was doubtful what sense ordinary hearers would put upon it. To satisfy himself on this head, he called up one of his servants and asked him what he meant by an avaricious man. The servant replied, "a mighty sly fellow." On calling up another and putting the same question to him, he answered that an *avaricious man* meant *"a good-natured jolly dog;"* for which reason the Dean altered the phrase in the sermon, putting the word *covetous* instead of *avaricious,* and on asking them what they meant by a "covetous man, " they readily told him. Molière, the famous French comedian, used to read all his works to an old woman who was his housekeeper before he offered them to the public, and he never retained any phrase or term which she mistook or did not understand. The late Mr. Pope constantly used the same method with regard to his poems, with regard to perspicuity and clearness of conception. [81]

The pith of the lectures would come up again in drill on the "Questions and Answers." Davidson delighted in rote, was made glad by hearing an echo of himself, but this other professor, as young Taney bears witness, would urge them on in kindly fashion and show most pleasure when the answer came back in the student's own words. "His object was to teach the pupil to think, to reason, to form an opinion, and not to depend merely upon memory . . . . He undoubtedly succeeded in fastening our attention upon the subject on which he was lecturing, and induced us to think upon it and discuss it, and form opinions for ourselves." [82]

It will be impossible ever to introduce Learning
into this Country, till this Plague of Trustees is extir-
pated from among us.

> Charles Nisbet to Alexander Addison,
> February 23, 1797

It is calculated for the improvement of mankind
and god Knows they have much need of improvement.

> John Montgomery to Francis Gurney,
> August 23, 1799

6

NISBET IN LIMBO AND

AMONG THE BLEST

FOR fifty years after the enactment of its charter, Dickinson College was, substantially, a state-supported institution. From the very first, Dr. Rush had counted upon public money, while planning to begin operations and to expand them by private benefactions. He and others expected an era of prosperity to follow the war, a mood of national optimism grievously disappointed. Grievously disappointing too was Nisbet, who attracted students but not gifts. Yet Rush, while he had done his project great harm by involving it in ridiculous controversy, had also made himself a leading spokesman for republican education, that patriotic hope so enduring and so dear to every loyal citizen. His essays on the subject, read everywhere and greatly admired, served to stimulate and direct an acknowledged obligation to the future. Direct church support was not asked, nor given. Nonetheless, this was a Presbyterian college, and he had wisely urged Presbyterians—so long a political power—to think less of capturing offices and more of education. Granted that a majority of his Board of Trustees attended its meetings rarely or not at all, yet they had been selected as men of influence over a state-wide regional pattern, and they valued the distinction. The state responded early to the needs of Dickinson College, first with sporadic grants, then regular income, then income with the first elements of public control.

In its opening "Whereas," the *Act for the Present Relief and Future Endowment of Dickinson College,* passed on April 7, 1786, quoted in full that clause in the constitution of 1776 enjoining that "all useful learning shall be duly encouraged." [1] It was a duty which later state constitutions would reaffirm. The provision for an endowment had been withdrawn from the act of incorporation, September 9, 1783, but only with the intention of applying for one later. Now, on the eve of Nisbet's reelection, this maneuver was justified to the tune of £500 ($1,333.33) and ten thousand acres of land (then valued at about 20¢ per acre). The grant, furthermore, gave substance to a viewpoint long to be cherished by Dickinson's trustees, that by enacting its charter the state had assumed a measure of responsibility for the solvency and continuing operation of the College.

Four years later, this beginning was followed by an act authorizing a lottery which was to raise $8,000 toward the building of Philadelphia's city hall on Independence Square and $2,000 "for the use of Dickinson College." [2] Boldly, the trustees purchased fifty of the $4 tickets, investing what was then a quite substantial sum in their hope of gaining, perhaps, the $3,000 top prize. [3] This brought them only a loss of $140, a warning not to accept implicitly Dr. Rush's confidence in the "peculiar care of heaven." [4] Even before the drawing, they were voting to petition the state for "some further assistance," and this was received by an act of September 20, 1791: $4,000, to be applied to faculty salaries and other needs. [5] Thus heartened, and eagerly anticipating further legislative aid, they appointed a committee at their next meeting to examine the charter for amendments "proper [to be] made by the Assembly." [6] In 1794 an act authorizing a lottery to raise $7,500 "for erecting a suitable College-House" [7] failed to pass, but in the next year $2,000 was granted outright for the payment of debts, with $3,000 to be invested for permanent income. [8] With the "College-House" their main objective, the trustees set up a legislative lobby, September 28, 1797, of their three most influential members, Dr. Rush, Pennsylvania Supreme Court Justice Thomas Smith and General William Irvine. [9] When the building, completed by prolonged and varied effort, burned down on the eve of occupancy in 1803, the assemblymen responded as promptly as private donors were doing, and voted $6,000 to replace it. [10] Three years later, with the new building "nearly finished," they passed a supplement authorizing $4,000, "to be applied to the purchase of suitable books and philosophical apparatus." [11] Both sums were loans, free of interest for two years, and secured by the lands granted in 1786. Both sums were to come from the arrears of state taxes owed by Cumberland County, so that the trustees by no means received prompt relief. The trustees on their part never paid any interest, and the mortgage was cancelled in 1819 [12] —a merciful and reasonable measure, as the College had been closed since 1816 for lack of funds.

That gesture of 1819 encouraged a local movement to reopen, underway in 1820. By an act of February 20, 1821, the state assigned $6,000 to clear the institution of debt and repair its building, taking in return full title to the College lands. [13] In addition—and as a first step toward that state endowment expected by Rush—$2,000 was to be paid each January 1 for the next five years, without condition, for the "support of the institution." This was continued in the act of February 13, 1826, establishing an annual subsidy of $3,000 under closer state supervision and control. [14]

Of the two universities and fourteen colleges chartered by the legislature in this half century, the lion's share of state aid went to the college at Carlisle. [15] In all, Dickinson received $56,193.33, almost a quarter of the total. It was an experience significant in the development of public higher education. The grant of 1795 had carried a condition that the sum provided for endowment be used for the education of not more than ten boys in the three R's, for two-year periods—standing as a somewhat indirect support of higher education. State aid and the hope of it tended to keep tuition fees low. The fees alone never met expenses. There was always an annual deficit, and the appeals for private gifts were increasingly in competition with those of other institutions. In its act of 1826, the state at last sought to secure fundamental premises of public education. One clause repealed the charter's provision that every clerical member of the Board of Trustees should be succeeded by another of the same profession. Only one-third of the membership could be clergymen. At each payment of the annual subsidy, the Board was required to report in detail upon operations of the year before. This was a not unreasonable provision, considering what had happened to previous state aid. It was unfortunate, however, that the reports must be made not to a knowledgeable education department, but to active partisan politicans, whom the trustees, on their part, tended to cajole and extol as if they were individual donors. [16]

The famous Dartmouth College case, 1815 to 1819, establishing a college charter as a contract with the state, not to be altered except by mutual consent, had stimulated college founding and discouraged state support of private institutions. In Pennsylvania, however, the Dickinson trustees were ready to agree to anything, and were approaching the point at which they would willingly hand over the whole operation to others. The state officials on their part were coming to realize—and in the end would clearly see—that appropriations had been far in excess of benefits derived, and that the long-envisioned state system could only succeed as a full and coherent public responsibility.

That was a responsibility for which the voters at large were not yet ready. Later, it would be remembered with delight how Governor George Wolf's old father, back in 1785, had been asked to contribute to one of the new academies and had replied darkly, "Dis ettication und dings make rascals." Reminded that his own son, with such an advantage, might become governor he had only extended the doubt: "Vell den, . . . ven my George is Gofernor it vill be queer times." [17] Queer times there would be indeed in George's tenure, 1829 to 1835.

So much for Dickinson's early days as a state college. Look now at the strange patterns of internal conflict in the midst of which—somehow—this success with the political system had been achieved. The perennial aims and conflicts of a college community can be seen on this early campus, bare and raw. Here are trustees following their narrow path of ideal, compromise and expediency ("expedient," the most frequently recurrent word in Dickinson's and other minutes of the time).

The need for money is always on their side of the balance, while the value of the degree is on the faculty's. Here we have Principal Nisbet, who put the academic standard above all else and saw it as the true key to financial stability, and Vice-Principal Davidson, with that warm spirit of accommodation.

A spirit of accommodation was a necessity in almost all business dealings in the America of this day. Nisbet was outraged by the late and partial payments of his salary. But his salary from the Church and Davidson's church and college salaries all were in arrears, and professors elsewhere suffered the same. [18] Money was short, and credit must needs be long. So also with subscriptions from private donors to the College. Speculation was rife. Dr. Rush, as College money came his way, was tucking it hopefully into the state certificates based on soldiers' pay, an investment related to the great land speculations which would reach their peak in the 1790's. That land fever undoubtedly did influence Philadelphia and Baltimore donors, as it had John Armstrong and Robert Morris, though Morris's $1,000 subscription may never have been paid. A college in the west would bring settlement, development, rising values. Publicity was essential to spur the thing along, and Rush, who had done so much to damage the good name of his "brat," was keenly promoting it. Davidson gained a warm accolade for his Baltimore visits and collections, 1785—"Show me a man that loves and serves our College, and he is my brother"—and he may have written the publicity which ran in Philadelphia newspapers and magazines through the winter of 1786–87. [19]

This statement, drawn up "By Order of the Board" and printed over the signature of John Armstrong, President pro tem, seems reasonably factual. The College building (which Nisbet did not hesitate to describe as a "hogpen") is precisely pictured as sixty feet by twenty-three, with three rooms for classes and a fourth, still unfinished, for the Library (2706 volumes in *"Greek, Latin, English, French, German, Low Dutch and Italian"*) and the philosophical apparatus ("a complete Electrical machine, a Camera Obscura of a new construction, a Prism, a Telescope, a Solar Microscope, a Barometer and Thermometer upon one Scale, and a large and elegant set of GLOBES"). In this milieu, "The Senior Class, consisting of twenty students, are studying Natural and Moral Philosophy, having already studied the Classics and Mathematics, and other Branches usually taught in other Colleges."

Compare this, however, to some excerpts from the Principal's report to the trustees, drawn up at about the same time, November 13, 1786:

> The mean Appearance, the small Dimensions, & dirty Entries to the Building proposed, but not yet prepared, for the Accommodation of Students, must create a considerable Prejudice against this College in the Eye of the Public, who are commonly led by Appearance . . . .
>
> If one Master continues to have the Care of Forty, or a greater Number, entering at different times, the utmost Capacity, Care & Vigilance on his part can not enable the Boys to make that Progress which their Parents will naturally expect, and which is attained in other Seminaries by the help of more Masters & better Accommodation.
>
> If the Trustees expect that this Seminary should thrive, or increase, the Grammar School must be separated from it, & put under the Care of a proper Master, under the Inspection of the Professor of Languages, that the Noise of the inferior Classes may not distract the Attention, & hinder the Progress of those that are farther advanced, and able to read the Greek & Latin Classic Authors.
>
> Besides those that belong to the Grammar School, only twenty attend the Professor of Mathematics, and have begun the Study of Natural Philosophy.
>
> The same twenty attend the Professor of Geography, Chronology & History, as much as their Attendance on the other Classes will permit, & have lately begun the Study of Logic & Mataphysics as a Preparation for that of Moral Philosophy.
>
> The Students are generally in great Want of Books, as none fit for their Use are sold here, and to commission them from distant places is impracticable & precarious. This Want must be supplied, either by commissioning a proper Assortment, or engaging some Person who is willing to take the Risk of their Sale.
>
> The Library, which might already be of some Use to the Students, is shut up & rendered useless, no Keeper being appointed to take Care of the Books, or to take Receipts for Books borrowed out of it, and of late a Communication has been opened, that admits the Boys to go in and out of it when they please, so that the Books are in danger of being totally spoil'd or lost.

He adds a suggestion that College administration by regular
Board meetings is not efficient:

> Besides their stated meetings, it might be proper for the Trustees to
> appoint a small Executive Committee of their Number, residing in or
> near this Town, fully empowered & enabled to make due Payments at
> stated Times, to give necessary Orders, & transact incident Business in
> sudden Emergencies. [20]

It should be noted that in the press release the twenty
select students are a "Senior Class," while in the report they are
given no such designation. They are Seniors by trustee fiat
alone. Here, as at other new colleges, trustees ("the trusties," as
Colonel Montgomery invariably and engagingly spells it) had
been pressing the faculty to have a commencement—a formal
culmination and exhibition of young talent which was sure to
be echoed widely in the papers and (so they believed) to attract
new students in greater numbers than the departing group.
Here, as in most American colleges, there were two month-long
vacations, in May and October (planting and harvest), with commencements most often, appropriately, in September. In their
impatience to make progress, the trustees resolved on November
16, 1786, "that a number of the students in the Philosophical
Class [*i.e.,* those studying for a degree] be separated according
to the Judgment of the faculty in order to be prepared for a
Commencement against the second Wednesday in May next &
that a public examination of the said Class be held on the
second Wednesday of April." However, on April 10, the day
before the examination, Nisbet and Davidson reported the impossibility of awarding any degrees after less than a year of
college classes. [21] Davidson would certainly have managed the
thing, but Nisbet was obdurate, and remained so, in his contempt for trustees who would graduate students by a mandamus
based only on their own sense of expediency.

Yet he held them off for only four months. On Wednesday,
September 26, 1787, the first commencement of Dickinson College was held. Nine young men, rather than the "Senior Class"
of twenty, delivered their orations and received their honors
before the rustle of ladies and gentlemen sitting it out in the

Presbyterian Church. The affair lasted all day, with morning and afternoon sessions. The salutatory was in Latin, on the "Advantages of Learning." Orations in English extolled the "Excellency of Moral Science," "Taste," the "Greek and Latin Classics," on the "advantages of Concord especially at the present crisis of the United States of America" (surely an allusion to the Constitutional Convention which had been meeting in Philadelphia all that summer) and more. Steel Semple, a grandson of old John Steel, spoke on the Nature of Civil Liberty and the Evils of Slavery and Despotic Power. Robert Duncan, who had done so well in that poetic dialogue between Philemon and Eugenius, August, 1785, delivered the valedictory, pouring libations upon "Science," and on "the worthy patrons of literature" seated there beside him. [22]

Within this conventional framework, however, the first commencement held rumblings of disaster. Few of the worthy patrons of literature had taken the trouble to come. Only the familiar—to Dr. Nisbet too familiar—trustee faces were there, and in his commencement address he drew the students' attention to the fact:

> Your further progress in learning, and especially your good be-
> havior, may recommend this infant seminary, now abandoned by the
> far greater part of its pretended friends and those who made the
> greatest noise about its establishment. Though greatly deficient in
> funds, payments and accommodations, it may yet flourish, if it
> abounded in students. [23]

Next day, the trustees would be buzzing like hornets over this, writing to Rush, discussing "a process in the nature of a summons" which would force their absent colleagues to appear or face removal. [24]

But there was more. Dr. Nisbet told the commencement throng that he had no further hope of state aid, and enlarged upon this in a personal vein, saying that he and his family had been "made the song of the drunkards, and the mob of the Capital of this State were entertained with feigned stories of our behavior, and our pretended enmity for a country for which we had long suffered persecution . . . . When I forget thee, O America, for whom I have already suffered so much, may my tongue cleave to the roof of my mouth and my right hand forget its office!"

Yet he would continue, he told them, to champion its learning and culture. Himself reared "in the most learned nation of Europe," he knew how it had risen to that stature from a beginning not unlike that of America, and in America he stood prepared to shine a guiding light. But to the few listening trustees no gleam appeared. To them, Rush's repeated *"All will end well"* had become an ironic jest. To Rush, John King was writing, November 5:

> The College is becoming a painful business. Instead of having our hopes realized, our fears are more & more increased. I see certain ruin before us—we are sinking every year, and must fall ere long. The gentleman on whom we depended so much, is accumulating debt upon us by so high a salary—we cannot possibly support him. It is said he supports himself with the hope of recovering off our private fortunes. No subscriptions can be collected. All is darkness—& if it should yet *end well*, it will be strange indeed. [25]

Look now for a moment at this campus in its setting of local, national, world events. The Constitutional Convention met in Philadelphia in that summer of the first commencement. Dr. Rush's *Address to the People of the United States* urging a "Federal University" had been favorably discussed. The proposal was omitted only in a belief that no constitutional authorization was needed. [26] That winter, Carlisle's respectable minority planned to celebrate Pennsylvania's ratification with salutes of cannon in the public square. Rioters spiked their gun and hanged James Wilson and Chief Justice McKean in effigy. [27] Frontiersmen had little regard for the new national order and, more, looked darkly upon the College as a cradle for Federalist tyrants of the future. [28] Nevertheless, a new state constitution followed in 1790, including those conservative provisions for which Rush and Wilson had fought so long. The University, too, was returned to its original foundation, though the hated Ewing remained as Provost.

All this while, to the west, Indians were on the warpath again, and troops were mustering at Carlisle. Harmar's campaign of 1790 was a failure, and St. Clair's of 1791 a disaster of blood and horror. Nisbet had seen enough to express highly uncomplimentary opinions of both general officers, and to predict what occurred. The prospect of transforming the Works into a campus vanished, and in 1793 the trustees moved their Principal to a house in town. He now averred that the change in his residence, made "under Colour of Friendship," had been delayed from spring to fall "in a hope that the foul air of the Marsh might have an opportunity of working its proper Effects on us." [29] He seems to have guessed what had long lain in the mind of Benjamin Rush, "that God will change his heart or take him from us." [30]

Not so. The Almighty Disposer of Events kept Charles Nisbet in his place, meeting his classes day by day, watching Carlisle and the world afar from under angry brows. News of France in turmoil brought him obsessive apprehensions of reechoing revolution, the rise of satanic powers. The French declared themselves a republic in the fall of 1792, their victorious armies on the march, and the brooding Principal could hear the bells of Carlisle ringing in jubilant response. [31] Carlisle, neglectful of its college, raised money and a cargo of flour for France. George Kline of the *Gazette* reprinted Paine's *Rights of Man*. Vice-Principal Davidson, readily identifying France's humbled prelacy with the Beast of the Book of Revelations, shared his parishoners' joy. [32]

In August, 1794, Wayne's victory over the Indians at Fallen Timbers on the Maumee relieved Dr. Nisbet's anxiety for his daughter, who had been living with her husband near the Ohio line. Yet all that summer the whole country from Cumberland to the west was in a ferment of insurrection against the whisky tax. Carlisle's "whisky or Liberty Pole" stood, gaunt and idolatrous, on the public square. A caustic sermon brought upon Nisbet imminent danger of tarring and feathering. [33] Then, like an avenging host to his rescue, came the massive federal army. Soldiers and rebels rubbed elbows in the crowded village. For two weeks, Washington was the guest of his friend John Armstrong in Carlisle. He sat in the Presbyterian Church with the governors of Pennsylvania and New Jersey at his side and heard the Blessed Peacemaker preach on "order and good government, and the excellency of that of the United States." [34] It was well received by all, but Dr. Nisbet's homily in the afternoon, on the "Guilt of Rebellion," nearly provoked a riot. [35]

Spring came, with federal power vindicated and secure. The paved turnpike from Philadelphia to Lancaster had just been completed, stimulating like improvements elsewhere and lessening the provincial remoteness of Carlisle, as in mid-twentieth century the completion of the Pennsylvania Turnpike would do. A move was afoot to bring the state capital from Philadelphia to Lancaster, with Carlislers pressing for a location still farther west. [36] The Presbyterian General Assembly met at Carlisle in this spring of 1795, with John McKnight presiding. It had met here three years before, on each occasion the College shining brightly in a piously convivial setting. [37] Yet this period shows a weakening of the church relationship. At trustees' meetings the legal, medical and businessmen were taking over from the once-dominant clergy. This changed Board would succeed in the long-sought goal of constructing a new building, but first must deal with a new and formidable crisis, long in the making—student power.

It was not, alas, student pressure for a curriculum such as Benjamin Rush desired, more relevant to American life, but for that other object of student partiality, the quick and easy degree. It culminated in what has been called "one of the most remarkable episodes in the history of higher education"—the Dickinson College student strike of 1798. [38] The boys knew that without their presence, and tuition fees, the institution would collapse. Trustee and faculty discord must also have encouraged their own partisanship. One can trace the origins of the trouble back to the commencement of 1792, when thirty-three young men had been graduated—not by class standing or examination, but by selection and vote of the Board. This apparently prosperous commencement was then played up fulsomely in the press. Nisbet was furious. He tried to entice a friend in Philadelphia into publishing a correction.

> We had so many Students at our late Commencement, that we are much at a loss for Recruits. Our Trustees gave a great many Degrees by Mandamus, to whom they chose, but concealed this Circumstance in the Account they gave in the Papers, to throw the whole Infamy of the thing on the Masters . . . . They never deign to talk with me of

Business. How miserable it is to be subject to the meanest of Men!
The Insolence of Office is more discernible here than in Great Britain.
Could you venture to cancel this in Mr. Dunlap's Paper by a
Note . . . ? [39]

For the next two years the Board kept no minutes, Davidson apparently managing affairs by occasional consultation with
trustees as he found them in town. When they finally met, April
16, 1794, General Irvine had succeeded Armstrong as President
pro tem, and their minutes foreshadow the crisis to come. The
students were in rebellion against prelection.

> It has been represented to the Board that the Institution is likely to
> suffer very much by the Complaints of many of the Students who
> have had their Education here on account of the Labor of writing so
> great a number of Lectures on the various branches of Literature, that
> the Dread of this Circumstance has deterred many Young Men from
> coming to this place, and occasioned their going to other Colleges for
> compleating their Education, and that an ungenerous use has been
> made of the Copies of these Lectures in some Instances, which have
> been communicated to others to be written out under the care of
> private teachers so [as] to obviate the necessity of attending any
> public seminary.

Five charter trustees were present then—King, Black, Dobbin, Samuel Waugh, John Linn—with two newly-elected colleagues, Robert Cathcart and Nathaniel Randolph Snowden. All
were Presbyterian ministers. General Irvine had brought his
friend, Johnston, late of the faculty. Dr. McCoskry and lawyers
John Creigh and Samuel Laird were there. These gentlemen met
the crisis very much as administrators of a century or more later
might have done. They held a conference with the faculty, urging that the students' burden be lightened "without abridging
the Plan of Education, or the Time of Attendance in College,"
and appointed a committee to review and regularize the situation. The committee reported a year later, May 26, 1795, with a
code of laws, duly adopted, printed and distributed, the first of
a long series of published *Rules and Regulations.* Prelection
ends. There are no more volumes of student notes on Nisbet
lectures. The tacit yielding on this is balanced by stated requirements. Before the May and September vacations every student

must stand examination before the faculty (as always, viva voce), and professors were permitted to examine classes quarterly if deemed proper. The largest emphasis, of course, is on discipline, though the roster of offenses and prohibitions, when compared for instance to that at Yale, shows either less inclination to mischief or, more probably, a greater indulgence. For the rest, students were to be admitted only after examination by the faculty, and none would graduate "untill the Faculty shall certify that he hath made sufficient progress in the course of his Studies, and shall have paid all Demands due to the Institution." [40] There had been some laxity, as this last implies, in collecting tuitions.

Irvine stepped down as President pro tem of the Board in 1795, and old John Montgomery, staunch champion of School and College through so many years, took the chair. Also made Treasurer two years later, he would be, till his death in 1808, the dominant figure in Dickinson affairs. Here the Board is changing. The meetings of 1796 had only two clerics faithful in attendance, John Linn and Samuel Waugh. With them were Dr. McCoskry, Dr. James Armstrong, son of the General, businessman Charles McClure, Michael Ege the ironmaster, and then the gentlemen of the law, Creigh, Laird, Thomas Duncan and James Hamilton. Judge Hamilton since his election in 1794 had been typical of the new trustee spirit. He, as Dr. Nisbet saw it, "torments us with Meetings, Prospects of Innovations, Speeches & Examinations, & other mechanical Modes of Education." [41]

Linn and Waugh brought in a "Regulation of Classes" in 1796—an attempt again to form three clearly-defined classes above the Grammar School with specified studies for each. [42] It was discussed with the faculty, and Dr. Nisbet had an opportunity to speak again on the effect of students being awarded degrees without full and well-founded faculty approval.

Appeals to the legislature continued. Tuition was raised from £5 to £6. These practical men were themselves coming to that sense of desperation which the clerics had felt. Sixteen resolutions passed on June 21, 1797 reflect "this period so alarming to the interests & existence of the College." They are a mélange of good intentions thrown in from around the table, focused on that hope of legislative aid. An annual library budget is here, and a determination yet to achieve that goal set at the first meetings of 1783, "a proper edifice." Most significant of all, there is a warm appeal to the faculty for cooperation, and especially to Nisbet, not as a money-raiser (they had given up all thought of that), but for his advice to them and his greater intervention in the conducting of classes and examinations. Here was a vindication of the Principal's view at last, a brief moment in which one can imagine the unschooled old Indian fighter and the "walking library" from "the most learned nation of Europe," advancing together.

In Dr. Nisbet's report to the Board meeting of June 20, 1798, we have a glimpse of the student body whose predecessors had rebelled against prelection and among whom trouble was brewing and soon to break out again:

> This Seminary now consists of Seventy Six Students, a greater Number than it has had at any time hitherto . . . .
>
> The Philosophy Class [*i.e.* degree candidates] at present contains Twenty Seven Students, of whom four & twenty have attended the other Classes, & the Lectures on Criticism, Logic & Metaphysics. The remaining three have been permitted to join the Class at the Beginning of the Lectures on Moral Philosophy, but cannot expect to receive a Degree at next Commencement, as they have neither attended the other Classes, nor the former Lectures delivered in the Philosophy Class.
>
> A few Students decline entering on the Study of Languages & Philosophy & apply themselves only to Mathematics & Geography, an Account of whom will be given by the Masters whom they attend.
>
> Some Students are negligent in their Attendance on the public Lessons, & take the Liberty of absenting themselves when they please, for which some silly excuse is never wanting. On Monday last five were absent from the Philosophy Class. Others show an Inclination to trifling & Indolence, which the Masters do their utmost to correct.
>
> It is to be apprehended that Reading & private Study is too much neglected by many Students, tho' Exhortations to that Purpose have not been wanting, but the Masters can not judge of the private Employments of Students, which do not fall under their Inspection. [43]

"Private study," or homework, could be enforced only in a dormitory, and the Board was working on that. As its final resolution of this meeting, this overwhelmingly lay group passed a measure in support of sound doctrine—political rather than religious. The Professor of History was enjoined to lecture four times a year on "the preeminence of the Republican Form of Government to all others—to display its virtues and Energies—its moral and intellectual excellence—the Grandeur & Perfections of our Foederal system & State Institutions & to point out any practicable Improvements—to exhibit the defects of the ancient Republicks compared with the enlightened principle of Representation which pervades the American codes, & which now renders this form of Government commensurate with any extent of Territory."[44] This was beamed, of course, toward the General Assembly of the state of Pennsylvania. Though cited by Historians as an outstanding example of trustee interference in the academic program, it must be added that Davidson, ever willing, may even have suggested the thing himself.

Conservative patriotic fervor was riding high. Adams had succeeded Washington, an enemy of French radicalism even more to Nisbet's taste. Mary Nisbet Turnbull had moved to Philadelphia, where her father saw her sometimes in vacation, or wrote her at "No. 229 Market Street, Opposite tho' not opposed to the President of the United States."[45] In the war fever of 1798, Dickinson students pledged loyalty to Adams as "the patron of science, liberty and religion," and the President responded with blessings upon them and their college.[46] This exchange had taken place at their return from the spring vacation. It was a week after their reassembling from the September recess that the blow fell.

At his home on the morning of Wednesday, November 7, 1798, Dr. Nisbet examined a group of new boys to determine their entrance standing. He then walked down to Liberty Alley to meet his first class, but no class appeared. Something worse than usual was in the wind. Only too well aware that others of the faculty often knew what he did not, he spoke to Thomson in the grammar school room. Professor Thomson knew. The faculty could, if it wished, meet with the students at two o'clock, but the boys had unanimously determined to leave college at once unless the whole degree course be restricted to one year.[47]

Administration yielded. Nisbet, never reticent in giving an

opinion, endured the "literary quackery" for three successive one-year terms. Classes continued as before, seven hours a day, but he threw at the trustees the absurdity of expecting a student "to read Cicero, Juvenal, Lucian, Homer & Xenophon, & to learn Geography, Astronomy, Chronology, History, Oratory, English Grammar, & Natural Philosophy, Arithmetic, plain Geometry, Trigonometry, Navigation & Algebra, Criticism, Logic, Metaphysics, & Moral Philosophy in the space of ten Months," all this without taking notes in class. [48] He stood his ground. It has been said that when Dr. Nisbet had a point to score his whole face would light up, bright and aggressive, with an expression all its own. We may imagine old Colonel Montgomery facing up to this, his gray mouth pulled down at the side, one eye closing slowly as it would have done behind a rifle barrel in the Indian wars.

Time would prove Nisbet in the right. Dickinson graduates lost standing among college men and with employers. This early experience shows well the tie between academic standards and the standing of the alumnus. Some other events were moving his way. Deism had become an influence in American colleges and the Presbyterian Assembly of 1798 (taking its cue from the Methodists) had sounded a warning against the danger. [49] Nisbet was reading John Robison's *Proofs of a Conspiracy*, hair-raising revelations of the menace of infidelity from a learned Scottish source which had become very popular in America. [50] When, only a fortnight after the student strike, news came through of Lord Nelson's victory of the Nile, he set a team of boys to ringing the College bell all day long, to serve a notice on Carlisle, "this trifling place," of how the winds of the world were blowing. [51] The rye crop in the valley, he reported to Mary, May 13, 1799, had been again attacked by the Hessian fly— "which threatens us with a Famine of Whisky. And if this is taken away, what have we more?" [52]

As he had foretold, students did not flock in to get the quick degree. The College lost both money and repute, and the trustees must needs return at last to the program they had affirmed so short a time before the rebellion. [53] They would find, however, that it is far easier to weaken a standard than to regain it. It would be a long road back, with a lesson learned— for a time—in the necessity of trustee-faculty cooperation.

Desperate yet determined, the Board was now giving its all to the perennial hope and concern of all trustees—its building program. Back in 1784, it had been the opinion of John Armstrong that "there never will be any Building erected at Carlisle that should deserve the name of a College, these seven years to come." [54] It would take twenty. Yet this alone could bring unity, status, permanence. Only Benjamin Rush believed that academic intangibles might be a firmer foundation than brick or stone: "It is said that before the time of the Emperor Constantine the churches had wooden pulpits but golden ministers, but after he took Christianity under his protection, the churches had golden pulpits but wooden ministers. The same," he assured his colleagues, "may be said of literary institutions." [55]

The trustees did not accept this as a necessary alternative. They had still the plans for a building drawn for them by John Keen in 1792. [56] Then they had had money from the lottery of 1791 and other sources, £1,700 to be exact. Montgomery had pressed in vain for a start, while inertia and the tides of debt took over. [57] But now, with the Colonel both President and Treasurer of the Board, a seven-acre lot was acquired from the Penns, just west of the village across High Street from the house that Dr. Nisbet had bought. Bids were being taken in November, 1798. [58] John Dickinson expressed joy that "a proper Edifice" was at last to be erected, trusted that it might have "an elegant simplicity" and prayed for success. [59] In response to a suggestion that prayer was not enough, he subscribed $100. [60] It was his first gift to the College in many a year. Nisbet had visited him in 1792, perhaps to solicit funds for the building, and would learn on his return to Carlisle that Dickinson had deposited $500 in a Philadelphia bank, subject to his personal order, and in a hope of receiving further visits. [61] Obviously, the Principal rather than the College held Dickinson's heart and conscience.

"New College," built of brick, rose slowly above the grass and bushes and outcroppings of the gray native stone. In July, 1799, the beams of the first floor were being laid; in August, the second floor; but money was running low. Periodically, the work would stop while subscribers in the county and the cities were being harried for payment. On May 26, 1800, it was voted to borrow $2,000, with the state land grant as security. It was the first step in the dissipation of capital held as permanent endowment, with others soon to follow. In 1800, the old Colonel suffered a long illness, prostrated by pain and worry at his home, "Happy Retreat." By 1801, he had a roof on his building, but work was at a standstill again.

Nisbet, who learned of trustee doings only by rumor, wrote John Dickinson on November 21, 1801, of mismanaged funds for which he was blamed, and of a plan to force his return to Scotland upon some pretext—"I am now in the condition of the Lion in the Fable of Aesop who in his Old-age was kicked by the Ass." [62] It was only too true, as Nisbet also readily declared, that the one-year course "had taken away two thirds of the Tuition Money & reduced the Reputation of the Seminary more than three fourths"—yet this error does seem to have led on to some improvement in trustee-faculty consultation. [63]

On December 24, 1802, Colonel Montgomery reported to Colonel Gurney, his aide in the intricacies of finance, "The new Building is so far finished as to accommodate the Proffors and Student." [64] Three rooms were in use, but Library and apparatus had not yet been moved in when, on the night of February 3, 1803, disaster struck. Montgomery poured out the terrible news to Benjamin Rush:

> . . . was nearly finished had a grand appearance was ornamentall and Elegent had 12 Large apartments but as all things are uncertain in this world and that our Joys and Comforts can not be Compleat or parmient that noble fine house was yesterday redusced to ashes by accidence occassioned by putting hot ashese in the Sellar about 11 oClock a Voulant snow storm from the west attended with a Bold wind had Blowen Sparks to Shavaing or other stuff and not Being Decovred in time the whole Building was instantly in flames and thus my friend after all our trouble and Exspence in Erecting an Elegent and Comfortable house for Dickinson College our hops were Blasted in a few minutes my Eies Beheld the Disstroying flames with an ackening Hart . . . . [65]

This from the Indian Fighter. The Walking Library turned a cooler eye upon the scene of desolation:

> We had been bothered by the Trustees to make our College conform to Princeton College. We have now attained a pretty near Con-

Top left: Robert Davidson. Copy, by Margaret F. Winner, after an oil by an unidentified artist. Top right: John Ewing. Copy, by Edward Dalton Marchant, of life portrait by Charles Willson Peale, 1788. Bottom left: General Willism Irvine. Copy, by James Reid Lambdin, of life portrait by Robert Edge Pine, c, 1784. Bottom right: Francis Gurney. Lithograph, c. 1835, after a contemporary silhouette.

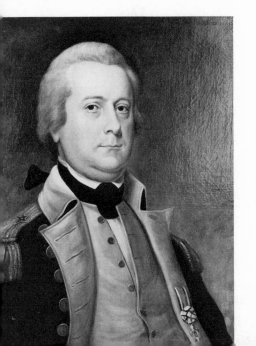

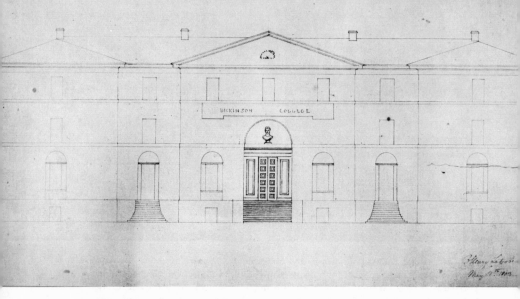

West College. Elevation and basement ground plan from first proposal by Benjamin H. Latrobe, 1803.

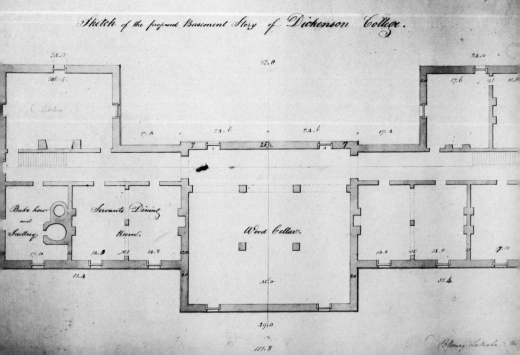

formity to it by having our Building burnt down to the Ground. But
it could not stand, as it was founded on Fraud & Knavery. The
Trustees in order to procure Money for finishing this Building sold the
Certificates that furnished the Salaries of the Masters, cheated your
humble Servant out of two thousand six hundred and twenty Dollars . . . . [66]

The burning of Princeton's Nassau Hall March 6, 1802, had
given the Dickinson trustees an example of a dramatic and inspiring swift recovery. Carlisle had subscribed generously to the
new building fund at once, and as soon as the spring thaws had
come and roads were firm they moved out with their appeal to
the surrounding counties and to the cities beyond. [67] Dr. Nisbet
was dispatched to Philadelphia and New York, where, as may
have been anticipated, he did poorly. [68] Robert Cathcart covered Philadelphia a year later with better success, though he raised
only $500. [69] Wisely, they had not sent Nisbet to Washington,
where Jeffersonian democracy was now in power. That field
went to the Rev. John Campbell, Carlisle's Episcopal minister,
and Judge Hamilton, a supporter of the new regime and a re-
puted free-thinker as well. Their collections of March, 1803,
included sums from the President, Vice-President, Chief Justice
Marshall, cabinet members and congressmen, even the embassies
contributing to the cause of American education.

Hamilton was one of a committee to secure plans for rebuilding and, with things going so well, wrote to his friend,
Judge Hugh Henry Brackenridge, then on circuit at Easton,
setting off a new chain of responses. The genial Brackenridge
rode "with the speed of an express" to Philadelphia, where
America's foremost architect and engineer, Benjamin Henry
Latrobe, was on the point of leaving to take charge of the
building program at the new capital. [70] Latrobe responded at
once with a letter of advice, preliminary elevations and ground
plans—to be followed later with working drawings as his contribution to the cause. The new "college house" would be on the
site of the other, but larger. Use stone, not brick, Latrobe advised, "the lime stone of your Valley" for indigenous character
and appearance of strength [71] —advice which has been followed
with fair consistency ever since, giving definition to the campus

as the town crept up around it. To accent his design he specified horizontal sill courses of cut stone from York County, a reddish brown in contrast to the gray.[72]

It was to be a long building, with a tall central chamber in which the whole college could assemble. Some features were new in academic design. Instead of dark central corridors, the corridors would be on the north, while most of the rooms, ranged along the southern front, would gain heat from the sun as well as their fireplaces—reinforced, as Latrobe sagely observed, by "the concourse of students." Latrobe recommended interior walls of brick and an iron roof, a new thing, also adding a safeguard against fire. Reminded that a college must have a cupola for its bell, he brushed through his Stuart and Revett *Antiquities of Athens,* and gave his simple design of columns and dome something of the aspect of the Athenian Tower of the Winds by adding its figure of a little fish-tailed god as weathervane—a feature which the Carlisle coppersmith (ignorant of the triton as a species but familiar enough with mermaids) would alter into the small feminine deity who has turned with the winds over Dickinson College for so many years.[73]

The cornerstone was laid on August 8, 1803, and in their notice of the event published in the *Carlisle Gazette* it is clear that the trustees well appreciated their good fortune:

> . . . The plan of the building has been furnished by Mr. Latrobe, surveyor of the Public Works of the U. States, and unquestionably the first architect of the age. The donation is considered invaluable as no price can be set on the efforts of the scientific mind. Simplicity and adaptation to the purposes of the Institution are its excellence. As a public building it will do honour to Pennsylvania.[74]

On November 4, 1805, students first assembled for classes in the "New College" of Latrobe. Only a bare sufficiency of rooms was finished. Montgomery's jubilant hope of having all the boys living and working together under the one roof brought a stern rebuke from Dr. Rush: "unfriendly to order and hurtful to morals."[75] He was alone in this view. Montgomery went right ahead with his plans, writing John Dickinson, November 20, 1805, that in the spring they would be able to employ a steward and board and lodge about forty students—

praying him to come and see for himself what their long labor
had wrought: "Built of stone has an Eligent and Grand appar-
ance has a hansome Coupulae." [76] Yet long labor still remained,
and five years would pass before any students had rooms. The
work of flooring, partitioning, plastering went forward, room
by room, as money could be found. [77] Classrooms, library, laboratory and society halls must come first.

It was in the first winter of rebuilding, January 18, 1804,
that Charles Nisbet died of a winter cold turning to pneumonia,
his life fading out on a whispered, "Holy, Holy, Holy." [78]
Trustees, faculty and students wore black crepe on the left arm
for thirty days. [79] His funeral filled the church where so often
he had preached strong doctrine to reluctant ears. There was
that sudden looming sense of a greatness that had shone and
passed. Rush and Montgomery joined at last in his praise. James
Ross, now at Franklin College, published a Latin ode, Charles
Keith of Edinburgh his "Monody," and Isabella Oliver, poetess
of Cumberland, her laurel wreath from the banks of Conodoguinet:

> ALAS! another luminary's gone!
> "Whence rays of truth and science brightly shone."
> Great NISBET'S dead! He too from Scotia came,
> His soul inspired with thy sacred flame,
> O Liberty! [80]

A learned successor would crown all this with a long epi-
taph in Latin, spelled out in marble at the center of the Old
Graveyard of Carlisle, [81] but no successor would have Nisbet's
fame for learning or his success as a teacher. Those who follow
the minute and regular march of Nisbet's sharply-whittled quill
across the page rarely see beyond the mood of pessimism and
contempt—unwilling citizen of a nation hastening to ruin, intellectually divided into "two great Parties, the Anything-
arians . . . & the Nothingarians." [82] Yet he had his own ideal of
freedom in the western world, patterned and belligerent though
it might be. "O Liberty!" Only a few—the poetess for one—were
aware of this. Nor does one see the humanity of the man; so
real to his close friends, or his hand in community welfare.
Early in his tenure, Nisbet had headed the managers of a school

for the education of the children of slaves,[83] and he had responded well to the Earl of Buchan's injunction to found a
neighborhood library.[84] Under his brash condemnations, too,
there lay the terrible humiliation of a father whose eldest son,
once so promising, had become a hopeless, notorious drunkard.

As for the trustees, Dr. Nisbet's passing ended the accumu-
lation of arrears of salary, but left them with a well-secured
obligation for a very formidable sum.[85] It left them also with
the problem of finding a successor who would attract students,
finish the building, achieve a balanced economy. At the trustees' meeting two days after Nisbet's death, Dr. Davidson had
proposed some curricular changes in evidence of his expecting
to rise from Vice-Principal to Principal. "O Providence, supply
his vacant chair!" Isabella Oliver had exclaimed, perhaps sure
that Davidson, her friend, would be the choice. But most of the
trustees demurred. At last, it being obvious that no perspica-
cious educator would take over the task of paying his predecessor's salary at the risk of his own, Davidson, the ever-willing,
was given the job under a conditional title, "President of the
Faculty."[86]

As such, he would continue with the College for five years
more. The previous years had really been his administration as
well, since there had been no effective rapport between Nisbet
and the trustees. He would now be running a smooth and undistinguished operation of three professors, forty to fifty grammar
school boys, and twenty to thirty degree candidates in a two-
year college course, Junior and Senior Classes. William Thomson, whom he had hired in 1794 to replace the young and
irreverent Henry Lyon Davis in the key position of Professor of
Languages, had left in 1802 for a more comfortable post at
Princeton. He was a casualty of the annual commencements,
when dwindling attendance forced a reduction in salaries and
even the Grammar School could not support an experienced
master. John Borland, a younger man, had replaced him, and
now, in 1805, Borland was replaced by the still younger John
Hayes, who had just graduated with that year's class, a ministerial candidate and (under Davidson's influence) a poet.[87]

Here was a student with whom Davidson had no trouble;
but it must be noted that student opinion, more than any other

factor, had prevented his appointment as Principal. [88] Student notes show his lectures on history, criticism, even science, to have been more than a cut above the level of *Geography Epitomiz'd,* but as poet and pedagogue he stood firm upon the little book, which every boy must purchase, memorize and revere. Woe to him who did not—and one who did not, it seems, was Dickinson's most famous alumnus of later years, now a sandy-haired, blue-eyed six-footer, with a wry neck which was to characterize him for the rest of his life, and a cockiness to be seen later as a sedate self-confidence. In his Junior year with the Class of 1809, James Buchanan enjoyed himself to the full while meeting perfectly every requirement of the college course, as his notes on science and mathematics for Professor McCormick bear witness. [89] At the end of that year, he was staggered to receive notice that he would not be permitted to return. So much for the gay life and a spirit of levity toward the author of *Geography Epitomiz'd.*

Actually, Buchanan's expulsion seems to have been no more than a disciplinary measure set up to have a sobering effect upon him. He was advised to seek clemency from the new President of the trustees, Dr. John King. John King, who had been pastor of the church of Upper West Conococheague, Mercersburg, since 1769, had baptized this boy and watched over him ever since. He delivered an admonitory lecture and sent James, chastened, back for the final year. In this more earnest mood, James made himself again a problem as commencement approached by trying to get both honors, valedictorian and salutatorian, for his own society, the Union Philosophical. Here the faculty saw fit to intervene, taking the decision from the students and awarding first place to Belles Lettres and second to a U. P. boy, while ignoring Buchanan, the top student, altogether. James struck back at this gross injustice with a student protest and threatened a strike—no orations at all from U. P. It was the Blessed Peacemaker, of course, who restored order, if not calm, and Buchanan, seething inwardly, delivered his oration with the others, its title *The Utility of Philosophy.* [90]

This was the young man who would move from Congress to cabinet, to the great embassies and to the presidency of the United States, always kindly and tactful, vain and precise, always seeking solutions first of all by friendly agreement—in statecraft and diplomacy, as his biographer has pointed out, a perfect pattern of the Blessed Peacemaker.[91]

In 1805, the *Rules and Regulations* of ten years before were republished with additions to insure due order within the new building—classes regularly seated together, hats removed on entrance and hung on their pegs, no knives, "segars," glass breaking, writing on walls or driving nails into them, no ball playing either in or outside the edifice.[92] Judge Hamilton and Dr. McCoskry were appointed a committee to supervise the removal of the scientific equipment and library, and $200 was appropriated for "maps and additions to the philosophical apparatus."[93] Since the state grant of that year specified apparatus and library, the trustees' meeting of March 13, 1806, instead assigned the $200 toward the claims of the Nisbet heirs. Dr. McCoskry, who had married a Nisbet daughter, was one of the administrators of the estate, and one can sense the rather desperate maneuvering to hold off that obligation until New College could stand complete and unencumbered. John Dickinson died, February 14, 1808, leaving no bequest to the College. Rush and Montgomery had been hoping to the last that this estate might do something to offset the demands of the other.

Dr. Rush was given charge of spending the state money assigned to laboratory, and in the fall of 1808, with over $1,000 in hand, he added an air pump, "a small chemical apparatus for showing the composition of air and water," and a large static electricity machine built in Germany ten years before, "the most complete and splendid thing of the kind ever imported into our country . . . . It will add much to the reputation of our College."[94] All his old enthusiasm for the College had returned, and his mind was again upon the need for a new Principal, a man of great eminence, but this time an American. To old John Montgomery, who had borne the battle for so long and who was now in the last months of his life, he could close a letter with the old bold assurance, "Adieu! my deal friend. Keep up your spirits. *All—All will end well.*"

"All will end well." Upon this confident note a new chapter in Dickinson College history begins. In politics, Jeffersonian democracy had the ascendancy, with Rush, at least, in sym-

pathy with its ideals. Beyond that, Jacksonian democracy would change the face of American life. But in academic life, the reaction against eighteenth-century rationalism and freedom of thought was in full swing through all these years, and would pose problems and forces of which the two old friends seemed unaware. Innocently abetted on both sides by Rush, the College would become a furious battle ground of piety and freedom fought out until it closed its doors in 1832, both sides abandoning the field.

The earliest view of West College. From the *Dickinson College Almanac for the Year 1807*. Astronomical calculations by David Pringle, Class of 1806.

During the Presidency of Dr. Atwater, and at the time of Judge Cooper's nomination to the Professorship of Chymestry, &c. there began to be an opposition in the Board to clerical influence.

A Narrative of the Proceedings of the Board of Trustees of Dickinson College . . . 1830

Knowledge is threefold: Physical, Moral and Religious. Physical is that which explains the laws, &c. of matter. Moral, explains the laws which rule men, as sociable and gregarious beings. Religious, teaches man his duty to God. We shall treat only of the first.

Thomas Cooper, opening of Second Course in Chemistry, 1812

7

SATAN'S SEAT

AT the commencement of September 27, 1809, the student discontent sparked by young James Buchanan and his fellow "Unions" might not have been kept under cover so well but for a new element of drama. The despised Davidson was retiring, and a new Principal, Jeremiah Atwater, had come in to hold the center of attention. Before the polite assemblage of College fathers, townfolk and students on that day of promise there stood a tall lean figure, to their eyes the typical New Englander, angular, nasal and sanctimonious, looking, in the spirit of this solemn hour, older than his thirty-five years. This was the type "from the East" old Colonel Montgomery had so despised. The newcomer's view of them was condescending, and they would be prepared to see in him the cunning meanness of the Yankee of stage and story. They heard now an inaugural address which opened with a long sophomoric review of the branches of learning. "How sweet is mathematical knowledge!" A sweetness, it seems, tempered by the sad fact that "it leads to scepticism on religious subjects."[1] He expressed an unctuous diffidence as successor to Dr. Nisbet, and there must have been some present who observed the contrast.

After the graduating orations had been spoken, two students recited "a dialogue in blank verse . . . complimentary to the Trustees, Faculty and all the friends of learning." Here was a far echo of the colloquy between Philemon and Eugenio at that first College forgathering of 1785—and undoubtedly from the same hand. Robert Davidson, the ever-willing, the ever-tactful, was doing his best, as he retired from the office whose full honors had been denied him, to make the occasion a success. He himself closed the ceremonies with what the editor of the *Carlisle Herald* called "a very appropriate and pathetic *Address* to the Graduates." [2] When the trustees met that afternoon, they would have his letter of resignation before them. They then responded with a hope that he might continue teaching, and added to this the high compliment of electing him to their body. It was a safe move, for administrative expediency rather than academic standard had always come first in his thinking. [3] As a trustee, he would attend meetings regularly, both enjoying and exercising the superiority of his position over that of the new Principal, toward whom he seems to have felt from the first an understandable coolness.

As for the Rev. Jeremiah Atwater, he was at the moment unaware of the thorns and pitfalls in the path before him. This was to be Dickinson's first experience with a new chief executive, burning to accomplish complete renewal. That flame, always so hopeful, so transitory, was fated here to a short and flickering life. Atwater had not been first choice. The search had been initiated in 1808 with the setting of the Principal's salary at $1,000 and then with a resolution to consult the heads of other colleges. [4] Spurred on by Rush, the trustees had elected the learned and active Samuel Miller, later Nisbet's biographer. He had declined, perhaps from an awareness of the size of the debt to Nisbet's heirs. So also had Andrew Hunter, an old friend of Rush who had taught mathematics and astronomy at Princeton. [5] James Patriot Wilson, an eminent Philadelphia divine, was approached by Rush and his committee. "Providentially"—the word is Dr. Rush's—when the group was at Wilson's they found there Timothy Dwight, President of Yale, whom Rush had already consulted by letter. To him they appealed again, and were told that "Mr. Atwater, President of Middlebury College, . . . was dissatisfied with his situation, and wished to leave it." [6]

Dr. Dwight may not have been aware that Middlebury, was no less dissatisfied with Atwater. But Mr. Atwater came of an old New Haven family. His father had been a steward at Yale, and the son, in Yale's Class of 1793, had won a three-year graduate scholarship for excellence in classics. He was a tutor at Yale when Timothy Dwight came in as President, turned to the study of theology under him, and thus became at the outset a protégé and disciple of the leading figure in that crusade against the eighteenth century's liberal intellectualism that revival of Faith, which was to have such appalling effects upon educational advance. Jeremiah Atwater, like an opening rocket in the war, reveals in his brief career all that can—and cannot—be accomplished by an inflexible piety. He had left Yale in 1799 to head the Addison Grammar School in Vermont, which became Middlebury College the following year. At Middlebury he had soon found himself overshadowed in every respect by Frederick Hall, a teacher of mathematics ("leading to scepticism on religious subjects") and natural philosophy, a brilliant teacher, widely travelled, urbane and popular.[7] To Atwater, the invitation from Dickinson College was providential indeed. He took an immediate and cursory leave of Middlebury, August 16, 1809, happily unaware that his past trials were soon to be repeated in the same pattern and in greater measure.[8]

On September 11, the Reverend Jeremiah, his wife and three children and his wife's sister, were in Philadelphia as the guests of Dr. Rush. To Rush, the new Principal "appeared to be learned, well read, pious," and he foresaw in him "a blessing to Science, Religion, and to all the best interests of our Country!"[9] Atwater may have declared his conviction that a career in education should be "subservient to the cause of Christ" and its success be measured in "bringing forward young men for the ministry."[10] He did not mention (since he confided this at a later date) his belief that education had not reached a respectable standing so far south even as Philadelphia, and that he "was going upon a business of experiment, the success of which I considered problematical; that my whole confidence of success (under Providence) depended on introducing some of the regulations of the New-England Colleges, particularly those relating to the all-important point of discipline, without which a College is a pest, a school of licentiousness."[11]

Discipline, we know, was discussed, and Atwater brought forward the unusual provisions in the Dickinson College charter by which this responsibility was vested solidly with the trustees, and not only that, but the Principal was denied any ex officio place on the Board. Other college presidents, in accepted practice, were in the chair at trustee meetings. "Dr. Rush," he recalled later, "mentioned to me with much approbation his agency in causing the charter to be as it is, and that it was occasioned by his dislike to the ascendancy which Dr. Ewing had gained over the Trustees of the Inst. in Phila." [12] That a feud with this college head of the past should now be limiting his own prerogatives must surely have been disturbing to Atwater, but he must now needs take the sour with the sweet.

Sweetness he found in his first meeting here with Dr. Rush's brother-in-law, Ashbel Green, pastor of Duffield's old church in Philadelphia, a man of commanding presence, amiability and charm. Dr. Green had also been eyed by Rush as a possible candidate for Dickinson. [13] He was, however, a trustee of Princeton and all his interests lay in that direction. Working through theological students at the College, he was endeavoring to make Princeton just such a province of Christ's kingdom as Dwight was fashioning at Yale, gradually destroying the influence of Princeton's able President Samuel Stanhope Smith, whom he would force from office and replace himself in 1812. Green brushed all educational theory aside. Sunday schools, Bible and tract societies and religious revivals were the thing. [14] The Princeton Theological Seminary is his monument in a career marked by the decline of the College and harassed by student turmoil. He was now happy to find in Atwater a kindred spirit, and when, a year later, he manifested his confidence by sending his own son to Dickinson, the bond was complete, and Jeremiah opened his heart to this new friend in a series of letters which inform us in detail of the turmoil and decline at Carlisle. [15]

Approaching Carlisle, the Atwaters had taken a wrong road, and so missed the delegation of citizens which had come out to escort them into town, the honor accorded Nisbet so long before. [16] Ignoring this ill omen, the new Principal reported to Rush a pleasing impression of the town—which, indeed, with its stone houses along wide, grassy, tree-shaded streets with flagstone footways, had a look of age and solid substance.

Latrobe's building, too, he admired; yet glimpsed alas that school of licentiousness—"the young men their own masters, doing what was right in their own eyes, spending their time at taverns & in the streets, lying in bed always till breakfast & never at the College but at the time of Lecture"—he had feared to find. [17] He had come, as he wrote back to Rush, to "a city broken down and without walls. I find that almost everything is to be begun anew." [18] To its predominantly southern student body he must now bring the standards of New England morality and order. [19]

The trustees responded, and gave him a record of initial accomplishment. It is respectable in character, and might have been more so had their support continued. First, a large new bell, symbol and instrument of institutional regularity, was purchased in Philadelphia. [20] Orders were then given to level the campus and plant trees, perhaps with the trim New Haven Green in mind. [21] Learning that no college catalogue had ever been issued, the Principal himself compiled one, listing all trustees, faculty and students from 1783. It revealed vacancies on the Board, and enabled him to have his new friend, Ashbel Green, elected to membership. [22] The first catalogue, 1810, was followed by others in 1811 and 1812, all in broadside form. For the commencement of 1810 he wrote a short history of the College which was published in revised form in the *Port Folio.* [23]

Atwater's catalogue of 1811 lists 118 students in four classes, counting the Grammar School as one. In the next year, however, a college population of 124 is divided into the four classes we know today, with a separate list of Grammar School pupils. Here we see solved the problem of standing with which Nisbet and Davidson had wrestled in vain, though there is some evidence that the reform was not yet secure. [24] Complementing the catalogue, Atwater brought in another innovation, the first printed *Laws of Dickinson College.* It is the successor of the earlier "Plans of Education," and it is probably the "code of Laws" submitted by the faculty to the Board and confirmed, with sundry amendments, on December 20, 1810. [25] It is a credit to Atwater's persuasiveness that its opening paragraphs were allowed to stand without moderation:

1. The government of the College shall be vested in the Principal and Professors, and shall be styled *The Faculty of the College.*

The Principal was to preside at faculty meetings, which either he or any two professors might call. Matters would be decided by a majority vote, with the Principal voting to break a tie.

The nine chapters of this little work cover every aspect of the college operation below the superior level of the trustees. The emphasis is strongly upon morality and discipline—to be maintained by monitors, tutors, and, over these, the faculty. The curriculum is outlined as a four-year course:

> The *Freshmen* class shall be instructed for one year in the learned languages and arithmetic; and the study of the languages shall be continued in part during the whole of their standing in College. The *Sophomore* class shall be instructed for one year in English Grammar, Geography, Algebra, Geometry, the mensuration of Superficies and Solids, and Conic Sections. The *Junior* class, for one year, in Chronology, and History, Trigonometry, Navigation, Surveying, and Natural Philosophy—and the *Senior* class, for one year, in Astronomy, Chymistry, Rhetoric, Ethics, Logic, Metaphysics, Civil policy, and the law of Nature and Nations—With these studies, shall be intermixed, frequent essays in Elocution, Composition and Forensic disputation. On the evenings of Tuesday and Friday, the students, about four each time, shall declaim immediately after prayers; nor shall any student be exempted from it, except on account of natural impediments, or other disqualifications, of which the Faculty or Principal may judge. It is recommended to the Senior class, more especially to pronounce orations or declamations of their own composition—Saturday forenoon shall also be principally employed in essays of Elocution, by the respective classes. The several classes shall frequently read specimens of their composition to their respective Teachers; and the three higher classes shall, once or twice a week, dispute forensically on some question previously appointed.

At about the same time as the first catalogue, a broadside statement of College finances from 1783 to 1809 was issued, a trustee document bringing the somewhat arcane operations of past treasurers into the open as well as could be done from the records at hand. [26] This may be counted as an Atwater reform and it may have influenced Rush in insisting that the Principal take part in the new effort to obtain a legislative grant, a matter which the trustees had felt that they could best handle themselves. [27] When it failed, Atwater turned to the pursuit of private benefactors with a somewhat desperate ardor. He now knew how desperate the need. Early in 1810 the trustees had voted to liquidate endowment sufficient to meet half of the Nisbet and other debts—and at the same time they voted $1,250 for new scientific equipment, entrusting selection and purchase to Dr. Rush. As it turned out, Rush himself was the only significant private donor, sending a gift, munificent indeed for those days, of $500. He placed no restrictions on its use.

> I request only,—nay, I *insist* upon no notice public or private being taken of it. Should I hear of my unworthy name being stained upon any of your walls, I shall employ a person to deface it. Tell Mr. Atwater I demand his interference to prevent it. The dread of seeing a record so calculated to feed vanity will forever keep me from fulfilling my promise to pay one more visit to Carlisle, in order to pronounce my parting blessing upon our College before I depart hence and am no more. [28]

Atwater saw here an opportunity for the completion of his plan. With this money the still unfinished upper floors of his building could be partitioned into dormitory rooms and the big central hall on the main floor made suitable for all-college assemblies. [29] He wrote President Dwight in a hope of getting young Yale graduates to serve as tutors, living with the students as overseers of work and morals. None came from Yale, but the University of Pennsylvania gave him Samuel Blanchard How, aged twenty, a youth of piety and charm, who became Principal of the Grammar School, a tutor in the College, and a trusted Atwater confidant.

Atwater was also seeking a professor of chemistry and natural science, an area in which McCormick of Mathematics was then doing double duty. Rush recommended a young German, Dr. Charles Frederick Aigster, whom he had not met but who had certificates of character from Dr. Nicholas Collin "Mr. Vaughan of Maine" and others. [30] Rush concurred warmly in the Principal's plan to reform not only the College but the town (where, as Atwater had apprised him, "Drunkenness, swearing, lewdness & dueling seemed to court the day"), [31] but the plan for a dormitory brought a prompt explosion. Atwater wrote back plaintively, September 18, 1810, that the trustees had agreed to hire "the German gentleman," but that especially with an increasing student body, "I know not how we shall succeed in having them under proper discipline without having them lodge in the College under the inspection of tutors." [32]

Many students had been living in the homes of faculty and trustees, and in these circumstances the system so strongly preferred by Rush must have been better than regimented dormitory life. But in other homes where students might lodge little interest would be taken in keeping them at their studies. We can imagine Atwater thanking Providence that this founder and prestigious trustee, so friendly to him but of such decided views—an exponent of mysticism as an exact science—dwelt afar and did not come to meetings. The Doctor's money was applied to a kitchen and other aspects of the plan than the actual living quarters. [33] More—Rush at this very time was reopening with fresh verve his war upon the study of the classical languages. [34] The only evidence of his having brought it to bear at Carlisle, however, is the trustees' appointment, November 10, 1810, of Claudius Berard, a young Frenchman, as "Teacher of the French, Spanish and Italian Languages"—the first foothold of modern languages in the curriculum. [35] One suspects that his fellow trustees, in turning to Rush for the purchase of library books and laboratory apparatus, may have hoped to cover their divergence in polity. It is clear from the first that they did not regard the arrival of Jeremiah Atwater as entirely "providential." Add to this that Aigster, the young German scientist, plausible at first acquaintance, was soon discovered to be insane and dismissed at the cost of a year's salary. [36]

As for Atwater, he would soon be wholly engrossed in a losing battle with the devil. After the catalogue of 1812, the student body declined, partly due to the outbreak of war with Britain, and no new broadsides were printed. "My wish," he confided to Ashbel Green, "is to be kept humble & to be prevented from seeking my own glory. . . . I ought to be thankful that the door has been opened for so much to be done. I am thankful for the praying society, religious library, Magazine &

association for distributing tracts." Yet, he added, Henry
Rowan Wilson, appointed "Professor of Humanity" (i.e. Greek
and Latin) at the same time as himself had become a constant
disputatious opponent. [37] Wilson was a Presbyterian minister, a
graduate of Alexander Dobbin's school of Gettysburg and of
Dickinson's Class of 1798, a man whose later pastoral career
was to be marked by controversy. [38]

As for Atwater's trustees, the small group now meeting
regularly stands out as exceptional for its anti-clerical bias.
These men may be seen as a sort of last stand against the rise of
a new, powerful and highly emotional religious orthodoxy, a
movement which, by every means of persuasion and condemnation, would in a few years dominate American life and education. Their phalanx numbers twelve, and they are listed here in
Jeremiah Atwater's own order of diminishing infamy, with a
few observations from other sources to brighten the picture
which his sombre eye had seen. [39]

Judge Brackenridge comes first, that amazing, amusing,
brilliant, learned, caustic and comical man—knee breeches flan-
nel frock coat and old-fashioned cocked hat, the satirical humor
of *Modern Chivalry* in his jaunty walk, his quizzical eye and
mouth. Atwater had found him an enemy from the very first.
"An apostate himself, he is virulent against any thing that sa-
vours of religion."

David Watts is next, a lawyer and "an open scoffer against
religion & the presbyterian church & clergy." The opening
charge seems a bit off the mark, since Watts is remembered as
one of the few forward spirits who spoke out all the responses
in the Episcopal Church service. It is said that in court he did
not study his cases as thoroughly as Judge Duncan, but could
often carry a jury with him by the confident, loud assertion of
his opinion. For years, he and Thomas Duncan were matched
against one another in pleading causes before the bench at Carlisle—Watts, large, forceful and sometimes rough, Duncan a
short, delicate, scrupulously neat man with a remarkably large
head, powdered hair, and silver buckles at the knee. His voice
would rise to a shrill note, just as the other's would deepen in
an impassioned plea. Though opponents in court, as trustees
they stood together. Duncan would go on in time to the state

supreme court, where Brackenridge pronounced him "the best that ever sat" on that bench. Atwater, too, had a tribute of sorts for Thomas Duncan as a Dickinson College trustee—"the most influential of any but is no friend to religious matters. . . . His brother James D. is determined to prosecute me to the very last as he had declared." Brother James had been a trustee only from 1807 to 1808, and it is not known how this hostile intention was to be carried out.

John Campbell, the large and phlegmatic Rector of the Episcopal Church, was seen as another inimical force, "very bitter at heart." He certainly stood solidly with those already named, and would vigorously defend them from the accusations of unchristian, infidel and immoral conduct so readily put forward by the Principal. It should be noted that Mr. Campbell had with him in this group several pew-holders at St. John's, and that, partly no doubt because of its dependence on the legislature the Board had lost its denominational character. The Episcopal infiltration, not now the cause of any particular remark, would later become a subject of acrimonious attention.

Also of Mr. Campbell's flock was Judge James Hamilton, who had married a daughter of the Rev. William Thomson, Anglican minister at Carlisle in Colonial days. To Jeremiah, however, "He is a Priestleyan in sentiment & is very hostile to religion." He was a large fat man, careless as to dress, well-read, social and with a courtly manner. On the bench he was inclined to be heavily dignified and prolix, displaying that minute insistence on detail which had so infuriated Nisbet when he had first become a trustee in 1794. In 1812, he would persuade the Board to authorize the granting of a master's degree after one year of graduate study—a commendable innovation in American academic practice but one which Atwater would successfully fend off, as a dangerous break with the accepted tradition of a "second degree" after three years of good behavior only. [40]

Dr. McCoskry, who had married Nisbet's daughter Alison, was likewise an Episcopalian. Here was a portly, dignified presence, powdered hair worn in a queue—still, at sixty, the town's most active physician, and still seen occasionally on parade as Captain of the troop of horse. Atwater dismissed him briefly— "has nearly become a sot & goes with the rest"—while another

West College. Photograph, 1861.

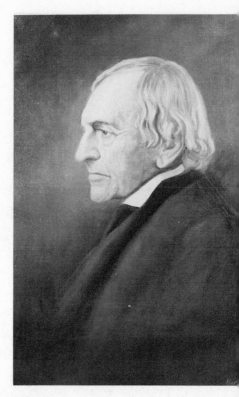

Left: Thomas Cooper. Enlarged copy, by Jane Hays Jones, of life portrait by Charles Willson Peale, 1819. Right: Jeremiah Atwater. Copy, by Margaret F. Winner, after an unidentified artist.

man of pill and powder on the Board, James Gustine, was put down as "a young physician of loose moral character—supposed to be fond of gambling."

Atwater thought that the President of the Board, Dr. James Armstrong, "would do well if not too much under the influence of Messrs. D. & W." In his heart he must have admired the old General's son, a commanding figure more than six feet in height, keen gray eyes and an imperious aquiline nose—always well dressed in the finest black broadcloth and wearing an old-fashioned dark wig with a queue—well-educated, widely-travelled, a superb horsemen, an austere aristocrat.

To Robert Davidson, Atwater could concede religious principles, though he "has never been a friend to me." Then there was old John Creigh, who "has many principles in favour of Presbyterianism but opposes experimental religion." Here, though unaware of it, he was seeing the Old Side spirit of the Latin school of Colonial times.

General William Alexander was pronounced an irreligious man, but at least not a tool of Watts and Duncan. The General had been a lieutenant in Irvine's first command of January, 1776, had served throughout the Revolution and was now employed as a surveyor of military lands. Jacob Hendel was lightly dismissed as "a well meaning German." Hendel, jeweler and maker of clocks and watches with a shop in Hanover Street next door to Thomas Foster's tavern (and so convenient to trustees' meetings), was a practical man—long face, long aquiline nose, large double chin reposing between the wings of his collar—a man steadily useful to the College in the area we would now style "Buildings and Grounds." And so on down to the few who were at hand but exerting no influence—all confided to the sympathetic ear of Ashbel Green, *"inter nos,"* a favorite Atwater interjection.

With such lords and masters, the Principal could nonetheless add that he was looking up to God and enjoying inward peace. Probably thanks to Green and Rush, the University of Pennsylvania had crowned him with its D.D. on May 30, 1811. Yet only a fortnight after that had come the terrible news: Thomas Cooper was elected "Professor of Chemistry and Mineralogy" at Dickinson College! Atwater had accepted from the first the trustees' determination to place a new emphasis on science. It was always popular with the students, and the lectures attracted community interest. It had the full support of Dr. Rush. Their vote, July 19, 1810, "That a Professor of Natural Philosophy and Chimistry be appointed," marks the establishment of a scientific department. Rush's candidate for the chair had been a costly failure but now, by a series of highly remarkable (if not Providential) events, these trustees had a man of their own—Cooper, the friend of Priestley, and since the deaths of Priestley and mad Tom Paine the world's most notorious infidel! He was to receive Dickinson's top professorial salary, $800, and Atwater's mind would roll back to Middlebury, where Frederick Hall had been raised to a salary double his own.

Dr. Cooper, aged fifty-one, stood barely five feet tall, a figure as short and plump as Atwater was tall and lean—a large head and a face marked by that aggressive intelligence which characterized his whole career. He was a humanitarian idealist dedicated to progress in this world rather than the next, an inveterate agitator and reformer. In religion he was a Deist, a philosophy which the clergy were now denouncing as "infidelity," atheism and the road to criminal degradation of every sort. He had had a classical education at Oxford, and was learned in medicine, law and science. He had toured America as a British observer in 1793 (passing through Carlisle, where he found the people "unsociable"), and in the next year had come back as an immigrant with Joseph Priestley. [41] Years before, Priestley had nominated him for membership in the Royal Society, where, however, his political radicalism made him unacceptable. He had lived and worked with Priestley in Northumberland. As editor of the Northumberland *Gazette,* he was brought to trial under John Adams' Sedition Act, and in 1800 had been imprisoned for six months. In 1804, he had become president judge of the district in which Northumberland lay, and here his precise and rigorous procedures turned his radical supporters against him. Charges were brought, and he had been removed from the bench in April, 1811. The counsel for his defense before the state legislature had been Judges Hugh Henry Brackenridge, James Hamilton and Jonathan Hoge Walker, with Thomas Dun-

can and David Watts—all trustees of Dickinson College. [42] These
gentlemen had certainly a large share in persuading Cooper to
transfer his learning and talents to the academic arena. There is
concrete evidence that, even while the trial was in progress, they
were seeking to force Atwater's resignation so that Cooper
might succeed him. [43]

There has been a recurrent conflict, from these early days
of Dickinson College history to the present, between those who
seek eminence and progress on the scholastic scene, and those
whose goals have been adjusted to a comfortable provincial mediocrity. Parents, by and large, seem to prefer to entrust their
children to conservative administrations and that would be particularly true of these years, with the clergy sounding trumpets
of alarm on every hand. Yet these men who met at Foster's
tavern to oversee the affairs of Dickinson College were now
bringing in a man of higher capacity than Nisbet, a liberal educator in the fullest sense, later to be remembered as one of the
few truly successful college presidents of his time. Here, in
Thomas Jefferson's opinion, was "the greatest man in America
in the powers of the mind and in acquired information, and that
without a single exception." [44] Jefferson would soon be enlisting Cooper as the "cornerstone" of his University of Virginia
faculty, a plan frustrated largely by clerical opposition. [45]

Had the clergy been forewarned they might well have mustered strength enough to prevent Cooper's election. [46] Davidson, Creigh and Alexander had opposed at the show of hands,
with the nine others in favor. A vote by ballot had been unanimous. Dr. Atwater was stricken by the news—"a fatal blow." He
dashed off an appeal to Rush—"Judge C. is said to be a man of
violent passions, & haughty, (some say intemperate). He has just
been dismissed by the Legislature. . . . He is supposed to be in
religious sentiment with Priestley, & to put such a man into a
seminary to poison the minds of youth . . . would be fatal. . . .
It would all at once blast all our hopes of Legislative aid."
More—it was illegal. That meeting of June 17, 1811, had been
called on adjournment only, without the required public notice,
and with the apparent intention of taking the opposition by
surprise. [47]

Cooper arrived on August 7 and took the oath of office. He

then sat down to compose the public *Introductory Lecture* with which new courses, in the sciences particularly, were launched in these days. It was delivered on the 16th, with the entire Senior and Junior Classes in attendance, and many from the Carlisle community as well. The trustees rightly expected that Cooper's presence would not only attract students but bring others in as subscribers to his course. [48] At their request the *Introductory Lecture* was published, a book of 236 pages, more than half of them "Notes and References " In it he presented his case for the scientific method, with a survey of chemistry and mineralogy. It was an expository sermon with its text at the end—"KNOWLEDGE IS POWER." [49]

Such doctrine, such a flood of demonstrable information, was sure to appeal to the students. Yet Atwater, a regular attendant at Cooper's lectures and watching like a hawk, could see no effort to corrupt young men, though sure that the new professor was "disposed to do so." [50] Cooper even reciprocated the Principal's attention by occasionally appearing in church. Actually, Cooper had a conservative methodology in education, as he had had in holding court. He believed firmly in a classical foundation, sharply at odds here with Benjamin Rush, although he agreed with Rush on the value of modern languages, particularly French. [51]

Dr. Rush, on his part, must surely have had some mixed feelings as to the Cooper appointment, though he took a position solidly with the clerical party. Atwater was his own appointee, Ashbel Green his relative and friend, and in Princeton affairs he was supporting Green's one-sided emphasis on theology. At the regular September trustees' meeting, Dr. Robert Cathcart came armed with a letter from Rush which "feelingly" described the danger to be anticipated from infidel professors, and the clergy were with him in force. They only succeeded, however, in having a declaration of their own that the June 17 meeting had been illegally read into the minutes, and exacting a promise of three weeks' notice in the future. [52] Old John King, foreseeing that an ouster would fail, had written at length to Cooper pleading eloquently for the presentation of science as subservient to religion. Atwater sent a copy of his letter to Rush, carried by young Samuel Blanchard How, whose departure for theological study would deepen the Principal's embittered loneliness and increase his despair of ever establishing full disciplinary control.[53]

In Philadelphia, in October, we find Rush summoning the Rev. Drs. Green and Muhlenberg into a conference intended "to preponderate over impudence and infidelity."[54] It may have sprung from a hope that Muhlenberg, a trustee of both Dickinson and Franklin, could bring needed new life to the Lancaster institution by placing Atwater at its head.[55] At the same time, Dr. Rush continued to cooperate in the search for new laboratory equipment, which included the purchase in December at Cooper's request of Joseph Priestley's reflecting telescope, burning glass and air gun.[56]

"We are now," Atwater had written to Rush on September 29, "completely in a house divided against itself"—a familiar enough situation at Carlisle, and one that had existed from the beginning of his administration since he had had Brackenridge and Davidson against him from the first and Henry Rowan Wilson almost as long. On May 21, 1811, the Board had named Davidson, along with its President, Dr. Armstrong, the Rev. Mr. Campbell, Hamilton, Watts and Duncan a committee to consult with the faculty on the state of the College, and then immediately had vested this group with the supervisory "power of visitors." This gave Davidson virtual control over every aspect of college life, an authority which the group exercised faithfully and frequently. Atwater, in establishing New England standards, must reckon first with the Blessed Peacemaker. A year later, at the trustee meeting of July 3, 1812, we find this committee correcting a "misapprehension" of the Principal as to his duties, which were then defined as those of "a general superintendent of communication," an advisor to the Board, and no more.

The same meeting returned Davidson to the classroom to teach "natural philosophy, the use of the globes and geography." Once more Dickinson students were to wrestle with the hated little book of rhymes—once more, but not for long. Davidson died on December 13, to the Rev. Jeremiah's outspoken relief.[57] Wilson resigned from the faculty in 1813 to take a neighboring parish, leaving the issue clearly between Atwater and Cooper. "The officers of the College are at sword's points with each other," a visitor from Vermont reported back. "The students are lawless as the whirlwind." [58]

In February, 1812, Atwater had confided to Green:

> The increase of students is the only thing that has saved me from being banished from this place long since. In the meantime, the persecution of the tongue has been pretty bitter. Carlisle has literally and emphatically long been Satan's seat. There pride & irreligion have long been enthroned & enjoyed undisputed dominion. The plain truths of the gospel have not been preached here with pungency & rich sinners have triumphed with impunity. The higher class here have been little better than infidels. Some of our lawyers & judges had read & admired the writings of Thos. Cooper. His coming here was, therefore, on every account to be dreaded. I put my own place at stake in vigorously opposing his coming, for I did not consider that it would be worth retaining if Mr. C. should gain an ascendancy in the affairs of the College. I hinted to the trustees my willingness to resign rather than be considered as approving the appointment of Mr. C. While their passions were up, they appeared to be almost willing to risk this & even went pretty far in giving hints themselves to the same effect. [59]

In the same letter he gives us his revealing picture of Cooper's behavior in a serious disciplinary case. In the period of the War of 1812 there was an epidemic of duels at the military post at Carlisle, [60] and the students caught the contagion. George Oldham, of the Class of 1813, was a principal in such a meeting, and another student his second. Oldham fled, and Mr. Watts, for the trustees, thought that the second should be let off lightly. Wrote Atwater:

> In looking into this affair, the Faculty judged it prudent to invite Mr. Cooper to sit with them—though still it was not done without much aversion. It happened that our meeting was in the evening after Mr. C. had been dining & drinking wine with Mr. W. Of course Mr. C. was not very well fitted to attend to business. But, after showing much aversion to looking into the affair of the duel, he finally agreed to sit with us. I must say that at the meeting he treated the Faculty quite disrespectfully. He would not consent to let the young men be questioned as to their guilt, as is the custom of all colleges in such cases. He threatened, if the question was put, to interfere & prevent their answering it. Tho' requested to speak in a lower tone, he persist-

ed in speaking so loudly as to be overheard by students without. Of course he has become much of a toast with those students who are disaffected to good government. In short, it has turned out very much as Dr. Rush prophesied, who declared that Mr. C. would in any difficult matter attempt to make himself popular at the expense of the other teachers. [61]

Dr. Rush was also kept informed. "He takes much pains to ingratiate himself with the students, inviting them to make chemical experiments in his room. He spends his Sabbaths there instead of going to church. He drinks wine pretty freely. . . ." [62] Rush was writing on the deleterious effects of alcohol at this time, and Atwater eagerly distributing the work. Then, in one of those experiments, nitric acid and bismuth exploded in Cooper's face, threatening his eyesight—this also quickly reported to Rush as evidence of divine disfavor. [63] But in June, 1812, Cooper had moved from Foster's tavern to a room in the College building, into the very heart of the student body. Dr. Rush, reading of all this with sorrow, thought of resigning his trusteeship, but agreed to remain as long as Atwater did so. [64] That was in February, 1813, and his death two months later went almost unnoticed at the College.

Two nephews of the President of the United States were among the boys sent to Dickinson because of Cooper's presence there. [65] Robert Madison was to study not only science but law, which the Professor of Chemistry and Mineralogy was adding to his repertoire. [66] At the same time, June, 1813, Cooper had revived John Redman Coxe's *Emporium of Arts and Sciences*, maintaining it with the Carlisle imprint as a leading scientific journal. Problems of weaponry were referred to him from Washington, and we find him advising the President on a shell that would explode after piercing a ship's side. [67] His articles on subjects in both science and art had been appearing frequently in the *Port Folio*, indicating a breadth of view and learning such, indeed, as a college president should possess. [68]

In further evidence of the general disintegration of good order expected by the clerics, there was, in the spring of 1813, a case of "wanton mischief and disgracefull filthiness," involving damage to the College building. [69] It was Dickinson's first ex-

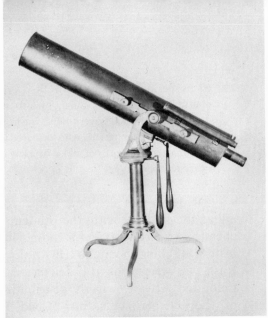

Scientific apparatus of Joseph Priestley, acquired by Dickinson College, 1811. Top left: Burning Glass. Top right: Reflecting telescope, made by W. & S. Jones of London. Bottom: Static-electricity machine, made by F.A. Boht of Hamburg, Germany, 1798. "The most complete and splendid thing of the kind ever imported into our Country. . . .It will add much to the reputation of our College." (Benjamin Rush to John Montgomery, July 5, 1808).

perience of an outbreak familiar elsewhere, and particularly so at Princeton under the administration of Ashbel Green. Dr. Rush would certainly have taken it as supporting his condemnation of dormitory life. In July, a more significant rebellion occurred. A substantial number of the boys formed a "combination to resist the endeavor of Professor Shaw for their improvement in classical learning." [70] Here was a very early manifestation of student—and public—dissatisfaction with the traditional classical course. [71] The trustees took stern measures, forcing some recalcitrants to "acknowledge error" and expelling others. It is inescapable that the discontent must have been caused by the contrast between Cooper's teaching, in our present-day term so "relevant," and the irrelevance of the other subjects, to which overwhelmingly the largest part of a student's time must be devoted. Yet Cooper himself stood solidly with the classics. Joseph Shaw, a Scottish pedagogue, had just arrived at the College, and may have introduced a stricter standard than had prevailed under the Dickinson alumnus, Wilson. One result may have been the trustees' promotion of Claudius Berard, September 28, 1814, from "Teacher" to "Professor of the Modern Languages," though it remained upon a fee rather than a salary basis.

By 1814 it was a Cooper faculty, with Shaw, Berard and Eugene Nulty, a brilliant new man in Mathematics, all united in their hostility to the Principal. If discipline was lax, they blamed Atwater for it, since this was the Principal's charge. They condemned Atwater's teaching, particularly his strong emphasis on declamation. They held his learning in contempt. In Cooper's hot-tempered statement, which at least reflected the belief of others as well, Atwater was "so grossly deficient in classical and other branches of education" that he had never dared put a question himself at the examinations, taught geography "from some trifling elementary book," and could not himself explain "the import of Latitude and Longitude." [72]

In this diatribe of June 15, 1815, Cooper makes clear his eagerness for a more congenial and better-paying situation. Atwater, equally exasperated, heard rumors of his leaving but felt sure he would stay "if he could throw me off." [73] The impending climax has been laid to "trustee interference," particularly a resolution in which the Board demanded that faculty report to it, weekly, "all delinquents or absentees." [74] This indicates laxity as to classroom attendance, but does not explain the faculty resignations. The impasse lay in the inability of Cooper's dominant party to remove Atwater, who was drawing the largest salary, scarcely earning it—and, as they discovered to their disgust, supplementing his income by running a livery business for the students. [75]

To the students, war within their own small world and war in the nation at large had brought excitements enow. They had their freedoms still. At the commencement of 1814 some of the Senior Class, with others, had marched to Philadelphia to resist an expected British attack, and received their degrees in absentia. [76] On July 4, 1815, patriotic and party fervor found expression at two elaborate banquets, one a decorous affair set up by the young Federalists, the other a formal hullabaloo given by the Democrats. At the latter, after young Julius Forrest's oration, and after Robert Madison had read the Declaration of Independence, a rousing round of toasts was drunk—twenty-one prepared, and twenty-seven "volunteers," with a blaze of music and no doubt a burst of song to follow almost every one. "Dickinson College! The brightest luminary of Pennsylvania—may its rays emanate with effulgence that characterized its founders," was followed by "The College Hornpipe," and "Thomas Cooper! The profound philosopher, the genuine patriot, and the endeared friend," by "Life Let Us Cherish." [77]

"What can the matter be?" This question headlined its final paragraph when the Carlisle *American Volunteer* of September 28, 1815, printed its news of the Dickinson College commencement, and the resignations, immediately afterward, of the Principal and most of the faculty. Only Nulty remained, with Mr. Trimble, a new man just hired to take over the Grammar School. "Something uncommon must have occurred," was the editorial surmise, adding tartly that nothing less was to be expected after all those Fourth of July toasts—enough to damn any college.

Atwater and Cooper went their ways, the one to a northern obscurity, the other to a southern flowering. For those who would have a box score in the contest, the figures could be

56-7. Atwater, to whom a college existed essentially for the production of ministers, had produced seven of them. The alumni in Cooper's fields of medicine and law were twenty-three and thirty-three respectively. By the same rating, Nisbet had been a ministerial winner, 67-65. [78]

Among the trustees who now met to wrestle with the problems of the hour there was a newly reelected member, the Rev. Dr. John McKnight. He had been born near Carlisle sixty-one years before, son of an officer in the French and Indian War, and had probably been prepared for Princeton at the old Latin school. He held a pastorate in Adams County in 1783 when he was named a charter trustee of Dickinson. He had resigned in 1794 on moving to New York, where he had been both trustee and professor at Columbia College, teaching moral philosophy and logic. [79] Here was a man, surely, who could bring a working unity at last to the discordant worlds of trustee and professor. It took his colleagues until November 1 to persuade him to assume the post of Principal.

Principal McKnight might have managed well had he been given the means for a fresh start. But payments to the Nisbet estate and other creditors had exhausted the treasury and prevented his bringing together a competent faculty. He had been in office only a month when another student duel shocked College and town. One lad was killed and three others fled. [80] The story was repeated in newspapers everywhere, with bitter condemnation, and Dickinson's repute seemed to have vanished with its funds. The *Volunteer* of December 28 tilted an eyebrow and observed that "The College has been a source of profit to this place," but now, "like the Baltimore turnpike road, is in *a very sickly* condition," and summoned community interest to its support.

No prompt aid, however, was forthcoming, and at their regular meeting of September 27, 1816, the trustees voted "to suspend the business of this College for the present." On November 5, in a mood of final despair, they appealed to the legislature "to take the College immediately under the protection, Patronage and Government of the State." [81] With a change in state administration the plea would be renewed, as Robert Cathcart, a leader of Atwater's party, joined with James Hamilton of Cooper's in seeking a revival.[82] In these dismal straits, as year followed year, the College building itself gave hope and a shred of living continuity. Here, as the petitions pointed out, was an "edifice," equipped with libraries and scientific apparatus of much value, waiting to be used.[83] And, in a small way, they were used, local alumni returning as had been their wont to the society halls for recreation or study.

Now the departed presence weighed heavily upon the little town. There was not only the loss of business income and of prestige, but the old fear that rising Harrisburg might establish a college in the area. And there was the silence of the College bell which for so long had rung the hours from dawn to dark, bringing its steady tempo to the life of the village. The boys and young men were missed, the lectures, the gossip, the commencement pageantry. The revival, when it came at last, was a community affair. The trustees had met once in 1817, once in 1819, and then gathered again on formal call, May 5, 1820, with a bare quorum of nine. Their first act was to fill twelve vacancies in the Board—all the new trustees were substantial citizens of the valley, and all were ready at the door to take their seats. Four were clergymen, six were lawyers, all were locally prominent in public service, professions or business. With this reinforcement, they voted to borrow money to pay taxes on the College lands and other debts, and then to launch a drive for funds that would enable them "to resuscitate the operations of the College."

Dr. George D. Foulke, Class of 1800, Chief Burgess of Carlisle and Captain of the Carlisle Hussars, issued a call for a "Town Meeting," May 26, 1800. From this came resolutions and appeals supporting the drive, and committees were appointed to carry it out.[84] Nearly $3,000 was raised that spring, a respectable sum for a rural community of about that many people, and the canvassers extended their efforts to the country at large. These successes paved the way for the state aid granted on February 20, 1821. By then the ball was rolling, hopes were high, a joint program with a proposed theological seminary of the German Reformed Church had been debated and approved.[85] Much time, thought and emotion were being given, too, to the election of a new Principal—a post of honor to be

filled only by one of the great figures of Presbyterian pulpit and
polity. And through it all, already and once more, fair poesy
had come with throbbing metre to the shadow of the campus
trees. "Philo," in eighty "Lines, on the Revival of Dickinson
College," describes the first rise of culture

> In early age, when lawless passions sway'd,
> And gloomy horror rang'd the desert's shade,

tells how first "The goddess; *Science,* wing'd her angel flight,"
enlightened Greece, and then, with all her retinue, our western
wilderness, where

> Fair *Freedom* rose to guard the rising world,
> And from her shores the raging Despot hurl'd.
> When carnage ceas'd, and Liberty was won,
> Fair Science rear'd her stately DICKINSON:
> Left for the winds of Fortune to engage,
> She, tottering, sunk beneath the tempest's rage,
> But not to sleep: Again her columns rise,
> Reflecting brilliant as they mount the skies;
> And Science, seated on her throne of light,
> Invites her children to inhale delight. [86]

Besides, without the least intended imputation to you or to your worthy Colleagues, as Trustees of Dickinson College, I may truly observe that I have experienced greatly more Satisfaction as well as practical success, when Unshackled with the regulations of any corporate Body, than otherwise. Such Bodies are but too prone either to Invade the province of the faculty of professors, or otherwise to Neglect it altogether.

Samuel Knox to Judge Hamilton, December 30, 1816

8

THE DUFFIELD YEARS

THOSE twelve new trustees elected on May 8, 1820, were all successful men living within a day's ride of Carlisle—ministers, lawyers, merchants, members of the legislature, a Member of Congress. The name of the Rev. George Duffield heads the list. Duffield, at twenty-six, was the youngest of them all, a little man, sharply intelligent, warmly emotional, afire with a personal concern for souls and causes. It may be assumed that he had been active in the reopening of the College, and may even have initiated it. He would be a constant, pervasive influence through these last ten years of the Presbyterian affiliation—rarely self-assertive, yet a power simply by virtue of his readiness with ideas, his willingness to work. He seems to have been aware that an inconspicuous leadership meets less resistance; and, indeed, as his own ruling place became obvious, opposition did arise. Three Presbyterian divines would now succeed one another in the Principal's chair, each of less capacity than the one before, and the decline of their influence would be matched by the increase of Duffield's. This is a Duffield era.

Duffield bore no title on the Board. All his varied influence in College and town was exerted simply as pastor of the Presbyterian Church. He stood in the pulpit from which John Steel had controlled the old Latin school. This was a vindication of his grandfather, the George Duffield whom Steel had so sternly opposed. From this pulpit, Nisbet and Davidson had spoken for the College. He must have seen, surely, the hand of Providence in his rise to this eminence. He had been born in neighboring Lancaster County, July 4, 1794, son of George Duffield, Comptroller General of Pennsylvania. After taking the University of Pennsylvania's degree in 1811, he had moved on through the full four-year course at the theological seminary of the Associate Reformed Church in New York, under its founder, John Mitchell Mason, "the prince of American preachers and expounders of the Scriptures." He was licensed to preach in the Presbyterian ministry, April 20, 1815, and passing through Carlisle on his way to attend to some business of his father's, he had found himself among his grandfather's friends and relatives of a former day.[1] He was invited to preach, and charmed all. The Carlisle congregation, which had been divided upon whether or not to issue a call to Henry Rowan Wilson, then had united upon Duffield, and he had been formally installed on September 25, 1816.

Thus had John Steel's flock come under the sway of the namesake and spiritual heir of his ancient enemy. It was a triumph at last for New Side, since this young George Duffield leaned toward the view that sin might be banished and salvation attained, simply by acceptance of Christ as master in preference to all worldly things. As he went on in parish work, the seminary's sharp doctrinal definitions were blurred and the direct upbuilding of God's kingdom on earth and enlisting souls for paradise became his paramount concern. In America, since his grandfather's time and before, the winds of religion had been blowing in this direction. The Methodists had built an impressive power upon their simple formula of "saving grace," and an organization easy to enter but firm in surveillance. It was not possible for Presbyterians now to look down on the Wesleyans as Nisbet had done. Duffield would meet the competition head-on, startling the Carlisle gentry with his Sunday school (their first), his Bible classes, prayer meetings and a hard line of "abstinence from worldly and sinful amusements." He distributed books by the dozen, tracts everywhere, a finger always on the pulse of holiness.[2] Now, after four years in Carlisle, the revived college was added to his curacy.

The new Board had been chosen with an eye to political as well as divine favor. Andrew Boden, Carlisle lawyer and Member

Top left: George Duffield (1794–1868). Painted and engraved by John Sartain. Top right: John Bannister Gibson. By Asher Brown Durand, *c.* 1830. Bottom left: Samuel Allen McCoskry. Copy, by S. George Phillips, after a miniature by an unidentified artist, *c.* 1836. Bottom right: Robert Coleman. By Jacob Eichholtz, *c.* 1812.

of Congress was one. Isaiah Graham, Carlisle tanner and self-made man, a judge and state senator, was another. Jacob Alter, a Quaker of French descent, had been twenty-two years in the legislature. The Board was now a bloc based on local interests rather than Rush's state-wide pattern. Four of the new men were ministers, with Duffield and John Moodey of Shippensburg in the lead, the one small and quick, the other large and benign. A fifth and sixth were elected on March 21, 1821: William Radcliffe De Witt of New York, now at the Presbyterian church in Harrisburg, and John S. Ebaugh of the Reformed Church, Carlisle. De Witt, another product of Mason's seminary, became a close ally of Duffield. Ebaugh represented a hope that a theological seminary of his denomination, Calvinist also, might be set up on the Dickinson campus. Judge Hamilton of the old Board had died in 1819, but his son reported these new developments to Thomas Cooper, now President of South Carolina College and at last no longer troubled by what he chose to call "the inveteracy of the *odium theologicum.*"

"I am glad to learn," Dr. Cooper replied, "that the college at Carlisle is likely to be resuscitated, but I fear, that with so many bigots among your trustees, and under compleat clerical guidance, it will have but a feeble existence." [3]

It was now up to this new Board to choose a principal, a man whose name and fame would restore all that the College had lost. They knew that, with the right man and a good salary scale, all the other faculty places could be filled well. The name of the redoubtable John Mitchell Mason was put before them at once. But perhaps in the knowledge that Dr. Mason had suffered a mild stroke the year before, they elected James Patriot Wilson. Wilson, as he had done in 1809, declined. Then the vote went to Dr. John Brodhead Romeyn of New York, Presbyterian cleric, friend and associate of Mason. He also declined, but Mason himself, elected on August 9, 1821, accepted the charge as an escape from the intense activity which had worn him down in body and mind. "It will employ me usefully in a work to which I find myself adequate, but which will not oppress me." [4]

To New Yorkers especially, Mason was "the great theological thunderbolt of the times." [5] He had graduated at Columbia in 1789, finished his studies at the University of Edinburgh, returning to found, in 1804, the seminary of the Associate Reformed Church, forerunner of the Union Theological Seminary. In his classroom, from his pulpit, through his *Christian Magazine* and his travels abroad, he had become a power. With Dwight and Green, he was a general in the great reaction against "infidelity." In 1800 he had stood up against the election of Jefferson, declaring a man who refused to believe in the Deluge or that God ever had a Chosen People unfit for the Presidency.[6] Yet within the boundaries of Biblical revelation, Mason was broad-minded, ecumenical, an enemy of pomp and pretense, a champion of individual freedom in studying and propounding the sacred texts.[7]

He had been a trustee of Columbia, 1795 to 1811, and Provost from 1811 to 1816, seeking this last position much as Ashbel Green had at Princeton. Like Green, he was less successful with college than seminary, but he came to Dickinson with his high repute as an academic figure intact.[8] With the gifts from the community topped on February 20, 1821, by a state grant of $6,000, a sense of confident prosperity awaited him at Carlisle, where workmen were repairing and painting the building all through that summer. A salary of $2,000 had been voted for him, setting a scale upon which he could readily summon a competent faculty. Tuition charges had been upped to match.[9] This was to be quality education. An inquiry from Mason had brought the trustees' first statement on tenure: "That the Principal and Professors hold their appointments during good behaviour." [10] He seems not to have suspected that he might have a trustee committee every moment at his elbow, but so eminent an educator, with former students on the Board, could hardly fear this. In December, 1821, he arrived, a tall, heavy-set man with high forehead and deep blue eyes. He had still, past and threatening illness notwithstanding, a look of energy and daring—he sat his horse, it has been said, "like the commander of an army." [11]

In his inaugural address, January 15, 1822, he appealed to the "delicate, noble sensibility" of the students: "If you shall bear us out in our hopes respecting you, then shall our efforts be animated, our labours sweetened, our success cheering: and Dickinson College revive from her desolations, a phoenix of renewed life, and spreading her lustre over your county, your state, your country, be a source of mild and enduring glory in ages to come." [12] He had with him a faculty of three to share this hope. Henry Vethake had the chair of Mathematics and Natural Philosophy, and would teach chemistry also till another could be found. Vethake, a portly, fresh-faced young man of thirty, had taught at Rutgers and Princeton, and had been attracted to Dickinson probably both by the salary offer and to escape the riot and turmoil prevalent under the rule of Ashbel Green. He was a professional educator with a distinguished career before him as teacher, author and college president. [13] Alexander McClelland, Professor of Belles Lettres and the Philosophy of the Mind, was a Presbyterian minister, a former student of the Associate Reformed seminary in whom Mason had recognized potential as a teacher. He was a small man with a strong, resonant voice, lecturing enthusiastically, with a flow of anecdotal humor which his ministerial colleagues deplored. Yet his anecdotes were to the point, often touched on well-known contemporaries, and surely held attention and awakened interest. He cited also Plato, Descartes, Newton, Locke, along with the leading Scottish philosopher Thomas Reid and his pupil Dugald Stewart. He turned constantly to the poets for illustration. [14] He would strike back sarcastically at the vague or superficial, and, like Mason, he encouraged independent thinking. With his start at Dickinson, he would remain a teacher for the rest of his life. Also from New York came John C. Slack, teacher of classical languages, "a young man of talents and repute," who had charge of the Grammar School. [15]

It remained only to find a classicist for the College. The original choice, John Burns, a Scot and an experienced teacher, had failed to agree with the trustees as to salary and returned to New York. [16] It would help, in seeking state bounty, not to have a solidly Presbyterian faculty, and a young Episcopal minister, educated in Philadelphia, was called to this post from the academy he had been conducting in his native county of Maryland. [17] The Rev. Joseph Spencer arrived in February, 1822, and in June became Rector of St. John's Church on the square—a pleasant, mild-tempered person whom the Church would remember with the gratitude due him also from the College. [18] At college, his part would be to live in the building and supervise student life, a task to which his courtesy and gentleness were not wholly adequate.

The courses of the new regime were topped off by Mason with the traditional Moral Philosophy for Seniors, and another, Truth and Evidences of Divine Revelation. [19] A student body of about one hundred had soon been recruited. As Yale had been Atwater's model, so now we find admission requirements and a curriculum similar to Columbia's, with commencement in July, followed by vacation until September. [20] The issuance of a regular printed report twice a year to parents and guardians was begun. [21] The new curriculum and code of regulations submitted by Mason to the trustees was passed and ordered printed in February, 1822. A new catalogue was printed. John Bannister Gibson, for the trustees' financial campaign, had pointed out the wisdom of appealing for a specific objective. "Additional buildings" became the choice, and was taken to the public and, once again, to the legislature. [22] A loan was authorized for the purchase of books, a mineralogical collection, chemical and other scientific apparatus. [23]

And, of course, there must be a commencement with all the attendant fanfare. It was held on June 26, 1822. In procession from the College to the Presbyterian church on the square came the Grammar School pupils, the students of the four classes, the faculty, the trustees, and Dr. Mason with two high officials of the state government, James Duncan, Auditor General, and Andrew Gregg, Secretary of the Commonwealth. Only two degrees could be awarded, one to James Hall Mason, the Principal's son; but eight other boys, including James' brother, Erskine, delivered orations. One can only imagine what consternation may have followed the trustees' "*General* order," hurriedly issued on that gala day, "prohibiting all Bands of music or professional singers (i.e. those who sing for hire) all Balls and dances and all dinners and suppers" which had been planned to mark the event. [24]

The tenure of John Mitchell Mason, launched so auspiciously, was to have rough, sad going, all in all. The trustees, in a front-page newspaper announcement in January, had promised the community that "Everything like PARTY POLITICS will be carefully excluded"—yet the Union Philosophicals, in one of their first "public exhibitions," extolled Napoleon Bonaparte and recited "the oration of General Harper on the murdered Lingan," bringing down the wrath of the *Carlisle Gazette* and throwing the trustees into a dither of prohibitory resolutions. [25] With this, we find the *American Volunteer* printing the veiled threats of *"Lex Talionis"* against "The holy crew of Dickinson College," and promising a retribution from which "their smooth and oily tongues shall not screen them." [26] With all this Mason was ill prepared to deal. Early in 1822 he had suffered a broken hip in a fall from his horse, and had barely recovered by commencement.

That summer was one of drought, failure of crops and then a typhus epidemic. Mason's young alumnus son, James, who had been teaching in the Grammar School died of the fever, November 6, 1822. College and town alike were stirred by the tragedy. Revivalists were always alert to catch and prolong the tense emotions of the funereal hour, but Mason at first would have none of that. He disapproved on principle of graveside eulogies. Yet when the student pallbearers lifted the coffin to bear it away he had cried out to them in anguish, "Young men! Tread lightly—ye bear a temple of the Holy Ghost!" and then begged an old friend who had come from New York to "say something which God may bless to his young friends." [27]

Dr. McCartee did so at the grave, and George Duffield carried on from there the work of revival. The story is told statistically in the number of additions "by profession" to the Duffield congregation: in 1822, 17; in 1823, 109; in 1824, 24. [28] For Dickinson, it was the first notable example of a culmination eagerly sought, year after year, in American colleges; and, indeed, it left its mark in Dickinson history. Eighteen students entered the ministry, not all impelled by the tragedy alone, but looking back to it as a basis of their dedication. One was George Washington Bethune, who would gain note also as a litterateur. He had come from Columbia for his Senior year at Dickinson, Class of 1823. He was a grandson of the Presbyterian philanthropist and saint, Isabella Graham, who had been a parishioner of Witherspoon in Scotland and of Mason in New York. George's sister, Isabella Graham Bethune, was now the young wife and helpmeet of George Duffield. John Miller Dickey, Class of 1824, who tells of the revival in his diary, went on to become an antislavery leader, founder and president of the trustees of Lincoln University. [29] His classmate, Daniel McKinley of Carlisle, would win his way from great poverty through college and seminary in answer to the ministerial call. Daniel, grandson of Henry Makinly of the Colonial school, "a young man of unexceptionable character," had been voted a full tuition scholarship by the trustees before the reopening of the College, the first instance of such recognition. [30]

It had become a feature of American life, this revival spirit, this unburdening of sin, embracing of salvation in a welter of self-exposure, joy and tears; and within the little world of campus life it was an ardently sought convulsion. Its curious affinity with the new political trend has been remarked—equally democratic, alike in their all-embracing appeals to faith. [31] As in politics, the spiritual fervor had the devil with it too, the rowdy and rebellious. On the night of May 27, 1823, two Dickinson students climaxed the revival season with a roaring blast of gunpowder which set the College building on fire. [32] Duffield's "Cumberland County Bible Society" had on campus his "Auxilliary Bible Society of Dickinson College," and his "Young Men's Missionary Society" was organized in the fall. [33] But while Erskine Mason, Daniel McKinley, George Bethune and the others were carrying their banners here, less pious youths had become boisterously critical of the fare offered by the college steward, and by fall this protest had an organization of its own. An inner circle of Union Philosophical, "The Turkey Club," undertook to provide in better fashion for the inner man. One clause in its constitution (that the turkey must be honestly come by) stands as evidence of the prevailing spirit of righteousness. The Turkey Club maintained a precarious existence through that winter, ending apparently when its secrets were betrayed by Matthew Spencer, the professor's younger brother. [34] With the warmth and fairness of all young men, whether holy or profane, U.P. also met in support of Greek independence and raised $50 for the cause. [35]

In the meantime, as Dr. Mason's health declined, the trustees became watchful and authoritative; the teachers resentful.

There was a direct clash in March of 1823, when rules for the Grammar School were enacted without faculty consultation and in disregard of the newly published regulations which gave the faculty control of all discipline, expulsion alone excepted. [36] The reply to the teachers' protest was that the Board had acted "in strict conformity with certain inalienable powers and authority vested in them by the charter." [37]

A year later, Dr. Mason resigned, delaying his return to New York only to be present at commencement, June 29, 1824, where he offered a prayer. Henry Rowan Wilson delivered the commencement sermon. The lion of the day, however, was His Excellency, the Governor of the state, John Andrew Shulze, accompanied by the Surveyor General, Gabriel Hiester. Solemnly attentive, they heard the Latin salutatory, the English salutatory, young McCoskry's oration "On Virtue as the Principle of a Republican Government," the "Dialogue on Colleges," and the "Conference" on the conspiracy of the crowned heads of Europe against the rights and liberties of mankind. [38] In the previous year a bill to appropriate $9,000 for the College had narrowly failed of passage, and the continuation of state support was much in the minds of all. [39]

Internal unanimity, on the other hand, was fragile. On June 8, the Board had returned the commencement date to the fall and passed other new regulations, topping them off by electing McClelland Principal at a salary of $1,600. Professor McClelland, whose use of wit and irony in class has been noted, and begun to manifest a sharpness of temper, out of class as well as in. He agreed to serve only pro tem, and on July 27 the Rev. William Neill of Philadelphia was chosen. [40] The call came as a complete surprise to Neill, who suppressed a first impulse to decline, and would soon regret his acceptance. He had held a comfortable pastorate in the city for eight years, and on his arrival at Carlisle in September, "found things in rather a low and unpromising state." [41] For almost two months following his formal installation on November 9, 1824, he was ill, depressed by the change much as Nisbet had been. [42]

The new Principal was a Princeton graduate of 1803, lean of face and body, tall, dignified and gentle. Sidney George Fisher, who takes a deprecating view in most of his diary char-

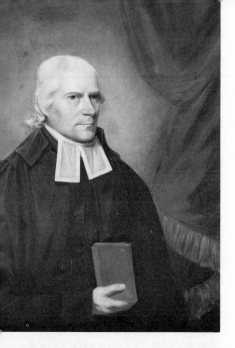

Top left: John McKnight. Copy, by Margaret F. Winner, after a portrait attributed to John Paradise. Top right: John Mitchell Mason. Copy, by John Wesley Jarvis, after Gilbert Stuart, 1809. Bottom left: William Neill. Copy, by Margaret F. Winner, after an unidentified artist. Bottom right: Samuel Blanchard How. Copy, by Margaret F. Winner, after an unidentified artist.

acterizations, describes him as "a worthy man, learned, I suppose, according to the ordinary use of the word, but of no great force of mind or character. He was very kind to me at college." [43] His regular teaching load was lighter than the others'—bringing Seniors Natural Theology and Evidences of Christianity—but he filled in as an assistant elsewhere constantly. [44] It was a type of classroom service which won him more gratitude than respect.

The Duffield family, meanwhile, had moved from "Happy Retreat," Colonel Montgomery's old home out on the Shippensburg road, to the larger house near the College where Dr. Mason had been living. It stood back from the street among trees, at the center of what was to be famous later as the Mooreland deer park, and is now the "Benjamin Rush Campus." [45] Not far away, on High Street facing the college, stood the German Reformed Church, a plain, square brick building, soon to become a focal point of interest in the educational picture. It had been built in Atwater's time, financed in part by "The German Presbyterian and German Lutheran Churches Lottery in the Borough of Carlisle." [46] The German Reformed synod had long been debating establishment of a theological seminary, and in 1820 had been invited to make it an adjunct of Dickinson College. On September 9, 1824, the invitation was more explicitly renewed, and in terms of manifest eagerness. [47] The College would provide the Seminary's professor with a home, in return for his acting as its "Professor of History and German Literature." Seminarians might take appropriate College courses and have full use of its Library. Should the Seminary plan a building, the College would grant title to a part of its campus. The offer was accepted. The new institution assembled on March 11, 1825, with five students, a library of a hundred volumes and a capital of $300. [48] Its professor, Dr. Lewis Mayer, was formally installed on April 6 in ceremonies in the College chapel. [49]

After Nisbet's course in theology and Cooper's in law, this began a third venture into professional and graduate training. Some months later, the Lutherans would be invited to bring in their proposed seminary. [50] It would locate at Gettysburg instead, although its head, Samuel Simon Schmucker, later became a member of the Dickinson Board, where the German

Reformed interests were already well represented. In 1823, and again in 1827, the College was invited to join in medical programs.[51] Similar offers came to other colleges of this day: medical men solved the difficulties of obtaining a charter by sending their students to the related institution for their diplomas—sometimes their only appearance there. Both offers were rejected, though both had respectable sponsors and one included a Dickinson professor, John W. Vethake, the medical studies in this case to have been pursued in Baltimore.[52] One is left in doubt as to whether the trustees rightly disapproved of such tenuous connections, or whether they acted in the spirit of Duffield's plea to a student who had gone on into medical study: "Do not allow your mind to be polluted and your heart to be debauched by the investigations of science."[53]

As for the Seminary, it was soon involved in smouldering contentions of its own. Lewis Mayer, with his blonde hair curling freely over his high forehead, his lean, sensitive face, long nose, deep-set eyes and thin, tight lips, was a man of great learning, inflexibly severe in its application. He was liberal for his time: "Theology as a science ought to be progressive, but its progress ought to be in harmony with itself and its past."[54] Here was the antithesis of the Seminary's next most influential figure, the Rev. John S. Ebaugh, pastor of the Carlisle congregation and a Dickinson trustee since August, 1821. Ebaugh, with his "good round honest German face and gay open countenance," and his old-fashioned plain thinking, had worked tirelessly for this cause and continued to do so.[55] Yet his temperament and Mayer's would come in time to open war.

Meanwhile, the college boys ridiculed and teased the seminarians. To get them out of the College building, Ebaugh raised money and built a new church at High and Pitt Streets, so that the old one could be divided into classrooms. He had the Seminary incorporated by the state to give it independence and permanence but its large board of trustees, like that of the College, was dominated by a local group, and Mayer found them intolerable.[56]

On October 7, 1826, Mayer resigned his Dickinson professorship. He had been expected also to teach German, but the course was not required and probably few boys, if any, elected it. In these years, modern languages—French, Spanish, Italian—were taught on a fee basis by Jacob Frederick Huber, a member of the German Reformed Church, an earnest man of Swiss descent who was to have the unique distinction in academic history of retrogression in rank, from full professor to instructor. [57] The Seminary's second year brought an increase of students, then a dropping off. Financial success, achieved by the hard work of Ebaugh and others, brought, as so often occurs, new elements of dissension; and in 1829 Mayer, bitter against all around him, arbitrarily moved with his students to York, a way-station on their progress to Lancaster. [58]

On January 14, 1825, with the prospect of the Seminary's coming before them, a special meeting of the trustees had approved a plan for general development, of which one feature, at least, has historic significance. The proposal had been the work of the Executive Committee: Judge John Reed, Chairman, Duffield, Knox, Hendel and William N. Irvine. The faculty had been consulted. Duffield presented the plan to the Board. Its first provision is the unusual one:

> To create a species of stock of which there shall be an indefinite number of shares, each share to be valued at fifty dollars, and to entitle the purchaser to the privilege of educating a young man for the space of two years at Dickinson College free from all charge for tuition, provided application be made for said benefit within ten years from the date of the certificate. The money raised by the sale of these shares to constitute a fund the interest of which shall be applied to the support of the professors.

Here is the germ of that scholarship certificate plan which twenty and thirty years later would sweep many colleges into a brief and heady expansion, to be followed by years of regret.

The new plan also embraced the erection of new buildings, expansion of the Library, apparatus and mineralogical collection, and the endowment of professorships, all this to be accomplished by gifts and bequests. A subscription paper outlining the whole was ordered printed, and President Neill was authorized to open the campaign. We have no record of sales of shares of stock. However, one notable result was the bequest by ironmaster Robert Coleman of $1,140 in bank stock and interest, received on February 15, 1827. [59] And a year before that, "by dint of hard pleading and perseverance," as Neill put it, and no doubt helped along by the broad appeal, the state had finally granted a continuing income. [60]

The Act of February 13, 1826, providing an annual income of $3,000 for five years, made the College in effect a state institution, with all the rights, privileges, hazards and headaches thereunto appertaining. Included was an amendment of the charter: not more than one-third of the forty trustees could be clerics. Two clerical trustees, one of them Ashbel Green, were therefore asked to resign. Also, the trustees must submit annual financial reports—and, as they well knew, be prepared for a critical examination of them.

One can see how students and curriculum had had a part in bringing matters to this culmination. We see almost all of the four classes present in the Senate chamber at Harrisburg, guests of the state for the official reception for General Lafayette in February, 1825. Samuel McCoskry, Class of 1824, later an Episcopal bishop, came forward to declare that the old General's life had been lived "in obedience to the manly dictates of a noble and generous heart," and Lafayette returned to the boys his "most affectionate and friendly thanks." [61] On August 30, 1826, the trustees approved two faculty recommendations. The first, which would certainly have had weight with politicians of the Jacksonian era, permitted students to take a course free of Greek and Latin, denying them "academical degrees or honors," but promising "a certificate . . . of their proficiency & attainments." [62] With the second came an admission which would have pleased Dr. Rush, that in dormitory life "the young men become coarse & rude, & awkward by being penned up together for years." At their parents' option, therefore, they might again live with town families. [63] These changes were fully publicized, along with a summary of admissions requirements and the studies of each class—a curriculum in which we see the gradual relaxation of classical language standards prevalent throughout American education. [64]

Student discipline remained a vital concern of trustees and faculty, vital also to public relations, and, at the same time, the issue on which they were most at odds. From the *American*

Volunteer of September 14, 1826, we learn that Dr. Rush's idea
of a student uniform had been revived. The editorial disapproval
of its "gaudy and useless ornaments" probably reflects that of
the town. Infractions of the rules were plenty, for the Duffield
moral standard was no more safe in Carlisle than Atwater's had
been. This town, where a company of players or a dancing
master could always enjoy a run, offered temptations which
Duffield—over the votes of a few Episcopal colleagues—sought
to curb. [65] Dancing and parties were forbidden, but town families, including those of some of the trustees, were enjoying both
and were not averse to inviting students. As for the faculty, the
burden of the rising tide of disorder fell first on poor Spencer,
the classicist who lived in the building and had the whole duty
of keeping order there. He was one of those who can mete out
punishment without inspiring respect. In 1825, anonymous letters were warning him of "something foul about," of an "impending storm" and even "a severe flagellation." [66] Three years
later, raids upon his rooms and the destruction of his clothing
had brought him nearly to nervous prostration, and he gave
notice that he must live elsewhere as the others did. [67]

The trustees then reverted to Atwater's plan of engaging
tutors, but to this faculty promptly objected that a tutor would
be an abecedarian, probably less able to deal with mischief than
Spencer, and that such an expense would further delay what
was most needed—the appointment of a professor of chemistry
and natural history. [68] Here they carried their point, bringing in
John Knox Finley, M.D., as lecturer in chemistry in November,
1827; yet when the establishment of a full professorship came
up in May they were barely able to get the place for Finley,
rather than another of whom they disapproved. Neill wrote a
strong letter on the subject, adding, acidly, "In prescribing the
course of instruction to be given, the Faculty request that care
may be taken not to interfere with other departments of college
study." [69] One can now taste the sharpening acerbity of faculty-
trustee communications. By the statutes of 1826, examinations
should "be conducted by the faculty in the presence of the
examining committee." [70] Yet the faculty minutes, which are
largely concerned with examinations and special conditions imposed upon individual students unable to meet required stand-

ards, also note the absence or laggard attendance of trustees. [71]

"The government of the College," those statutes declare, "is essentially vested in the Faculty. 2. It shall be administered as nearly as possible, after the manner of a well regulated family. 3. Private advice, affectionate entreaty, and frequent admonitions shall always precede the more stern measures of public admonition, and exclusion from the institution, except when offences are flagrant and publicly committed." [72] So far so good, had not the trustees constantly intervened, fearful that faculty leniency might lead to more sin or faculty severity arouse the wrath of influential ·parents, and eager always to assert their own authority. Repeatedly, they reaffirmed the teachers' prerogative only to violate it.

There was a juridical obsession throughout the little community. Each student society had its "court." That of Belles Lettres was a committee of three, levying fines for non-attendance and sitting in judgment on more serious breaches of order. Here, in fact, was student government, operating effectively within a limited range. Their minutes show earnestness, maturity, pride in a coherent and smoothly functioning organization, in a growing library and in an intellectual program whose periodic "exhibitions" must command public respect. All this, to be sure, was maintained by emulation of the rival society with its duplicate program. Yet in favorable circumstances these young men (younger than the students of today) could manage their own lives well. With trustees and faculty themselves rivals in imposing "discipline," the circumstances were not favorable. Disorder was spreading everywhere. On February 24, 1827, Thomas E. Buchanan appealed to the Society from a decision of Belles Lettres court—pleading for acquittal but, if condemned, determined to "support myself with the consciousness of having acted in strict conformity to what I deem right." Faced with this:

> The court resign with pleasure the arduous duties which have been imposed upon them. They have watched with trembling anxiety the spirit of tumultuousness which of late has shown itself in this Hall. But may we not hope that the members of our society will take a decided stand against every thing like anarchy and confussion? Order & proper respect to the chair are indispensable to our very existence—

when these are sufficiently impressed on every mind our beloved
society may rise superior and set at defiance the hand that would
cloud its rising glory. [73]

By August, Thomas was in deeper trouble yet. Faculty and
trustees alike had found him guilty of sundry "outrages," including the destruction of Professor Spencer's boots. Two others, William Maclay Lyon and John Norris, were also before
these bars of justice for "card-playing in the College edifice, . . . profane and obscene language, . . . riotous behavior." [74] The faculty recommended that Buchanan be expelled,
and imposed a sentence of dismissal on the other two—only to
learn that the trustees had already come to a conclusion according to their own concept of "a well regulated family." Their
idea had been to expose the culprits to the full terrors of the
law by haling them before a justice of the peace. If contrition
resulted, the Board would then be ready with what a twentieth-
century president of the College called "executive clemency." It
recalls a disciplinary practice of the Revolutionary armies, a
pardon at the gallows' foot. Buchanan fled the town. With Lyon
and Norris it worked. But when both reappeared in class, fully
restored, a sharp protest came from faculty to trustees, echoed
and reechoed in hard words and soft. [75]

Small wonder that the students felt more than ever the
urge to manage their own affairs. By the end of the year both
societies were cherishing wild hopes of independent charters of
incorporation, with buildings owned by themselves. By January,
1828, they had prepared their petitions to the legislature. They
sent them in March, with what result can be imagined. The
trustees took advantage of their enthusiasm to make these
buildings part of their program, offering to pay two-thirds of
the cost if the students could raise the rest. [76]

It was student initiative that built the "ball alley," the first
evidence of a much-needed athletic program, at this time. It
became popular at once, though the faculty found themselves
hard put to it to limit the activity to students, and students in
good standing only. When Johnston Moore, a student in trouble
for window-breaking, refused "with foul and profane language"
to leave the place, he was suspended. In this verdict the trustees

(in a chastened spirit after the Lyon-Norris case) agreed, though the boy came of a wealthy local family. [77]

Spencer had fled the scene. Most boys were boarding in town, and the office of steward, once lucrative, was no longer so. [78] The final departure of this official was spurred on by the threats of the "Invisibles:"

> Sworn by all—a warning voice from the Invisibles. Beware, beware, unfortunate man—thy doom is fixed, and death awaits thee. It is decreed by the Invisibles that you shall be secretly, horribly, and cruelly slain! Your body is doomed to be exposed to the fowls of the air, and devoured by the beasts of the field, and your soul doomed to everlasting perdition, if, within one week, and no more, you do not leave the college, and no longer pollute the sight of gentlemen with your hated physiognomy. If you dare to divulge this letter you shall be strangled instantly; therefore take the warning voice, death-devoted man! Depart and live!
>
> A Warning Voice. [79]

Chapel in the cold light of dawn began the round of classes; then evening chapel; then mischief running wild through the night. In the dark hours of November 24, 1828, the janitor was driven out. The trustees consoled themselves with the fact that they had been trying to get rid of him anyway. [80] But, left unprotected, the building suffered heavy damage in the next affair, a riotous December night marking the final collapse of the spirit of sanctity which had come in with the revival of five years before. [81]

Ironically, in these post-revival years, charges of overt sectarianism were brought against the College authorites. Unsympathetic taxpayers probably realized that this was the best calculated way to alienate state support. It began a few months after the Act of February, 1826, when Mr. Duffield, by detective work of his own, felt that he had discovered the author of one of those "incendiary and diabolical" anonymous letters to the steward, and had sought to awaken remorse in his suspect by pleading for his soul. This the boy's father interpreted as proselytizing, and the *Lancaster Gazette* of January 16, 1827, drew a dark conclusion from the story: "That institution has leant to monkishism for years, and if it has sunk into a school for religious intolerance and persecution the sooner it is levelled with the dust the better."[82] Election campaigns were spiced with similar insinuations, and the broth was kept a-bubble by Presbyterian suspicions that the Episcopalians on the Board planned a coup d'etat. Here the Episcopalians began to drop out.[83] On November 19, 1827, Edward James, Benjamin Stiles, Alexander Mahon and Redmond Conyngham resigned in a body. All, like Conyngham, were men of "lettered tastes and liberal feelings," and ready to support the College on such terms only.[84] The state Senate, taking note of the rumors, called for an investigation to determine whether the annuity should be withdrawn, and the Board of Trustees, December 11, 1827, invited it.[85] The ordeal, so familiar to later state colleges and universities, was then awaited with the usual well-founded apprehension. Most significant is the action of the faculty at its meeting of January 22, 1828, appointing Professor McClelland as its representative and instructing him "to use all fair means to secure a decision, in relation to the Faculty, distinct from that which may be had, in regard to the Board of Trustees."[86] The Senate committee's report, March 25, 1828, found no evidence of bad faith and recommended that the subsidy continue, yet the mere fact that an investigation had been held tended to keep suspicions on the prowl.[87]

The trustees now move forward into a dream world of solution-by-buildings. There would be a dormitory, a commons, the two society halls.[88] We find initiative in academic matters coming—and rather tartly—from the faculty.[89] The rule, by a resolution of Duffield's,[90] that faculty must submit its minutes regularly to trustee examination, and then that near-successful move to replace Dr. Finley, had brought the professors to a mood of open exasperation. All this sets the stage in perfect fashion for the entrance of Mrs. Anne Royall of Washington, her skirts swishing boldly along, bright eyes under the bonnet seeing all.

Mrs. Royall had written a novel, *The Tennesseean,* but was best known for her *Black Book, or A Continuation of Travels in the United States.* Her works of local description combine sharp and accurate observation with much humor and one overriding bias. All those sordid deeds and motives which religious people then imputed to "infidels," she applied to the religionists themselves. Presbyterians ("blue skins") were her particular aversion. She also reversed their charge of a plot to overthrow our government: "It is useless to repeat a fact too well known, that these Presbyterians, glutted with women and money, have become not only beastly wicked, but are in every part of the U. S. aiming to overturn our government and establish the reign of terror." [91] Small wonder that Neill and the others fled or hid from her. She caught only the long-suffering Spencer, whom she found "afraid to speak above his breath." However, he invited her to visit his class. "He is a gentleman of young appearance, tall and slender, dark complexion, oval face, soft blue eyes, and of mild and engaging manners." [92] She was four days in Carlisle, where she found "more churches, more old maids, and more wickedness . . . than any town of the same population in the United States. It leaves Pittsburgh and Newburyport far behind." [93] At the end, a deputation of about thirty students called at her rooms—"sprightly and entertaining, and bestowed on me all the honor a going at Dickinson." [94]

From Anne Royall we learn that the College was affectionately known in Carlisle as "Old Mother Dickinson," and that Mr. Duffield bore the soubriquet of "Pope." But Pope Duffield, who had seemed to cringe when he saw her in his congregation, had now another enemy who troubled him more, a fellow member of the College trustees. The precise theology Duffield had brought with him from seminary had yielded to the warm personal approach of a revivalist, a deviation highly offensive to his fellow trustee and distant relative, George Armstrong Lyon. Mr. Lyon, lawyer, bank president, president of the trustees of Duffield's church, was a son of one of the patentees of 1773 and a man as rigid in principle as ever John Steel had been. From his lean and deeply-lined face, gray hair curling at top and sides and lantern jaw below, his small eyes watched Mr. Duffield's every move at meetings, and at home his fine script filled page after page with evidence of heresy. [95]

With College affairs become a patchwork of cross purposes, once, at least, we find Board and faculty in unison. General Gabriel Hiester, a state official, had sought and obtained election as a trustee solely in order to rebuke the teachers, who had refused to sign his son's diploma. Young Augustus Otto Hiester,

it seems, had alluded critically to the faculty in his commencement oration of 1828. The General's motion lost, ten to one—
"singular and pitiable displays of character," was the comment
he got from George Duffield.[96] Yet so tender were feelings
everywhere that when, in January, 1829, a student read in class
a mock-serious review of the nursery rhyme, "Cock Robin,"
and McClelland derided it as abounding "more in threadbare
conceits than in genuine attic humour," hurt feelings rolled
from students to Principal to trustees.[97] The trustees, condemning the faculty's "system of discipline, if *system* it can
properly be called," dealt in their own ways with mounting
disorder.[98] At last, on August 1, 1829, they launched an investigation of teaching loads, methods and competence, with a
reduction of salaries in view.[99] Here Dr. Neill, at odds with
McClelland since the "Cock Robin" affair, resigned.[100]

As for the future, all their turgid effort had produced nothing but the state subsidy. Vethake was leaving, Finley too. They
elected McClelland Principal, but he refused the honor, then
resigned. Spencer would go in a few months. Again, Carlisle was
asking, "What can the matter be?" The trustees would respond
with their eighty-three page *Narrative,* authorized in May, 1830,
and published in the fall. It would be countered promptly by
Henry Vethake's *Reply,* printed at Princeton, where he was
then teaching. The *Reply* attributes past failures and their inevitable continuance simply to operative procedures "unconnected
with the particular individuals to whom, as Trustees or faculty,
the administration of the college is confided." In Vethake's
concise and sensible view, the faculty's lack of ultimate power
in discipline necessitated the constant presence and vigilance of
a quorum of trustees who, as he wrote, "can hardly avoid being
seized with a spirit of legislation," and he cited the year 1826
when "no less than forty meetings" had been held. With no
regular faculty representation they would act often on "inaccu-
rate and prejudiced statements of some one of their number."
He cited also a propensity of college governing boards which
will reappear from time to time in this history until well into
the twentieth century: "When the trustees transact their business entirely apart from the Faculty, they will often be disposed
to make a mystery of their proceedings to the latter, and thus

impair that mutual confidence, which it is important should always exist between the two bodies." [101]

In a hopeful vein, at the commencement of September 23, 1829, it was announced that Philip Lindsley, one of the truly great educators of the day, had been elected Principal—though he had not accepted, and would not. [102] Duffield had not been altogether happy with the Lindsley choice, but then Nathan Sidney Smith Beman, preacher and teacher in his wing of Presbyterianism, also declined. At this, Duffield, putting warmth of Christian feeling above all else, brought in the name of his university classmate and Dickinson's former Grammar School master, Samuel Blanchard How—a man who "depends on God alone." [103] How was elected, to be formally installed March 30, 1830.

Vethake's departure made a drop in enrollment certain. Junior John Weidman wrote home on Christmas day that only ten students remained—"Dickinson has burnt unsteadily and has been entirely blown out." [104] Yet at that last commencement there had been, besides the name of Lindsley, one other ray of hope. "The Alumni Association of Dickinson College" appears, and is permitted by the trustees, mirabile dictu, to entertain the graduating class at dinner. [105] It had appointed a committee— Richard Rush, the Doctor's distinguished son; James Buchanan, now in Congress; and William Price, '15—to seek help from others. [106] Williams College had formed such an association in 1821 and Columbia in 1825, and Princeton's, founded in 1826, was at this very time conducting an active campaign which would meet successfully a desperate need for funds. Dickinson had long had some of this element of strength in the two societies' "Graduate Members," those nearby often in active association, and those at a distance retaining their interest and loyalty. At the next commencement, 1830, the Association sponsored an oration by Price, followed by a debate between two lawyers, Benjamin Patton and Judge John Reed, on the proposition, "Would it be expedient for the United States to establish a national university?" [107] But a year later only How was there to address the group, pleading for support. [108]

How's leadership would be much on a par with that of his friend Atwater, now again in touch with him from New Haven.

Soon after his coming, the campus ball alley was removed. [109]
A new edition of the statutes, more stringent than the last, was
compiled and printed, to be sold to all entering students at
12½¢. At least, by the spring of 1830, How had a working
faculty on campus, with himself as "Professor of the Moral
Sciences," and another Presbyterian minister, Alexander W. Mc-
Farlane, as "Professor of the Exact Sciences." [110] This last department embraced "Mathematicks and Natural Philosophy,
demonstrative," while young Henry Darwin Rogers, aged twenty-two, supported it as "Professor of the Natural Sciences," that
is, "Chymestry, Natural History and Experimental Philosophy."
The fourth addition was, like Rogers, a young career teacher,
Charles Dexter Cleveland, "Professor of Languages." [111] With
no one in the fields of history or literature, Cleveland would
enter these on his own inititative within the wide scope of
Greek and Latin.

Behind that sense of concern for their institution which the
Dickinson College trustees had been manifesting with such grim
zeal, there had been, throughout these years, in America, Britain and Europe, a rising concern with education as a whole. It
brought, as would the population explosion of the 1950's, an
interest in techniques of mass instruction—teaching machines—
the Lancastrian system of making pupils the subalterns of a
single master. [112] Joseph Lancaster's coming to America in
1818 had stimulated interest, bringing a Lancastrian school to
Carlisle soon after. [113] Dickinson's Grammar School, after a
shuffling life in a rented building so shabby "that it tempts the
boys to commit violence upon it," had been given to the master
on a fee basis in 1829. [114] Six months later, in March, 1830, it
reopened as Henry Duffield's "Carlisle Institute" in the old
Seminary building opposite the College, with an ambitious program for boys from seven to fourteen. [115] Another boys'
school, "The Old College Seminary," was operating under capable teachers in Liberty Alley, where Nisbet had taught. [116]

With public education, that dream of Rush and so many
others, becoming an accomplished fact, educational theory
aroused fresh interest everywhere. In 1806, Dr. William Maclure
had brought to Philadelphia an assistant of the Swiss innovator,
Johann Heinrich Pestalozzi. Pestalozzi's reforms—a bond of un-

derstanding and sympathy between teacher and pupil, the presentation of facts from a basis of the child's own observation and experience with no intrusion of meaningless rules and tables—would not be widely accepted in America until after the Civil War. Though a few, among them Horace Mann and Henry Barnard, were promoting them in the 1820's and 1830's, our theologically oriented professors had small regard for new modes of exposition or for transforming the classroom into a place of mutual understanding, comfort and joy. On the college level, these new notions pointed toward more courses and some freedom in course election. This would be expensive, and would inevitably mean a weakening óf the traditional emphasis on Latin and Greek. In New Haven warm discussion of this issue brought forth the famous *Yale Report on the Classics,* written by President Jeremiah Day in 1827 and published in 1828—a forceful and tremendously influential defense of the established curriculum. If the old learning did not meet all practical needs, it was still the best "mental discipline." After that tough grind, the young man could readily pick up what interested him more. Classical learning marked the gentleman. More, it marked the school as standing in the mainstream of timeless Christian erudition.

Here and there some deviation occurred, but most colleges, like Princeton, rallied promptly behind the "Yale Plan." The Presbyterian schools were having too much trouble with their "Pelagian Controversy" to give this matter front place. Where Old Side and New Side had once engaged, now Old School was trumpeting its forces out against New School's promise of the soul's regeneration by confession and good works. In Carlisle, Lyon of Old School, supported from afar by Ashbel Green, leads the attack on New School's Duffield.[117] Duffield, entrenched and tightly organized, fights on two fronts: Lyon on his right, and on his left those so-successful rivals in the field of emotional religion, the Methodists.[118]

When it came to the attention of the Dickinson College trustees that the youngest member of their faculty was a Pestalozzian, supporting an alien faith by the spoken and written word, a formal resolution made clear that his resignation would be accepted.[119] They might have read a lesson—but apparently did not—in the character of the students who chose to depart with him at the end of the session. [120] Henry Darwin Rogers was a friend of Henry Vethake, and would go on to a career in teaching and in science even more influential and distinguished than the older man's. From August, 1830, until he left Carlisle the following July, he published a magazine, *The Messenger of Useful Knowledge,* with the influential amateur of science, James Hamilton, Jr., as his backer and collaborator. It combined original articles with "a register of news and events" in the learned world. It was Rogers who, in the lead article of the December number, had daringly stated that Americans, though aware of the paramount importance of education, "have not yet ascertained what education must be, to be judicious and to answer our wants. . . . The wordy learning of our schools imparts unfortunately almost no information that a youth can apply when he issues upon engagements of manhood." [121] From this he had gone on to extol "that unsophisticated philosopher of nature," Pestalozzi.

The Principal (or President, since the old title was by now used only when legal formality required it) was grateful for the advice of his Professor of Languages on how to replace Rogers. In an unguarded moment, How had confessed to Cleveland that the University of Pennsylvania in his day had been little better than an academy, and that his teaching experience had been on the school level only. [122] He was grateful for guidance, and the other only too eager to give it. Cleveland was a young fellow of much charm—a calm, open countenance with an abundance of curling hair almost shoulder length. He had graduated from Dartmouth College in 1827, older than most students, but with a warm dedication to scholarship and teaching, and to an idealism embracing international peace and the abolition of slavery. [123] At Dartmouth, he had written a text on *Grecian Antiquities,* and at Dickinson rewrote and republished it. [124] Later in life, as author and educator, he would join his friend Rogers as a member of the American Philosophical Society, a rare honor for a humanist. Cleveland was now openly promoting the example of the New England colleges, but from a different viewpoint than Atwater's. In August, 1830, he brought his case to the trustees, pointing out also the advantages of giving a college president ex officio status on the Board. How himself pressed this point, which the trustees mulled over distastefully and tabled. [125] Cleveland had obtained architectural drawings, giving a flutter of substance to the dreamed-of new building. [126] At his persuasion, the master's degree was made subject to the delivery of an oration as evidence of progress. [127] With the initial advantage of being on the scene before McFarlane or Rogers, Cleveland had found himself in a power-behind-the-throne situation, cheered by How's grateful "Sir, I depend upon you," and "Sir, without you I would leave the institution." [128]

Yet the Carlisle trustees were no more friendly to Dartmouth as a model than to Yale, and by February, 1831, How was keeping a little book in which he noted down all the sins of Cleveland, brought to him by the watchful McFarlane. [129] Blissfully unaware of this, Cleveland had given his heart to Alison Nisbet McCoskry, the old Doctor's granddaughter. They were married immediately after the spring examinations, March 29, 1831, by Mr. Duffield, and set out for a honeymoon tour, going first to Baltimore where the groom had taught before coming to Carlisle, then to the New England colleges. They would stop at Yale to interview Dr. Silliman's assistant, Charles U. Shepard, the man whom How had agreed would make an excellent replacement for Rogers. [130]

An incident during the examinations might have given a hint of trouble. McFarlane, having put the Freshmen through their paces in algebra, had given his colleagues the usual opportunity for questions. How asked a few. Then Cleveland called on one youth for "the reason" of the solution he had worked out on the blackboard. "This he could not do. I therefore went with him from statement to statement, sometimes telling him and sometimes drawing out his own mind by questions, till we came to the final result." Here McFarlane blurted out an angry, "It is the same thing!" [131] Cleveland, as they must have realized then, had simply given the others a demonstration of the Pestalozzian method. When he returned a month later, it would be to learn that the honeymoon with How, also, had ended.

How, ignoring the negotiations with Shepard, had persuaded the trustees to appoint Lemuel Gregory Olmstead, a pleasant youth from neighboring Perry County, who had taken the course at the new Rensselaer Polytechnic Institute but had not yet earned a bachelor's degree. [132] More, and worse: in Baltimore, Cleveland had discussed Dickinson affairs with Dr. William Nevins, Judge Alexander Nisbet's pastor and a man of much influence in Presbyterian affairs. Nevins, emphasizing his personal friendship for George Duffield, was disturbed by the prevalent belief that Duffield "governed the College, and governed it only for sectarian purposes." Duffield should be persuaded in a friendly spirit to resign. All this, brought by Cleveland to How *"in the strictest confidence,"* was taken by How to the pastor, and in a less amicable light. [133]

Once more, animosity filled the institutional veins; once more, paralysis was setting in. Now Cleveland (academically worth all the others put together, though perhaps a little too keenly aware of the fact), was at swords' points with How and McFarlane, leaving Olmstead an embarrassed neutral. Only Cleveland had the respect and affection of the students. He held them so, pleasantly confident, oblivious of the others' problems with discipline. To the young men who must spend four years with a faculty so small, such a presence was the College's one redeeming feature, and sensing the outcome, they began to drift away. Meanwhile Cleveland, assigned the chore of Librarian, had taken it up with his wonted earnestness, reclassifying and recataloguing the whole, and adding new books partly at his own expense. Students had been assessed a fee for the use of a library inferior to the holdings of their own societies. Now they would have some return for it. Cleveland's report of September 27, 1831, marks the opening of the Library's first reference room, and a general collection directly serving the curriculum. [134] One is reminded of the work of Bertram H. Davis in 1953 to 1957 to expand the Library's frontiers; but Cleveland's work was given a shorter term, as How, on September 26, came to the trustees with his little book and its charges of dereliction in inspecting and disciplining the students. [135]

By this time the student body had shrunk to five Seniors, no Juniors, seven Sophomores and eleven Freshmen. [136] Some action was imperative, and two trustees Judge Frederick Watts and the Rev. John Moodey, had a plan ready, supported also by How. Classics would be taught in the first two years only. Upperclassmen would take only mathematics, with natural and moral philosophy. Boys could enter as Juniors, thus bypassing Latin and Greek entirely. [137] From experience with the certificate students, they could gauge how popular this would be—certain to attract young men seeking practical rather than "literary" preparation. Here was a bold flouting of the Yale Report, and a generous yielding to what was then known as "the spirit of the age." The plan had a modern, pioneering aspect; yet there was no supporting program to redeem the loss of academic respectability in what, for most students, would be a return to the two-year college course. It was probably true, as Cleveland suspected, that he was to be replaced by How in a downgrading of the classical program. [138]

A trustee committee brought the proposal to the faculty on September 30, but by that time faculty and trustees alike were involved in so intricate a pattern of controversy that no progress was possible. George Duffield was opposing the new curriculum, having no doubt that it would bring students, and none that it would "bring the College down to a mere academy." [139] The proposal that he be asked to resign had had, interestingly, the effect of strengthening his friendship with Cleveland. They had stood together ever since in the steamy winds of others' hostility. *The Presbyterian, The Expositor,* the Carlisle papers are spotted with shadowy insinuations against McFarlane and Duffield, followed by recriminations and denials. [140] It had been a high year for Duffield: 108 additions to his flock "by profession," as against 8 the year before and 17 in the next. All through it he had been writing a book, and by fall must have been reading proof on its six hundred pages, for the volume appeared in the first weeks of 1832—awaited by the hostile Mr. Lyon, voracious and ready to spring.

Duffield on Regeneration (its binder's title) is a work now difficult to conceive as dangerous or controversial. [141] The author's dedication "To the members of his charge," however, apologizing for errors imbibed in theological school and now "REPUDIATED," was confession enow of deviance. Presbytery placed the book, rather than the writer, on trial for heresy in a long, indeterminate wrangle reflecting the larger church division. [142] Lyon, with some seventy families, broke away to found the Second Church, a return to the rival congregations of Colonial days. Duffield would stay on the scene only till the trial was ended, leaving in 1835.

The Dickinson trustees, meanwhile, waded through McFarlane's complaints against Cleveland and Cleveland's rebuttals, wrangled heavily, gave the enraged McFarlane a grudging vote of confidence and then, on February 18, 1832, wearily called a halt: "That as this Board believe they will be compelled by circumstances to suspend the operations of the College at the end of the present session, they therefore deem it inexpedient to investigate the charges preferred against Professor Cleveland."

The students faced the crisis with emotions in shining contrast to the defeatism of the Board. Belles Lettres took inventory of its beloved library (2,607 volumes, with recent purchases listed: Buffon in five volumes, Percy's *Reliques* in three, the six volumes of William Beloe's *Anecdotes of Literature and Scarce Books* and Burlamaqui's *Principles of Natural Law*) and elected five resident alumni as interim librarians, so that:

> . . . the books may be preserved from damage and loss. Where is the member of the Belles Lettres society who does not feel an inward regard for her name and interest and a longing desire to protect that which has been and, if preserved, will ever be the source of her honour; will point out to posterity the remnant of a body which stood and shone as long as Dickinson College remained in existence. It is the anxious desire of the Librarians that the Belles Lettres society may not remain in name and recollection only, but that it may rise again in full splendor and adorn the Institution to which it belongs. [143]

More than anything else, it would be the alumni of the student societies who would maintain continuity with the past. The trustees did act to keep the Grammar School open, giving another graduate member of Belles Lettres the Rev. Daniel McKinley, permission to live in the "College Edifice" as caretaker and to conduct a "classical school" there—a reversion of sorts to the names and status of 1773. [144] McKinley, soon to be called as pastor of the new Second Presbyterian Church, would be prompt in enrolling the next President of the College, Methodist John Price Durbin, as an honorary member of Belles Lettres, and other society men were equally forward in maintaining the rights and dignities of the past.

As for the public at large, the reaction to the closing of the College was one of shocked surprise, reflected well in the brief comment of *Niles' Weekly Register:*

> Dickinson College, which has been the peculiar object of state patronage, and had the advantage of location in the beautiful village of Carlisle, in the center of Pennsylvania, has ceased operations. *Reason*—too much sectarianism, and too little true piety. [145]

Pallas and the Muses. Design for Belles Lettres Society "diploma" by Thomas Sully, engraved by George Murray, 1815.

From that little knowledge I possess of the History of Seminaries, in such parts of this Country as I am best acquainted with, my impression is, that their Success does not so much Depend on publick endowment, as on the capacity and conduct of the principal professors.

Samuel Knox to James Hamilton, October 25, 1816

I think you will bear me witness, young gentlemen, that the faculty of this college has endeavored to resist this tendency of our times [to enter professional life inadequately prepared], and to maintain a high standard of education. We know our present interests suffer by this course, but we hope for our reward in future. We look to the character you will sustain and the influence you will exert to demonstrate to our countrymen the wisdom of our views.

William Henry Allen, Baccalaureate Address at Dickinson College, July 8, 1840

9

A METHODIST NEW DAWN

"Too much sectarianism, and too little true piety"—a sharp rebuke, coming at a time when public awareness of educational needs had been sharply revived. The early 1830's were a season of school and college founding. Now the leading provision in the will of Stephen Girard had just become known: a fabulously endowed institution which promised to become a model for all others. The public school systems would soon be an accomplished fact, with their promise of better stabilized college preparation than ever before. Jacksonian democracy was transforming American society along bluntly practical lines, and with it an era of imaginative and ardent reform movements was coming in—forces to which the colleges would respond gingerly, while endeavoring to stand as rocks of intellectual probity among the flowing tides.

For Dickinson College the answer would now be an avowed sectarianism, and piety in due proportion. At special session on March 12, 1833, the trustees discussed an enquiry from the Rev. Edwin Dorsey of the Baltimore Annual Conference of the Methodist Church as to their willingness to retire in favor of Methodist control and a program of expansion and endowment They pronounced it "worthy of consideration."

Methodism had mushroomed in America since its first small meetings in New York in 1766. Methodists had rooted themselves in the cities and swept out through the countryside everywhere, setting the frontier aflame for holiness. Nisbet had watched their progress in Carlisle with a sharply contemptuous eye. They had a kinship with New Side Presbyterianism, but this was all-the-way and inordinately successful. They combined a doctrine of unusual ease and warmth with a remarkably tight and effective organization. From bishop to class leader to member, each with his tender or burning recollection of "conversion," they were a united brotherhood, and "Brother" or "Sister" their common form of address. Their itinerant ministry reached out through the thinly settled lands. Their clergy's regular changes of location kept the spirit of inspiration fresh, as did their modest educational standard. They lived to shake down the heavenly fire, and left theological hair-splitting to their rivals.

Yet by 1830 they had education itself as a major issue of their own—warm inspiration against cold book-learning, a "God-made" against a "man-made" ministry. They were growing in numbers and social status, and the desirability of educational institutions of their own could not be denied, though any proposal of a theological school would still have met overwhelming opposition. That would not come until the founding of Drew University in 1867. This prevailing hostility put the intellectuals of the Church upon their mettle. They were determined to succeed and eager to win the respect of educators everywhere. The Baltimore Conference, central and strong, controlling a vast area from central Pennsylvania down into Virginia, had before it the example of the New England Methodists, who had taken over the buildings of Captain Alden Partridge's military school to found Wesleyan University in 1831. By June, 1833, the time of Wesleyan's first commencement, Baltimore had been joined by the powerful Philadelphia Conference in the Dickinson venture. With the growth of the Church, conference divisions would divide responsibility for the College—New Jersey separated from Philadelphia in 1836, Newark from New Jersey in 1857, and from Baltimore came East Baltimore, 1857, and Central Pennsylvania, 1868—but with the two original conferences still holding their endowment funds in trust. That same year, 1833, Pittsburgh Conference was taking over Allegheny College, also formerly Presbyterian. It all had the inevitablity of a rising tide.

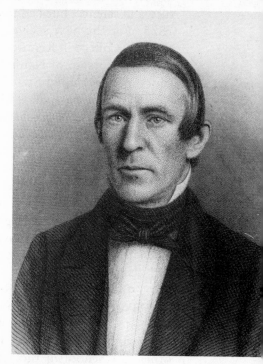

Top left: Henry Vethake. Lithograph by John H. Sherwin, *c.* 1855. Top right: Lewis Mayer. By Jacob Eichholtz, *c.* 1830. Bottom left: Charles Dexter Cleveland. Engraving by A. B. Walter from an ambrotype. Bottom right: Henry Darwin Rogers. By an unidentified artist.

The old Board was as ready to yield to events as it had formerly been to turn the burden over to the state. The seats of the half dozen who refused to resign were declared vacant as the Methodist majority moved in.[1] The old regime held its last meeting on June 6, 1833, and the new one its first on June 7. On that day, John Price Durbin was elected to head the new administration. An amendment to the charter was initiated to give the presidency of the Board to the Principal of the College. Durbin would be the institution's first actual chief executive, formulating policy for Board approval and carrying it out.[2] He was also one of those churchmen in Dickinson's history who saw the office as a step to higher ranges of ecclesiastical service.

Durbin was then thirty-two years of age, a Kentuckian of poor background, yet one whose conversion and call to the itineracy had been acts of deliberation rather than of the endemic emotional ecstasy. He was self-educated in classics, literature and science, but had taken a degree at Cincinnati College in 1825. For the next six years he was Professor of Languages at Augusta College in Kentucky. In 1831, he had a choice between the professorship of Natural Science at Wesleyan and the chaplaincy of the United States Senate. He chose the Senate.[3] The General Conference of 1832 elected him editor of the *Christian Advocate and Journal* and other publications. From this vantage point he supported the educational movement as giving Methodists a larger access to the professions, supporting both Dickinson and Wesleyan and even, in a final editorial of July 18, 1834, the idea of a theological seminary.[4]

Among the first acts of the new Board were building repairs, grading and planting the campus with trees and shrubs, property insurance and inventory.[5] More importantly, it provided for the immediate continuance of the Grammar School, and accepted the offer of Judge John Reed of Carlisle to establish a "law department." Reed had been a student in the Class of 1806, and a trustee from 1821 to 1828. "I would not contemplate," he wrote in his proposal June 8, 1833, "more than a nominal connection with the College." But since there was no other law school in the state, and his own new home would adjoin the campus, he could foresee a relationship of mutual advantage.[6] So indeed it would become. His first student was enrolled April 1, 1834, and the College would confer its first degrees of Bachelor of Laws two years later.[7]

By Durbin's arrival, April, 1834, the Grammar School had grown to nearly forty pupils, laboring over Caesar, Cicero, the Greek reader and New Testament and an assistant must be found for Mr. Dobb.[8] Thus primary and professional training preceded the College itself, which the conferences had resolved not to open until $45,000 had been raised. In May, word of an accounting of $48,000 in subscriptions came through, and the second Wednesday of September was set for formal opening.[9]

Avowed sectarian control would now remove the old charge of Dickinson's being covertly so controlled; while at the same time, as at Wesleyan and almost all other denominational schools, students of other faiths would be welcomed—as would, in careful proportion, faculty and trustees. The trustees of the new Board were primarily clergy and laymen of the two conferences, men who would speak for education and whose voices would carry weight in General and Annual Conference, in the crowded city churches, in the country circuits, down to that last unit of about a dozen souls, class and class leader. Persuasion would not be easy, yet an organization such as any modern development officer might envy was there. The first list of trustees included in their minutes, June 7, 1833, is headed by two names obviously so placed for their importance. The first is John Emory, a graduate of Washington College, a man of unusual ability who had turned from the law to the ministry and had been elected a bishop the year before. The second is John McLean, a rugged, self-educated newspaperman, lawyer and politician, who had refused a cabinet post under Jackson rather than agree to political dismissals. Jackson had responded by making him a Supreme Court Justice in 1829. Even so early, he was spoken of as a presidential possibility. Under Dickinson's Chief Justice Taney, Dickinson's McLean wrote the dissenting opinion in the Dred Scott case.

The Baltimore group included Dr. Samuel Baker of the College of Medicine, a fashionable practitioner,[10] and Thomas Emerson Bond, physician and editor, a man of great influence in the growth of the Church. Others were Bond's close friend the Rev. Alfred Griffith, whose sermons were described as "heavy artillery," ponderously declaimed from under shaggy brows, lightened with flashes of humor; preachers Stephen George Roszel, aging now, but a powerful influence in General Conference, and John Davis, tall and commanding "a prince in Israel." [11] Roszel at that first meeting nominated Daniel Webster for membership, no doubt mindful of the Dartmouth case and Webster's championship of the independence of college trustees under their charter, but the name lost by nine votes.

Philadelphia had strength of the same sort—old-line Methodists like Samuel Harvey, merchant and banker, and younger men of education and refinement. Harvey had watched and recorded the earliest growth of the American church and came to Carlisle ready to give this new enterprise the Midas touch of his personal success. The Rev. Pennell Coombe had also an interest in finance, as did another clergyman, Charles Pitman with his large head and sunken eyes, a dark, earnest, melancholy man. The Rev. Joseph Lybrand, with a florid face under dark hair and a "well-regulated cheerfulness," came (as the description would imply) from a well-to-do Philadelphia family. [12] John Miller Keagy, the brilliant physician and educator, author and disciple of Pestalozzi was there. He would be appointed to the College faculty two years later, just before his death. James Barton Longacre, the painter and engraver was another new trustee, as was the scholarly Englishman, Joseph Holdich, who would resign after two years to accept a professorship at Wesleyan. Holdich, nearsighted, would long be remembered by the Wesleyan boys for having tipped his tall hat to the President's cow as he crossed the campus, with a "Good morning, Madam." [13]

Carlisle was best represented by men of the old families and of other churches, elected, one may suspect, with an eye to a continuance of the state subsidies. William MacFunn Biddle would be an active member of the Board from 1833 until his death in 1855. When Charles Bingham Penrose presented his resignation, June 7, 1833, he was immediately elected Secretary of the Board. Penrose, who had married Biddle's daughter, Valeria, was a successful politician, a genial, attractive man of thirty-five, his bald crown surrounded by a bushy halo of yellow curls. [14] He was a trustee of the new Second Presbyterian

Church. Charles McClure of the Class of 1824 (and Turkey Club), an Episcopalian, would soon be elected to the state legislature, and would serve in Congress after that. [15] Frederick Watts, who collaborated with Penrose in the publication of law reports and stands as founder of the Pennsylvania State University, would be reelected a Dickinson trustee in 1841. [16]

This new Board met only once a year, at commencement Later, there would be a midwinter meeting also. Its executive committee, varying in title, powers and activity, would be present in the intervals. At Dickinson as at Wesleyan, the trustees were independent and self-perpetuating under their charter. Churchmen of seventy-five and a hundred years later would bemoan the failure of those of 1833 to initiate a charter change giving the Methodist conferences direct control of Board membership. Why they did not is obvious. They were a minority in a predominantly anti-intellectual denomination. The majority looked askance at higher education. Strong pressures to introduce elements of the trade school were exerted. These trustees had to deny any intention of setting up an educational standard for the ministry, though some cherished a hope that their program would lead in that direction. The two "patronizing conferences" took their own guarded view of the situation. Each would hold the endowment funds it raised for the College under conference-elected trustees, and they took up the old practice of sending "visitors" as official liaisons with the campus, where they continued to appear at commencement until 1925. [16]

From the first, the conferences would be watching the College with a sensitivity to the doubts and misgivings which have always confronted educators in one form or another. The two conferences subdivided, and conference representation on the Board became a matter of jealous concern. So also did loyalty to the Church. This could include acceptance of any favorite doctrine or practice, and we glimpse frequently the old-line clergy's distrust of soft-living intellectuals—of colleges and academies as "the high places of the devil." [17] In 1846 the New Jersey Conference, an offshoot from Philadelphia, demanded that students kneel rather than stand at prayer, and that faculty set the example. Faculty "respectfully" refused. [18] Baltimore took Durbin roundly to task for countenancing the reading of novels. [19] In all of this Durbin was well supported by his faculty, but the age of the College gave him an additional element of stability—"a network of custom and tradition more intractable, as more exacting and imperious, than written codes." [20]

The new sectarianism, Durbin had found, interested Carlisle more than any other feature of the reopening, and he brought the matter out in his inaugural address. *"What religious requisitions will be made upon the students?"* Only College chapel, he declared, and Sunday attendance at any church of their own choosing. "They will be received as Christian youth . . . and it will be the duty of this ancient and venerable institution to see that they lose not this character." [21]

His audience was listening to a rather small, angular, shrill-voiced man, with sandy hair over a receding forehead and sleepy hazel eyes which could become lustrous and commanding when aroused. [22] Durbin's renown as a preacher was based on what, in the religious jargon of the day, was called "the sudden change." Prosaic, thoughtful, informative, he would skillfully lay a foundation and then suddenly surge forward with it in a torrent of warmth and fervor. [23] Some students thought him a poseur, but Sidney George Fisher's estimate at their meeting in 1838, "a damned pompous fanatical Methodist & prig" is jaundiced to say the least. Even Fisher glimpsed in Durbin and his surroundings a refinement he would not have expected to find in a Methodist minister's home. [24]

Durbin, keeping the initiative, held both trustees and faculty to his will. [25] He would influence the town through his work at the College and with the new public school system. [26] He appears in 1840 on the executive committee of the National Convention for the Promotion of Education in the United States presided over by Alexander Dallas Bache, the new head of Girard. [27] That he was not elected a delegate to General Conference that year was attributed to his forwardness as an educator. [28] The organization would never realize that the religious life of a college must be exploratory, creative, combative, exciting a loyalty only to its ideals, if it would escape the contempt a tacit subservience deserves. Durbin's faculty breathed life and advance into orthodoxy—a function not rediscovered at

Dickinson until the 1960's—and the spirit of inquiry touched the classroom as well.

> The method of instruction in the College is by regular and careful recitation, accompanied with free and unrestrained enquiry and conversation on any or all points directly or collaterally involved in the subject. The students know that they are at liberty to make free enquiries or to propose and discuss any questions. They are encouraged to it. This process while it enables the instructor to satisfy himself of the knowledge of the students in reference to the particular subject calls into action his intellectual powers and accustoms him to think and investigate, while the communication with the Professor directs his thoughts and stimulates his investigation. Thus the true object of a collegiate education is obtained, viz. to develop and discipline the powers of the man. The books used in instruction are subject to change, but generally are the same as those used in the best colleges.

So Durbin informed his trustees, July 20, 1836. His own classroom was, as one student described it, "a place of pleasure," so ready was he to move from lecture to discussion, encouraging challenge and debate, even letting the young men believe they had lured him away from the routine of presentation and recital. [29] He was teaching as "Professor of Moral Science." The usual presidential course, "Moral Philosophy," was intended as a summation of all previous learning and its application to contemporary life. Content and approach were left very much to personal choice, and the altered title suggests Durbin's bias.

At the outset, Durbin had only two colleagues besides Judge Reed and the three men who were then handling the larger body of Grammar School pupils. That ever-central place in Latin and Greek had been taken by John Emory's son, Robert. Robert, just turned twenty-one, had graduated at the head of his class at Columbia in 1831. In that year his father had been elected President of Randolph-Macon and he its Professor of Languages. [30] The father became a bishop instead, while Robert, before coming to Dickinson, had been studying law under Reverdy Johnson in Baltimore. His students now saw a dark-haired young man peering at them through spectacles, an exacting teacher, always precise, a perfectionist, yet with a sweet

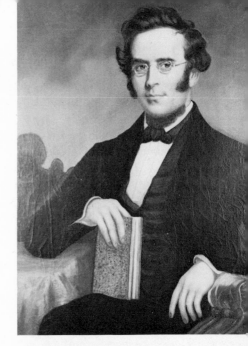

Top left: John Price Durbin. By an unidentified artist, *c.* 1835. Top right: Merritt Caldwell. By an unidentified artist, *c.* 1840. Bottom left: James Buchanan. By Jacob Eichholtz, 1834. Bottom right: William MacFunn Biddle. By Thomas S. Officer, 1834.

voice, a dignified charm and that remote intensity which so often characterized the young consumptive. [31] In Emory's classes a student called upon to recite must sit in a chair apart from the others, not led on by questions but merely directed to speak upon the subject—a situation in which success and failure were equally conspicuous. The practice encouraged sound preparation. President Herman Merrills Johnson followed it, and we see it in the 1890's, vestigial and ineffective, in the classroom of Emory's student, Dr. Henry Martyn Harman. [32] Emory left after five years for a tour of duty in the ministry, then returned to assume the acting presidency and presidency of the College.

At the outset, too, this faculty had only one experienced professional teacher, Merritt Caldwell. He was a native of Maine, and had been Principal of the Maine Wesleyan Seminary from 1828 to 1834. The appointment may be traced to trustee Thomas Sewall, another New Englander, a graduate of the Seminary, a man of refinement and scholarly tastes. [33] Durbin turned to Caldwell for advice, and received sound, dispassionate counsel. Caldwell's publications include a *Conjugation of the English Verb, A Practical Manual of Elocution,* a volume of Christian biography and a study of the psychological principles of Christian perfection. His commencement address of 1835 refutes the prevalent doctrine of separate "powers of the mind," calls for more widespread "female education" and attacks the insistant utilitarianism of the times. [34] He had come to Carlisle at the age of twenty-eight, he and his wife Rosamond living in West College, where their son, later a Dickinson alumnus, was born. Here was a confident, unruffled figure in the milieu which Joseph Spencer had found so difficult—a face framed in dark brown hair and side whiskers, with calmly observant eyes behind the steel-rimmed spectacles. He was a successful but not a popular teacher, patient, impersonal, always strict and fair within the rules. When the students who had been directed to step forward for recitation, first bowing to the professor, chose instead to rush up and prostrate themselves, kissing the floor at his feet, we see Caldwell, unmoved, noting down the minus marks in his book as he nods to them to proceed. [35] He did laugh at the dramatization of Thomas Campbell's poetic dialogue between the Wizard and Lochiel, Chief of the Camerons, when Lochiel, at the climactic, *"Down, soothless insulter!"* stamped his foot so hard that the stage all but collapsed. "Well, Spottswood, you ought to be emphatic just where you were, but don't you think that your emphasis was a little too pronounced?" [36]

Caldwell, like Emory, was tubercular. In 1841 he was too ill for a full schedule, but he recovered and lived another seven years. Moncure Conway learned from him "the importance of weighed words, exact statement, and tones sympathetic with the sense. His criticism of our compositions, or of our accentuation in reading, was uttered with such sweetness that the effect was always encouragement." [37] And Conway always remembered his announcement in class that there would be "no more Monday morning recitations, as he was going away." They learned of his death soon after. [38]

Within three years, college enrollment had risen from thirteen Freshmen and five Sophomores to over a hundred, and the first Seniors of the new regime graduated in 1837. That level was maintained till the Civil War years, while the crowded grammar school population was allowed to drop to a lower figure. These developments brought new faculty to the College, and began the practice of using recent graduates of high standing, such as Thomas Bowman or John Zug, as instructors for a year or two in the preparatory work.

With Keagy dying of consumption before he could take over his duties as "Professor of Chemistry and Experimental Philosophy," a new man of indubitable health and vigor was found in the state of Maine. William Henry Allen, a twenty-six-year-old Bowdoin alumnus who had attended Caldwell's academy at Readfield, and had been teaching Latin and Greek. He wrote frankly that he could teach the sciences acceptably (though not "to equal my predecessor until after long experience"). He would do so for ten years, following with three in English literature. [39] "Bully" Allen, sturdy, round-faced, bald, was immensely popular and effective. Dr. Richard A. F. Penrose of the Class of 1846, looking back from his chair in Medicine at the University of Pennsylvania, thought his lectures "the clearest and most philosophical I have ever listened to. They possessed also a quality not common in lectures on such subjects, which I might designate by the word 'adhesiveness,' that is, the student somehow *could not* forget them; and hence it was that the graduates of Dickinson knew more about these sciences than any of the other young men of their day." [40] In Caldwell's illness, Allen took over rhetoric and logic, which were being taught from Archibishop Whately's texts, and carried his students enthusiastically beyond Whately. [41] "Corpus," as they also called him because it suited that ruddy rotundity, took his Methodist background lightly and was more ready than anyone else to assure them that good novels were "always worth reading." [42] When in 1849 the telegram came informing him of his election as President of Girard College, he and Mrs. Allen invited them all in to "have an oyster," an evening of warm congratulations, refreshments and cigars. [43]

"Bully" had turned over his work in the sciences to young Spencer Fullerton Baird, an alumnus of 1840. Baird would leave a year after Allen to join Joseph Henry in setting up the new Smithsonian Institution. He was the youngest of this young faculty, and was, as young Conway saw him, "the beloved professor and the ideal student . . . . All that was finest in the forms he explained to us seemed to be represented in the man." [44] He had prepared himself with the study of medicine and languages and with exhaustive reading; he stood high with other naturalists, among them Audubon, whom he assisted in the identification of the birds he was painting. [45] Baird was still the passionate boy collector and had come to the College with a wealth of materials, demonstrating his value by working for a year without pay. Suddenly, the Museum became as large as and more used than the Library. He made field trips a part of the regular course—a startling innovation in the higher education of that day.

Baird was the faculty's only non-Methodist—actually a member of no church. He and Allen, close and congenial, cared little how the College's religious sponsorship might fare. Their colleagues John McClintock and George R. Crooks were on the other hand profoundly concerned and would profoundly influence the Church's new intellectualism. McClintock, a Philadelphian, arrived in 1836, a year after his graduation from the University of Pennsylvania at the age of twenty-two. A decade before, Joseph Holdich, his pastor, had recognized the boy's unusual promise. At Dickinson he would teach mathematics for four years, then Greek and Latin until 1848. In appearance he was the teacher and scholar only, though he was soon to have notoriety as a man of action. He was short and slender, with a small body and a large head, its features delicate, youthful and engaging. As Professor Allen put it, "McClintock had a head as large as Daniel Webster's poised on a body half his size." His carriage and manner were always graceful, frank and easy. His swiftness of thought and warmly sympathetic responses made him, to some, "the most magnetic and inspiring" of the faculty. [46] "If there is such a thing as a universal genius," Durbin said, "Mack is one." [47] There was a genuine idealism here, with a radiance long remembered. Crooks, younger, and a classmate of Baird, saw McClintock as an Apollo, "amazing us by the energy with which he quickens our minds." Crooks, after a stint as assistant in the Grammar School, taught classics in the College for two years and left in the same year as McClintock, whose biographer he eventually became. The two collaborated on a wide range of works and ended their careers at Drew, McClintock as President, Crooks as Professor of Church History.

The revived Dickinson had assembled a faculty which Moncure Conway saw in retrospect as unsurpassed in any American college. The national importance of seven of this small group is attested by their inclusion in the *Dictionary of American Biography:* Durbin, Keagy, Allen, Baird, McClintock and Crooks. One only was palpably a failure, Thomas Emory Sudler, teacher of mathematics from 1840 until he was eased out in 1851. "Colonel Sudler" to colleagues, "Jimmy Sudler" to students, could flash through to mathematical solutions with as much skill—and as little comprehension on the part of his audience—as a prestidigitator. He would swing into class in his blue military cloak, and watch like a hawk to be sure that the lad at the blackboard got no surreptitious help—"Every gentleman must stand on his own bottom." [48]

This faculty was a tight unit, meeting formally once a week (largely on disciplinary matters), and as regularly if less formally for intellectual discussion. We see Durbin, Emory and Allen fascinated by Caldwell's solid defense and McClintock's light-

ning thrusts at "that great *crux philosophica,* the human will,"
as expounded in the new treatise by Professor Upham of Bowdoin. [49] Caldwell, senior educator, held forth among them and
in public on educational progress, and lured them as well into
the new borderlands of psychology, phrenology and mesmer-
ism. [50] He was a stern advocate of temperance, recognized by all
as a vital social reform, though the medicinal value of alcohol
was not denied, and was sometimes invoked by a student in
trouble. Faculty, like the students, were not wholly free of the
vices of smoking and chewing. The professors, young men all,
joined in walks, horseback rides, fishing and shooting, would
meet again in "soirees" and suppers often with a cheerful crowd
of college boys, and girls from the young ladies' academy.

The influence of the state of Maine upon this scene appears
once more in the Carlisle Female Seminary, an attendant feature of the new Dickinson, whose preceptresses, the Misses
Phoebe and Sarah Paine and Mrs. B. H. H. Stevens, had come
from the Maine Wesleyan Seminary. Its curriculum included all
the "common English studies," along with botany, chemistry,
astronomy, mental, moral and natural philosophy, the French,
Spanish and Italian languages, music and drawing. [51] This liberal
program gave the College faculty an additional source of income, and sometimes brought the girls into college classes, with
Allen's, again, the most popular—"What student of that day will
ever forget our electrical circles there? How tenderly we took in
ours the soft, white hands of the blushing maidens! How tightly
we held them, trembling when the shocks from the battery
waxed heavy, and the fair ones wriggled and twisted and strug-
gled in vain to get free, squealing as only girls can squeal!" [52]
The Female Seminary was incorporated in 1838 under seven
trustees, of whom Durbin was the only Methodist, though it
had strong Methodist endorsement. [53] It would be for many
years a crowning feature of the schools clustering about the
College—by 1843 fifteen of them, with about eight hundred
pupils. [54] Among these the old Grammar School shone for a
while as "Dickinson Institute," intended no doubt to give it
equal status with the New Jersey Conference's Pennington
Seminary of 1837 and the other academies from which boys
were coming. Thin, sharp-chinned Levi Scott, later a bishop,

catalogued the growing library of the Oratorical Society, the Institute's equivalent of Belles Lettres and Union Philosophical. [55] Here one must credit also the enthusiasm of John Mc-Clintock, Librarian of the College from 1840 to 1848.

McClintock, from his first arrival in 1836, found college life wholly congenial and predicted that its regularity would be "very serviceable to my health."

> The order is as follows:—First bell, half past five A.M. ; prayers, six A.M. —breakfast immediately after prayers; recitations, nine, ten, eleven, or nine, ten A.M. and four P.M. , or ten, eleven A.M. , and four P.M. , never exceeding three recitations a day. The students generally are moral, studious, and well-behaved, and many of them are pious. Evening prayers at five P.M. —tea immediately after prayer. Last bell, nine P.M. Thus the bells are:—First, half past five A.M. , second, six A.M. ; third, eight A.M. ; fourth, nine A.M. ; fifth, ten A.M. ; sixth, eleven A.M. ; seventh, twelve M. (dinner); eighth, two P.M. ; ninth, three P.M.; tenth, four P.M. ; and five, seven, eight and nine P.M.
>
> On Sabbath, after breakfast, two classes meet at eight o'clock; preaching, eleven; dinner, half past twelve; Bible class, . . . three; preaching, half past six, as usual. On Tuesday evening we have a social meeting for literary conversation, etc. On Wednesday, Faculty meeting; Thursday, preaching; Friday, prayer-meeting; Saturday, debate; so that the days and evenings are pretty well filled up. [56]

The old German Reformed Church building, facing West College from across High Street, had been purchased from schoolmaster Henry Duffield in 1835, refurbished as "Dickinson Institute," and made a part of this little world under the rule of the College bell. Burned in December of the next year, it was promptly rebuilt in better style. This was South College, complementing the rambling, shambling North College of 1822, on the other side of West. Meanwhile, the long, tall walls of East College were rising, four sections four storeys high with fire walls between, the fourth section at the east end designed to be the home of the President. Otherwise, it was a typical college dormitory of the time, strikingly similar to Princeton's East College, completed two years earlier.

But Yale was now Dickinson's model of academic respectability, as it was for Princeton and others throughout the land. [57] The Dickinson *Statutes* of 1834 are merely a revision of those of 1830, but the edition of 1836 is patterned directly on *The*

South College I, *c.* 1860, as rebuilt in 1838.

South College II, *c.* 1900, as enlarged in 1886.

Laws of Yale College. The marked difference is only in Yale's section on "Crimes and Misdemeanors" with its hilarious reflection of student life in New Haven, as against Dickinson's "On the Deportment of Students" which reflects Methodism's larger flow of redemption and grace, and a new faculty's hopefulness. Deportment at Dickinson would soon be approaching Yale's. "Old East" was finished and filled with students in January, 1837—fresh paint, brightly carpeted floors, three rooms for each two students, two for sleeping and a third where "chum and I" could study. [58] Yet only a few weeks later the first desecration had occurred.

Faculty minutes for the time are lacking, and scattered notes on the disciplinary cases of March, 1837, present a confused picture—Purnell driving a stick into the door of Mr. Roszel, Grammar School master, a strange business of Wright's having found money hidden under Professor Caldwell's carpet, but more palpably guilty of noise and disrespect—Waters and Owens also up for noise. Dreadful to relate, there had been "whooping" in East College attic, and logs of wood rolled recklessly down the stairs with damage and din, greeted from below by young voices raised in the song,

> I've oftentimes been told
> That ye. British sailors bold . . . .

Only so much of the lyric was noted down in the tight, shocked script. No more was needed. Professor Caldwell moved that Wright, Waters and Purnell be dismissed forthwith, Owens suspended for the rest of the year. After discussion, the severity of this proposal was somewhat modified. Three of the culprits disappear from the Dickinson scene. John Armstrong Wright, who was to become a dedicated trustee, regained status by making a full apology. [59]

Soon after, some vengeful student pen labored out a touching tribute to Caldwell, forged the signature of John Price Durbin at its close and dispatched it to the *Christian Advocate and Journal* which, mirabile dictu, printed the whole, filling a half column of the huge sheet. Professor Caldwell was dead, his last moments before his "soul departed to the land of spirits" feelingly described. And finally, "It became my painful duty to address the weeping and afflicted assembly at the grave, when I discoursed on the words, 'Well done, good and faithful servant.' " [60]

A year later, looking forward to graduation, John Wright had chosen the career, engineering, in which he would attain eminence. "It is the wish of my friends, of Prof. McClintock, Durbin & Allen & I think it will suit my turn of mind." [61] He saw the College as flourishing, Belles Lettres "in the height of her glory"—better than "the Unions." [62] Belles Lettres minutes show the society at this time using its "Court of Inquiry" as an instrument of student self-government, yet with a leniency unlikely to attract faculty approval. Wright, on January 25, 1837, had been fined only 25¢ for intoxication and "unnecessary noise." On January 4, for "frequent intoxication," Freshman Henry W. Nabb had been fined $1 and ordered to sign the pledge. On appeal, a week later, the pledge was remitted and the fine increased by 50c. Faculty frequently resorted to the signing of pledges, and in the case of John Quarles of the Class of 1850, bright and popular Secretary of Belles Lettres, accepted the pledge of a group of his friends to stand with him on the straight and narrow. It was given, alas, in vain. "Squabbles," repeatedly guilty of "criminal conversation" with "girls of dissolute character," and in East College, no less, did not graduate. [63]

To enter the Freshman Class at Dickinson (or Yale) a boy must be at least fourteen years of age. [64] As Judge Reed put forward from the first, they should be entering, not graduating, at eighteen. [65] Up to fourteen or fifteen the influences of piety tended to prevail. McClintock found his small brother, aged ten, in the Grammar School, "getting a little *too* religious: for half the time when I go to my room in College I find some half a dozen youngsters holding a *prayer meeting,* and it incommodes me not a little." [66] But later, the forbidden delights and excitements would appear—disruptive classroom tricks (as early as January, 1840 it had been discovered that pepper sprinkled on the stove top in winter made the atmosphere almost unendurable, especially for a teacher with weak lungs or throat), card-playing, alcohol and the girls sure to be found at night on the dark streets of a garrison town. The faculty, to protect the virtuous, were kept busy with surprise visits to dormitory rooms and the back rooms of taverns, and with sifting the evidence on which suspensions or dismissals would depend. As in the Presbyterian regime, room-visiting was a duty which the faculty abhorred and inclined to leave to the President, with his larger salary and greater responsibility.

Riots and rebellions continued to enliven the scene. In the spring of 1843, a hundred students armed with pistols, knives and clubs held the campus wall against the "Carlisle Infantry," until other soldiers arrived from the post and raised the siege. [67] Rebellion against faculty authority had appeared early, and would continue. "The young gentlemen," President Durbin reported to his trustees in 1839, "took a resolution which left the Faculty no alternative but to yield to their peremptory demand in a question of administration of discipline, or to send them home if they did not yield." [68] They had been sent home.

Only the societies could raise student objections and maintain dialogue in terms of academic courtesy. At the start of the Methodist regime they had opposed any invasion of ancient practices, and would continue to meet issues in this fashion. [69] Yet faculty was far more apprehensive of organized opposition than appreciative of the value of independence. The *Statutes* made clear that society property belonged, in fact, to the Board, and that meetings were held under faculty authority and only at authorized (never nocturnal) hours. The students, aware of the value of their libraries, their public "exibitions" and their invited speakers, all at a considerable cost borne by themselves, still yearned for true autonomy in buildings, or a building, of their own. By 1840, class loyalty was vying with loyalty to the society. [70] The fraternities would follow. Yet these teachers did maintain a friendly rapport with their students, benign and more lenient than their predecessors. How else could the young naturalist Baird, Class of 1840, capable of trudging sixty miles in a day with pack on back, have been excused from early morning chapel because of "palpitation of the heart?" [71]

Similarly, what is gained in class depends far more on the character of the teachers than on a published curriculum. Comparing the *Statutes* of 1828 and 1834, one does see an advance in standard and goals. The quality of the new is supported also by the Grammar School schedules, where a thorough foundation for the college years was being laid. The new Board in its first scheme, approved September 25, 1833 and published at once in the Carlisle and other papers, promised professorships of (1) "Intellectual and Moral Philosophy," embracing both "Political Economy" and "Evidences of Natural and Revealed Religion" (Butler's *Analogy*); (2) "Exact Sciences," that is, mathematics; (3) "Natural Sciences," including chemistry, mineralogy, geology, botany, physiology; (4) Greek and Latin, the languages, literature and "antiquities"; (5) "Belles Lettres," English literature, with rhetoric and elocution; and (6) French, Spanish, Italian and German. [72]

The modern languages were taught at first on a fee basis as formerly, but with no regular professor until 1846. They were being offered, the *Statutes* of 1834 inform us significantly, "to meet the demands of the age, and enable the institution to offer every facility to a complete education." Durbin's vein of caution and respect for respectability were hostile to "the spirit of age." Emory, succeeding him as President, would find the faculty more ready to accept experimental changes.

In Methodist thinking, the fine arts rated only a milder condemnation than works of fiction, but music was another matter. Here there was a tradition stemming from the Wesleys themselves, a source of inspiration and unity, though to have an organ or piano in church was still unusual. Durbin proposed a regular course in Music in 1837, and a teacher was engaged for those who "voluntarily associate for this purpose." [73] Four years later, Edward L. Walker appears in the catalogues as Professor of Music, holding that post until 1847. [74]

Anatomy and physiology were taught on a fee basis, 1842 to 1844, by Dr. James McClintock, John's older brother, and efforts were made to continue what was, in effect, a pre-medical course. [75] John McClintock, at the same time, was making an effort to launch a pre-ministerial course on Sunday afternoons in the Chapel, he lecturing on the Pauline writings and Durbin on the Old Testament. [76] The course has a note in the catalogues from 1841 to 1843. Judge Reed's law school, the while, may well have had a sounder, if less insistent, appeal than the ministry to young men seeking careers. Certainly then, as in later years, the Law School was a strengthening and maturing influence.

As Durbin was aware and Emory would soon learn, special courses and electives evoke the perennial problem of where to find the money. This had been a first concern of the Methodist trustees, knowing as they did the low income level of their constituency, as well as the hostility of most of it to higher education. Carlisle, grown to a lovely country town of four thousand inhabitants, was grateful, as it had been before, for the revival of the College, and a trustee resolution of June 8, 1833, had welcomed the "spirit of mutual friendship." From this good beginning the two parties settled into the mutual exacerbations of town and gown. Methodists had long been partial to the "manual labor system" in education, by which students worked to support the school, not a little like prisoners at labor. It had prevailed at Cokesbury College, derided by Nisbet. Both Wesleyan and Dickinson perforce made gestures and broke promises in its behalf.[77] Its false economy had been demonstrated at the Maine Wesleyan Seminary.[78] It was thought degrading by professional educators, which may have been one reason why the constituency approved it. It was an even more unwelcome idea to the tradespeople of Carlisle, who preferred college students as customers rather than competitors. Years later, after giving a few poor students rooms in which to work at their trades, the College would respond to town complaint and forbid the practice.[79] Durbin experienced all the sensitivity of a college president to local feeling. When he turned for advice to Caldwell, vacationing in Maine, it was given in terms he scarce dared follow:

> You know I have always been more indifferent to the feelings which the good people of Carlisle might please to indulge toward the college than you have. We ought to do right & then ' *go ahead;*" if they love us, well; if *not, well*. I don't think our college would go down if all the borough east of West Street should be swept away by some flood, or if all the people east of that street should die of the cholera . . . .[80]

In the last year of Durbin's administration the College, by order of the borough, built pavements along the West and High Street sides of the campus, an insistence upon conformity with the requirements imposed on all residents to be repeated in later generations, and with chronic ill feeling on both sides. [81]

That initial $45,000 was to have come from collections in the churches and among the laity and from the sale of scholarships. On payment of $500 to the conference fund, the donor received a certificate entitling him and his heirs forever to send one student to Dickinson College. [82] A minister who raised $100 could send one minister's son. [83] In addition to the itineracy and other preachers, agents were employed to solicit. College sessions began at last in a spirit of jubilation, yet the drive, over the top on paper, had actually far from achieved its goal. Agents signed up subscribers readily, but were slow in collecting cash. [84] Scholarships were sold without proper record. They were given for both cash and kind. [85] Durbin hoped to launch his Music Department with a $350 piano which had been given in part payment for a $500 perpetual scholarship, but the trustees voted to try, at least, to get the money. [86] Many purchasers elected to pay only what would be the interest on $500 until they could afford the principal, and sums were coming in undesignated as to whether they were interest or principal. [87] By Durbin's first commencement, 1837, they had in cold truth received less than $20,000 of the stipulated endowment. [88]

A month later, auguring future prosperity, the Cumberland Valley Railroad's first train smoked and rattled into the village at the market house and square. Yet already the panic of 1837 had brought the smouldering presence of hard times, to last for a decade more. Durbin's report of 1843 shows the combined funds at only $41,793, and income from every source barely meeting the annual expenses of over $9,000. Writing, pleading, collecting in churches and camp meetings, he and his professors still might not have weathered it but for state aid. The new Board, not without effort and delay, was able to get the final $3,000 installment of the grant of 1826, and—pleading that the College now "bears more directly on the great middling class from whence our common schools must derive their teachers" became one of the schools to which $1,000 a year was granted 1839 to 1843. [89]

This new willingness of the state to support the College

despite its sectarian bias emphasized the insecurity of church support, and we see faculty looking elsewhere. Emory resigned in July, 1840, to enter ministerial work. McClintock, replacing him in languages, was replaced in mathematics by Sudler. Durbin, at the same time, asked and was granted a six-month leave to visit Europe. Then, in May, 1841, he stood for election as secretary of the Missionary Society, an important church office which he would hold later, from 1850 to 1872. He was defeated by one vote only, friends of the College opposing his leaving it. [90] He had done well as a money-raiser, and there was still a debt of $15,000 borrowed from the conferences to build East College and rebuild South.

The trip to Europe was made in 1842 and 1843, with Emory brought back as Acting President. Durbin was allotted $1,000 to purchase books and apparatus abroad. He was, quite obviously, following the example of President Wilbur Fisk of Wesleyan, who had crossed the ocean in 1835, returning with scientific apparatus and specimens and then bringing out a popular book on the tour. [91] Durbin would write two similar books of travel, published by his son-in-law's firm, Harper and Brothers. [92] He would be welcomed back to Carlisle with a procession, speeches, an illumination of the College buildings. [93] Yet faculty morale had been low since before his departure. [94] He lingered two more years and then resigned to reenter church work. [95]

Caldwell, to whom the acting presidency would have come by seniority, was grateful for Emory's return. Both were slowly dying of consumption. Now, for two years, there would be an Emory administration characterized by that stern inner vitality. Faculty by-laws were adopted at once to remedy past laxity: faculty would meet every Friday evening and attend all prayers. No class would be dismissed until the ringing of the bell, and none omitted without prior notice to the President. That ever-unpopular chore of visiting student rooms would be a scheduled duty of each, once a week, "the President to visit them all." [96] The rampant drinking and card-playing declined under this watchfulness. In 1847, Emory could report not a single dismissal for discipline—not even Charles Wesley Carrigan, who had had liquor in tavern and in his room, but whose fellow students had intereceded for him in thirty-six lines of melodious appeal, "Forgive that Erring Youth":

> Deep is the *anguish* of his heart!
> O add not to its wo,
> Lest black despair should o'er his mind
> Its fatal influence throw. [97]

Examinations in the new regime continued to be oral and open to the public by invitation. Finals in 1837 ran for five afternoons, one for each professor, from two o'clock to five. Durbin had set the example of writing questions on slips, to be passed out, giving each student time for consideration before he would be called upon to speak. Samples, on Butler's *Analogy*:

> Why can we not conclude death will be the destruction of the living powers—"from the reason of the thing"—nor from the analogy of nature? Explain.
>
> State & illustrate the argument in favor of the moral govt of God, founded upon the "necessary tendencies of virtue."
>
> Apply these principles to the temptations of the Christian and of Christ—& show how the latter was "without sin." (Not in the author but in our conversations.) [98]

With the written questions, alas, we have our first records of cheating. McClintock's slips were obtained from "his beautiful sister, Annie," and Sudler's filched at dinner time from inside his tall hat. [99]

After Durbin's return from abroad, Allen introduced a new grading system which continued for many years. Class performance and general deportment were figured together in a plus and minus record. [100] Following a student request of 1845, the sums were announced at the end of the year. The top student of 1846 had a score of 5,657, and the lowest, 1,004. [101] Ultimate standing was dramatized in the commencement program: the Valedictorian in first place, then the opening Salutatory, the "Philosophical Oration" coming third and the other addresses arranged in order of standing—each mercifully short and blessedly interspersed with music by the military or some other band.

College catalogues and trustee pronouncements do not always tell us precisely what was being learned in class. In his first report as Acting President, Emory gave in more dependable detail a description of the work of the year just passed. In a summary, it appears that

Freshmen,
> with Emory, studied William Smellie's *Philosophy of Natural History* (Boston, 1838).
> Caldwell led them through a course in English grammar and composition, probably from his own text, and a basic course in geometry.
> With McClintock, they read Sallust's *Conspiracy of Catiline,* Horace's odes, Xenophon's *Cyropaedia,* studied Charles Anthon's *Latin Prosody,* "Grecian antiquities" and Greek exercises from Sophocles.
> Sudler confronted them with "decimal fractions and algebra to its highest branches."

Sophomores.
> Emory introduced the class to Thomas Hartwell Horne's *Introduction to the Study of the Bible,* and lectured on ecclesiastical history.
> Caldwell carried his English grammar course into elocution, completed the study of geometry and went on to Charles Davies' text on plane trigonometry.
> Allen took the class through Lord Woodhouselee's (Tytler's) popular two-volume *Universal History from the Creation of the World to the Beginning of the Eighteenth Century* (Boston, 1838, but also to be had in a Harper set of six volumes, 1839).
> McClintock's young classicists had taken up Cicero's *De Oratorio,* more Horace, with Theophrastus, Xenophon and Euripides.
> Sudler was laboring along in trigonometry, and one wonders whether Caldwell's math class may not have been intended to make up for his colleague's poor presentation.

Juniors. Emory, in the presidential course usually reserved for Seniors, used the work of a great American educator and contemporary, Francis Wayland's *Moral Science.* This was reinforced by Archbishop Richard Whately's *Elements of Logic,* with declamation every Saturday, and by
> Caldwell's work with Wayland's *Political Economy* and Whately's *Elements of Rhetoric,* and a written composition every three weeks.
> Allen taught French grammar and reading (he had confessed him-

self inadequate with the spoken language), beginning with new texts by Alexander G. Collot and Arséne Napoléon Girault. The Juniors attended his science class for Seniors. McClintock had reached the *Medea* of Euripides, Sophocles' *Oedipus Tyrannus,* lectured on the Greek drama, and filled in with Cicero, Juvenal and Perseus.

Sudler's classroom, in turn, was threading the mazes of analytical geometry, spherical trigonometry, surveying and differential calculus.

Seniors. Emory, in addition to Bishop Butler's *Analogy of Religion, Natural and Revealed,* so long to be a staple and a terror to Dickinson Seniors, took them through Caleb Sprague Henry's *Epitome of the History of Philosophy,* a translation (with additions) from the French of Bautain recently published in two volumes of "Harper's Family Library." This fare was punctuated, as was his work with the Juniors, by Saturday speeches and debates.

Caldwell introduced them to Upham's *Mental Philosophy,* for a modern view, and then to William Paley's *Evidences of Christianity,* a complement to the work with Butler. He delivered also a short lecture course on the history of the English language.

Allen's texts were William Augustus Norton's *Elementary Treatise on Astronomy* (Philadelphia, 1839), John Johnston's *Manual of Chemistry* (Philadelphia, 1839, a popular text by a Methodist author), Sir David Brewster's *Treatise on Optics* (Philadelphia, 1835) and John Lee Comstock's *Elements of Mineralogy* (Boston, 1827), with lectures twice a week on heat, electricity, mechanics, pneumatics, hydrostatics, chemistry and other aspects of "natural science." Like Durbin, he had class discussions of a "colloquial form, in which points which had been too hastily passed over while the experiments were in progress, were more fully and familiarly explained. I regard these conversations as the most profitable as well as the most pleasant exercises which the Seniors have had in my department." [102] Going afield as the others so often did, he worked into all this a course based on James Bayard's *Brief Exposition of the Constitution of the United States* (Philadelphia, 1834).

McClintock was now leading the way through the *Prometheus Bound* of Aeschylus, Tacitus' *Germania* and *Agricola* and Terence's *Andria.*

Sudler, at his peak, led the class through analytical mechanics and "Civil Engineering embracing the theory of Mathematics applied to practical problems," the use of mathematical instruments, with lectures on the principles and history of mathematics.

As President, Emory obtained trustee approval of an improved modern language program, with a first appearance of electives. Juniors could choose between Greek or German; Seniors, mathematics or French. [104] Charles E. Blumenthal joined the faculty as "Professor of Modern Languages and Hebrew," teaching at first on a fee basis, and without a graduation requirement in his subjects. [105] Yet the change was popular with the more serious students, who had their eyes already on study in Germany and travel in Europe. [106] Wesleyan University had had from the beginning a "Literary and Scientific Course" leading to the Bachelor of Science degree. [107] This concession to "the spirit of the age" appears briefly under the same heading in the Dickinson catalogue of 1846–47. In line with earlier Dickinson practice, however, it had only three years' duration and led only to "a certificate of proficiency under the seal of the College." [108] It seems to have been a compromise between Durbin's condemnation of partial courses, [109] Emory's more progressive view, and a respect for the older conservative traditions of the College.

One of Emory's proposals of 1846 is a credit to his leadership only in that he was able to impose it on a reluctant faculty. He integrated Grammar School and College, bringing all classes together in the main building and spreading the teaching loads to include both. Crooks, Principal of the School, was a brilliant young fellow, well able to sustain the post of Adjunct Professor of Languages, and he foresaw that the College faculty, Baird particularly, would do well with the younger boys. Their salaries would be duly increased. The real saving would be in space. [110] The College Library, rearranged and catalogued by Emory and McClintock back in 1837, was moved into South, along with the natural science lecture room and laboratory and Baird's large and rapidly expanding Museum. [111] Thus Emory met space needs which the trustees had refused to grant Durbin at their 1845 meeting. The Board had put Durbin off by raising the vision of an entirely new building housing laboratory, Museum, the society halls and all the libraries. Emory hoped to

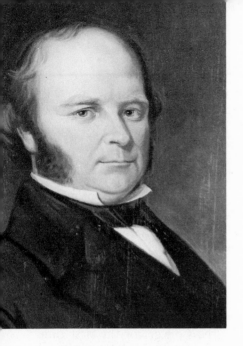

Top left: William Henry Allen. Copy, by Margaret F. Winner, of life portrait by Jeremy Wilson, 1854. Top right: John McClintock. By James Barton Longacre, 1850. Lower left: Alexander Jacob Schem. Lithograph by John H. Sherwin and Louis N. Rosenthal, *c.* 1855. Lower right: Spencer Fullerton Baird. Photograph, *c.* 1855.

achieve this too. The societies were clamoring for larger halls, and were ready to appeal to their graduate members (the only alumni organization of the time). At the 1847 meeting he proposed that the societies raise $6,000 for their share, and the conferences at least $4,000 more. [112] He was eager to launch a broad drive for funds. [113] Yet in 1847 he was only reimbursed the $300 he had spent to refurbish old North College with those workshops for poor students which were to alarm the town and then be used for dormitory and other purposes. [114] And even as he advanced his plans and hopes he must needs ask for a possible leave of absence because of failing health.

It had been an exhausting year for the President, topped off by a sudden catastrophe of fury, bloodshed and death only five weeks before commencement and the trustees' meeting. "The McClintock Riot" brought the College for the first time face to face with the issue of slavery in its most hideous aspect. It brought human values, with which College and Church should be so deeply concerned, into the balance with property values, also of such urgent concern to both. We now see Dickinson's most brilliant professor standing out for the moral issue, and the President doing his best to bring money and morality into an accommodation.

Money and morality—the murder of Lovejoy, the gag rule in Congress, had been followed closely by the Panic of 1837. With the years of hard times, as so often occurs, intellectual and religious idealism simmered and surged. In 1844 the Methodist Episcopal Church, South, had separated itself from the main body upon the issue of slavery. Durbin, heading the Philadelphia delegation in that famous General Conference, had brought forward a "Plan for the Removal of Slavery" by indemnification of owners and colonization in Africa, but withheld it from publication until it appeared in the *Christian Advocate* of February 10, 1847. The end of the Mexican War and the rise of the Free Soil Party had then brought the battle into national politics. "A Southern Methodist" approved the "Plan," while "A Virginian" raised reasonable doubts as to the feasibility of transporting to Africa five million Negroes, Americans for generations and, as experience had taught, unwilling emigrants. [115] President Olin of Wesleyan and others of the northern conferences, though predominantly antislavery, were even less ready than Durbin to act. [116]

Not so McClintock. He was reading law and watching Congress, alert for the attack. Close after Durbin's came his own articles in the *Advocate*, "Slavery, No. I" of February 24, followed by II, III and IV—bold, clear condemnation, scornful and provocative. [117] Judas had sold his Master for the price of a slave. Slave-money was the price of blood. Slavery, root of the ruin of republican Rome, had been brought to republican America and "thrown upon the spotless shoulders of Christianity." [118]

The *Advocate*, under a storm of protest, balked at the fifth article, observing primly that "we ourselves differ with him, *toto c[o]elo*, in respect to the good which he supposes has been done by the abolition societies." [119] McClintock's first book, a Latin text in collaboration with Crooks, had just been published. He had offers from the University of Pennsylvania, from a church, from Harper's for an editorship. He knew he would be considered for the presidency of Dickinson should Emory fail to go on, and was prepared to decline it as he would later decline the presidencies of Wesleyan, Alleghany and Troy. In a mood of great issues and a widening career, he was looking beyond the schoolroom, beyond Carlisle, when, on a calm day in early summer, June 2, 1847, the little town began to buzz with the affair of James Kennedy and Howard Hollingsworth. They had come up from Maryland in pursuit of runaway slaves and were now at the courthouse with their prisoners, Lloyd Brown had his ten-year-old daughter Ann, and Hester, wife of a Carlisle man, George Norman. As McClintock would soon become acutely aware, the "aristocracy" and the "rabble" of Carlisle were hotly proslavery, a feeling not shared by "the substantial middle class." [120] Black citizens had the aid of such men as Jacob Rheem, later a trustee of the College, and lawyer Samuel Dunlap Adair in forcing Kennedy to answer for the manner of the capture he had made and the legality of holding his prisoners in the county jail. This had filled Judge Samuel Hepburn's courtroom with excited spectators, black and white.

Meanwhile McClintock, stepping into the post office, met the ebullient Charles Wesley Carrigan and learned what was happening. George Sanderson, Postmaster and printer, confirmed it. The student no doubt expected a strong reaction from this professor. It came. McClintock denounced the seizure as illegal under a new state act against slave hunting in Pennsylvania, passed March 3, 1847. He brushed aside Carrigan's suggestion that federal law would nullify that of the state. Together they hurried to the courthouse, where Judge Hepburn was himself making haste to settle the matter in Kennedy's favor. Kennedy had a carriage waiting for his prisoners at the door. As the two came in, Mr. Thorn, the hot-tempered and occasionally hard-swearing Episcopal minister, told them of doubts that Hester and the little girl were slaves at all. McClintock, hearing the Judge order the three to be delivered to their master, came forward indignantly to present the fact of the new law. His Honor denied knowledge of it. McClintock promised at once to bring his own copy, and then, as Carrigan remembered, "pressing hurriedly to the dock, in an excited manner," told the prisoners that under the law they were free to go where they chose. [121]

McClintock was not present when the three, aided by their friends, made a break for liberty at the door. Shouts were raised; stones flew. Kennedy, dashing in pursuit, was knocked down and trampled, suffering injuries from which he died soon after. When McClintock returned with his document, his only part in the melee was to warn off a white man threatening a black woman with a club. Back at the College, however, he found an excitement almost as great as that in town. The students were shocked by the thought of an abolitionist in their midst. Those from the South were packing to leave. Next day they held a meeting on the stone steps and in the Chapel, with Edwin Webster, later a lawyer and Congressman, presiding. "We were all stormy until the door opened and the face of McClintock was seen, serene as if about to take his seat in the recitation room." Young Moncure Conway never forgot the transformation wrought by "the calm moral force of that address in the Chapel, the perfect repose of the man resting on simple truth." [122] A resolution of approval was passed, echoed by one from the faculty praising their resistance to popular clamor and loyalty to the College. [123]

With the press aroused, with shocked and angry letters pouring in, a typical college-president circumspection overcame any finer feeling in President Emory. He could, of course, honestly clear McClintock of any violent action or illegal intent: " . . . the reports are grossly false, & may be traced to some of our most corrupt citizens. The Professor's presence on the occasion was purely accidental & he is incapable (whatever his views about slavery) of any illegal interference with a master's rights." [124] But when he faced his trustees on July 7 it was with a careful oral statement "on the subject of slavery and abolition," to which McClintock, serving as secretary, must have listened with mixed feelings. The Board, however, heard it with satisfaction and resolved that he "commit the same to writing for publication."

That summer, during vacation, McClintock would be brought to trial before Judge Hepburn for "inciting to riot." He would be acquitted over an abundance of perjured testimony, faring somewhat better than his Negro co-defendants. "The truth of the case," he confided to his diary, "was that my human and Christian sympathies were openly exhibited on the side of the poor blacks—and this gave mortal offense to the slaveholders and their *confreres* downtown." [125] His *Advocate* articles, no less, along with his willingness to advise the Judge, had helped to make him an unwelcome presence.

The year that followed, with Allen as Acting President, was difficult. Emory was in London to attend the Evangelical Alliance, returning by way of Havana to Baltimore where he died, May 18, 1848. Caldwell, teaching but little through the year, died in Maine on June 6. Early in the year, evoking the authority of the Board's executive committee, Allen had called a halt to faculty absences and irregularly scheduled classes. Professors must provide substitutes at their own expense. [126] Conversely, at year's end he urged the trustees to authorize the treasurer to borrow, so that faculty might be freed from doing so on personal security. He recommended also returning the Grammar School to South College under its own teachers (Library and Museum remaining there also) and strengthening Baird's department to meet his "reputation as a Naturalist and skill as a teacher." Blumenthal's also must be reinforced: "In the present state of education the department of Modern Languages is very important, and a knowledge of French and German almost indispensable." [127]

As to the presidency, there was no thought of electing Allen, an educator, to an office tacitly open only to a clergyman. By late June there were a dozen candidates in view, led by Stephen Montfort Vail, Principal of the New Jersey Conference Seminary, and Herman Merrills Johnson, professor and Acting President at Ohio Wesleyan. [128] A week before the election it had narrowed down to two, Joseph Holdich and Jesse Truesdell Peck. Holdich wrote to Allen that he would accept if it were "a cordial election." [129] It was not. Peck won by two votes.

McClintock, resigning from the faculty, was elected to the Board of Trustees. Thus Dickinson retained a figure of recognized eminence, within the pale of a safely conservative majority. McClintock was accepting the editorship of the *Methodist Quarterly Review,* a position which would become, in his hands, a far greater influence in the intellectual advance of the Church than a college presidency could have been. His wife had written in January, "Some of the trustees say John *must* be President next year, but we are not very much inclined to anything of that kind." Students, she reported then, were crowding the College, even from the South—"riots and all." [130] John, on his part, was not only disinclined but felt that his convictions on slavery unfitted him: "I might become an incendiary . . . I am too impulsive, too unsteady, to be made a model for young men." [131] Emory's success in recapturing the southern constituency had tarnished McClintock's standing elsewhere and brought out the problems he would have had in Emory's place. [132]

But the students of that long-remembered year of the riot had seen the force of an open commitment to truth. Young Conway would go out upon that "earthward pilgrimage" of a long and memorable life. John Fletcher Hurst, scholar and churchman, as a flaxen-haired, boyish-looking student in the Class of 1854, would lead the U. P. debate on the resolution "That the interests of the United States would be conserved by the abolition of slavery," and win it. [133] In the College, lethargy, equivocation, that mental paralysis imposed upon so many

by this overwhelming issue, could not again be a safe, unchal-
lenged, respectable surrogate for truth.

"Old Dutch delivering a speech to this society." Pencil drawing in Belles Lettres
minute-book. Professor Blumenthal spoke "On the Study of Languages," April 28,
1847.

Never was there a more good-natured set than the students generally. Fighting was unknown, quarrels very rare, and a spirit of justice prevailed. Hazing had been reduced to a very mild attempt at fun, the last instance I ever heard of being that of Bonbright. This beautiful blond youth, whose flaxen hair made him look very young indeed, was introduced into a solemn conclave in West College (the room I think of Theodore God-bless-my-soul Primrose), for a ceremony necessary, he was told, for his admission to the college. He was questioned about his home and family and gave unexpectedly piquant answers with a deliciously childlike simplicity. The fun was immense until someone asked, "What advice did your mamma give you when you left?" The bland boy replied, "She told me that if any fools tried to haze me I should tell them just such a pack of lies as I've told you!" There was a roar, the lights were put out, a sound heard of scampering feet, and Bonbright awoke next day to find himself a hero.

Moncure D. Conway, "Reminiscences of '47-'49," *Dickinsonian*, October, 1899

10

FROM CONWAY TO CONRAD

JOHN MCCLINTOCK meant to vote for Holdich for President in 1848. He was persuaded at the last minute to switch to Durbin's candidate, Peck—a younger man, with a cheerful vitality and large heart, one who had spoken out against slavery at the famous General Conference of 1844.[1] It was a decision he soon regretted.[2] Peck was from upper New York State, where he had grown up as "a jolly buoyant youngster," the youngest of ten. Now, at thirty-seven, he was a tall, massive figure, a florid face under a high bald dome, brown hair and whiskers hiding his ears, a mild gray eye, a warm and genial spirit. Allen remembered him as "a man of commanding presence" and good voice. "But he had not received a collegiate education and his want of acquaintance with what may be called the unwritten law of colleges subjected him to numerous embarrassments."[3] Peck himself in his first report mentions "the embarrassments of untried and oppressive responsibilities," and his gratitude to his faculty in easing them.[4] In the four years of his administration faculty initiative prevailed. In finance he was untidy and, though he visited churches and camp meetings, he had no fund-raising magic at a time when magic, surely, was needed. His experience as an administrator had been as principal of two New York academies, and the students sensed in his manner a willingness to regard them as children.[5]

From the first, too, everyone saw Peck in contrast to Emory, that dedicated spirit, beloved and admired, by the students most of all.[6] Peck's favorite phrase, "high moral tone," was ridiculed. Young Moncure Conway, angered at having his much older "chum," Henry Gere Smith, summoned before the faculty for drinking and card-playing, dashed off the letter which caused the President's detention in an asylum for the insane—Dickinson College's most renowned student prank. Peck was due to make his initial appearance before the Baltimore Annual Conference, meeting at Staunton, Virginia, March 7, 1849. This was home country to the boy, who was also well equipped to write a mature and urgent letter to the superintendent of the asylum there: a deranged relative had escaped from his attendants and would arrive by the cars at Staunton. Could Dr. Stribling meet him at the station and detain him? A physical description was given, together with the fact that the patient, as soon as approached, would announce himself as "Jesse T. Peck, D.D., President of Dickinson College." The ruse succeeded, much to the amusement of Conference and College. [7]

Inevitably, there was more trouble. The students drowned Peck's voice in chapel by scraping their feet, and "coughed him out" in class. In September the faculty tightened the rules—minus marks for bad behavior could cut down academic standing.[8] Peck himself was strongly inclined to be lenient. "No tender heart," it was said, "beat more keenly in sympathy with the student than his." [9] He would much prefer simply to read a formal statement in chapel, deploring the fault, as in his *Reprimand to Seniors for Burial of Butler:*

> . . . But the formal organization of a class or a number of students for such a purpose to be executed in the dead of night—accompanied by procession, torch lights, addresses &c. is in a high degree disorderly. It has led as you see, however much you may regret it and however carefully you may guard against it directly to rude & boisterous hallooing, the firing of pistols, ringing of the bell, and thus disturbing families, exciting public resentment and bringing odium upon the college. [10]

Peck even tried the effect of ironic humor in a case of

> Rolling the cannon ball
> Down West College hall. [11]

Yet in vain. Always there was trouble. In December, 1849, it was the famous nocturnal "Oyster Hunt" among the freight cars standing on the High Street tracks by the College. The President, aware that students were searching the cars for a rumored barrel of the delicacy, was lured into one by voices which were actually under, rather than in it. The door slid to and was fastened, while ready hands rolled the car away to a more remote and darker spot. [12] In January, 1850, a student "shot the old Doctor's dog," and that was probably when he demanded the public surrender of all firearms. They all came laden into chapel and dumped tongs, pokers and shovels from every stove on campus at his feet. Mrs. Peck was suspected of spying, and washbasins were emptied from high windows upon her. [13]

Every spring, of course, brought its own rash of disorder. In 1850, it was girls in East, with Peck himself dragging one out from under the bed; Quarles was in deep trouble again, not to mention "Irregular Sophomore" W. H. Backhouse (the young secretary of the faculty amusing himself by spelling the name phonetically here and there among its numerous appearances, "Bacchus"). In 1851, it was a full-scale "rebellion" of the Sophomore and Junior Classes—the most dreaded of all breaches of discipline. They had attended the funeral, at the Catholic Church, of Jacob Faust, a popular Carlisle storekeeper, after asking, and being refused, permission to do so. In a final impasse, twenty-three Juniors rejected the demand that they apologize, signing a pledge that "the fate of one . . . be the fate of all." Suspension or dismissal was voted upon them all, and all were adamant. It just so happened that on April 14, in the midst of wild excitement at the College, James Buchanan, President Polk's Secretary of State and now a leading candidate for the presidential nomination in 1852, was stopping over at Major Patton's hotel, and someone thought to ask this alumnus, adept at diplomatic compromise, to mediate. Buchanan wrote a statement for the students in which their feelings were vindicated, while denying any attempt to usurp the faculty right to govern. A catastrophe was averted. [14]

Yet when the trustees met in July, Peck announced his intention to retire at the end of one more year, "determined to . . . seek *rest* from cares and labors to which I feel myself poorly adapted." No rest was given him during that year. Persecution continued in one form or another up to May, 1852, when the students set fire to "the privy connected with the President's dwelling," even as the President was composing his swan-song commencement address, later to be published as *God in Education.* [15]

As for Peck's performance in class, we have only a Junior's notes outlining his course in Moral Science, eloquently subscribed at the end, "A bore is finished. C. S. Pennewill, December 5th, 1849." Yet some students in an act of tardy appreciation sent to Peck's final trustee meeting a petition that he remain. The Board voted that he be given a copy of it. But his successor, elected at a special midwinter meeting, was ready to take over.

Dr. Charles Collins had had fourteen years' experience as President, Treasurer and Professor of Natural Science at Emory and Henry College in Virginia. Here again was a native of the state of Maine, a small figure in ministerial black, white wing collar, stock and tie, a tight, firm mouth, dark brown hair and brown eyes behind octagonal gold spectacles. He had gone from Maine Wesleyan Seminary to Wesleyan University, graduating there in 1837. Now thirty-nine years of age, "Old Specs" would be eight years at Dickinson, leaving in 1860 for a better livelihood as president and proprietor of a young ladies' academy in Tennessee. He came with no such accolade as earlier presidents had received, and he inherited all the difficulties of his predecessor. [16] The Board did not accord him the distinction of printing his carefully prepared inaugural address. [17] When an outbreak of smallpox occurred a few months later a writer in the *Carlisle Herald* blamed Collins—surely an extreme example of implied presidential culpability. [18] Mischief was still afoot by night and day, but there were no insane asylum or boxcar incidents with Collins. A steadier and more purposeful hand had come in. Buildings and equipment were improved, the library fee was applied to the purchase of books, prize medals were introduced for oratory and composition. [19] The student body, which had been declining under Peck, rose again to an average of about 140 for the College, 65 for the Grammar School. The curriculum was strengthened slightly—as much as could be in the face of financial problems on the one hand, student unrest on the other.

With Peck, two young adjunct professors had been added. The Rev. Otis Henry Tiffany of the Class of 1844 was rosy-cheeked, portly and elegant, a growth of beard just where it would conceal his double chin, an epicure famous for his skill in dressing a salad. [20] Mathematics was his province, but he took Latin classes also. [21] James William Marshall, just graduated in 1848, would be promoted to Professor of Latin and Greek two years later. Marshall long served as secretary of the faculty and took other administrative duties also in his fifteen years at the College, going on into the consular service, the Post Office Department and a year as Postmaster General under Grant.

The departure of Allen and Baird and the death of Judge Reed in 1850 took away the last of the Durbin faculty. Natural science went to the Rev. Erastus Wentworth, who had taught at both of Peck's academies and had been an 1837 classmate of Collins at Wesleyan. His flair and originality made him a popular teacher. He would leave in 1854 for the mission field in China, and would be known in later life as an author and editor. Also under Peck, in 1850, Herman Merrills Johnson came in as Professor of English Literature. He was a New Yorker who had been a pupil at Cazenovia with Peck, and had gone on from Wesleyan's Class of 1839 to informally scheduled post-graduate work in languages. He had been teaching Latin and Greek at Ohio Wesleyan since 1844, and came to Dickinson as distinctly a unique personality—a thin, slight figure, a thin, deeply-lined, Lincolnesque face with dark hair and brows, deep-set eyes, a mouth lined to humor or sarcasm. [22] Here was a scholar-teacher with a working knowledge of Greek, both ancient and modern; Hebrew; Anglo-Saxon; Gaelic; Arabic; Syriac—a Methodist minister who could expound the doctrines of Buddhism with admiration, had numerous articles and one book to his credit, owned a large private library, and regarded its library as the heart of any college. [23] He shared his delight in English literature with a lively family, including a daughter who would become a successful novelist. [24] A good deal of business sense came along with all this, and we find Johnson handling sales of books and stationery to the students and investing his savings meticulously. [25] Charles Francis Himes, a student in his day, thought him "unsurpassed as a suggestive and stimulating teacher," working from broad knowledge and less tied to textbook assignments than any other. [26] Surprisingly, in spite of this competence and his sympathy with the new fraternity movement, Johnson was unpopular with most of the students. [27]

Languages were a basic issue in the liberalization of the curriculum in American colleges. Peck's first report to his trustees reveals faculty dissatisfaction with the teaching of French and German at irregular times and a special fee. [28] Reform was only gradually achieved. When Charles E. Blumenthal was replaced in 1854, the new man was paid $400 in salary, plus $4 for each tuition-paying student, or about $750. The new man was Alexander Jacob Schem, who had left his native Germany and the Roman Catholic priesthood three years before, and whom Rufus Shapley, Class of 1860, remembered as a "tall, ungainly, bent, yellow-haired, dreadfully nearsighted" figure, "whose broken English was our delight, and whose French pronunciation was a thing to be shunned." [29] In 1855, Collins extended the study of modern languages to all four classes, increasing the salary to $600 with a lower student charge, making a total of about $1,000. [30] Schem suddenly disappeared in mid--term, February, 1860. During the night a large number of cannon balls had rolled down from the attic of East, thundering against his door. He was seen the next day on the road to Harrisburg, hatless and coatless, green umbrella under one arm and Greek lexicon under the other—later to emerge in New York, where he attained national eminence as an encyclopedist and author. [31] Faced by this emergency, Collins began the practice, long continued, of having the Professor of Latin also teach French, with Greek and German somewhat less aptly combined. [32]

It is hard to discern, but undoubtedly there was student pressure behind this development. In 1854, the Seniors petitioned for the substitution of French for astronomy, but were denied, "inasmuch as the scheme of studies has been fixed by the Board of Trustees." [33] Fifteen months later, Belles Lettres was debating the superiority of ancient literature over modern, and deciding in favor of the modern; and in 1860, faculty granted a student group permission to organize their own class in German. [34] Meanwhile, since 1858, a trustee committee set up on motion of John A. Wright and consisting of Allen, Mc-Clintock and Collins, had been preparing a report "on the adaptation of the present course to the wants of the age"—in short, a larger invasion of the old static curriculum by electives of contemporary interest. Of its deliberations, unhappily, we have no record, and its report, postponed in 1859, passed out of mind with the Civil War crisis. [35]

There were still pressures for Biblical study on a higher level. Peck's report of 1851 had shown the faculty's willingness to allow electives for this purpose. [36] The coming of the theologically-trained Schem as "Professor of Modern Languages and Hebrew" stimulated this move toward a fuller understanding of the great religious texts. By 1860, both Dickinson and Allegheny had pre-ministerial courses—a prelude to the establishment of the first Methodist theological seminary at Drew in 1867. [37] But the groping toward an educated ministry and a more intellectual religion widened a growing rift between the College and the Methodist Church of Carlisle. In 1833 the town's faithful had been worshiping in an unpretentious building set back among stables in Chapel Alley. A better home, one where College functions could appear to advantage, was clearly indicated, and in 1835 the former German Reformed Church at Pitt and High Streets was purchased for $5,000. Of this sum, which the parish could ill afford, $1,550 came as a loan from the College endowment funds, a friendly gesture from which much unfriendliness would follow, as principal and interest remained unpaid. [38]

The faculty, doing all it could to discourage "heat and rant" in religion, had been from the first at odds with the town congregation, where men and women sat in opposite pews and enjoyed old-fashioned noisy worship in the old-fashioned way. [39] In 1844 the Church forbade Belles Lettres to decorate its building for an anniversary oratorical exhibition, and the professors, in view of other incidents of the same sort, declined to mediate. [40] In 1852 there was open disucssion of forming a separate church. For over three years thereafter a congregation of professors and students, wives and friends, met in the College chapel. The First Presbyterian Church was host to student exhibitions. In July, 1857, commencement exercises were in the courthouse, and in that same year the cornerstone of the Emory Methodist Episcopal Church was laid at the corner of West and Pomfret Streets. It would rise in elegant Victorian Gothic, designed by Thomas Balbirnie, whose work still characterizes the Franklin and Marshall campus. [41] The separation would bring satisfactions, along with costs which were hard to bear and which weakened the academic program. That Emory was built on a town rather than a campus site.signaled a hope of reunion, long to be cherished on both sides yet not met for many years.

In 1854, Collins had proposed building a chapel on campus between West and East, with a new dormitory to create an ensemble of "completeness and magnificence." [42] He did add an observatory in the cupola of South College for William Carlile Wilson, Wentworth's successor, a Dickinson alumnus of 1850 and a layman. Wilson had studied at the research institute of Frederick Augustus Genth, the brilliant German chemist, in Philadelphia. [43] The policy of seeking pastors for Emory who could help with College classes brought in Dr. Thomas Daugherty, formerly a professor of anatomy at the Baltimore Medical College. [44] The wonders of water and gas mains came to Carlisle in 1855 and 1856 and were duly, if sparingly, introduced on campus. [45] The buildings were painted, the presidential residence at the end of East got a new porch, and a college portrait gallery was begun, "to create a monument to the noble men whose lives and labors constitute" its history. [46] All these changes were related in one way or another to a new system of college financing causing a great stir elsewhere and taken up at Dickinson just before Collins had come in.

President Peck had arrived to find the original endowment goal of $45,000 still unachieved. Through his administration and long after, each year's deficit must be met by a loan. West College needed a new roof. [47] An act of legislature freeing the College of all but state taxes on real estate seems not to have improved relations with the borough, now increasingly insistent on compliance with its ordinance on sidewalks. [48] It was in an atmosphere of mounting crisis that Professor Johnson brought

Top left: Robert Emory. By James Pine, from a daguerreotype, 1848. Top right: Jesse Truesdell Peck. By an unidentified artist, 1854. Bottom left: Charles Collins. By an unidentified artist, c. 1860. Bottom right: Herman Merrills Johnson. Lithograph by John H. Sherwin and Louis N. Rosenthal, 1854.

to the trustees at their meeting in June, 1851, the new scholarship plan. In brief, he argued:

1. Endowment should pay at least half the cost of a college education.

2. Such an endowment would never be achieved by small collections "within our patronizing territory."

3. It could be raised by the sale of scholarships in large numbers, cheap, and for a given term, i.e.,

Four years tuition,	$25
Ten years tuition,	$50
Twenty-five years tuition,	$100

These would represent "a loan without interest payable in tuition." An endowment of $100,000 from about two thousand purchasers he thought an easy minimal goal. At the very most, this would bring in two hundred college students at one time. The larger the sales, the smaller the percentage of students and the more certain that endowment income would cover the cost. [49]

Johnson added a characteristic suggestion of his own: that $10,000 of the capital be invested in building a superior library, the interest to be provided by an increase in the library fee to $3.

The trustees, taking a highly favorable view of all but this last provision, assigned the plan to a committee and called a halt on any further sale of transferable or perpetual scholarships. [50] The plan was actively promoted for the next three years. In January, 1854, as one instance of his activity, Collins spent ten days in Baltimore, achieving sales and promises of nearly $10,000. [51] By the Board meeting in July, however, when the attainment of the minimum goal of $100,000 was announced, he had a larger deficit than ever to be met; and it still remained to have the handsome scholarship certificates engraved, collect the cash, and invest it—after which "a year must transpire before it can yield a support. How to throw a bridge over this gap is a direful problem." [52]

Other direful problems there would be, and Dickinson, where the scholarship idea seems to have had its birth in 1825, would now share them in various ways with Allegheny, De Pauw, Jefferson, Oberlin, Princeton and other schools and colleges over a wide area. Here was the heady draft of sudden riches. Some institutions spent the money at once without even a thought of investment. Himes may be right in saying that, with tight, conservative management, the plan had merit. [53] However at Dickinson, with its large force of faculty, friends and paid agents, it was not so managed. Expenses were heavy, many certificates never paid for, and the actual receipts far below the goal figure. [54] For two years there were boom times on campus, students swarming in, plans for new buildings and a rosy future. [55] Then the spectre of deficit reappeared; the price of scholarships was raised; and Collins and his Board persuaded the Education Fund trustees to invest heavily in a Milwaukee land speculation at 12 percent, which soon, with the panic of 1857, defaulted on interest payments. [56] By 1860 it was openly admitted that the plan had been a failure, and that annual collections in the churches, so long inadequate, must be resumed. [57]

The new scholarship certificates did not cover Grammar School tuition. This resulted in poorly prepared arrivals being entered as irregular students of the College instead of in the School. Parents, spurred on by this situation as well as by the hard times, began garnering in the older certificates, and with such success that by 1858 the School was operating at a loss. [58] Two other schools had been regularly preparing boys for Dickinson—the Dickinson Seminary, far to the north at Williamsport, Pennsylvania; and Pennington, the older academy of the New Jersey Conference. [59] Williamsport Dickinson was to become virtually an arm of the Preachers' Aid Society of the Central Pennsylvania Conference. [60] Similarly, the effort of Emory and Johnson to set up a loan program for indigent students, after languishing through the years, was given financial support by the Baltimore Conference only as an agency to aid sons of ministers. [61]

Now at least the problem of student enlistment was solved—solved with a bang whose reverberations would still be heard years later. The scholarship system went into operation in 1854, and the class entering in the fall of that year "brought together," in the words of one of its number, the President's nephew Horatio Collins King, "as great a variety of boys and men as was ever seen outside of Castle Garden." Here were 110

Freshmen, many totally unprepared for college, many sent in a belief that the certificate covered all expenses. They came, he goes on, from as far south as Georgia, but "Maryland contributed a lively set of rollicking blades, whose fathers believed they had made a successful speculation and would have their sons educated, boarded, fed and clothed, for the paltry sum of six dollars and twenty-five cents a year." [62] Some had to return at once, and the class was halved by Sophomore year. The remainder soon caught the spirit of college life, set the regulations at defiance and gave "Old Specs" many a sleepless night. "I think," as Professor Wilson acidly remarked after climbing the stairs to his recitation room and finding a calf at the desk, "your class is large enough already." [63]

It all belonged to a new era whose tempo was felt in all the American colleges, and would be for many years to come. Rigid discipline supporting a rigid and outmoded curriculum was creating a student world more and more apart from the faculty's. Senior William Charles Ford Reed dwelt upon the frustrations of "College Life" in a chapel speech of 1851:

> . . . Sports of all kinds, companions agreeable and disagreeable, disputes and reconciliations, whiskey and stolen chickens, society elections and disappointed candidates, and *last*, though not *least*, chapel speeches—all go to make up the experience of college life. A new regulation is made! And, immediately, there is a meeting of a class, motions are made and clamorously debated, a remonstrance is sent to the faculty, the Doctor meets the class in some lecture room and talks around the point a while, the class settles down like a mass of wilted cabbage-leaves, and the members find themselves, at last, just where they started.
>
> But, notwithstanding this diversity and the excitement attending some of these circumstances, how tedious does college soon become. To go through the same round of duties one week after another, to be always busy, to be under continual restraint, to be under the necessity of rising at an hour appointed by others, to be answerable for your whereabouts even on Sunday—*all this* is excessively unpleasant. [64]

"Borous" it was, but on the other side, sports, parties, "spreeing," "getting tight," and the fellow-feeling that went with the breaking of rules, created delight. Resistance centered upon class recitations and between-class restrictions. To shine as an orator at society anniversary or commencement remained a treasured goal, but there was little or no other intellectual response, and the rift became so wide that a student who turned to any professor for advice or assistance might be lastingly ostracized. [65] Collins, bemoaning class loyalty, seeing his charges "dragooned into submission to a tyrannical majority," tightened the rules and forbade any unauthorized meeting. [66] Unauthorized meetings, wild and high, went on. It was an era of student diaries, which somehow must have been kept hidden from pervasive faculty watchfulness, for they tell all. None makes more delightful reading than that of "Rache" King over his four years. It is bright with music and song, and dreams of love in gorgeous detail, the thrill of Mattie Porter's first kiss (and a Latin blessing whispered in her ear), February and valentines both amorous and comic, taking Mattie to hear Uncle Charles lecture on "The Democratic Tendencies of Science," examinations even in such abstruse subjects as Paley's theology passed with éclat and left with a triumphant yell—"and here my eternal borosity ends." Horatio, an earnest Freshman, joins "a reading club" whose members astonish the College by "wearing the Shakespeare collar." Uncle Charles nods approval. But as a Sophomore, inevitably, the "borous" vie with the "bunkum times," with much midnight revelry, lively hours at the Lager Beer Saloon, and Dr. Collins announcing a sense of sad betrayal. There was racing through tollgates, stealing signs and nailing them on the presidential porch, tampering with "the old engine Nicholas Biddle" on the railroad tracks, organizing "the Viginti," a "Calathumpian band" to serenade selected victims, and a smaller, more temperate musical group to perform in neighboring towns. [67]

One sees still a pleasant personal relationship between faculty and students at parties and elsewhere, the dissidence of the young men being directed particularly against the classes they found dull, chapel exercises and the manifold rules laid down to maintain a safe and orderly routine. The College bell, the voice of that routine, suffered every imaginable interruption and abuse. [68] All made common cause, for while class loyalties had formed, class rivalries had not. Hazing had not come in, though a renegade would suffer, and a "green" new arrival might be subjected to "facultyizing," a form of mock trial in which dreadful penalties were imposed by a group of ridiculously costumed judges. As ever, a weak financial structure increased the students' sense of power. With so many on scholarships, wholesale dismissals could not be quite so ruinous, yet were no less sure to be met by student action. "Another College 'hellibeloo'," McClintock noted in his diary, February 6, 1856, "some 70 or 80 students having combined to dictate to the faculty in the case of Hulsey, Hepburn and Maglaughlin who were dismissed. It is the old, ever-recurring contest, 'Who shall rule, Faculty or Students?' "[69]

The three students had been found guilty of tarring Professor Tiffany's blackboards. Indignation sprang from the fact that three should be made to suffer for an act in which a score or more had been happily engaged.[70] Rendering blackboards useless with grease or tar, and making the classroom air unendurable by putting red pepper or asafetida on the stove were the most oft-repeated disruptive devices.[71] No professor was immune from harrassment, though Wilson and Johnson were favorite targets. Modern Languages fared best, though "Old Dutch" Blumenthal felt insulted in the spring of 1854 when Tucker came to class "fantastically decorated with flowers in his hair," was sent from the room and then (the testimony indicates) hurled in garbage at the professor.[72] A high point in Wilson's vexations came when one of his regular classes was billed throughout the town as a public lecture on new scientific discoveries.[73] Wilson accepted defeat in 1858 when all copies of an unpopular text persistently disappeared, and he quietly substituted another.[74] The obsequies accorded "Scotch" Johnson's text, Asa Mahan's *Intellectual Philosophy*, included specially-composed pieces in prose and verse, English and Latin:

December 15, [1856], Monday,

Junior Class met in Gordon's room at 1 and made a few more arrangements—invited the Senior Class, &c. &c. . . . At 11 o'clock the officers elect met in Slape's room, and in a few minutes marched to South College, where we took up the bier (a white window shutter) on which in a black box lay Mahan's Intellectual Philosophy shrouded in black. We marched into Prof. Wilson's room, which was brilliantly illuminated, every gas-light going in full blow. A greater part of the

Seniors and Junior Class were present. W. J. Stevenson opened the services by an oration on the life and services of Mahan, which was very good. After this Gough read a very appropriate poem, with a number of good bits. The procession then re-formed, bier supported by six pall-bearers in front, Cloud and myself next, the Juniors as chief mourners, and then the Seniors, about half of them with lamps and candles, and marched with solemn tread down Main Street to the Campus gate, which entered, we proceeded towards West College up the main path, thence down the North and South path, to the S. W. corner of the campus, where were Hulsey—the sexton—standing by the open grave. The first Ode, to the tune of "Auld Lang Syne" was sung with spirit, after which I read my Sermon of fifteen minutes length: during which the coffin was lowered and the earth dropped lightly in. At the conclusion, Cloud delivered an appropriate Latin Prayer, which by the by was very good indeed. We then sang the 2nd Ode, to the tune of "Massa's in the cold, cold ground," I singing the solo, and all joining in the chorus. I then pronounced a blessing and we all started toward our rooms yelling and howling most piteously. During the exercises we were of course occasionally interrupted by sobs and loud wailing. All—Seniors included, concur in saying that the exercises were splendid throughout: and especially so, as the time for preparation was so short. I was dressed in my long, patriarchal cloak, formerly father's, and a black sailor hat fixed in imitation of a priest's three-cornered affair, with a long black cape entirely concealing all my head, save the face: looking quite priestly and awful solemn . . . . P.S. The Philosophy buried belonged to Prof. Johnson, who teaches it, and was stolen from him yesterday by Ali Slape, while Johnson was at church: and forsooth he missed the book, and concluded that he had mis-laid it: however it is not mis-laid, but deposited in the fit receptable for such an abominable bore, which now to think of, makes the blood run cold: but to think of as defunct, sends a thrill of pleasure to the heart. Farewell old Mahan: may you lie forever in that chilly grave, undisturbed, unchanged. [75]

Mahan, however, did not lie long undisturbed. A few days later, a German laborer known to history only as Fred discovered the little grave and at once notified the town authorities of an apparent infanticide. In the presence of a coroner's jury and in full expectation of culminating evidence of college-student wickedness, the ground was opened. Marshall was the only faculty member present, hesitating to summon others as he noticed a gleam in the eyes of young men around him, and remaining to enjoy alone the denouement, with the cry of *"Sold!"* as the little black box was opened.[76]

As faculty firmness enhanced the challenge to mischief, so faculty methods of seeking evidence aggravated it. Collins was said to have trained his new telescope atop South on the window of the bell room in West, where card-playing took place, and to have used it in attempting to discover the site of a rumored student duel. The duel was a hoax, staged entirely for his benefit, and with such contagious gusto that when the town constables finally arrived, exhausted, at the scene, they were persuaded to join in the fun, bearing an ostensibly wounded combatant, smeared with chicken blood, back to his bed at the College—a unique instance of town-gown cooperation.[77]

Intoxication rated one hundred minus marks, and anything over a hundred brought dismissal from college. The plus and minus ratings seem to have been administered with a good deal of convenient flexibility. The accounting was announced only at year's end, then to be received by the students with mingled surprise and unconcern. "Rank injustice," Horatio King noted in his diary, July 10, 1856, "but 'let 'em rip.' "

The faculty had as yet no thought of diverting student energies into an athletic program. Of the games played the most popular was a rough-and-tumble, old-fashioned kind of football, the ball kicked only, by as many players as chose to join in, and each side working to drive it over the opposite campus wall.[78] In 1838, Judge Reed had declared the sport "as valuable in a college as the black board. Collision knocks out the sparks of wit, and prepares the mind for action," but two years later Durbin had restricted all games and forbidden football altogether. It was back under Peck.[79] Collins forbade it again after four players were dismissed for fighting.[80] William I. Natcher, Freshman of that famous Class of 1858, seems to have been the lad who died after kicking the ball over the roof of West College—and sparked another "rebellion" in the demand for a suitable period of mourning.[81]

We find Charles Francis Himes on "the Ten Pin Alleys" with other students in the spring of 1853. He invested 12½¢ in a pair of sixteen-pound dumbbells, recommended by Professor Johnson "for strengthening and enlarging the chest. My chum has a 25 pound ball," with which he exercised, tossing it up and catching it again. A student-organized "Military Department," an activity forbidden by earlier regulations, flourished in the late 1850's. The "Carlisle Junior Cadets," turning out smartly with the other town militia companies, should not be mentioned apart from their opposite number in the College, the "Schweitzer Guards," who exercised with pretzels, beer and fried oysters at Schweitzer's Lager Beer Saloon. [82]

As the student diaries bear witness, the boys and young men found ample time for amusement. The very rigidity of the ordained, familiar studies made them less onerous. The year's course filled forty weeks, and Seniors were allowed four weeks in which to prepare their commencement addresses (of from ten to fifteen minutes each). Collins' prizes (a stimulus, here as elsewhere, indicative of academic apathy) were attracting little competition. [83] Society prize oratorical contests fared better, and one of them, in 1857, inspired the first of the burlesque programs that would live on as a college custom for many years. [84] By the 1850's the rift between students and faculty had become so wide that it stood as an unwritten law that one must not, under penalty, apply to a professor "for assistance or advice in anything." [85] Students had an intellectual life largely their own. The society library circulation records show independent reading. A chess club met at Mrs. Hall's boarding house. [86] So also did the Shakespeare Club, a flourishing group which attracted even such bright spirits as Billy Bowdle, "the incarnation of mischief and jollity." [87] A dramatic association played Shakespeare, though officially theater attendance rated ten minus marks. [88] The election to honorary society membership of such authors as Melville and Hawthorne is evidence that the contemporary novel was both read and appreciated. [89]

The two old literary societies still dominated student life, each with its "anniversary" exhibition of oratory for College and town, its exciting elections for office, its debates (in which interest seems to have waned somewhat), and its "Court of Inquiry," that germ of self-government. Four years after Judge Reed's death the students were granted a room for a moot court, and Union Philosophical joined in meeting this need. [90] Only the societies had the capital for printing a student paper, and *The Collegian* of 1848–49 (almost wholly a Moncure Conway production) was sponsored by a committee of three members from each, setting the pattern for the *Dickinsonian* of 1872. The old hope of building society halls, such as had long existed at Princeton and for over a decade at Franklin and Marshall, was reawakened in 1857, but again in vain. [91] Belles Lettres had followed the Unions' lead in organizing alumni and both were ready for a campaign. [92] It might have succeeded had independent incorporations been granted, yet already that urge was being met by the new fraternity movement. The influence of the fraternity upon society life is seen at once in the new gold badges of B. L. and U. P., and in a renewed emphasis on secrecy and ritual. [93]

The fraternity movement had begun with Kappa Alpha at Union College in 1825. Two years later came the Yale Report, manifesto of that faculty conservatism against which students posed this new force of their own. Francis Wayland observed in 1842 that young people herded together under a distasteful regimen will form a social system of their own. [94] This the fraternities did. "Among the barbarians, we are the Greeks." The Greek-letter designations might be seen as an ironic nod to the outmoded classical course. Here was brotherhood, unencumbered by external rule or duty. Faculties rose in opposition to the evil. Just as the Anti-Masonic furor was receding, they found this new web of secrecy rising in their midst. Church government had always been hostile to the rival, secret rituals. Here worldly savoir faire was substituted for spiritual grace, the polished gentleman of affairs for the exemplar of Christian piety. [95] At Dickinson, some might even have seen the parallel between the chapter networks and the Methodist organization, each with its emphasis on brotherhood, loyalty and joy in life— but joy in two quite disparate patterns.

Brotherhood of this new kind first appeared at Carlisle, May 12, 1852, when Professor Johnson and three students organized the "Eclectic Society of Dickinson College," a chapter of Wesleyan's Phi Nu Theta. [96] No matter that this had been founded, and remains, a society with a particular regard for scholarship. At Wesleyan both Johnson and Charles Collins had belonged to it, and to Phi Beta Kappa as well. A Dickinson faculty meeting promptly responded to Eclectic by condemning any group "to whose meetings members of the faculty may not at all times have access." The trustees, "with closed doors," as promptly reinforced the edict by a stern mandate. [97] This was one of Peck's last acts, and it remained for Collins, in the next year, to uncover and erase the chapter of Zeta Psi, exacting solemn pledges from the membership and burning all records. [98]

Phi Kappa Sigma followed in 1854, at first as an inner circle among members of Belles Lettres, whose hall was well adapted to secrecy. When discovered by the faculty and ordered to disband it gave, but by no means kept, its acquiescence. [99] After all, in this same period some of the professors had been active in the Know-Nothing movement setting an example of undercover politics and action. [100] Long before that, moreover, faculty had been conspicuous in Carlisle's flourishing Masonic lodge. [101] Phi Kappa Sigma had a friend in Johnson, and it is probable that others were beginning to realize the futility of opposing this new development. [102] On April 8, 1858, the supposedly nonexistent chapter rolled out to Carlisle Springs in a four-horse omnibus for a glorious banquet, with addresses, odes, toasts and intermissions for "pumping ship." [103] Sigma Chi and Phi Kappa Psi came in 1859. Others followed, but the factor which made fraternities not only acceptable but necessary, their assumption of boarding and lodging functions, would come later at Dickinson than elsewhere.

The Peck regime had opened with a rule perhaps derived from the Doctor's boarding school experience. All students living in college, and all unmarried faculty, must eat in the College commons. [104] The result was not only an overcrowded dining hall, but surpassed all precedent in impromptu and planned disorder. More and more students sought parental permission to eat elsewhere, and the faculty contingent finally gave up when a young adjunct professor, eyes lowered in the act of giving thanks, received a bowl of hot mashed potato full in his face. [105] Student-managed boarding clubs appeared in 1856, and multiplied when the Civil War inflation made private boarding expensive. [106]

A high point in that year of 1856 had been the election of James Buchanan to the presidency of the United States—with a

constant whirl of torchlight processions, bonfires, and, on election night, old North College itself going up in smoke and
flame. [107] In the campaign, southern students had openly
talked of secession if Frémont won. [108] Horatio King dug back
in U. P. minutes and was delighted to find that as an undergraduate the famous bachelor statesman had read "an essay on
the Danger of a too frequent connection with the Fair Sex." [109]
Buchanan, prudent compromiser whose diplomacy had settled
the student "rebellion" of 1851, would now be expected to
unite the nation. Four years later, on the edge of the emerging
crisis, Dr. Collins resigned, and the College also had a crucial
presidential election before it. Collins, who had declined two
other college presidencies, would head the State Female College
near Memphis, Tennessee. [110] One of his final recommendations, bluntly turned down by the trustees, was a concession to
student feeling which might have made things easier for his
successor. He had suggested that instead of holding prayers and
recitations before breakfast (during the winter by candlelight),
these begin at 8:45, and that evening prayers be omitted altogether. [111] His successor must continue to deal with the situation in which, as "Rache" King had it in one of his songs,

> Prayers and imprecations,
> Fly to heav'n together. [112]

The election was hurried through with a sense of crisis and
urgency. Mary Johnson, watching her father pace up and down
the parlor of their rooms in West College, suddenly found the
place alive with a merry, laughing crowd, come to bring him the
news of his elevation. [113] He did not, actually, face a rosy prospect: the floating debt was larger than ever, faculty salaries
unpaid, endowment interest in arrears; and there was every
reason to expect continuing "pecuniary embarrassment." At the
electoral meeting, trustee the Rev. Pennell Coombe, a man given
to morose extremism, had moved that Dickinson College put up
its buildings for sale and remove "to some other locality." [114]
He may have had Williamsport in mind, or the motion may have
been simply a threat to the borough, with its persistent claim on
the College for sidewalks.

With the war crisis of 1861, the student body was suddenly

reduced to about half—seventy-two in College, thirty-two in Grammar School in that year. Faculty and trustees united in refusing to close the institution, though it was agreed that salaries must be paid only from revenue received. East Baltimore Conference established an annual "Day of Prayer for Colleges" (long continued through the years), and approved Johnson's suggestion of an appeal to the Pennsylvania legislature for aid, promising to match any appropriation with scholarships for "meritorious pupils of the common schools." [115] Johnson also advised, and his trustees approved, extending the scholarship certificates to Grammar School tuition. [116] This would remove a long-standing complaint—though it later resulted in the closing of the School as a continuing financial loss. In Philadelphia, there was an appeal to selected donors for funds. [117] The 1861 commencement must have had something of the air of closed ranks marching into dubious battle with unshaken esprit de corps. Seventeen Seniors (aggregate grades for their four years ranging from 11,549 to 7,400) made their meticulous little speeches—the "literary oration" in Greek, the salutatory in both Latin and English—all with the rounds of polite applause and the intervals of music.

Through the Civil War, Johnson had a teaching staff of four, all Dickinson graduates. Wilson, in science, was the senior. William Laws Boswell, formerly in mathematics, now taught Greek and German. The other two were new arrivals. John Keagy Stayman would have ancient and modern languages, philosophy and English literature in his repertoire during his years at the College. "Johnny" Stayman was the easy-going, jovial, ever-popular type. Let his class "raise a doleful howl" at the length of an assignment and he would shorten it. His own texts were marked with the jokes interjected every year. [118] Samuel Dickinson Hillman had mathematics and astronomy—"keen and merry . . . and the best chess-player in a faculty of chess-players." [119] Faculty met less often, and encountered only such minor disciplinary problems at the "tick-tacking" of a window. There were secret midnight dances with screeching fiddle and whirling forms that "made the mermaid tremble on her throne." One of these brought a lecture from President Johnson, candle in hand, "thin lips drawn tightly over his teeth in a

sort of sickly smile"—he then losing his way in the dark, as the
tale goes, to be found at morning in Boswell's pantry, held at
bay by the professor's big Newfoundland dog. [120] But the old
student-teacher impasse had melted away before the larger conflict—or had been transferred to it. Conrad and Cloud, as spies
of the Confederacy, with their secret line of communication to
Richmond and their plan to kidnap Lincoln and send him south
along it, were only enlarging the bold spirit and major preoccu-
pation of student life. [121]

In 1862, the Law Department was revived with the appointment of Judge James H. Graham, Class of 1827, as Professor. To this was added an honorary LL.D., but he seems to have
taken the whole as an honorary distinction, since no law students are known to have graduated in his twenty years' tenure. [122] We see Judge Graham briefly among the "wrathy" citizens when soldiers from the camps at Carlisle wrecked the office of the *American Volunteer* for having called Lincoln a des-
pot. [123] A more significant event of the year was Congress'
passage of the Morrill Act (vetoes in 1857 by Buchanan), bringing the rise of the land-grant universities, and stirring a hope of
Federal aid in the small colleges as well.

With 1863 came the war itself to Carlisle, Rebel troops
pouring through, "the dirty, ragged, lousy & harelip rascals
from Georgia and Virginia," and cavalry who had "fine-cut
faces & looked every inch fighting men." [124] The Barracks were
burned; the town was shelled on July 1 by Fitzhugh Lee; and
then the tide drew backward into the holocaust at Gettysburg. [125]

The invaders had bivouacked on campus, and we have a
glimpse of President Johnson exchanging Masonic signs with
their commander, and gaining a promise that no damage would
be done. [126] Johnson was proud of the patriotic ardor of
"about twenty of our students, including young gentlemen
from the states of Virginia & Maryland & Delaware" who at the
first news of invasion had "rushed to arms in the common
defense of their country." Governor Curtin, an alumnus of
1837, had granted at once his request for their discharge after
the battle. [127] Federal authorities had then taken over the College buildings for hospital and other purposes. [128]

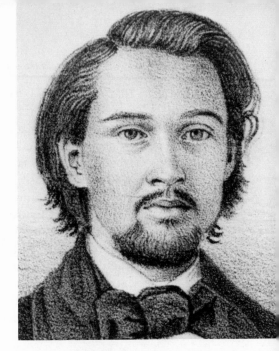

Top left: Thomas Nelson Conrad. Lithograph by John S. Sherwin, 1857. Top right: Daniel Mountjoy Cloud. Lithograph by John H. Sherwin, 1858. Bottom left: Moncure Daniel Conway. Lithograph, *c.* 1855. Bottom right: Horatio Collins King. Lithograph by John H. Sherwin, 1858.

In that fall of 1863, "Emory Female College" was opened, with Emory Church as its classroom building. [129] Lasting only three years, it was a new, and nearer, move toward coeducation, as well as providing added income for hard-pressed faculty and some easing of the financial burden of the church.

At war's end, Johnson could announce to his trustee meeting of 1865 that the student body had returned to about three-quarters of its former figure—not counting the abnormal crowding from "the scheme of scholarships, that is, about 1854-57." Also, there were fewer of the irregular students whose presence had characterized the scholarship inundation. [130] The President's report reveals a sense of a new era and new opportunities in education. He stressed again the need for a library building. He brought forward the elective principle which, a few years later, was to be given such prominence by Eliot at Harvard.

> We think that the time has come for a partial reorganization of the College Course of Studies. There is a demand for something more practical, which we are not at liberty to ignore. We think the first two years of the College Course should be devoted mainly to the elements of Classical learning, & the pure Mathematics; and that after that there should be divergence, that the young man may choose those studies best adapted to qualify him for his calling. [131]

A first step in this broadening program, Johnson told them, should be the pre-ministerial course adopted in 1851 but not long continued; and, "not less imperative," new science offerings embracing analytical and agricultural chemistry, geology, mining, metallurgy and natural history. His recommendations were referred to a committee which included the forceful and forward-looking churchman Matthew Simpson and John A. Wright, the engineer who had served on that earlier committee to consider adaptation to "the wants of the age." [132]

The Board voted approval insofar as funds would allow, and agreed to publicize the "Enlarged Course of Study for the use of Agents." [133] The agents were those of the new Centenary Campaign, and the most active of them was the Rev. Pennell Coombe. [134] American Methodism would reach its hundredth anniversary in 1866, with the exhilarating realization that it was now the largest religious society in the land. $100,000 was the goal of the "centenary endowment of Dickinson College."

Coombe asked James Buchanan to endow a professorship and was turned down sharply. [135] He found a more likely prospect in Jacob Tome of Maryland. Coombe was also quick to see that professors of high reputation were the fund-raiser's best talking point, and turned a critical eye on Dickinson's little faculty—its salaries still pro-rated on receipts. Actually, in this drive small contributions counted most. Each Sunday school pupil bringing a dollar received a medal with West College shown on one side, on the other Mrs. Susanna Wesley with little John at her knee, and the legend, "Feed my lambs." [136]

Johnson had another proposal for expansion at that Board meeting of 1865. Mr. A. M. Trimmer stood ready to establish, at his own expense but subject to "the general authority" of the College, a school of business. The College would receive half of all proceeds in excess of regular overhead. [137] Thus came into being the Dickinson Commercial College, which within two years was operating with over a hundred students and a faculty of five, including Martin Christian Herman, a young lawyer and Dickinson alumnus of 1862, later a trustee, as its Lecturer on Mercantile Law; and, as Instructor in Phonography, the Rev. William Trickett, an Englishman who would graduate with Dickinson's Class of 1868 at the age of twenty-eight, and follow with a year as Principal of the Grammar School.

The Grammar School was moved again into West, to make room in South for the Commercial College, but it was closed entirely at the end of the 1868-69 term. The extension of scholarship privileges had made it a losing proposition, and its presence in college classrooms had been as disturbing as when Emory had brought them together. [138] Some professors did preparatory tutoring privately, but the School, Dickinson's link with its remotest history, remained closed until 1877.

When Professor Wilson had died, March 2, 1865, a new emphasis on science had been under discussion for some time. Wilson himself had recommended the appointment to the faculty of Charles Francis Himes of the Class of 1855, who had taught at Troy University, and taken advanced study at the University of Giessen. [139] Thomas Daugherty, back in Carlisle with an eye on Emory Female College, was also a candidate for this chair, but Himes was elected. [140] Thus began, in 1865, thirty-one years of singularly dedicated service to Dickinson College by a man who might well have risen to national stature had he not identified himself so completely with the establishment of a pre-eminent scientific course on this one small campus. His teaching from the first was successful and popular, in spite of the dismally deficient laboratory in the basement of South and a laboratory fee of $25. [141]

"Dutchy" Himes was fully alert to the educational thinking of his day, and particularly to Herbert Spencer's on the value of scientific training, its advantages over the obsolete classical course both for practical purposes and as "mental discipline." [142] He put Dickinson at the front of a modern trend, doing all in his power to maintain that position by hard work, persuasion, personal expenditure and even (alas) political maneuvering. At the Board meeting of 1866 Johnson announced good results in permitting the substitution of analytical chemistry for Greek in Junior year, or in Senior year for either Latin or Greek (with Hebrew, French and calculus as other Senior alternatives). That meeting granted Himes authorization "to solicit and receive specific donations towards the erection and furnishing a suitable building"—a goal not to be achieved for nearly twenty years. By 1867, Himes had added a course for prospective teachers, and had organized his students into "The Scientific Society," under student officers but with himself as "Director." With its seal, its motto of aspiration, *"Nunc ad sidera,"* it stood on a par with B. L. and U. P., though more closely tied to the curriculum. It had twenty members in its first year, with Jesse Bowman Young, a war veteran and ministerial candidate, as President. [143]

Himes was too astute ever to permit his program in science to appear to conflict with that advance in theological training simultaneously put forward at the Board meeting of 1865. His classmate of 1855, the Rev. Shadrach Laycock Bowman, came in soon after as Professor of Biblical Languages and Literature, promoting this side with much of Himes' energy. [144] Yet the newness and verve were all on the side of science, while the founding of Drew Theological Seminary would soon supply the Church's need amply well, and Bowman himself would end his teaching career at Drew. In 1868, the trustees voted to extend "the elective system of studies" to all but the Freshman Class and to give Science the space in South from which the Commercial College was withdrawing. [145]

Meanwhile, the glowing prospect of the Centenary Fund contrasted sadly with present stringencies. Professor Boswell, after resigning in 1865 had brought suit for arrears of salary, obtaining a judgment still unsettled three years later. [146] Johnson had hoped for an endowment of $200,000 from the conferences, Baltimore, East Baltimore, Philadelphia, New Jersey and Wyoming, but at the final accounting the College received half that sum, and must then wait for income to accrue. [147] Pennell Coombe startled the 1867 meeting of the Board by moving that the new endowment justified an immediate "reconstruction" of the faculty, a position with which his colleagues did not agree. [148]

The faculty deserved better than this in view of past hardships, and none more than Johnson, who had travelled constantly in pursuit of funds, exhausted his own means, even borrowed from Belles Lettres in order to keep going. Worn out by it all, he died suddenly after a brief and apparently slight illness, April 5, 1868. [149] Hillman, as senior professor, took his place, and when the trustees met two months later they heard Mr. Coombe's renewed motion for "a private session, to take into consideration the election of College President & the reconstruction of the Faculty." [150] It did not, again, prevail.

The election was held at a special meeting in the Methodist Book Rooms in Philadelphia, September 8, 1868, giving Hillman a full year as Acting President. He was not, however, considered as a candidate. William Henry Allen could have had it, but was held back by a crisis at Girard. [151] Pennell Coombe was for Dr. George Beniers Jocelyn, President of Albion and with long experience as a college administrator. [152] From the first, however, a majority seems to have leaned toward the selection, for the first time, of a Dickinson alumnus. These defeated another move to postpone the decision and, at the end of a long day, by a vote of 22-3, elected the Rev. Dr. Robert Laurenson Dashiell, of the Class of 1846.

The age is groping half blind but conscious of a great want, for *a system of practical education.* We go stumbling and blundering on, mistaking our way, retracing our steps, trying again, dissatisfied with our selves and with our doings, yet not disheartened, having strong faith that the right way will be found some time, if not by us, by our successors, and that errors and failures have their uses in achieving ultimate success.

William Henry Allen to Charles Francis Himes,
January 5, 1866

I I

McCAULEY

A returning alumnus may tend to see the problems of college
life in terms of his own day. The Rev. Dr. Dashiell came back to
Dickinson after twenty-two years to continue the work of Robert Emory, whose exemplary student he had been.[1] We see
him now, with his pale blue eyes and sandy hair, a handsome
and successful pulpiteer eagerly confronting a situation far removed from Emory's. The fraternities had become a part of
college life, the interdicts against them ignored and forgotten.
His student body included older men, veterans of the war such
as Jesse Bowman Young, who had risen from private to captain
and was now a leader in undergraduate organizations, editor of
the first yearbook.[2] In his faculty, too, there were new ideas
and a new idealism, with Himes as their champion.

From the moment of his election he had been soliciting
funds. He came to the campus with a fortune in promises, and
with plans to continue the harvest. There would be new buildings, an endowed chair of Biblical Language and Literature, and,
as an extension of Himes' good work, courses in engineering,
mining and metallurgy.[3] He began a chain of alumni clubs in
New York, Philadelphia, Baltimore, with annual dinners to promote the fair name and prosperity of the College.[4] He made a
first move toward a reunion of the town and College churches,
an objective which would relieve the financial stringency of
both and make the Emory Chapel building available for educational use.[5] Yet the golden promises given him would not be

honored. The newly-formed Central Pennsylvania Conference praised in the same breath his plans for an endowed "Biblical chair" and for reducing the costs of education.[6] No endowed chair came his way, and at the end of four years all that had come of his building program was the so-called "pagoda," an ornamental bandstand in front of Old West, together with more practical improvements in the way of walks, gates, an extension of indoor plumbing and general repairs.[7]

Not only was the new President an alumnus, but so also all of his small faculty. There is a convenience in recruiting a professor who returns to home ground, and without the critical eye of wider experience. Himes had both the loyalty and the wider experience, Hillman and Stayman the parochial view. Through Johnson's administration, Hillman had been Treasurer of the Board of Trustees. When Hillman became Acting President in 1868, Himes succeeded him as Treasurer, and at the same time succeeded Stayman as Secretary of both the Board and the faculty. This brought "Dutchy" into a position of influence, with opportunities to promote the pattern of advance he had been commending. The more modern of Dashiell's first recommendations, such as a further extension of electives, are evidence of pressure from Himes. Stayman retained only the post of Librarian he had had since 1865, and we note that within three years he had only $30 for general book purchases, while $100 had been budgeted for natural science.[8] Himes, by his success in classroom and laboratory, by his public lectures on topics of major contemporary interest, held the academic reputation of the College in his hands. His classmate, Bowman, left the faculty in 1871 with his ambitious program in biblical studies unrealized. His place was taken by Henry Martyn Harman of the Class of 1848, coming with a solid background of teaching and scholarship in Bible, Greek and Hebrew—long a respected and beloved figure, a warm friend and ally of Himes.[9]

Himes and Harman, close as they were, are reflected in very different student attitudes. Himes' enthusiasm for his discipline as a whole, his excitement in those aspects, such as photography, where he had pioneered, his high aspirations for the College, all were contagious. So was his loyalty to his fraternity, and throughout his career he would have Phi Kappa Sigma staunchly behind him. All this commanded respect, while Harman, a giant of a man, remote and gentle, won love. To the students' delight, he was as gullible as he was learned, and became more so through the years with the failure of his hearing and eyesight. One could always wrap up the rest of any hour by asking him the question, "What was the value of the penny in the time of Christ?" [10] A student called upon to recite must sit in a chair by the Doctor's desk in the old-fashioned way, but for all that could still be coached by his "chum" at the back of the room. When George H. Bucher, '95, sitting in the chair, found himself at a loss to name the Church Fathers, Paul Appenzellar, from behind, prompted—"Athanasius."

"Yes, yes," says the Doctor. "Very good. Go on."

"Gregory," came next, Appenzellar to Bucher to the professor.

"Good. Good. Go on."

On came Arius, then Polycarp, but the line broke down and the class broke up in laughter when Dionysius came hesitantly through as "Diabetes." [11]

Dashiell, as a student, had known only the two literary societies. Now he found around him a rising tide of undergraduate organization, with the four fraternities; two student-managed boarding clubs; their chess club; the old Shakespeare Club; two religious groups, the Society of Religious Inquiry and the Missionary Society; an Orphean Glee Club with six members; and the Dickinson Base Ball Club with twenty-three. [12] Two years after his inauguration, the boarding clubs had increased to six, including *"L'Hôtel des Bons Mangeurs," "Hôtel de Boeuf,"* and "Worshippers of the Fleshpots of Wetzel." With these had come a boat club, a second baseball club, the "Eclipse," and— farthest yet from Emory's time—the open practice of card-playing, a Whist Club. [13]

Dashiell had come to the campus with a determination to enforce discipline as Emory would have enforced it. His first order of business in faculty meeting was to revive the old, unpopular ritual of visiting student rooms. [14] "The colleges of this country," he declared, "are passing through a severe test, the restless spirit of our young men, impatient and restive under control, the concession of parents permitting their sons to select their own college & leave for another when things do not please them, enabling them to hold over their institutions a threat." He met "the sneer and cry of tyranny, unnecessary humiliation of students," but stood firm in his belief that "moral conduct must be given equal weight with scholarship and the two graded together." [15]

That sneer and cry was topped by one long-remembered crisis, "The Rebellion" of the spring of 1870. On Tuesday, April 26, Carlisle celebrated the passage of the Fifteenth Amendment with a parade, alive with color, bands of music, eloquence. Black citizens were out in full force, and one of their banners bore the legend:

> IN MEMORY OF DR. McCLINTOCK,
> PERSECUTED FOR OUR SAKE. [16]

White friends were among them as before, though the newspapers' flouting of "the darky amendment" hardly bespeaks a universal warmth of feeling. However, the Sophomore and Junior Classes wanted to be in on it, and when their request was denied, they went anyway. Faculty met, imposing five hundred minus marks on each of the absentees. With a storm of resentment taking shape, faculty met again the next day and reduced the penalties, but on a varying scale which seemed only to increase the injustice. [17] The two classes informed Dashiell on April 30 that "they, to prevent all further aggravation, will absent themselves from all duties until the Faculty & Students come to an understanding." [18] The stern penalty of suspension followed. The students, bitter and unrepentant, left for home. It was not until then that the faculty, faced with disaster, found a pretext to withdraw its action, issuing a printed notice of reinstatement on May 17, 1870. [19]

"The Rebellion" was not a solitary incident. Just before Dashiell's arrival, the two old literary societies had once more moved to obtain independent charters—with William Trickett active in the attempt. [20] Repulsed in this, the societies were now assailed from within as fraternity men hatched a plan to control the offices of both. The Independents responded with a scheme to make themselves dominant in U. P. at least. This brought members of Belles Lettres transferring their allegiance en masse to the Unions, an unheard-of thing, and in the Union Hall, long dedicated to orderly debate, brawling fist fights became the last recourse. [21] This spring, as Dashiell reported to his trustees, June 6, 1871, had been one of "more than ordinary care & anxiety."

> Immediately following the election of speakers for the anniversaries of the Literary Societies, seasons always of great excitement, an unhappy difficulty arose, which very soon divided the U. P. Society into two irreconcilable parties & greatly reduced the numbers of the B. L. Society. So fierce and threatening was the attitude of these toward each other, that after repeated efforts to harmonize, the Faculty felt that the order and peace of the College demanded the suspension of the U. P. Society until these differences could be settled. Those of you who have been students will appreciate the difficulties attending these struggles, especially when you remember that since our day a new element has entered college life & association. From present indications we shall lose a part of our number. No temporary loss of students can retard the progress of this institution so much as these contentions. We hope to close the matter before your Board shall adjourn.

It was, indeed, with Harman's help, settled soon after. [22] In the meantime, tempers at this commencement had been sharpened still more by the last-minute refusal of a degree to Orson D. Foulks, a Senior of low standing but high popularity, who had composed for the occasion a Class History characterized, in the official view, by "insult and defamation." This in turn brought down upon Dashiell all that the young man's father could muster by way of insult, defamation and legal threat. [23]

A year later, June 25, 1872, Dr. Dashiell presented his resignation to the trustees. He had had this step in mind, he told them, for two years. "Circumstances have hastened my purpose in this matter." The Church, aware of his intention, promptly elected him Missionary Secretary, succeeding Dr. Durbin. He would live on in this office until 1880, remembered best in after years as a "dynamic" preacher and "a successful dedicator of churches." [24]

The mantle fell, as promptly, on another alumnus of Emory's day, James Andrew McCauley. He had gone from the Class of 1847 into teaching and had risen to Principal of the

Wesleyan Female Institute at Staunton, Virginia, but had been in the ministry of the Baltimore Conference from 1854 to 1872. [25] The College had elected him Professor of Greek and German in 1865, but, after six months of hesitation, he had declined. A meagre face, bald, spectacled, with long nose, thin lips and pale sidewhiskers of a distinctly clerical cut, he was noted for a winning manner, scholarly tastes and kindness. [26] "Even an infirm body," we are told, "& certain peculiarities of utterance resulting from sickness in early manhood, could not obscure his rare powers as a preacher." [27]

Professor Himes noted his new chief's "want of physical vigor," found his reserved manner greatly in contrast to Dashiell, "one of the most magnetic of men"—but was to be surprised by McCauley's capacity for work and his attention to detail. [28] The College letterhead of the coming years carries the names of "J. A. McCauley, D.D., President," and "C. F. Himes, Ph.D., Sec'y. and Treas'r.," and between them they ran the entire college operation, in addition to their teaching. It is an administration memorable for the appalling and mischievous blunders of 1874, which were to cast a shadow over all of McCauley's long presidency and echo far beyond it. In this awful brew, Himes, though not the prime mover, gave acquiescence and support and must share in the blame.

At least, in a charitable view of the matter, both were moved by a wiser primary objective than new buildings—the need for a faculty of recognized eminence. This was what Pennell Coombe had long been emphasizing as a first condition of liberal financial support. Twice Mr. Coombe had called for a meeting behind closed doors to "reconstruct" the faculty. McCauley and Himes were now using the same term and preparing their reconstruction with the secrecy of a coup d'état. Of the teaching staff of six, three were to be removed, Hillman, Stayman and Trickett, leaving McCauley himself, Himes and Harman. That McCauley wished to replace those three with congenial clerical types more responsive to his will was undoubtedly also a motive. Hillman had been with the College for twenty-three years, and it is apparent in this chronicle that new presidents often find past administrators as well as older faculty an encumbrance. The first ten years of his tenure had been as

Principal of the Grammar School, and he had remained a competent, active teacher on that level. [29] Stayman, Class of 1841, had been an assistant in the Grammar School in 1845, and had been dropped on the advice of Durbin. [30] He lived in Carlisle, and it is obvious that his appointment as Adjunct Professor of Latin and French, 1861, had simply served to fill the place at a difficult time.

With Trickett it was quite another matter—a brilliant younger man, precise and aggressive in the new Germanic style. In class he was the direct opposite of the easygoing Stayman, a dragon figure to inattentive students and, it would seem, to McCauley as well. Trickett had been absent for two years of study in Europe when he was elected Professor of Modern Languages in 1872. The circumstances are revealing. There had been another nominee, Dr. John Moore Leonard of the Class of 1855, a man whose record in college teaching stands equal or superior to Trickett's. The trustees were equally divided between the two, with discussion centered upon "the theological soundness of Mr. T's views." After one tie vote, the matter had been decided by a trustee who had arrived late and voted entirely by happenstance. [31]

The plan to "reconstruct" must have matured early in the academic year 1873-74. Only a majority of trustees sure to favor the change would be informed. At the June meeting, all faculty seats would be declared vacant and a new faculty elected. McCauley was selecting replacements for the professorships of modern languages (ex-Trickett) and philosophy and English literature (ex-Stayman), making discreet inquiries among the clergy. To Himes he gave the freedom to choose his own man for Hillman's place. Mathematics and astronomy were closest to Himes' own field, and McCauley may have considered also that this replacement was likely to bring the strongest reaction from friends and former students of Hillman. Hillman, after all his years of service, living in West College with his wife and three children, would lose both home and livelihood.

The limitations of the two older professors were well known, but a stronger case was needed against Trickett. The faculty minutes of November 10, 1873, record that a committee of one each from the Freshman, Sophomore and Junior

Classes had been received, "saying that they wd. not hereafter recite in Prof. Trickett's recitation room." No reason is given, but Trickett's standards of promptness and performance may be inferred. The President stated that he had made "some remarks to the classes in the Chapel at Prof. Trickett's request," and the faculty took no action, trusting that this would settle the affair. So it did, the students voting by a small majority to end their strike. [32] In his report to the trustees at the end of the year, however, McCauley, would enlarge darkly upon this incident as "a serious disturbance . . . in one department of the College. As this combination embraced more than 3/4 of the students in College, and among them many of the most mature in years and excellent in general character, . . . it was extremely difficult to manage." [33]

Professor Himes, casting about for a colleague in mathematics ready to take the post on the modest salary allowed him, $1,600, wrote on February 10, 1874, to William Righter Fisher, a young alumnus of 1870 who had just returned to Philadelphia from study at Heidelberg and Munich. Fisher had not yet fixed upon a life career, but had the law in mind, and was moved by a "dream of . . . the amelioration of the miseries of our common brotherhood." [34] Receiving no reply, Himes wrote again in March, in both letters discreetly saying no more than to suggest a meeting in Philadelphia. It was not until June 5, with the zero hour barely three weeks away, that he wrote again, revealing—in reiterated "Strictly Confidential" terms—precisely what was in the wind. His anticipation of commencement was, this year, he wrote,

> rather tinged with sadness, for whatever may be the faults or short-comings of the individuals mentioned we have been long associated together & our relations have at least not been unfriendly, but I cannot but feel at the same time perfectly free from any responsibility in the matter and also that it is perhaps the best thing that can be done for the college, provided that the places are filled with men calculated to impart greater strength internally & externally to the institution. I regard Dr. McCauley as a most admirable man for his position & for this crisis, as he is fully equal to it in scholarly ability, & had the fullest confidence of the friends of the college & the heart of the church with him, and with the changes indicated the college

under him may begin a new era. The selection of the individuals to fill any vacancies that may occur will be largely, indeed to a certain extent almost exclusively in his hands, as it should be. He has in mind several first class men, at least as far as endorsement by leading men in the church goes as well as his own judgment.

The chair of mathematics was one of the most difficult to fill, but he felt certain of Fisher's appointment. He lauded McCauley as "an honorable, honest, Christian gentleman," in whose belief the change could best be "accomplished quietly." [35]

Fisher at last agreed, with assurance that he would have leisure for his study of law. But having also his own concept of honesty, he had already shown Trickett the ultra-confidential letter. The two had been warm friends since college days. From this and other leaks, the victims of the scheme became aware of the threatening storm. They alerted their friends on the Board and elsewhere. They went at once, of course, to the President of the College, who calmed their fears with assurances that "as far as he knew there was no foundation for the rumors." This was the answer given both to Hillman and his father-in-law, Dr. Wing of the First Presbyterian Church, and yet their uneasiness was kept alive by small incidents such as the young man (Fisher) spirited out of McCauley's office as Hillman came in, to prevent a meeting. [36]

With an electric tension in the air, the trustees met in South College on the afternoon of Tuesday, June 23, 1874. They attended to routine business on the coming commencement, and heard the President's annual report, where difficulties with his faculty received only an indirect allusion. Aided by Colonel Wright, the President had been successful in quieting fears on the one hand and mustering a majority for change on the other. [37] Pennell Coombe could not attend, but had written McCauley urging him to "meet the case boldly." [38]

The storm broke on the next day. A committee on lack of harmony in the faculty offered a resolution expressing confidence in McCauley, declaring all professorships vacant and naming a committee of three, with McCauley as chairman, to reconstruct. McCauley, eager to keep up some semblance of not having been concerned in the matter, asked to be included in the

resolution and excluded from presiding or discussion. This was
tabled. Himes and Harman were then quickly returned to office,
and the Rev. Aaron Rittenhouse, of Wesleyan's Class of 1861,
elected Professor of English Literature. But things were not
going as smoothly as planned. Though the approved nominee
for modern languages was the Rev. Joshua Allen Lippincott,
Class of 1858, General Rusling now nominated Fisher for this
chair instead of for mathematics. It was a move that made
Fisher, the young man who had betrayed the secret, the one
who would displace his friend Trickett. James H. Lightbourne
then moved the substitution of Trickett for Fisher, and a petition from forty-nine students was read, urging Trickett's retention, "believing the chair to be most acceptably and ably
filled." [39] The Lightbourne motion was lost and Fisher elected.
Hillman was then moved as a substitution for Lippincott. "On a
rising vote the substitution was lost, 13 ayes, 13 nays." [40] As a
sop to the loser, one quarter's salary was voted him—it would be
deftly subtracted from Fisher's. [41] The business ended with
laudatory resolutions on those who appear in their opponents'
private correspondence as "the discomfited," or "the non-
elect."

"The Board of Trustees seemed to be very much in earnest
& have reconstructed," Himes wrote to Fisher, describing the
events. "Their action meets with general approval," he noted in
conclusion. "There was of course excitement in town but it is
softening down." [42] McCauley, trusting that it would be so, had
sought rest and refuge in a tour of England, leaving Himes as
Acting President to deal with whatever might arise.

Any softening the Acting President may have observed was
only a lull before the storm. An article in the *Shippensburg
News* extolling the deposed professors was echoed with heightened indignation in the Philadelphia *Sunday Mercury* of July
12. Dickinson College, "one of the leading educational institutions of the United States," had violated every principle of law
and equity by "an intrigue to obtain position, which we had
hoped would be confined to pot-house politicians." A young
alumnus, "One of '73," replied, conceding the "intellectual
qualifications" of the three, but stating that Hillman's "loud
complaints and denunciations" had begun in Johnson's adminis-

tration, had reached virulence in Dashiell's, and had been renewed against McCauley—echoed by Stayman and Trickett. [43] "Veritas," an older alumnus using pertinent lines from "The Heathen Chinee" as his text, struck back at this "bunch of abominable trash, inconsistencies and misrepresentations." Himes himself, he said, had once opposed Johnson and had consistently opposed Dashiell, while under McCauley there had been no dissension. [44]

So the battle went on. [45] Early in its course, Rittenhouse had declined his appointment, frightened away by the "furious tilts" in the press. [46] Himes was able, however, to find an excellent replacement in the Methodist theologican Charles Joseph Little, a University of Pennsylvania graduate recently returned from study in Berlin. He came as Professor of Philosophy and History. The entering Freshman Class of that September, in the opinion of one of its number, James Henry Morgan, was both small and poor. [47] Yet when McCauley returned on the 20th, Himes had a "Grand Ovation" prepared, the Carlisle Brass Band to conduct him from the depot to the Chapel, speeches, applause, introduction of the new professors, hand-shaking all around. [48]

All this, before "a fashionable and brilliant audience," covered the now-known fact that Professor Trickett's attorneys would appear in court with a writ of quo warranto demanding that Professor Fisher be made to show by what right he occupied his friend's chair. The case was heard on October 6, and on the 17th decided in Trickett's favor. [49] The other two non-elect at once took similar action. Here was humiliation indeed for the gentlemen of the cabal, yet the College charter was explicit, authorizing only "removal for misconduct or breach of the laws of the institution." [50] Charges against the three were then prepared, but were so palpably insubstantial that the decision to pay each a year's salary in return for his resignation easily followed. [51] The Board sought solace in discussing a future amendment of the charter, to erase so dangerous a provision.

Obviously, the College needed more than a grand ovation to recover from the damage that had been done. It would not now be easy to attract teachers of professional eminence who would in turn attract students and generous benefactors. The reconstruction had at least brought in one good man. Dr. Little, brilliant and learned, would be remembered by many alumni as their most stimulating influence in college life. [52] Himes, elected to the American Philosophical Society in 1874, expanded his plans for the future, his public lectures and his strong position in the curriculum. [53] The College catalogues, listing the texts for each course, show Himes as the only professor who specified also required reading in current journals.

Aaron Rittenhouse would join the faculty as Professor of English Literature and History in 1883—satisfied at last that he was not entering a nest of "pot-house politicians." A faculty of six at the beginning of McCauley's long tenure had grown to ten at its close. At the beginning only Himes had a Ph.D. (honorary, but well substantiated by graduate study and publication) while at the end there were seven, with only the Rev. Lyman J. Muchmore, the new "Director of Physical Training," without a doctorate of some sort. All but Muchmore and Harman became charter members of Pennsylvania's Alpha Chapter of Phi Beta Kappa, which held its first meeting, April 13, 1887, consolidating the effort of these years in this newly-revived bastion of academic respectability. Dr. Harman, increasingly conservative in all matters, had been invited to join, but refused. [54]

It had been a hard road back from the sorry events of 1874. McCauley and his trustees had been jolted into injured dignity as much as the old Board of the 1820's. Two years later, with Pennell Coombe present and active, they were discussing charter revisions, including the power to remove professors for any "cause that may seem good & sufficient to the said Board (with trial or otherwise as may by them be deemed most prudent)." [55] When it came, the revision of June 20, 1879 simply eliminated all reference to faculty tenure, while adding one useful reform, the division of trustee membership into four classes, one to be elected or reelected each year. The election of alumni trustees had been discussed in 1876, but did not come until 1891. [56]

Since the "reconstruction" of 1874 had so obviously repelled rather than attracted students, more must be done. Two years later General Rusling moved that the Board waive entrance examinations and admit Freshmen and Sophomores on certificate from the academies at Williamsport, Pennington, Wilmington and the Wyoming Seminary at Kingston, Pennsylvania. After considerable debate it was agreed to admit only Freshmen on these terms. [57] In the next year the old Grammar School, now the "Preparatory School," was reopened. The two Methodist congregations had at last been brought together, and this freed Emory Chapel for use by the School. [58] In 1877 also, a three-year "Latin-Scientific Course" was set up, leading to the Bachelor of Philosophy degree, a widening of electives which followed Wesleyan's lead as far as this smaller faculty could accomplish it. [59] By 1884, with the new Scientific Building, a Professor of Chemistry would be added, leaving the Physics Department to Himes; and in 1885 the Ph.B. course increased to a four-year program. [60] At the same time, an "English-Scientific Course," also dubbed a "Modern Language Course," marked a further retreat from the classics. Increased English studies were to be combined with German and one other modern language. [61] Classics remained prominent in preparatory work, Freshman and Sophomore years, and with candidates for the B.A.

The first notable event of McCauley's administration had been the founding of the *Dickinsonian,* September, 1872, a joint project of the two literary societies "for the purpose of advancing the interests of the institution; and uniting more closely the Alumni to their Alma Mater; and promoting Science, Art, Literature and Religion." [62] At the outset the monthly issues contain a large infusion of faculty and alumni productions. McCauley wrote benignly on Christian aspects of education, Himes explicitly on Herbert Spencer or the radical new ideas being tried out by Eliot at Harvard. [63] A year after graduation, Edwin Post of '72, who would attain eminence as a classicist at DePauw and elsewhere, was contributing a series of thoughtful pieces on "Higher Education: Results and Tendencies"—hot issues such as the elective system and coeducation. [64] A student contributor to the *Dickinsonian* of December 2, 1873, has his own appraisal of that perennially controversial subject, "The Marking System":

> It is, perhaps, a Utopian idea to advocate an institution where no marks would be made; where no honors would be distributed, and

where one would study for the love of study. To such an institution
no man would come except for the pursuit of knowledge, and to such
no worthless son would be sent by an indulgent father for the mere
name of going to college. . . . We chafe against the restrictions of a
college life, because our inclinations are forced into certain paths.
Hence it is that when we neglect our studies we think we injure the
Professors because they hold the reins of government. Away with
such nonsense! If we are men let us act like men, study for love of
study, and for our own self good, leaving the marking system to take
care of itself, and holding fast to the precious grains of truth.

Student contributions would soon come under the same watchful supervision as the public orations. [65] Yet the student reporting and presswork are good, while at the same time one can
occasionally glimpse through the veil of dignified journalism the
prevailing spirit of *Gaudeamus igitur, Juvenes dum sumus.*

One can admire the spirit of independence shown by the
literary societies in inviting Walt Whitman to "act as poet" at
their affair on the evening of June 17, 1876. The faculty must
have been deeply shocked, and vastly relieved when the poet
was obliged to decline. The letter of invitation had been written
by Sophomore James Monroe Green, who left Dickinson at the
end of that term, but went on to later eminence as an educator. [66]

It is in these last years of the century that one sees the
flowering of the "collegiate" way of life—four years of group
rivalries, whole-souled and violent, of intense friendships, hates,
the union of heart in song, yells, underclass scraps and upperclass masculine elegance, all frozen into "college customs"
around the slender supporting stem of the curriculum. It is the
young man's introduction to both life and learning. Tobacco
and alcohol are more than ever to the fore. [67] College professors
everywhere might be distressed by so many anti-intellectual preoccupations, but those with an administrative viewpoint soon
learned that this was the way to make a happy, contributing
alumni body, its loyalty sustained through life by the team
games and commencement high jinks.

The *Dickinsonian* of March, 1884, announces the formation of the Dickinson College Athletic Association. Dr. Fletcher
Durrell, who had come the year before as Professor of Mathe-

matics and Astronomy, was the moving spirit here, bringing with him also American rugby football as he had found it played at Princeton. [68] By 1889 football was the dominant sport, with baseball in the spring, tennis, track and gymnasium active—the College bell and the College yell signalling every jubilant hour—*"Hip! Rah! Bus! Bis! Dick-in-son-i-en-sis! Tiger!"* [69]

Youthful high spirits made for a constant undercurrent of violence. An appalling amount of property damage was done from day to day—all recorded in the bills of Samuel J. Fells, who made a very decent living through a long life putting things together again. [70] One can tell when Carlisle had had snowballing weather by the recurrence of replaced glass. It was no doubt in part with a hope of restoring earlier concepts of discipline that Dickinson, with other colleges, introduced a Department of Military Science after the war—that, and the lure of a government-supported program. [71] This came in 1879, the year of the establishment of the Indian Industrial School at Carlisle Barracks. Lieutenant E. T. C. Richmond, Second Artillery, assigned to the Dickinson College Cadet Corps, had been at the Barracks, active in turning the post over to Captain Richard H. Pratt and his young Indians. [72] The government provided swords, muskets, two cannon, equipping two companies of Cadets in their smart gray uniforms. [73] The faculty, however, refused to require participation by the three lower classes, and insisted upon treating military science "in the same manner as any other elective study." [74] Richmond, unable to enforce West Point discipline under these conditions, resigned in 1881, ending the experiment.

College students, here as elsewhere, were not only often setting faculty authority at defiance, but assuming disciplinary functions of their own. The "facultyizing" of the 1850's had become a regular processing of Freshman and fraternity initiates—vainly deplored and resisted from above. An effort to stamp out the evil brought McCauley and his faculty into a hassle and humiliation very similar to that of 1874. On the night of November 9, 1886, they were meeting in the President's office, taking evidence of hazing from Freshmen, while other students, outside, expressed their indignation by hooting, jeering, shouting and rowdy song, the clamor rising at last to a climax of flying stones. When a rock large enough to have inflicted death (in the considered opinion of the nine professors) crashed through a window and crossed the room above their heads, Morgan, the young adjunct Professor of Greek, dashed out and, among the figures fleeing before him into darkness, recognized Sophomore John Martz Hill. Questioned the next day, Mr. Hill pleaded a measure of innocence: "Well, Doctor, I threw no stones." [75] The faculty, consulting among themselves, decided on dismissal from college, and ordered him to leave Carlisle within twenty-four hours.

In this plight the young man bethought him to consult William Trickett, who had been for ten years now a member of the Cumberland County bar. On Trickett's advice he wrote to McCauley, demanding reinstatement, but refusing to be tried by the faculty, from whom he could not expect fair treatment. Only a court of law would do. To court the case came in the January term, and Judge Sadler's verdict was much the same as Judge Junkin's had been in the case of the three professors. Hill had been denied orderly presentation of evidence, the right to question witnesses; in short, as he had been punished without trial, "the court of common pleas will order his restoration by the writ of mandamus." [76] The court went on to express astonishment that men "trained in the languages and sciences" should have so imperfect a conception of the rules of evidence, citing in particular the faculty claim that Hill had acknowledged his guilt. Professor Rittenhouse, questioned as to the words of the confession, had replied that it had been without words: "He turned white." [77]

Student diaries are fewer in these years, and the student albums coming in—filled with evidence of a gayer, more active social life. In the late seventies lecture rooms were still being rendered useless with grease or oil, cannon balls rolling, the walls of the privy knocked down. A decade later, games, music, dramatics (farce and mock trial prevailing at first), class fights, banquets, kidnapping of class officers, were parts of a new pattern of students' involvement with themselves, and faculty· coming to be regarded with a tolerant affection rather than enmity. Regulation of this new order, or disorder, would be a first concern of student government when it came. It was a thoroughly

Emory Hall, the former Emory Church, 1858, as remodelled for the Dickinson School of Law, 1900.

Ladies' Hall, as it appeared in 1905, when renamed "Lloyd Hall."

West College and the "Pagoda," *c.* 1880.

Dickinson College Cadet Corps Band, *c.* 1880.

masculine milieu, and understandably hostile to any intrusion by the gentler sex.

The spectre of coeducation had arisen as part of the trustees' recovery effort of 1876. General Rusling had moved a committee with Colonel Wright as chairman. The committee had moved, 1877, that young ladies be admitted on the same terms as men, and the Board had promptly tossed the hot potato to the faculty for a report at its next annual meeting. [78] The faculty voted in favor (Dr. Harman dissenting), but advised delay (Professor Lippincott *contra*) until the buildings could be suitably renovated. "They must be protected from all that might be indelicate." [79]

Coeducation was inevitable. It had ample background in the College's philosophy and experience. Rush, Neill, Caldwell and others had shared enlightened ideals of "female education," there had been and still were close ties with the young ladies' academies of Carlisle. McCauley himself had been the principal of such a school. Nearby Wilson College, Wellesley and others were setting women's education on a scholastic equality with the bastions of masculinity, though the fear of weakening standards would persist into the twentieth century. Old George Metzger, Class of 1798, died in 1879, and his will, dated January 29, 1872, left $25,000, his home and library, "for a Female College, wherein to have taught useful and ornamental branches of education." The Metzger Institute, which in 1913 would be merged with Dickinson's coeducational program, might conceivably have been a part of it from the start, had the trustees been looking to the future in a more alert and liberal fashion. Metzger classes began in September, 1881, the girls greeted soon after by a score and more of boys with the Cadet Corps cannon—a foretaste of what feminine invaders of Old West and Old East might expect. [80] Yet in 1882 the faculty voted that campus improvements had removed their only objection of 1878. Presumably by an oversight, the trustees did not give final authorization until 1884. [81] Girls had already been enrolled in Preparatory School classes, but now a direct application had been made for admission to the College.

William H. Longsdorff, a physician living near Carlisle, had come to McCauley with a proposal. He was the father of four daughters. The eldest, Zatae, was a Freshman at Wellesley. Let Dickinson come to a decision on coeducation and he would provide a vanguard of girls able to cope with male opposition in whatever form it might take. It was done, and Zatae arrived as a Sophomore in the Class of 1887. Dr. Longsdorff had fought through the whole of the Civil War as an officer of cavalry, and his daughters matched him in intrepidity and determination. "We were outdoor girls," as Zatae's sister put it, unperturbed by finding mice or garter snakes slipped into their pockets or by the sudden appearance of any other supposed female repellant. Zatae faced open hostility, and it reached a crescendo in her Junior year when she competed for the College's most coveted honor, the Pierson Oratorical Prize, a gold medal, and won it. So much harrassment had been brought to bear before the actual event that when the night arrived her father hired special police to watch the campus. It was a tense moment as the little figure stepped up before the audience in her black silk dress with bustle and train, at her throat the pin of gold mined by her father in the West, with her little sister, Persis, standing by to turn the pages of her oration—*Hand Workers versus Head Workers.* Persis trembled when the hooting outside began, and then the soul-rocking tocsin of the College bell. Some pages were lost altogether when the gaslight faded and went out and had to be restored. But the Prize was fairly won. Zatae went on from graduation to the Woman's Medical College of Pennsylvania, earning her M.D. in 1890. Through a long life in her father's profession she would seek and meet every challenge with that same verve, that same determination never to be outdone. [82]

At Zatae's graduation, Dickinson had come a long way from the doldrums of a dozen years before. This had been an era, to be sure, of academic expansion everywhere. Former peers, such as Presbyterian Princeton or non-denominational Pennsylvania, were becoming great universities, while the campus at Carlisle remained small, compact, conservative, its growth on a far more modest scale but with a respectable academic standard and its ancient traditions somehow still intact.

McCauley had an alumni body thinly united by occasional meetings and the *Dickinsonian's* monthly column of alumni news. Its potential had been greatly weakened by the war. The students who had come in such numbers from the South were now in no posture to be benefactors of education, least of all to a northern institution. At the same time, the College's appeal to its sons was still largely parochial. When one southerner, Moncure Conway of Virginia, wrote from London in 1877 to ask what service he could render "Old Mother Dickinson" he was given scant encouragement. [83] Conway, erstwhile Methodist, erstwhile Unitarian, now minister of an ethical society in a foreign land, was, for all his success as an author, a dangerous renegade in the sight of many. Few in Carlisle could appreciate his concern for life, his "Earthward Pilgrimage" back from the heavenly city to the human heart. In America, the churches were characterized as never before by crowded pews, increasing wealth and a deepening theological atrophy. [84] Loyalty was a first demand upon a denominational college. Dickinson, independent and nondenominational by charter, was suspect. In 1873, a move for Church control of the election of trustees was defeated. [85] In 1875, the Central Pennsylvania Conference considered removal from Carlisle to "some larger centre of Methodism," but balked at the expense. [86] The larger center must have been Williamsport, where Dickinson Seminary, without any change in curriculum, was already granting college degrees—over Professor Himes' strenuous public protest. [87] Come 1879, the Conference must needs be reassured that at Dickinson College, "though the heathen classics are read, and the researches and speculations of skeptical authors considered, the Christian dogmas are taught and the God of the Bible proclaimed and honored." [88] Five years later, the Conference was endeavoring unsuccessfully to endow a chair which it itself would fill, while on campus the *Dickinsonian* raised the universal student complaint against required religious attendance—was it valid? "We think not. The majority of students before entering college are connected with the M. E. church; after entering you cannot tell where they belong." [89] Chapel was already an ebbing tide— moved from 7 A.M. to 9:15 in 1875, with evening sessions discontinued altogether in 1878. The catalogues long continue to list that "Society of Religious Inquiry" for student soul-searching, but not until the Rubendall years of the 1960's would there be a free and imaginative exploration of religious thought and practice, such as Conway could have approved.

Religionists in these years of theological stagnation reveal unusual reverence for the magic number, and among Methodists "Centenary" held magic. England's "Centenary Fund" to mark the hundredth year since Wesley's ministry began had more than doubled its goal in 1839. Wealth had been poured out for the American fund of 1866. By 1881 the trustees were planning a financial drive to mark the centennial of the College charter. The conferences joined in, but with 1884, centennial of the organization of the American Church, as their point of emphasis. [90] It was high time to do something, since for years the reports of the United States Commissioner of Education had shown a massive flow of treasure into college coffers, with only the paltriest share for Carlisle. [91] Friends and alumni responded, making possible in 1882 long overdue repairs and modernization in East and West Colleges. The centennial year brought finally that Science Building for which Himes had labored so long and which he had envisioned as carrying past traditions into a glowing future. He had launched his campaign for it in Washington, June 26, 1878, at a meeting with Spencer Baird, Ira Remsen of Johns Hopkins and other distinguished men. The building, financed by banker Jacob Tome, was a far more modest accomplishment than the domed museum and classroom complex presented at the Washington meeting by Montgomery Cunningham Meigs, architect of the Smithsonian. [92] But it was a long step forward from the outmoded conditions in South, and at last made possible the division of "natural science" into departments of chemistry and physics. The scientific museum must needs remain in South, as did the observatory with its "excellent achromatic telescope . . . adapted to research as well as instruction." [93]

The College centennial brought other substantial gifts, notably Thomas Beaver's of $30,000 in 1882. Moreover, funds coming in to the trustees rather than to the conferences marked an advance in responsibility and independence. [94] And inflow increased as the centennial year went by. Most notable was the gift of a library building by the widow of James Williamson Bosler, Class of 1854. As seems so often to have been the way of young men who have fallen short of a college degree, he had gone on to make a great fortune—in banking, real estate and on the cattle ranges of the Far West. Before his death he had

James Williamson Bosler Memorial Library Hall, built in 1886.

Bosler Hall, as remodelled, 1941.

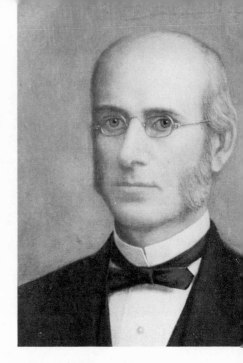

Top left: Robert Laurenson Dashiell. Photograph, 1871. Top right: James Andrew McCauley. By Robert Wilkinson, 1882. Bottom left: Samuel Dickinson Hillman. Lithograph by John H. Sherwin, 1858. Bottom right: William Trickett. Photograph, *c.* 1870.

pledged $10,000 to the alumni working toward a McClintock memorial professorship. [95] Mrs. Bosler cancelled this obligation and agreed instead to the Library, to cost nearly seven times the sum. McCauley, eager to include other facilities in the new edifice, proposed enlarging the plan, with cheaper materials. "The lady, however, treated this suggestion with disfavor, declaring her intention to build, if at all, with material the most durable, and the least liable to fire." [96]

Bosler Hall, with its tower and arched portal guarded by twin cherubs, libraries on the main floor and the large hall for chapel and assemblies above, was completed in 1885. Here was indeed a noble advance from the Reading Room in Old West which McCauley had set up in the first flush of his presidency, collecting from eight donors enough money to buy reflectors for the lamps, matting for the floor, green baize table covers, chairs, and six spittoons at $1.50 each. It had been intended for periodical literature, and proved a failure for lack of just that. Two years later, the students were suggesting that a billiard table might make it of some use. [97] The society libraries, meanwhile, were active and crowded, in their fiction sections at least, but had long outgrown their rooms. [98] The chronic situation of the College Library may be seen in a typical Librarian's report:

Gentlemen:
    There is nothing special to report concerning the College Library. Only about a dozen volumes of Public Documents have been added to it.
                                        Very Respectfully,
                                        Henry M. Harman. [99]

Now the books, though still in three distinct entities, were together in one place; nearly thirty thousand volumes, or, allowing for duplication, about twenty thousand titles. Morgan, the young Adjunct in Greek, was busy with a new arrangement and catalogue—time not altogether well spent in the opinion of some trustees. [100]

A gymnasium, for which the students had long been pleading, followed quickly, built at a modest cost of $7,000, the gift of Clemuel Ricketts Woodin of Berwick, Pennsylvania; while equipment was provided by another manufacturer connected with railroading, William Clare Allison of Philadelphia. Soon after, South College was remodeled and enlarged for the Preparatory School. With all this, endowment was growing with some four- and even five-figure gifts, such as the $5,000 for prizes and scholarships from Delaplaine McDaniel of Philadelphia and a $10,000 memorial to Clarence Gearhart Jackson, '60, of Berwick.

The successes of the McCauley years must be credited in part to the leadership of trustees with a clear concept of educational values, and particularly to two high-ranking veterans of the war—Brigadier General James Fowler Rusling, lawyer, author and traveller;[101] and Major General Clinton Bowen Fisk, founder of Fisk University. Rusling had been a classmate of James W. Bosler, and after graduation, while preparing for the bar, had been at Dickinson Seminary as "Professor of Natural Science and Belles Lettres."[102] He had been elected to the Board in 1861, resigned in 1883, but was reelected in 1904, serving until his death in 1918. Fisk, elected in 1883, was an active participant until the year before his death in 1890.

McCauley was to learn that the successes as well as the failures of a long tenure can bring rivalry and opposition. As Treasurer and Secretary, Himes had given him strong support at the outset through his broad educational outlook, and, for instance, his promptness and energy in bringing other Pennsylvania college administrators together and securing an act of exemption from state taxation.[103] Yet Himes gradually emerges as a rival, clearly so at the Board meeting of 1881 when his friend and fraternity brother, James Hepburn Hargis, proposed "consideration of the Centennial Presidency of the college."[104] McCauley promptly resigned in protest to "the proceedings of today with their antecedents," gaining votes of non-acceptance and confidence.[105] In the next year Himes resigned as Treasurer, leaving in the following summer for the third of his five European visits.[106] Opposition to McCauley increased. Rumors flowed freely, some of them in print, spinning a web of financial scandal. In 1886 the Board was asked to investigate charges of "serious mismanagement and internal dissensions," hurriedly conducted a hearing, and contented itself with a resolution regretting the want of harmony.[107]

When McCauley presented his final resignation, June 27 1888, things had come to such a pass that Thomas Green Chattle, New Jersey physician, teacher and legislator, moved to receive also "the resignation of all the members of the present faculty with a view to the reconstruction of the same." Under the revised charter it could now be done. Prudently, however, his motion was tabled and the administration of the College turned over, ad interim, to the senior professor, Himes. McCauley, wan and embittered, here leaves the field to his enemies, a man long remembered by many with affection and respect as "a Christian gentleman," and by others derided as a perversion of just that. "McCauley," as William Trickett put it, "has a talent for piety." [108]

"Dutchy" would have less than a year as Acting President, though long enough to prove his popularity and efficiency. [109] College opened with a large enrollment and the only untoward event of his administration, the riot of Halloween night, 1888, brought students and faculty into a new and rare moment of rapport. He had given permission for a campus bonfire made of the old picket fence on the north side. The event had been cleared with the town firemen, who, however, returning late and merry on the railroad from their picnic, saw fit to leap from the cars and attack both fire and students. Students were reinforced by faculty, stones flying, fence pickets dangerously wielded. At next morning's chapel, black eyes, cuts and bruises showed how they had stood together in the melee. [110]

No such healthy uproar could dissolve the factions that had been growing in trustee, faculty and alumni circles since 1874. The Board saw the need for a new president who would stand unencumbered by all that, and looked to Clinton Fisk, who had the widest connections of any, to find an answer. The General, though in ill health, was about to achieve something of a triumph in the presidential election of this year, rolling up an impressive vote as the Prohibition Party's candidate. It was at New Haven on September 8, soon after the opening of his campaign, that he met George Edward Reed, minister of Trinity Methodist Church, a vigorous, determined man in his early forties, and in their conversation remarked that he had a roving commission to find a president for Dickinson College, and, "I think I have found the man . . . ." [111]

Above all, I have been anxious to realize the will of God concerning me in a matter involving departure from the particular line of work to which hitherto my life has been consecrated, and in the prosecution of which I should count it but honor and privilege to spend the remainder of my days.

George Edward Reed, February 2, 1889, accepting
the presidency of Dickinson College

One cannot help feeling that man is the crowning glory of creation when "Dockie" tramps by.

Microcosm, 1907

12

REED

GEORGE EDWARD REED, a native of the state of Maine and a graduate of Wesleyan, Class of 1869, knew nothing of Dickinson College, nor had he ever thought of leaving his chosen profession. But when General Fisk went on to describe Carlisle, "in the glorious Cumberland Valley, the gateway to the south," and then the "long and honorable history" of its small but ancient seat of learning; and on top of this, most persuasive of all, the potential for a brilliant future with a right, strong hand at the helm, the thing took hold. He spoke to others. General Horatio C. King gave him his first glimpse of the alumni's strong affection for their college. Invited to visit the campus, Reed found a brass band and yelling students at the station as his train drew in. He addressed them in a crowded chapel. There was a reception, with faculty and prominent trustees, among them William C. Allison and Wilbur Fisk Sadler. Such a welcome, to a man of decision and strong will, his eyes on the future, held high promise. He was unanimously elected, and the College had once more a New Englander at the helm, armed with enthusiasm, noble vitality and minimal experience—prominent forehead with hair parted in the middle, narrow, commanding eyes over a large moustache and strong cleft chin.

General Fisk came to Carlisle for his inauguration, the only trustee from a distance to do so. He presided "with genial manner and frequent sallies of wit" at the ceremony in Bosler Hall.

The student choir sang. "Dutchy" Himes spoke for the faculty, dwelling on its individual merits, and Senior Charles Wesley Straw for the students. To Reed, who had hoped for the pomp and circumstance of academic pageantry, it seemed barbaric.[1] Yet when he himself stepped forward to speak and the whole assembly rose, applauding, waving hats and handkerchiefs through the awful din of the *"Hip! Rah! Bus! Bis! Dick-in-son-i-en-sis! Tiger!"* and the four class yells, he had at least the assurance of a devout following. "His resonant voice and musical cadences," we are told, "thrilled the vast audience present as he in glowing terms pictured Dickinson's future."[2]

He presided at his first faculty meeting on the next day, April 26, 1889. It included invited guests, and opened with a prayer, beginning this custom.[3] Its purpose was to plan a celebration of the centennial of George Washington's presidential inauguration, with Metzger Institute and the Indian School participating. Clearly, the College was in for a change of pace, a break from slow tradition. Reed had already made the round of the five "patronizing conferences," Baltimore, East Baltimore, Philadelphia, New Jersey and Central Pennsylvania. The conferences, like the older members of the College community, may have felt a chill at the new wind a-blowing. Only the students were jubilant:

> We like his pluck in the declaration that we need a million dollars. . . . Sentiment alone will not build up a college. Ready cash and plenty of it is most necessary. Give us the million.[4]

Here is the key to the long administration of George Edward Reed. He came to transform a small college into a great university. He would soon find a coolness in faculty and alumni who held old ways and traditions dear, an indifference among trustees, with only the students wholly on his side, and he would end with a small college still, but a better one. From the first, things were changed by swift fiat. Chapel services, the most ingrained routine in college life, were given a new look, with all faculty participating. Suddenly, to Himes' indignation and distress, the old Chapel gallery was torn out.[5] The President gloated over the amount of rubbish ("225 cart loads") he had had hauled away.[6] This attitude was hard to bear, but it was on

Left: Zatae Longsdorff, wearing the dress and gold pin worn when she won the Pierson Medal in 1886. Right: George Edward Reed. By Louis Hasselbusch, 1902.

Library Reading Room in Bosler Hall, c. 1935.

the empire-building in the curriculum that faculty could turn a more critical eye.

Two months after his inauguration, Reed came to his first trustee meeting with a program for the College—"popularization of its aims and methods, reforms in its conditions of admission, enlargement of its various curricula, the establishment and development of departments of instruction . . . having no existence at the present time, and improvements in the buildings and upon the campus." [7] He had already added a third year to the Preparatory School course in anticipation of new entrance examination requirements. Admission standards for the Modern Language Course must be as strict as for the Latin-Scientific and the Classical, and its graduates should receive the Ph.B. A School of Engineering would be his first step toward university status. The Board approved all this and more, giving him a completely free hand.

He met at once with his faculty, and the introduction of an earned master's degree and doctorates in philosophy and science was voted. [8] By fall, however, the M.A. received hesitant but unanimous support, while on the Ph.D. and D.Sc. Reed had five with him and three against, Himes and Harman being joined in opposition by Ovando Byron Super of Modern Languages. [9] Morgan, who voted with the majority, readily admitted later the impossibility of maintaining the doctoral program. [10] When it was put in operation, it would be found necessary to accept off-campus work, and with this easing of the strain on the small faculty and Library, four young men, from 1893 to 1898, did receive the Dickinson Ph.D. The M.A. "with examination" continued as a thin stream among the larger number of students coming to receive the traditional and perfunctory one. [11] The School of Engineering, possibly conceived as something that might appeal to railroad car manufacturer Allison, never came into being.

One enduring element of graduate study was achieved, but not on Reed's initiative. It was the project of William Trickett, seconded by his friend Sadler. The Dickinson School of Law came into being, a revival of the old Law Department, but now an affiliated corporation with Dr. Reed as President of its forty-four incorporators. [12] In the aura of this formidable backing, Trickett would run the whole operation in a very personal way for nearly forty years. Judge Graham's long, inactive tenure had brought the College into some disrepute, as students, attracted by the continuing catalogue announcements, found no substance in them. [13] The new Law School was inaugurated with "an appropriate and interesting ceremony" in Bosler Hall, September 30, 1890, and classes began in the former Emory Church, refurbished for the purpose by the ever-generous Allison. [14] Trickett, with the prestige of his books and articles published through the last eight years, [15] easily mustered a faculty and returned to teaching with all his former strictness of standard intact. Reed had acted boldly to add what would prove a broadening influence of lasting value to the College, and in doing so had lost favor with trustee and alumni partisans of McCauley. McCauley did not hesitate to pronounce the new operation "a fraud." [16] Trickett, unperturbed, would continue in Emory until 1918 and then on his own campus, renowned for his learning, for the learning imparted to others in his high, squeaky voice, and for his biting insistence upon precision and punctuality. A life-long bachelor, he had few friends. Judge Sadler, on his faculty from the first, was the closest. Rumor had it, as rumor often will, that they had once been rivals in love and that the girl had chosen Sadler. A new co-ed, 1886, would long remember her first glimpse of Trickett on the street—taut figure, glittering glasses, bristly moustache and goatee—and how the older girls had quickly warned her of a sinner passing by. [17]

In the Law School Reed had some compensation as his dreams of expansion faded. It had been a shock, after arrival, to find a debt of $16,000 of which he had not been informed. [18] Now a floating debt would be with him throughout. His frequent trips afield—largely a continuation of his career as a popular preacher—did not rally rich donors as expected. When he brought to Jacob Tome, "multimillionaire of Port Deposit," his vision of "Tome University," with Dickinson College as its autonomous college of liberal arts, it was brushed aside as far too ambitious a scheme. [19] In his frank way, he faced the trustees June 4, 1894, with his failure:

> The fashion of the time seems to be to elect to the Presidencies of Colleges, Gentlemen—generally laymen—of independent fortune,

Gentlemen to whom the question of salary is of no particular importance, who themselves are able to lead in the making of subscriptions,
and who, by reason of business associations with men of wealth are,
presumably, capable of exercising a wider influence in financial lines
than is possible to a clergyman dependent upon a meagre salary, and
whose song, ordinarily, [is] that of the old itinerant,

"No foot of land do I possess,
Nor cottage in the wilderness."

The new departure seems, in many instances, to have worked
admirably, and perhaps is the thing now needed in Dickinson College.

As matters now go in our Colleges, the great desideratum here is
money. To get money would appear to be the peculiar business of a
College President, and if in this he does not succeed, the proper
thing—the only thing, indeed—is that he step down and out.

My own success in the line of money-getting has not been so great
as I had hoped, largely, it may be, because of inability to give the
matter the required time and attention, possibly because my genius
does not work in that line . . . .

But for the persuasion of members of this Board, coupled with the
fear that something of harm might come to the College through any
sudden action on our part we should have retired from the position
we now hold, six months ago. If the needed increase in the resources
of the College shall not soon be forthcoming, our conviction is that a
man with larger money-getting power should, in the near future, be
secured. [20]

It was a suggestion which might have applied equally well to the
Board; and the Board remained content with things as they
were.

The professors, on their part, watched the fading of the
dream with some evident relief. They were slow in warming to
this new president, whose role in teaching was minimal, and
concept of his office overreaching. Soon after arrival, Reed had
moved from the east end of East, where earlier Presidents had
lived, to the former home of Judge John Reed at the corner of
High and West Streets. He bought the house himself for the
College, and the cooperative Mr. Allison enlarged it for him to
double its former size, at a cost of $5,500—and "very sore
about it," as Harman informed Himes, "and told Dr. Reed he
need not come back. I cannot write more. You can read between the lines, until we see you." [21] East had lacked elegance

and had been too close to student uproar for the Doctor. He also separated his office from the "faculty room" in East—"a very undesirable arrangement, as I learned from sad experience."[22]

Younger as well as the old alumni were disturbed by Reed's disregard of traditions. John M. Rhey, '83, led a bloc which saved the campus wall from demolition.[23] At this point Reed had not even that student support he enjoyed so long. His quick denunciation of the constant, carefree window-breaking and other destruction had brought out the old threat of organized rebellion.[24] In the face of it, he instituted a damage account to replace the system of a general charge upon everyone for "incidentals." (The students referred to the sport of smashing things as "taking out incidentals.")[25] In 1890 there had been a coalition of both students and faculty against him. The Juniors had felt it necessary to purge their class of women. The four girls appealed to the President, who promptly demanded that the action be rescinded. Faculty support of the class was met by Reed with a threat to resign, and those who fain would have had him do so yielded rather than have it conditioned upon their response to the matter at issue.[26]

What emerged from these first conflicts was the loyalty, admiration and love of the student body. If his tours afield failed to bring money, they did bring students and students with that lasting affection which a friendly admissions officer can inspire. The student population nearly quadrupled in his time. In 1890 he had 152 undergraduates and 100 in Preparatory School. At his retirement the figures were 351 and 124, plus 77 in Law. Here at least was one element of stability.[27] Here was Reed's constituency, and it was sustained by more than personal warmth. He improved student living, and permitted, as he tells in that report of 1894, "great liberty of action" in comparison to the strict regulation of the past. He found himself at times at odds with faculty in this area, always yielding when he must with good grace—content perhaps to let the onus rest with them.[28] He was not eager to visit condign punishment upon the guilty, as witness the experience of Raphael Hays, '94, working as a student assistant in his office. A constable came stalking in from Lewistown with a warrant for the arrest of a student charged with having "done wrong by our Nell." "Docky" Reed, severe in aspect as befitted the President of the Board of the School of Law, expressed in clear tones his doubt as to the validity of the papers and advised that they be checked at the courthouse. Raphael slipped out to bring a timely word of warning to the culprit. Next morning brought the following brief interchange:

Reed: Raphael, did you overhear what I said to that officer?

Hays: No, sir.

Reed: Good. I'm glad you did. [29]

Still later, in interrogating the participants in a riot which had, of all things, grown out of the theft of the co-eds' ice cream in "Ladies' Hall," we find Reed asking one youth the astonishing question, "Was it against me?"

"Oh! No, Doctor! We all love you! We wouldn't do a thing like that against you!"

This reassurance, given in all earnest sincerity, brought from the Doctor an admission that if the to-do had been "against" him he would have resigned. [30] That offer to resign seems to have been consistently effective with trustees, faculty and students.

As a first thing, Reed had moved to improve the comforts and dignity of student life. He replaced the old stoves at once with steam heat. His insistence on respect for property went hand in hand with making it respectable—cutting the grass, resetting the stone steps of Old West, that favorite lounging spot of students even in later years when chapel must needs be held in Bosler. [31] In short, he brought in both well-being and an air of distinction. No less appreciated, he brought the College teams from the fairground to an athletic field of their own— land in the open lots to the west, between High and Louther Streets. [32] In 1909, two years before his retirement, it would be replaced by the present Biddle Field. [33]

Team sports had all begun with intramural contests. Intercollegiate baseball had been played since 1876, football since 1885. Football, rougher and more popular, met tragedy in its second season with the death of Sophomore E. Herbert Garrison in the Swarthmore game. Faculty minutes reveal a tight

Beta Theta Pi Chess Club, 1892. Clyde B. Furst and James H. Baker *vs* Vergil
Prettyman and Paul Appenzellar; Frederick S. Still *vs* Robert E. McAlarney.

Left: Lacrosse, *c.* 1890. Right: Student Group, 1871.

Football, 1889.

In the new Gymnasium, *c.* 1887.

supervision after that, due in part to the perils of the game, and in part to the spirit of mayhem and mischief which attended it on nearly every campus. In 1883, students "in their football suits" had been laughed at, but by January 29, 1898, pride in the local warriors of the gridiron had come to life and we find the *Carlisle Daily Herald* giving space to the College's new football caps—"light in color, containing the letters D. F. B. T." No mention here of the College colors, though in *Songs of Dickinson*, 1900, they are recognized in spirited pieces by one young alumnus and three undergraduates. The University of Maryland's Maroon and Black came in 1897—adopted, it is said, after a Dental Department professor won a prize with plates made of maroon and black rubber. The folklore of Bowling Green traces its Olive and Brown to the Dean's admiration of a lady's hat. In more dignified fashion, Dickinson's Red and White go back to the rival red and white roses of the old student societies. [34] Intercollegiate basketball and tennis came to Dickinson in 1900, soccer not until 1932.

Meanwhile, if football seemed rowdy and dangerous to many, it could still compare favorably to a cane rush or any of the other "class scraps." These ran high and wild through fall and winter, the lowerclassmen pitted against one another in furious melee, sometimes in an announced battle royal for cane or flag or pants—but always with Juniors abetting the Frosh, Sophs urged on by the Seniors—the struggle seen as part of their initiation into manhood. So also the greater and more dangerous evil of hazing. Hazing did not attract students, and carried always the threat of further trouble, as when the father of John Gibson Cornwell, '97, talked of bringing suit against the College, sounding his anger in the press. Young Cornwell had been bound and gagged by masked students, his head partly shaved and daubed with molasses, and then his whole suffering frame "deluged" with lager beer. [35] Reed had first come upon the "evil and barbarous" custom one night soon after his arrival in 1889—following a crowd of boys into a dark room where he saw a Freshman tossed in a blanket to the College yell. [36] At the opening of the next academic year it was announced that "hazing will not be tolerated under any circumstances." [37] Yet in the face of every prohibition it continued, supported, after all, by precisely the same principle which had guided college faculties and trustees for so many years—the idea that stern discipline is the one sure mold of acceptable behavior.

Hazing, often with sadistic byplay, was increasing on almost every American campus. At Carlisle it had its point of concentration in "The Sophomore Band," highly secret, terrorizing Frosh, faculty and the community at large. This organization had even, in time, its official journal, *The Onion*, "Greatest of all the Dickinson publications," and, as Vol. 1, No. 1 proclaims, "Published in Hell by His Majesty the Devil." *The Onion* ran from about 1907 to 1911 (all surviving issues are undated). As far as George Edward Reed could make out, all of this organized virulence had grown out of the celebrations of Admiral Dewey's victory at Manila Bay. The Band staged "a night of riot and disorder. To accomplish their purpose the first objective was the demolition of every electric lamp on the campus that under cover of darkness they might conduct their operations without fear of capture or detection. This accomplished, the next objective was to make attacks upon other students and, as usual, to make assaults upon two of the most venerable of the College buildings; then to kindle bonfires upon the campus, and similar outrageous efforts. To check these performances was a very difficult if not impossible task." They were finally checked—if no more—by enlisting a counter force of "resolute upper classmen." [38]

Multiple student conflict and rivalry made the faculty somewhat less an object of combative attention. Yet in February, 1908, when the faculty punished four Sophomores for "Insubordination and Conspiracy," nearly the whole student body seemed about to join them in these odious sins, and forced a lessening of the penalty. Students themselves were beginning to feel a need for regulation. Student self-government emerged from faculty-encouraged efforts to bring some order to counteract the fighting and hazing. The first Pan-Hellenic League voted to dissolve in 1907 after two years, the majority dashing out on campus and giving "a yell to show their satisfaction." [39] November 4, 1908, brought the Student Assembly, its stated purpose "to organize the male students of the college into a body so that they may intelligently and in an orderly manner consider

the problems affecting them." Its representative Senate would
have lost at once all semblance of authority but for the physical
prowess of its President, an older student from the neighboring
farmland, "Dad" Peters. [40] Completely responsible student
government would remain an unrealized dream. An attempt to
set up an honor system in 1895 had quickly collapsed. [41] It was
followed by an "Honor Guild" which Freshmen were encouraged to join, a more gradual approach, persisting for some years
but failing to reach its goal. [42] Yet Reed's faculty did achieve a
situation in which many examinations were unmonitored, with
other evidences of a healthy rapport between student and
teacher.

A college may well seem one of the most over-organized
bodies in existence. In Reed's small but growing group of young
people there were more facets of activity than can be detailed
here. Everyone belonged, of course, to Belles Lettres or Union
Philosophical—girls excepted. The girls had their Harman Society, founded in 1896 and named, with truly feminine sweetness
and whimsicality, for coeducation's staunch opponent. [43] It had
been the year of his retirement, and the old Doctor was enormously pleased and complaisant when the young ladies came to
ask his permission. From then on three groups met on Wednesday afternoons, the time set aside over many years for literary
society business, and, when the societies had faded out, still
kept free of class assignments because of use of the time by
faculty committees. There would not be enough girls for a rival
to Harman until the McIntire Society was founded in 1921 in
the twilight years of this ancient aspect of college life.

Ten fraternities and two sororities were on campus by the
close of Reed's administration. Chapter houses had come in.
The ever-fluctuating organization of the small group of independent men had begun. The four classes no longer had the
solidarity of pre-fraternity days, but were held together by the
imminence of battle and by their occasional banquets or other
affairs—always planned with great secrecy in order to frustrate
attempts at disruption or the kidnapping of speakers and officers. The Class of 1896 had the first Freshman banquet, carried off successfully with the class flag flying from the roof of
the Hotel Wellington, despite rumors that the Sophs, aided by

Law and Preps, meant to break it up; and in 1905 the tradition was still maintained, with Professor and Mrs. Filler and the co-ed guests arriving in closed carriages. [44] Nineteen Two rich in Phi Betes and hedonists, a class which "never left anything untried," revived the old custom of funereal rites, this time for Walker's text in economics, taught by Major Pilcher—the participants in costume, the songs printed for the convenience of mourners. [45] Seniors ended their four years with song and ceremony, including the "class ride," leaving at an early hour for Doubling Gap, tin horns blowing, and back at night after a full day in the hills. [46]

With all this, there were the Glee Club, College Quartet, Mandolin and Guitar Clubs, and other groups continually rising and fading. The Department of Music, begun with the 1907-08 academic year on a promise of financial support that was not made good, was so successful that Reed recommended its continuance. [47] In his determined enthusiasms, Reed was only too ready to start a project at once and hope for the means later, but here it was carried along on the enthusiasm of others also. The Y.M.C.A. was a pervasive hazy influence over a long period, allied to that of the Honor Guild. Small and steadfast, the students' Prohibition League stood as an island among the streams and currents of the time. The professors, as an escape from the duties which otherwise brought them together, had a Faculty Club, social but with a "literary flavor." [48] The athletic field was a social meeting place for all as well, and the teams important elements in the complex pattern of the academic body. Over it all the faculty maintained its watchful supervision—a faculty now more loved and respected than ever before, sharing this esteem with such other focal points of familiar affection as Noah Pinkney, waiting outside East with his basket of "Dickinson Sandwiches" ("Fine as silk! Bo'n today, sah!"), and Dick, the lumbering and beloved Great Dane who was photographed with the teams and attended every chapel, occasionally melting the services into gales of laughter by an enormous yawn during prayer or Scripture. [49]

Alien and fond, the co-eds were a coherent group in the midst of all this, and more so once they were established in "Ladies' Hall," the former Hepburn residence in Pomfret Street

Henry Martyn Harman. Photograph by Charles Francis Himes, *c.* 1897.

Harman Literary Society, 1897.

("Lloyd Hall" after 1905). Zatae had set a standard for those who came after, and by 1909 a masculine "irritation of feeling" that 25 per cent of the student body was winning "an altogether disproportionate share of College honors and prizes" reached trustee level. [50] A committee, on sober consideration, found "intellectual superiority" equally to blame with "the fact that the women in the College have fewer distractions, by far, to encounter than the men." A strict limitation to 25 per cent was recommended. To most young men, the studious girl was still an object of mingled awe and repulsion. Clyde Bowman Furst, '93, later Secretary of Teachers College, Columbia University, put it in a song with a ponderous refrain:

> Osteology, morphology,
> Biology, histology,
>   And sciences which make the brain in furious frenzy whirl,
>   In furious frenzy whirl, in furious frenzy whirl,
> Conchology, geology,
> Ichthyology, zoology,
>   Are some of the minor studies of the Dickinson College girl. [51]

Amy Fisher was the first woman to teach, taking classes in the Preparatory School for two years after her graduation in 1895, where she had delivered one of the commencement "Honorary Orations," *Post Tenebra Lux.* Gallantly, the *Dickinsonian* felt the same way:

> When Dickinson as a university has her Colleges of Liberal Arts, Medicine, Fine Arts and Law the new woman will also have the opportunity of occupying the executive position in the line of Nisbet, Durbin and Reed. [52]

The *Dickinsonian,* still edited by a board drawn from the old literary societies, surely led all extra-curricular activities in endurance and value. We may marvel at its restrained journalism, in the face of all else that was going on. Beginning with both news and literature on a monthly basis, it had now reached biweekly status, and from 1896 to 1902 separated the functions and published a "Monthly Edition" as a literary magazine. [53] The twin operation reached a climax under the editorship of Boyd Lee Spahr—"Yodeler" Spahr, a Phi Beta Kappa student of

1900, nicknamed for the most conspicuous of many talents. As with Moncure Conway's *Collegian,* failure to maintain the full standard brought whip-cracking—in this case a publication by the retired board, *The Deadly Parallel.* [54] *Microcosm,* the yearbook, almost always a project of the Junior Class, was another perennial flowering, beside which *The Onion* and other more highly perfumed blossoms briefly shone.

Drama—legitimate drama—had flourished early at Dickinson, with high tragedy the thing for sophisticated Carlisle—"The Fatal Discovery," 1786, "The Fair Penitent," 1797. Yet the curtain of ecclesiastical displeasure had soon descended. It rose again, if only briefly, in the liberation of Reed's years. A drama group was formed in 1894, the year of the downfall of the traditional "Oratorical Burlesques." Those popular entertainments had ended at the Carlisle Opera House, June 1, 1894, when Freshman Ray Zug, draining his beer bottle, had hurled it at a Sophomore, striking a townswoman in the face and severely injuring her. The new group, active through 1895, revived in the spring of 1901, was organized at the opening of the next term as the Dickinson Dramatic Club. [55]

Faculty watched with concern. Some professors reported a lessening of attention to study. Anxiety and unease prevailed. On October 19, 1903, "The President of the College was instructed to take such measures as will prevent the ladies of the College from appearing in public as members of the Dramatic Club." [56] It was a lady of the College, Mrs. Lucretia Jones McAnney, Matron at Lloyd Hall and later Instructor in Oratory, who revived the flagging activity, and with new brilliance. The Dramatic Club was pulled together once more in response to her incredible proposal of Shakespeare at commencement. Through many discouragements, both incidental and deliberately applied, it was done—"A Midsummer Night's Dream" was staged in front of East College, and with resounding success. So much so that President Reed asked the lady to direct another production for the hundred and twenty-fifth anniversary commencement in 1908. "As You Like It" delighted again a large audience. But alas. One of the many Methodist clergy present, a strict constructionist on the *Discipline,* voiced complaint and Reed, aware of rising hostility, responded. The curtain fell once more, but would rise again after the election of a new President three years later. [57]

Debating, so long fostered in the literary societies, had now too much else in competition with it. We find faculty setting debate subjects, a sign of flagging interest. Fresh impetus came in 1902 with a Debating League for intercollegiate contests—and these were further enlivened by the presence of cheerleaders, alert to call for a yell at every telling ratiocination. The Contemporary Club of 1908, an early independent men's organization, was formed around a debating program. [58] Debating was still a feature of college life which, more than anything else, brought contemporary issues face to face with the traditional curriculum.

Thanks to the amazing hardihood of academic tradition, the eighteenth century's emphasis on oratory had its peculiar and not too happy effect on the standards of this later day. The commencement oration of Dickinson's early years was a public demonstration of the candidate's learning and competence. Yet as class size increased, orations were cut down in time to five minutes or less, and then the alternative of a senior essay was allowed the same brevity. Under Reed, Seniors had a free month for this final effort, but their productions have all the thinness of a ten-minute oration. Only occasionally, among the hundreds in the College archives, does solid substance appear, as with Guy Carleton Lee's *Development of the Council. A Chapter from English Judicial History,* or Clyde Furst's *Study of the Robin Hood Ballads,* and these are thin indeed in contrast to an honors paper of recent years. [59]

In the curriculum, Reed found students clamoring from the first for more electives. His larger faculty could meet the demand, with due attention to distribution requirements. No one, as Morgan observed, can ever deprive the student of "his God-given right to complain," and here grades and examinations were a prime target from the first. [60] Even this late, oral examinations had not been replaced entirely by written ones. The "exemption system" of examination was urged, and rejected, in 1896. [61] Letter grades were introduced the next year, replacing professorial comment. [62] Hebrew was dropped with Harman's retirement, and while a full course schedule of Greek and Latin went on, he had taken with him an element of scholarly appreciation that would not easily be replaced. [63] Science gained ground with a "Medical Preparatory Course" in 1895 and a Biology Department in 1899, under Henry Matthew Stephens, '92, returning from study at the Massachusetts Institute of Technology. [64] The faculty of ten, at Reed's arrival, had become twenty-one by 1911, in addition to the ten masters in Prep School and Trickett's corps of seven.

A first act of Reed's had been the dismissal of Aaron Rittenhouse, Thomas Beaver Professor of English Literature, judged incompetent on the basis of disorderly classes. One of the few advantages of enlisting teachers from the ministry was that they could be returned with ease and honor to the Church. Two of Reed's appointments in English became famous campus figures. The Beaver chair was taken in 1890 by a scholarly Down Easter who had left the faculty of Merritt Caldwell's Maine Wesleyan Seminary to earn his Ph.D., Bradford Oliver McIntire. Montgomery Porter Sellers, Class of 1893, had joined McIntire as adjunct that year, becoming full professor in 1905 and Dean in 1928. A shy and industrious bachelor, he long carried half the work of the department at a minimal salary. [65] Trustee Wilbur Fisk Sadler, dedicated to the idea of a quality faculty, had resigned from the Board in 1892 over Reed's policy of aiming at the lowest possible salary figure. [66] Yet by and large the members of Reed's faculty did honor to themselves and their profession. One finds them feeling concern on the quality of honorary degree recipients, and frowning darkly at the mere rumor that the Athletic Association was enlisting "promising men" upon standards of its own. [67] Individually, Reed's faculty was a mélange of men with impeccable academic background and achievement, such as Robert William Rogers, Professor of English Bible and Semitic History, or John Frederick Mohler, '87, Professor of Physics; of solid young alumni like Cornelius W. Prettyman, '91, and Mervin Grant Filler, '93; and among these one finds some energetic spirits from other professions, ranging from the brilliant Swiss theologian Michael John Cramer (his wife was a sister of General Grant) to the versatile Major James Evelyn Pilcher (his wife a niece of Mrs. Reed). [68]

In 1893, Reed organized his faculty under a board of four class deans, with himself as chairman. This group, later the "Committee on Government and Discipline," superceded the senior professor (now Himes) in controlling affairs during the President's absences. [69] Three years later, Himes resigned. He had prepared resignation statements in 1892 and 1894, their tenor suggesting an expected alumni reaction that might unseat Reed. [70] Some response came, but brought no action. When "Dutchy" resigned, so also did his friend and ally, "Dad" Harman. Himes was fifty-eight, Harman seventy-four. Both had enjoyed student popularity of a more solid sort than Reed's, and Himes long continued the rapport with fraternity affairs, his annual party for Seniors, and the like.

Also in 1896, Reed promoted "Jim Henry" Morgan to Dean of the College. Morgan cites this among evidences of Reed's impartiality, as he had been a supporter of McCauley, while Reed was rated an ally of Trickett. [71] There was a more obvious reason. Reed, always lenient, needed a firm hand, and had found it. Morgan was a big man, rough in manner, in class maintaining a precise standard, warm to a good student, harsh to others. In vacation, he hunted, fished, hiked for miles. Now he took up the duties expected of a college dean in that day with all his thoroughness and all the ardor of his own undergraduate career. He was hated—"Reed's penny-dog and doer of dirty work in snooping on students." [72] His fame was sung, most of the verses too ribald for preservation, but we have snatches:

> There is no flesh in Morgan's stony heart;
> It does not feel for man. [73]

Newspaperman Dean Hoffman, '02, recalled:

He prowled about the campus at all hours, and the students who could pull a fast one without his interference felt they had reached the heights of achievement. . . . Being somewhat of a physical giant, Dr. Morgan seemed utterly fearless. Sometimes I think he enjoyed the old-fashioned class rush as much as the rest of us. Certainly he did not hang about the fringe of the melee when the two phalanxes collided. He was into it, pulling out boys and tossing them aside or grabbing them by the collars long enough to catalogue them for subsequent

Top left: Charles Francis Himes, *c.* 1900. Top right: Physics, "Exercise No. 108," Class of 1889. Bottom: Laboratory in Tome, *c.* 1901. Professor William Birckhead Lindsay and Instructor Leroy McMaster.

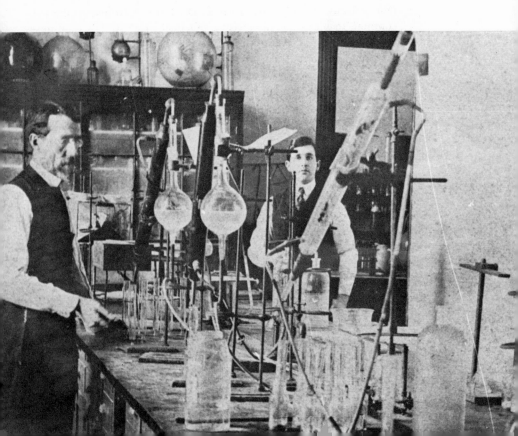

citations or maybe just for the lust of battle. Despite his interference I think the students admired him for the guts he had in mixing up in these physical combats. [74]

In addition to the Greek of his professorship, Morgan had been teaching Freshman English, Rhetoric, Logic and Political Economy, the latter including "Constitution of the United States" on a discussion basis—"and I am pleased to believe that this has been one of the most pleasant and profitable features of the class. It is a plan I am developing yearly . . . . " [75] Succeeding Harman as Librarian, we find him pleading, as so many had done before, for modern books. [76] Another editor, Robert Emmet MacAlarney, '93, gives us a still nearer picture of this new force in Reed's faculty:

> He was tall, gaunt, with humorous twinkles behind his glasses as he regarded us. Other memory details are: diagonal "cutaway" coat with braided edges, lean and knuckly fingers continually playing with a heavy gold watch chain from which depended a Phi Beta Kappa key, a genuinely warm smile and an equally impressive frown when some of us inept students floundered. And he was a swell Grecian. Not the rapt, dreamy scholar type, such as Dr. Harman (whose memory I continue to bless) but the incisive, practical coach. Unless I am mistaken there was a vivid appreciation of pagan beauties beneath Dr. Morgan's classroom carapace. In any event I like to think there was. But since we were a very primitive minded little Methodist college from 1889 to 1893, naturally an instructor did *not* expatiate on the love of life of the Olympians, or those who frequented the Painted Stoa. But Dr. Morgan cued us, and library digging did the rest. Furthermore he was a square-shooter. Severe, when discipline was at stake—and many of us were unlicked cubs—he "played the game" as a faculty member. I sat under some fine men at Dickinson. In addition to Morgan: Dad Harman, Robert W. Rogers (gallant gentleman, much too fine to waste his time on us), Flip Durrell (math., later of Lawrenceville) and Dutchy Himes. I remember. [77]

Credit for the founding of the Library Guild, March 3, 1903, a Friends of the Library group dedicated to raising a permanent fund for the purchase of books, should go to McIntire, aided by Filler. [78] The need had been recognized by Reed since 1892. [79] He was that rara avis, a library-minded

president. Later, aided by the ubiquitous Pilcher, he served a
term as State Librarian of Pennsylvania, and was invited by
President McKinley to become Librarian of Congress. [80] In
1900, he appointed for the first time a Librarian of the College
with no other duty, Leon C. Prince, a faculty son and later
faculty member; and in 1905 he recommended that the
$10,000 from the Alexander E. Patton bequest be added to the
Library endowment. [81] Prince was succeeded by Captain Alfred
John Standing, a former teacher at Indian schools in the West,
who doubled as "Curator of Buildings and Grounds," a newly
established office. [82]

Administration could no longer be a faculty sideline. The
first Registrar, Chester A. Ames, appeared in 1900. [83] In 1906
the President was given an assistant in his development work,
and later Morgan, as Dean had to be relieved of some teaching
duties. [84]

President Reed owed most of his success in development to
his brethren in the Church, notably to the Rev. Dr. William
Wilson Evans, for a time pastor at Carlisle and long a friend and
trustee of the College—a man of means and influence, with the
portly frame and down-flowering moustache of the turn-of-the-
century executive. W. W. Evans had arranged the bequest that
brought William Weidman Landis to Dickinson in the Susan
Powers Hoffman Chair of Mathematics, and persuaded the Rev.
J. Z. Lloyd to transform "Ladies' Hall" into "Lloyd Hall." [85]
The Central Pennsylvania Conference, and individuals in it, contributed generously but always insufficiently, and always with
that possessiveness which discouraged donations from outside
the denomination. To Evans and his confreres education must
always be secondary to worship. The first major building of
Reed's administration, largely an Evans accomplishment, was
the Allison Memorial Church, dedicated on March 6, 1892. [86]
Here was a long-awaited consummation for Carlisle Methodists
and yet—at a cost of $40,000—a very minor contribution to the
intellectual growth of the College. [87] William Clare Allison had
had, at Reed's arrival, plans of his own for educational expansion at Dickinson. He would make other gifts, but the long-
range plan did not reappear.

Two years earlier, Himes had sounded out Miss Matilda

Wilkins Denny and Mrs. Mary O'Hara Denny Spring of Pittsburgh, and found them favorable to the idea of the old Denny
homestead, across West Street from the campus, becoming a
College memorial to the family.[88] Here was the site, if funds
for building could be found. In 1895, work was begun on a
large classroom edifice to cost the same as the church. It was
completed a year later, largely on borrowed money. At a meeting of December 2, 1896, Reed suggested a subscription, to
open with a contribution of $50 from each trustee. General
King, newly elected and a man of large ideas, announced himself as in favor and ready to give his share. "No motion being
made to carry out this suggestion of the Pres. the matter was
dropped." The Rev. Dr. David Henry Carroll spoke for a loan,
but against a large loan. General King stood stoutly for borrowing: "Without debt there is no progress. The Building should be
finished."[89]

After eight years of use, Denny Hall was burned to the
ground, March 3, 1904. Freshman George Briner, sitting near
the door in a third floor classroom, heard a hesitant knock, and,
welcoming any interruption, leapt to open it. The shy Adjunct
Professor Sellers was there, saying something about smoke coming from Professor Landis's office—not too unusual in the face
of Landis's heavy addiction to cigars. However, class was dismissed and all went tumbling down the stairs. Briner and Frank
Green ran back up with pails of water, but when they opened
the door it was to find the office a mass of flame which swal-
lowed each bucketful with only an angry hiss.[90] Rebuilding on
an expanded foundation was authorized in June, to be financed
by the $17,000 insurance and a campaign based on a complex
of memorial elements.[91]

In 1900 Reed had recommended a new dormitory as "an
imperative necessity."[92] In its stead, as offering a surer financial return, the flourishing Preparatory School was given a huge
but thriftily designed structure, completed in June, 1902. At
that time $55,000 was still owing on the work, and Reed was
"looking far and wide" for the sum.[93] He was still looking
when Denny burned. Among those to whom he turned in this
desperate plight was Moncure Conway—regarded by Central
Pennsylvania's faithful as a mad and dangerous infidel. Conway

Denny Hall I. Preliminary drawing by Thomas B. Langsdale, architect.

Denny Hall II, as rebuilt, 1905.

had been awarded an L.H.D. in 1892, and while on campus had helped judge the Junior Class orations, insisting upon an "Especial and honorable mention" to William M. Watts for his on Walt Whitman—an author generally regarded (like Conway himself) as suspect and fearsome.[94] But now Conway met the crisis. He turned to his friend Andrew Carnegie, with whom he had been working in the cause of international peace. Carnegie, hearing the story of the fire, responded with an offer of $50,000 if the new building could stand as a monument to Conway. Reed, in anguish at a condition that could not be met, told of the commitment to a Denny memorial—and then deftly advanced the cause of the "Collegiate Preparatory Building." The gift came. Reed would always remember his walk through that morning's brilliant sunshine to the home of trustee Edward William Biddle—meeting the Judge outside his door—holding up the envelope—drawing out the letter and check with a trembling hand.[95]

Later, he asked permission to carve on the facade under Conway's name, "The Gift of Andrew Carnegie." Mr. Carnegie replied tersely that he never allowed his name on a building unless he had paid for the whole of it. Equal to this, Reed replied that its full cost was $63,480. Back came a check for $13,480, and the stone was inscribed.[96] So came into being Conway Hall, an excellent boarding school with a complete high school program, from commerical course to college preparatory; beside and within the College, an almost duplicate world of study, teeming with battle and delight, its banners waving overhead, its alma mater devoutly sung to the tune of "Fair Harvard":

> The hours we have spent within thy dear walls
> Are pearls in the setting of life . . . .[97]

Carnegie's was the largest gift the College had ever received. A heady draft! Freethinker Moncure Conway had opened wide a door, and George Edward Reed's situation was like that of the college student suddenly confronted by satisfactions and opportunities never tasted within home walls. He had made contact with a great new influence in American education, the philanthropic trusts. They were teaching college presidents the value of the earned Ph.D., and to think in terms of scholarly standards as never before. Nearest at hand to Reed was the Carnegie Corporation for the Advancement of Teaching, founded in 1906 with a capital of $31,000,000. He applied for a place in its pension program, and learned—as had Dickinson's Presbyterians of earlier years—that "sectarianism" can be an encumbrance. Thirteen trustees were present in Philadelphia, February 14, 1907, when Reed proposed a startling declaration:

> Resolved, That the Board of Trustees of Dickinson College heartily endorses the action of the President of the College in making application for recognition by the said Carnegie Foundation for the Advancement of Teaching.
>
> Resolved, second, that the President of the College, who is also ex officio President of the Board of Trustees, be instructed to forward to the President of the Carnegie Foundation for the Advancement of Teaching, the following statement of facts:
>
> 1. That Dickinson College is under the friendly auspices of the Methodist Episcopal Church, but has never been owned or controlled by any church body.
>
> 2. That by the Charter of the College the Board of Trustees is a self-perpetuating body and fills all vacancies in its membership, save such as are filled by Alumni Association organized under a plan for alumni representation sanctioned by the Board of Trustees.
>
> 3. That no religious organization, as such, has or can have, representation in the governing body of the College.
>
> 4. That under section 9 of the Charter of the College no denominational test is, or can be, imposed in the choice of trustees, officers or teachers, or in the admission of students; neither are denominational doctrines or tenets taught to the students.
>
> 5. That the publication in any periodical of any church, or in any secular year book, or in any educational report, or elsewhere, that Dickinson College is under denominational control is not in harmony with the facts and is made without authority of the Board of Trustees.
>
> Resolved, third, that in order to avoid misunderstanding on the part of the public, the President of the College is herewith directed in the future to report the College as non-sectarian.

This alone might not have passed, as it did, had not Reed combined it with explicit farther objectives of bright promise. It was a play for escape from debt into his vision of the future, a mingling of artfulness with that imaginative but fully sincere idealism. Dickinson College must have a "Department of Peace and Public Service," grandly housed in a "Temple of Peace," otherwise to be known as "The William Penn Memorial Hall." Conway helped to detail its proposed curriculum, while his son, Eustace, contributed plans for the Temple. [98] Conway came to Carlisle and delivered, April 25, 1907, an address jointly celebrating the 225th Anniversary of William Penn's Frame of Government for the People of Pennsylvania, and "the department founded here this day—Peace and Public Service— . . . the first of its kind in any institution." [99]

His address was the long and weighty effort of an old man, but his massive body, flowing hair and beard, gave it a patriarchal and prophetic cast. Six months later, alone in Paris, his life of searching ardor would end, but now, with final eloquence, he appealed to the single benefactor and to the world:

> *Implora pace,* O my friend from whom I now part. Entreat for peace not of deified thunderclouds but of every man, woman, child thou shalt meet. Do not merely offer the prayer "Give peace in our time," but do thy part to answer it! Then, though the whole world be at strife, there shall be peace in thee.
>
> Farewell! [100]

But when the plans for the department and temple were brought to the hard-headed little man at Castle Skibo, he turned them down. He had done enough for Dickinson College, and that was that. [101] Reed went on. He had at least the pension plan. The February meeting had authorized also a financial campaign, and he would keep his temple in prospect still. Three years later he did find a professor, George A. Crider who took, without salary, the "Chair of Social Problems and Business Institutions," defined as "the first section of the Department of Peace and Public Service." [102] He was determined, as Benjamin Rush had been, to balance the hell of war with a heaven of peace—though unable to see it with Rush's glint of ironic humor. [103]

He was not amused when, striding down the walk to morning chapel, he found a large privy, torn from among the lilacs in some neighboring yard, set up in front of Bosler Hall and identified by a sign, "DEPARTMENT OF PEACE AND PUBLIC SERVICE." That would have been easier to bear had he not had so many other critics as well. On June 3, 1907, trustees Evans and Carroll moved to reconsider the February statement, as disturbing to the church relationship. This was tabled. [104] But opposition to Reed had long been present in the local conference, with charges of loose morals among students, loose doctrine in class and the like. Reed's declaration of 1907 on independence from church control was seen as a crowning perfidy and would be a sore point between Conference and College for the next thirty years. [105] At the commencement of 1908 a commission headed by the Rev. Hiles C. Pardoe, author of a novel based on Dickinson history, was investigating, and would report an insoluble "moral" bond. [106] Reed's involvement with Moncure Conway was at the same time highly suspect, for all of Judge Biddle's reassurance "that the world of mammon and frivolity possessed no attractions for this serious thinker." [107] Reed was more vulnerable on the slow progress of the financial campaign and that continuing annual deficit of $6,000 to $7,000. [108] No wonder, then that the harried President yielded so tamely at that commencement of 1908 on the issue of "As You Like It."

Yet in the Board meetings of that year, on King's motion, he was given a rising vote of confidence. One other action also augured well. The young lawyer, Boyd Lee Spahr, was elected "to fill a vacancy in the Philadelphia Conference representation." Here, as at other colleges in these years, we see the young alumni exerting pressure for control, for scholarship over piety, for the professional over the clerical educator. Alumni-elected trustees had come in in 1891, insuring alumni spokesmen on the Board, but these might come and go with their terms. [109] Here was the new viewpoint more solidly represented by a man of twenty-eight, as successful in life as he had been in college, not a Methodist, inordinately proud of his school and determined to place and hold it among the best.

Having gained this new blood and promise, the trustees closed their deliberations and went out to the rites and fanfare of Commencement Day. The procession had become more formalized since Nisbet's faculty, trustees and scholars had paraded out from Liberty Alley to the church on the square so long ago. From Civil War days and for many years, trustee William Ryland Woodward had led it out as Marshal, followed by "Judge" Watts, head janitor, arrayed for the occasion in ministerial black with a tall silk hat and bearing the red-ribboned diplomas on a silver salver, and after him the band, and then the trustees, faculty and the class. Now Horatio King was Marshal, big body, big moustache and sparkling eye. When Reed had first come, only he had worn a gown, then the students followed suit, and now (forced into it by long-applied student pressure) all the faculty moved with him in a flutter of black poplin and the panoply of academic colors. [110]

On February 16, 1911, Dr. Reed presented his resignation, ending twenty-two years of service, and at their June meeting the Board elected Eugene Allen Noble to succeed him. They acted with three criteria:

1. A Methodist, "preferably a minister."

2. "A man of scholarly attainments, a good business man, with executive ability, capable of managing a large corporation; and able to bring money to Dickinson College."

3. A man "capable of acceptably representing the College in public, preferably an educator."

Noble was an alumnus of Wesleyan, 1891, where he had won the commendation of Caleb T. Winchester as a student of literature. He had headed Centenary, a Methodist junior college for women in New Jersey, from 1902 until 1908, when he had become President of Goucher College. [111] There he had been the personal choice of John Frederick Goucher (a Dickinson alumnus of 1868), and later it would be rumored that Goucher was not unwilling to pass the acquisition on to his alma mater. [112] Noble's name had been on a list of ten submitted to the meeting by Reed. Experience would show that he measured up to the three criteria well—with the exception of the rather prolix No. 2. He had found grave financial problems at Goucher, found Dickinson's almost as bad, and he lacked the necessary Midas touch.

Immediately after the election, on the motion of Boyd Lee Spahr, a charter revision was approved, authorizing the Board to

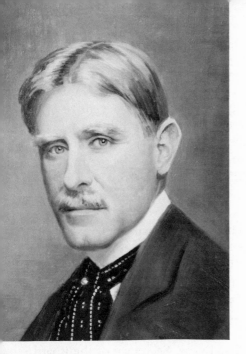

Top left: Eugene Allen Noble. By Margaret F. Winner, 1930. Top right: Mervin Grant
Filler. By Wilbur Fisk Noyes, 1931. Bottom: The academic procession on Founders
Day, *c.* 1910, going to Nisbet's grave in the Old Cemetery, Carlisle.

elect its own President. The President of the College would continue as a member ex officio, but not as its executive officer. [113] This, May 27, 1912, brought the Hon. Edward W. Biddle, President Judge of the Cumberland County Courts, into the new office. Let the President of the College be a Methodist minister. The President of the Board, his superior, was now a layman of conspicuous ability, living within the fold of the Second Presbyterian Church.

Dr. Reed, in looking back upon his own inauguration as primitive and barbarous, may well have been comparing it to Noble's. That took place on Tuesday afternoon, May 28, 1912. General King fired the opening guns with a speech on Dickinson's long history. John K. Tener, Governor of Pennsylvania, administered the "civil oath of office" with an appropriate introduction. A "religious oath" followed, with a delegate of Bishop William Burt officiating. Dr. Evans, Secretary of the Board of Trustees, presented seal and key. Judge Biddle, aided by the Presidents of the Senior and Junior Classes, invested Noble with "the official hood." Dr. Morgan spoke for the faculty, and then the new President came forward with the culminating address, later to be published, a revival of those formal statements on educational policy with which Nisbet and others had begun their careers. [114] He pled for "the old discipline," as "a form of educational pragmatism worthy of modern exposition," and in his peroration extolled John Dickinson. Commencement followed on the next day, with honors to prominent men in the scholastic world, to men of wealth and affairs, and even—a quite new departure—to an artist, Timothy Cole.

For the new President was a man of culture before all else—sensitive face, large, thoughtful eyes, the trimmed moustache of the new century. The artistic tastes, the dignity, the emphasis on ceremony, did not appeal widely to college men of this day, although there was one present at this time, Freshman William Wilcox Edel, who watched it all with ardent admiration and would become one of the few student friends of Eugene Allen Noble. [115] Happy, too, was Lucretia McAnney, back again at once with Shakespeare. When Noble left, so would she, advancing to the Morningside Players of Columbia University. [116]

Noble had great personal charm, was delightful in conversation or an after-dinner speech, and imparted to College affairs a
new dignity and taste. His commencement ceremonies were
models of grace, the fewer orations interspersed not with the
blare of a band but with selections such as Franz von Suppé's
"Light Cavalry March" or Verdi's "Sextette from Lucia di Lam-
mermoor." Such matters as student recruitment, pursued so
ardently by Reed, he left to others. The enrollment declined
sharply—a fatal reversal. He had not yet won the faculty allegiance which Reed had only with some difficulty been able to
command. Nor could Reed's popularity with the students be
passed on to another. Noble sought to create a new image, and
some faculty, some students, did not take to it warmly. A deri-
sive printed sheet, *Revelations*, 1911-12, went the rounds. Here
we learn that Noble's concept of "The Dickinson Type" had
brought upon him the detestation of "half the college." He was
accused of padding the student damage account to add luxuries
to the President's House. One senses a background of faculty
murmuring similar to that Reed had faced at first. Morgan,
unlikely to have had much personal rapport with the new sophistication, comes in for equivocal praise—"We want to say a
few words in behalf of Morgan, we all know what a janus faced,
truth juggler he is [but] when he was in college he was a good
sport and some what of a hell-raiser not at all the 'Dickinson
Type.' "

Financially, the new President was already in trouble. By
1911 a debt of $120,000 had accumulated, against an endow-
ment of $320,000, and uncommitted investments were being
applied to it, reducing income.[117] On May 27, 1912, eve of
Noble's inauguration, Treasurer John S. Bursk reported an operating deficit of $4,867, with no funds for urgently needed re-
pairs—"I venture to hope that something will be done to relieve
the situation."

Noble gained some relief when the trustees of the Metzger
Institute, August 15, 1913, agreed that their building and income should be used henceforth "for the advantage of the students of Dickinson College."[118] Lloyd Hall would be sold, and
Metzger Hall begin its long term as a dormitory for co-eds. But
the financial crisis deepened. Without money for maintenance,

equipment everywhere was falling into deplorable condition. In September, representatives of other colleges were forbidden to visit Conway Hall. [119] Noble reported to the Executive Committee, December 5, 1913, that he had appealed to Rockefeller's General Education Board for $50,000. [120] There was small chance of such a grant with the burden of debt increasing. Now Morgan, who had made caustic comment at the outset when Noble added four bathrooms to the President's House, was joined by ten other full professors in protesting their unpaid salaries. The Committee met to deliberate on this ten days later, at the Hotel Commonwealth in Harrisburg. A meeting of the Board was called, January 20, 1914, at the University Club, Philadelphia. There Judge Biddle would announce $4,500 owed to faculty, and borrowing power exhausted. [121] The places of meeting speak of the crisis. The imminence of bankruptcy and closing must not be noised abroad, or loss of students would bring certain ruin. On April 22, at the University Club, President Noble and nine trustees met in emergency session with eight professors, Morgan McIntire, Mohler, Gooding, Filler, Landis, Prettyman and Stephens. It was William Lambert Gooding, Professor of Philosophy and Education ("a great teacher and every inch a gentleman") who put the trouble in a nutshell: President Noble "lacks the will to do." [122]

Noble gave his resignation to the Executive Committee, May 8. [123] The Board, on the Committee's recommendation, elected Morgan Acting President. There had been pressures for an outsider, but they yielded to the will of the Dean's colleagues; and, indeed, it would have been difficult to find an outsider willing to take over. One glimpses the tensions of the final hour, lightly taken, when Leonard Stott Blakey, short-term Professor of Economics and Sociology, dashes off a letter to "Miss C.":

> Commencement is on but its going to prove to be a pretty tame affair. The fireworks are not going off. The powder must be wet. I'm glad President Noble was at his best in the baccalaureate sermon this morning. I wish you might have heard it. He spoke from John 12:21 pointing out the greatness of Hellenism both past and present and showing that its weakness then and now lay in its neglect of the religious, if we may call it that. It has been a hot summer day which

makes it perfectly delightful for commencement. The old campus is beautiful and will no doubt arouse much enthusiasm in the old grad that happens to get back. I love the old building myself.

Tomorrow night the trustees determine upon the future for pres. & policy of the college. So many petty men are busy having their interests pushed by their little group of friends on the board that the old guard on the faculty have become frightened lest they get a figurehead for President and have oiled all wires for Dean Morgan. The Dean has the support of the faculty, for Shadinger and I could see no reason for opposing such a move on the part of the old guard. Its their college, they are its alumni to a man and here they will wait until the first stipend comes from the Carnegie Foundation. [124]

It was, as Blakey said, an unruffled gathering of alumni and parents. Lucretia McAnney, bless her, did introduce a note of surprise by producing Euripides instead of Shakespeare. It was *"Iphigenia in Tauris"* in the Gilbert Murray translation. [125] Perhaps she sensed this as a time when Artemis must intercede to prevent the inhuman sacrifice. So, after a fashion, it had come to pass. The Olympians had spoken. A strong, rough hand of their own, "a swell Grecian," would hold the fasces and make destiny.

The Belles Lettres and Union Philosophical emblems.

There's a tall thin man named Morgan.
He makes as much noise as an organ,
And when he is vexed
Says, "Look at your text!"
And glares at a man like a gorgon.

Anonymous

13

MORGAN

PRESIDENT NOBLE had been absent from campus through all
vacations—"in the mountains," as Dean Morgan had put it, making clear also that he himself had been on duty throughout.[1]
President Morgan would leave town only on College business,
generally the recruiting of students, staying on the job until,
after fourteen years, a breakdown brought him to hospital. Like
the hero-dictator of some ancient city-state, he rode into power
at a time of crisis, and went on to rule with an absolutism which
left its impress on the scene long after he had departed from it.
It is a story of one man's amazing strength and disquieting
limitations. He was above all a teacher, a scholastic drillmaster,
and he now extended this character to every part of the college
operation. He set goals he knew he could reach, and within
those limits held to a tough and honest standard of academic
excellence. His teaching of Greek had stood firmly on the text,
but with readiness to criticize "the author, his logic and rhetoric, to call attention to the customs of antiquity, to the geographical references; . . . in short, to compare the ancient world
in its politics and religion with the modern."[2] He would have
no truck with graduate work.[3] He wanted his liberal arts program as clean as possible of special-interest courses such as Business. "My judgment," he said, in sharp opposition to Himes'
thinking, "is decidedly against the technical in connection with
the liberal arts. It is good for the technical, but it is bad for the
liberal arts."[4] He was hostile even to the Law School, because

of its low admissions standard. Alumni athletic scholarships must be geared to all academic principles. His correspondence shows constant, and tactful resistance to largesse in honorary degrees.

At the end of Morgan's regime William Righter Fisher wrote to congratulate him on a college and faculty of high quality—recalling his own experience of 1874, when he had found most of his colleagues "intellectually flabby" and the "managerial background" no better. [5] Yet curiously, to Morgan McCauley was the beau ideal. "His influence upon me was as ointment poured out. He was my college president." [6] The affinity was sacramental rather than actual. One need only compare McCauley's policy statement on the "mild and parental" institution cultivating "intellectual pursuits" with Morgan's:

> It is the policy of the College to be a teaching institution, and its first aim is to furnish wise and expert teaching leadership. To attain this end the College has steadily exalted the teacher, and its policy has been to have mature and experienced teachers in its corps of instruction, without inexperienced tutors. [7]

Long after Morgan's retirement, and with more sophisticated statements of policy in the catalogues, its faculty would still be declaring Dickinson "a teaching college," undiluted by any responsibility for expanding the boundaries of knowledge. Restricted course offerings, with library acquisitions rarely ranging beyond them, were coupled with the admirable determination to achieve excellence within those bounds.

It all ties in with the background of a boy who had been born on a farm in southern Delaware and at the age of thirteen had been taken to Philadelphia by his widowed mother to be educated. She worked as a seamstress while he prepared for college at Rugby Academy. "Harry"—the "Jim Henry" came later—became president of the Dickinson chapter of Phi Kappa Psi, and one of the U. P. editors of the *Dickinsonian*. He won the coveted Pierson gold medal for oratory in his Junior year. At commencement in Emory Chapel, 1878, he delivered the Latin Salutatory—"elocution . . . good, though his manner was somewhat too forcible." [8] With further study in mind, perhaps for the law, perhaps a course at Drew and the ministry, he turned to teaching, as many have done, to earn a living while making up his mind. He became professor and vice-principal at Pennington, teaching English and the commercial course, 1878 to 1881; then a year at Rugby; and in 1882 to Carlisle as Principal of the Dickinson Preparatory School. Two years later, McCauley brought him into the College at Adjunct Professor of Greek, partly as an antidote to Harman's gently lackadaisical teaching, partly to supervise removal of the libraries to the new building, involving problems with which "Dad" could not be expected to cope. Harman had not been consulted in this, first learning of it from the newspapers, an error of tact which did not make for a warm relationship.[9] The *Dickinsonian* spiced the news with its advice to the two new professors, Morgan and Super: "Don't see too much. If you suspect anything irregular, yet not in your line of business, don't make your eyes sore watching too closely," and also, "Don't show a partiality to the co-eds."[10] Both points were wasted on Morgan. He concerned himself with every aspect of student life; and on December 30, 1890, was married to a former co-ed, Mary Rebecca Curran, '88, like himself a winner of the gold medal.

The students planned a "Grand Calathumpian Serenade" for the newlyweds.[11] They approved of Morgan's "rare enthusiasm, ability and skill," and his involvement in everything gave him a unique authority.[12] In the dispute as to the victor of an impromptu cane rush in 1891, the *Dickinsonian* averred that it could be left to Morgan, "who was on the spot," as to which class had the most hands on the cane.[13] In 1890 Reed promoted him to full professor, and in 1892 Bucknell's honorary Ph.D. placed him, outwardly at least, on a par with Super of Modern Languages, who had come with a Boston University doctorate. From 1892 to 1895 Morgan went though the steps of admission to the Methodist ministry.[14] Then followed that career as "Reed's penny-dog and doer of dirty work" already described—he was Dean in the old sense, with disciplinary control as the primary concern.

Here was Morgan's preparation for the presidency, developing a thorough and recognized competence within a limited range. As early as 1892, when he addressed the Association of the Colleges and Preparatory Schools of the Middle States and

Maryland, meeting at Swarthmore, on the effective use of college libraries, he was Dickinson's frequent spokesman. [15] He was an elected school director of Carlisle from 1896 to 1904. [16] Force of character brought leadership. At Reed's retirement in 1911 he had commended Morgan to the trustees as the man to run the College till a successor could be found. In 1914 he was the faculty's choice for President as the only man deemed able to stave off the threat of bankruptcy. [17] He refused the title of "President Pro Tem," took that of Acting President for the first year, and in it demonstrated his ability to overcome the crisis.

Student recruiting was his first recourse. Despite rumors of closing, he added 35 to the student body of 257 in his first year. Four Seniors were refused graduation because of low grades. "This," declared Morgan, "was effective announcement that good academic standards would be maintained at any cost." [18] Each entering class, except during the war years, was larger than that before. On Morgan's recommendation, June 4, 1921, the trustees set a limit of "500, planning no increase in the enrollment of women, but for a small but very gradual increase in the number of men, from 295, the enrollment this year, to 350 or 375, and that this plan to limit the size of the College be announced as our policy—quality rather than quantity being our goal." [19] As so often occurs, the figure crept inexorably beyond the limit. It was 566 at Morgan's retirement in 1928, with an increase in faculty from sixteen to thirty-one.

He ran a tight ship. Reed's imaginative vision went out the window along with Noble's languorous refinement. All was close, shrewd management within close boundaries, setting a pattern of parsimony which lasted right through the boom times of the twenties. There was method in his miserliness. When students came with those $25 scholarship certificates for four years' tuition, Morgan would tell them, as Reed had done, that they were good for $6.25 on each annual bill, no more. But then, on occasion, he would recall his feeling for the original purchaser, making a special small exception for a higher sum and so enlisting a grateful student who might have gone elsewhere. [20]

In the long, slow retreat of classical studies in the American colleges, Morgan's Dickinson kept up a remarkably spirited rear guard action. The studies are more selective but cover a wider range than in Durbin's and Emory's day, and are better designed to give a comprehension of life and literature as a whole. Filler, heading Latin, was promoted by Morgan from class dean to Dean of the College in 1914. Morgan, after his first year as Acting President, gave all his time to administration. His faculty of three in Greek was completed in June, 1916, with the arrival of Herbert Wing, Jr., Harvard, '09, fresh from his Ph.D. at Wisconsin and a year in Greece. Wing, stepping into Denny Hall, was mistaken for a prospective Freshman by Senior Raymond R. Brewer, who in later years would represent Dickinson on the faculty of West China Union University at Chengtu. [21] So began, for that newcomer, an association of more than fifty years, and for the College a stalwart influence in teaching and in academic policy through the changing pattern that lay ahead.

In its President and Dean the College had now a mutually congenial, warmly effective administration. Morgan continued his very immediate—and often athletic—involvement in student deeds and doings, leaving his colleague free to develop a more sophisticated and stimulating curriculum. [22] Fiercely proud of policies which put scholastic achievement before all else, Morgan did not fail to acknowledge the Dean's part in their success. [23] Morgan, as his own admissions officer, had begun the practice of selecting only students of promising rank in high school. [24] It lessened what he called "the problem of infant mortality." So did his program for helping Freshmen adjust to college life—frequent reports, reinforced by "counsel, advice and admonition. Most of those in danger change. Others do not, and within two or three weeks an occasional Freshman may be dropped as not trying to meet conditions. This helps tremendously the morale of the rest. Their withdrawal is a steady tonic for those who remain." [25]

The College was already sectioning classes according to ability, to give brighter minds full play and challenge. Class absences were allowed only to those with A and B grades. [26] A committee on "special work looking toward special honors at commencement" was set up in 1919 to replace the now-vestigial A.M. *in cursu.* [27] Filler, attending the inauguration of Aydelotte at Swarthmore in 1921, was pleased to note that much of Aydelotte's program for academic advance was already present at Dickinson. Honors courses based on the new program at Swarthmore followed in 1922, together with the system of majors and minors to insure a wiser choice of electives. [28] Small recitation sections, never to exceed thirty, had long been fixed policy. [29] All this was crowned in the spring of 1926 by the first of the now-traditional "A Dinners," a convivial honoring of Phi Beta Kappa and all other top-grade students. [30] We find the *Dickinsonian* at the same time pleading for greater student participation in planning the curriculum, and reproving the Senate for failure to advance the student potential. [31] In 1915 faculty and Student Senate had reestablished an honor system, that perennial ideal and effort of many ups and downs, which in the upsurge of 1922 Morgan could report as "working very well indeed." [32]

Morgan's insistence that progress toward a liberal arts degree should be undiluted by special interest courses was not carried to an extreme. Courses preparatory to business, medicine and law were retained. Following a trend among other colleges, a course in education to meet "the growing high school demand for college trained teachers" was added in 1915, and in the next year a course in engineering. [33]

It cannot be denied, when one takes a broad view of the campus scene, that the Dickinson School of Law has been an element of strength and maturity in the life of Dickinson College. After Reed's retirement a committee of trustees, President Noble, Frank B. Lynch, Horatio C. King, Boyd Lee Spahr and Charles K. Zug, had examined the College-Law School relationship and made plans for a formal integration of the School as a department of the College. Virtually complete at Noble's resignation, the final integration was opposed, successfully, through the years by Morgan, and their efforts only led on to a more complete separation. [34] The formal agreement between Board of Trustees and Board of Incorporators that the Law School was a department of the College only had the effect of admitting the "undesirable law men," as Morgan called them, to the College fraternities and teams. [35] A student like bottle-hurling Ray Zug could be dimissed from College only to turn up in Law, as much a part of the scene as ever. Worse, bright young men were transferring in mid-course from College to Law. The liquor problem entered in. And beyond all this one must infer the personal clash: Trickett was running his operation as an even more absolute dictator than Morgan in his—Trickett, the enemy of McCauley, the scoffer at the Church. Morgan threw it all into one safe generalization: "I believe a good condition for the liberal arts student is a school without professional or technical associations." [36]

More rightly questionable was the maintenance of a preparatory school as part of a college operation. This solved itself. With the improving high school systems, and particularly the Carlisle High School's Lamberton building, completed in 1914 and far superior to Conway Hall, the end of a fairly profitable adjunct was in sight. Two years later Morgan suggested closing, with 1918 in mind, but the declaration of war in 1917 hastened the action. The end came suddenly, bringing sharp pangs and some long-lasting bitterness. Many had come to love the School, where "school spirit" had been more frankly fostered and avowed than in the College. William Albert Hutchison, Headmaster from 1904 to the closing, had run it with all of Morgan's vigor but with the added élan of a more freewheeling athletic policy. "I remember the days," his son wrote, years later, "when Conway Hall had not done too well on a Saturday and on Tuesday when the 10:45 steamed majestically down Main Street on its way to Harrisburg, Docky Hutch would break loose from the main door of Conway Hall with his little black bag, race down the street (he always caught the 10:45) and off he would go. A few days later he would return from the mining country [and] with him might be a pretty good sized boy (who just had to have an education) . . . ." [37] The old building, offered for government use and declined, was refurbished when peace returned as a Freshman dormitory, and in this role unified the entering classes and the faculty's work with them. [38]

The Great War came as only a brief interruption of college life. Morgan at once announced an early closing in May, and the granting of full credit to students entering essential places in the labor shortage. [39] In the fall a Students' Army Training Corps unit of 252 was added to a regular student body, diminished from the 381 of the year before to 277. Because of the influenza epidemic, SATC had only just begun its program at the armistice, "and the men who had come to prepare for the army lost heart in their work." [40] Of the faculty, Landis was on the Italian front with the Y.M.C.A., Filler associate secretary of the Y.M.C.A. Personnel Board, and "Rusty" Norcross of Psychology a first lieutenant in the Sanitary Corps. With the year 1918-19, all was back to normal—Freshman rules, class scraps, literary societies—all greeted by the *Dickinsonian* among "signs of this return of the happy days." [41]

There followed, throughout the educational scene, a refreshed idealism and search for improvement. Morgan writes to Senator Boies Penrose in favor of the League of Nations and proposes to his Executive Committee that Dickinson join other colleges in giving a free education to two French girls. [42] The Committee responded, but with a measure of restraint, "Protestant girls approved." Morgan made Dickinson one of the first participating institutions in Teachers Insurance and Annuity Association, 1918. In that year, Lemuel T. Appold, accepting a trusteeship which was to be active and fruitful through the years, told him that faculty salaries, which had had no significant increase for twenty-five years, ought to be "at least $3,500. I almost gasped at the thought." [43]

Morgan was proud of his growing faculty and departments expanding solidly within his concept of the liberal arts. [44] "Baldy" Sellers had become one of its legendary figures, with his "Unity, Coherence and Emphasis," and, when pleased by an answer, his "Precisely so!" ' Feathers" Landis (so dubbed because of the light growth on cheeks and chin) had been teaching a survey course in fine arts, given recognition in 1928 by a Carnegie Foundation gift of books, study photographs and original works. [45] Ralph Schecter, joining the faculty in 1922 as an instructor in English, "showed himself," Morgan wrote, "a genius in music." [46] He organized a thirty-five piece College orchestra and continued it with distinction for twenty-five years. It played every day in chapel, valued by Morgan because it kept his restive congregation quiet. [47] Schecter's "Appreciation of Music" course began in 1926, by student request. [48] Mulford Stough, coming as instructor in 1927 and quickly promoted to associate professor, brought new verve and emphasis to the

The Sophomore Band, with Dick, 1901.

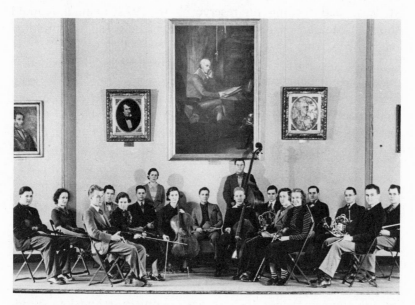

The College Orchestra, *c.* 1935.

teaching of American history. Stough met student contempt
and resistance at first. It was all too wide of the text. Being sent
repeatedly to the Library to read this or that did not sit well
with a student body some of whom went through their whole
course without ever crossing the Library threshhold. Later, converted, they were telling one another that college was not
worthwhile without "a Stough course." Here was a contrast to
the teaching of Bradford O. McIntire, slowly dictating the same
lectures, year after year, to be taken down word for word in the
manner of Nisbet's "prelection." Yet his each lecture was a
skillfully organized essay and a lesson, in itself, on the presentation of a scholarly theme. [49]

It is true that some students in the forepart of the century
went through Dickinson without knowing there was a Library,
and that Edwin E. Willoughby, '22, later Chief Bibliographer of
the Folger Shakespeare Library, received a faculty reprimand
for spending too much time in it, rather than with his texts. [50]
Yet for some years the *Dickinsonian* had been printing lists of
the books bought with the Guild endowment. In 1916 a trained
librarian was first employed, and in the next year some courses
at least had reading on reserve. [51] In 1922 Lemuel Appold
shocked Morgan again by noting that a new Library building
might be in order. [52]

Over all this scene of academic growth, Morgan presided as
a bearish but benevolent tyrant. When some of his faculty conceived a scholastic project of their own, he called them in and
told them bluntly that their function was to teach, his to run
the College, and if the matter went any further they would
leave. [53] As he aged, his frequent noisy throat-clearing bore out
the character:

> "Dockie" Morgan coughs and sneezes like his collar gave him pain;
> And he struts and snorts and sizzles just to show he runs the school,
> But he justifies the co-eds tho they've broken every rule . . . . [54]

Partial to the co-eds he was, standing against continuing
pressure for their removal led by Spahr, Appold and Zug. These,
in turn, his most active and influential trustees, were motivated
by the then prevalent feeling that coeducation and low standards went together, and that Dickinson must stand as a peer of

the eastern quality colleges for men. It was in this spirit that Rutgers was resisting siege by Mabel Smith Douglass and the New Jersey Federation of Women's Clubs, and Wesleyan shooing away its "quails" from the "Quails' Roost." But for the much-needed income they brought in, the Metzger girls might also have been proscribed. [55]

In 1914, when Morgan had sallied forth to save the day by enlisting a sizeable incoming class, the abolition of hazing had been a primary need. In Reed's later years the practice had become increasingly brutal. By 1911, faculty was fulminating against "the present system of hazing by the use of paddles and bludgeons as conducted by the Sophomore Band." [56] It had continued into Noble's administration, with the added refinement of branding with nitrate of silver. [57] The trustees passed a vote of condemnation. Morgan appealed directly to the students, who "took drastic action to abolish hazing from the College." Actually, only the nighttime raiding and molesting, deeply rooted in Dickinson mores, was abolished. Penalties would now be inflicted by daylight upon Freshmen who had overstepped a Sophomore list of proprieties. Thus, the sentences on Freshmen Frank E. Masland and James B. Stein were carried out at the old stone steps. The culprits had accompanied "certain young women about promiscuously." For this they were "treated" with corn syrup, made to run "a sort of bloodhound contest" on a course covered with molasses and were given haircuts, after which "sudden thunder showers" descended upon them from a clear sky. [58]

An early effort was made, with the help of the Student Senate, to regulate rushing. An effort to end all class fights, triggered by a fatality in the "Bowl Scrap" at the University of Pennsylvania, fell through. [59] By 1923, the "Student Tribunal" had fixed a scoring system for class rivalries: Flag Scrap, 20; Pants Scrap, 10; Football Game, 15; Basketball, 20; Baseball, 15; "any new scrap," 10. Tug of War (with the Letort Spring between) brought winners 20 points, the losers a ducking. [60]

The kidnapping of rival class members, often with a view to abandoning them in some remote spot beyond the mountains, was continued with such constant, watchful opposition from the President of the College that one must needs infer that he had become simply an accepted hazard in the game. It was a familiar campus spectacle in these years to see Morgan dash out from Denny, perhaps to stop some innocent-looking wagon, seizing the horse by the head, ordering the prisoners hidden within unbound and released. [61] He must have had a constant lookout from his window on an upper floor, must have known every livery stable nag and rig by sight. Nothing escaped Morgan, champion of fair play. When the picture of Negro student Dorothy Anna Davis was placed at the end of all others in the 1924 *Microcosm* with a patronizing notice, he had the editor-in-chief up before the faculty, and then before the deans for discipline. [62]

Morgan, a trustee and member of the Headquarters Committee of the Anti-Saloon League, prided himself upon a campus where drinking, though common before 1914, had become, he said, "practically non-existent." [63] One may suspect that the "Jazz Age" of the twenties, while not a prevailing force at Dickinson, was far more so than the President chose to admit. Skull and Key was widely known as a drinking club, and an estimated 20 per cent of the co-eds "loose as a shoestring." [64] Morgan, running the College as if it were personal property, was surely aware of everything. He is seen right on the spot as a known bootlegger comes out of East—"You get off my campus and stay off." He storms the office of a physician known to oblige students with whiskey by prescription. [65]

It was much the same with the "metzkirts" at Metzger learning to smoke. From 1919, they lived under the sharp eye of a practical no-nonsense Dean of Women and Professor of English, Mrs. Josephine Meredith. It is said that Mrs. Meredith made the young ladies returning from a party pass by her close enough for her to smell their breaths. She allowed them no male visitors save Dickinson students, and these must pass the same close scrutiny. [66] With legalistic efficiency she enacted and posted rules to fit every contingency. Dean Russell Thompson, looking into affairs at Metzger in 1947, was both awed and charmed. He suggested a simplification of the code, yet cherished it in memory, particularly Rule 124, stating that when crowded conditions in an automobile obliged a young lady to sit upon a young gentleman's lap they must be physically separated by a newspaper, and that the newspaper must be of at least the thickness of the regular daily edition of the *New York Times.* [67]

Yet we have here one of the stalwarts of Dickinson history. Josephine Meredith lived and worked precariously between, on the one hand, the Methodist powers, watchful and rigorous in their judgments of the young, and, on the other, those enlightened enemies of coeducation in any form, including women on the faculty. If she protected her girls against hazards, she herself faced greater ones, and did so with determination, fairness and humor. She caught and held the lasting admiration of many. Estelle Bernard, '49, would always remember that friendly, staunch involvement with a shy student's problems and the sparkle in the eye. When Mrs. Meredith laid down a law, as in her "ANTI-BIFURCATION ACT" of 1944 against "freakish costumes" outside the dormitory, the decree would be accepted with an answering sparkle.

Morgan, on his part, frankly confessed that social rules must be "largely a question of expediency," and reduced all rules to one—conformity with "the requirements of good morals and good citizenship." [68] He had long cherished a hope of enlisting the fraternities not only in protecting these standards, but in the cause of scholastic excellence. He declared that he had from the first "encouraged student participation in the conduct of the College." [69] Yet to share power was not Morgan's way, and in the November following that statement of June, 1923, we find the Senate resigning in a body as a protest against the prolonged curtailment of its powers, declaring that student government had come to exist in name only. [70]

Morgan's presidency was characterized by thrift. At the outset, as he put it, "No advantage was small enough to be ignored." [71] In later years this former Librarian and aging President would tour the Library alcoves, each lighted by a single bulb, and turn it out if no reader was there. This was a rebuke to Librarian May Morris, who had come in 1927, bringing a more liberal concept. [72] In responding to a request for advice Morgan confessed to President George L. Omwake of Ursinus that "We have no budget. I am afraid that I would have to confess that I am the budget. I suspect this College is exceptional in this." [73]

He was right. Furthermore, for financial development in the large, he had neither talent nor taste. He relied upon Mother Church, with the Rev. Dr. John William Hancher as his guide throughout. Hancher, Assistant Secretary and financial expert of the Board of Education of the Methodist Episcopal Church, had met with the trustees just before Noble's resignation. Wisely, he had then advised "a harmonious background" as a first condition in launching a campaign. [74] Hancher was with the Church organization until 1930, when he had his own agency for "Philanthropic Finance" in Chicago. He collected honorary honors along the way, prizing especially his election, 1918, to Phi Beta Kappa, Alpha of Pennsylvania. [75]

In 1915, with the Central Pennsylvania Conference planning a "Jubilee" drive for funds for education and with Reed's resolution of February 14, 1907, still rankling some minds, the trustees deplored its language and reaffirmed loyalty to the Church, while still declaring "the lack of formal, legal, sectarian restraint." [76] This campaign, in the midst of the war effort, could hardly have reached its goal of $125,000 for Dickinson, but it enabled Morgan to pay off $12,000 of debts and add $16,000 to endowment. [77]

When plans for a major campaign on the part of the College were taking shape in 1919 and 1920, this last experience had only increased Morgan's trepidation. "Some things I can do," he confessed to Charles Zug, "others are hard, almost impossible for me. Among the latter is a definite and direct approach for money." And to Bishop McDowell, "This financial problem . . . is a new one . . . for which I feel no special fitness and certainly for which I have no appetite." And again, "Dr. Hancher is going to supervise our campaign, but I have the feeling that the President of the College ought to do and be more in such a campaign than I know how." [78] He did try, and with little success. When trustee Charles E. Pettinos, New York manufacturer, took Morgan to his club for lunch he found this college president simply an embarrassment, with his harsh loud voice and raucous breathing. [79]

A start was made, June 8, 1920, with the General Education Board's appropriation of $150,000, to be matched by $300,000, the total to be held as endowment in support of faculty salaries. [80] With this from the Rockefeller organization,

Hancher staggered Morgan by raising the campaign goal from $500,000 to $1,000,000. In the face of the post-war depression this seemed astronomical. It was finally raised again, however, on the initiative of Bishop Joseph Flintoft Berry, to $1,600,000, with the Pennington School brought in as a co-beneficiary. Dickinson's share was to be $1,250,000 and Pennington's $350,000. [81]

Final plans were made on November 8, 1921: "Launching Sunday" would be on May 14, 1922; "Review Sunday" on May 28; "Gleaning Sunday" on June 25; and July 3 the Closing Day. At that time, expenses had come to $11,500, and $20,000 had to be borrowed to carry on. [82] The campaign took longer than planned, and even then failed to reach its goal. Dickinson College benefited by this, its first great financial drive, but to many it was a near-fiasco. Some of its literature is catechistical in form, and all awash with piety, becoming more prayerful toward the end—"The silver is Mine and the gold is Mine saith the Lord of Hosts," and "Honor the Lord with thy substance and with the first fruits of all thine increase." The colorful little leaflet, *To My Mother*, could hardly have been very helpful. [83] Pennington failed to cooperate. So also the preachers and district superintendents—though Morgan in an effort to mollify them had had the trustees, June 3, 1922, authorize the five conferences to nominate one trustee for each fifty thousand members. [84] This action brought him a sharp inquiry from Clyde Furst of the Carnegie Foundation. [85] It was just at this time that Goucher College was the scene of a determined effort to escape from exactly the same element of sectarian control. Poor Morgan! He had pressures from the other side as well, such as a veiled warning that "the relations of the school to the Carnegie Founding . . . is not keeping with the last clause of the fourth verse of the fifteenth psalm." [86]

The campaign ended in November, $225,000 short of its objective, with a welter of uncollected subscriptions and unsettled questions on the division of debt and benefit with Pennington. [87] The cost of the "Dickinson-Pennington Movement," at one point estimated at 18 percent was probably well above that, and after two years Morgan was only just beginning to receive income from it. [88] Moreover, during the campaign the General Education Board had seen fit to reduce its subsidies. [89]

The experience did have certain fruitful side effects. Alumni like Paul Appenzellar, interested in College but not in Church, felt challenged to show their own supporting power. [90] During the campaign Appold had sparked a revival of the General Alumni Association. He would serve as its first President, to be succeeded briefly by Edward M. Biddle and then by Boyd Lee Spahr from 1928 to 1931. Appold's banking experience was already reflected in the stability of College investments. Now he underwrote half the cost of *The Dickinson Alumnus,* starting publication in 1923. [91] Gilbert Malcolm, '15, who had been an assistant in the campaign, and during the war had been on the board of *The Stars and Stripes,* took over as editor. He was given the collection of campaign subscriptions as a sideline. The campaign had shown beyond peradventure that church support would be inadequate in itself and a deterrent to giving from other sources. By 1927 even Morgan was proclaiming that he headed a college "free from denominational control," although he continued to measure his success by the number of his boys who had become teachers or preachers, with district superintendents as the crowning achievement. Spahr had taken him bluntly to task in July, 1923, on these points and on undue assumption of authority—reminding him that Dickinson was not a normal school or a theological seminary. [92]

The campaign had also intensified alumni interest in winning teams. In 1915, the faculty had given serious consideration to abandoning football. [93] By 1920, the activities of the Campus Club in hiring athletes and pressuring for a more aggressive coach than the scholarly Forrest Craver had aroused Morgan's ire. They could give scholarships to players, but the players must meet his academic requirements. [94] A peak came in 1922 with the engagement of Glenn Killinger, outstanding athlete, as football coach. Killinger's will to win outraged Morgan and alienated even some of his players. [95] He lasted a year only, and Morgan settled down to the promotion of eligibility rules and the Eastern College Athletic Conference. A decade later he was begging the Carnegie Foundation to take the initiative, and onus, of "what seemed to me to be the next step in any vital reform, that those colleges who stand for scholarship and are disgusted with our present football situation might well unite and for a given period of years eliminate football." [96]

The 1922 campaign had had the building of a new gymnasium and the renovation of East and West Colleges as stated goals. Its results precluded any thought of a new building and in the dour outlook Morgan used to say that if offered a new gym as a gift he would decline it, as he had not enough money to pay the electric bill. [97] With East, where broken plumbing overflowed the floors and bursting steam pipes wrought havoc, where a rat ran out across the floor at the Kappa Sigma dance, something had to be done. [98] The renovation of East, authorized in June, 1924, was accompanied by an increase in the tuition from $160 to $200, and in the charge for women from $475 to $550. [99] Students cooperated that year by reseeding the campus grass and laying a new path. [100] For West College, Appold contributed $18,000 to transform the old chapel into Memorial Hall, and then added the McCauley Room on the floor below as a memorial to the President of his and Morgan's day. In the next year, 1926, the trustees launched the campaign that would build the Alumni Gymnasium on the site of old South College, torn down to make way for it in the spring of 1927.

Morgan, at his seventieth birthday, came to chapel to find the students ready with a great bouquet of roses in the Dickinson red and white. [101] He had retirement in mind now, and would bring it up at the 1927 trustee meeting. It had grown hard to keep up the pace. Louis A. Tuvin, '10, sometime in these last years had come upon Morgan in the club car of a train, puffing a cigarette, a spectacle never seen on campus. Amused, the young man sat down, and learned that Camels were the President's favorite brand. "Tuvin," Morgan observed after a while, "you are in the drug business." And then, having put the matter on a semi-medical basis, "The aroma of a good whisky excites me no end." Could Tuvin by any chance meet such a need? Tuvin could. They retired to his compartment where a strong dose was prescribed and poured. [102]

Such things might help, but the strain was growing heavier, and in January, 1928, on his return from another trip, a breakdown came at last. Convalescence was slow. When the trustees met, his resignation was in their hands, to take effect on July 31. On August 1, they elected Dean Filler to take his place, an act which invited the continuance of Morgan's influence, if not his activity. William Trickett died on that same day, ending an era at the School of Law.

For Morgan, there followed a trip through Europe to Greece. He left laden with gifts from students and alumni, in a stateroom banked with flowers. [103] On his return the trustees established the "James Henry Morgan Lectureship," setting aside an endowment of $25,000 for its continuance. [104] Morgan, with his new leisure, turned to the writing of a history of Dickinson's century and a half.

"Baby Boy" Filler was, if we make an exception of Himes' brief tenure. the first layman to head a Dickinson College administration. A first act was that of many another incoming college president, a professional survey of the school. It must be taken also as recognition that after so long a span of Morgan's highly personal type of management more modern and more regular procedures were in order, and this was a tactful and compelling way in which to present the fact. The Church's Commission on Survey of Educational Institutions sent a staff of four for the purpose, headed by Floyd Wesley Reeves, Professor of Educational Administration at the University of Chicago. Its 374-page report was received in the fall of 1930, with copies for all faculty and trustees. Boyd Lee Spahr found it full of valuable information and recommendations, particularly on the Library and the investment of endowment. He bridled, however, at the thought of turning Old East into a co-ed dormitory in order to increase the proportion of women, and deplored the fact that all comparative statistics were to small Methodist colleges, mostly in the Midwest. [105] Fifteen years later, to the shocked surprise of returning alumni, there would indeed be girls in Old East. The proposed expansion of the Library into the chapel area above would come only as a last expedient before removal to a new building—though the intention of doing so would have its profound effect on later events. The report, all in all, is a thorough and knowledgeable document, comparing very favorably to that pulled together by the Church's University Senate in 1962.

Filler acted upon his own experience as well. He, more than any other president Russell Thompson had known, sensed the need for more thorough and sympathetic student guidance. He therefore supplemented the class dean system, which had never met the problem adequately, by assigning a limited number of students to each member of the faculty. Assignments were made arbitrarily at first, then on a basis of presumed common interests of student and advisor. The plan "simply did not work," partly no doubt due to the continuance of heavy teaching loads, and after Filler's time there was a reversion to class deans as the only recourse. [106]

Filler's time was short. An alumnus, George M. Briner, '07, recalled that Dr. Filler "never seemed at ease," citing the comment of a campus visitor, "You took a perfectly good professor and made him into a poor president." So much for outward appearances. They did not know, nor was Filler himself aware, of the illness which would end in his death, March 28, 1931. In the brief period left to him, he completed the new gymnasium and renovated Conway Hall. He obtained the Carnegie Corporation grant for books for the Library ($2,000 a year, 1932 to 1937) which, wisely managed by May Morris, at last brought the collection within reach of modern standards and set the pace for future library budgets. He fought the pressures from the athletic enthusiasts and dealt with the manifold financial problems of the deepening Great Depression. He may have had Morgan at his side more than he would have preferred, but he had also Boyd Lee Spahr as a promoter-ally. With Morgan's retirement, Spahr's long years of close and intimate touch with Dickinson administration begin, unifying campus, alumni and trustees, and confirmed by financial support. By 1930 he was urging Filler to consider a new $1,000,000 endowment drive. [107]

With Filler's death, Boyd Lee Spahr offered the motion that Morgan take over again until a new choice could be made. The old man consented to do so, at less than half time "and without compensation." [108] When Filler had taken office, the influence of Spahr, John Rhey, Appold and Zug, in short, the more forward-looking group, became apparent at once in trustee minutes and other records, characterized by a precision and clarity not always present before. The Spahr interest had been manifested on campus by a "Dickinsoniana Room" in West

College and a concerted effort to bring together portraits of great College figures of the past. Now Judge Biddle, dying of cancer, had stated his wish that Spahr succeed him as President of the Board. Morgan summoned Spahr to his office and raised his objections. First, this was a Methodist college and the chief officer of the trustees should be a Methodist. The answer was equally blunt, "It is not a Methodist college in the way you think." A second objection, "Because you drink," received an equally cursory reply. Appold and Rhey then threatened to resign if the matter were not dropped, and it was. [109] Biddle's resignation and Spahr's election followed on June 5, 1931, with the election also of Gilbert Malcolm, another non-Methodist, as Treasurer. Morgan, in compensation, was given a four-year term as a member of the Board, an eminence he would use as best he could to promote the loyalties which now seemed to be slipping away. [110]

With handicaps in the distance between Carlisle and Philadelphia and the demands of his law practice, Spahr was determined to achieve advancing quality, with the Ivy League colleges of the East as his standard. Dickinson also must eliminate sectarian influences, while keeping historic ties intact. His first task was to find a new President. Few trustees had names to put forward. Spahr brushed aside the suggestions of Morgan and trustee John Rogers Edwards that faculty participate in the choice. Edwards even mentioned that some colleges had left it entirely in faculty hands. To Spahr it was thinkable to ask the opinions at least of department heads, but only "as individuals and not as a collective group." [111] As matters stood on campus, a faculty choice would certainly have been a Morgan choice, and it was time now for a president of broader background and outlook.

Bishop William Fraser McDowell, a trustee who had been a breezily healthy influence in Dickinson affairs since 1917, brought forward the man who was elected without opposition, October 10, 1931. Karl Tinsley Waugh, born in India in 1879, the son of a missionary, was neither a clergyman nor an alumnus. His academic credentials were impeccable: an Ohio Wesleyan B.A., 1900, and M.A., 1901, he followed with a Harvard M.A., 1906, and Ph.D., 1907. In that final year he had been a

Weld Fellow, and assistant to William James. He was an associate in psychology at the University of Chicago, 1907 to 1909, Professor of Psychology at Beloit until 1918, Dean and Professor of Psychology and Philosophy at Berea till 1923, and Dean of the College of Arts and Sciences, University of California at Los Angeles, at the time of his election.

Due to a temporary commitment on the faculty of Long Island University, Waugh did not begin his term until January 1, 1933. In November, Miss Euphemia, the last of the Moores of Mooreland, had died, and Boyd Lee Spahr had embarked at once on his long-cherished project of doubling the size of the campus by adding that tract to it. Contributions added to his own of $10,000 brought it about, and it was announced to the trustees by Dr. Waugh, October 20, 1932. A small segment was purchased by the Law School, with whom the discussion of integration with the College was still continuing. Spahr envisioned at this time a large auditorium as a central feature of the new campus, replacing the old chapel and leaving Bosler Hall entirely free for library expansion. [112]

Chapels by this time were reduced to three per week, and even at that a majority of the students, according to the 1930 survey, found them insipid or tedious. The *Dickinsonian*, in a spirit of mild protest, printed excerpts from Anne Royall in order to contrast "the religious tone which pervades Dickinson to this day" with that of a century before. [113] All over the country student mores were changing again as the "Jazz Age" gave way to serious ideals for democracy and the social order, all highlighted against Depression suffering. Class scraps and kidnappings faded and vanished during Waugh's brief term. It followed that students would react with greater sensitivity than any other group to what was about to occur in campus inner circles.

Mrs. Waugh was happily settled in the President's House, proud to be the first to entertain the whole faculty at once. Occasional faculty meetings were held there, followed by a social hour, always with a program of some sort, and all accomplished with only one maid. [114] Dr. Waugh had attended his first trustee meeting on February 20, 1932, with twelve basic recommendations to add to the numerous small procedural re-

Top: Presidents Morgan and Waugh, 1931. Bottom left: Russell Irvin Thompson. By Ben Kamihira, 1955. Bottom right: Herbert Wing, Jr. By Ann Didusch Schuler, 1958.

forms he was making. One was the presentation of a tentative budget for the coming year. "This, I understand, was a new feature in Dickinson procedure."[115] But all, actually, were established factors in the management of colleges which had not had the single-minded attention of a James Henry Morgan.

Morgan, at Waugh's first coming, had been prompt with a warm welcome. He had then made it his habit to drop in regularly at the President's office to see how the new man was doing, and to offer advice.[116] He liked less and less what he found.

At the first faculty meeting of the next term, September 16, 1932, new regulations had been adopted, with student standing based on the ratio of grade points to semester hours, and provision for "Degrees with Distinction." Modernization of the curriculum came March 6, 1933, approved, like the earlier actions, on the motion of Herbert Wing, Jr. On March 27, rules for special and departmental honors were passed, the departmental to be justified by a thesis. At the same time, Waugh introduced a new plan for student government, to include both men and women and with each living unit represented in proportion to its size.[117] He devised a new scholarship loan plan, based on endowed units of a revolving fund, from which he anticipated improvement and growth in the student body.[118]

It is here that this *History of Dickinson College* could well emulate *Tristram Shandy* and draw a printed curtain over its page. Morgan, incensed that his counsel, so freely offered, was neglected—objecting particularly that his own nominees for the Curriculum Committee had not been appointed—was using his position as trustee, with faculty and town, to launch a campaign of appalling vilification.[119] Dr. Waugh, knowledgeable and assured, lacked the other's firm decisiveness and passion. The smear spread, a whispering campaign imbued with preposterous charges of vice and dishonesty. If Waugh himself was anywhere at fault it was only because, as a psychologist, he had failed to diagnose and salve the rage of the power-proud old man, to satisfy in some way that continuing sense of proprietorship, and to realize in time what influence Morgan still held among faculty and trustees and how he might use it. Morgan, frustrated in his hope of having a churchman as President of the Board, could only discern dark motive and decay in the conduct of this new-comer. He was ending his Dickinson career in a spate of partisan bitterness worse even than that he had seen about him in his Freshman year, deeply damaging to the good name of the school and similarly an impediment to the search for competent leadership. Dr. and Mrs. Waugh soon found themselves isolated socially. Friends of Morgan did not go to the house, and instructed all others to avoid it. A few bold and fair-minded spirits such as Horace Rogers, Elmer Herber, Chester Quimby and Mary Taintor refused to accept the ban. Malcolm, Meredith, Milton Eddy of Biology, were among the hostiles, Eddy so forward in spreading obloquy that he was forced to make a public retraction. [120]

When Morgan came at last to the trustees it was with an irreparable breach between his party and the President—the President supported only by those, younger for the most part, who could recognize sound policy and found the undercover attack repulsive. At the meeting of June 9, 1933, a committee of Morgan and four others was commissioned "to consider the finances and general welfare of the College and report . . . in the near future." On June 24, Waugh read a list of further constructive recommendations for the future, at the close of which he was persuaded to make an "oral resignation." [121] The committee of his enemies took over, and Morgan was once more installed as President.

He called a special faculty meeting, June 26, which, with ten members conspicuously absent, erased all reforms and restored the old ways. Spahr wrote him on the same day, suggesting a revision of the bylaws to set up "a trustee committee on the selection of members of the faculty." [122] Waugh had reappointed—and the Board at its June meeting dismissed—Dr. Gerald Barnes, a freewheeling but thoroughly competent professor of sociology. This would come under AAUP investigation. [123] Morgan had been successful in creating distrust of Waugh, without adding conviction of his own trustworthiness. Yet he was in the saddle, as of old. At a faculty meeting, September 12, he read "A Brief Statement of Facts," followed by informal remarks, and, on Landis' motion, was given "a unanimous standing vote of 'heartfelt gratitude.' " Ten days later,

Bishop McDowell resigned from the Board of Trustees, sending both Morgan and Wing notification of the fact. [124]

All of the Waugh reforms were now reversed or contemptuously brushed aside. Most of them would, to be sure, return as Dickinson more gradually caught up with the times. At the time, all seemed odious to the old guard. One of the first had been to divide the College funds between the two Carlisle banks, a reasonable provision in a time of bank failures. [125] One offended banker had been a member of that committee on College finances. Waugh's last recommendation, that honorary degrees come through a joint committee of faculty and trustees, now in effect, was offensive to those who had been concerned in awarding the laurels in a more summary manner.

The retired President had gained one condition, continuance of salary for a year. This had included occupation of the President's House, and there he remained despite efforts to evict him by force or persuasion. Dark condemnation could not be spoken so easily with its object still in Carlisle and his daughter a student at the College. Eleanor Waugh was elected President of the McIntire Literary Society that spring—one evidence of the student response to what had happened and was happening. The effort to conceal all details of the affair soon fell through. Student indignation seethed. The *Dickinsonian* of November 2, 1933, called on "those in authority to treat the student body with the consideration it deserves and not subjugate it to a condition it is not willing to accept." That of May 10, 1934, printed an editorial, "The Re-birth of a College," sent in from the Morgan camp, but the student editor blue-pencilled every reference to Morgan, reducing it to ten almost incomprehensible lines. Others, extolling Morgan as the "savior" of Dickinson in every hour of crisis, did appear, but student opinion held firm, and they sent to Waugh himself a summary of their own view of his accomplishment: a modernized curriculum; the solution of problems in student activities, fraternity rushing and athletic organization; a budget system bringing economy and open accounting; the advocacy of scholarship loans rather than gifts. [126] A survey team from the Methodist Board of Education, ostensibly studying student opinion on World Missions, found much to report on Waugh and brought an angry counterblast from Morgan, with his contemptuous, "the Adullamites all flocked to them." [127]

Alumni reactions were the same. Was it not devious, Professor Carl Hartzell of Franklin and Marshall inquired of Morgan, to speak of a "serious financial condition" resulting from Waugh's short term, and then immediately present Dickinson as one of the few colleges without a deficit? By the spring and summer of 1934 Morgan was contending with both adverse national publicity and aroused and hostile alumni clubs. [128]

Needless to say, Dr. Waugh continued his active career as an educator after leaving Carlisle. He left with statements from some faculty, such as that of Horace E. Rogers, which did much to relieve the bitterness of the Dickinson debacle:

> His ideal for Dickinson was to make it rank among the best Liberal Arts colleges. He was doing his utmost to bring this to pass. His progressive administration here at Dickinson was terminated all too soon, which does not dispute the fact that he is well qualified to undertake the duties of a college administrator. [129]

Hopes were now fixed upon a formal sesquicentennial celebration in 1933 that would draw all together again and help to obliterate what had occurred. There would be a convocation with twenty-one honorary degree recipients, among them John Charles Thomas, once of Conway Hall and now of the Metropolitan Opera, and former Carlislers William Rose and Stephen Vincent Benét. Josephine Meredith was composing an historical pageant. Morgan was laboring on his history of the College, his first book, indeed his first scholarly publication of any sort. It was completed, and in very respectable form, though not entirely without help. Newspaperman Dean Hoffman, "Red" Malcolm, Boyd Lee Spahr and others had been hard put to it to persuade the "Old Master" to accept assistance and get it out in shape and on time. While this was going on, Prohibition was up for repeal, a sad turn of events for old stalwarts of the Anti-Saloon League, and one glimpses the hectic scene in the letters of the brilliant, madcap general of the Engineer Corps, James G. Steese, '02, to Spahr:

> I cannot understand Morgan's stubbornness with respect to the proposed so-called History. One would think he would want to put

his best foot forward and welcome assistance. . . .

As I recollect, the College has only two representatives in Congress at this time, Kurtz and Rich, and both voted against the submission of the repeal amendment to the people yesterday. Of course, Kurtz is an old woman, and Rich a half-baked fool, but if that represents the college's 100% contribution to leadership in these dire times, maybe that explains our difficulty in working up Morgan's history so as to give the college some reason for existence, or show it has ever played any important part in moulding public opinion. [130]

All came through on schedule, and 1933 went by with attention focused on the heroic past. By the close of the academic year, the future could be faced with a new strong hand in the President's office. As an alumnus of 1917, Fred Pierce Corson had witnessed the crisis of the Noble-to-Morgan years, had gone on through Drew University to the Methodist ministry and had become one of those district superintendents whom Morgan watched in the twilight of his life with such pride. In President Corson the Church had its solidly efficient champion on campus, unprejudiced by any previous experience in college administration, one of Morgan's boys, and yet also more than ready to work harmoniously with the new President of the Board of Trustees toward widening goals.

And when the trustees transact their business entirely apart from the Faculty, they will often be disposed to make a mystery of their proceedings to the latter, and thus impair that mutual confidence, which it is important should always exist between the two bodies.

Henry Vethake, 1830

Due to the generosity of its benefactors and due to the high academic standard which its faculty has maintained there is today no better small liberal arts college in the country than ours. That happy situation can be maintained with the continued and increasing loyalty of the alumni, who, since Mr. Appold's challenging leadership in the early '20's have responded generously to the needs of the College, and this is as it should be, for, after all, while the Board of Trustees are the legal owners of the College, the equitable owners are the great body of its alumni.

Boyd Lee Spahr, at Alumni Luncheon, June 3, 1950

14

THE SPAHR YEARS

IN the twenty-five years 1934 to 1959, three presidents succeeded one another on campus: Corson for a decade, Prettyman
in a brief climax to his forty-four years as Professor of German
Languages and Literature, and the thirteen stormy seasons of
William Wilcox Edel. But it is a quarter century dominated
throughout by Boyd Lee Spahr.

The charter amendment of February, 1912, had created
the new office of President of the Board. The President of the
College remained as an ex officio member, but subordinate to
whatever authority the other chose to exert. It is inescapable
that this change, moved and put through by young Spahr,
leader of the progressive anti-denominational group, was conceived as a means of escape from the parochialism of the past.
The first incumbent, Presbyterian Judge Biddle, had remained
benignly inactive while Morgan strove in his vigorous way to
prove that a college of impeccable academic standing could be
developed in close alliance with the Central Pennsylvania Conference of the Methodist Church.

Spahr entered the office in 1931, "against the tearful protest of Dr. Morgan," as anti-church stalwart Paul Appenzellar
described it, and with the support of all those who desired
complete independence.[1] Through the years he had been constantly active in trustee and alumni affairs. His relationship with
Morgan had been outwardly cordial, though he was aware of
Morgan's opposition to some of his favorite projects, such as the

union of Law School and College. He would now combine more constant attention with more generous giving. The President of the Board would become the real executive authority of the College, a busy lawyer at a distance of more than a hundred miles, yet with a finger on virtually every detail of its administration.

This control became complete with the final retirement of Morgan. Spahr had agreed to the Waugh dismissal, probably because Morgan had brought campus tensions to a point that seemed to preclude any other solution. The peak years of the Spahr era begin with the election of Fred Pierce Corson as President of the College, June 8, 1934—Methodist clergyman whose classmates of '17 had recognized his ministerial dedication and executive talent in the nickname "Bishop." He had earned his B.D. at Drew in 1920 and served various pastorates for a decade before becoming District Superintendent of the Brooklyn South District, New York, an eminence which his alma mater had crowned with a D.D. in 1931, his first of a score of honorary degrees.

Corson, with no previous experience in academic administration, readily accepted the Spahr role. Spahr's interests ranged everywhere, from fundamental policy down to athletic control, fraternity rushing or some detail in the alteration of a building.[2] Letters flowed back and forth between the Presidents, sometimes two or three in a day. The telephone, certainly in later Spahr years, was much in use.[3] Spahr's success in the law brought not only more and more munificent giving but the capable management of estates willed to the College, sometimes under complex terms. Always a keen amateur historian, he gave much time to tracing Dickinson figures of the past down to potential donors of the present, performing this service with thoroughness and skill. By the same token, he was filling the chapel and other walls with portraits of the Dickinson great, so that the campus itself would speak to all comers of its long history. Through the years, he would continue to seek manuscripts and rare books for the Library's Dickinsoniana Collection, which had had its curatorial staff since 1932.

Every year throughout these years the proofs of the College catalogue were sent to Spahr, who meticulously read and revised them, thought and phrase, colon and comma. The President of the Board, annually reelected, was apparently oblivious to rising alumni resentment of one-man control, and certainly there was no alumnus ready to give an equivalent in time and money.[4] The large Board had its majority of Methodists, the one necessary condition to receiving the conference funds, with Spahr seeing to it that as many as possible were men who put College loyalty first.[5] In Board as in College, each president appointed all his committees. Spahr's large and congenial Executive Committee soon became responsible for all major decisions, which were then regularly endorsed by the full Board. All opinion was represented on it, all were in friendly consultation; and yet Spahr, adroit and tactful, not unwilling to compromise, remained always the deciding voice.

In Duffield's day the few local trustees had run everything. Now they were campus observers for Spahr. Most of the total of forty or fifty had little to do and little to contribute. Spahr himself deplored the general concept of membership as purely honorific.[6] In 1936, thirty-nine trustees gave $5,680, Spahr, Appold and Appenzellar each having put in $1,000. Many sent only token sums and seven nothing whatever.[7] Appenzellar, succeeding Methodist Appold as Finance Chairman in 1935, dourly estimated only 20 per cent of all giving as from church-related sources.[8]

In Corson the anti-denominational group felt that it had found a clergyman wholly dedicated to academic administration—a precise, efficient, budget-minded manager and, to cheer their hearts, a Methodist willing to concede that many of his faith lacked the intellectual ideals which must sustain a front-rank liberal arts community. On these terms he won cordial acceptance by the militantly anti-clerical business executive Appenzellar, banker and Chairman of the Board of the Dictaphone Corporation, who was bringing new order and promise into the financial structure of the College. Appenzellar expressed his immediate approval by remodelling the President's House.[9] Thus began a cordial relationship which, considering this trustee's explosive temperament and habit of peremptory command, must have been something of a strain on the President of the

College, jarring also at times the nerves of the President of the Board.

Corson, with what most college presidents would consider an overdose of trustee prompting was at least left almost wholly in charge of the curriculum. Here he could make his own mark in the educational world—as long, of course, as it brought no additional expense. History indeed repeats itself and these Dickinson presidents of the Spahr era would see the repetition of some of the phenomena of the Duffield years, 1821 to 1832. Historian Boyd Lee Spahr was fully aware of the past evils of "trustee interference." Morgan—surely with his own situation in mind—had been at pains to emphasize them in his 1933 *History*. Yet here again we find the same legalistic interpretation of trustee duties and prerogatives taking hold. Trustee authority becomes increasingly remote, until meetings cease altogether to be held on campus. There was but one token point of contact. Beginning in 1935, two professors met with a trustee Committee on Honorary Degrees, a reform originally proposed by Waugh. Beyond this the rift was complete and, as in former days, was reflected in on-campus distrusts and divisions.

These years bring also the emergence of aggressive student opinion, hostile to administration, critical of faculty, and at times more effective than either in bringing advance. The student body continued at about 550, dropping sharply during the war years, and at the peace rising steadily beyond 1,000. Part of this growth would come from a gradual relaxing of the limitation on co-eds to 25 per cent. [10] The women had Metzger, spacious and archaic, as their only domain until Old East was given a quick face-lifting and opened to them in 1946. At the same time, Biddle House became a men's dormitory, but there would be no further progress here until Morgan Hall was completed in 1955. Corson established a student health service in 1936. [11] The need for a student union, acknowledged in 1935, had token recognition with the building of South College in 1947, but social life remained centered in the fraternities and sororities throughout this period. [12]

The fraternity spirit permeated everything through these years, with separate, competitive loyalties which often outweighed any feeling for the College as a whole. [13] Here drinking and other convivialities of *dum vivimus vivamus* were sheltered and fostered. President Corson at once addressed himself to the problems of control. New rules for chaperonage, along with the point system on extra-curricular activities, added unwelcome duties for the underpaid faculty. [14] "Hell Week" was curbed for a while after the death of a student in 1935. [15] Yet by 1940 Corson must needs acknowledge that drinking involved the women as well as men, and we have, deep in the shadows of this past, the awesome spectacle of Mrs. Meredith redoubling her vigilance. [16]

Dickinson, still fearfully and devoutly conservative in social regulations, had moved ahead of many colleges in the problem of subsidized athletics, so worrisome to Morgan. The Board of Athletic Control (President, Treasurer, Dean of the Law School, two faculty, two alumni and one Senior student) had been established by trustee action June 8, 1934. Primarily intended to control the increasing athletic budget, the Board brought other forms of regulation as well. Limited scholarship inducements would be offered, but with no relaxation of academic requirements. In November, 1934, Spahr, who when younger had supported athletic subsidies, was strongly protesting the Board's decision to remain in the Eastern Pennsylvania Athletic Conference. It imposed a choice between full subsidies or consistently losing, and he urged the scheduling only of schools equal in standards and size. [17]

It was in this period that football fire and fury earned Dickinson's brightly jerseyed players the title of "Red Devils"-- deplored by Corson, who vainly sought to substitute a more temperate soubriquet, "Colonials." [18] "Mac"- Richard Henry McAndrews, former professional baseball player—had been the bright centering force in Dickinson athletics for more than twenty years, as he would continue to be for more than twenty. Mac would lose all control of himself in the excitement of a game. Morgan was his apologist when a Philadelphia coach complained of his "antics" in 1934—the "strictures not unmerited," Jim Henry confessed, but "a fine man at heart and the soul of kindness and helpfulness to the boys." [19]

"Old Mac" has a stellar role in the lore of all these years— Old Mac, who, "taking his morning swim in the pool found

"Mac" and the "Red Devils," *c.* 1938.

Class Scrap, 1910.

that he had company in the form of a baby shark, brought from Baltimore by fast car, by students with the shark's interests at heart." This from John Nicholson, whose long academic career reached its peak in the Library at Kent State, recalling fondly the Mermaid's goings and comings, the white horse holding center stage in chapel, a host of vivid and affectionate memories of this campus.

> What is Dickinson? It is made up of all these things, for me, for all Dickinsonians. It is made up of many more things like these, as well. Its ancient past, its mellow middle years, its merry, warm-hearted modern times, its rich tradition, its willingness to venture into new, still-to-be-explored ways, its resistance to change, and yet its willingness to accept change when change is for the good of Dickinsonians and for Dickinson herself. Dickinson is, for me, a memory, and a very happy one. Dickinson is a ghost for me. I have said to myself, time and time again, "I cannot go back to Dickinson, for it will have changed, and will not be the same as the memory I have of a richly blessed campus." And yet I have come back, over and over again to Dickinson, and found her still the same . . . quiet, and filled with comfort; unchanged and unchanging; and yet always somehow renewed. This is part of the mystery which makes a great college great for all men and women who come within her influence. [20]

Nicholson's tender recollection was supported by a librarian's precise insights, notably in the meticulous study of undergraduate reading which he had made in collaboration with Russell Thompson. [21] This was a recognition of the expanding emphasis on library use in higher education. At Dickinson, where active growth had been delayed until the Carnegie grants of 1931–36, the collection expanded from 52,192 volumes in 1933 to 63,300 in 1938; the budget from $6,050 to $15,027 in the same period. This was being achieved by Librarian May Morris, in office since 1927. At her retirement in 1956 the figures would be 102,326 volumes and $48,576. Here "Maisie," who reckoned a sense of humor and "a glint in the eye" among the essential qualifications for librarianship, was building her own little empire in open alliance with the younger and more progressive faculty.

These were a minority, but an active one. In the Spahr era we see the gradual disappearance of the small, perennial faculty group, known to generations of alumni accepted into their lore with love or friendly derision. Ernest Albert Vuilleumier of Chemistry had succeeded Baldy Sellers as Dean in 1933. Sellers, of limited genius but transcendent devotion, had somehow accumulated a small fortune on his miniscule salary, and left it all to Dickinson. His will, penned late one night near the end on an English Department memo pad, opens quaintly, "If I should die before I wake . . . ", and goes on to particularize the disposal of $60,000. [22] Vuilleumier's faculty, as John Nicholson remembered it, was made up of "sound scholars and devoted teachers. Very fortunate are those of us who remember Mulford Stough and his provocative history classes; and Russell Thompson with his wry and dry humor, and his continuing good-natured feud with his long-time friendly enemy Mulford Stough. That happy feud enlivened a good many classes for students who will remember the long-distance arguments which transpired between the two. There was Dean Vuilleumier's benignant way of handling all students. There was the encyclopedic memory of Herbert Wing, and his astonishing book and paper filled office. There was Whit Bell with his students crowding around him at the end of class. And there were so many more." [23]

The scientists led in publication—"Vooley," Herber, Rogers, Parlin and Eddy. Dr. Eddy's expertise in hair classification had launched him toward fame in 1934 with his solution of the "Babes in the Wood" murder case. [24] In the humanities, Dr. Doney's wide influence is reflected in the new literary magazine, *The Hornbook,* founded in 1932 with Craig R. Thompson as a student editor. Doney and Wing applied Harvard standards to their work, but there were those on this faculty whose success as professors ran far ahead of their formal credentials —Charles Lowe Swift, in English, ex-schoolteacher and newspaperman, friend and drinking companion of H. L. Mencken; or the equally original Stough, whose response to a Middle States questionnaire on himself is barren indeed but does include, on background experience, the debonair, "Fishing over the continent has helped me much in geography." [25]

Corson, efficient and thorough, was a perfect trustees' man on campus. His control over the faculty was complete. In those dark Depression years he kept the institution solvent. Salaries were minimal and based on each individual's absolute need. They were now reduced but, as in Civil War days, with the reduction contingent on a deficit. Corson therefore must have earned some faculty gratitude by keeping his accounts in the black. [26] In the year 1933-34 expenses had equalled income at $165,804, but in 1940-41, costs of $264,126 came well within the $299,000 income—statistics which go far to explain trustee approval of the Corson regime. A favorite story of Dr. Paul Herbert Doney told of his summons to the President's office to be informed that his services—certainly outstanding—were to be rewarded by a raise in salary. The raise, not specified at the time, turned out to be $50 for the year. Carlisle merchants were cudgeled into giving college and faculty discounts an effort long to be echoed in town resentments. [27] New trustee bylaws of June 7, 1935 regularized faculty rank and made a step toward tenure for full professors. As young Professor Mary B. Taintor recalled, Corson rarely if ever gave the answer one wished to hear, but at least it was always uttered with unmistakable precision.

In setting out to modernize the curriculum, the President took and held the initiative, organizing faculty committees to do the work but keeping his own superior coordinating role before them. An honors program supported by oral and written examinations and a thesis, similar to but more stringent than Waugh's, came first. [28] On September 12, 1936, Corson asked and was given faculty authorization to appoint a committee "to study the correlation of work during the Senior year." This brought into being the "Committee of Eight" and a two-year study resulting in a long advance toward the ideal of academic excellence. Its chairman was Herbert Wing, Jr., who had been carrying much of the programs in both Greek and History; his colleagues were Carver, Doney, Landis, Prettyman, Sellers, Thompson and Vuilleumier. By June, "a definite change in academic policy" could be announced, though the work of formulation continued. [29] In September, 1938, it was virtually ready for application to the Class of 1942. Freshman and Sophomore work was to be a liberal preparation for the more specialized Junior and Senior years, and sophomore comprehensive examinations would determine fitness to enter the upperclass program. Seniors must take two broadly conceived courses, World Literature and Philosophy of Life, and must pass comprehensive examinations in their majors to graduate. Some freedoms, such as unlimited class absences for A students, offset the rigidity of the requirements. "Independent study" existed in the form of reading periods in lieu of class, followed by testing or papers. [30] After Freshman year, participation in at least one extracurricular activity was expected, with more dependent upon each student's standing. [31]

Favorable comment in the *New York Times* sealed the College's commitment to quality education along these new lines. [32] Yet factors were present or approaching which would limit or defeat much of the effort. While World Literature, first taught by Swift and more lately by Amos Benjamin Horlacher, became one of the most popular and effective courses, Philosophy of Life never got off the ground, due to opposition in the Department of Religion. [33] It was a proposal in which the President had taken a warm personal interest, and he would have been one of the fourteen faculty involved in teaching it. To the historian it is interesting as a modernized revival of the old presidential Moral Philosophy course, intended to top off everything else with a guide to right living. [34] The plan for senior comprehensives, adopted by the faculty on March 31, 1941, would be postponed soon after for the duration of the war, and the war would bring with it new influences affecting the whole program.

The shadow of world conflict had first been felt in 1938 when Chinese students ceased to come from Fukien Christian University, held back by the crisis of invasion. [35] Oblivious to turmoil abroad, a new major financial campaign was launched in 1940, only to be brought to a sudden halt by the Japanese attack in December, 1941. [36] It had two accomplishments in that brief period. About $15,000 was raised, and a new founding date, 1773, acquired.

"I guess I put my foot in it a little with President Hutchison of Washington and Jefferson at the Harrisburg luncheon," Boyd Lee Spahr had confided to Corson, January 25, 1939. He had ridiculed the practice of adopting an official founding date based on that of "an earlier academy," only to learn afterward that his fellow guest had done exactly that. Nine months later, representing Dickinson at the inauguration of Haverford's new president, he found W. and J. called out and marching to the fore, with rank as the second oldest college in Pennsylvania. This Spahr's devotion to his school, always alertly competitive, could not brook. Here was a point of prestige, as he told Corson, "which I think we should conserve." Others might "smile tolerantly at it," but "I am not going to yield second place to Washington and Jefferson and I think you agree with me." [37]

He had already given, in advance of the campaign, $7,500 toward completion of property holdings on the Mooreland campus, and $10,000 toward the renovation of Bosler Hall. Bosler must be expanded for library purposes and, in keeping with his ideal of a coherent architecture for the whole campus, given Georgian lines and a facing of the native limestone. Other contributors were mustered, and the work completed in October, 1940. [38] As affairs were managed at this time, no one dreamed of consulting Miss Morris, and the result, from a librarian's viewpoint, left much to be desired. Maisie, presented with a completely uncentralized addition, handled the situation well. Her new "Spahr Room" brought a warmer, more constant and more personal rapport between this trustee and the Library. Her "Sharp Room," dedicated to recreational reading, set for the whole campus a new standard of attractive furnishing and atmosphere and became the scene of her Thursday afternoon Library Teas, bringing students and faculty regularly together, the one place besides the President's House where a College guest could be graciously entertained.

In 1942 Dr. Wing first offered his course in The History and Interpretation of World War II, in effect a very wide-ranging background survey which was continued, with variations, until his retirement in 1961. A two-course offering in Aviation, under Dr. Parlin and sponsored by the Civil Aeronautics Authority, ended its second and last year in 1942. Beginning on March 1, 1943, a large segment of campus and faculty was taken over by the Thirty-second Training Detachment (Air Crew). A group of 140 entered each month for a five-month course, with a maximum student body of about 700. Conway and East were barracks. Classes were in Denny, Tome and West. The old gymnasium was converted into a mess hall. In all, 2,260 cadets passed through the program until its sudden termination, January 29, 1944.

The outbreak of war had brought grave anxiety as to the College's financial future. Now, with only 195 undergraduates and the war still in progress, there was a new sense of emergency. Plans were made to enlarge housing facilities for women students, and the alumni asked for $30,000 in contributions, more than doubling the recent Annual Giving figures. The President's statement of the case to the trustees, February 12, 1944, was published at once in the *Alumnus,* suppressing, however his revelation that the government occupancy had, in fact been remarkably profitable, accumulating a surplus of between $125,000 and $150,000. Nor was it published that salaries had dropped back from government to College level with appointments still on the emergency year-to-year basis. [39] Happily, not only did the alumni meet their goal, but Annual Giving continued to move upward from the $30,000 figure.

President Corson, having added a sense of crisis to plans for the immediate future, was now, simultaneously, himself a point of crisis. "Bishop" of 1917 was in line for an actual bishopric in the Methodist Church. The news broke in the late summer of 1943, shocking those trustees who had thought that Corson, like Reed, "would count it but honor and privilege" to serve the College through life. It was now rumored that "Bishop" had been actively seeking this consummation for the last five years. [40] Shocked or no, the Board might have responded simply and normally by casting about forthwith for an advantageous replacement. But "the fly in the ointment" (a phrase recurrent in Morgan's correspondence) was Paul Appenzellar. The Chairman of the Finance Committee had done wonders with the College portfolio, had arranged with the Chase Manhattan Bank for loans at 1½ per cent, and had given generously himself. Appenzellar, with that tight, nervous mouth in the large face, willful, domineering, had accepted Corson as a friend and as a convert to the idea of College over Church. He now sensed betrayal. At least four times already he had struck cold fear into his colleagues of the Spahr group by threats to resign, once because of the suggestion that a Democrat be given an honorary degree. [41]

Appenzellar and manufacturer Robert Rich, who favored

Top left: Fred Pierce Corson. By Wilbur Fisk Noyes, 1937. Top right: Cornelius William Prettyman. By Wilbur Fisk Noyes, 1945. Bottom left: Bradford Oliver McIntire. By Wilbur Fisk Noyes, 1947. Bottom right: Boyd Lee Spahr. By Wilbur Fisk Noyes, 1937.

Corson's elevation, became protagonists in a wordy battle. Spahr, who in September had been mildly urging Corson to decline any bishopric, by April, 1944, was warning him that acceptance would mean instant termination of his college presidency—at the same time reminding both contestants of "an old tavern in Philadelphia where there was a large sign on the wall, 'Gentlemen must not discuss politics or religion.' "[42] There followed negotiations with Corson in which the trustees enacted salary and retirement benefits to offset the economic advantages of the episcopacy. Appenzellar felt certain and Spahr reassured that this action included an agreement on Corson's part to decline. The correspondence leaves one with an impression that Dr. Corson was as eager for the new office as any churchman might be expected to be, but pursued it hoping that if successful it would appear as a draft, an irresistible call to duty. He seems also to have regarded it as one which could be successfully combined with a college presidency. On Sunday, May 28, 1944, he himself delivered the commencement address marking his tenth year as President and wearing for the first time the purple gown in which Dickinson Presidents still appear.[43] Less than a fortnight later he became, on second ballot a Bishop of the Church—and the storm broke.

As early as December 6, 1943, Appenzellar had contemplated using Corson's new ambition to "begin a movement to take the College out of any church connection"—let the Board simply tell the managers of the two conference funds to discontinue payments and that would be that, small loss and a final liberation. Spahr, however sympathetic, saw it nonetheless as profitless contention.[44]

Corson, triumphant at his election by the Jurisdictional Conference at Ocean City, opened one telegram which was far from congratulatory. Bob Rich, standing near, saw the flush of anger as the Bishop reached its conclusion:

> ...SUCH A STANDARD AS YOU HAVE SET PROBABLY IS SATISFACTORY FOR A CHURCH OFFICIAL. IT ISN'T HIGH ENOUGH FOR ME SO CONSIDER OUR PERSONAL RELATIONS COMPLETELY SEVERED. I HOPE NEVER TO SEE OR HEAR FROM YOU AGAIN. AM RESIGNING FROM COLLEGE BOARD.
> PAUL APPENZELLAR[45]

Treasurer Gilbert Malcolm received, as promptly, a demand that Appenzellar's $1,000 check be returned and daring him to sue for the remainder of his $20,000 subscription.[46] Sumner Drayer, mild-tempered manufacturer of Miss America Candies, was staggered by a "terrific" letter.[47] To Spahr came ink-splashed longhand letters blasting all Methodists and hinting at a willingness to withdraw his resignation in return for an all-out fight, seasoning rancor with poetry—from Tennyson, "His honor rooted in dishonor stood," and from Milton's "Lycidas," "a favorite of mine . . . this line which took on new meaning as I recall our recent.'mess,' 'As killing as the canker to the rose'— There's church control to a college!"[48]

Spahr hastened out to Carlisle. He would not break with the Church, but he would instantly erase the possibility, for which Corson had already provided, of combining presidency and bishopric. He met with the Board of Deans and passed on to the Executive Committee its recommendation that Will Prettyman take over as Acting President.[49] He then urged Appenzellar to reconsider his resignation—ventured to "suppose" that the next President would be a Methodist, "but I am certainly gunshy at selecting a clergyman . . . . I don't propose to have the College act as a nursery for bishops."[50]

In his last trustee meeting as President, Corson had recommended a Committee on Student Life—two faculty and two trustees to survey the communal situation as a whole rather than from the fraternity and other viewpoints Spahr appointed Russell I. Thompson as chairman, Arthur V. Bishop and trustees Lloyd W. Johnson and S. Walter Stauffer. He had in his hands Thompson's "View of the Future of Dickinson College," written in that spring, a personal appraisal of the institution and its potentials, a full and lucid statement by a professional educator and devoted alumnus. It may well have been the first such thing he had read. Thompson's reports to the Committee were equally perceptive and clear.[51]

Simultaneously, the Middle States Association of Colleges and Secondary Schools, while continuing accreditation, was pointing out to Prettyman areas of serious weakness in the structure he had inherited—in the program of objective and comprehensive testing, in a preponderance of high grades, inadequacy of laboratories, the summer session, the lack of a policy on faculty tenure, the financial structure. Prettyman reported to Spahr, who advised him upon what answers to return. [52]

Raphael Smead Hays, Carlisle manufacturer who figures in this history as the discreet student assistant of "Docky" Reed, was the first to suggest that in recognition of his long service the new President be elected without the pejorative "Acting." [53] This was done. Thompson could well have been the right choice of a younger man. But "Dutch" Prettyman, old-timer, heart and soul a professor, humorous eye and lounging walk, possessed an experience and commanded an affection that promised well. Here, as one of his students, Dr. James Morgan Read, '29, has described him, was "a tremendously large human spirit," a teacher who taught, for the most part, "by the simple force of his personality," in love with his discipline and yet always with the whole range of learning and culture in view. That was not all. Prettyman had been an innovator in the use of teaching aids, the first to play records to his language classes and show films. Read had been the first to benefit by the student exchange program with German universities which Prettyman had inaugurated and financed by money-raising departmental events.

Characteristically, Prettyman dedicated his administration first of all to a blessed release from rigors of the past. "A new President—A New Spirit"—so the students hailed him in a newspaper keyed to progress, *The Free Dickinsonian.* Its mimeographed pages took a bold stand for mature journalistic responsiblity, rejecting both the old *Dickinsonian's* carefully supervised reporting and the carefree abandon of that "low obscene scandal sheet" recently published for the first time, the *Drinkinsonian.* [54] It made a plea as well for mature and responsible student government. Prettyman actually consulted the students on their needs and desires. He reactivated the health service, relaxed the rules on smoking and opened the door to frequent dances which, as he sagely observed, "put them all in a very good frame of mind." [55]

To Spahr, he recommended two policy reforms: the adoption of a faculty retirement plan, and that Dickinson become coeducational "in the true sense of the term," that is, three hundred women in the student body of six hundred. [56] He must have known that neither stood a very good chance of Board approval, but could readily concur himself with Spahr's first proposal, a D.D. for "the Reverend Howard L. Rubendall, '31, a Presbyterian clergyman who has recently become Headmaster of the Mt. Hermon School in Massachusetts," another teacher known for his popularity with students. [57]

On March 13, 1945, before he had been a year in office, Prettyman suffered a severe heart attack. He would remain an invalid, dying on August 7, 1946, soon after the long-delayed election of a successor. In the interval, the College was run by an "Administrative Committee" of Spahr, Malcolm and Vuilleumier, a triumvirate whose reign accomplished little and left one of its members, "Vooley," much embittered. [58]

Spahr's long-standing effort to integrate College and Law School was renewed. [59] The basement of Tome was renovated, and Prettyman had thought this would stave off the need for a chemistry building. [60] Spahr was for making the old gym and army mess hall into an attractive college commons such as Haverford and Swarthmore had, but not to replace the fraternity dining rooms. Edna Appenzellar, Paul's wife, had promised "a dining hall on the English university plan" a year before, but now it must be done without her help. It was authorized on December 15, 1945, together with a new women's dormitory to be built on Mooreland and replace Metzger. [61] Yet alas, in the midst of these pleasant preoccupations new factors were beginning to emphasize the lack of trustee-faculty accord. Faculty elected a committee to codify bylaws and committee structure. Wing opposed any change, and Spahr enjoined the committee to drop the matter pending the election of a president, yet giving an impression that he considered any action by an elected committee a threat to constituted authority. [62]

Students, meanwhile, were present in greater force than ever before, more than half of them the older, purposeful veterans of the war. Here, as at other colleges, they had lost touch with tradition, the songs, customs, high-jinks. Efforts were made repeatedly to arouse interest in the mores of college life, in particular those which had given this college its individuality, but to little avail. [63] A rigorous schedule of "Attendance Regulations," with an accompaniment of penalties, enacted February

1, 1946, had to be purged of its system of demerits in October. [64] In March, 1946, the Student Senate, out since 1943, was revived with both men and women members, a reform first proposed by Waugh. [65]

These students wanted the leadership of a president, and he must be a "recognized educator." [66] The stormy "demonstration" of December 7, 1945 (a day for the veterans to remember) had made clear that they wanted much else besides: abolition of "faculty politics," responsible student government, more and better courses, a relaxed and well-defined social policy, vocational guidance and placement, a new Dean of Women. [67] But the president came first, and the Harrisburg *Patriot* confidently predicted that one would be elected when the Board met at the Union League in Philadelphia, December 15. [68]

High on Spahr's list of candidates was Arthur Sherwood Flemming of the Civil Service Commission, who would later become President of Ohio Wesleyan and then enter Eisenhower's cabinet as Secretary of Health, Education and Welfare. He had visited Dickinson and expressed a very definite interest, and yet, deeply involved in war and post-war programs of the government, at last declined. [69] Spahr continued his search. No choice was made that winter, and only rumors reached the campus. One had it that Charles S. Swope, President of West Chester State, had visited Carlisle and made a particular survey of the President's House to be sure it suited him. Cornelius Fink, the only AAUP man on the faculty, brought his copy of the *Bulletin* to May Morris with its account of West Chester's place on the censured list, condemning Swope's administration. [70] Whitfield Bell and Russell Thompson, casting about for some trustee who might present a counter case, brought the article to Dean Hoffman, Harrisburg newspaperman, and were deeply relieved to learn of Swope's removal from the list. [71] The search became desperate. Then came Malcolm to the rescue with the name of his classmate of 1915, Bill Edel, who was due for retirement after thirty years' service as a Navy chaplain. Here was a Methodist clergyman, but one with a fresher, broader ministry behind him, a man experienced in dealing with young men, a new outlook, new view of disciplined living. Instantly approached, he instantly accepted, and his name was presented and approved, June 7, 1946.

It cannot be said that those who had hoped for a "recognized educator" were happy in the choice. This new man—friendly eyes behind thick lenses in a round, earnest face—had been Superintendent of Education on Samoa from 1924 to 1926. He had received a Dickinson D.D. in 1935. At the first Dickinson ceremony attended by the author of this chronicle, September 18, 1949, he delivered "The Sermon-Theme, 'HOW DIZZY CAN YOU GET' "—a question which, as it then seemed, only time could answer. Yet the mantle of Morgan and Corson had fallen upon a very different sort of fellow. No professor with ideas or ideals of his own would now be confronted with an abrupt threat of dismissal. Edel fully accepted the trustee concept of an authoritarian chain of command, but it would now be administered on campus by a man with a highly sensitive ego, conscious of his share of the poetic-artistic temperament, greatly eager to be loved and admired, and determined to prove himself a great college president.[72] To be able to confer a benefit of any sort gave him joy. He rejoiced to find dates, names, personal relationships falling into patterns that seemed to give a special sense of order to the world. He faced his whole task with the duties of obedience and command in mind, and with a ritualistic piety. He himself must preside at every meeting, introduce every speaker, appear in every photograph. The conferring of degrees gave him a solemn pleasure, careful in the formation and utterance of the words by which the transformation was wrought. Every College gathering took on the character of a religious service, opened with a prayer and generally closed with a blessing. Chairing faculty meetings, he always stood when speaking on behalf of the trustees.

He made himself perhaps the hardest-working president the College had ever had, his office always open to faculty concerns, reviewing (and at times amending) committee recommendations, reading and initialing the minutes of student groups—keeping a finger on everything, his West College light often burning far into the night. Displeasure might be expressed in a friendly question, in non-appointment to a committee (there were committees enough to take in everyone), or non-adjustment of salary. Faculty rank was honorary, occasionally a compensation for low salary, and at least once promotion to Associate was made to ease the hurt of dismissal. This gentler management was to be exercised over a changing faculty and student body, each group with its own growing ideals and spirit of independence; and in an era, too, of educational experimentation in ever wider and more fluid patterns. Edel must deal with these trends on the one hand, and on the other with an increasingly conservative Board of Trustees.

Vuilleumier, Chairman of Chemistry, suave and popular professor, had not been happy as a member of the administrative triumvirate with Spahr and Malcolm. He gladly yielded the Dean's office to Russell Thompson, whose experience contributed much to the successful launching of the new regime. Horlacher, Navy colleague, critic and friend of the President, came in as Dean of Men. Library staff was admitted to the faculty with the status of an instructional department, and a regularization of faculty ranking begun—notably with McAndrews; "Mac" became Assistant Professor of Physical Education after thirty-four years as Instructor. [73] In response to those earlier student demands the curriculum was modernized, with courses in Russian language and literature among the innovations. These last were authorized by the trustees, 1947, "because of the development of the United Nations and the new political alignments," over the recorded negative votes of Rich and Feroe, and survived only until 1950. [74] Greek and Latin had been dropped as requirements for graduation just before Edel's election, with Dickinson the last college in Pennsylvania to take this step. [75] The quality-credit system of grading was adopted, and senior comprehensives ordered to begin in 1949. [76] The Ph.B. disappears with the Catalogue of 1946-47.

The Middle States Association, still with an eye askance at Dickinson, had sent President Levering Tyson of Muhlenberg to interview Edel, November 15, 1946. Edel a month later proposed a self-evaluation by his faculty, a reappraisal which led up to the visit of the Association's accreditation team, March 7-9, 1949. The Middle States report attested to "a well-organized liberal arts program," though inadequate in speech, music and fine arts. Languages overemphasized grammar and composition,

giving too little attention to literature. A separation of Philosophy and Religion into two departments was advised.[77] There
were other criticisms but it was, as Dr. Edel reported to the
trustees, "generally favorable." The report, however, was not to
become a basis for faculty action or discussion. Like the College
Charter and Bylaws, it was kept out of general circulation in
that defensive withdrawal of administration behind boundaries
of its own.

A group of thirteen faculty members brought in a chapter
of the American Association of University Professors, December
10, 1948. The Swope incident had created an appreciation of
the value of AAUP, but the leadership came from a newcomer,
Dr. William Lonsdale Tayler of Political Science.[78] Tayler's response to the question, "Do you recognize any responsibility
that has a religious connotation resting upon you as a teacher?"
had been, "Yes, indeed. To try to practice what I teach—World
Citizenship. International understanding and good will to all
people."[79] It was a doctrine which he would continue to promote with freshness and cheer.

In December, 1946, Edel had asked Spahr for a committee
to bring faculty salaries into line with those of other institutions
and with the cost of living. He wanted men with a fresh viewpoint, suggesting Stauffer and Masland as experienced employers and William C. Sampson, a superintendent of schools.[80]
Three years later he shocked the Board with a faculty tenure
plan, but was persuaded to withdraw it without formal presentation.[81] Crowning all this effort, at the start of the year
1950–51, the trustees granted a bonus of one half of one
month's salary in "recognition of faculty assistance in economi-
cal administration."[82] Salary improvement, when it came,
would be under AAUP pressure.

To the Board, first things must come first, with a revival of
the deferred financial campaign. A preliminary conference, November 25, 1946, had set primary goals: a women's dormitory,
a student union (generally in later references, "student center,"
"union" being a controversial term in Carlisle) and increase of
endowment by $2,500,000.[83] The monetary goal was a much
smaller, unnamed sum when the "Ten Year Development Program" was launched in a four-day convocation, complete with

parade and honorary degrees, celebrating the College's 175th Anniversary, April 22-25, 1948. [84]

A survey by the firm of Marts and Lundy, 1947, was viewed by the trustees with an optimism it hardly justified. It shows rather that the cultivation of potential donors had been long neglected and reveals a divided, unenthusiastic constituency. Simultaneous campaigns by both Church and Law School darkened the picture. [85] The new President was far behind in the personal contacts which require long cultivation, but forward in creating occasions and distinctions. He joined enthusiastically with Spahr in regularizing the named professorships, creating a core to which others could be, and were, added at $50,000 each—celebrating them in bronze outside his office door. [86] Memorial tablets and memorial names flowered everywhere. The vernal celebration of Founders Day was revived. The two top upperclassmen were dubbed Junior and Senior "Sophisters," a word culled from the historic past, and rewarded with scholarships, a place in convocation ceremonies and their names in bronze.

The President came back from a trip to England in the summer of 1951 with refreshed zeal and the idea of chairings. Now each inward and spiritual chair would have its outward and visible one. The professor, after delivering an address on his discipline, would be seated in it by presidential pressure on the shoulders, and at that moment by prearrangement a group of "chairmen" would rush forward to bear seat and seated from the Chapel platform to the faculty section below. This novel "custom" was accepted by faculty with mixed feelings, but by the students with delight and derision, roaring with laughter at the presidential antics and professorial response.

To offset all this with a fixture of ceremonial dignity came the "Great Mace of Dickinson College," carved in wood to Edel specifications and surmounted by a bronze mermaid, the gift, 1951, of Frank E. Masland, Jr. In the same year the Mary Dickinson Club enlisted the women of the College community in its support. [87] Here also came the first "Joseph Priestley Celebration," to become an annual occasion of high distinction. In 1954 Mary Dickinson Club pressure brought the Board of Trustees its first woman member, Mary Sharp Foucht, already a long-time supporter of the College Library. [88] That same year valuable support came with the formation of the Parents Advisory Council, a group of forty fathers, ten for each class, selected by the President. Yet a huge job of personal research and solicitation remained undone. Also in 1954, George Shuman, Jr., who had remained with the College in administrative posts since graduation, was called to the Spahr office and given the direction of a reactivated Ten Year Development Program— leaving it to him to inform Edel of the changed situation. [89] The spadework of college development followed, searching and thorough, arousing new interest, such as that of Homer C. Holland, '13; bringing into the Board such stalwarts as Rolland L. Adams, '27; and achieving steadily mounting financial figures. [90] The supporting Development Council, organized May 4, 1956, included five trustees, five alumni, three parents, three "friends," two faculty (Taintor and Tayler) and two students. [91]

In 1950 Dr. Edel would occasionally remark good-naturedly that he had now completed a four-year course in college management and was prepared to carry the torch unaided. From this declaration of independence one could date the rising spirit of faculty resistance to the President and the invisible trustee authority. Or, if you prefer, the opening might be set in 1949, when a young instructor had put his job on the line by openly inviting his colleagues to "A Cocktail Party." [92] Certainly, the opposition came from new faculty and from students with more sophisticated backgrounds than those of the Central Pennsylvania Conference. Carlisle itself was changing as Turnpike and expressways brought the cities nearer. Always the Law School, and then the coming of the Army War College in 1951, fostered a more liberated social life. More and more, the trustees felt themselves confronted by a conspiratorial threat to legitimate power. More and more on the other side, the neglect of basic educational progress in favor of "window dressing" was deplored. A primary irritant here came from administration efforts in behalf of the few Seniors failing their comprehensives. Against stout resistance, the requirement was at last "temporarily suspended," due to "present world conditions." [93] It would not be restored. Faculty bylaws were adopted to forestall smooth control by prearrangement and from the chair, including a rule on secret ballot when voting on any name, or when requested. [94]

On March 5, 1951, the nomination of a close friend of Boyd Lee Spahr for an honorary degree was voted down, and the name of William Faulkner substituted. Faulkner, to older shepherds of the Dickinson community, was not an admired author. Others, however, had lost all patience with the easy bestowal of these honors and had taken alarm at the President's view that hónorary degrees might reasonably be awarded to the number of 10 per cent of the graduating class. The Faulkner vote was rescinded, and a special meeting called to restore the Spahr friend. [95] Immediately after making its concession on Faulkner, the faculty voted, "That a Committee on Academic Standards be instituted; that the committee consist of four members of the faculty (one from each rank), chosen by the faculty, and of the Dean of the College, ex officio; that the members of the committee be elected at the next faculty meeting; that the chairman of the committee be elected by the members of the committee." [96]

An elected committee! It was a crossing of swords. Happily, the President did not invoke—as he would later—that by-law which enjoined him to submit to trustee approval any faculty action which might be thought to affect "fundamental policy of the College." [97] A special faculty meeting followed, March 24, to discuss "The State of the College," with Edel warmly denying a lack of any sense of direction and Ben Horlacher bluntly presenting faculty dissatisfaction with administrative concealment of policy and action and with the lack of a tenure policy. The new committee was elected on May 9: Eric W. Barnes, Benjamin D. James, Walter T. James, Bertram H. Davis.

Dr. Edel's characteristic response to these events was an eloquent plea at the trustee meeting of June 6 for an increase in faculty salaries. The average of $4,120 was, as he pointed out, "less than a common laborer can earn in many parts of the country." The Board met this with what was intended, apparently, as incentive rather than immediate benefit. It raised all maximum figures, "but without any change in the lower limits." [98] The action was widely publicized and some professors found themselves subjected to increased charges by town creditors who did not understand that the Corson regimen remained intact. No one received any actual raise.

At this same time, student power was stirring from its winter's sleep. Demonstrations reminiscent of 1945 were followed by an open hearing on student complaints, filling Bosler Hall, March 5, 1952. Grumbling was loudest and most effective in the matter of compulsory chapel, twice a week, with its vestigial dusting of religion and its "cultural" programs geared to strict economy. There was a response at the May 5 faculty meeting when Horlacher moved that the trustees be asked to set aside certain student fees "as a fund to be used for projects suggested by the Student Senate and approved by the Faculty." The reply from Dr. Spahr was couched in terms which were to become increasingly familiar: "It should seem apparent upon reflection that the trustees acting through the College administration cannot abrogate their functions in this matter." [99] Administration then followed Horlacher's cue to a more effective solution. Let the students themselves pay a $10 fee in support of a cultural affairs program managed by a joint student-faculty committee. It was done, and at a stroke it changed for the better the character of both College and town.

Independent student comment continued in The *Drinkinsonian,* the fraternity skits and, brighter yet, "The Dickinson Follies." The "Follies," born in 1949, now celebrated rumors of an Edel deficit with "Out of the Red," full of song-and-dance comment such as "Higher Education is a Mess!" [100] "Let's face reality," the *Dickinsonian* editorialized, May 12, 1954. "Queen Victoria died over fifty years ago, but the social concepts formed in her time seem to live on at Dickinson." The old standards, old ideas of "discipline," were in slow retreat. At times the President would speak out against "vulgarity, obscenity and sacrilege," and then balance that with an intervention which he liked to call "executive clemency." Executive clemency was assuredly a disturbing factor, and nearly wrecked the newly formed Student-Faculty Judicial Council in 1958, in the dreadful case of the Phi Kappa Psi brother who had been sniping at professors with the house air gun. [101]

President Edel, with segments of faculty and student body

pitted against him, faced also a triple threat which he christened, in poetic imagery, "the three Black Beasts"—inflation, the draft and a paucity of students reflecting the low birthrate of Depression years. [102] In 1950 he had succeeded in enlarging the quota of co-eds as an emergency measure of the Korean War of 1950 to 1953. [103] The Reserve Officers Training Corps unit, hurried through under this impetus in 1952, became a favored Edel project, adding military glamor to the commencement ceremony and replacing one of the older College traditions, the "Doll Show" (later "Doll Dance"), with a Military Ball. [104]

Edel was aware that the population explosion would, in the course of time and nature, remove one Black Beast from his view. He must hold his faculty together through the lean years. [105] The faculty with which he had come into office was well worth the effort. It had a good corps of veterans. Whitfield Bell was back from war service. Eric Barnes, in whose appointment Spahr took justifiable pride, had brought together a new English Department, coherent and able. There were unusual younger men such as Walter Thomas James and John Wesley Robb, both of Philosophy and Religion, a group whom Edel characterized to the trustees as "among the most brilliant and valuable teachers we have." [106] Yet as the faculty-administration rift widened many would go, much of the coherence would be lost, and a new emphasis on "loyalty" as a condition of employment would not better the situation.

Illness took Russell Thompson from active service in 1950; Frederic W. Ness, '33, succeeded Acting Dean McCullough in 1952. For six years he had been Assistant to the Vice Chancellor of New York University. His functions were to be all of those usually assigned to a college dean: admission policies, curriculum, departmental organization, library, faculty enlistment, promotion, separation. They were detailed by the President in a letter to all faculty. [107] It was not long, however, before Dr. Ness learned that all matters "related to money" would remain with the President. In short, Edel would still wield the scepter of Morgan and Corson. Barnes went on leave in 1951, submitting his final resignation two years later. A professional actor as well as a brilliant scholar, he has left his mark upon the College with the Mermaid Players and in the Library's

Top left: Ernest Albert Vuilleumier. By Wilbur Fisk Noyes, 1949. Top right: Mulford Stough. Bottom left: Eric Wollencott Barnes. Bottom right: Whitfield Jenks Bell, Jr.

superior section on Shakespeare. [108] Bell, Boyd Lee Spahr Professor of American History, left in 1953, returning as an alumnus trustee and attempting, more fully than Barnes though with no better effect, to convince Boyd Lee Spahr that all was not well on campus. Bell left a continuing contribution in the Boyd Lee Spahr Lectures in Americana, inaugurated on March 7, 1947, with Lyman H. Butterfield. They were placed under the aegis of "Maisie's" Library to protect their scholarly character from administrative pressures. Kuebler, a classmate of Ness who had been openly deploring the decline of the standards set by the Committee of Eight and had once presented a motion consigning all honorary degrees to a limbo of trustee decision alone, left in 1955. [109]

Explicit criticism of the President was coming to Spahr from these men and from others. Barnes' was perhaps the most devastating. His view was broad, his statements made with diplomatic precision. He had "gathered that the College felt that the quality of the individual instructor was a secondary matter." Edel, "without academic awareness of the problems involved," insisted upon making all decisions himself. Corson and Edel, neither an educator, had alike failed to develop "a real atmosphere of learning on the campus." To complaint from the campus, Sydney Kline added the viewpoint of a parent and trustee. Spahr referred all this to Edel, disturbed and yet content to accept the presidential rebuttals. [110] With the chain of command still apparently frank and strong, criticism of Edel was criticism of the Board. Not until a break in that chain appeared would his feeling change.

Buildings, always the happiest area of trustee endeavor and accomplishment, brighten the Edel years. Renovation of the old gym as a commons had been completed in 1947, to last until the collapse of one wall in 1953. South College, acquired from the Federal Works Agency, went up in 1948. The long-projected women's dormitory was opened on the Benjamin Rush campus four years later, bearing the name of Sumner M. Drayer, "largest single subscriber of any living person to the Ten Year Development Program." [111] Metzger would remain, for Freshman women. Mathews House, for women, came in 1957, the year when the mysterious Nickel Potato Chip building was ac-

Alumni Gymnasium, built in 1929.

Drayer Hall, built in 1952.

quired. In 1953, old Colonel John Montgomery was honored in the naming of faculty apartments, added to an early mansion with the area's only authentic Greek Revival facade. Morgan Hall, 1955, for men, gave Dean Ness an opportunity for an improved Freshman program, with a step away from dependence on fraternity housing. [112] Spahr gifts of 1956 and 1958 added the squash courts to South and relieved a desperate situation in the Library with new stack space, study space and lighting. A gift of C. Scott Althouse had made possible the new chemistry building of 1957, and in the next year the interior of Tomé was entirely rebuilt.

It depends upon one's point of view whether the new Allison "Church-Chapel," opened in 1957, should have crowning achievement honors or be rated a "fly in the ointment." Stately, well-designed, it was from the very first a point of contention and would remain resolutely moot. On the night of January 20, 1954, the church at the corner of High and West had been swept by fire. President Edel, an opportunist of the first order, was at work on plans for a new and greater edifice even before the ashes were cold. An acute illness of the aging President of the Board gave Edel more freedom in developing a scheme by which the College would exchange a section of the Rush Campus for the old Allison site and would agree to contribute a substantial sum to the new building and to share in its maintenance. Spahr was in basic agreement, believing that his twenty-year-old hope of giving the Library all of Bosler would be realized. [113] Not so, though he would not be informed of it until long after the fait accompli. The Church fathers were determined to have a temple in which no secular voice would be raised. This brought up sharp questions as to the justification of Dickinson's $200,000 contribution—answered by statements that the money would come entirely from "Methodist sources." [114] Yet as with the earlier church, its value to the broad educational program remained a debatable issue.

Administration and trustee organization, meanwhile, were being consolidated. By 1954, Class Deans had been gradually eliminated, and the Deans of the College, of Men and Women, were coordinating their work with that of faculty advisors. [115] Middle States had recommended such a change five years before. A trustee Committee of College-Fraternity Relations, authorized on December 4, 1954, enunciated "general principles" which would take the brotherhoods under the wing of the Board and away from "College rules and regulations." This brought a prompt and pungent objection from Edel, with a reminder of the confusion such trustee involvement had caused in the 1820's. Edel won his point on this, but the Committee was continued through 1956 after a faculty attack on racial discrimination by national fraternities, sparked by Julien Ripley of Physics, had brought old and new concepts of brotherhood into collision. [116]

The Board meeting of June 10, 1955, was the scene of a carefully prepared Spahr effort to smooth out all troubles for a fresh start. It was preceded by a trustee-faculty dinner, on campus. This had been suggested by the AAUP chapter six months before, and Spahr, as soon as he had heard of it. had begun to prepare his address on the subject assigned to him, "The Trustees' Vision of the Dickinson College of 1965." [117] Chapter President Davis spoke on the character and ideals of the Association. No immediate rapport was established, but it was certainly an historic confrontation of the two groups. Next day, out at the Masland Company's guest house on King's Gap where the summer trustee meeting was currently being held, a charter amendment was authorized admitting Shuman and Ness to Board membership as Financial and Academic Vice Presidents. [118] Vice President Malcolm, formerly Treasurer and Alumni Secretary, had been in this position since 1947. The three (none eligible for President of the Board) were intended to bring a closer, firmer liaison with the campus. In operation this change would be found only to increase frictions within the Board, and would be eliminated in the revision of 1966. For the faculty, salaries and tenure now received positive action. A survey conducted by the Chapter of AAUP had revealed all the inequities of a continuing thrifty paternalism. President Roger E. Nelson had brought them to Edel's attention in a lucid and forceful way in the spring of 1953. [119] New faculty had been of necessity taken on at better salaries, and in one case a department chairman inadvertently learned that he had an Instructor, without doctorate, receiving more than himself. [120] Edel's appeal for a $1,000 to $1,500 rise in base pay for the four ranks and of $500 in top par for Instructors was couched in terms very close to those of President Davis' address at the dinner:

> I am proud to be able to bring the College to the place where it can be among the leaders in restoring to the profession of teaching its proper standing in the competitive economy, and to the individual teacher the sense of dignity and self-respect that rightly belongs to him. The college professor, at the peak of his profession, stands on a level with the lawyer or the physician at the peak of his, and deserves comparable remuneration. [121]

In 1954, at the Chapter's urging, Edel had renewed his earlier recommendation on tenure. It had gone to committee, and now, at this meeting, had favorable action at last with "indefinite term of office for Professors and Associate Professors." [122] President Edel, with the dignity and self-respect of his own office much in mind, topped off his report with a statement on "This Year of Accomplishment," followed by "A Personal Word" deploring the derogatory statements of some present and departed members of faculty and "by an equally small group of alumni." To this the Board responded with a rising vote of "complete confidence." [123] Complete confidence is not indicated, however, in the creation at this meeting of a Committee on Educational Program. Its chairman would be Dr. Carl C. Chambers, '29, Vice President for Engineering Affairs at the University of Pennsylvania, and the only university professor on the Board. Later, when Spahr was pressing again for trustee participation in the selection and promotion of faculty, Chambers' reply would be a resounding negative. "Dr. Chambers is very much on the faculty side on all questions," Merle Allen reported to Spahr in reply to an inquiry. "He is tainted with AAUP." [124]

In this way, with spotlights and music, the stage was set for the climactic events of the spring of 1956. All that fall and winter the drums of anti-Communist hysteria has been beating. Curtain rises upon Dr. Laurent Raymond LaVallee, in his first year as Assistant Professor of Economics, informing Dr. Edel that he had been named as a Communist and summoned before the House Committee on Un-American Activities, where he would invoke the Fifth Amendment. That was on December 23. He appeared before the House, March 1, and was suspended from the faculty by Edel on the 19th to await, as the bylaws provided, a hearing before the Executive Committee of the Board. [125] In the meantime, a faculty Committee on Academic Freedom and Tenure had been elected and active: Davis, Flaherty, Ripley and Taintor. A special faculty meeting, March 21, approved the Committee's report asking LaVallee's release from suspension, the submission of the President's charges to the faculty for a hearing, and a revision of the bylaws to accord with AAUP recommended procedure. [126]

The nervously legalistic psychology of the Board was in full flower at its hearing in Harrisburg, April 20, 1956. Its charges were "Insubordination," "Incompetency," and "Disloyalty to the Government of the United States and Dickinson College." Spahr, overriding Judge Woodside, would not accept pleading the Fifth Amendment as evidence of guilt. [127] The other charges sufficed to the satisfaction of the Board, though not at all to that of the faculty, some of whom found it particularly odd that a colleague should be dismissed on the basis of evidence which had shown him to have been, in his teaching, entirely competent and unbiased. [128]

So began a chain of events which would change the history of Dickinson College as no other had done. Immediate reactions are always interesting. Even before the hearing Bishop Corson, a trustee since 1944, had declared it certainly justifiable to dismiss atheists as having no "place on the faculty of a Christian College," advocating "a full investigation" and hinting darkly that Dickinson's troubles could be traced to "violation of the no-liquor rule." [129] It had, indeed, been a year of heavy student drinking. Edel, oblivious to these implied reproaches, was busy with his speech to honor the College at one of the Newcomen Society's publicity-oriented luncheons. [130] It was held in Morgan Hall, May 10, and climaxed by everyone downing a health to her Majesty the Queen—with fruit juice in plastic cups. Trustee Woodside was demanding that Christopher Miniclier be penalized for his *Dickinsonian* editorial of April 13, admonishing the Board in stiff, plain language on the LaVallee case—"Gentlemen, this cannot go on if Dickinson is to remain a college of any reputation." Spahr checked that punitive impulse as he would do time and again—recalling how he himself, as the student editor of fifty-six years before, had faced up to the anger of Dean Morgan. [131] He was now out of patience with the whole matter, wishing that Edel had simply refused reappointment to LaVallee and so escaped all the expense and bad press. [132]

This had been, Dr. Edel reported to the trustees foregathering again at King's Gap, "in several ways a very difficult year." He had, however, glad tidings to announce: a Ford Foundation gift of $406,400, to be held as endowment for the increase of faculty salaries. Of this, $135,466 was an "Accomplishment Award" for the recent advance in salary scale—something for which the AAUP Chapter could surely claim its due share of credit. Edel, however, recognized the benefaction in two named chairs, one for Henry Ford in Education, one for Edsel Ford in Economics. [133] The first went to Edgar M. Finck. "We had a fine 'Chairing' ceremony for Ed Finck today," the President wrote to Spahr, February 20, 1958. "When the 'chairmen' carried him from the platform there was tumultuous applause." Ford's Director of Educational Affairs attended the ritual and "seemed very much impressed." [134]

Finck, who pronounced AAUP 'a blatant, 'pinkish,' intransigeant pressure group employing many reprehensible tactics of a labor union, including academic blackmail," [135] was sharpening a faculty rift which Wing, with a single-handed program of dinners and evenings, was laboring more conscientiously to heal. Two parties, one loyal to administration, the other to professional ideals, were now nearly equal in a balance any incident might overset.

On June 19, 1956, Bertram Davis, President of the Chapter of AAUP, received notice that his contract would not be renewed. For six years he had been one of the English Department's most scholarly and effective teachers, and Chairman William Sloane had recommended promotion to Associate with tenure. Edel informed Spahr of this action, casually, at the close of a newsy letter of August 24. Some faculty, he predicted, would be "very much upset," but he anticipated no "serious trouble." Yet Sloane had instantly resigned his chairmanship in protest—serious trouble had already come, and would grow. A month later, yielding to an aroused faculty, the departmental recommendation was followed. But bitterness and divisions continued. Davis resigned, leaving at year's end to join the Washington staff of the Association, rising to its top post of General Secretary in 1967. [136]

The Edel star had begun to wane when "Sputnik" of October 4, 1957, gave a positive aspect to rivalry with Russia and in American education a new impetus to the sciences—promptly reflected in Roscoe Bonisteel's gift of the planetarium in Tome. [137] Two months later, Edel announced that he would retire on his sixty-fifth birthday, March 26, 1959. Spahr had initiated this move and would have been content to have had it earlier. Faculty, too, had touched upon the idea in presenting a silver plate, 1956, marking the President's tenth year in office: "Long ago another sailor wandered the wine-dark, loud-roaring sea. He, too, was beset by monsters, but he after ten years was safely at home in Ithaca." [138] Now, with the spring of 1958, the most threatening monster of all reared its head above the waves. In March the AAUP *Bulletin* published its committee report on the LaVallee case, and at the Association's annual meeting in April censure was voted upon the Dickinson administration. The professor was not held blameless in his refusal to answer questions, but "this factor does not remove the serious breach of procedural due process that occurred or remove the justification for faculty concern in regard to its continuing damage to the College." [139]

The first strong reaction to censure came from the students, again exciting trustee ire, and again with Spahr showing a defensive partiality for the student editor. [140] On campus, desultory months followed the announcement of a presidential change a year and a half away. A remedial chapel series "America at the Crossroads," with Robert M. W. Welch, Jr., among its highlights, seems not to have affected outlooks or moods. Administration took from AAUP the initiative in surveying educational problems, first with the autumn study sessions at Camp Shand, followed by panel discussions in faculty meetings. Horlacher, Sloane and others led faculty efforts to improve the curriculum. [141] The establishment of Art and Music Departments came on May 29, 1958. Art studio had begun on a non-credit basis under Mary Virginia Snedeker in 1955, with regular courses in the next year taught by Joseph Sherly Sheppard. In Music, Dr. Lloyd Ultan joined Ralph Schecter whose courses in appreciation and history had been popular for many years. [142] Both innovations, filling a lack noted by Middle States in 1949, had been delayed by faculty fear of credit courses in "skills" set up on an economy basis.

The President won faculty applause and gratitude with his plan for "Refresher Leaves" at full salary for all who had given ten years of service. Yet faculty unrest and frustration remained. [143] Warlow and Bowden appealed to Chambers as the Board's only "higher education pro" to intervene somehow in the continuing inequities and questionable appointments. Chambers was sympathetic. He sent a copy of their letter to Spahr with a plea that something be done, though himself at a loss as to what it might be. [144] All depended, really, on the coming of a new President; and here, with faculty excluded, pressures of church affiliation were uppermost. Spahr, working with a representative committee of the Board, was nonetheless intent, as before, upon making his own decision.

William Wilcox Edel, the while, was gliding toward retirement upon a long wave of testimonial dinners and gifts. Most memorable of these was the "Arts Award," a companion piece, in humanities, to the Priestley Celebration and endowed by the contributions of nine trustees totalling $32,155. [145] By special request of the Board he continued in office from his birthday to commencement, where he was borne on high through the heart of the throng of students, parents and alumni in a self-imposed "chairing." Home, then, to California, while his classmate, "Red" Malcolm, always ready to meet an emergency, would take over the presidency until Spahr's choice of a younger successor, already approved in committee, could be confirmed.

With Gilbert Malcolm, familiar to all the College through so many years, there would be, at long last, a release from the unpredictable. Heavy ceremony would go by the board. So it did at his installation in that commencement of 1959. First they draped him in the purple gown. Then they laid in his hand the huge ritual ring attached to a golden chain and intended to be passed from Dickinson President to Dickinson President until the end of time. This gem had been the offering (since restored to him) of a California clergyman, inventor of the "Telephone Prayer," and was associated in some arcane fashion with the name of King Solomon.

But the ring is too much for "Red." Up it goes in the air to the limit of his long arm—"What am I bid?"

Roars of delight! The cool, sweet breath of change.

The College Bell.

In a word let the College be the grand centre of intelligence to all classes and conditions of men, diffusing among all the light of every kind of knowledge, and approving itself to the best feelings of every class of the community.

Francis Wayland, *Thoughts on the Present Collegiate System in the United States,* 1842

To a very great degree the only individual that has a real vested interest in Dickinson College is the student; the only group, actually, that has inalienable vested interests in this college is the student body. Therefore the student, while he is in residence and after he becomes an alumnus, should be the center or focal point of all the planning, all the effort of Dickinson College.

Russell I. Thompson, "View of the Future of Dickinson College," 1944

15

RUBENDALL

IN that commencement of 1959, behind robe and ring and laughter, Malcolm's successor was a speculative presence, undefined, a focus for the hopes and doubts of all who felt a concern for the future of the College.

He was still a speculative presence in the Board of Trustees, although its committee, after more than a year in the consideration of forty candidates, had reached a unanimous decision seven weeks before. Doubts and hesitations, too, had lingered in the mind of the nominee himself. As usual, Spahr had worked with a committee of his own appointment: Frank Masland and Merle Allen of Carlisle; two Harrisburg lawyers, David Wallace and Judge Robert Woodside; C. Scott Althouse and Congressman S. Walter Stauffer. Althouse, suddenly incapacitated by a stroke, had been retained in deference to his large gifts and promised bequest. Stauffer, a Methodist, replaced Dr. Ketterer, the only Methodist clergyman named, who had died before he could serve. Pressures from the Central Pennsylvania Conference and elsewhere for the inclusion of Bishops Corson or Oxnam had been tactfully resisted.[1] Well-founded fears of Spahr's dislike of the Church affiliation were disturbing Corson, foreshadowing his withdrawal from the Board in 1967.[2] A faculty offer to participate in the selection had been rejected with a cool rebuff, insuring a long period of conjecture and unrest on campus.[3]

Spahr's choice, Howard Lane Rubendall, '31, a Presbyterian clergyman, had been Headmaster of the Mount Hermon School since 1944 and President of the combined Northfield Schools since 1955. On December 10, 1958, after his first interview with the Nominating Committee, he had written Spahr that he had sensed at the meeting an "air of extreme conservatism" which might hamper a new administration, one of whose aims should be to create an environment of "free and open inquiry." On March 4, 1959, he had asked that his name be withdrawn, pleading his commitment to a program of reorganization at Northfield. This sparked a flurry of promotion for other candidates, but Spahr adroitly fielded the names as they came in, and in April he obtained Rubendall's agreement to come at the end of a second year. Rubendall was elected at the Board meeting of December 11, 1959, to take office on July 1, 1961. This, however, was to be kept secret for a time, both Rubendall and Malcolm wishing to cut as short as possible any "lame-duck" period.[4]

But at Carlisle the interim character of Malcolm's administration could not be ignored. It was only to be hoped that these two years would bring a receptiveness to change beyond what Dr. Rubendall had observed at that first interview. Change there must be, and soon. Men's housing, dilapidated, overcrowded, with the ever-present peril of fire, was at a point of crisis. New buildings and the safeguarding of the fraternity system were interrelated, prime trustee interests, and at that December 11 meeting the Board had authorized two committees to work together upon it: one of five trustees, of which Spahr named Samuel W. Witwer of Chicago as chairman, and the other of representatives of the ten fraternities.

To faculty the crisis was even more apparent and vastly more complex—heightened on the one hand by the long period of conflict and repression, and on the other by their sense of an impending era of advance in the academic world as a whole. In the decade of the Sixties, responding to influences already well formed, the Dickinson community would become a coherent entity as never before. Old prevailing rules of status among students, teachers and even trustees had been disappearing from American college life as it became more representative of the population and less of elite groups. All four classes were merging into a lively, awe-inspiring whole. A similar change would occur in faculty, with rank and length of service diminishing in importance.

The Sixties would open also a new chapter in the long story of curricular adjustment to the individual student and to the world he must enter. There would be a new emphasis on the old dictum of learning to learn as superior to any mere marshaling of facts. A cycle of almost feverish innovation and experiment was coming in, recalling Mulford Stough's sardonic quip from the day of the Committee of Eight, "Stay right where you are, and every twenty years you'll be leading the pack!"[5] The small colleges, once so complacently content with their smallness, now sensed dangers of inadequacy and isolation and were turning ardently to cooperative relationships at home and abroad.

To Malcolm, thoroughly committed to the older trustees' viewpoint, censure by AAUP was only one of a complexity of problems he must face, rather than a lever by which to restructure and strengthen the community. He had his own vision of the future, and his own profound regret that the opportunity to realize it had come so late. The long years had brought him confidence in himself as an "old pro" of academic management. He had been an undistinguished student in the Class of '15, and as a Sophomore suspended for his part in the first severe hazing incident of Noble's administration.[6] It was in his nature to become friend and advocate of students wherever friend or advocate was needed—a troubleshooter at all levels—in addition to his work with alumni. He long remembered Morgan's reply to a query about the persistence of irksome presidential problems, "Young man, if we didn't have the trouble, we wouldn't need you." For years he served as advisor to pre-medical students, taking much pride in their numbers and success. His personal acquaintance with the whole Dickinson constituency became encyclopedic.

Throughout, he had been a hard worker in a breezy, easy fashion. The early and tragic death of his young wife had brought an aura of sympathetic interest. Whatever he himself felt was covered up in rough good nature, chain-smoking, a vein of cynicism. He was a loyal Lutheran Church member. His cheerful human interests everywhere made him an excellent second in command to the Methodist clergymen in the presidential chair—a little too ready at times to say "Yes" to a petitioner, but on the whole an antidote to upper-level pontificating. When Spahr informed him that the co-ed author of a "damnable article" in the *Dickinsonian* should be turned over the knee and given "a thorough spanking," there could be no doubt of the genuineness of "Red's" ready offer to carry out the sentence himself.[7]

Now the President's House acquired a fresh charm from the paintings and other furnishings given from the collection of "Patsy" Potamkin, '31, whom its new occupant had befriended in student days.[8] "Red" was happily aware that he had something here beyond what his art-conscious classmate and predecessor had achieved, but took it all in a mood of levity, stoutly refusing to surround himself with any hint of presidential grandeur. The image of his administration must be one of direct, no-nonsense application to practical problems.

Of these it had a plenty. Faculty committees, appointed by Edel in October, 1958, were preparing for the visit of a Middle States reaccreditation team early in 1960. This group could scarcely be expected to concur wholeheartedly with the view that AAUP censure had been imposed by a "union" plotting to unsurp the power of the trustees, though hope lingered in some hearts that it might do so.[9] Much faculty time and thought was being given to the drafting of a statement on Academic Freedom and Tenure, and its submission to the trustees. [10] This issue could be pursued in a spirit of tact and compromise, but not that which suddenly arose beside it—the non-Communist affidavit required under the loan program of the new National Defense Act. A majority of the faculty voted to join the other colleges refusing to participate under that condition. The vote was checkmated as Malcolm invoked that bylaw on fundamental policy which transferred the decision to the trustees. [11] On its part, the Board had had faculty salaries under consideration since Malcolm's accession, using (tacitly) the AAUP scale and hoping to raise Dickinson's·standing from the low-level D to a C. [12] It was having second thoughts about the Refresher Year program and its costs. [13] It had become disillusioned with the

Allison Church agreement, bemoaning the chariness of the Allison trustees to permit student use. A plan to acquire the old Carlisle Opera House ("The Bucket of Blood," in student parlance) for concerts and assemblies fell through. [14] On top of all this, the trustee-faculty dinner of January 9, 1961, still the one point of rapport between these groups, was given over to the showing of an anti-Communist movie, "Operation Abolition." Afterward, responding to faculty protest and persuasion, "Red" issued a disavowal of the film's authority.

In 1959 George Shuman, heading Development, had sought to create unity and excitement with the announcement of a $15,000,000 financial campaign; a trumpet call which had only emphasized the disjointed character of an interim regime. [15] The students once more were demanding liberalized rules on drinking to replace those now constantly ignored. [16] A student "Committee on Racial Integration" took up the challenge offered by an incident of co-ed snobbishness, demanding liberalization and unity in this fundamental area. [17] This was in the spring of 1960, with trustees and administration pondering the final report from Middle States. It had, they agreed, "an AAUP undertone." [18] At least accreditation was not denied. The Association had merely voted to defer that final decision until April, 1962, requiring the submission of two interim progress reports. The critique had specified needs for greater efficiency, liberalization and unity, with recommendations for achieving them. Happily, the report was not kept in a semi-secret category, as had been the case a decade before, but went out at once to faculty, trustees and press.

At the close of Malcolm's first year Dean Frederic W. Ness went on to greater responsibilities, and was replaced by Admiral Roger E. Nelson, a professor of mathematics with a record of distinguished service in the Navy through World War II. Old hands are well enough, but a new administration needs a new verve and this one now had it in quarterdeck clarity of command. The College Purpose must be redefined, as a first basis for action. More to the point, faculty committees must be reconstructed toward simplicity, directness and genuine participation. Their number was cut from fourteen to six, and membership became largely, if not wholly, elective. It was a long step forward in policy and management, and the grudging trustee agreement something of a triumph. Voting rights were extended to instructors, the trustees acceding to this, interestingly, on the ground that these young persons would prove more amenable than "the hard core of A.A.U.P. members with tenure." [19] The faculty was becoming, as was the student body by an equally inevitable evolution, a community of peers. Malcolm, who seems to have anticipated some "hard core" opposition to this packet of reforms, wrote jubilantly of their prompt acceptance at the Faculty Meeting of November 7, 1960, "It exceeded our fondest dreams." [20] This to Rubendall, who had visited the campus shortly before, and was following developments with lively interest.

At that same meeting, along with the College Purpose and in line with the whole concept of mission and mission control, a Steering Committee of trustees, administration and faculty was approved. [21] This group could make a synthesis of findings and opinion available to Witwer's Special Committee on Fraternity Housing, to the fraternity representatives and, finally, to the Board. It could also press action on that oft-fought issue of unified living arrangements against the separate entities of the fraternity houses. A national trend was running strongly against the fraternity system, and at Dickinson its defenders were, again, making ready to hold the line. All agreed that some campus expansion, with new and modern houses, would be necessary. As to land, that on the west of Conway Hall owned by the Pennsylvania Railroad and by trustee Merle Allen's firm could be easily acquired, though one segment of the tract, the Lawrence property, was being held for an exorbitant sum.

A year went by, and Spahr proposed an alternative: build the new houses on Biddle Field. One may guess the rationale: remote from main campus and any new commons, fraternity men would live and dine together as before. He put this plan, prolix and persuasive, to the Executive Committee in Philadelphia, January 5, 1961, and carried his point as he had so regularly done. Witwer's plea for the railroad and Allen property was to no avail. At the seme time the Committee authorized acceptance of the "Indian School Farm" from the Federal government. Those sixty-five acres, a mile to the east of the campus, would provide a new athletic field. [22]

Top left: William Wilcox Edel. By Wilbur Fisk Noyes, 1950. Top right: Gilbert Malcolm. By Ann Didusch Schuler, 1957. Bottom left: Howard Lane Rubendall. Bottom right: Samuel Weiler Witwer.

Here was a decision certain to bring its own train of doubts, problems and delays. It is memorable only in marking the end of the pattern of carefully prearranged Executive Committee decisions, automatically endorsed by the Board. Witwer, whose committee had faced "filibustering and dilatory tactics" rather than the "full and careful debate" he sought, was in a mood of understandable asperity: "the problem has been shunted back and forth for the last two years between various and sundry groups to the extent that Tinker, Evers and Chance were pikers. I am too busy in my office to establish a pattern of flying East once a month to participate in a round robin, never-ending procedure." [23]

The Executive Committee met again, February 10. Witwer moved for a beginning of five houses, to be built on the rail-road-Allen site. It was defeated, 6–3, and the whole matter referred back once again to the Steering Committee. Witwer, returning once more from Philadelphia to Chicago, resigned his chairmanship. The Steering Committee on its part also met the Spahr opposition head-on, with recommendations to acquire the railroad and Allen tracts immediately and start fraternity house construction there. [24] This was confirmed at a Special Meeting of the Board, held on campus, April 8. In the aftermath, Spahr continued a proponent of the Biddle Field site. Champions of the old order watched with anxiety, fully aware of the wretched condition of men's housing and the need for modernization, yet fearful of the changes it might bring, and alarmed by Dean Nelson's driving hostility to delays, to threatened disruption of the athletic programs, to fraternity traditions and power. [25] But with this, more than ever before, trustee rebellion against Spahr control was emerging—in much the same progressive spirit that had been Spahr's three decades earlier. [26] The Board's regular meeting, June 1, 1961, brought one new factor into the issue, the authorization of Howell Lewis Shay and Associates, a Philadelphia firm of architects and engineers, to survey the entire college plant and recommend a program of building and renovation.

Such was the uneasy state of affairs when Rubendall came into the president's office, and Malcolm retired, as Provost, to the opposite end of the West College hall, his long rapport with the alumni still an immense advantage. [27] It is significant that two alumni of the Nominating Committee, Spahr, '00 and Spahr's friend and fraternity brother, Woodside, '26, were closer in viewpoint than the man they had selected. There could be a wide gap between '26 and '31. At Rubendall's graduation the full impact of the Great Depression had come, and a pre-ministerial student would see and feel clearly its effect on human values. He was teaching at the American University in Cairo, Egypt, 1931 to 1934, its "blonde" player of rugby. There one observer noted what was to be central to his character as an educator throughout:

> Bud immediately caught the fancy of the fellows in college, and with that spontaneity of good fellowship of which only "Rube" is capable, he quickly became a friend of the students. Not to mention his other valuable contributions to the life of the College, Bud has done his best work in the field of student relations. [28]

Cairo was a broadening experience. Even more so was the influence of Reinhold Niebuhr and others at Union Theological Seminary, where he earned his B.D. in 1937. Ordained in the Congregational Church, his pastoral work before going to Northfield was Presbyterian. Now, finally, some parts of the Dickinson community were cherishing a lively hope that a tenuous Methodist tie would reassert itself—but Bud had "never been much attracted to denominational Christianity," least of all its political aspects. [29]

At about the same time word had seeped back from Northfield to Carlisle that Dickinson's new President had brought new life and dedication into the Northfield board of trustees. Be that as it might, Dickinson's Board would watch and wait. A leader of its denominationally-minded old guard, Robert F. Rich, looked sharply askance at the appointment of Arthur D. Platt as "Executive Assistant to the President" in 1961. Presidential authority must be watched and controlled. "We learned our lesson from Dr. Waugh and Dr. Edel and I am not interested now in having it happen the third time, so we should approve step by step the actions of the President before we give blanket authority at the College." [30] Cool and efficient, knowledgeable and experienced, Platt would be a mainstay of the Rubendall years, remote from controversy, a determining factor in all its successes.

Let it be for some Froissart of the future to chronicle in full the victories, retreats, the zealous counterthrusts of these years, the battling in background and shadow. Advance toward academic and social maturity was achieved. Religion, so long a matter of banal acceptance on campus and of emotional concern in the governing body, was there, in the vaward, with banners. To be effectively "church-related" a college should, as Durbin's young faculty had shown, enter this realm with wide-open and exploring eyes, relate principle to life with frank consistency and bring to the Church elements of progressive strength not to be expected from the congregations.

The *Dickinsonian,* supporting the new President, called for "critical judgment" and challenge of the relevance of Christian faith. [31] Inevitably, the "double standard" of conduct, with the venerable and explosive issue of alcohol, appeared. Trustees Corson and Rich, who had made short work of an Edel proposal to restudy the drinking problem, were still present and more firm than ever. [32] One June, 1, 1961, responding to an appeal by Dean of Women Barbara Wishmeyer, the faculty went "on record as being willing to receive with interest and objectivity proposals about possible liberalization of the drinking rules." A constructive liberalization of the entire religious program, meanwhile, was under way—to hostile eyes a process of deterioration which reached its climax in the social rules of the spring of 1963. To bring the old problem into line with sophisticated adult mores, it had been conceded that social drinking among students over twenty-one would be acceptable. Those under age must abide by state law. Upon every occasion there must be freedom of choice. The students would regulate this new order themselves, faced with the alternative of security police to do so.

The Philadelphia Conference, meeting at just this time, reacted instantly. The income from the old endowment funds would be withheld "until such time as the College shall revoke any permission for the use of alcoholic beverages in Fraternity Houses of the College." Rubendall, first learning of the action in its blaze of newspaper publicity, protested in vain. In vain was the offensive permission withdrawn. The Church funds would remain in implacable escrow for six more years while further concessions were sought—application of the money only

to the education of Methodist students, Conference right to
appoint trustees, division of the money among other causes.
These were resisted successfully. What began on the moral issue
of alcohol ended on the moral issue of breach of trust, that
point conceded at the last with the payment of all accrued
interest. [33]

The Methodist National Board of Education had been on
the scene in these years, notably with substantial gifts to the
growth of the Library. Its University Senate, by invitation, had
sent a survey team in the spring of 1962, supplementing that of
the Middle States. Both reports, as an objective mirror of current problems and conflicts, prefaced the full-scale Academic
Study launched by the faculty in September, 1962, and continuing for two and a half years. Ben Horlacher was its Coordinator, with a Steering Group of three others: Howard Long for
"The Liberated Student," its committee on curriculum; Warren
Gates chairing that on the learning process; and Bruce Andrews,
that on the academic community. Under these, faculty, administration, students, alumni and trustees all were involved. The
Study's major recommendations, adopted at the faculty meetings of March 16 and April 13, 1964, included trial of the 5–5,
4–4 course plan, "Independent Study options for all Dickinson
students" and raising the graduation requirement from 1.75 to
2.00 credits. [34] In addition, it had brought to all the community
a sense of self-realization and new health with which to meet
the removal of AAUP censure that April and the final Middle
States reaccreditation in July.

AAUP censure had ended just before the official displeasure of the Philadelphia Conference had been imposed. Association and Conference were alike in procedure—having acted in
response to a single incident, each then took all activities and
attitudes of the offending administration under review. Professor LaVallee had gone his way, making no demands for compensation, but the demand for clearly acceptable and affirmed policies of freedom and tenure, for full faculty participation in all
educational matters, were being pressed to make sure that no
repetition would occur. Trustee and administration response to
overtures from local chapter and national office had come slowly. One sees the ice of cold defiance gradually thawing. In Feb-

ruary, 1960, Herbert Wing, Jr., senior member of the faculty and so often an intermediary between opposing camps, had visited Washington to discuss the matter. [35] A year later we find Spahr reading in the *Dickinsonian* of Dr. Peggy Heims' talk to the chapter on salaries, and then writing cautiously to Malcolm that something should be done to raise the level and correct the inequities. [36] Dean Nelson had moved into direct negotiation. A committee from Washington visited the campus, October 17, 1961.

"Perhaps," Ken Bowling of the *Dickinsonian* had editorialized, April 28, 1961, after removal of censure had been denied, "the fundamental problem has been, and is, the unhealthy relations between the faculty and the administration and the faculty and the Board." This the Board would warmly deny, while agreeing nonetheless to further liberalization. [37] These concessions brought the certainty of success a year later, with an immediate easing of tensions and sighs of relief that the long hassle was over. Soon after, the Admiral, taut and purposeful, stepped back into the classroom, and the Rev. Samuel Hays Magill, red waistcoat and large cigar, stepped boldly forth from the Chaplain's office to the Dean's.

All these changes had been anticipated by the resignation of Boyd Lee Spahr as President of the Board, December 15, 1962, ending an era of thirty-one years of close personal control in the office he himself had created. His place was taken by the affable Sidney D. Kline, '24, banker and lawyer of Reading. Spahr had held onto the position only until he could feel assured that the new President of the College was firmly in the saddle. That, surely, was an optimistic view of the situation of a Dickinson President committed to progress in an environment of "free and open inquiry," or of any college president in this era of campus unrest. Yet the Rubendall program would go forward, responding to its own forces and the issues of the day.

"Set your sights high," trustee Roscoe Bonisteel had said, advising the Librarian to distribute a brochure on Yale's new Beinecke Library to every Board member—if only to startle them with the idea that Dickinson might conceivably, one day, possess and maintain such a treasure house. That old, long-prevailing concept of sound ideals within a framework of littleness and parsimony fell with the Rubendall years—an historic change underlying all its other achievements. For the first time, a fully staffed Development Office appeared where in the past there had been only a presidential assistant or the redoubtable George Shuman rising with the dawn to stir his mixed brew of projects and duties. Shuman, with his experience and contacts of many years, continued an effective parallel effort in Development. In its first decade, 1961 to 1971, total assets nearly quadrupled and endowment rose from 6,000,000 to 11,000,000.

In 1964 the old Ten Year Development Program, with all its ups, downs and extensions, was replaced—these things always are, and should be, launched with grandiloquence—by The Third Century Development Program, with an initial goal of $6,000,000 by 1970. [38] Two years later came the Ford Foundation Challenge Grant—$2,000,000, if it could be matched three to one, by an additional $6,000,000. Its target date, June 30, 1969, was met successfully. The Ford Challenge Grants were not given on a basis of need, but of merit and promise. As intended, this award stimulated the whole forward movement.

Observers of the future will see the transformation of Dickinson College first of all in its most obvious manifestation, the new gray limestone walls. Adams Hall honoring a great supporting trustee and his wife, opened in 1963, a new dormitory for women adjoining Drayer. A year later, the newly acquired campus to the west with its ten residence halls for men was occupied, completing that long-fought reform in fraternity housing. A volume of significant social and educational history could be written since the Kuebler Report on Fraternity-College Relations had been adopted by the faculty, June 2, 1953, and sent on to the Board of Trustees. At the same time, and as an integral part of the same plan, the Holland Union Building brought dining and recreational facilities for the whole College. [39] Homer C. Holland is gratefully remembered by the author of this chronicle as a donor whose benefactions began with a truckload of books for the Library—expanding thence to this long-sought achievement.

Two new dormitories, Malcolm and Witwer Halls, came in 1966. The Charles A. Dana Biology Building of that year coincided, by a happy circumstance, with the establishment of the

Florence Jones Reineman Wildlife Sanctuary, three thousand acres in Perry County, held by an independent trust but under the management of Dickinson's Biology and Geology Departments. [40] In the next year came the climax of the longest-projected effort of all, the Boyd Lee Spahr Library, appropriately dedicated as the College's center of scholarly activity at all levels. Through all his years as President of the Board, the Library had been that trustee's first and most constant concern. Librarian Emeritus May Morris had helped to break the ground, but did not live to see the structure in which her competence and devotion to the College are likewise memorialized.

A new dormitory followed in 1969, honoring a married couple of the Class of 1908, Helen Kisner and Hugh B. Woodward, from whose estate the largest gift ever received by the College would be coming. Its two wings would stand together as a monument also to Dickinson's acceptance of the idea that young men and women might live healthier and more congenial lives without the rigid separation once thought so necessary. [41]

That government and foundation aid, for so long and over the whole national scene, had been concentrated on stimulating scientific advance, stirred a reaction at conservative Dickinson. Students and faculty began in 1962 an annual drive for their "Dickinson Humanities Fund," moving toward an undetermined goal at about a thousand dollars a year. [42] This small effort, and the far more formidable Ford Humanities Grant of 1968, were followed by a separate, culminating project, the transformation of East College into the Bernard Center for the Humanities. [43] It was completed in 1971, and soon after the traditional liberal arts were again reinforced by the opening of the Anita Tuvin Schlecter Auditorium.

These are the high points in a program of campus expansion and modernization such as no previous Dickinson administration had dared even to imagine. The whole, or most of it, may be found set forth with statistical restraint in the final appendix to this work. Its lesser aspects extend from the acquisition of town residences for use or demolition, to facilities such as the locker and training building at Biddle Field—that last a long-felt need financed from contributions made by the Washington Redskins football team in return for pre-season use of the field.

A foundation for these accomplishments and the academic growth that would come with them was laid by the trustees in the two-year presidency of Sidney Kline. Such a beginning could not have been made under a Board preoccupied with fears of Communist infiltration or declining Church influence. Kline was succeeded in June, 1964, by Samuel W. Witwer of Chicago, Class of 1930, Harvard Law, 1933, he who had already been so instrumental in setting the pattern of future campus expansion. Prominent in law and politics, he had, since that time, seen his many years of effort for the reform of the Illinois court system crowned with success. An active and distinguished Methodist layman, he would now watch over and foster the growth of his college in a bland, engaging spirit far removed from the parochialisms of the past. The trustee-faculty relationship was blessed, at long last, with mutual confidence. As the *Dickinsonian* of September 18, 1964, announced in reporting the year's opening convocation, "the era of the New Dickinson" had arrived.

The Board, to be sure, had still that impediment to working efficiency which Benjamin Rush had fixed upon it—its large size. The good Doctor had been aiming at state-wide influence, and his quorum of nine shows what he expected the working body to be. In the Spahr years there had been frequent complaint of trusteeship without sense of responsibility. Now, as had rarely occurred in the past, a concern with constructive action was felt throughout. The charter revision of February, 1966, set the membership at between twenty-five and fifty in a step toward reduction. It also eliminated the triple vice presidencies of 1955, conceived originally as a firmer tie with campus affairs. More open communication had brought a far better, unformalized, rapport. [44]

Yet the campus, faculty and students, had been changing more rapidly through the years, in ways that were forcing readjustment everywhere. That faculty which once had been as settled and permanent a body as the Board itself had vanished. Since the war, comings and goings, new faces and ideals, had become frequent, the size of the whole slowly increasing with that of the student body. Dickinson's faculty of the Fifties was often critical of administration—not so much against the concentration of authority, for that left the teacher more free with the concerns of his discipline, as against the manner in which it was exercised. The faculty of the Sixties, at Dickinson as elsewhere, was involved in the total operation to an extent that would have been inconceivable at Carlisle in the Spahr years. Innovation and planning had become necessary virtues followed compulsively almost everywhere in academe, and in all graduations from the profound and original to baton-twirling imitation.

Other basic changes accompanied the experimental curriculum developed in the Horlacher study. A division of the Sociology Department into Sociology and Anthropology came in 1963; a major and minor in American Studies, first projected many years before, in 1965; and in 1966 the division of Philosophy and Religion into two departments, a Middle States recommendation of 1949. Compulsory chapel ended its anguished existence in 1965, to be replaced by a College Church and a Lecture Series, both voluntary. [45] But already a proliferation of departmental lecturers and other special events was emerging, among which the Public Affairs Symposium, scheduled annually by the Chaplain's Office, would have a front place. Here was a broad and flexible enlargement of the curriculum which recalls, in a way, the activities of the old literary societies in maintaining student contact with the issues, and the public, of their own time.

Even more characteristic of the Sixties was the reaching out to new disciplines, new alliances with other institutions, new direct contacts with foreign lands and civilizations. In 1959 the faculty approved a course in Comparative Non-Western Cultures, to include "racial and cultural backgrounds of the current nationalistic movements and social conflicts in Asia and Africa." [46] Two years later, three Dickinson professors joined with others at five neighboring colleges in a program to develop teaching competence in Far Eastern studies. The group received Ford Foundation support in 1962. [47]

Looking back on institutional cooperation to the time of World War I, we find President Morgan becoming aware of binary programs with professional schools, "much the same as we have done in connection with the Law School." He told the trustees, "Frankly, I do not know what to recommend," but had asked that faculty be given power to act. [48] There the matter rested until the engineering program with Case Institute of Technology, 1950, and those with Rensselaer Polytechnic Institute (1951), University of Pennsylvania (1953) and Massachusetts Institute of Technology (1957). [49] The Curriculum Committee of the Fifties viewed these alliances with both interest and caution. [50] In another category, a "Tri-College Project for the Greater Harrisburg Area," worked out in 1951 by the Presidents of Dickinson, Elizabethtown and Lebanon Valley Colleges, had been dropped when it became apparent that the State University was not immediately setting up a Harrisburg branch. [51]

The Area College Library Cooperative Program initiated at Dickinson in the spring of 1964, made the resources of ten south-central Pennsylvania colleges, a total of over a million volumes, mutually available—with the support of the State Library's active program and great collection. When the Central Pennsylvania Consortium—Dickinson, Franklin and Marshall, Gettysburg and Wilson—came into being in 1967, again with Ford support, its most solid uniting factor was ACLCP, with its inter-library truck service worked out by Herbert B. Anstaett of F. and M. bringing a still wider range of libraries into the central orbit. [52] The Consortium was itself heir to the expertise developed under the Ford Institutional Service Program of 1962. The "India Institute" of its first year was followed by "South Asia Area Studies"—and then a new departure with its "Harrisburg Urban Semester," offering opportunities for study and direct involvement in urban problems.

Prettyman, as professor, had brought German plays and music to Carlisle, using the proceeds to send selected students to Germany for a year. After 1928, this had developed into a program of exchange scholarships. [53] Edel had moved at once to reopen this program, and in 1948 was exploring "area training," to be based upon reciprocal agreements with foreign universities. [54] It was not until the turbulent Sixties, however, that Dickinson followed the lead of other institutions and set up an educational enclave overseas. On November 2, 1964, the faculty approved the plan for "A Center of International Studies in Affiliation with the Johns Hopkins University Bologna Center." Its first year would be under the direction of Professor K. Robert Nilsson, and its students (like those of the Washington Semester at American University) would be "qualified political science majors" in their Junior year. The decade ended with four off-campus programs in operation: the old Washington Semester, Bologna, The Asian Studies program with the University of Pennsylvania, and the Institute of European Studies. Conducted tours by faculty members, sometimes sponsored by more than one college, had been on the Dickinson scene since the Fifties. Yet in the Summer Classical Institute of 1971 (a month in Greece and Italy under professors from Dickinson and Franklin and Marshall), the idea had become formalized with daily lectures, final examination, term papers three weeks after return and two course credits as laurel wreath at the end of the race.

Those academic prizes which flowered so conspicuously in the last century are now seen as an effort to stimulate the particularly desultory student scholarship of those days. [55] One can wonder how historians of the future may view Dickinson's two new and munificent prizes of the Sixties—both not for students, but for faculty. The Lindback Award for "distinguished teaching," the recipient to be selected by the President, was first given in 1961. [56] The Ganoe Most Inspirational Teacher Award, supported by a bequest of some $90,000, was first made in 1969. Its winner must be chosen by a secret ballot of the Senior Class, taken just before commencement. [57] Here is something new indeed, a student-to-faculty prize. Perhaps the recollection of familiar and beloved professors of the past had inspired the idea, bringing a hope of turning student attention once more to professorial virtues. Yet it is surely in tune with the spirit of the Sixties, when the student moves to center stage, becomes critical of faculty domination in the classroom and tends to identify himself with academic management.

The population explosion had reached college level, and this massive new generation looked out upon the world beyond with little of the old light-hearted hopefulness, with much disfavor and with an insistence not to be denied. The draft involved it in a brutal conflict without appeal to the ideals of youth. The old college joie de vivre was little seen. It was for the colleges, then, not only to inform, but to transform that blind, Luddite resentment into an understanding of ideals and a passion for rebuilding.

Russell Thompson's report of 1944, with its determined emphasis upon the students' central place, might have been held against him had he been considered then for the presidency of Dickinson. The student demands of 1945 and 1952 brought the idea sharply forward. By the close of the Fifties, Malcolm spoke for many when he confessed to Spahr his weariness with continuing hassle and resistance. "I can understand that faculty who haven't had their own way or students who haven't had their own way should be rebelling against some decisions that have been made." [58] Six months later, the wave of young discontent swept right into Spahr's Philadelphia office. The Student Senate was formally demanding that it be informed precisely what criteria "are employed in rewarding, retaining or dismissing faculty members," and citing evidence to show that no criteria existed. It was a delegation of six young men, with the Secretary of the Senate, Ruth Kean, "who also had a good deal to say." [59] Between the lines of his account of the affair to Edel one can see the venerable President of the Board standing, firm as ever, upon the legal prerogatives which these invaders held in such slight regard—inwardly bridling against their presumption, but loving them as flesh and blood of Dickinson. Their complaints, he suspected, were AAUP-inspired. As to that, it need only be observed that in the professors' long search for security, freedom and a right to determine educational policy, and then in the students' similar revolution, each had support from the other.

Slowly, a new coherence was emerging. At Dickinson as elsewhere, the traditional class "scraps," those wild convulsions of group rivalry and unity, had vanished in the serious mood of the Great Depression. The singing and the yells faded with World War II. Freshmen rules and hazing diminished after the student clamor for "a new spirit" in 1945, a change welcomed by Edel and his faculty. [60] There were resurgences, but Freshman indoctrination had become vestigial by the early Sixties and had vanished entirely at the end of the decade. Every student, every faculty member too, then had equal voice.

With this came the erosion of the fraternity system. Faculty had been long harassed by the problem of regulatory rules, constantly changed, never wholly effective. But now, at last, the envy of outsiders was turning to disdain. Racial barriers in national charters made the whole picture of selectivity offensive. Brotherhood had wider boundaries. From 1960 to 1962, years of the Freedom Riders, of the Bay of Pigs, of gathering crisis in the East, the old small values fell rapidly. The publication at Dickinson, 1959–60, of *The Journal of Student Research* attracted much interest and underlined a new student feeling for scholarship. [61] After 1964, when the pouring of military might into Vietnam began, the old campus issues seemed petty indeed. Fraternity membership was declining—85 percent of the men in 1960, 45 percent ten years later. In 1964 an independent was elected President of the Student Senate, and a new constitution was drawn, ending its domination by the Interfraternity Council. [62] Holland Union was completed in that year, followed by the fraternity men's prolonged but futile boycott of its use as a social center.

Under "Docky" Reed, students in the mood of that delegation to Spahr's office might have been called before the faculty for Conspiracy and Insubordination. President Morgan had from the first "encouraged student participation in the conduct of the College," and by 1923 could assess the result with pride. [63] It largely consisted, to be sure, of a well-ordered student activity budget financed by the students themselves. Student self-discipline as a premise to genuine participation in the conduct of the College came slowly and late. In 1953, in a motion which reviewed the historical background and concluded that the faculty as a whole was "not organized to administer discipline," Roger Nelson proposed giving the Dean entire responsibility. [64] This was done, and Dean Ness created what was to become the Student-Faculty Judicial Council. Six years later, a still more responsible group was proposed by John W. Dixon on the principle that "self-government· and self-control are a part of the rights and privileges of mature persons as well as an essential part of the process of attaining maturity." This was returned to committee on Edel's objection that it would take discipline entirely out of the hands of the incoming president. [65]

Students had long held some regular committee memberships—one on the Board of Athletic Control since 1934 (increased to two, a Junior and a Senior, in 1955), others on Shuman's Development Council of 1954 and the Cultural Affairs Committee, where in 1952 student protest and financial assessment had brought so sudden a transformation from the drab offerings of the past. In Cultural Affairs students would move—as Nelson had insisted from the first they should—from participation to the decisive role. Not until 1966, with other college faculties admitting students to regular faculty committee membership, did Dickinson follow suit. [66] Voting privileges waited three years more. [67] On November 7, 1969, ten years after Ruth Kean and the others had said their say in the Spahr office, student leaders met with a committee of the Board, some fifty individuals in all, for a pioneering discussion of campus affairs. [68]

At last it had become possible for students to move on from the resentfully negative attitudes of the past into constructive participation. As with other liberated groups, to be sure, negative criticism came as a first impulse from the new position with students casting a doubtful eye on faculty in course evaluations and raising questions as to the right of tenure. [69] Again in 1964, year of the Berkeley turmoil, Dickinson's new curriculum had brought sharp condemnation of the enlarged classes in certain core subjects, a wide deviation from the boasted faculty-student ratio of 1 to 14. [70] At that same time, aroused students forced a change in the Spahr Library architecture, a much improved (and more expensive) exterior design. [71] Dickinson students were in the South that summer, working for civil rights. [72] Racial equality had its eminent champion on campus in the newly-appointed Chaplain, Joseph Reed Washington, Jr. The number of black Americans in class was increasing until, in 1971, it was exceeded in Pennsylvania only at Swarthmore. [73] Protest against the Vietnam war was bitter and profound, with a downgrading of ROTC not long before the nation-wide student protests of the spring of 1970. [74]

In all this, students and President were standing together in a manner unique at Dickinson, where "Docky" in the past had received only a patronizing or conditional affection, if any at all. Here now he moves in a glow of admiration and gratitude. A letter to Rubendall, 1970, from a young alumnus thanking him for "your tremendous leadership of and love for Dickinson," might have been one voice speaking for all:

> As Dickinson prepares to graduate another class, we find it is an ever more increasingly difficult world into which they enter. It has been only two years since I graduated but in that short space of time the situation in this country has changed tremendously. Not only that but it is my generation which I believe is the most greatly affected by these events. It is we who must go to fight in Southeast Asia, it is we who in the next twenty years face the results of today's pollution. It is we who must still face a race that has been discriminated against and still is. It is we who face a world in which millions are starving yet we can afford to spend billions upon billions of dollars to wage a war and destroy homes, a country and a *people.* This is a bleak picture that Sunday's graduating class have to look forward to.
>
> There is a bright side or at least a gleam of light to this dismal and frustrating situation. There are such institutions as D'son and such administrators as you and your staff. This past year most especially has been a difficult one for the colleges and universities of our country. In this period I have been most proud of the stance Dickinson has taken in regard to these pressing issues. You are a concerned college that desires peace in the world, that is concerned about ecology and is not afraid to stand up for those principles in which it feels it is right.
>
> I know that the college and you have come under attack for the position that has been taken by Dickinson in these matters. I know that there are very disgruntled alumni (to use a mild adjective) and a very angry town of Carlisle at this moment. I'm also aware that it will be a most trying Trustee meeting this weekend . . . . [75]

True it was that there were those, in a town so traditionally conservative as Carlisle and in so traditionally conservative a Board of Trustees, to whom this new Dickinson seemed to sound the rumbling tremors of a broken world. The Students for a Democratic Society, having torn one great university asunder, set up a Dickinson chapter. We can only wonder how an earlier Board might have received the explanations so candidly offered to this one. President Rubendall pictured the SDS as "not a group of Communists or Stalinists, rather it is a group of interested and concerned humanists who are intrigued by the philosophy of the early Marx." And the President of the Board:

> Mr. Witwer stated that as distressing as the present situation with SDS may seem to some, it represents nothing really new in Dickinson's history, as revolution was in the air on the campus from time to time since the earliest days. [76]

Dickinson's "Declare Day," March 3, 1969, had brought a concerted outpouring of opinion and emotion based upon perennial student concern with the grading system—all sparked by the unsubstantiated belief of one young professor that if he announced in advance an A for every member of one large class, all would respond by matching performance to evaluation. [77] The Haverford College professor who at this same time and in a more restrained expression of the same spirit regarded "teaching in the light not so much of knowledge imparted as of the mind and heart made larger," was uttering words familiar to educators long before his time. The difference lay in his new concept of "self-scheduled examinations, a modified grading system, student presence on standing committees of the faculty," all to bring about a transmutation of the college into "a true community." [78]

That goal had come to Dickinson, as elsewhere. Student unity encouraged, even enforced, unity of the whole. Administrative officers were urging faculty to assume larger responsibilities and yielding them also to students. Either would have been incredible a few years before. The Sixties had become an era of change and emergence, of concern with both the small immediate and the great issues, of realization that all issues are one web. Release from class distinctions was bringing not only the little campuses but the stubborn nations of the world a little closer to that ideal of "true community."

"Tuta Libertas"—rampart and counterscarp safeguarding the treasures of mind and spirit against surrounding wickedness. In the broad picture, that protective impulse has been a Dickinson College trait from the first—marked out long ago in those sharp lines of cancellation drawn by some unknown hand across certain venturesome passages in Dr. Rush's *Plan of Education.*

There is a refreshing breath of escape from it in the intellectual vigor of the first Methodist faculty, though Durbin and his young men were very conscious of Dickinson's past and willing to deviate only in what stood out as static or unsteady educational practice. George Edward Reed's visions of a university, of a Department of Peace and Public Service, shine through a mist of dead pan parochialism. Even here in the Sixties, Dickinson's greatest era of advance and change, Dean Wanner could speak to the trustees of a pattern of progress achieved without the disruptions of experimentation.[79] There has been a solid continuity of growth—the years of stagnation balanced by forward surges full of storm and promise.

The ancient dictum that education without religious guidance and restraint is a force of vast potential evil was strong in the mind of Benjamin Rush. Jim Henry Morgan echoed it long after. "The selfish tool sharpened by education may prove very dangerous"—and he saw the dangers multiplied by the moral relaxation of his time.[80] Morality had been coupled too long with the idea of automatic adherence to a religious society. The *Dickinsonian* of Morgan's day bubbles and flashes with the students' cynical rejection of just that. Yet the old correlation of morality and learning is with us still, fundamental and refreshed. We have learned that unimpeded truth has its own moral and persuasive force, more sure, less malleable than any other. It will not only produce techniques of destructive exploitation, but prove the need for controlling them. It can pose a new morality against the self-perpetuating, brutalizing accompaniments of military power, a new unifying force for the fusion of nations and races.

It is the essential duty of a college to preserve, impart and increase knowledge. Turbulence and ferment are needed from time to time to clear off traditional patina and give a new clarity to the old design. This has occurred again, and the student's mind and will are more free than ever in the past. "Self-taught" is a phrase that has long been applied to learning or skill as a badge of honor. Yet learning and skills are always self-taught. The teacher can only stimulate by word and example, by discipline and demand, and then, as best he may, assess the result. The ultimate success or failure is the student's own.

Dickinson's young men and women, pondering this, have joined others in questioning the value of grades, and even avowing that the degree itself might be discarded. [81] Partisans of that idea should look back to Charles Nisbet, who emerged from the University of Edinburgh as one of the most learned men in Britain's isles, disdaining, as did many others of his day, to take its degree.

Education in this century, in grade and high school has assumed more and more of the preparation for life once expected of the family. The college Senior is taking leave of a school system as much as of home ties, and one can sometimes see in student attitudes of the Sixties some of the young adult emotions of resentment, rejection, demand, transferred from parent to college. Graduate school protracts the term for many. This long involvement will increase. The students' new influence on campus augurs a closer, more reciprocal relationship as alumni. At Dickinson there is a long background here. One sees it moving from the first alumni associations of the 1830's to the election of alumni trustees in 1890, and the expansion of the process in 1930. Some cautious restraint follows that, but by 1950 Boyd Lee Spahr must needs couple a firm affirmation of trustee ownership with an avowal that the "equitable owners" are the great body of alumni.

One of the student demands of December 7, 1945, had been for vocational guidance and placement, services in which Dickinson had fallen far behind the pace-setting institutions. A response, alas, with a policy statement that "the interest of the College in its students does not terminate with graduation," was nine years in coming. [82] It was not until still later, in that crucial year 1964, that the College's Placement Bureau acquired a Director of Counseling. Here was a foundation, at least, supporting both choice of careers and continuance in them.

Continuing rapport with alumni in the perennial learning process is one only of the new frontiers. It is supported by the advancing trend in institutional cooperation. The interlocking systems with points of specialization such as the state colleges have been developing strengthen it. The foreign programs, too, are becoming a constellation all around us—broad ideals lighted also by the allure of escape and adventure. A world system of

Student Protest and Demand.

PEER.

education is still far indeed from reality—yet what a vision for the volatile heart of Benjamin Rush!

Back to the microcosm on the campus at Carlisle, and one sees the widening circle reaching out to enfold both the wide and far, the small and near. This expansion of our new community has come (inconceivable as it would have been in former administrations) from the Chaplain's office. The Public Affairs Symposium was one of the innovations of 1964. It has involved the curriculum and the whole College community in larger issues of the day far more effectively than the literary society debates or the old chapel programs were ever able to do. Student participation has been an essential feature. Speakers have included figures of national and international importance. Its planners, finally, have been singularly successful in scheduling in advance topics headed for front-rank urgency in public discussion:

1964, *The American Purpose in World Revolution.*
1965, *Urbanization and the American Society.*
1966, *The New Morality?*
1967, *The Power of Persuasion.*
1968, *Television: The Eye that Never Blinks.*
1969, *Dissent.*
1970, *Science and Public Policy: Environmental Pollution.*
1971, *Privacy?*

That of 1970 led on to the interdisciplinary courses, "Environmental Studies," and to constructive student action in neighboring lands, waters and politics.

On a quite different level came PEER, in 1968. President Rubendall had appointed an ad hoc committee to explore the possibility of a student-staffed program to aid disadvantaged elements of the Carlisle community. Children of the eight to twelve age group were selected as the least well provided from other sources, and with the best promise of success. PEER, the summertime lessons and games of the "Program of Enrichment, Education and Recreation" have a foundation, of course, in the social service projects long, and still, fostered by the fraternities, yet with a vastly greater impact on student body and community alike.

These newcomers to the campus scene are symbols of change and of a coming era. They are new ranks in the unending march of life, philosophy, exploration. After PAS the old controlled voices will not be heard again. Those PEER children, too, little groups, wide-eyed, are (where they would love to be) part of the parade. They move with us forward. They are one with the faculties of the past, the black broadcloth, those faces, stern, benign, amused, one with the flow and overflow of student life, the aspiration in all its variant hues and flame, timeless as the shining rivers.

The academic procession! Out from the shadows and on beyond us it will go, the generations of the young, the lords and prophets, mimes and pipers, bearing the banners of battles won before, bringing the color and the music out beyond the ramparts of the world.

NOTES

Abbreviations:

DAB   *Dictionary of American Biography* (N.Y., 1946).

DCA   Dickinson College Archives, Carlisle, Pa.

HSP   Historical Society of Pennsylvania, Philadelphia, Pa.

PMHB   *Pennsylvania Magazine of History and Biography*

SL 1   *Bulwark of Liberty. Early Years at Dickinson. The Boyd Lee Spahr Lectures in Americana. Volume One, 1947–1950* (Carlisle, 1950).

SL 2   *"John and Mary's College." The Boyd Lee Spahr Lectures in Americana* (Carlisle, 1956).

SL 3   *Early Dickinsoniana. The Boyd Lee Spahr Lectures in Americana* (Carlisle, 1961).

SL 4   *The Spahr Lectures, Dickinson College. Volume 4* (Carlisle, 1970).

Chapter 1. Plot and Cast

1. Vicesmus Knox, *Essays, Moral and Literary* (London, 1803), vol. 2, pp. 103 ff., laments a situation at Oxford deserving "not only the severity of censure but the utmost poignancy of ridicule." Sir Alexander Grant, *The Story of the University of Edinburgh* (London, 1884), vol. 1, p. 270, compares the wealth, beauty and stagnant intellectual life of eighteenth-century Oxford with the intellectual vigor of "the small, poverty-stricken, ill-housed University of Edinburgh."

2. To Richard Price, April 22, 1786. Lyman H. Butterfield, ed., *Letters of Benjamin Rush* (Princeton, 1951), vol. 1, p. 388.

3. George P. Schmidt, *The Old Time College President* (N.Y., 1930), p. 75.

4. The Presidents of Dartmouth and of Trinity, North Carolina, quoted by Frederick Rudolph, *The American College and University: A History* (New York, 1962), p. 139.

5. George P. Schmidt, *The Liberal Arts College* (New Brunswick, N.J., 1957), p. 35.

6. Sensation, Retention, Perception, Association, Observation, Attention, Abstraction, Memory, Understanding, Wit, Ratiocination and Imagination, as listed by David McClure in *A System of Education for the Girard College for Orphans* (Phila., 1838), chart opp. p. 16.

7. *The Centennial Memorial of the Presbytery of Carlisle* (Harrisburg, 1889), vol. 2, p. 167.

8. Schmidt, *Liberal Arts College* p. 53.

9. Julian P. Boyd, ed., *The Papers of Thomas Jefferson*, vol. 7, p. 686.

10. To Charles Wallace, Sept. 2, 1790. *Bulletin of the New York Public Library*, vol. 1 (1897), p. 119.

11. In a letter to Principal-Elect Nisbet, Aug. 27, 1784, Rush describes the newly designed seal of their college: "The device consists of a Bible, a Telescope, and a Cap of Liberty—the two last placed over the first. The motto is *Pietate et Doctrina tuta libertas.* This Excellent sentiment was suggested by our worthy governor Mr. Dickinson." Butterfield, vol. 1, p. 335.

Chapter 2. Curtain Raiser

1. *Records of the Presbyterian Church in the United States of America, embracing the Minutes of the General Presbytery and General Synod, 1706–1788* (Phila., 1904), p. 171.

2. Richard Webster, *A History of the Presbyterian Church in America, from its Origin until the Year 1760* (Phila., 1857), p. 484.

3. Presbyterian Historical Society, Phila.

4. The history and background of the school are reviewed by Thomas Clinton Pears, Jr., "Colonial Education among Presbyterians," *Journal of the Presbyterian Historical Society*, vol. 30 (1952), pp. 115–26, 165–74.

5. On Tennent: Horace Wemyss Smith, *Life and Correspondence of the Rev. William Smith* (Phila., 1879), vol. 1, p. 103.

6. In a religious denomination where thought and concern are equally alive, innumerable shades of opinion will appear, and one finds men of these two parties sometimes nearly of the same complexion, at others radically different. Pelagius, a British monk who fl. 400 A.D., denied Original Sin. Few New Siders went as far as that, but many Old Siders were willing to imply that they did. Benjamin Rush, explaining the situation to Charles Nisbet in Scotland, Aug. 27, 1784, is more temperate: "The Irish are in general Presbyterians. They compose about 1/6 or 1/8 of the state, and as they are a modern society and not very remarkable for industry, they possess not more than 1/20 of the wealth of the state. They are subdivided into four lesser sects, *viz.* Old Lights, New Lights, Seceders and Covenanters. The Old and New Lights agree in all the essentials of the Westminster Confession of Faith. The former are thought to be more attached to the doctrinal, the latter to the practical parts of Christianity. The ministers of the former are in general the most learned. The ministers of the latter are the most animated but least connected in their public discoveries. Both parties belong to our synod, and both sides claim many able divines and pious ministers. The Seceders and Covenanters are the same kind of people here as they are in Scotland." Lyman H. Butterfield, ed., *Letters of Benjamin Rush* (Princeton, 1951), vol. 1, p. 336.

7. As described by Saul Sack, *History of Higher Education in Pennsylvania*

(Harrisburg, 1963), pp. 39–40, an excellent and definitive work to which the author of this is more largely indebted than footnotes will declare.

8. John S. Brubacher and Willis Rudy, *Higher Education in Transition* (N.Y., 1958), p. 17.

9. MS. Presbyterian Historical Society, Philadelphia.

10. George Morgan, "The Colonial Origin of Newark Academy and of Other Classical Schools from which arose Many Colleges and Universities," *Delaware Notes,* vol. 8 (1934), pp. 26–30, states that Newark trained some 5,000 boys, but names only a few of the Colonial period, notably the Signers, Thomas McKean, George Read and Col. James Smith. Edward D. Neill, "Matthew Wilson, D.D., of Lewes, Delaware," *PMHB,* vol. 8 (1884), p. 46n, includes John Dickinson in a list of 17 students of the early period. Pears, p. 169, more conservative, omits Dickinson from the list of 9 for whom he has found positive evidence of attendance.

11. Obituary of Alison by Matthew Wilson, *Pennsylvania Journal,* April 19, 1780.

12. William A. Hunter, *Forts on the Pennsylvania Frontier, 1753–1758* (Harrisburg, 1960), pp. 176–77. Conway Phelps Wing and others, *History of Cumberland County, Pennsylvania* (Phila., 1879), p. 51. Rev. D. K. Richardson, *A Historical Discourse delivered in the Presbyterian Church of Greencastle, Penn'a., August 9th, 1876* (Chambersburg, Pa. 1876), p. 13, recalls Captain Steel as "a brave and fearless man," yet "not unmindful . . . of the higher commission he held as messenger of the Prince of Peace," and illustrates this synthesis with a remembered incident: "It was the Sabbath. The congregation had assembled in a barn standing on the farm now owned by Mr. Adam Wingerd. They brought their arms with them. When Mr. Steele entered the rude pulpit, which had been erected, he hung his hat and rifle behind him. The male members of the congregation sat listening to the Gospel message with their arms at their side. While in the midst of his discourse some one appeared and quietly called a member of the congregation out, and told him of the murder of a family, by the Indians, of the name of Walter, at what is now known as Rankin's Mill. The awful story was soon whispered from one to another. As soon as Mr. Steele discovered what had taken place, he immediately brought the services to a close, took down his hat and rifle, and at the head of the members of his congregation, went in pursuit of the murderers."

13. Hunter, pp. 369, 406, 412, 564.

14. *Ibid.,* p. 431.

15. *Ibid.,* p. 432. Leonard W. Labaree, ed., *Papers of Benjamin Franklin,* (New Haven & London, 1963), vol. 7, p. 105. Wing, p. 58. Steel's letter of April 11, 1756, calling upon Gov. Robert H. Morris for arms and equipment for 54 men, is at HSP.

16. Smith, vol. 1, p. 137.

17. *Edinburgh Magazine,* vol. 3 (1759), p. 179.

18. Mrs. Duffield and Mrs. John Armstrong were sisters, daughters of Archibald Armstrong (d. 1775) of New Castle County, Del., and so identified in his will.

19. Minutes of Donegal Presbytery, Presbyterian Historical Society, Philadelphia.

20. Allan D. Thompson, *The Meeting House on the Square* (Carlisle, 1964), p. 29, citing Thomas Penn's letter of June 4, 1760, to John Armstrong (Penn MSS, HSP), in which Penn states that he has granted the land on the square and supposes that the church is now being built. Three years before, Armstrong had obtained stone for "a Meeting House on the North Side of the Square," an incident noted in all histories of the Carlisle church as establishing its date of origin, though no building was then erected. It is, however, evidence of the Colonel's primary voice and influ-

ence in church affairs. Now, coincident with Armstrong's application for a deed for the site, Steel had obtained permission from the provincial authorities to hold a lottery to finance his own building program (p. 30.).

21. Duffield's opposition had a head start. Steel had been called to the churches of Upper and Lower Pennsborough (Carlisle and Silver Springs), April 3, 1759, and installed on April 17, according to Duffield's letter to Blair. Carlisle was to have two-thirds of his time. Duffield, whose call was laid before the Presbytery on Aug. 21, 1759, and who was installed on Sept. 19, nevertheless claimed prior rights which a secretly and hastily contrived conspiracy had invaded. Webster pp. 484, 672. Conway Phelps Wing, *A History of the First Presbyterian Church of Carlisle, Pa.* (Carlisle, 1877), pp. 67–71. *The Centennial Memorial of the Presbytery of Carlisle* (Harrisburg, 1889), vol. 1, p. 69. Joseph A. Murray, *A Contribution to the History of the Presbyterian Churches, Carlisle, Pa.* (Carlisle, 1905), pp. 6–9. Thompson, pp. 33–34.

22. George Duffield, *One Hundred Years Ago: An Historical Discourse Delivered . . . during the Centennial Celebration of the First Presbyterian Church of Carlisle,* July 1, 1857, p. 11.

23. *Records of the Presbyterian Church,* p. 297.

24. The Bureau of Land Records, Harrisburg, records lands in Bedford County, warrant of June 8, 1762, and on Shawnee Creek, May 16, 1767. A Bedford County plantation is mentioned in Steel's will, Court House, Carlisle.

25. Pears, p. 137. Morgan, p. 20, gives Alison's first salary as £20, Steel's as £15, later raised to £40 and £20.

26. John Steel, MS sermons. Presbyterian Historical Society, Phila. Wing, *First Presbyterian Church,* p. 109.

27. P. 333. Sypher's MS, HSP, gives no source.

28. Wing, *Cumberland County,* p. 151.

29. The boy was the Rev. William Linn (1752–1808) (*Centennial Memorial,* vol. 2, p. 56); and the theological student, the Rev. Robert Cooper (c. 1732–1805), who was licensed to preach, Oct. 24, 1764. William B. Sprague *Annals of the American Pulpit* (N.Y., 1858), vol. 3, p. 270,

30. *PMHB,* vol. 29 (1905), p. 366.

31. MS. Presbyterian Historical Society, Phila.

32. *Colonial Records,* vol. 9, p. 464. Charles A. Fisher, *The Snyder County Pioneers* (Selinsgrove, Pa. 1938), p. 91.

33. Wing, *First Presbyterian Church,* p. 85.

34. Steel's prompt and eager response to the summons, dated Carlisle, Feb. 27, 1768, is at HSP. His report for himself and the three other commissioners, Fort Cumberland, April 2, 1768, is at the Public Record Office, London. They met with both settlers and Indians and persuaded a few of the settlers to leave. The others, however, determined to await the making of a treaty and move only if the Indians should "appear dissatisfied."

35. Alfred Nevin, *Churches of the Valley* (Phila., 1852), p. 70. The agreement is printed, pp. 327–28.

36. Wing, *First Presbyterian Church,* pp. 75–76.

37. *Records of the Presbyterian Church,* pp. 366–67. On May 21, 1767, the Synod of Philadelphia received a letter from John Elder and John Steel, "as moderator and clerk of the Presbytery which they call the Presbytery of Donegall," threatening to leave the jurisdiction of the Synod unless granted separate status. This met with flat rejection on the next day. On June 23, 1767, the official Presbytery of Donegal gave "serious consideration to the danger threatening" and to its duty "as

Watchman on the wall of this part of Zion." Minutes, Presbyterian Historical Society, Phila. The Synod of the next year, May 25, 1768, attached Steel, Elder and other dissidents to the Second Presbytery of Philadelphia. *Records*, p. 384.

38. Lyman H. Butterfield, *John Witherspoon Comes to America. A Documentary Account based largely on New Materials* (Princeton, 1953), p. 3. This work is the primary source for the events centered at Princeton.

39. Donegal Minutes, 1773. Typescript, p. 313.

40. James Seaton Reid, *History of the Presbyterian Church in Ireland* (Belfast, 1867), vol. 3, p. 305.

41. To Ezra Stiles. Butterfield, *Witherspoon*, p. 13. Samuel Purviance, Philadelphia merchant and ardent Old Side politician, was pushing to have "4 able professors appointed & Dr. Alison at their Head" (p. 4).

42. Butterfield, *Witherspoon*, p. 59.

43. *Ibid.*, pp. 87–88.

44. Wing, *First Presbyterian Church*, p. 92.

45. Webster, p. 480.

46. Wing, *First Presbyterian Church*, p. 105.

47. Murray, pp. 49–53, printing the contracts in full.

48. Thompson, p. 32.

49. MS, Presbyterian Historical Society, Phila.

50. Murray, p. 13.

51. The announcement was first quoted by James Mulhern, *A History of Secondary Education in Pennsylvania* (Phila., 1933), pp. 86–87.

52. Wing, *First Presbyterian Church*, pp. 93–96. The original charter is in the Cadwalader Collection, HSP.

53. *Maryland Gazette*, Aug. 13, 1761.

Chapter 3. The Latin School at Carlisle

1. Recorder of Deeds and Register of Wills. Cumberland County Court House, Carlisle.

2. *Records of the General Synod of Ulster from 1691 to 1820* (Belfast, 1890–98), vol. 2, p. 491. David Stewart, *Fasti of the American Presbyterian Church, treating of Ministers of Irish Origin·who Laboured in America during the Eighteenth Century* (Belfast, 1943), p. 16. James Seaton Reid, *History of the Congregations of the Presbyterian Church in Ireland* (Belfast and Edinburgh, 1886), pp. 205, 289.

3. Charles A. Hanna, *The Scotch Irish . . .* (N.Y., 1902), vol. 2, p. 382.

4. Henry McKinley, sadler, died in 1814, and is recorded in a deed to the schoolmaster's house as his son. The others appear in Carlisle records as of right age at a time when no other family of the name was present. John became a country schoolmaster. Isaac McKinley, a neighboring physician, may also have been of the family.

5. *Centennial Memorial of the Presbytery of Carlisle* (Harrisburg, 1889), vol. 1, p. 343. Dr. T. C. Stevenson on his father's life, Murray Papers, DCA, describes the school as "a select Classical Academy here under the direction of the Rev. Mr. McKinley."

6. David Elliott, *The Life of the Rev. Elisha Macurdy* (Allegheny, Pa., 1848), p. 14.

7. *Biographical Sketch of Rev. Thomas Creigh, D.D., read before the Presbytery of Carlisle* (Chambersburg, Pa. 1881), p. 3.

8. Cumberland County Historical Society, Carlisle.

9. _Ibid._

10. George Chalmers, _Life of Thomas Ruddiman_ (London, 1794), p. 274.

11. The new and successful Wilmington Academy had moved, 1773, from the town hall to a building of its own (_PMHB,_ vol. 49 [1925], pp. 317–18), and a spirit of emulation may be inferred at both Newark and Carlisle.

12. Lucy E. Lee Ewing, _Dr. John Ewing and Some of his Noted Connections_ (Phila., 1924), p. 18. Ewing's letters, Feb. 20, June 24 and July 5, 1774, are in the Van Pelt Library, University of Pennsylvania.

13. Lyman H. Butterfield, ed., _Letters of Benjamin Rush_ (Princeton, 1951), vol. 1, p. 299.

14. _Ibid._, p. 299n.

15. "In County Committee, Carlisle, May 3d. 1776. Resolved that the Reflections thrown out by Mr. Henry McKinly on Col: William Irwin's Character by giving Coll. Irwine for the author of his slanderous report on Col: Wilson, in the Course of his Defence, appear to this Committee to be false and scandalous." Irvine Papers, HSP, vol. 1, p. 39. Congress joined in the defense of James Wilson, twenty-two of his fellow members certifying, June 20, 1776, that he had "declared it to be his opinion that the Colonies would stand justified before God and the World in declaring an absolute Separation from Great Britain forever," and that he had merely urged postponement of the measure. U. S. Revolution Papers, Library of Congress.

16. _Pennsylvania Archives,_ 5th ser., vol. 3, pp. 671–76, 679–80, 683–88, with history and muster rolls of the regiment. _Colonial Records,_ vol. 10, p. 756. Originals are in the Pennsylvania State Archives and the National Archives. Of the two sheriffs of Cumberland County whose election was announced, Nov. 5, 1776, Henry Makinly received 170 votes and his brother-in-law, Robert Semple, 490. _Pennsylvania Archives,_ 6th ser., vol. 11, p. 157.

17. Pension Rolls, National Archives.

18. Francis Alison, Sr., to his son on obtaining the appointment, _PMHB,_ vol. 29 (1905), pp. 495–96.

19. Pennsylvania State Archives, Harrisburg. There is a sequel in John C. Fitzpatrick, ed., _The Writings of George Washington_ (Wash., 1931–44), vol. 8, p. 425. From General Orders, July 18, 1777, we learn of the court martial of Private Robert Story, charged with desertion from "the 11th Penn: Regt., and inlisting into Capt McKinley's Company of the 12th Pennsylv: Regiment." The court declared him entitled to pardon by the Commander-in-Chief, upon returning the bounty to Captain McKinley.

20. To the Committee of Correspondence at Carlisle, Aug. 13, 1775. Founders Collection, DCA.

21. _PMHB,_ vol. 41 (1917), p. 258.

22. Thomas G. Tousey, _Military History of Carlisle and Carlisle Barracks_ (Richmond, Va., 1939), p. 93.

23. John Creigh to John Hay, Aug. 25, 1777. Cumberland County Historical Society, Carlisle.

24. F. B. Heitman, _Historical Register of Officers of the Continental Army_ (Baltimore, 1932). He is also cited as having resigned because of the depletion of his regiment. He was later a member of Assembly and a justice for Northumberland County. _PMHB,_ vol. 3 (1879), pp. 320–21.

25. "A true state" of the Twelth Pennsylvania at the time when it was combined with the Third, National Archives. See also _Pennsylvania Archives,_ 5th ser., vol. 2, p. 910; vol. 3, p. 683.

26. Sept. 12, 1778. Cumberland County Historical Society, Carlisle.

27. *Centennial Memorial,* vol. 2, p. 221, giving him the rank of lieutenant-colonel of militia. Conway P. Wing, *History of Cumberland County* (Phila., 1879), p. 91n. *Pennsylvania Archives,* 5th ser., vol. 6, p. 155.

28. Wing, pp. 90–91.

29. *History of Cumberland and Adams Counties* (Chicago, 1886), p. 95. *PMHB,* vol. 66 (1942), p. 23.

30. *Centennial Memorial,* vol. 2, p. 221.

31. Samuel Postlethwaite to Col. John Davis, Aug. 27, 1779. Davis to Gen. William Irvine, Sept. 8, 1779. John Davis Papers, Library of Congress.

32. To John Agnew, March 30, 1780. Cumberland County Historical Society, Carlisle.

33. Register of Wills and court records, Cumberland County, Pa. Henry Makinly was involved frequently in litigation up to July, 1784. The surviving tax lists do not record him as deceased until 1787. Letters of administration were issued to John Steel, Jr., Feb. 7, 1792, and account filed, June 15, 1796.

34. Recorder of Deeds, Cumberland County, vol. 1, Book F, p. 28. The house was on the south side of High Street, Lot No. 36.

35. Personal recollections of Ross by George Chambers, a Dickinson College trustee who had been his pupil at Chambersburg, and by "W. D." and "J. S. F." appear in *Historical Magazine,* ser. 1, vol. 6 (1862), pp. 324–25, 261–62, 357–58. See also Joseph Henry Dubbs, "James Ross, Latinist. An Early Lancaster Pedagogue," *Papers Read before the Lancaster County Historical Society,* vol. 9 (1904), pp. 32–36; and U. L. Gordy, "The Chambersburg Academy," *The Kittochtinny Historical Society Papers,* vol. 9 (1923), pp. 568–69, 578–80.

36. Joseph Smith, *History of Jefferson College* (Pittsburgh, 1857), p. 70, giving the recollection of James Power, Princeton Class of 1766, who described Ross as a "class mate." They were together at the Faggs Manor school but it has not been substantiated that Ross was at Princeton.

37. *Historical Magazine,* p. 357.

38. Undated. DCA.

39. Luther Reily Kelker, *History of Dauphin County, Pennsylvania* (N.Y. and Chicago, 1907), vol. 2, pp. 573–74.

40. *Historical Magazine,* p. 357. The story is typical of the often apocryphal anecdotes which garnish a teacher's reputation. Another version appears, *ibid.,* p. 261.

41. Ross to William Young, April 26, 1786, DCA, on a Latin prosody to be added anonymously to Young's forthcoming edition of Ruddiman's *Rudiments* (Phila., 1786). Later, Young and Nisbet enjoyed a long and friendly correspondence, perhaps initiated by Ross.

42. An announcement in the *Carlisle Gazette,* Sept. 24, 1800, states that Ross has been a teacher of Greek and Latin "for more than 30 years."

43. Princeton's degree is recorded in the Trustees' Minutes, but the *General Catalogue* of 1906 mistakenly identifies the recipient as the Pennsylvania Senator, James Ross.

44. *Historical Magazine,* p. 357.

45. Presbytery Minutes, Presbyterian Historical Society, Phila. The Minutes also record the appointment of committees to examine the school on April 11 and August 17, 1782.

46. Bill to "The Trustees for Erecting the Latin School-House in the town of Carlisle to John Creigh." DCA.

47. Edward W. Biddle, *The Old College Lot* (Carlisle, 1920), pp. 6–9.

48. Whitfield J. Bell, Jr., "The Other Man on Bingham's Porch," SL 2, p. 36.
49. Butterfield, vol. 1, p. 309.
50. To John Montgomery, *ibid.,* vol. 2, p. 834.
51. Lyman H. Butterfield, "Benjamin Rush and the Beginnings of 'John and Mary's College,' " SL 1, p. 39.

Chapter 4. The Charter

1. Owned by Mrs. T. Charlton Henry, Philadelphia. Described and illustrated in C. C. Sellers, *Portraits and Miniatures by Charles Willson Peale* (Phila., 1952), pp. 186–87, 294.

2. Medal, 1808, illustrated in Lyman H. Butterfield, *Letters of Benjamin Rush* (Princeton, 1951), vol. 2, opp. p. 780.

3. See Donald J. D'Elia, "Benjamin Rush, David Hartley, and the Revolutionary Uses of Psychology," *Proceedings of the American Philosophical Society,* vol. 114 (1970), pp. 109–18. Hartley's theory that the brain, as inert matter and therefore incapable of self-motivation, is activated by impulses from a divine source, postulated a direct relationship between the deity and the devout soul, eminently satisfactory to Rush. It could serve to refute the deistical belief, popular among his enemies, in the present remoteness of God the Creator, and the dependence of events upon human reason. Hartley's best-known doctrine, "the association of ideas," stressed the importance to each impression of those preceding it, thus presenting education as a necessarily unified structure—an essential element of Rush's proposals for an American educational system.

4. Richard H. Shryock, in *DAB:* "He was . . . the victim of a certain credulity about diagnoses and cures which characterized much of his work." Lyman H. Butterfield, "Benjamin Rush and the Beginnings of 'John and Mary's College,' " SL 1, p. 37: "Rush possessed that sometimes useful but very disconcerting faculty of self-hypnosis which enables a person to believe that he cannot possibly be wrong." And Carl Binger in *Revolutionary Doctor* (N.Y., 1966), p. 164, an eminent psychiatrist's opinion on one of the founders of his science: "With all his many gifts and at the height of his intellectual powers, Benjamin Rush lacked the talent for what we call insight. This has been true of many great men—especially of men with sensitive introversive natures who hide what they wrongly consider their weaknesses behind restless and aggressive outward activity."

5. It is worthy of note that here also Scotland was leading America. Scottish educators had long faced a rising demand for a curriculum attuned to contemporary life, and were meeting it with academies in which science and other practical subjects vied with the classical course: Alexander Morgan, *Rise and Progress of Scottish Education* (Edinburgh and London, 1927), p. 93; Martin L. Clarke, *Classical Education in Britain, 1500–1900* (Cambridge, 1959), p. 146. Scottish-born William Smith, in his *General Idea of the College of Mirania.* (N. Y., 1753), advanced the ideal of education for citizenship with a clarity instantly appealing to Benjamin Franklin and others, and laying the foundation for his long and successful career in American education.

6. Butterfield, *Letters of Benjamin Rush,* vol. 1, p. 388. May 25, 1786.
7. *Ibid.,* p. 292.
8. Jan. 16, 1785. DCA.
9. To John Montgomery, June 6, 1801: "The millenium . . . will probably be brought about by natural means. Civilization, human knowledge and liberty must first pervade the globe." Butterfield, *Letters of Benjamin Rush,* vol. 2, p. 834.

10. To Charles Nisbet, Aug. 27, 1784. *Ibid.,* vol. 1, p. 339.

11. Rush to John King, April 2, 1783, on winning Presbyterian support for the college: "Firmness and decision will carry all before them. Remember the Duke of Rocheficeau's maxim, 'The only way to *be* established is to appear so.' " *Ibid.* vol. 1, p. 300. And in 1808, again seeking a college president: "Offer him a generous salary, and trust to providence and the Doctor's talents and character to pay it." *Ibid.* vol. 2, p. 969.

12. Rush Papers, Library Company of Philadelphia, on deposit at HSP.

13. Oct. 15, 1782. Butterfield, *Letters of Benjamin Rush,* vol. 1, p. 290.

14. *Ibid.,* p. 293.

15. Lamberton Collection, HSP, vol. 2, p. 41.

16. Butterfield, *Letters of Benjamin Rush,* vol. 1, p. 338.

17. Edward Potts Cheyney, *History of the University of Pennsylvania* (Phila., 1940), p. 176.

18. Burton Alva Konkle, *George Bryan and the Constitution of Pennsylvania* (Phila., 1922), p. 295n.

19. Armstrong to Rush, Jan. 6, 1783; and John King to Rush, Jan. 9, 1783. Rush Papers.

20. To Charles Nisbet, Aug. 27, 1784. Butterfield, *Letters of Benjamin Rush,* vol. 1, p. 337.

21. John Black to Rush, April 16, 1783. Rush Papers. Rush in *Pennsylvania Packet,* Feb. 17, 1785.

22. Ernest J. Moyne, "The Reverend William Hazlitt and Dickinson College," *PMHB,* vol. 85 (1961), pp. 291, 297.

23. *Ibid.,* p. 299.

24. *Ibid.,* p. 300. A consolatory but unlikely conjecture. We find Armstrong writing to Rush, Feb. 28, 1784, Rush Papers: "Pray is Mr. Hazlet employed? and are his Evening lectures designated for the establishment and defence of the Christian religion? I make no doubt that gentn. is capable of saying many proper things in opposition to Deism, but is he equally opposed to the Arian & Socinian heresie?"

25. "Mr. Wilson will draw up our charter. His education in a British university and his perfect knowledge of all the charters of the American colleges will qualify him above most men for this business." Rush to John King, April 2, 1782. Butterfield, *Letters of Benjamin Rush,* vol. 1, p. 300.

26. " . . . a majority of them are Presbyterians, but the charter of the College allows of no exclusive privileges to any one religious society." *Ibid.,* p. 322. This readiness to bring together under sectarian control scholars and teachers of different faiths had long been established—it was a practical view embodied in the first announcement of King's College, 1754. Louis Franklin Snow, *The College Curriculum in the United States* (N.Y., 1907), p. 56.

27. Saul Sack, *History of Higher Education in Pennsylvania* (Harrisburg, 1963), vol. 1, p. 44.

28. Rush to Armstrong, March 19, 1783. Butterfield, *Letters of Benjamin Rush,* vol. 1, pp. 294–97. Armstrong withdrew his opposition in a letter to Rush, April 16, 1783. Rush Papers.

29. George H. Morgan, *Annals, Comprising Memoirs, Incidents and Statistics of Harrisburg* (Harrisburg, 1858), pp. 71–72, 76–77.

30. Butterfield, *Letters of Benjamin Rush,* vol. 1, p. 310. He was elected to the Board in 1787.

31. "Of Dickinson's manner of speaking I have some recollection—he possessed, I think, considerable fluency, with a sweetness of tone and an agreeable modulation

of voice, not well calculated, however, for a large audience. His law knowledge was respectable, though not remarkably extensive, for his attention was more directed to historical and political studies." John Fanning Watson, *Annals of Philadelphia* (Phila., 1891), vol. 1, p. 319.

32. Rush Papers. In repeating the story in the *Pennsylvania Packet,* Feb. 17, 1785, Rush capitalizes the horrid word, "SOCINIAN." Socinus, a sixteenth-century Italian, had denied the Trinity, the divinity of Jesus, original sin, propitiatory sacrifice and the depravity of man; and, his mind cluttered with all this devastation, had found only the virtues of Christ for guidance.

33. Moyne, p. 298.

34. "The sweepings 'of their studies will be very acceptable in our illiterate wooden country." Rush to John Coakley Lettsom, April 8, 1785. Butterfield, *Letters of Benjamin Rush,* vol. 1, p. 351. Dr. Lettsom responded with the largest and most valuable gift to come from Britain, 30 volumes of the Journals of the House of Commons, a set still preserved at the Library despite Rush's determination to have it removed: "a student of Dickinson College . . . would find nothing in them but such things as a scholar and a gentleman should strive to forget." *Ibid.,* p. 382. To Granville Sharp, Rush had written, Nov. 28, 1783: "It will make me happy to record your name in the archives of the college as a friend to this nursery of humanity." *Journal of American Studies,* vol. 1 (1967), pp. 20–21. Sharp responded liberally with books, including all his own writings.

35. Thomas Jefferson Wertenbaker, *Princeton, 1746–1896* (Princeton, 1946), p. 65.

36. Butterfield, *Letters of Benjamin Rush,* vol. 1, p. 339.

37. Samuel Miller, *Memoir of the Rev. Charles Nisbet, D.D.* (N.Y., 1840), p. 308.

38. James G. Low, *Memorials of the Church of St. John the Evangelist: being an Account, Biographical, Historical, Antiquarian and Traditionary, of the Parish Church of Montrose and Clergy thereof* (Montrose, 1891), p. 70.

39. Dec. 5, 1783. Butterfield, *Letters of Benjamin Rush,* pp. 315–16.

40. Thomas Smith to Rush, Jan. 23, 1785. Rush Papers.

41. June 30, 1784. Trustee Minutes, DCA.

42. The story of the Tod letter and all the events surrounding it is best told by Alfred Owen Aldridge, "Dickinson College and the 'Broad Bottom' of Early Education in Pennsylvania," SL 3, pp. 93–114.

43. Lyman H. Butterfield, ed., "Dr. Benjamin Rush's Journal of a Trip to Carlisle in 1784," *PMHB,* vol. 74 (1950), pp. 451–52.

44. John Dickinson Papers, R. R. Logan Collection, Library Company of Philadelphia, on deposit at HSP. James Henry Morgan, *Dickinson College* (Carlisle 1933), pp. 25–26.

45. Butterfield, *Letters of Benjamin Rush,* vol. 1, 319.

46. Montgomery to Rush, May 7, 1784. Rush Papers.

47. DCA.

48. Butterfield, "Dr. Benjamin Rush's Journal " p. 452.

49. *Ibid.,* p. 453.

50. Butterfield, "Benjamin Rush and the Beginnings of 'John and Mary's College,' " SL 1, p. 49.

51. Butterfield, *Letters of Benjamin Rush,* vol. 1, p. 323.

52. *Ibid.,* 334–35.

53. Miller, pp. 104–11, 121–23.

54. Michael Kraus, "Charles Nisbet and Samuel Stanhope Smith—Two Eight-

eenth Century Educators," *Princeton University Library Chronicle,* vol. 6 (1944), pp. 17–36.

55. Miller, p. 109.

56. Boyd Lee Spahr, "Charles Nisbet, a Portrait in Miniature," SL 1, p. 59.

57. Dickinson to Nisbet, Oct. 25, 1784. Roberts Collection, Haverford College. Dickinson to Rush, same date. DCA.

58. To Montgomery, Nov. 13, 1784: "Whether he purchased the vote that lately made him president of the state by this secret act of treachery to the last hopes of the republicans, or whether he wished to anihilate our College and thereby prevent any future drafts being made upon him for its support, or whether he is under Quaker influence as to the future power of the Presbyterians, I know not," Butterfield, *Letters of Benjamin Rush,* vol. 1, p. 341. Absurd as the allegation of bribery is, there may have been a shred of truth in the others. The confidence of potential donors had vanished in the bickering, and Dickinson stood alone, his own confidence shaken. Further, he was moving closer to Friendly ideals. He would give again, not to the College, but to safeguard Nisbet's position. His final large benefaction was in support of a Quaker school.

59. *Ibid.,* p. 338. Other contemporaries saw a "sober and temperate," solid and edifying individual, who could "become the companion of innocent mirth and happy gayety," his temper "not often ruffled." Lucy E. Lee Ewing, *Dr. John Ewing* (Phila., 1924), pp. 14–15.

60. Nov. 28, 1784. Butterfield, *Letters of Benjamin Rush,* vol. 1, 345.

61. Dec. 10, 1784. *Ibid.*

62. Jan. 4, 1785. *Ibid.,* p. 349.

63. Francis Hopkinson, *Miscellaneous Essays* (Phila., 1792), vol. 2, pp. 142–43. Quoted by Alfred Owen Aldridge in "Dickinson College and the 'Broad Bottom' of Early Education in Pennsylvania," SL 3, pp. 112–13.

64. Edward Potts Cheyney, *History of the University of Pennsylvania* (Phila., 1940), p. 134. Davidson is said to have been a brother of Professor James Davidson, teacher of classics at the University, who was one of William Hazlitt's Philadelphia friends, and had long been known in college and academy as "Old Wiggie," from the habit he had of snatching off his wig and beating his pupils with it. This personal detail, and much of the portrait drawn here, is from the sketch of Robert Davidson by his son in William B. Sprague's *Annals of the American Pulpit* (N.Y., 1858), vol. 3, pp. 322–26.

65. In his teaching, Davidson blended the second and third items of this title into the first, telling his students that Chronology "has such an intimate connection with the study of history, that no progress can be made to any good purpose in the knowledge of facts and events without it. These two sciences, *Geography & Chronology,* have been called the *eyes of history.*" Lecture notes, DCA.

66. *Two Hundred Years in Cumberland County* (Carlisle, 1951), p. 93.

67. Butterfield, *Letters of Benjamin Rush,* vol. 1, pp. 351–54. Original in DCA.

68. *Ibid.,* p. 356.

69. To William Linn, May 4, 1784. *Ibid.* pp. 332–33.

Chapter 5. Nisbet in his Prime

1. Samuel Miller, *Memoir of the Rev. Charles Nisbet D.D.* (N.Y., 1840), pp. 299–300. William B. Sprague, *Annals of the American Pulpit* (N.Y., 1858), vol. 3, pp. 458–59.

2. Nisbet to Jedidiah Morse, Oct. 24, 1799. Yale University Library.

3. George Hay Kain and others, *A History of the York County Academy, York, Pennsylvania* (York, 1953), pp. 28–29.

4. Solomon Drowne to his wife, Oct. 31, 1788, John Hay Library, Brown University: Reading a very pretty town, but Carlisle "still more beautiful, containing some of ye most elegant stone buildings in the state." Robert Davidson, 1791, DCA, describes Carlisle as having 13 boarding houses, 27 shops and 400 dwellings.

5. David Wilson Thompson, *Early Publications of Carlisle, Pennsylvania, 1785–1835* (Carlisle, 1932), pp. 2 ff.

6. "JUNIOR," on p. 2, col. 3.

7. Rush to John Montgomery (?), July 1, 1785. Rush Papers, Library Company of Philadelphia, on deposit at HSP.

8. Miller, p. 136.

9. *Pennsylvania Gazette,* Oct. 27, 1784, states Dickinson had selected "about 1500 volumes." The bill for work on Nisbet's house, DCA, "195 feet Boards for Doctr nisbets Librerry," suggests about 1,100 volumes. Nisbet estate inventory, Cumberland County Court House, 1804, gives 1,425 volumes.

10. His salary was two to three times that of a professor. Philip Freneau derided it in rhyme:

> It seems we have spirit to humble a throne,
> Have genius for science inferior to none,
> But hardly encourage a plant of our own:
> If a college be planned,
> 'Tis all at a stand
> 'Till to Europe we send at a shameful expense,
> To send us a book-worm to teach us some sense.

Poems, written and published during the American Revolutionary War (Phila., 1809), vol. 2, p. 207.

11. Nisbet to Witherspoon, April 3, 1784, HSP: "The most offensive Letters to Government that I ever writ, have been those published in Newspapers during the War, & some of them have been reprinted in London, Edinburgh, Newcastle & Glasgow itself, some of them eight times over, without the least Censure & I never was a Prisoner of State for any private Letter, except two to Lord George Gordon, which on Examination were found to be perfectly innocent, though I was the first Person in the British Dominions that was delated to Government for favouring the Cause of America." John Kay, *Series of Original Portraits* (Edin., 1877), vol. 1, p. 94n, cites Nisbet's opposition to Robertson. Miller, pp. 75–77, repeats anecdotes of Montrose.

12. Nisbet to Buchan, June 13, 1785. Miller, p. 133.

13. John Jamieson (1759–1838), philologist and poet, author of *Etymological Dictionary of the Scottish Language,* etc., to Samuel Miller, Aug. 5, 1805. HSP.

14. Now owned by a direct descendant of the Nisbets, Mrs. Harry Sisk.

15. Rush to John Erskine, Oct. 25, 1785. Rush Papers.

16. July 23, 1785. Rush Papers.

17. Sept. 29, 1786. Miller, p. 148.

18. Rush Papers.

19. Rush to Montgomery, Nov. 15, 1783, Rush Papers: "I am preparing some thoughts to lay before the board of trustees upon the subject of education proper for a college in a new republican state." These would reach final form in his *A Plan for the Establishment of Public Schools and Diffusion of Knowledge in Pennsylvania; to*

Which are Added Thoughts upon the Mode of Education, Proper in a Republic (Phila., 1786). This is printed also in his *Essays, Literary, Moral and Philosophical* (Phila., 1798). Lyman H. Butterfield, ed., *Letters of Benjamin Rush* (Princeton, 1951), vol. 1, pp. 491–93, prints his "Plan for a Federal University" as first published in the *Federal Gazette,* Oct. 29, 1788.

20. Rush, *Essays,* p. 19. Olive Moore Gambrill, "John Beale Bordley and the Early Years of the Philadelphia Agricultural Society," *PMHB,* vol. 66 (1942), p. 429, mentions a plan for the endowment at Dickinson of a professorship in "the chemical, philosophical and elementary parts of the theory of agriculture."

21. The attack began with his "Enquiry into the Utility of a Knowledge of the Latin and Greek Languages, as a Branch of Liberal Education, with Hints on a Plan of Liberal Instruction without them," published anonymously in *American Museum,* vol. 5 (June, 1789), pp. 525–35; and in *Essays,* pp. 20–56. American opinion was strongly utilitarian, and Matthew Carey thought Rush would have won his point had he been less vituperative. Saul Sack, *History of Higher Education in Pennsylvania* (Harrisburg, 1963), vol. 2, pp. 608–09. "Offal learning," from Rush to John Adams, Feb. 4, 1811, in John A. Schutz and Douglas Adair, *The Spur of Fame* (San Marino, Cal., 1966), p. 178.

22. DCA.

23. Rush, *Essays,* p. 70.

24. Hampden-Sidney classed its grammar school as freshmen until 1812. Princeton had long had the full four classes. Pennsylvania conferred its degree at the end of the third year until 1826.

25. From the minutes of the Coetus, German Reformed archives, Lancaster Pa., courtesy of J. Stuart Prentice. Coetus replied to the College, April 28, 1785, regretting that it could not contribute its "Mite to this usefull undertaking." DCA.

26. The same requirement prevailed at the University of Edinburgh, where the idea had been borrowed from the faculty of Medicine. Alexander Grant, *The Story of the University of Edinburgh* (London, 1884), vol. 1, pp. 277–78. Rush may therefore have been advocating a requirement he himself had met as a student of medicine at Edinburgh.

27. Rush to the trustees, Oct. 21, 1786. Rush Papers.

28. Having adopted the *Plan* on Aug. 11, the trustees appointed a committee on Oct. 19, 1785 to review it, and the Minutes of Nov. 15, 1786, DCA, record its debate and adoption as revised.

29. *Carlisle Gazette,* Aug. 17, 1785. The news release had probably come direct from Rush, as had similar publicity in the *Pennsylvania Packet,* March 31, 1786.

30. Butterfield, vol. 1, pp. 374, 378. Rush had pronounced Mr. Tait to be "a man of great piety and formerly well acquainted with the business." Tait gives his own view of his troubles in a letter to Rush, May 20, 1786, Rush Papers. Here he mentions three Irish teachers of English and writing, "besides women's schools established for a number of years past in this town."

31. Rush Papers. The "Dialogue" may be attributed to Davidson, who had been much acclaimed for a similar performance at the College of Philadelphia, 1775. It had been spoken earlier at the public examination of June 15, an account of which was sent by John King to the *Maryland Gazette,* Aug. 5, 1785.

32. Minutes of the Presbytery of Brechin. Scottish Record Office, Edinburgh.

33. Thomas Nisbet to Rush, Aug., 1785, Rush Papers: "Dr. Nisbet's mental faculties are quite decayed & he talks more like a child than the man he was sometime ago." Nisbet to Rush, Dec. 5, 1785, *ibid.,* describes his continued suffering. Rush to Richard Price, May 25, 1786, Butterfield, p. 389, gives his view in retro-

spect: "The letters written by Dr. Nisbet to his friends soon after his arrival in America, from which so many extracts have been published in the Scotch papers, were written under a deranged state of mind occasioned by a fever which fixed itself upon his brain. The Doctor has since perfectly recovered his health and reason, and is now perfectly satisfied with our country."

34. Whitfield J. Bell, Jr., "The Other Man on Bingham's Porch," SL 2, p. 44.

35. "Besides it might involve Dr. D in some Deferticulty if he shoud now accpt and afterwards be under the nessecety of resigning (perhaps in a short time) having some one placed over him in the institution who as yet has no connection with it and no pretensions to be his superior for I do not hesitate to give it as my opinion that one who has gone thro' the several Grades in teaching from a tutor in an accademy to a proffesors chair in a University is in all probabilly better qualified for and has a better claim to the Chair of a Principal than one who may not have had litle or no experience in teaching." Montgomery to trustees, undated. DCA.

36. Rush to Montgomery, Feb. 20, 1786. Butterfield, pp. 379–80.

37. *Ibid.*, p. 376.

38. Miller, pp. 140–42. Nisbet's letter to Buchan, June 22, 1791, DCA, has at its head the Earl's dry comment, "Exaggerated account of affairs."

39. Nisbet to Rush, Jan. 9, 1786. Rush Papers. Apparently Rush, in a new and foredoomed effort to inspire, had urged his Principal to be a St. John and a Lycurgus. Nisbet adds "St. Job."

40. Jan. 30, 1786. Rush Papers.

41. Feb. 15, 1786. *Ibid.*

42. Edited and translated by David Wilson Thompson, *Dickinson Alumnus*, Feb., 1947, pp. 20–21.

43. Butterfield, p. 383.

44. Both from the press of Kline and Reynolds of the *Carlisle Gazette*, 1786.

45. I. H. M'Cauley, *Historical Sketch of Franklin County, Pennsylvania* (Harrisburg, 1878), pp. 120–21. Trustees Minutes. Information from Marion D. Neece.

46. Belles Lettres Society Minutes, Sept. 9, 1786, DCA: Mr. Cochran was admitted, "after signing an acknowledgement of Secrecy, & the Laws of the Society." On April 8, 1800, Mr. Hillyard was expelled, for he "not only divulged the secrets of Society, but had ridiculed & reprobated the proceedings."

47. *Carlisle Gazette*, Jan. 4, 1786. *Pennsylvania Packet*, Jan. 20, 1786.

48. *Catalogue of the Union Philosophial Society, Dickinson College*. Second edition (Carlisle, 1896), p. 3. Almost all the original records of the Society have been destroyed by fire.

49. Belles Lettres Society Minutes, March 2, 1793. DCA.

50. John Shippen's composition of Aug. 8, 1789, was published as a little book, *Observations on Novel-Reading* (Phila., 1792). It is dedicated to Charles Nisbet, whose philosophy, in a less happy aspect, is clearly reflected in its opening lines: "Although at first sight it appears natural that virtue should flourish in direct proportion to the advancement of knowledge, the contrary, it is to be feared, is too well founded in experience to admit a contradiction. Men, as they gain knowledge, invent new species of wickedness; and thus alas! the seeds of immorality and libertinism have found a very fruitful soil among mankind for the two or three latter generations."

51. Taney's own recollections of his life as a student are given in Samuel Tyler's *Memoir of Roger Brooke Taney, LL.D.* (Balt., 1872), pp. 37–54.

52. Carl Brent Swisher, "The Education of Roger B. Taney," SL 1, p. 155.

53. Thompson, *Early Publications of Carlisle*, pp. 62–63. *The Western Almanac*

was printed in 1791–99 by Archibald Loudon, who also brought out the *Dickinson College Almanac*, 1807.

54. The whole affair is recounted in a more-than-Nisbetian diatribe, DCA, *An Address to the Students of Dickinson College. By Henry Lyon Davis. Qua dies tam festa ut cesset prodere Furem, Perfidiam, Fraudes, atque omne ex crimine lucrum Quaesitum. Juvenal.*

55. A valuable glimpse of the early curriculum is given by Samuel Brown in a letter to John Coulter, Oct. 5, 1788. Library of the College of William and Mary. Admitted to the College in November, 1787, Brown had read 12 books of Homer and 3 of Cicero. With Davidson he had studied English grammar, Rhetoric, Chronology "and part of Natural Philosophy." With Nisbet he had written 180 lectures on languages, history of philosophy, criticism and logic. He had been reading books in English in the College Library. In mathematics he had taken Euclid, arithmetic, trigonometry and part of surveying.

56. "A Reminiscence of Doctor Charles Nesbit of Dickinson College. By James Duncan," *PMHB*, vol. 5 (1881), p. 103.

57. Charles Nisbet, *An Address to the Students of Dickinson College, by the Rev. Charles Nisbet, D.D. On his Re-election to the Office of Principal of said College* (Carlisle, 1786), p. 12.

58. *Ibid.* p. 10.

59. Student transcript of commencement address, Sept. 26, 1787. Library of Centre College.

60. Nisbet to Alexander Addison, May 11, 1792. Darlington Library, University of Pittsburgh.

61. *Ibid.* Herbert F. Thomson and Willard G. Bloodgood, "A Classical Economist on the Frontier," *Pennsylvania History*, vol. 26 (1959), pp. 195–212, give the best analysis to date of Nisbet's teaching, dealing only with this one aspect. Nisbet divided Moral Philosophy into three parts, Ethics, "Oeconomics" and Politics, "corresponding to books in the Aristotelian corpus, and to divisions that were frequently adhered to in the Scottish universities." His lectures on "Oeconomics" moved from family relationships, to contracts, to "Political Oeconomy" and to government. "Political Oeconomy" dealt with the principles of economics, resources, manufactures and money, commerce, taxation (pp. 197–98).

62. Charles Nisbet, "Hints on Education," *Port Folio*, vol. 8 (1812), p. 259, distinguishes between the "schoolmaster" who teaches by "extempore and repeated admonitions," and the "humanist, by premeditated and continued discourse." Miller, p. 320, quotes Matthew Brown, Class of 1794: "His plan of instruction in College was by Lectures, which the classes were expected to write in full. He delivered them with so much deliberation and with such pauses, that, after some practice, we were able to take down the whole . . . . There were, however, few classes, all the members of which would consent to sustain the labour of doing this. His lectures were thought by some to be too voluminous; but they were exceedingly rich, and excellent in their kind. Besides a thorough and philosophic investigation of his subject, it was always illustrated by appropriate anecdotes, characterized by that wit and vivacity for which he was so distinguished. He seldom finished a lecture without some exhilirating anecdote, and some brilliant flashes of wit and humour, electrifying the whole class." "Glimpses of Old College Life," *William and Mary Quarterly*, vol. 8 (1900), p. 213, cites similar student notes on Bishop Madison's lectures with separate questions and answers.

63. Some contrasting definitions help to characterize the teacher:
Nisbet: "Moral Philosophy has for its object the direction of the will & human

actions. It is the province of moral philosophy to regulate human actions." John Young notes, 1787. DCA.

John Witherspoon: "Moral Philosophy is that branch of Science which treats of the principles and laws of Duty or Morals. It is called *Philosophy*, because it is an inquiry into the nature and grounds of moral obligation by reason, as distinct from revelation." *Lectures on Moral Philosophy and Eloquence* (Phila., 1810), p. 5.

Nisbet: Natural Philosophy is "That which treats of matter & investigates the Nature & Properties of Bodies." "Questions and Answers on Logic," c. 1787 Cumberland County Historical Society, Carlisle.

Davidson: "*Natural Philosophy* is that science which instructs us in the properties & operations of the material world, helps us to look into the secrets of nature to see the beauty of creation, & to please ourselves with the wonderful works of God." Lecture notes of John Creigh, 1787. Cumberland County Historical Society.

64. Tyler, p. 41.

65. Edwin Augustus Atlee, *Essays at Poetry, or a Collection of Fugitive Pieces; with the Life of Eugenius Laude Watts* (Phila., 1828), pp. 34–35.

66. Sprague, p. 457.

67. *Ibid.* Also Miller, pp. 340–41.

68. *Historical Magazine*, ser. 1, vol. 6 (1862), p. 357.

69. DCA.

70. Among the students taking the course were David Denny, Samuel Mahon, Nathaniel Randolph Snowden, John Thompson, Samuel and William Woods and John Young. Perhaps also Alexander Porter. Of these, only one received an advanced degree, Snowden's M.A., 1790.

71. Miller, pp. 211–12.

72. *PMHB*, vol. 3 (1879), p. 291.

73. As still remembered by Taney, many years later. (Tyler, p. 43.) He notes that all boys were made to buy the book, bringing us a very early example of this requirement and the resulting student grudge.

74. Moral Philosophy, Lecture 29, Feb. 23, 1787. DCA. Transcript by John Young, then aged 25, the most accurate recorder of Nisbet's lectures.

75. Philosophy, morning lecture, July 16, 1788. DCA. John Young.

76. *Ibid.*, afternoon lecture.

77. Nicolas Malebranche (1638–1715), author of *De la Recherche de la Verité*.

78. Thomas Reid (1710–1796), *An Inquiry into the Human Mind, on the Principles of Common Sense* (Edinburgh, 1764).

79. Joseph Priestley (1733–1804), *Examination of Dr. Reid's Inquiry into the Human Mind on the Principles of Common Sense* (London, 1774). Priestley's study, *Hartley's Theory of the Human Mind*, followed in 1775.

80. Philosophy, June 24, 1788. DCA. John Young.

81. *Ibid.*, June 27, 1788. Conclusion of the lecture.

82. Tyler, p. 40.

Chapter 6. Nisbet in Limbo and Among the Blest

1. James T. Mitchell and Henry Flanders, eds., *The Statutes at Large of Pennsylvania* (Harrisburg, 1896–1915), vol. 12, pp. 221–25. The trustees had appointed a committee, June 14, 1785, to petition the legislature for "an Endowment for the College". Trustee Minutes, vol. 1, p. 139. DCA. On Nov. 28, Rush wrote Montgomery that it would mean hard work even to get a few hundred pounds and a few thousand acres. "They consider a Presbyterian College only as a nest for vipers and

Bryans and Ewings to engender in." Lyman H. Butterfield, ed., *Letters of Benjamin Rush* (Princeton, 1951), vol. 1, p. 377. Montgomery had more opimistic aims. To Benjamin Franklin, Dec. 6, 1785. Franklin Papers, American Philosophical Society.

2. Philip Gardiner Nordell, "The City Hall and Dickinson College Lottery," *Dickinson Alumnus,* Oct., 1962, pp. 5–8. Mitchell and Flanders, vol. 15, pp. 276–82. C. H. Haskins and W. I. Hull, *History of Higher Education in Pennsylvania* (Wash., 1902), p. 49. The drawing was announced in *General Advertiser,* April 25, 1791.

3. Trustee Minutes, Sept. 28, 1790.

4. *A Statement Exhibiting the Receipts and Expenditures of the Trustees of Dickinson College, from March, 1785, till October, 1809.* Broadside, DCA.

5. Mitchell and Flanders, vol. 14, pp. 123–24. Trustees' petition, Trustee Minutes, Sept. 28, 1790.

6. Trustee Minutes, May 2, 1792. Dr. Nisbet, catching a rumor of this action, suspected a further invasion of faculty prerogatives. To Alexander Addison, May 11, 1792. Darlington Library, University of Pittsburgh.

7. *An Act for Raising by way of Lottery the Sum of Seven Thousand Five Hundred Dollars for erecting a suitable College-house in the Borough of Carlisle.* (Harrisburg, April 1, 1794).

8. April 11, 1795. Mitchell and Flanders, vol. 15, p. 282.

9. Trustee Minutes.

10. March 24, 1803. Mitchell and Flanders, vol. 17, pp. 352–53. The Hon. (not Prof.) James Ross opposed: "It was placed in a bad soil, it could not produce good fruit; that it had sent forth a parcel of fellows to prey upon the public, and that if it did not flourish it ought to be moved to another place; that it was an ungrateful county that would not pay their taxes, that they owed $97,000 and if they had paid the interest it would have built two such colleges." Philip S. Klein, "James Buchanan at Dickinson," SL 2, p. 163.

11. Feb. 24, 1806. Mitchell and Flanders, vol. 18, pp. 94–95.

12. March 23, 1819. Pennsylvania, *Laws, 1818–1819,* p. 152.

13. Pennsylvania, *Laws, 1820–1821,* pp. 47–48. Franklin College, recipient also of 10,000 acres, had cleared over $12,000 from the sale of 4,771 acres by 1828. Joseph Henry Dubbs, *History of Franklin and Marshall College* (Lancaster, 1903), p. 92.

14. Pennsylvania, *Laws, 1825–1826,* p. 27.

15. Saul Sack, "The State and Higher Education," *Pennsylvania History,* vol. 26 (1959), pp. 244–45.

16. Trustee Minutes record, e.g., a vote of Feb. 17, 1826, that the names of all members of both houses of Assembly "be transcribed in a neat style and suspended in the College Library."

17. James Mulhern, *A History of Secondary Education in Pennsylvania* (Phila., 1933), p. 312.

18. Salaries remained in arrears throughout their tenure. Dr. Nisbet's sarcasm on the subject only echoes more sharply that of Dr. Ewing, who wrote on behalf of the faculty to the University of Pennsylvania trustees, June 12, 1783: "We hear indeed that your Committee have settled our Accounts, but we know not how[eve] r if it can be called a Settlement of an Account, for one Party to determine how much they will pay, and have the other at Liberty to receive it, or let it alone." University Papers, I, 24. University of Pennsylvania Archives.

19. Butterfield, vol. 1, p. 376. Rush had suggested that John King write the announcement. *Ibid.,* p. 383. It appeared with the date, Dec. 19, 1786, and gave "great pleasure in our city." *Ibid.,* p. 411. Philadelphia saw it in the *Pennsylvania*

Journal, Feb. 10, 1787, and on the reverse of the front cover of the dignified *Columbian Magazine,* Feb., 1787.

20. DCA.

21. Trustee Minutes, April 10, 1787.

22. *Carlisle Gazette,* Oct. 3, 1787. James Henry Morgan, *Dickinson College* (Carlisle, 1933), pp. 133–34.

23. Sept. 26, 1787. Copy by John Young. Library of Centre College.

24. Trustee Minutes, Sept. 27, 1787.

25. Rush Papers. Library Company of Philadelphia, on deposit at HSP.

26. Edgar Bruce Wesley, *Proposed: The University of the United States* (Minneapolis, 1936), pp. 4–5.

27. Joseph B. Smith, "A Frontier Experiment with Higher Education," SL 1, p. 93. Charles Page Smith, "James Wilson and the Era of the American Revolution," SL 2, pp. 90–91. John Montgomery to William Irvine, Jan. 9, 1788, Irvine Papers, HSP. Dickinson student John Shippen to his father, March 3, 1788, in *Two Hundred Years in Cumberland County* (Carlisle, 1951), pp. 66–67.

28. William Petriken to John Nicholson, May 23, 1788. Nicholson Papers, Pennsylvania State Archives.

29. Nisbet to Alexander Addison, Oct. 29, 1793. Darlington Library, University of Pittsburgh.

30. Nisbet to John Montgomery, Jan. 21, 1787. Butterfield, vol. 1, p. 410.

31. Smith, SL 1, p. 98.

32. David Wilson Thompson, *Early Publications of Carlisle, Pennsylvania, 1785–1835* (Carlisle, 1932), p. 14.

33. Samuel Miller, *Memoir of the Rev. Charles Nisbet, D.D.* (N.Y., 1840), pp. 228–29.

34. John C. Fitzpatrick, ed., *The Diaries of George Washington* (Boston and N.Y., 1925), vol. 4, p. 212. Printed as *A Sermon on the Freedom and Happiness of the United States of America, preached 5th Oct., 1794, and published at the request of the Officers of the Philadelphia and Lancaster Troops of Light Horse* (Phila., 1794), where we see, p. 23, that Dr. Davidson does not let so fine an opportunity pass without mention of the College, its "sons of science" and its promise of being "an extensive blessing to the Western Country, if supported by a generous public."

35. Robert Davidson, Jr., in William B. Sprague, *Annals of the American Pulpit* (N.Y., 1858), vol. 3, p. 324.

36. Petition of Dr. McCoskry, Robert Davidson, John Montgomery, John Creigh, etc., March 14, 1796. Pennsylvania State Archives.

37. Miller, p. 317; Conway Phelps Wing, *History of the First Presbyterian Church of Carlisle, Pa.* (Carlisle, 1877), pp. 135–36.

38. Richard Hofstadter and W. P. Metzger, *The Development of Academic Freedom in the United States* (N.Y., 1955), p. 218.

39. Nisbet to William Young, June 9, 1792. DCA.

40. *Rules and Regulations for the Government of Dickinson College, adopted by the Board of Trustees the 26th May, 1795. Carlisle, Printed by George Kline.* This broadside was reprinted with additions as a pamphlet, 1805.

41. Nisbet to Alexander Addison, Feb. 23, 1797. Darlington Library, University of Pittsburgh.

42. Trustee Minutes, April 27, 1796. Grammar School pupils were to study the Latin texts from Cordier's *Colloquies* to Ovid and Virgil and the Greek Testament. Freshmen would move on to Lucian, Horace, Cicero, Juvenal, Xenophon, Homer and a seasoning of arithmetic. Juniors would move into the higher mathematics, with

rhetoric, chronology and history. Seniors were to go further in mathematics and have the culminating courses in natural and moral philosophy, logic, metaphysics and criticism. The two upper classes would continue to review the classics.

43. DCA.

44. Trustee Minutes, June 20, 1798. The minutes of Sept. 26, 1798; Sept. 29, 1799; April 23 and Sept. 23, 1800, at odds over the wording of the commencement formula.

45. DCA. Reproduced in Archibald Douglas Turnbull, *William Turnbull, 1752– 1822* (privately printed, 1934), p. 43.

46. The incident, which had been sponsored by trustee William Bingham is fully described, but without date, in Morgan, pp. 162–65. Bingham must have been inspired by the march of 1,200 young men of Philadelphia in support of Adams, May 7, 1798. The address of the Dickinson students was widely publicized—*New York Spectator,* July 14, 1798, and elsewhere.

47. Nisbet to Rush, Nov. 12, 1803. Rush Papers.

48. Nisbet to trustees, July 29, 1799. DCA. Miller, p. 283. The one-year graduates had a record of ill success in after life, e.g., March 6, 1801 when the faculty was unable to recommend any prospective teacher to the York Academy. George Hay Kain and others, *A History of the York County Academy* (York, 1953), pp. 34–35.

49. Herbert M. Morais, *Deism in Eighteenth Century America* (N.Y., 1934), pp. 160–62. G. Adolph Koch, *Republican Religion. The American Revolution and the Cult of Reason* (N.Y., 1933), p. 277.

50. Miller, pp. 256–57.

51. Nisbet to William Young, Nov. 23, 1798. DCA.

52. DCA.

53. Nisbet reported to the trustees, Dec. 4, 1799, DCA, a year after "this imperious Requisition of the Students," that his colleagues were attempting to break the new pattern by "raising a Junior Class in Masquerade." On the afternoon of the commencement of Sept. 23, 1800, the trustees rescinded "the regulation regarding a commencement once in every year," and directed the faculty to present students for graduation only as they had made sufficient "proficiency in learning." Trustee Minutes. Nisbet's report, Oct. 8, 1800, DCA, complained that this offered no real solution and asked the restoration of the rule on three classes. He was still pleading for this in his report of April 27, 1802, "tho' it is to be feared that the Students will not submit to this at present." On Oct. 18, 1802, DCA, he reported that the faculty "had contrived to keep their last class for a year and a half," with a hope of the three-year course in view. It remained at two years, however, through Nisbet's and Davidson's administrations.

54. Armstrong to Benjamin Rush, Dec. 13, 1784. Rush Papers.

55. Oct. 21, 1786. Butterfield, vol. 1, p. 397.

56. Trustee Minutes, Dec. 18, 1792. A grant of land was to be solicited from the Penns, and bids then invited "for the building a college agreeably to the plan furnished by Mr. Kien." John Keen of the Carpenters' Company, Philadelphia, had been an apprentice of Robert Smith, architect of Nassau Hall. Whitfield J. Bell, Jr., "The Other Man on Bingham's Porch," SL 2, pp. 51–52

57. "If we don't begin soon we will not be able to get the Roof on nixt Summer." Montgomery to William Irvine, Dec. 19, 1792. Irvine Papers, HSP.

58. Bid of John Hunter, Nov. 24, 1798. DCA.

59. Dec. 11, 1798. DCA.

60. Montgomery to Francis Gurney, Aug. 23, 1799. DCA.

61. Miller, pp. 226–27. Alexander Nisbet, writing to John Dickinson, July 27, 1808, Rush Papers, describes him as "the *best friend* of my father."

62. HSP.

63. Nisbet to trustees, Nov. 8, 1803, DCA; to Rush, Nov. 12, 1803, Rush Papers. Trustee minutes, Oct. 27 and Nov. 29, 1802, show the Board calling for faculty advice on "the future of academic government." Unanimity here, however, seems to have been accompanied by a lack of it in faculty. Davidson to Judge Hamilton, Oct. 23, 1803, James Hamilton Papers, HSP, begs a glimpse of Nisbet's plan. Nisbet's plan, Oct. 18, proposes the three-year course on terms impossible without Davidson's full cooperation.

64. DCA.

65. Feb. 4, 1803. Rush Papers.

66. To Alexander Addison, Feb. 12, 1803. Darlington Library, University of Pittsburgh.

67. "A Sketch of the Rise, Progress and Present State of Dickinson College," *Port Folio,* vol. 5 (1811), p. 243.

68. Montgomery to Rush, June 22, 1803. Rush Papers.

69. Including a second $100 from Dickinson. (Report on collections, Aug. 22, 1804. DCA.)

70. Brackenridge to James Hamilton, May 19, 1803. DCA. The Judge's extended novel, *Modern Chivalry,* touches upon college-burning as a possible manifestation of frontier anti-intellectualism. (Quoted by Smith, SL 1, pp. 76, 84–85.)

71. Latrobe to Brackenridge, May 18, 1803. DCA.

72. Two of Latrobe's preliminary drawings are extant (DCA), basement ground plan and elevation of "proposed North Front." The sill courses are shown here. In his sketch of the building at the Maryland Historical Society, made when he first saw it in 1813, Latrobe has indicated the horizontal lines of his original plan—evidence that he was not satisfied with the trustees' substitution of coigns for sill courses.

73. Paul F. Norton, "Latrobe and Old West at Dickinson College," *Art Bulletin,* vol. 33 (1951), pp. 125–30. The source of the mermaid vane was first identified in Charles F. Himes' pamphlet, *The Mermaid of Old West* (n.p., c. 1917).

74. Quoted in Morgan, pp. 94–95.

75. Butterfield, vol. 2, p. 867.

76. Rush Papers.

77. According to the broadside *Statement* of expenditures from 1785 to 1809, DCA, $12,000 had been spent on rebuilding, and $7,000 to $8,000 would be needed to "perfect the design of Mr. Latrobe, who furnished the Plan, and to enclose and improve the College grounds in a suitable manner."

78. Miller, pp. 288–98.

79. Trustee Minutes, Jan. 20, 1804.

80. Isabella Oliver, *Poems on Various Subjects* (Carlisle, 1805), pp. 20–21. Robert Davidson wrote the introduction to the book.

81. Miller, pp. 298–99. In translation in Sarah Woods Parkinson, *Memories of Carlisle's Old Graveyard* (Carlisle, 1930), pp. 182–83.

82. Nisbet to Charles Wallace, Oct. 31, 1797. *Bulletin of the New York Public Library,* vol. 2 (1898), p. 285.

83. 1788. DCA.

84. Miller, p. 193. Thompson, pp. 20–23.

85. $6,693.37 from the College, $1,206.20 from the church. (Inventory of estate, Cumberland County Court House, Carlisle, Pa.)

86. "Sketch," *Port Folio,* vol. 5 (1811), p. 244.

87. John Hayes, *Rural Poems, Moral and Descriptive* (Carlisle, 1807). Thompson, pp. 57–61. Of Borland, Montgomery had written to Rush, June 22, 1803, Rush Papers: "Our new Grammer Master is a Compleat scholar and has an Excellent Metode of speaking and is a Decent good looking man. The young men are highly Pleased with him and the trusties feel no loss in the change of his being in the place of Mr. thomson."

88. John Linn to John McDowell, 1804, Presbyterian Historical Society, Phila: "His character as a teacher never stood high either with ye students or with persons of information at home or abroad."

89. DCA.

90. Philip S. Klein, SL 2, pp. 166–70.

91. *Ibid.*, p. 179.

92. *Rules and Regulations for the Government of Dickinson College* (Carlisle, 1805), pp. 7–8.

93. Trustee Minutes, Sept. 25, 1805.

94. Butterfield, vol. 2, p. 969.

Chapter 7. Satan's Seat

1. Jeremiah Atwater, *An Inaugural Address delivered at the Public Commencement of Dickinson College, September 27th, 1809* (Carlisle, 1809), pp. 5–6.

2. *Carlisle Herald*, Sept. 29, 1809.

3. E.g., among many, a discreet little note to Judge Hamilton, James Hamilton Papers, HSP, on some Grammar School boys who had performed poorly at commencement, "as they are of those families whom it is of importance to please, I would suggest the propriety of saying nothing by way of discrimination."

4. The salary was voted, Sept. 29, 1808; the resolution on the importance of finding a Principal, March 10, 1809. A copy of the latter was sent to Rush as evidence of concurrence with him on the absolute necessity of engaging "on this side of the Waters . . . a learned & respectable Principal." Rush Papers, Library Company of Philadelphia, on deposit at HSP.

5. Rush to Miller, July 5, 1808. Andrew Hunter to Rush, April 10, 1809. Rush Papers.

6. George W. Corner, ed., *The Autobiography of Benjamin Rush. His "Travels Through Life" together with his Commonplace Book for 1789–1813* (Princeton, 1948), pp. 275–76.

7. W. Storrs Lee, *Father Went to College. The Story of Middlebury* (N.Y., 1936) pp. 43–48, 54. Atwater's letters to Jedidiah Morse, Jan. 6, 1807, and June 29, 1809, HSP, give his early and final views of Hall.

8. His letter of resignation has been frequently quoted, "To the Corporation of Middlebury College, Gentlemen, I now resign my office as President of Middlebury College, wishing that you individually and collectively may experience the Divine Blessing, Yours, Jeremiah Atwater."

9. Corner, p. 286.

10. Atwater to Green, July 20, 1811, HSP: "It is my final determination to make my situation in life subservient to the cause of Christ—to make my connection with a college useful towards bringing forward young men for the ministry."

11. Atwater to Rush, March 11, 1811. Rush Papers.

12. Atwater to How, May 13, 1831. Copy in Murray Papers, DCA.

13. Whitfield J. Bell, Jr., "The Other Man on Bingham's Porch," SL 2, p. 58.

14. Thomas Jefferson Wertenbaker, *Princeton, 1746–1896* (Princeton, 1946), p. 164.

15. Atwater to Green, 22 letters, 1810–15. HSP.

16. Atwater to Rush, Oct. 2, 1809. Rush Papers.

17. Atwater to Rush, March 11, 1811. *Ibid.*

18. Atwater to Rush, Oct. 2, 1809. *Ibid.*

19. Atwater, Inaugural Address, p. 23, in an appended statement over the signature of James Armstrong, President of the Board of Trustees: "A system of education and rules for the regulation and discipline of the College, on the plan of the New–England Colleges, will be adopted." Not only were the students largely from the South, but a vote of the trustees, Sept. 25, 1805, shows a particular effort to publicize the College in that area.

20. Trustee Minutes, Oct. 23, 1809: "That Genl. Gurney be authorized immediately to purchase a Bell for the College." This must have replaced the bell rung by Nisbet for the Battle of the Nile.

21. Trustee Minutes, Nov. 2, 1810. "The College Ground will be levelled and forest Trees planted." Townspeople were invited to lend their aid. Samuel Knox, 1796, had made his plea for the college campus as a place of recreation, a botanical garden. Frederick Rudolph, ed., *Essays on Education in the Early Republic* (Cambridge, Mass., 1965), p. 362.

22. Atwater to Rush, Sept. 18, 1810, on his catalogue. Rush Papers. The next letter, undated, reports the election of Green, recorded also in Trustee Minutes, Sept. 27, 1810.

23. *Port Folio*, vol. 5 (1811), pp. 239–45.

24. Trustee Minutes, March 29, 1814, with a resolution that "at the commencement of the next session a class shall be formed to be called the Freshman Class."

25. 12 pp., printed by Alexander and Phillips, Carlisle, but without date or title page. DCA.

26. Showing a balance of $5,850.75 as Atwater came into office.

27. Atwater to Rush, Dec. 27, 1809; Feb. 4, 1810; April 22, 1810. Rush Papers.

28. Rush to James Hamilton, June 27, 1810. James Hamilton Papers, HSP.

29. Trustee Minutes, July 19, 1810, with vote for immediate action in making student accommodations with the Rush gift. The matter had been discussed, May 17. Minutes of a year before, March 10, 1809, show that a few students were living in the building, under Mrs. Mitchell's eye. Atwater refers to the present Memorial Hall as "our hall for public worship," while to the trustees it is "the Hall for Exhibitions."

30. Rush to James Hamilton, Aug. 7 and Sept. 1, 1810. James Hamilton Papers.

31. Atwater to Rush, April 22, 1810. Rush Papers. Also to Green, Feb. 22, 1810, HSP: "The poor are always intemperate & immoral, & the rich luxurious and dissipated." Col. Simonds at the Barracks "is supposed to be an infidel and does not make the soldiers attend public worship." Atwater to Rush, May 21, 1810, Rush Papers, responds to Rush's approval of the plans for reform.

32. Rush Papers.

33. Trustee Minutes, Oct. 26, 1810.

34. See Corner, pp. 345–47, for Rush's notes, 1809, for the renewal of his attack of 1789.

35. Atwater to Rush, July 4, 1810, Rush Papers, lists $400 (the sum a tutor would receive) among "Present salaries" as that of the "Professor of French." The title of Professor of the Modern Languages was given Berard by the trustees, Sept. 28, 1814.

36. Aigster's condition was soon to be obvious but the first warning note is

interesting: "Dr. Nisbet over again in some respects." Atwater to Rush, Oct. 16, 1810. Rush Papers.

37. Atwater to Green, undated. HSP. Atwater to Rush, March 11, 1811, Rush Papers, defends himself against charges brought by Wilson to the trustees.

38. *Centennial Memorial of the Presbytery of Carlisle* (Harrisburg, 1889), vol. 2, pp. 96–99, 152.

39. Atwater catalogues the trustees in his letter to Green, July 20, 1811. HSP. Others' descriptions of them appear in the *History of Cumberland and Adams Counties* (Chicago, Warner, Beers, 1886), pp. 150–51; *Two Hundred Years in Cumberland County* (Carlisle, 1951), pp. 92–95; *Centennial Memorial,* p. 373; *Sketch of the Character of Dr. James Armstrong,* James Hamilton Papers.

40. Hamilton to Rush, Feb. 2, 1812. Rush Papers. Trustee Minutes, Sept. 30, 1812. Atwater to Ashbel Green, April 26, 1813. State Historical Society of Wisconsin. No M.A's. were awarded in the remainder of Atwater's tenure.

41. Thomas Cooper, *Some Information Respecting America* (London, 1794), p. 93. David Wilson Thompson, *Early Publications of Carlisle, Pennsylvania* (Carlisle, 1932), p. 64. Harold A. Larrabee, "Truculent Thomas Cooper," SL 2, pp. 192–93.

42. Thompson, p. 65. Larrabee, pp. 198–200.

43. Atwater to Green, March 22, 1811, HSP, refers to a plan to "oblige me to quit, thro' mortification & disgust," in which Judge Brackenridge, Henry Rowan Wilson and Robert Davidson were involved. Cooper to James Hamilton, undated, James Hamilton Papers, writes with icy contempt of "principal Atwater, whom I understand the Trustees wish to get rid of, on acct. of his incapacity."

44. Dumas Malone, *The Public Life of Thomas Cooper, 1783–1839* (New Haven, 1926), p. 237.

45. Larrabee, p. 206, quoting Jefferson: "It will give our young men some idea of what constitutes an educated man."

46. Atwater to Green, July 8, 1811. HSP.

47. Atwater to Rush, June 17, 1811. Rush Papers. The minutes show that an adjournment date had been set at the May 21 meeting, then erased and June 17 substituted.

48. Trustee Minutes, Aug. 10, 1811.

49. *The Introductory Lecture of Thomas Cooper, Esq., Professor of Chemistry at Carlisle College, Pennsylvania. Published at the Request of the Trustees. With Notes and References* (Carlisle, 1812). C. W. Peale's Museum Accession Book, HSP, was inscribed by Cooper, 1803, with the sentiment, "Knowledge is Power."

50. Atwater to Rush, Feb. 6, 1813. Rush Papers.

51. Thomas Cooper, "Copy of a Letter to a Friend on University Education," *Port Folio,* vol. 5 (1815), pp. 349–50. To Cooper, it would "admit of no controversy, that a young man turned out into the world with an intimate knowledge of the Latin, Greek and French languages, a readiness at Latin composition, and with a competent knowledge also of mathematics, algebra and fluxions, is better qualified both for active life and literary pursuits, and will have attained more facility in acquiring other branches of knowledge, than by any other possible mode of education in use at the present day."

52. Whitfield J. Bell, Jr., "Thomas Cooper as Professor of Chemistry at Dickinson College, 1811–1815," *Journal of the History of Medicine,* vol 8 (1953), p. 78. The Episcopal minister's endorsement of Cooper as a scholarly "friend to Christianity" was appearing in the papers at just this time. The hostility of the legislature to clerical control must also have tended to restrain the orthodox party.

53. Sept. 29, 1811. Rush Papers.

54. Oct. 15, 1811. DCA.

55. Atwater to Green, May 11, 1812. HSP. To Rush, Feb. 6, 1813. Rush Papers.

56. Trustee Minutes, Dec. 17, 1811. Rush, receipt, Jan. 12, 1812. Rush Papers, Bell, "Thomas Cooper," p. 79. The apparatus is now in the Morris Room, Spahr Library.

57. Atwater to How, Feb. 13, 1813. Copy, DCA.

58. James Henry Morgan, *Dickinson College* (Carlisle, 1933), p. 186.

59. Atwater to Green, Feb. 23, 1812. HSP.

60. Paul E. Zuver, *A Short History of Carlisle Barracks, 1757–1934* (n.p., 1934), p. 65.

61. Atwater to Green, Feb. 23, 1812. HSP. Trustee Minutes, Feb. 22, 1812 record Oldham's expulsion, but with a statement on his otherwise exemplary character.

62. Feb. 23, 1812. Rush Papers.

63. Feb. 12, 1812. *Ibid.*

64. "I read with satisfaction, that you will defer resigning your trusteeship while I am here. I feel grateful for this expression of your friendship." Atwater to Rush, Feb. 6, 1813. Rush Papers.

65. Ralph L. Ketcham, "Uncle James Madison and Dickinson College," SL 3, p. 174.

66. *Ibid.*, pp. 178–79. Cooper's law courses are advertised under the heading, "DICKINSON COLLEGE" in the Georgetown *Federal Republican,* Nov. 19, 1813, as due to open with the spring session, May, 1814.

67. Cooper to James Madison, Feb. 18, 1813. Library of Congress.

68. Bell, "Thomas Cooper," p. 80.

69. Trustee Minutes, May 14, 1813.

70. *Ibid.,* July 31, 1813.

71. Richard J. Storr, *The Beginnings of Graduate Education in America* (Chicago, 1953), p. 29, dates the rise of serious controversy on the relevance of the classical course at 1815–1830.

72. Atwater to Green, June 24, 1815, HSP, names Shaw and Nulty as in alliance with Cooper. Cooper to David Watts, June 15, 1815, Cumberland County Historical Society, Carlisle, gives the general denunciation of Atwater.

73. Atwater to Green, June 24, 1815. HSP.

74. Trustee Minutes, June 12, 1815. So cited first by Merritt Caldwell, "Historical Sketch of Dickinson College," *American Quarterly Register,* vol. 9 (1836), p. 123.

75. Cooper to Watts, June 15, 1815, Cumberland County Historical Society.

76. Trustee Minutes, Sept. 28, 1814.

77. For the Federalists: David Watts Huling, *Oration Delivered before the Students of the Belles Lettres Society of Dickinson College, and a Number of Ladies and Gentlemen of Carlisle, assembled at the College to Celebrate the 4th of July* (Carlisle, 1815). For the Democrats: Julius Forrest, *Oration Delivered before the Republican Students of the Belles Lettres and Union Philosophical Societies of Dickinson College, July 4, 1815* (Carlisle, 1815).

78. Morgan, pp. 396–97.

79. *Centennial Memorial,* vol. 2, p. 55. *American Volunteer,* Nov. 2, 1815.

80. Trustee Minutes, Dec. 18, 1815. The Terrell Carr Papers, University of Virginia, contain additional light on the affair. John T. Corbin, Class of 1816, was killed in the encounter. Dabney Carr Terrell, '16, his opponent, received a letter from Edward Govan, '15, stating that a jury had brought in a verdict of first degree murder and advising him not to return. Terrell completed his education at Geneva, "under

the auspices of Albert Gallatin, Minister to France." He met Mme. De Stael and Lord Byron, wrote and published poetry. He became "a great favorite" of Byron, who, noting his enjoyment in chewing tobacco, tried it himself, but with an unhappy result. Terrell later practiced law at New Orleans, where he died Aug. 26, 1827.

81. Trustee Minutes, Sept. 27, 1816.

82. Cathcart to Hamilton, Jan. 18, 1818. James Hamilton Papers.

83. Printed petition, Jan. 17, 1817. Cumberland County Historical Society, Carlisle, Pa.

84. *American Volunteer*, May 25, 1820. Trustee Minutes, June 1, 1820.

85. Trustee Minutes, Dec. 13, 1820.

86. *American Volunteer*, Jan. 31, 1821.

Chapter 8. The Duffield Years

1. *Centennial Memorial of the Presbytery of Carlisle* (Harrisburg, 1889), vol. 2, pp. 149–51.

2. *Ibid.*, p. 153. Duffield to W. W. Woodward, bookseller, March 3, 1821, HSP, shows him ordering Isabella Graham's life, Dobell's Hymns, etc. by the dozen "to circulate them among the people of my charge."

3. James Hamilton Papers. HSP.

4. Jacob Van Vechten, *Memoirs of John M. Mason* (N.Y., 1856), p. 516.

5. Dr. John W. Francis, quoted by G. Adolph Koch, *Republican Religion* (N.Y., 1933), p. 238.

6. *Ibid.*, p. 270. John Mitchell Mason, *First Ripe Fruits* (London, 1803), pp. 265, 271. Jefferson based his reasoning against the Deluge on "insufficieny of water."

7. Van Vechten, pp. 528, 530.

8. *A History of Columbia University, 1754–1904* (N.Y., Columbia University Press, 1904), pp. 97–102.

9. Trustees Minutes, Dec. 12, 1821. Tuition was $36 and room rent $8 per year, boarding $2 per week, plus incidental fees and charges, including use of the Library.

10. *Ibid.*, Sept. 8, 1821. Trustee by-laws enacted June 29, 1824, state: "No professor or officer of the faculty shall be removed untill an accusation shall be preferred by the Board specifying the charges alleged against him of which he shall have notice and due time to prepare and make his defence."

11. Van Vechten, p. 524.

12. John Mitchell Mason, *Address delivered at the Organization of Dickinson College . . . . January 15th, 1822* (N.Y., 1822), p. 16.

13. *DAB*. Pronounced "Vetick."

14. Thomas Creigh notes. DCA. *Centennial Memorial*, vol. 1, p. 16; vol. 2, pp. 163–67.

15. Carlisle *American Volunteer*, Oct. 18, 1821.

16. *Ibid.*, Dec. 13, 1821. Trustee Minutes, Jan. 7, 9, 11, 1822.

17. Trustee Minutes, May 6, 1822, citing a letter from James Ross on the vacancy. Henry Vethake, for the faculty, to the trustees, May 28, 1822. DCA.

18. Alan Carter Smith, *A History of the Anglican Community at Carlisle, 1746–1829*, MS, 1968, pp. 45–48. St. John's Church, Carlisle.

19. *Statutes of Dickinson College . . . February 15, 1822*, (Carlisle, 1822), p. 5. William B. Sprague, *Annals of the American Pulpit* (N.Y., 1858), vol. 4, p. 23, adds that Mason lectured on rhetoric using as text Horace's *Art of Poetry* and Longinus' *Treatise on the Sublime*.

20. *Columbia University*, pp. 87–91, 107. *American Volunteer*, Feb. 28, 1822.

21. Trustee Minutes, Sept. 8, 1823. The earliest surviving report, DCA, April, 1827, lists grades from 1, the lowest, up to 5, with 3 representing "a decent mediocrity."

22. Trustee Minutes, Jan. 29, Nov. 5, 1822.

23. *Ibid.*, Aug. 31, 1822.

24. *Ibid.*, June 26, 1822.

25. Promise to eschew politics, over signature of James Armstrong, President of the Board, *American Volunteer*, Jan. 17, 1822. Recital of Robert Goodloe Harper's oration on the murder of Federalist James Maccubin Lingan, 1812, *A Narrative of the Proceedings of the Board of Trustees of Dickinson College from 1821 to 1830* (Carlisle, 1830). p. 5.

26. *American Volunteer*, July 11, 1822.

27. Sprague, vol. 4, pp. 12–13.

28. Conway P. Wing, *A History of the First Presbyterian Church of Carlisle, Pa.* (Carlisle, 1877), p. 166. "By profession" signals an experience and public avowal similar to the Methodist "conversion."

29. George B. Carr, *John Miller Dickey, His Life and Times* (Phila., 1929), pp. 76–78.

30. Trustee Minutes, Dec. 15, 1821. Evidence supports strongly, but does not prove, the descent from Henry Makinly. Young Daniel appears as a Duffield protégé but, when the church split, would go with the Old School party.

31. Koch, p. 281.

32. Trustee Minutes, May 29, 1823.

33. Duffield's religious organizations supported, and are chronicled in, the weekly *Religious Miscellany*, a publication put out by George Fleming of his congregation, Jan. 17, 1823 to July 2, 1824, after which it continued, on a broader basis, as the *Carlisle Adviser*.

34. Turkey Club Minutes, Nov. 11, 1823 to Feb. 14, 1824. DCA. Matthew Spencer defected to Belles Lettres but is not entered in the published roll of either society. Oswald Tilghman, *History of Talbot County, Maryland* (Balt., 1915), vol. 2, p. 403, describes his later tumultuous career as a teacher at Princess Ann. The organization of Duffield's "Young Men's Missionary Society," Sept., 1823, is reported in *Religious Miscellany*, vol. 2 (1823), p. 155. On Oct. 3, 1823, the trustees had empowered their Executive Committee (Duffield, Hendel and Isaac Brown Parker) to deal with student complaints.

35. July 17, 1823. *Religious Miscellany*, vol. 2, p. 365.

36. *Statutes, 1822*, p. 7.

37. Trustee Minutes, March 29, 1823.

38. *Carlisle Gazette*, July 6, 1824.

39. *American Volunteer*, Feb. 6, 1823. The bill had passed the House, but had been defeated in the Senate, 48–33. *Ibid.*, April 10, 1823.

40. Trustee Minutes, June 8, 22, July 27, 1824.

41. William Neill, *Autobiography* (Phila., 1861), p. 47.

42. *Ibid.*, p. 48. The *Carlisle Gazette*, Nov. 9, 1824, describes in detail the inauguration procession, headed by the Janitor, bearing the keys of the College, then the Grammar School pupils, then College students, then the Principal Elect, with the faculty, clergy, judiciary and other prominent citizens bringing up the rear.

43. Nicholas B. Wainwright, ed., *A Philadelphia Perspective. The Diary of Sidney George Fisher Covering the Years 1834–1871* (Phila., 1967), p. 311.

44. Neill, p. 50.

45. Wing, p. 168.

46. J. Stuart Prentice, *The History of the First United Church of Christ, Carlisle, Pennsylvania. 1763–1963* (Unabridged MS of work published Carlisle, 1963), pp. 101–02.

47. Trustee Minutes. H. M. J. Klein, *The History of the Eastern Synod of the Reformed Church in the United States* (Lancaster, 1943), p. 136.

48. Klein, pp. 137–38.

49. Trustee minutes, March 12, 1825. Lewis Mayer, *Inaugural Address delivered by the Rev. Lewis Mayer, at his Inauguration as Principal in the Theological Seminary of the German Reformed Church, in Carlisle, Pa. On Wednesday, April 6, 1825* (Carlisle, 1825).

50. Trustee Minutes, Dec. 8, 1825; Feb. 15, 1826.

51. *Ibid.,* June 25, 1823; Jan 17, 1827. A third offer was rejected, March 31, 1832.

52. Dr. James Henry Miller, Class of 1808, was also involved in this project. The trustees solaced Dr. Vethake with an honorary A.M., 1827. For background, see George H. Callcott, *A History of the University of Maryland* (Balt., 1966), pp. 52–53, 69.

53. William Cohen, *James Miller McKim: Pennsylvania Abolitionist* (Ph.D. dissertation, New York University, 1969), p. 29.

54. Prentice, p. 154.

55. Anne Royall, *Mrs. Royall's Pennsylvania, or Travels continued in the United States* (Wash., 1829), vol. 1, p. 214.

56. Prentice, pp. 143, 151–52.

57. The course appears in the College catalogue of 1827, and Huber is by name in that of 1828. He was Professor of Modern Languages at Wesleyan University, 1831–42, resigning at the time of the Millerite excitement, and following his disillusionment was taken back with lowered rank.

58. Theodore Appel, *Recollections of College Life, at Marshall College, Mercersburg, Pa., from 1839 to 1845* (Reading, Pa., 1886), pp. 75–76. Klein, p. 145. Theodore Appel, *The Beginnings of the Theological Seminary of the Reformed Church in the United States, from 1817 to 1832* (Phila., 1886) publishes correspondence on the Carlisle period, pp. 42–81.

59. Memorialized since 1948 in the Robert Coleman Chair of History.

60. Neill, p. 49.

61. *American Volunteer,* Feb. 10, 1825.

62. First proposed by Neill, for the faculty, to the trustees, April 25, 1825. DCA.

63. Neill, for the faculty, to the trustees, Aug. 30, 1825, and Sept. 6, 1825. DCA. *Narrative,* p. 7.

64. *American Volunteer,* Oct. 13, 1825. In addition to the studies of the four classes, admission requirements are given: geography; arithmetic as far as fractions; Latin and Greek including prosody; translation of Virgil, Cicero, Greek Testament and Dalzell's *Collectanea Minora.*

65. Report of a committee of trustees, Sept. 25, 1826. DCA. Trustee Minutes, Sept. 27, 1826.

66. Anonymous to Spencer, Feb. 27, 1825. DCA.

67. Spencer to the trustees, Dec. 8, 1827. DCA. Trustee Minutes, Dec. 10, 11, 13, 17, 1827. *Narrative,* pp. 11–16.

68. Trustee committee report, Dec. 10, 1827. DCA. Faculty Minutes, Dec. 12, 1827.

69. May 21, 1828. DCA. Finley to James Hamilton. James Hamilton Papers.

70. Trustee Minutes, April 1, 1826. *Statutes of Dickinson College* (Carlisle, 1826), p. 13.

71. E.g., Faculty Minutes, Aug. 13, 1827, and Trustee Minutes, Sept. 26, 1827, acknowledging the duty but urging faculty to give examinations "in a shorter period," but "with no abatement in the strictness."

72. *Statutes, 1826*, p. 8.

73. Belles Lettres Minutes. DCA.

74. Trustee Minutes, Aug. 11 to Sept. 14, 1827. Faculty Minutes, Aug. 17 to Sept. 17, 1827. DCA.

75. Faculty protest to trustees, Aug. 27, 1827, DCA. Report of trustee committee on communication from the faculty, Sept. 7, 1827. DCA.

76. Belles Lettres Minutes, Jan. 26, 28, 31, 1828. Trustee Minutes, March 3, 4; April 2, 5; May 18, 24, 31, 1828.

77. Faculty Minutes, March 28, May 14, 15, July 16, Aug. 18, 22, 1828. Trustee Minutes, Aug. 28, 1828.

78. *Narrative*, p. 57.

79. Royall, vol. 1, pp. 205–06. *Narrative*, p. 9.

80. *Narrative*, p. 58.

81. Faculty Minutes, Dec. 13, 1828.

82. *Narrative*, pp. 9–10. *American Volunteer*, Jan. 25, 1827.

83. *Narrative*, pp. 23–24.

84. "Redmond Conyngham," by Alonzo Potter. MS, American Philosophical Society. Bishop Potter's obituary was written without an awareness of a less prepossessing aspect of Conyngham's "lettered tastes." See William A. Hunter, "Substitute for Truth: Hazard's 'Provincial Correspondence,'" *Pennsylvania History*, vol. 29 (1962), pp. 278–90.

85. Trustee Minutes, Dec. 11, 17, 1827.

86. Faculty Minutes, Dec. 24, 26, 1827; Jan. 22, 25, 1828.

87. *American Volunteer*, April 3, 1828.

88. Trustee Minutes, April 2, 1828.

89. Faculty Minutes, March 21, 1828.

90. Trustee Minutes, Sept. 26, 1827.

91. Royall, vol. 1, p. 190.

92. *Ibid.*, p. 193.

93. *Ibid.*, p. 202.

94. *Ibid.*, p. 216.

95. Lyon Papers. DCA.

96. Diary of George Duffield, Feb. 2, 1829. Burton Historical Collection, Detroit Public Library.

97. *Narrative*, p. 65. The incident is described in detail by John Linn McKim, Class of 1830, "A College Riot," *Dickinsonian*, Monthly ed., Oct., 1899, pp. 13–16.

98. Trustee Minutes, Feb. 16, 1829. Faculty Minutes of 1829 reflect "the spirit of rebellion . . . particularly at evening prayers," with some students dismissed and others, like W. Bishop, admonished ("for carrying a chicken into the prayer hall"), while by summer the whole situation was complicated by "some animosity apparent between the students and the mechanics of the town."

99. Report of Committee on Present State and Prospects, Aug. 1, 1829. DCA. The committee interviewed the faculty, compiling a revealing statement on teaching loads and methods. Faculty minutes, Aug. 3, 1829, record a request to the trustees for a copy, and, Aug. 14, their refusal. *Narrative*, pp. 70–71, records the trustees'

final decision that faculty had fallen into "a *habit of disregard to rules,* which are essential to the existence of the institution." Salaries would be reduced.

100. Neill to trustees, Aug. 1, 1829. DCA.

101. Henry Vethake, *A Reply to "A Narrative of the Proceedings of the Board of Trustees of Dickinson College, from 1821 to 1830"* (Princeton, Dec. 15, 1830), pp. 9–11.

102. Samuel Hazard, ed., *The Register of Pennsylvania,* vol. 4 (1829), p. 239. Lindsley had had experience enow with trustee interference at Princeton.

103. Diary of George Duffield, Jan. 22, 1830.

104. To his father, Jacob B. Weidman, Dec. 25, 1829. DCA. Belles Lettres Minutes, May 30, 1829, had attributed diminishing support of library acquisitions "to the unfavourable prospects of the College in losing our best professor."

105. Trustee Minutes, Sept. 22, 1829.

106. *Narrative,* back cover.

107. *Messenger of Useful Knowledge,* vol. 1 (1830–31), pp. 14, 46.

108. Samuel Blanchard How, *An Address delivered to the Graduates of Dickinson College, on Wednesday, September 28, 1831.* (Carlisle, 1831), p. 20.

109. Trustee Minutes, April 16, May 13, 1830.

110. *Ibid.,* March 30, May 26, 1830.

111. *The Statutes of Dickinson College.* (Carlisle, 1830), p. 9.

112. *Port Folio,* vol. 6 (1815), pp. 412–13.

113. *Carlisle Republican,* Aug. 15, 1820.

114. William Neill to trustees, Aug. 30, 1825. DCA.

115. Trustee Minutes, Sept. 9, 1829. *American Volunteer,* March 11, 1830.

116. *American Volunteer,* March 18, 1830.

117. Green to Lyon, Sept. 16, 1831. DCA.

118. *An Appeal to the Christian Public from the Unprovoked Attacks of the Rev. George Duffield, against the Methodist Episcopal Church. By A. G., Elder in the M. E. Church* (Carlisle, 1828). *A Review of "An Appeal to the Christian Public . . . "* (Carlisle, 1828).

119. On motion of Frederick Watts, Trustee Minutes, Feb. 10, 1831. Rogers resigned Feb. 15, his resignation to take effect at end of the spring term.

120. One of the number was the distinguished scientist, Samuel S. Haldeman.

121. Rogers to Hamilton, Oct., 1830 to Aug., 1831. James Hamilton Papers. *Messenger of Useful Knowledge,* pp. 66–67.

122. Charles D. Cleveland, *To My Friends* (Carlisle, April 16, 1832), p. 23.

123. Student records, Dartmouth College Library.

124. Charles D. Cleveland, *An Epitome of Grecian Antiquities. For the Use of Schools* (Boston, 1827), and *A Compendium of Grecian Antiquities* (Boston, 1831).

125. Trustee Minutes, March 7, 1831. Cleveland had written the trustees on the matter in August, 1830 (*To My Friends,* p. 27), and Atwater, after reading Vethake's *Reply,* had urged How to press the matter.

126. Trustee Minutes, Dec. 15, 1830. $1,500 had been subscribed for the "additional edifice" when How issued a printed appeal, DCA, announcing that it would bear the name of any donor of a like sum.

127. Cleveland, *To My Friends,* pp. 28–29.

128. *Ibid.,* p. 23.

129. *Ibid.,* p. 3 n.

130. Charles Upham Shepard, already well launched on his distinguished career, had been recommended to the trustees as professor of chemistry and natural history by Edward Hitchcock of Amherst, May 13, 1828 (James Hamilton Papers).

131. Cleveland, *To My Friends,* pp. 2–3. McFarlane, complaint to the trustees, Feb. 15, 1832. DCA.

132. Cleveland, *To My Friends,* pp. 4 n, 34. A letter from Olmstead to Joseph A. Murray, July 13, 1864, Library of the Cumberland County Historical Society, describes his brief professorial career—"I was a green boy."

133. Cleveland, *To My Friends,* p. 26.

134. DCA.

135. How, report to trustees, Sept. 27, 1831. DCA. Cleveland, *To My Friends,* pp. 14–15, 20–22. The most curious and revealing of How's charges (as stated to Cleveland himself) was that he had revealed the secrets of the faculty to Mr. Duffield.

136. How to trustees, Sept. 27, 1831. DCA.

137. Moodey to Andrew Carothers, Oct. 29, 1831. DCA. Trustee Minutes, Sept. 28–29, Nov. 5, 1831.

138. Cleveland, *To My Friends,* p. 29.

139. *Ibid.,* pp. 5–9. George A. Lyon, statement, Sept. 29, 1831. DCA.

140. Lyon to Duffield, Aug. 26, 1831. DCA. *Carlisle Herald,* Sept. 8, 16, 1831. Ashbel Green to George A. Lyon, Sept. 16, 1831. DCA. Trustee Minutes, Sept. 28, 1831.

141. George Duffield, *Spiritual Life: or, Regeneration, illustrated in a Series of Disquisitions, relative to its Author, Subject, Nature, Means, &c.* (Carlisle, 1832).

142. *Remarks upon the Report of the Committee appointed by the Carlisle Presbytery to review the Work entitled Duffield on Regeneration; together with some Additional Extracts from the Minutes, not listed in the Official Extracts* (Phila., 1832). Andrew Carothers, John Creigh, James Loudon and Samuel Elliott, *The Principles of Presbyterian Discipline, unfolded and illustrated in the Protests and Appeals of the Rev. George Duffield . . . in which his strict Adherence to the Confession of Faith and the Standards of the Church is fully shown* (Carlisle, 1835). Samuel John Baird, *A History of the New School and of the Questions involved in the Disruption of the Presbyterian Church in 1838* (Phila., 1868), pp. 462–67.

143. Belles Lettres Minutes, March 17, 1832.

144. Trustee Minutes, Feb. 18, Aug. 20, 1832.

145. *Niles' Weekly Register,* vol. 42 (1832), p. 83.

Chapter 9. A Methodist New Dawn

1. The trustees refusing to resign were George Chambers, Isaiah Graham, David McConaughy, John D. Mahon, John Moodey and W. R. DeWitt. Trustee Minutes, May 9, 1834.

2. Trustee Minutes, Sept. 25, 1833. *Charter and Bylaws of Dickinson College* (Carlisle, 1966), pp. 9–10. The amendment enacted April 10, 1834 made the Principal President of the Board, empowered the Board to declare vacant seats not occupied for two years and vested all discipline except expulsion with the faculty.

3. John A. Roche, *The Life of John Price Durbin* (N.Y. & Cin., 1889), pp. 58–59. Durbin was zealous to promote the study of science, but he was a churchman first. His chief work in the field is a liberalized edition of the *Mosaic History of the Creation of the World* by the English Methodist, Thomas Wood, and his chief contribution to science at Dickinson the acquisition of apparatus and materials, notably the collection of Prof. Walter R. Johnson of Philadelphia in 1834.

4. *Ibid.,* pp. 95, 102–03. James Penn Pilkington, *The Methodist Publishing House. A History. Volume 1* (Nashville & N.Y., 1968), pp. 225, 281.

5. Campus arboretum, Trustee Minutes, Sept. 27, 1833; May 9, 1834.

6. *Ibid.*, June 8, 1833. Saul Sack, *History of Higher Education in Pennsylvania* (Harrisburg, 1963), vol. 2, pp. 437, 440.

7. Sack, pp. 440–41.

8. Trustee Minutes, June 7, Sept. 27, 1833; May 8, 9, 1834.

9. *Ibid.*, May 8, 1834. "Statement showing the number of subscribers, amounts subscribed, and sums received . . . March 14, 1835," DCA, lists $39,546 in subscriptions, with $1,741 paid at time of printing. H. M. Johnson, circular letter, DCA, states that $30,000 had been realized from a hoped-for original endowment of $100,000.

10. George H. Callcott, *A History of the University of Maryland* (Balt., 1966), p. 23.

11. J. W. Hedges, *Crowned Victors. The Memoirs of over Four Hundred Methodist Preachers* (Balt., 1878), pp. 542–45, 351–53.

12. The Papers of Samuel Harvey are at HSP, and his sketch of the rise of Methodism in DCA. Coombe and Pitman both served as College financial agent. Sketches of Pitman and Lybrand are in William H. Sprague, *Annals of the American Methodist Pulpit* (N.Y., 1865), vol. 7, pp. 603, 521.

13. Carl F. Price, *Wesleyan's First Century* (Middletown, Conn. 1932), pp. 46–47.

14. Joseph Alexander Murray, *A Contribution to the History of the Presbyterian Church* (Carlisle, 1905), p. 31. Penrose was elected to the state senate, where he was Speaker through most of his three terms. He is described in the Carlisle *American Volunteer,* June 17, 1823, as a leader of the Shillewallee wing of the Democratic Party.

15. Trustee Minutes, May 8, 1834, record his appointment to make application for continuance of the state grant.

16. First listed in the Catalogue of 1840, with representatives from Baltimore, Philadelphia and New Jersey.

17. *Christian Advocate and Journal,* Feb. 5, 1845.

18. Trustee Minutes, July 18, 1846, p. 54.

19. Wilson Lee Spottswood, *Brief Annals* (Harrisburg, 1888), p. 50. Roche, p. 204.

20. Roche, p. 219.

21. John Price Durbin, *Inaugural Address, delivered in Carlisle, September 10, 1834, upon the Re-opening of Dickinson College* (Carlisle, 1834), p. 12.

22. Roche, pp. 192, 354.

23. Spottswood, pp. 7–8. George R. Crooks, *Life and Letters of the Rev. John McClintock* (N.Y. & Cin., 1876), pp. 69–70. James Andrew McCauley in *Dickinsonian* Jan. 7, 1873.

24. James Henry Morgan, *History of Dickinson College* (Carlisle, 1933), p. 252. Wainwright, Nicholas B., ed., *A Philadelphia Perspective. The Diary of Sidney George Fisher* (Phila., 1967), p. 53.

25. Charles Francis Himes, *A Sketch of Dickinson College* (Harrisburg, 1879), p. 61, quoting W. H. Allen.

26. Thomas E. Vale, *The Public Schools of Carlisle* (Carlisle, 1935), p. 13.

27. *Proceedings of a National Convention for the Promotion of Education in the United States* (Washington, 1840), p. 2. Thomas Sewall was also a member.

28. John McClintock, diary, April 5, 1840. McClintock Papers, Emory University.

29. Spottswood, pp. 6–7.

30. Herbert B. Adams, *Thomas Jefferson and the University of Virginia* (Wash. 1888), p. 241.

31. Morgan, pp. 273–74.

32. *Ibid.* Richard A. F. Penrose in *Dickinsonian*, May, 1877, p. 58. J. F. Rusling in *Dickinsonian*, May 13, 1914, p. 8.

33. Hedges, pp. 533–35.

34. Merritt Caldwell, *An Address delivered . . . July 16, 1835* (Hallowell, Me., 1835).

35. Spottswood, p. 8.

36. *Ibid.*, p. 4. *Dickinsonian*, May, 1882, p. 10.

37. McCauley, p. 25.

38. Moncure D. Conway, *Autobiography* (Boston & N.Y., 1904), vol. 1, p. 48.

39. Allen to Caldwell, Augusta, Me., July 25, 1836. DCA. Cheesman A. Herrick, *Girard College Worthies* (Phila., 1927), p. 24.

40. Penrose, p. 58.

41. Conway, vol. 1, p. 48.

42. *Ibid.*, p. 49.

43. David D. Leib in *Dickinson Alumnus*, vol. 15 (Sept., 1937), p. 20.

44. Conway, vol. 1, p. 49.

45. Elmer C. Herber, "Spencer F. Baird—World-famous Naturalist," SL 2, pp. 212–32.

46. Roche, p. 221. McClintock is described by W. H. Allen, "Dickinsoniana," address delivered June 4, 1870, McClintock Papers; R. M. Henderson in *Dickinsonian*, Nov., 1898, p. 309; *National Magazine*, vol. 2 (1853), p. 3.

47. Spottswood, p. 9.

48. Conway, vol. 1, p. 47. Penrose, p. 58.

49. McClintock, diary, Nov. 30, 1839. McClintock to Robert Emory, Jan. 19, 1841. McClintock Papers. Thomas Cogswell Upham's *Philosophical and Practical Treatise on the Will* (Portland, Me., 1831; N.Y., Harper, 1841), with its psychological rather than theological approach, seems to have been misjudged by McClintock as a Calvinist document.

50. Stephen Montfort Vail, "Merritt Caldwell," *Methodist Quarterly Review*, vol. 34 (1852), pp. 574–93.

51. *Christian Advocate and Journal*, March 16, 1838. McClintock, diary, Oct. 20, 1837.

52. Spottswood, p. 9.

53. Act No. 95, *Laws of Pennsylvania*, (1838), p. 617.

54. Sherman Day, *Historical Collections of the State of Pennsylvania* (Phila., 1843), p. 265.

55. Record book, April 8, 1841, and library catalogue, 1844–59. DCA.

56. Crooks, pp. 72–73.

57. Merritt Caldwell, "Historical Sketch of Dickinson College," *American Quarterly Register*, vol. 9 (1836), p. 129.

58. Charles G. Murray to his brother, Joseph, Carlisle, Jan. 11, 1837, HSP: "Our new College is finished and fild with students." "Extract of a Letter from a Student of Dickinson College," *Christian Advocate and Journal*, Feb. 17, 1837.

59. Faculty memoranda on the student case of March 21, 1837. DCA.

60. *Christian Advocate and Journal*, May 12, 19, 1837. Vail, p. 579, notes that Caldwell in this year had made himself a "tower of strength" for the temperance cause in the Cumberland Valley persisting fearlessly though "the movement at this time was very unpopular."

61. John A. Wright to J. A. Murray, April 20, 1838. James Hamilton Papers, HSP.

62. *Ibid.,* March 3, 1838.

63. Faculty Minutes, Nov. 2, 9, 1849; March 25, 27, 1850. DCA.

64. *Statutes of Dickinson College* (Carlisle, 1836), p. 7.

65. (David McClure), *A System of Education for the Girard College for Orphans* (Phila., 1838), p. 17.

66. To his father, Jan. 11, 1837. McClintock Papers.

67. C[harles] F[orce] D[eems] in Hollidaysburg, Pa., *Democratic Standard,* June 2, 1843.

68. Trustee Minutes, July 11, 1839. Herber, p. 215, and Roche, pp. 193–94, give accounts of the uprising by S. F. Baird and Thomas Bowman.

69. E.g., U. P. Society to the President, May 4, 1836, DCA, objecting to an "authority never exercised before."

70. Herber, p. 217.

71. *Ibid.,* p. 215.

72. Trustee Minutes, Sept. 25, 1833.

73. *Ibid.,* July 19, 1838.

74. *Ibid.,* July 7, 1841. Faculty Minutes, Sept. 26, 1841.

75. Catalogues, 1842–44. *Carlisle Herald,* June 7, 1843, announcing lecture course. Trustee Minutes, July 10, 1844.

76. McClintock to Robert Emory, Jan. 19, 1841. McClintock Papers.

77. Trustee Minutes, May 9, 1834, contain a resolution that the manual labor system will be introduced "in compliance with the recommendation and request of the Balt. and Phila. A. Conference" as soon as funds are available "and other necessary arrangements made." Durbin's report, *ibid.,* July 12, 1835, recommends introduction of the system and cites "numerous applications from young men of limited means . . . referring mainly to the manual labour system." The *Christian Advocate and Journal,* May 1, 1835, contains a "Report on Education" by Charles Pitman and Edmund S. Janes, "agents of the Philadelphia Conference for Dickinson College," promising the establishment of the system and forswearing any design to set up a theological school at Carlisle. The professors took an opposite view. Durbin, Emory, McClintock were eager to advance theological training. None wanted the manual labor system. McClintock, writing to Emory, Jan. 19, 1841, McClintock Papers, deplores the fact that it had gotten "into the heads of the preachers again." He had thought it a dead issue. With Pestalozzi and others and in the view of Benjamin Rush, manual skills had been seen as an extension of educational practice, but the "system" belonged to the democratic revolt against upper class's monopoly of education. James Mulhern, *A History of Education* (N.Y., 1946), pp. 274, 356, 375, 381, 401–03.

78. Matthew Simpson, ed., *Cyclopaedia of Methodism* (Phila., 1881), p. 559.

79. Petition, 1849. DCA. Trustee Minutes, July 11, 1849.

80. Caldwell to Durbin, Aug. 24, 1836. DCA.

81. Trustee Minutes, July 10, 1845. Morgan, pp. 304–06.

82. Trustee Minutes, May 9–10, 1834.

83. *Christian Advocate and Journal,* Oct. 3, 1834.

84. C. R. Fite to Durbin, Dec. 9, 1837. DCA. Trustee Minutes, July 18, 1838.

85. Trustee Minutes, July 12, 1843, p. 7, and July 11, 1846, p. 47.

86. *Ibid.,* July 19–20, 1838, pp. 311, 317.

87. Notice on subscriptions, *Christian Advocate and Journal,* June 10, 1836.

88. Durbin, printed appeal for funds, Nov. 25, 1837. DCA.

89. Petition to House of Representatives of Penna., Jan. 8, 1838. Rush Papers, Library Company of Philadelphia, on deposit at HSP. Morgan, pp. 289–90. Thomas

H. Burrowes, *Fourth Annual Report of the Common Schools, Academies and Colleges of the Commonwealth of Pennsylvania* (Harrisburg, 1838), p. 65.

90. Thomes E. Bond to his son, May 31, 1841. Bond Papers, DCA. McClintock, diary, May 12, 1841; and to his sister, Jane, June 9, 1841. McClintock Papers.

91. Price, pp. 52, 54–55. Both brought back books, scientific apparatus, models of the "Giant's Causeway."

92. *Observations in Europe, principally in France and Great Britain* (N.Y., 1844). *Observations in the East, chiefly in Egypt, Palestine, Syria and Asia Minor* (N.Y., 1845, 1847, 1854).

93. Faculty Minutes, Sept. 22, 1843.

94. John McClintock, diary, March 25, 1842: " . . . the College . . . evidently on the decline in discipline, scholarship and character."

95. Resignation, Trustee Minutes, July 10, 1845. Roche, pp. 141 ff.

96. Faculty Minutes, Sept. 20, 1845.

97. DCA.

98. DCA.

99. William H. Allen in *Dickinsonian*, April 6, 1875, p. 81. James Fowler Rusling in *Dickinsonian*, May 13, 1914, p. 8. Wilson Lee Spottswood in *Dickinsonian*, May, 1882, pp. 10–11.

100. Faculty Minutes, Sept. 20, 1844. "Rules and Regulations," Sept. 20, 1844. DCA.

101. Faculty Minutes, July 9, 1845.

102. William H. Allen, report to Emory, July, 1846. Trustee Papers, DCA.

103. Emory report, Trustee Minutes, July 8, 1846.

104. Faculty Minutes, June 27, 1846.

105. Trustee Minutes, July 8, 1846, p. 52; July 7, 1847, pp. 70–71, 76–77.

106. Samuel D. Hillman to Thomas E. Rogers, March 31, 1847. HSP.

107. Price, p. 48.

108. "The Faculty recommend that no student under sixteen years of age be permitted to pursue the partial course." Trustee Minutes, July 7, 1847, p. 69. On Aug. 20, 1845, Gov. Francis Rawn Shunk had inquired about entering his two sons at Dickinson, not to graduate, but "to acquire useful knowledge to fit them for performing their duty . . . . They are pretty good English scholars. They have read in Latin Caesar, Cicero, Ovid, Livy, Sallust and four books of the Odes of Horace. In Greek, Greek reader, Greek Testament, 4 books in Xenophon and 4 books in Homer. They have studied Algebra, Geometry, plane and spherical trigonometry and made some progress in Rhetoric and Evidences of Christianity . . . . I want to send these boys another year to School to revise and expand their knowledge of the Latin & Greek languages, Mathematicks &c. and to study natural philosophy, chemistry, astronomy, Geology and the French and German languages. I name these, as my object is to reach as far as I can, practical results." To James Hamilton, James Hamilton Papers.

109. Durbin's reports, Trustee Minutes, July 12, 1835 and July 19, 1838.

110. Emory report, *ibid* July 8, 1846.

111. Librarian's report, *ibid.,* July 19, 1837.

112. *Ibid.,* July 7, 1847.

113. Durbin to Emory, Nov. 10, 1846, DCA, declaring without obvious conviction his strong faith "for your College building." Emory appeals in *Christian Advocate and Journal,* June 2, 1847: "Where are the Lawrences, the Williams, and the Horries of the middle states, that will by one noble benefaction bless the College and embalm their own names?"

114. Trustee Minutes, July 7, 1847, p. 74. S. D. Hillman to T. E. Rogers, Feb. 7, 1847, HSP: "The old hall back of the 'den' has been converted into rooms."

115. *Christian Advocate and Journal*, March 10, 31, 1847.

116. Price pp. 53, 80. Lewis M. Purifoy, "The Methodist Anti-Slavery Tradition," *Methodist History*, vol. 4 (1966), p. 9.

117. *Christian Advocate and Journal*, Feb. 24, March 31, April 21, 28, 1847.

118. *Ibid.*, April 28, 1847.

119. *Ibid.*, May 19, 1847. The fifth article is in the McClintock Papers.

120. McClintock to his brother-in-law, Edgar B. Wakeman, June 16, 1847. McClintock Papers.

121. Charles Wesley Carrigan, . . . *Centennial Anniversary of Dickinson College. "An Incident which marked a crisis in her history."* (leaflet, Carlisle, June 27, 1883), p. 3. For other accounts of the riot and trial see Conway, vol. 1, pp. 52–53; Crooks, pp. 143–83; McClintock to Caldwell, June 3, 1847, McClintock Papers. A newspaper account appears in *Two Hundred Years in Cumberland County* (Carlisle, 1951), pp. 165–67. The most recent study is Martha C. Slotten's *The McClintock Slave Riot of 1847* (MS, DCA).

122. Conway, vol. 1, p. 52.

123. Faculty Minutes, June 7, 1847.

124. Emory to David Creamer, June 8, 1847. Manuscripts Collection, Morristown National Historical Park.

125. McClintock Papers.

126. Financial Committee Minutes, Sept. 29, 1847. DCA.

127. Trustee Minutes, July 12, 1848.

128. McClintock to Mrs. Caldwell, June 26, 1848. McClintock Papers.

129. Trustee Papers, July 7, 1848. DCA.

130. Mrs. John McClintock to her mother, Jan. 17, 1848. McClintock Papers.

131. To Stephen Olin, May 21, 1848. *Ibid.*

132. McClintock to Emory, Aug. 2, 1847. *Ibid.*

133. Albert Osborn, *John Fletcher Hurst* (N.Y. & Cin. 1905), pp. 301, 49.

Chapter 10. From Conway to Conrad

1. McClintock to Stephen Olin, Sept. 12, 1848. McClintock Papers, Emory University. *First Fifty Years of Cazenovia Seminary, 1825–1875* (Cazenovia, N.Y., 1877), p. 67.

2. To Olin, Oct. 16, 1848. McClintock Papers.

3. William H. Allen in *Dickinsonian*, April 6, 1875, p. 81.

4. Trustee Minutes, July 12, 1849.

5. Gouverneur Wesleyan Seminary, Oneida Conference and Troy Conference Academy, Poultney, Vt. Peck's article, "Conference Academies," appears in the *Christian Advocate and Journal*, Jan. 7, 1845.

6. Moncure D. Conway in *Dickinsonian*, Monthly Edition, Nov., 1899, p. 43.

7. *Ibid.*, pp. 43–44. Smith's case appears in Faculty Minutes, Feb. 12, 23, 1849. Smith had become intoxicated "under the impulse of the moment," and was returned to his class after a plea from his mother and a pledge of good behavior. Conway, in *Dickinsonian*, Feb. 2, 1875, states that the trick was concocted during a card game, and that he signed the letter, "Hugh Blair." It may be surmised that this reflects his feeling toward the *Lectures on Rhetoric and Belles Lettres* of Nisbet's countryman and contemporary, long republished in America as a school and college

text. According to Wilson Lee Spottswood, *Brief Annals* (Harrisburg, 1888), pp. 77–78, members of the Conference at Staunton thought the incident "a very amusing joke," a feeling not shared by Peck. See also Boyd Lee Spahr, *Dickinson Doings* (Mount Holly, Pa., 1900), pp. 15–29.

8. Faculty Minutes, Sept. 13, 1849.

9. Albert Osborn, *John Fletcher Hurst* (N.Y. & Cin., 1905), pp. 27, 247.

10. Oct., 1850. DCA.

11. Conway in *Dickinsonian*, Monthly Edition, Nov., 1899, p. 44.

12. Thomas G. Chattle, "The Oyster Hunt in Cumberland Valley," *Dickinsonian*, April, 1877, pp. 49–50.

13. *Ibid.* David D. Leib, "Student Diary Tells of Days before Civil War," *Dickinson Alumnus*, vol. 15 (Sept., 1937), p. 21. Horatio C. King, "Reminiscences," *Dickinsonian*, April, 1882.

14. Faculty Minutes, April 10, 12, 1851. Statement by the Junior Class, April 16, 1851, DCA, "through Mr. Buchanan to the Faculty, admitting their fault." *American Volunteer*, April 10, 17, 24, 1851.

15. Board of Trustees, Executive Committee Minutes, May 11, 1852. DCA. Jesse T. Peck, *God in Education: A Discourse to the Graduating Class of Dickinson College* (Wash., 1852).

16. Horatio C. King, "Mother Dickinson," *Dickinsonian*, Oct. 4, 1875, tells how they "undertook to scrape him down as they had Dr. Peck," at his first evening chapel. The scraping feet drowned his voice, but the voice went on until, with the supper hour long past, it prevailed. Charles Collins, diary, Sept. 12, 1852, DCA, describes his first sermon: "What a field to cultivate! I want the hearts of these young men. How shall I win their affections & how acquire that influence over them that shall enable me to lead them to Christ? Let this be my study. For this great work, O God, prepare me." See also Horatio C. King, "History of Dickinson College," *American University Magazine*, vol. 6 (1897), p. 31.

17. Collins, diary, July 14, 1853.

18. May 11, 18, 1853.

19. Trustee Minutes, July 13, 1853. Medals, *ibid.*, July 8, 1857, the gift of John Gregg of Philadelphia.

20. Mary Dillon quoted in *Two Hundred Years in Cumberland County* (Carlisle, 1951), p. 224.

21. Christian Philip Humrich, Class of 1852, to Samuel K. Davis, DCA, "We recite latin to Tiffany and he does not explain it. While I recited latin to Prof Crooks I got along very well and understood it also . . . . We recite Greek to Crooks and he explains it and makes us studdy hard . . . . He makes us translate and wright out all the parsing."

22. Rufus E. Shapley, "Dickinson of Forty Years Ago," *Dickinsonian*, April, 1900, p. 234.

23. His *Heroditi Orientalia Antiquiora; comprising mainly such portions of Heroditus as give a connected History of the East to the Fall of Babylon and the Death of Cyrus the Great* went through five editions, 1854–68. "The Library therefore," Johnson states in a draft for an article, DCA, "is the essential foundation of the College. This is first. Every thing else is secondary & subordinate."

24. Mrs. Mary C. Dillon, author of eight novels, 1904–20. *In Old Bellaire*, 1906, has Carlisle as its romantic background.

25. E.g., accounts of James H. Graham's "Carlisle Land Association." DCA.

26. *A Sketch of Dickinson College* (Harrisburg, 1879), pp. 70–71.

27. Diary of Horatio C. King. DCA. Charles W. Super, *A Pioneer College and its Background* (Salem, Mass., 1923), p. 33.

28. Trustee Minutes, July 11, 1849.

29. Shapley, p. 234.

30. Faculty Minutes, June 20, 1855. Trustee Minutes, July 11, 1855.

31. Shapley, p. 235.

32. Trustee Minutes, July 11, 1860. Peck had suggested the idea to John McClintock, Nov. 2, 1850. McClintock Papers.

33. Faculty Minutes, Dec. 15, 1854.

34. Belles Lettres Minutes, April 23, 1856. DCA. Faculty Minutes, April 2, 1860.

35. Trustee Minutes, July 7, 8, 1859.

36. *Ibid.* June 25, 1851.

37. Saul Sack, *History of Higher Education in Pennsylvania* (Harrisburg, 1963), vol. 1, pp. 368–69.

38. Trustee Papers, 1837, Folder VI. DCA. Ruth E. White, *History of the Methodist Church in Carlisle, Pennsylvania. 1792–1954* (n.p., n.d.), pp. 14–17, 43.

39. "We were trained to write and speak with care, and to avoid anything like the heat and rant which so easily beset the preacher," Moncure D. Conway, *Autobiography* (Boston & N.Y., 1904), vol. 1, p. 54. Osborn, pp. 33–34, 38–39. *Two Hundred Years*, p. 227.

40. Faculty Minutes, Feb. 16, 1844.

41. Architect's drawings in DCA. "Such a grand building, with its Gothic windows and fine walnut wood-work and red carpets in the aisles!" Mary Dillon in *Two Hundred Years*, p. 227. A program of the dedication, Nov. 14, 1858, is in the James Hamilton Papers, HSP.

42. Trustee Minutes, July 12, 1854.

43. Himes, p. 110

44. King, diary, June 13, 1856.

45. Trustee Minutes, July 11, 1855. King, diary, May 20, 1857. *Two Hundred Years*, pp. 177–79.

46. Charles Collins, subscription book for painting and repair, 1857. DCA. Portraits of Nisbet, Peck, Emory, Caldwell, Trustee Minutes, July 12, 1854.

47. Board of Trustees, Executive Committee Minutes, July 1, 1851. Trustee Minutes, July 8, 1857, show $1,600 still owed for the roof.

48. Tax exemption in *An Act to Incorporate the German Reformed Congregation of Harbaugh's Church in Washington Township, Franklin County, and to Exempt the Real Estate of Dickinson College in Carlisle from Taxation,* signed by Gov. Francis R. Shunk, April 10, 1848; authorized copy, March 4, 1857. Sidewalk construction would be a long-standing issue with the Borough. In 1857 the College owed both construction and penalty charges.

49. *Endowment of Dickinson College. Argument Exhibiting the Basis of the Plan.* Submitted by H. M. Johnson to the trustees, Feb. 18, 1852. In this later summation he stresses the urgency of action (p. 5). Allegheny and three other Methodist Colleges have adopted the plan. "Jefferson College, at Canonsburg, heretofore a powerful rival, is full on the course. We shall soon be surrounded and eaten out if we remain as we are."

50. Trustee Minutes, June 26, 1851.

51. Charles Collins, diary, Jan. 26, 1854. DCA.

52. Trustee Minutes, July 12, 1854.

53. Himes, pp. 79–80.

54. King, "History," p. 26, states that $100,000 was subscribed but only $60,000 realized. H. M. Johnson, *Collegiate Education* (circular letter, Aug., 1863), gives the figure as "about $70,000."

55. Collins report, Trustee Minutes, July 11, 1855: "no embarrassment from excess of numbers & the financial difficulties have been provided for." Architects' plans for dormitories in DCA.

56. Himes, p. 80. James Henry Morgan, *Dickinson College* (Carlisle, 1933), pp. 302–04.

57. East Baltimore Conference Minutes, 1860, Report of the Committee on Dickinson College. DCA.

58. Trustee Papers, 1858.

59. Trustee Minutes, July 13, 1848, resolution recognizing Dickinson Seminary as "preparatory to this institution." Charles Scott Williams, *History of Lycoming College and its Predecessor Institutions, Williamsport Academy, Dickinson Seminary, Williamsport Dickinson Junior College* (Balt., 1959). Sack, pp. 164–67. John McClintock reported "double-dealing" to Robert Emory, Feb., 1845, McClintock Papers: "There will be an attempt made to disconnect Pennington Seminary from us—or, rather, to say that it never was connected with us."

60. Spottswood, p. 273.

61. John McClintock to Robert Emory, Aug. 30, 1845, McClintock Papers, suggested "An Education Society" to aid indigent young men, "preachers and others." Faculty Minutes, Oct. 28, 1851, appoint H. M. Johnson to draft a constitution. Draft of Constitution in DCA. Johnson, in Trustee Minutes, June 23, 1863, reports limitation to ministry. *Ibid.,* June 28, 1882, reports a balance of only $2.54, due to non-payment of loans.

62. Horatio C. King, "College Reminiscences," *Dickinsonian,* Feb. 4, 1873, p. 37.

63. King, "History," p. 33. The class entered with 108 regular and irregular students, in Sophomore year was reduced to 45 regulars and in Senior year to 36, as cited in *Dickinsonian,* April, 1878, p. 1.

64. DCA.

65. David Clarke John, "Dickinson in '59," *Dickinsonian,* Monthly Edition, Jan., 1900, p. 135. Charles W. Super in *Dickinsonian,* Dec. 2, 1915.

66. Trustee Minutes, July 13, 1853.

67. King, diary, Dec. 5, 1856, etc.

68. Trustee Minutes, July 8, 1840, record the recommendation of a new and larger bell by Durbin. In fact and legend, assaults on the bell, thefts of the clapper and other devices to silence it are legion. *Vide* Spahr, pp. 117–19; Super, pp. 30–31.

69. McClintock Papers.

70. King, diary, Dec. 7, 1855: "Greased Tiffany's boards with fish oil." *Ibid.,* Jan. 24, 30, 1856. King, "Reminiscences," pp. 16–17. Faculty Minutes, Feb. 1, 2, 4, 8, 15, 1856. William T. Kinzer, diary, Feb. 2, 1856, Virginia Historical Society: "Great times! A college rebellion! . . . I heard that the President said the College is in a critical condition." Albert H. Slape to James Andrew Munroe, Feb. 4, 1856, DCA: "Our Class Forever! Great excitement in old Dickinson! Students in direct rebellion. One hundred on the point of leaving for their homes!! . . . I don't suppose the walls of East College ever saw such a rebellion." Sophomores were accused, but Freshmen, Juniors and Seniors also took part. "I tell you Munroe we have a *bully class* numbering about fifty and they are all tip top fellows, *study hard and care for nobody.*" *New York Daily Tribune,* Feb. 5, 1856: "DIFFICULTY AT DICKINSON COLLEGE. One hundred of the students . . . have rebelled against the Faculty in consequence of the alleged unjust expulsion of four members."

71. Faculty Minutes, April 28, 1852: Johnson's room "so full of pepper as to require a dismissal of recitation." King, "Reminiscences," cites Marshall as braving it

out, and McClintock declaring asafedita inhalations good for his asthma anyway. "It was attar of roses to him."

72. Faculty Minutes, May 15, 1854.

73. King, diary, Feb. 22, 1856; "Got a good joke on him."

74. John, p. 135. King, diary, March 16, 1858, mentions the "Night Hawks" as active in the suppression of Smith's *Mechanics.*

75. King, diary.

76. *Ibid.* Horatio C. King, "The Inquest Adjourned," *Dickinsonian,* April 6, 1875, pp. 73–74. Spahr, pp. 127–33. It must be added that the book by Oberlin's first president, Asa Mahan, *A System of Intellectual Philosophy* (2nd ed., N.Y., 1847, Harper), hardly deserved the obloquy cast upon it.

77. The "duel" is recounted in *Dickinsonian,* June, 1883, and March 21, 1935. Collins' purchase "of a fine Achromatic Telescope, manufactured by Henry Fitz, Esq. of N.Y.," is reported in Trustee Minutes, July 8, 1857; and its use in the observation of students by King in *Dickinsonian,* Nov., 1882.

78. Osborn, p. 51.

79. J. P. Durbin, address to students, Sept. 19, 1840, DCA: "No play South of the Buildings, and no football at all on the Campus." John Reed in David McClure's *A System of Education for the Girard College for Orphans* (Phila., 1838), p. 18. Osborn, pp. 35–37.

80. Faculty Minutes, Sept. 24 and Dec. 12, 1853; Feb. 17, 1854.

81. King, diary, April 30, 1855.

82. Himes, letters home, May 2, June 10, 1853. DCA. Record book of Cadets, 1857–59. DCA. King, diary, March 14, 1847.

83. Faculty Minutes, April 7, 1857.

84. The idea originated with Horatio King, Al Slape, Tom Conrad and others, as related by King, *Dickinsonian,* April 28, 1915. See also Super in *Dickinsonian,* March 10 and Dec. 2, 1915.

85. Super, *Dickinsonian,* Dec. 2, 1915.

86. John Peach to James H. Morgan, Jan. 24, 1914. DCA.

87. James Fowler Rusling, "Class of 1854," *Dickinsonian,* May 13, 1914, p. 6.

88. King, diary, Jan. 26, 1857. "Romeo and Juliet" was in rehearsal, with Tom Conrad as Lady Capulet. Faculty Minutes, April 2, 1860, on minus marks.

89. Belles Lettres Minutes, May 26, 1852.

90. Faculty Minutes, Nov. 24, 1854.

91. Frederic S. Klein, *The Spiritual and Educational Background of Franklin and Marshall College* (Lancaster, 1939), pp. 171–72. Belles Lettres Minutes, April 27, 1857. Petition of the societies, July 8, 1857. Trustees Papers, DCA.

92. Catalogue of the Union Philosophical Society, Dickinson College (Carlisle, 1896), p. 6: "General Union Philosophical Society" organized, 1844, "in order to perpetuate the earnestness and enthusiasm in the breasts of our Brother Unions."

93. King, diary, Nov. 1, 1858: the initiation "a fiery ordeal." Himes, p. 85, describes the gold badges introduced in 1852.

94. Francis Wayland, *Thoughts on the present Collegiate System in the United States* (Boston, 1842), pp. 123–24.

95. Frederick Rudolph, *The American College and University: a History* (N.Y., 1962), pp. 148–49.

96. Constitution and Minutes, "Eclectic Society of Dickinson College." DCA. Carl F. Price, *Wesleyan's First Century* (Middletown, Conn., 1932), pp. 43, 246.

97. Faculty Minutes, July 3, 1872. Trustee Minutes, July 7, 1852, with Peck's report calling for a prohibition of unauthorized secret societies, p. 218, and trustee

discussion "with closed doors," p. 226. It may be assumed that Peck led an opposition in which he had support from the clergy of the conferences.

98. Faculty Minutes, June 10, 11, 13, 18, 22, 1853. Trustee Minutes, July 13, 1853.

99. King, diary, Oct. 31, 1856, and elsewhere, records initiations of Slape, Cloud and Conrad, furnishing of hall, etc. Faculty Minutes, Nov. 23, 30, 1857, on requirement to disband. Himes, pp. 9–10, 12.

100. *Carlisle Herald*, May 31, 1854: "We hear it whispered about that an association of the mysterious order of the *Know Nothings,* which has suddenly grown into such wonderful strength throughout the country and has turned the schemes of politicians topsy-turvy in so many places, has been organized in Carlisle." An address "To the Officers and Members of the American Party in the State of Pennsylvania," HSP, is signed, "O. H. Tiffany, President of the State Council of Pa.," and dated, "Carlisle, August 10th, 1855." In Carlisle, the *American Volunteer* fulminates against the order and the involvement of Prof. Tiffany and others of the College in it, and finally, Aug. 23, 1857, cites the ill will brought on the faculty "by their constant dabbling in politics, . . . But we gained our point which was to drive them from their Know Nothing lodges to their duties in the College."

101. *The Temple. A Monthly Magazine, devoted to Masonry, Literature and Science,* was published at Carlisle, 1851–52, with Prof. Blumenthal as co-editor, serializing his novel, "Ellen Fisher," his articles on Masonry in Portugal, and others by W. H. Allen, including Allen's account of the large delegation from Carlisle to the Masonic funeral of Stephen Girard.

102. William C. Round, diary, April 13, 1861. Louis Round Wilson Papers, University of North Carolina.

103. King, diary, April 9, 1858.

104. Trustee Minutes, July 12, 1848.

105. Chattle, p. 49.

106. James P. Sterrett to James A. Devinney, Sept. 13, 1845, DCA, with explanation of the boarding clubs at Jefferson College. Collins' report describing clubs at Dickinson, Trustee Minutes, July 9, 1856. Kinzer, diary, March 20, Oct. 3, 1856. Super, *Pioneer College,* p. 35.

107. Kinzer, diary, Nov. 4, 10, 1856. King, diary, Nov. 10, 1856.

108. John, p. 135.

109. King, diary, June 19, 1856.

110. Collins, diary, Dec. 2, 1854; Jan. 17, 1859; March to May, 1860.

111. Trustee Minutes, July 11, 1860.

112. Horatio C. King, *Songs of Dickinson* (N.Y., 1900), pp. 18–19.

113. *Two Hundred Years,* p. 229.

114. Trustee Minutes, July 11, 1860. The motion was tabled, and a committee appointed "on means of relieving the College from pecuniary embarrassment."

115. East Baltimore Conference Minutes, 1861. DCA. The legislature responded with its act of April 29, 1862, authorizing the College to borrow up to $15,000.

116. Trustee Minutes, Dec. 4, 1861.

117. H. M. Johnson, *To the Members and Friends of the Methodist Episcopal Church,* printed circular, Nov. 14, 1861. DCA.

118. Charles W. Super in *Dickinsonian,* May 5, 1909, p. 7.

119. *Two Hundred Years,* p. 226.

120. C. F. R., "How the Boys of '65 disposed of the Doctor," *Dickinsonian,* Nov., 1875, p. 3. Super in *Dickinsonian,* May 5, 1909, p. 7.

121. John Bakeless, "Captain Conrad's Spy Net," SL 4, pp. 159–72. Milton E.

Flower, "Dickinson College and the Civil War," *Dickinson Alumnus,* vol. 39 (Feb., 1962), pp. 1-8.

122. Trustee Minutes, June 25, 1862.

123. Jessie S. Colton, ed., *The Civil War Journal and Correspondence of Matthias Baldwin Colton* (Phila., 1931), pp. 84-85.

124. Charles F. Himes to Ogden N. Rood, Oct. 2, 1863. Himes Papers, DCA.

125. Burning of the Barracks and a tour of the College appear in the diary of Assistant Surgeon William W. Marston, C.S.A., June 27-30, 1863. Property of Henry Lee Curry, Richmond, Va.; citation courtesy of Bell I. Wiley from copy at Emory University. Himes, p. 73, cites several shells falling on campus, one penetrating Johnson's lecture room in East, another the roof of South.

126. Thomas M. Johnson to Fred P. Corson, Oct. 20, 1939. DCA.

127. Trustee Minutes, June 24, 1863.

128. Board of Trustees, Executive Committee Minutes, Sept. 19, 1863.

129. East Baltimore Conference Minutes, 1864, p. 232. DCA. Announcement in *American Volunteer,* Sept. 1, 1864, Rev. R. D. Chambers, President, assisted by Samuel D. Hillman. Rev. William C. Leverett's Mary Institute, founded in 1861, appears in *American Volunteer,* Aug. 26, 1869, as a more successful competitor.

130. Trustee Minutes, June 27, 1865.

131. *Ibid.* See also Sack, vol. 2, p. 610.

132. East Baltimore Conference Minutes, 1867, 1868, DCA, echo Johnson's recommendation on the "Biblical Department" with warm approval. Sack, vol. 1, pp. 329-30, quotes Acting President Hillman's report, Trustee Minutes, June 23, 1868, as evidence of the post-Civil War trend toward secularization in the colleges.

133. Trustee Minutes, June 28, 1865.

134. Board of Trustees, Executive Committee Minutes, Feb. 17, 1865. Pennell Coombe, correspondence and reports. DCA.

135. Coombe to Buchanan, April 29, May 3, 6, 1865; Buchanan to Coombe, May 2, 1865. Buchanan Papers, HSP.

136. Over view of West College, "Sunday School Centenary Offering" and "Religion and Science." Manufactured by Warner and Sons, Philadelphia. Trustee Minutes, June 26, 1867, offer two twenty-year scholarship certificates to Sunday schools contributing $500. Himes, p. 81.

137. Board of Trustees, Executive Committee Minutes, Sept. 20, 1865. Dickinson Commercial College was established Sep. 1, 1864, according to its catalogue, 1867. DCA.

138. Trustee Minutes, June 24, 1868. Himes, pp. 87, 130-31.

139. Himes, pp. 117-18.

140. Trustee Minutes, June 28, 1865.

141. Himes, pp. 118-19.

142. *Ibid,* pp. 112-14, 120-22.

143. *Ibid,* pp. 127-28. Dickinson College, *Microcosm,* 1867-68, p. 15.

144. Shadrach L. Bowman, *Special Report. Proposed Plan for the Enlargement of the Biblical Department of Dickinson College,* dated June, 1867, presented, 1868. Trustees Papers, June 23, 1868, Folder IV. DCA.

145. Trustee Minutes, June 24, 1868.

146. Board of Trustees, Executive Committee Minutes, Jan. 6, 1866; April 27, 1868.

147. Dickinson College, Board of Trustees, "Dickinson College's Interest in the Income from the Dickinson Fund of the Education Fund of the Philadelphia Conference of the United Methodist Church," 1969. DCA.

148. Trustee Minutes, June 25, 1867, pp. 216, 218.

149. Treasurers Papers, DCA, show Johnson travelling much in pursuit of funds. His own resources were exhausted and the College in debt to him at his death.

150. Trustee Minutes, June 24, 1868, p. 276.

151. William H. Allen to John Francis Bird, Sept. 4, 1868. DCA.

152. Erastus O. Haven, University of Michigan, to trustees, Aug. 29, 1868. DCA. Robert Gildart, *Albion College, 1835–1960* (Albion, Mich., 1961), pp. 94–96. Jocelyn was President of Albion, 1864–69 and 1871–77.

Chapter 11. McCauley

1. *Reception of Dr. Dashiell, President Elect of Dickinson College.* Broadside, DCA. In contrast to the formal inaugurals of an earlier day, here we see Dashiell given a welcome spiced with classical allusions but all in the cheerful spirit of an alumni reunion. Dashiell's response to the congratulatory speeches recalled his own student days with emotion. "He made a very happy allusion to Dr. Emory—that model man—whose heavenly deportment, pious and exemplary life had so inspired him (Dashiell) while under his (Emory's) administration, that as he stood before his (Emory's) portrait a few days ago, the involuntary prayer arose from his heart, 'O that his mantle may descend upon me.' " Dashiell's student days are more directly reflected in his "College ms.," DCA, with such pieces as "A History of the Greek Drama," a "History of the Reformation," 1844, dedicated to Dr. Durbin, and an essay, "Kindness—the moving force of Society."

2. *Microcosm*, 1867–68.

3. Trustee Minutes, June 22, 1869, pp. 297–308.

4. *Ibid.*, June 8, 1870, pp. 337, 351. *Microcosm*, 1867–68.

5. Trustee Minutes, June 8, 1870, pp. 340–41.

6. Central Pennsylvania Conference, *Annual Minutes* (Harrisburg, 1869), p. 38.

7. James Henry Morgan, *Dickinson College* (Carlisle, 1933), p. 327. Trustee Minutes, June 8, 1870, p. 338, list assets of $71,134 held by the Philadelphia Conference, $101,280 by Baltimore, "about $7,500" by New Jersey and $19,976 in the hands of the trustees as the basis of a reconstituted College endowment.

8. Trustee Papers, June 23, 1868, Folder V. DCA.

9. Harman's *A Journey to Egypt and the Holy Land in 1869–1870* (Phila., 1873) was followed in 1879 by his *Introduction to the Study of the Holy Scriptures* which was long in print as Vol. 1 of G. R. Crooks and J. F. Hurst's *Library of Biblical and Theological Literature.*

10. Information to the author from Merkel Landis.

11. George H. Bucher to Gilbert Malcolm, March 31, 1959. Spahr Papers 1003 A-C, DCA.

12. *Microcosm*, 1867–68.

13. *Ibid.*, 1871–72.

14. Faculty Minutes, Sept. 20, 1869. DCA.

15. Trustee Minutes, June 6, 1871, p. 358.

16. Whitfield J. Bell, Jr., "Highlights of Dickinson History," *Dickinsonian*, May 19, 1932.

17. Faculty Minutes, April 26, 1870.

18. *Ibid.*, April 30, 1870.

19. Trustee Minutes, June 8, 1870, p. 350. Morgan, pp. 331–32.

20. Executive Committee Minutes, April 27, 1868. DCA.

21. Faculty Minutes, Nov. 10, 28, Dec. 9, 13, 1870; June 7, 1871. Trustee Minutes, June, 1871, pp. 361–62, 371. Charles T. Dunning, "Reminiscences of College Days," *Dickinsonian*, Nov. 4, 1903, pp. 6–7. Morgan, pp. 333–34, 423. The Independents became a chapter of Theta Chi, Dashiell breathing his relief at this event to the trustees, June 25, 1872: "The young gentlemen of the independent persuasion have organized a new fraternity & wear with proper pride a beautiful badge as the symbol of their new order. This I think will finish for some years the war between fraternities and independents."

22. Trustee Minutes, June 6, 1871, p. 356.

23. Faculty Minutes, Oct. 11, 1870, May 30, 1871. Orson D. Foulks, depositions, etc, DCA.

24. Central Pennsylvania Conference, *Minutes,* 1880, p. 65.

25. McCauley, graduating with second honors, had been recommended to the teaching profession, July 9, 1847, by Allen, McClintock, Sudler and Baird. DCA.

26. Wilson Lee Spottswood, *Brief Annals* (Harrisburg, 1888), p. 81.

27. Obituary, Feb. 3, 1897, by James H. Morgan and Henry C. Whiting. DCA.

28. Obituary by Charles F. Himes, *Baltimore Methodist,* Dec. 16, 1897.

29. E.g., petition of 27 Grammar School pupils asking the "continuance of the services of S. D. Hillman as our Principal," Trustee Papers, Feb. 18, 1852, Folder IV.

30. John Price Durbin to Robert Emory, Jan. 19, 1846. DCA.

31. Trustee Minutes, Aug. 8, 1872. F. A. Ellis to Charles F. Himes, Nov. 29, 1874. Trustee Papers, Dec. 9, 1874, Folder I.

32. Morgan, p. 32.

33. Trustee Minutes, June 24, 1874, p. 14.

34. Dr. George Wilds Linn, '69, to William R. Fisher, Nov. 7, 1874. Fisher Papers, DCA.

35. Himes to Fisher, June 5, 1874. Fisher Papers.

36. Conway Wing Hillman, statement on his father's connection with the College. DCA.

37. *Ibid.*

38. June 18, 1874. Trustee Papers, 1874, Folder IV.

39. *Ibid.*

40. Trustee Minutes, June 24, 1874.

41. *Ibid.* Himes to Fisher, July 1, 1874. Fisher Papers.

42. Himes to Fisher. *Ibid.*

43. *Sunday Mercury* (Phila.), July 19, 1874.

44. *Ibid.,* July 26, 1874.

45. *Ibid.,* Aug. 2, 1874, "One of '73" replying to the reply, "In reference to the blarney-cant and windy nothingness contained in an article communicated to you last Sunday . . . ."

46. Thomas Green Chattle to Himes. Trustee Papers, Dec. 9, 1874, Folder III.

47. Morgan, p. 346.

48. *Carlisle Herald,* Sept. 24, 1874.

49. Details were reported in the *Dickinsonian* Oct. 6, Nov. 3, 1874.

50. Dickinson College, *Charter and Bylaws* (Carlisle, 1966), p. 7.

51. Trustee Minutes, Jan. 4, 1875. Hillman's case differed in that he had accepted severance pay. He joined the faculty of the new Cumberland County State Normal School, Shippensburg, vacating his West College rooms in April, 1875.

52. Morgan, p. 345. *Northwestern University Bulletin,* March 23, 1911. He had begun his teaching career as Professor of Mathematics, Dickinson Seminary.

53. Himes' *Lecture on the Telephone,* June 13, 1878, has been noted as perhaps

the first musical broadcast. After the lecture, music played in Philadelphia was heard by the audience in Carlisle.

54. Minutes, April 19, 1887. DCA.

55. Trustee Minutes, June 24, 1876, p. 71. Original draft in Trustee Papers, 1876, Folder II B.

56. Trustee Papers, 1876, Folder II. Dickinson College, *Charter,* 10–11.

57. Trustee Minutes, June 28, 1876, p. 66.

58. Charles Francis Himes, *A Sketch of Dickinson College* (Harrisburg, 1879), pp. 88–89.

59. Carl. F. Price, *Wesleyan's First Century* (Middletown, Conn., 1932), p. 121. Trustee Minutes, June 26, 1877, pp. 4, 13.

60. Morgan, p. 352. Trustee Minutes, June 23, 1885.

61. Faculty Minutes, May 14, 1877. Trustee Minutes, June 27, 1877, pp. 86, 95. Trustee Minutes, Sept. 4, 1884, record the establishment of a "course of four years with Modern Languages in place of Latin & Greek."

62. The paper was proposed by Wilbur Fisk Spottswood of U. P., according to Catalogue of the Union Philosophical Society (Carlisle, 1896), p. 6. There had been no student publication since 1849, when Moncure had transformed *The Bouquet* (manuscript, read in Chapel) in the five issues of his *Collegian,* 1849. Belles Lettres Minutes, Sept. 18, 1872, DCA, record the *Dickinsonian's* editorial organization and purpose.

63. Himes, "Introductory Lecture to Juniors and Seniors," *Dickinsonian,* Oct. 7, 1873, pp. 2–3.

64. *Dickinsonian,* Oct. 7, 1873, p. 3; Dec. 2, 1873, pp. 18–19; Feb. 3, 1874, pp. 34–35; April 7, 1874, p. 51.

65. Faculty Minutes, Dec. 21, 1876.

66. Collection of Charles E. Feinberg, Detroit, Mich.

67. Professor Stayman despised tobacco chewers in class, but took a tolerant view even on discovering that Elias Dunlevy Maine had cut a hole in the bench through which to spit. "Ah, Maine, how can you *expect to rate* high in my estimation when you act in this way?"—his pun greeted with the usual feet stamping. Duncan M. Graham, "Some Wayside Yarns of '73," *Dickinsonian,* Dec., 1882, p. 16.

68. Wilbur J. Gobrecht, *History of Dickinson College Football* (Carlisle, 1971), p. 7.

69. Oliver Mordorf, '89, "Social Life at Dickinson College," *Dickinsonian,* Feb., 1888, pp. 3–6.

70. Treasurer's vouchers. DCA. Executive Committee Minutes, Feb. 14, 1907, record Fells' retirement as a carpenter after more than fifty years of service.

71. Executive Committee Minutes, Jan. 27, 1864. Trustee Minutes, June 26, 1867, p. 220; June 24, 1879, p. 127; June 25, 1880, p. 155. Faculty Minutes, March 31, 1879.

72. Paul E. Zuver, *A Short History of Carlisle Barracks* (n. p., 1934), p. 126.

73. Dickinson College, *Minutal,* 1881. Treasurer's vouchers, 1880–81.

74. Trustee Minutes, June 23, 1880, pp. 145–46; June 29, 1881, pp. 164–65.

75. Carlisle *American Volunteer,* Feb. 23, 1887.

76. *Pennsylvania County Court Reports* (Phila., 1887), vol. 2, pp. 459–64; vol. 3, pp. 77–89.

77. *Ibid.,* vol. 3, p. 89.

78. Trustee Minutes, June 28, 1876, p. 66; June 26, 1877, p. 90.

79. *Ibid.,* June 25, 1878, pp. 114–15. Faculty Minutes, June 17, 1878.

80. Whitfield J. Bell, Jr., "Highlights of Dickinson History," *Dickinsonian,* Nov. 17, 1932.

81. Morgan, p. 350. Faculty Minutes, May 21, 1883. The trustees, June 25, 1884, stepped warily into the debatable ground: "Whereas application has been made to the Faculty to admit ladies to certain lectures in the College be it Resolved That the whole matter as to the admission of females to the College course be left with the faculty to determine, upon cases as they may arise." At least the step was taken more resolutely than at Middlebury, where women were admitted on equal status simply because President Cyrus Hamlin, an opponent, had not heard the trustee vote correctly.

82. Information from Mrs. Ernest W. Sipple (Persis Longsdorff), Nov. 10, 1968.

83. *Dickinsonian*, Nov., 1877, p. 11.

84. What Henry Steele Commager in *The American Mind* describes as a long flight from reason and from the realities of American experience came often as a shock to earnest church members, as when Lucy Holt Doney of the Library staff, summoned in 1958 to a meeting held by the Lecturer in Practical Theology, found herself in a circle, holding hands and singing, "Blest be the tie that binds."

85. Trustee Minutes, June 24, 1873, pp. 400, 410–11. Morgan, p. 337.

86. *Minutes*, 1874, pp. 46–47; 1875, p. 48.

87. Himes, speaking "at the Educational Anniversary held in Altoona, Mar. 23." *Dickinsonian*, April 7, 1874 p. 52.

88. Report of James C. Clarke for the Harrisburg District. Central Pennsylvania Conference, *Minutes*, 1879, p. 43.

89. Central Pennsylvania Conference, *Minutes*, 1885, p. 64. *Dickinsonian*, Jan., 1884, p. 6.

90. Morgan, pp. 347–48. Central Pennsylvania Conference, *Minutes*, 1885 p. 64.

91. Edwin Post in *Dickinsonian*, Nov. 4, 1873, p. 3.

92. Himes, pp. 131–33. Meigs' plans in DCA. In Trustee Minutes, June 25, 1878, pp. 117–18, Himes included a plea for erection of the building in his departmental report; and *ibid.*, June 22, 1880, pp. 139–40, reiterated his hopes, announcing publication of his history of the College at his own expense.

93. Himes, p. 134.

94. Gifts of over $200,000 were reported to the Central Pennsylvania Conference, *Minutes*, 1885, pp. 62–64, inspiring resolutions for the "enlargement and upbuilding of Dickinson College into an institution second to none in the land in educational appliances, facilities and opportunities," and renewed determination to try to raise $40,000 for the Conference professorship.

95. McCauley report, June 24, 1884. Trustee Papers, Folder III.

96. McCauley report, Trustee Minutes, June 25, 1885, pp. 280–81.

97. Treasurer's vouchers, 1872–73. DCA. *Dickinsonian*, Feb. 5, 1874, p. 37; March 3, 1874, p. 44; April 7, 1874, p. 52.

98. *Dickinsonian*, Jan. 6, 1874, p. 28.

99. Trustee Papers, 1876, Folder V.

100. Trustee Minutes, June 23, 1886, pp. 294, 304.

101. Rusling's works include *Across America; or, The Great West and the Pacific Coast*, 1874; *The Railroad! The Stock-yards! The Eveners! Expose of the Great Railroad Ring that Robs the Laborer of the East and the Producer of the West of $5,000,000 a Year*, 1878; *Men and Things I Saw in Civil War Days*, 1899; and *European Days and Ways*, 1902.

102. Matthew Simpson, *Cyclopaedia of Methodism* (Phila., 1881), p. 769.

103. Trustee Minutes, June 23, 1874, pp. 12–13.

104. *Ibid.*, June 28, 1881, pp. 168–70. Hargis to Himes, July 12, 1888, DCA, acknowledging D.D. conferred during Himes' Acting Presidency.

105. Trustee Minutes, June 29, 1881, p. 170.

106. *Ibid.,* June 28, 1882, p. 201. Trustee Papers, 1882, Folder VI. Executive Committee Minutes, Sept. 8, 1882.

107. Trustee Minutes, June 23, 1886, pp. 300–01. *Dickinsonian,* April, 1886, p. 10; May, 1886, pp. 5–6, 12; June, 1886, pp. 3–5. Morgan, pp. 352–54. *American Volunteer,* Feb. 23, 1887, describes an attempt to blackmail McCauley into paying hush-money.

108. Conway Wing Hillman statement. DCA.

109. Morgan, p. 357.

110. George Van Derveer Morris, *A Man for A' That* (Cin. & N.Y., 1902), pp. 271–76.

111. George Edward Reed, "Reminiscences of Dickinson," *Dickinson Alumnus,* Feb., 1925, pp. 7–8. Alphonso A. Hopkins, *The Life of Clinton Bowen Fisk* (N.Y., 1890), pp. 280–81.

Chapter 12. Reed

1. George Edward Reed, "Reminiscences of Dickinson," *Dickinson Alumnus,* May, 1925, pp. 13–14.

2. *Dickinsonian,* May, 1889, pp. 14–15.

3. Faculty Minutes.

4. *Dickinsonian,* April, 1889, p. 6.

5. Charles F. Himes to George D. Chenoweth, July 22, 1911. Himes Papers, DCA. George Edward Reed, *Alumnus,* Aug., 1925, p. 33, and Nov., 1925, p. 25.

6. *Ibid.,* Aug., 1925, p. 32. George Edward Reed, Annual Report, June 5, 1911. DCA.

7. President's report, June 25, 1889. Trustee Papers, DCA.

8. Faculty Minutes, June 29, 1889.

9. *Ibid.,* Jan. 14, 1890.

10. James Henry Morgan, *Dickinson College* (Carlisle, 1933), p. 359.

11. The first, Wilbur Morris Stine, '86, took both Ph.D. and D.Sc. in 1893, going on to a reputable career in teaching and practicing electrical engineering. The last course entry for the Ph.D. appears in the catalogue of 1894–95, specifying that the candidate must take a major (two years) and a minor (one year), the subjects offered being Assyrian, Hebrew, Latin, Greek, German, French, English, History, Philosophy and Mathematics; a minor, for resident students only, was offered in Physics and Chemistry. The D.Sc. had been abolished by the trustees, June, 1894. The catalogue of 1896–97 states that graduate work is provided only for alumni candidates for the M.A. The best-known to receive the "A.M. by examination" was Montgomery P. Sellers.

12. George Edward Reed, *Alumnus,* May, 1926, pp. 20–22. Burton R. Laub, *History of the Dickinson School of Law* (Carlisle, 1968), sec. II.

13. The catalogue of 1862–63 first lists J. H. Graham on the faculty, describing the Law "Course of Study," with texts, Moot Court and fees. *Ibid.* 1869–70 omits "Course of Study," 1875–76 omits Moot Court and fees, and after 1876–77 there is only Graham's name in the faculty list. *Dickinsonian,* Feb. 5, 1874, p. 37, reflects student discontent with "an *empty* department," but notes "the formation of a class in Blackstone."

14. *Dickinsonian,* Oct., 1890, pp. 17–18. Reed, *Alumnus,* May, 1926, p. 21.

15. Notably, *Law of Liens in Pennsylvania,* 3 vols., 1882; *Law of Limitations in Pennsylvania,* 1884; *Law of Assignments in Pennsylvania,* 1883.

16. James A. McCauley to James H. Morgan, Oct. 14, 1890. DCA.

17. Elizabeth Anna Low, '91, "I was a Coed." MS, DCA.

18. President's report, June 25, 1889. Trustee Papers, DCA.

19. Reed, *Alumnus,* Nov., 1925, p. 28, and May, 1926, p. 22. As late as 1923 the dream is reflected in Charles W. Super's *A Pioneer College,* with its references to "Dean of the College of Liberal Arts" and "Dean of the College of Law."

20. Trustee Papers.

21. Aug. 12, 1890. Himes Papers, DCA.

22. Reed, *Alumnus,* Aug., 1925, p. 30.

23. Information from Boyd Lee Spahr.

24. Reed, *Alumnus,* Nov., 1925, p. 25.

25. *Ibid.,* pp. 25–26. Faculty Minutes, Feb. 4, 1891. *Dickinsonian,* Feb., 1891, p. 5.

26. Reed, *Alumnus,* Feb., 1927, pp. 22–24. Morgan, pp. 359–60.

27. Morgan, p. 363.

28. *Ibid.,* p. 360.

29. Information from Boyd Lee Spahr.

30. Information from George M. Briner, '07.

31. Reed, *Alumnus,* Feb., 1926, pp. 22–24. Morgan, p. 361.

32. Trustee Minutes, June 6, 1892, p. 18. Reed, *op cit.,* pp. 21–22.

33. Trustee Minutes, June 7, 1909, pp. 468–70. Morgan. p. 440.

34. Willard Geoffrey Lake, '87, "Football Reminiscences," *Dickinsonian,* Jan., 1890, pp. 12–13. Horatio C. King, *Songs of Dickinson* (N.Y., 1900), pp. 12, 21, 29, 40–41. King's "Dickinson for Aye," first published in Benjamin J. Hinchman, Jr., *Songs of Dickinson* (N.Y., 1910), p. 78, hails "the white and crimson roses, Loving tho'ts each leaf discloses." George H. Callcott, *History of the University of Maryland* (Balt., 1966), p. 272. James R. Overman, *History of Bowling Green State University* (Bowling Green, State, 1967), p. 36.

35. Newspaper clipping with illustration. DCA.

36. Reed, *Alumnus,* Aug., 1925, p. 31.

37. Faculty Minutes, Sept. 10, 1890.

38. Reed, *Alumnus,* Feb., 1927, p. 25. Information from J. Clair McCullough, '09.

39. Pan-Hellenic Constitution, Bylaws and Minutes. DCA.

40. Student Assembly Constitution in Faculty Minutes, Nov. 4, 1908. Reed, *Alumnus,* Nov., 1925, pp. 26–27.

41. *Dickinson Quarterly,* vol. 1, no. 1, Dec. 18, 1895.

42. *Dickinson Students' Hand Book,* 1903–04, p. 34: "Although recently formed, it is already one of the largest organizations in the college. Every new student should join it."

43. Harman Literary Society, *Salmagundi,* 1906, p. 3.

44. *Microcosm,* 1896, p. 41. *Dickinsonian,* Feb. 15, 1905.

45. Whitfield J. Bell, Jr., in *Dickinsonian,* June 3, 1932. Francis Amasa Walker, *Political Economy* (N.Y., 1892).

46. As described in *Dickinsonian,* May, 1890, pp. 8–9.

47. Trustee Minutes, June 8, 1908, p. 439.

48. Reed, *Alumnus,* Feb., 1927, p. 25.

49. *Dickinsonian,* Feb. 3, 1904, p. 6. "Uncle Noah Pinkney Passes over Jordan," *Alumnus,* Aug., 1923, p. 21. "Dick," obit. in *Dickinsonian,* Jan. 21, 1903. Whitfield J. Bell, Jr. *Dickinsonian* Jan. 12, 1933.

50. Trustee Minutes, Feb. 25, 1909, pp. 448, 451–52.

51. King, p. 54.

52. *Dickinsonian,* Jan., 1896, p. 7.

53. Thomas L. Hoover, '00, in *Dickinsonian,* May 19, 1909.

54. Information from Boyd Lee Spahr.

55. *Dickinsonian,* March and Nov., 1895; Oct. 18, Nov. 8 and Dec. 6, 1901; Jan. 24, 1902. Reed, *Alumnus,* May, 1926, pp. 24–26. Faculty Minutes, June 8, 1894, deal with "Mr. Zug's offense." The culprit promptly transferred to the Law School, graduated LL.B. in 1897, went on to become first a chemist, then an artist.

56. Faculty Minutes, Oct. 19, 1903.

57. "A Brief Sketch of Dickinson's Theatrical Heritage," *Dickinsonian,* Feb. 15, 1917.

58. *Dickinsonian,* Feb. 12, 1908.

59. Student Orations, DCA.

60. *Dickinsonian,* June and Oct., 1890.

61. Faculty Minutes, March 10, 1896.

62. *Dickinsonian,* Jan. 30, 1897.

63. Reed, *Alumnus,* Aug., 1926, p. 37.

64. Trustee Minutes, June 3, 1895. Faculty Minutes, Sept. 23, 1895; Jan. 28, 1896. Biology Department established, Trustee Minutes, June 5, 1899, pp. 225–26. Stephens is commemorated by his students in a bronze plaque now in Dana Hall, "In labors indefatigable, in service abounding, in character steadfast, in influence persuasive and abiding."

65. Executive Committee Minutes, Aug. 10, 1904; Feb. 7, 1905.

66. Marts and Lundy Survey, 1947, DCA.

67. Trustee Minutes, June 4, 1894, p. 73. Faculty Minutes, Oct. 16, 1903.

68. Reed, *Alumnus,* May, 1925, pp. 14–16; Aug., 1926, pp. 36–39.

69. Trustee Minutes, June 12, 1893, pp. 8–9. Morgan, p. 360.

70. Himes Papers, DCA.

71. Morgan p. 362.

72. James Gordon Steese, '02, to Whitfield J. Bell, Jr., Nov. 7, 1936. DCA.

73. *Alumnus,* Feb., 1937, p. 27.

74. To Whitfield J. Bell, Jr., July 3, 1936. DCA.

75. Trustee Papers, 1890, Folder III A.

76. *Ibid.,* 1895, Folder II A.

77. To Whitfield J. Bell, Jr., July 25, 1936. DCA.

78. Trustee Minutes, March 5, 1903, pp. 323–24.

79. Dickinson College album of George Edward Reed, vol. 1. DCA.

80. *Alumnus,* Feb., 1930, p. 12.

81. Trustee Minutes, June 4, 1900, p. 276. *Ibid.,* Feb. 7, 1905, p. 14.

82. Thomas C. Battey, *The Life and Adventures of a Quaker among the Indians* (Norman, Okla., 1968), pp. 52, 61, 71–75. Trustee Minutes, June 2, 1902, p. 308, on employment of "a Curator of Buildings and Grounds."

83. Trustee Minutes, Jan. 11, 1900, p. 265.

84. Executive Committee Minutes, April 17, 1906. Trustee Minutes, June 3, 1907, p. 422; June 8, 1908, p. 438.

85. Trustee Minutes, Feb. 7, 1905, p. 16. Reed, *Alumnus,* Nov., 1926, p. 31.

86. *Dickinsonian,* Feb., 1892, p. 1. Ruth E. White, *History of the Methodist Church in Carlisle, Pennsylvania, 1792–1954,* pp. 18, 20–21.

87. It is hard to discern any liberalizing influence of College on Church, while the Church was offering such fare as William Maslin Frysinger's published sermon, *Is Romanism or Protestantism True?* (Carlisle, 1897), and his tract, *Is Evolution Fact or Fiction?* (Healdsburg, Calif., n.d.)—questions for which he had unequivocal answers.

88. Matilda W. Denny to Charles F. Himes, March 7, 1890. Himes Papers, DCA. Trustee Minutes, April 5, 1893, p. 44. Reed, *Alumnus,* Nov., 1926, pp. 27–31, fails to give credit to Himes.

89. Trustee Minutes, Dec. 2, 1896, pp. 145–46.

90. Information from George M. Briner, '07.

91. Reed, *Alumnus,* Nov., 1926, pp. 29, 31.

92. Trustee Minutes, June 6, 1904, p. 5.

93. Trustee Papers, June 2, 1902, Folder II.

94. Moncure D. Conway, Committee on the Junior Class Oration, June 5, 1892. DCA.

95. Trustee Minutes, Feb. 7, 1907, p. 364. Edward W. Biddle, *Moncure D. Conway and Conway Hall* (Carlisle, 1919), pp. 2–3.

96. *Ibid.,* p. 3. Reed to Morgan, Jan. 11, 1916. DCA.

97. Ralph W. Schecter, *Songs of Dickinson* (Carlisle, 1937), p. 28.

98. Reed, *Alumnus,* Nov., 1926, p. 31.

99. Moncure D. Conway, *William Penn Memorial Day, Dickinson College, Commemorative of the 225th Anniversary of the Frame of Government for Pennsylvania* (Carlisle, 1907), p. 12.

100. *Ibid.,* p. 27.

101. Reed, *Alumnus,* Nov., 1926, p. 31.

102. Trustee Minutes, Feb. 17, 1910, pp. 478–79 and Feb. 16, 1911, p. 501. Executive Committee Minutes, Oct. 14, 1910, pp. 135–36, 144.

103. Benjamin Rush, *Essays, Literary, Moral and Philosophical* (Phila., 1806), pp. 183–88.

104. Trustee Minutes, June 3, 1907, p. 426.

105. Trustee Minutes, June 5, 1900, pp. 283–84, record a vote of confidence in Reed. *Dickinsonian,* Dec. 13, 1901 and Jan. 10, 1902, defends him against attacks in the *Pennsylvania Methodist* led by the Rev. Silas Comfort Swallow of Harrisburg, Prohibition candidate for President in 1904. *Ibid.,* May 6, 1903, editorializes against the "brainless puppets" who insulted Reed. James Henry Morgan to George Gailey Chambers, Jan. 11, 1934, DCA, states that Reed's "denial of church control . . . has bothered me all through the years."

106. Central Pennsylvania Conference, *Minutes,* 1908, pp. 105–06. *Ibid.,* 1909, pp. 130–31.

107. Biddle, p. 12.

108. Report of the President, Trustee Papers, June, 1908.

109. *Charter and Bylaws of Dickinson College* (Carlisle, 1966), p. 12. Morgan, p. 448.

110. *The Class of 1870, Dickinson College, Carlisle, Pennsylvania* (Carlisle, 1903), pp. 26–27. Reed, *Alumnus,* Nov., 1925, p. 28 and Aug., 1926, p. 39. *Dickinsonian,* Jan., 1891, p. 5, editorializes that at least faculty and Seniors should be gowned. Trustee Minutes, June, 1893, p. 54: hood and gown recommended. *Dickinsonian,* May 27, 1903, p. 10 and April 27, 1904: faculty have agreed under student pressure.

111. Anna H. Knipp and T. P. Thomas, *History of Goucher College* (Balt., 1938), pp. 135–36.

112. Boyd Lee Spahr to Whitfield J. Bell, Jr., Oct. 20, 1936, DCA, mentions David Henry Carroll as a trustee of both Dickinson and Goucher, "and I suspect he was the most influential in having Dr. Noble named." Knipp and Thomas, pp. 159, 165–67, describe Dr. Goucher's unsound financial policy, and his coolness toward Noble for publishing a statement on it.

113. Trustee Minutes, June 5, 1911, pp. 532–33. *Charter,* pp. 12–13. W. F.

Sadler, Trustee Minutes, 1887, p. 325, had proposed a similar change. Cf. Boyd L. Spahr to Fred P. Corson, Feb. 1, 1935. Spahr Papers, DCA.

114. *Dickinson College Bulletin,* July, 1912, "Inauguration of Eugene Allen Noble as President of Dickinson College. The Commencement Exercises."

115. Information from Dr. Edel.

116. *Dickinsonian,* Feb. 15, 1917, p. 9.

117. Morgan, p. 373.

118. Executive Committee Minutes, Sept. 16, 1913, pp. 193–96.

119. *Ibid.,* p. 198.

120. *Ibid.,* Sept. 26, 1913, pp. 197–98 and Dec. 5, 1913, p. 200.

121. Trustee Minutes.

122. Boyd Lee Spahr to Whitfield J. Bell, Jr., Oct. 20, 1936. DCA.

123. Accepted by Board of Trustees, May 15, 1914. Minutes, p. 589.

124. DCA.

125. *Dickinsonian,* May 27, 1914, pp. 2–3.

Chapter 13. Morgan

1. James Henry Morgan, draft of address to the trustees, Jan., 1914; Boyd Lee Spahr to Whitfield J. Bell, Jr., Oct. 20, 1936. DCA.

2. Catalogue, 1888–89, p. 30.

3. Morgan to A. S. Downing, April 19, 1920, Morgan Papers, DCA: "One of the first acts of my administration was to stop this work for which I felt that we were not well prepared."

4. Morgan to W. M. Yeingst, July 3, 1920. Morgan Papers.

5. Feb. 23, 1928. *Ibid.*

6. Morgan to George D. Crissman, Sept. 7, 1922. *Ibid.*

7. Catalogues, 1924–25, etc.

8. Morgan's oration, *The Politician,* is reported in the *American Volunteer,* June 28, 1877; *Carlisle Herald,* June 28, July 5, 1877; and *Dickinsonian,* July, 1877.

9. James Henry Morgan, *Dickinson College* (Carlisle, 1933), p. 352.

10. *Dickinsonian,* Oct., 1884.

11. *Ibid.,* Jan., 1891.

12. *Ibid.,* Dec., 1885.

13. *Ibid.,* Oct., 1891.

14. Central Pennsylvania Conference, *Minutes,* 1893, pp. 10, 33. Admitted to full membership, *ibid.,* 1895, p. 29.

15. *Dickinsonian,* Jan., 1893.

16. *Carlisle Daily Herald,* Feb. 19, 1896; Feb. 17, 1904.

17. Frysinger Evans to Morgan, Dec. 12, 1924. Morgan Papers. Morgan, p. 375. Trustee Minutes, May 15, 1914. DCA.

18. Morgan, p. 376.

19. Trustee Minutes, June 4, 1921, p. 687.

20. George Edward Reed to William Hoblitzell, Dec. 19, 1901. DCA. Morgan to Miss Nannie Reich, Jan. 14, March 14, 1919; to Mrs. Mary E. Aregood, Aug. 11, 1920. Morgan Papers. Morgan to S. Carroll Coale, May 20, 1922, and statement on scholarship policy, July 24, 1935. DCA. Scholarship claims have continued to be a matter of occasional concern. Executive Committee Minutes, Feb. 3, 1956, DCA, place the value of an unused certificate as "an amount not exceeding the tuition fee of the College at the time of issue."

21. Information from Herbert Wing, Jr. Morgan on "Dickinson in China," DCA.

22. Filler to Dean Robert Williams, May 11, 1921. Morgan Papers.

23. Morgan, p. 388.

24. Mervin G. Filler, "Why They Quit Dickinson," *Dickinson Alumnus,* May, 1924, pp. 10–11.

25. Morgan to Robert Johns Tevorrow, June 23, 1922. Morgan Papers.

26. Mervin G. Filler, "The Last Decade at Dickinson," *Alumnus,* Aug., 1923, p. 25.

27. *Ibid.,* pp. 24–26. Faculty Minutes, June 23, 1919: agreement on "special work looking toward special honors at commencement," and termination of the A.M. *in cursu.*

28. Catalogue, 1922–23. Morgan, p. 382. Information from Herbert Wing, Jr.

29. Filler, "Last Decade," p. 25.

30. Phi Beta Kappa, Alpha Chapter, Minutes, June 5, 1926, p. 107. DCA.

31. April 24, 1926.

32. To Mr. Kellogg, c. June–Aug., 1922. Morgan Papers.

33. Saul Sack, *History of Higher Education in Pennsylvania* (Harrisburg, 1963), vol. 2, pp. 523–24.

34. Trustee Minutes, Jan. 9, Feb. 26, 1913. Boyd Lee Spahr to Eugene A. Noble, Feb. 16, 1914. DCA.

35. Boyd Lee Spahr to Mervin G. Filler, March 15, 1922. Morgan Papers. Trustee Minutes, June 4, 1923.

36. Morgan to President Emery W. Hunt, Bucknell, Sept. 26, 1924. Morgan Papers. Mervin G. Filler, letters to alumni on campus drinking, 1928. DCA.

37. Paul L. Hutchison to William W. Edel, May 14, 1959. Spahr Papers 1003–0–3. DCA.

38. Paul E. Zuver, *A Short History of Carlisle Barracks* (n.p., 1934), p. 135. M. P. Sellers, "Work of the Freshman Dean," DCA.

39. *Dickinsonian,* Feb. 7, 1918.

40. Morgan to Albert E. McKinley, Pennsylvania War History Commission, Dec. 20, 1919. Morgan Papers. Catalogue, 1918–19 lists SATC members.

41. *Dickinsonian* Feb. 6, 1919.

42. Morgan to Penrose, Oct. 3, 1919. Executive Committee Minutes, April 29, 1919.

43. Morgan, report, 1926. DCA. Morgan to Edward J. Horn, Dec. 22, 1919, Morgan Papers, states that there had been no increase in salaries for twenty-five years. Beginning then, he made regular small increases.

44. Morgan, pp. 381, 387.

45. Catalogue, 1916–17 and later. *Alumnus,* May, 1928, p. 10.

46. Morgan to George L. Omwake, Oct. 28, 1927. Morgan Papers.

47. Schecter to Morgan, Oct. 16, 1924. Morgan Papers. Information from Ralph Schecter.

48. Student petition, c. March–May, 1926. Morgan Papers.

49. Morgan to Stough, April 5, 1928. DCA. Information from Whitfield J. Bell, Jr. McIntire, information from D. Wilson Thompson, '21.

50. Information from Dr. Willoughby. "Were You Ever in the Library?" *Alumnus,* Feb., 1924, p. 18.

51. Trustee Minutes, June 3, 1916. Faculty Minutes, March 3, 1917. DCA.

52. March 15, 1922. Morgan Papers.

53. Information from J. Clair McCullough.

54. *Microcosm,* 1916, p. 199.

55. After the war, the proportion of women had increased from 1–4 to 1–3.

Serious opposition in 1923 is described by Morgan to Bishop McDowell, Aug. 9, 1923, Morgan Papers; and the whole matter covered by Josephine B. Meredith, "Women at Dickinson College," DCA. Admission of women to the faculty is discussed by Meredith. Morgan informed Dean F. Louise Nardin, University of Wisconsin, March 24, 1920, Morgan Papers, that women had been admitted to full faculty membership three years before.

56. Minutes, Faculty Committee on Government and Discipline, Jan. 26, 1911, pp. 6, 12–19. DCA.

57. *Ibid.,* Dec. 4, 1912, p. 25.

58. Trustee Minutes, June 8, 1914. Morgan, p. 375. *Dickinsonian*, Nov. 4, 1914 and Feb. 14, 1915.

59. *Dickinsonian*, May 2, 1916. *Ibid.,* Oct. 17, 1919, and Student Senate to Morgan, Oct. 3, 1919, Morgan Papers, on agreement to end after-chapel scraps.

60. *Dickinsonian*, Nov. 17, 1923.

61. Information from D. Wilson Thompson and J. Clair McCullough.

62. Faculty Minutes, June 1, 6, 1923. *Microcosm,* 1924, p. 66.

63. Morgan to George W. Williams on Anti-Saloon League, Dec. 12, 1921; to Franklin C. Southworth, May 2, 1922, and to Willis J. Abbot, May 8, 1924, on drinking; Morgan Papers.

64. Albert J. Bates, '28, to Filler, in Filler letters to alumni, Nov. 1928, on campus drinking. DCA.

65. Information from Ralph Schecter.

66. *Dickinsonian*, Nov. 8, 1928. Meredith gives the daily routine at Metzger. Meredith to Morgan, c. June–Aug., 1922. Morgan Papers. Morgan to Meredith, Nov. 4, 1919, *ibid.,* discusses rules for women and urges self-government.

67. Information from Benjamin D. James.

68. Morgan to Walter E. Harnish, Hedding College, May 6, 1924. Morgan Papers.

69. Morgan, report, Trustee Minutes, June 4, 1923. Morgan to Alfred C. Dieffenbach on fraternities and scholarship, Jan. 2, 1920. Morgan Papers. Faculty Minutes, March 3, 1920, p. 33. *Alumnus,* Nov., 1924, pp. 5–6.

70. *Dickinsonian*, Nov., 1923.

71. Morgan, p. 378.

72. Information from May Morris.

73. Nov. 1, 1927. Morgan Papers.

74. Trustee Minutes, Feb. 27, 1914, pp. 582–83.

75. Mervin G. Filler to Hancher, June 4, 1930, Filler Papers, DCA, declines to nominate a friend of Hancher for honorary membership, describing his resistance to undue liberality in this respect in the past.

76. Trustee Minutes, Feb. 26, 1915, p. 607. Extracts from Minutes, 1922. Morgan Papers.

77. Trustee Minutes, June 2, Dec. 14, 1917.

78. April 29, 1919. Morgan Papers. Morgan to Bishop McDowell, Feb. 10, 1920. *Ibid.* Morgan to John R. Edwards, Nov. 9, 1920. *Ibid.*

79. Marts and Lundy Survey, 1947, No. 126. DCA.

80. Trustee Minutes, June 12, 1920, pp. 672–73. Correspondence with Abram W. Harris, May 15 to July 6, 1920. Morgan Papers.

81. Morgan to Lemuel T. Appold, Nov. 29, 1920; to J. W. Hancher, Nov. 19, 1921; to F. B. Lynch, Jan. 23, 1922. Morgan Papers. Hancher to Henry W. Jordan, Feb. 5, 1924. *Ibid.*

82. Trustee Minutes, Nov. 8, 1921, p. 692.

83. Dickinson College, endowment, album of campaign literature, April–Nov.,

1922. DCA. Morgan to Clyde Furst, Nov. 16, 1922, defending the campaign literature. Morgan Papers.

84. Morgan, Report, June 3, 1922. DCA. Trustee Minutes, June 3, 1922, p. 695.
Trustee Harry L. Price to Morgan, May 31, 1922, "Conference representation will not
relieve the tension." Morgan Papers. Morgan to Charles K. Zug, Jan. 15, 1923; to
John W. Hancher, Oct. 3, 1921; to Lemuel P. Appold, Oct. 31, 1922. Morgan Papers.

85. Clyde Furst to Morgan, Nov. 3, 1922. Morgan Papers.

86. Anna H. Knipp and T. P. Thomas, *History of Goucher College* (Balt., 1938),
pp. 262–69. John W. Gailey to Morgan, June 26, 1922. Morgan Papers.

87. Dickinson College Endowment, Nov. 15, 1922, Papers on the Campaign.
DCA. James H. Morgan, "The Endowment Campaign," *Alumnus*, May, 1923, pp.
7–8.

88. Edward W. Biddle to Morgan, Jan. 2, 1923; Morgan to J. W. Sparks, May 9,
1923. Morgan Papers.

89. Morgan to A. W. Harris, Board of Education, Methodist Church, Nov. 7,
1924. *Ibid.*

90. Appenzellar to B. C. Conner, Jubilee Fund, May 9, 1921. *Ibid.*

91. Appold to Morgan, July 27, 1922. *Ibid.* Trustee Minutes, 1923, p. 706.
Alumnus, Sept., 1936, p. 20. Morgan, p. 448.

92. *Alumnus*, Aug., 1927, p. 11. Henry Logan, '10, in *Dickinsonian* March 28,
1969. Morgan, Report June 2, 1924, DCA, answering Spahr's criticism.

93. Faculty Minutes, Nov. 23, 1915. Morgan in *Dickinsonian*, Dec. 2, 1915.

94. Morgan to Roy Kauffman, Gilbert Malcolm and others, July 20, 1920; To
Frank E. Masland, Jr., Dec. 6, 1920; to Cornelius W. Prettyman, Jan. 23, 1921.
Morgan Papers.

95. Dickinson College Athletic Association to alumni, Jan. 4, 1921, on Killinger;
F. G. Jaggers to Morgan, Oct. 16, 1922; Morgan to President Fred W. Hixson of
Allegheny, Nov. 23, 1922; Morgan to Prettyman, Dec. 21, 1922. Morgan Papers.

96. Morgan to President Henry H. Apple, Franklin and Marshall, Dec. 4, 1920.
Morgan Papers. *Alumnus*, Nov., 1926, p. 12. Morgan to Appold, Jan. 6, 1931, DCA,
on proposal to Carnegie Foundation.

97. *Alumnus*, May, 1923, pp. 7–8. Information from Ralph Schecter.

98. Kappa Sigma to Morgan, Jan. 11, 1923. Morgan Papers.

99. *Alumnus*, Aug., 1924, p. 8.

100. *Dickinsonian*, April 4, 1925.

101. *Alumnus*, Feb., 1927, p. 6.

102. Information from Louis A. Tuvin.

103. *Ibid.*, Feb., 1929, p. 7. *Dickinsonian*, June 8, 1929.

104. Trustee Minutes, June 7, 1929, p. 14. The foundation was initiated by a
series of lectures on Roman writers and statesmen by Robert Seymour Conway,
1930, later published by Harvard University Press.

105. Boyd Lee Spahr to Mervin G. Filler, Dec. 29, 1930. DCA. Trustee Minutes,
June 8, 1925, p. 720, record the authorization of "an educational survey of the
College," on motion of Charles K. Zug, indicating an opinion then that procedures
needed up-dating.

106. Russell I. Thompson, "View of the Future of Dickinson College," pp. 6–7.
Spahr Papers 1003–73.

107. Spahr to Filler, June 23, 1930. Presidents Papers, DCA.

108. Executive Committee Minutes, March 28, 1931.

109. Spahr to Paul Appenzellar, June 17, 1944. Spahr Papers 1003–71.

110. Catalogue, 1931–32, p. 8. Morgan was a member of the Committee on

Trustees, and his correspondence shows his primary interest in the religious affiliations of the membership.

111. John R. Edwards to Boyd Lee Spahr, May 4, 1931; Spahr to Morgan, May 6, 1931. Spahr Papers.

112. Spahr to Morgan on his hope of acquiring the property, July 6, 1925. Morgan Papers. Spahr to alumni, appealing for contributions, Aug. 1, 1932; list of subscribers, Sept. 24, 1932; Karl T. Waugh to trustees, Oct. 20, 1932; Spahr to James G. Steese, Feb. 28, 1933; Spahr to William W. Emmart, architect, July 24, 1937. Spahr Papers 1003.

113. *Dickinsonian,* Feb. 27, 1930. Prompt and angry protest from Clark F. Hoban. Filler Papers, DCA.

114. Faculty Minutes, April 4, 1932 to Feb. 6, 1933. Information from Mrs. Waugh.

115. Trustee Minutes, Feb. 20, 1932; June 9, 1933.

116. Information from Horace E. Rogers.

117. Faculty Minutes, Sept. 16, 1932, pp. 82–85; March 6, 1933, pp. 94–95. *Dickinsonian,* April 6, 1933.

118. Waugh to Oril Brown, Sept. 23, 1932. DCA.

119. Spahr to Morgan, June 27, 1933, Spahr Papers, mentioning Curriculum Committee.

120. Whitfield J. Bell, Jr., notes on a conversation with Mrs. Mary Evans Rosa, '89, Aug. 10, 1936. DCA.

121. Trustee Minutes, June 24, 1933, p. 106.

122. Spahr to Morgan, June 26, 1933. Spahr Papers.

123. Correspondence with AAUP, Nov.–Dec., 1933. Spahr Papers.

124. Faculty Minutes, Sept. 12, 1933. McDowell to Morgan, Sept. 23, 1933. DCA.

125. Information from Dr. Waugh.

126. Dickinsonian, May 24, 1934. Karl T. Waugh, summaries of professional career. DCA.

127. Morgan to John R. Edwards on the visit of Mr. and Mrs. DeWitt C. Baldwin, Nov. 17, 1933. DCA.

128. Hartzell to Morgan, April 3, 1934. DCA. Trustee Minutes, June 8, 1934. *Dickinsonian,* Feb. 15, May 10, 1934. *Microcosm,* 1934. *New Republic,* Feb. 7, 1934, laments the decline of academic freedom at Rollins and Dickinson Colleges and calls for an investigation.

129. Waugh, summaries, June 28, 1934. DCA.

130. Steese to Spahr, Feb. 21, 1933. Spahr Papers.

Chapter 14. The Spahr Years

1. Appenzellar to Spahr, June 14, 1944. Spahr Papers 1003–71, DCA.

2. E.g., Corson to Spahr, Oct. 25, 1940: Miss Morris wants a tea closet in her recreational reading room, "a nicety but not a necessity." Spahr, Oct. 26: Will accept Corson's judgment. Spahr Papers.

3. Information from Mrs. Pauline Lay, secretary.

4. Marts and Lundy, survey report, 1947. DCA.

5. Information from Boyd Lee Spahr, to whom the requirement could be satisfied by Methodist parentage or baptism.

6. Spahr to Corson, July 17, 1940. Spahr Papers.

7. List of donors, June 5, 1936. Spahr Papers 1003–23.

8. Appenzellar to Spahr, June 14, 1944. Spahr Papers 1003–7. He quotes Spahr on the estimate of giving.

9. *Dickinson Alumnus,* Dec., 1936, p. 7.

10. Trustee Minutes, Dec. 17, 1938, p. 223. DCA.

11. *Ibid.,* Dec. 12, 1936, p. 183.

12. *Ibid.,* June 7, 1935, p. 156.

13. E.g., S. Walter Stauffer to Gilbert Malcolm, Sept. 19, 1928, DCA: "My allegiance to Dickinson is tied up largely with my fraternity." A loyal trustee through many years, he here makes his contribution conditional upon fairer treatment for Sigma Alpha Epsilon.

14. *Faculty Minutes,* Nov. 4, 1935; March 15, 1938. Corson to Guy L. Rohrbaugh, Dec. 18, 1936 and April 21, 1937. DCA.

15. *Dickinsonian,* April 18, 1935.

16. Address of President Corson, Faculty Minutes, Sept. 14, 1940.

17. Spahr to Corson, Nov. 21, 1934; Sept. 18, 1935; Nov. 22, 1935; Feb. 10, 1942, on "the obtaining of football boys who are also good students." Spahr Papers.

18. Wilbur J. Gobrecht, *History of Dickinson College Football, 1885–1969* (Carlisle, 1971), pp. 184, 214.

19. Dorothy E. Burns to Morgan, March 5, 1934, with reply. DCA.

20. John B. Nicholson, Jr., to George Shuman, Jr., June 6, 1959. DCA.

21. Russell I. Thompson and John B. Nicholson, Jr., "Significant Influences on General Circulation in a Small College Library," *Library Quarterly,* vol. 11 (1941), pp. 142–85.

22. Spahr Papers 1003–41.

23. Nicholson to Shuman, June 6, 1959.

24. Milton Walker Eddy, "Hair Classification," *Proceedings of the Pennsylvania Academy of Science,* vol. 12 (1938), pp. 19–26. Arthur Larsen, "Detective by a Hair," *American Mercury,* vol. 83 (1956), pp. 117–22.

25. Dickinson College Faculty, questionnaire for Middle States, Sept. 5, 1944. DCA.

26. Trustee Minutes, June 5, 1936.

27. Marts and Lundy Survey report, interviews 80, 82.

28. Faculty Minutes, Dec. 2, 1935, pp. 154–55.

29. Trustee Minutes, June 4, 1937, pp. 192–93.

30. Herbert Wing, Jr., Recommendations of the History Department concerning Reading Periods, Nov. 2, 1939. DCA.

31. Faculty Minutes, Sept. 12, Nov. 2, Dec. 10, 1936; April 7, May 20, 1937. *Alumnus,* Sept., 1938, p. 16. Information from Herbert Wing, Jr.

32. *New York Times,* July 3, 1938.

33. Information from Herbert Wing, Jr. Listed as a two-hour required course for Seniors in the catalogue, 1938–39, 1939–40, it last appears in the 1940–41 issue with the requirement omitted.

34. Dickinson College Curriculum, Jan.–April, 1940. DCA.

35. Correspondence, Corson and President Ching Juu Lin, 1935–38. DCA.

36. Spahr to Corson, Dec. 16, 1941. Spahr Papers. Trustee Minutes, Dec. 13, 1941; Dec. 15, 1945.

37. Spahr to Corson, Jan. 25, 1939; Oct. 21, 24, 1940. Spahr Papers. Brochure on founding dates, Spahr Papers 1003–B. Trustee Minutes, Dec. 14, 1940.

38. Spahr on the inadequacy of library facilities and plan for financing improvements, Trustee Minutes, Dec. 17, 1938, pp. 226–28. Completion of the work, *ibid.,* Dec. 13, 1941, p. 292.

39. *Ibid.,* Feb. 12, 1944, pp. 338–39. *Alumnus,* Feb., 1944, pp. 1–3. In Trustee Minutes, May 21, 1943, Corson had reported, confidentially, a contract "much more favorable" than those secured by other institutions.

40. Merle W. Allen in Marts and Lundy survey report.

41. Spahr to Corson, Dec. 11, 1937; Spahr to Paul Appenzellar, Feb. 5, 1940; Corson to Spahr, May 13, 1942. Spahr Papers. Appenzellar to Spahr, Feb. 21, 1943, in unusually explosive and revealing mood. Spahr Papers 1003–65.

42. Corson to Spahr, Sept. 14, 1943; Spahr to Corson, Dec. 13, 1943 and April 29, 1944; Spahr Papers 1003–65.

43. Trustee Minutes, Dec. 14, 1943. The change is said to have been inspired by a recent appearance of the President of Boston University wearing a unique presidential gown, and has also been related to the gift of "a Purple Silk Coat" described by Charles Nisbet in a letter of July 3, 1793. DCA.

44. Spahr Papers 1003–65.

45. Robert H. Rich to Spahr, June 14, 1944, *ibid.,* 1003–71. Appenzellar had accepted Corson's allowing his name on first ballot, since in Church as in secular politics that was a "favorite son" affair, never resulting in an election.

46. Appenzellar to Malcolm, June 9, 1944. Spahr Papers 1003–71.

47. Drayer to Spahr, June 15, 1944. *Ibid.*

48. June 9, 20, 26, 1944. *Ibid.*

49. Spahr to Executive Committee, June 12, 1944. *Ibid.* Trustee Minutes, June 30, 1944, p. 354.

50. June 23, 1944, Spahr Papers 1003–71.

51. Spahr to Thompson, July 6, 1944. Thompson report, Spahr Papers 1003–73.

52. Charles C. Tillinghast to Prettyman, Nov. 27, 1944, and related correspondence. DCA.

53. Gardner Hays to Spahr, June 19, 1944. Spahr Papers 1003–71.

54. *Free Dickinsonian,* July 17, 1944, p. 1.

55. Prettyman to Spahr, Sept. 20, 1944. Spahr Papers 1003–74. Information from Benjamin D. James.

56. Prettyman to Spahr, June 26, 1944. Spahr Papers 1003–71. Trustee Minutes, Dec. 9, 1944.

57. Oct. 10, 1944. Spahr Papers 1003–74.

58. Marts and Lundy report, interview with Vuilleumier.

59. Trustee Minutes, Dec. 15, 1945.

60. Prettyman to Spahr, Oct. 14, 1944. Spahr Papers 1003–74.

61. Corson to Spahr, May 31, 1944. Spahr Papers 1003–65. Trustee Minutes, Dec. 9, 1944, p. 356; Dec. 15, 1945, p. 382. Spahr to Executive Committee, Oct. 14, 1953. Spahr Papers 1003–75.

62. Correspondence, Nov., 1945. Spahr Papers 1003–25. Information from Whitfield J. Bell, Jr.

63. *Dickinsonian,* May 16, 1946; Oct. 29, 1948.

64. *Attendance Regulations,* Feb. 1, 1946, pp. 1–16, rules; 17–23, penalties. DCA. Faculty Minutes, Sept. 20, 1947, pp. 6–7, removal of fixed penalties.

65. *Dickinsonian,* March 28, 1946.

66. *Suggestions Considered Requisite by the Students of Dickinson College for the Improvement of the College,* Dec. 15, 1945. DCA.

67. *Carlisle Evening Sentinel,* Dec. 8, 1945. *Dickinsonian,* Dec. 13, 1945.

68. Dec. 10, 1945.

69. Spahr to Corson, Nov. 14, 1945. Spahr Papers 1003–25. Arthur S. Flemming to C. C. Sellers, Jan. 4, 1971. DCA.

70. "West Chester State Teachers College," AAUP *Bulletin*, vol. 25 (1939), pp. 44–72.

71. Information from Whitfield J. Bell, Jr.

72. Vide *Microcosm*, 1915, p. 56: "He came from Baltimore with the avowed intention of showing how the college should be run . . . . Bill is a born poet."

73. Trustee Minutes, Dec. 14, 1946, pp. 402–05. *Alumnus*, Feb., 1947, p. 1.

74. Trustee Minutes, Dec. 14, 1946, pp. 402, 405.

75. Faculty Minutes, May 6, 1946, p. 201. Saul Sack, *History of Higher Education in Pennsylvania* (Harrisburg, 1963), vol. 2, p. 615.

76. Faculty Minutes, Sept. 20, 1947; Nov. 1, 1948.

77. Middle States Association, Report, March 7, 8, 9, 1949. DCA. *Alumnus*, May, 1949, pp. 1–3. Trustee Minutes, June 3, 1949, pp. 467–68.

78. Dickinson College Chapter archives.

79. Marts and Lundy report.

80. Trustee Minutes, Dec. 14, 1946. Spahr to Stauffer, Sampson and Masland, Dec. 31, 1946. Spahr Papers.

81. Trustee Minutes, June 3, 1949, pp. 471–72.

82. Faculty Minutes, Sept. 9, 1950.

83. Conference with Ward, Wells and Dreshman, Nov. 25, 1946. Spahr Papers.

84. Trustee Minutes, June 4, 1948. pp. 441–42. Spahr Papers 1003–27–1.

85. Marts and Lundy report.

86. Spahr to Edel, Jan. 9, 1947, Spahr Papers. Trustee Minutes, June 4, 1948, pp. 440–41, 446.

87. William S. Heckscher, *Maces. An Exhibition of American Ceremonial Academic Sceptres* (Durham, N.C., 1970), with related papers. DCA. Mary Dickinson Club, Trustee Minutes, Dec. 4, 1954, pp. 97–98.

88. Catherine S. Eitemiller, '46, to Spahr, Feb. 3, 1953. Spahr Papers.

89. Information from George Shuman, Jr.

90. Shuman to Spahr, Dec. 4, 1958, Spahr Papers 1003–27–1; and Dec. 30, 1958, *ibid.* 1003–1.

91. Spahr Papers 1003–27–1. Trustee Minutes, June 2, 1956, pp. 169–72.

92. Said to have been Oscar Weamer Nestor, Instructor in Economics, 1949–50.

93. Faculty Minutes, May 12, 1950, pp. 262–63. *Ibid.*, Dec. 4, 1950, p. 19.

94. *Ibid.*, Dec. 3, 1951, pp. 98–99; March 3, 1952, pp. 114–16.

95. *Ibid.*, March 5, 1951, p. 35; April 2, 1951, p. 37; April 11, 1951, p. 38.

96. *Ibid.*, April 2, 1951, p. 37.

97. Dickinson College, *Charter and Bylaws* (Carlisle, 1956), sec. 20j, p. 23.

98. Trustee Minutes, June 6, 1952, p. 8.

99. Faculty Minutes, Sept. 15, 1952, p. 190.

100. *Dickinsonian*, April 8, 1949. *Microcosm*, 1951, p. 102.

101. Faculty Minutes, May 29, 1958.

102. Trustee Minutes, June 6, 1952, p. 3.

103. *Ibid.*, Dec. 9, 1950, pp. 511, 513.

104. Faculty Minutes, June 2, 5, 1952, pp. 158, 164. Trustee Minutes, June 6, 1952. "Doll Show," *Dickinsonian*, Dec. 18, 1953.

105. Trustee Minutes, Dec. 9, 1950, p. 513.

106. *Ibid.*

107. July 28, 1952. DCA.

108. Opening, 1949, with "Ladies of the Jury," followed by "The Tempest," 1950. The first Barnes production had been "The Coventry Nativity Play," Dec. 19, 1946.

109. Faculty Minutes, Feb. 2, 1953, pp. 222–23.

110. Spahr to Edel, Nov. 27, 1953; Edel to Spahr, March 23, 1954. Spahr Papers.

111. Trustee Minutes, June 6, 1952, p. 20.

112. Faculty Minutes, April 18, 1955, pp. 172–73.

113. Spahr to Edel, Nov. 27, 1953; Spahr "To the Students of Dickinson College," Aug. 16, 1954; Spahr to Edel, Oct. 30, 1956, admits that the letter to the students had been "largely your composition," although one point was certainly a Spahr insertion, "Also, it will enable the College, as soon as the church is built, to convert the present chapel in Bosler Hall into library space which is most urgently needed." Spahr Papers.

114. George Shuman, Jr., finally informed Spahr, March 4, 1958, that student assemblies and lectures could not be held in the church. The "Methodist sources" have not been published. Spahr was aware, June 30, 1959, of $110,000 borrowed by the College, of which $25,000 had been met by "six conferences or individuals." Spahr Papers 1003–27–1. Trustee Minutes, Dec. 12, 1959, show Malcolm's report of $25,000 from the Kresge Foundation ("I was touched when I turned over the check and found written in long hand, 'In the name and for the sake of Jesus Christ, Stanley S. Kresge.' "). Spahr to Malcolm, Jan. 13, 1960, Spahr Papers 1003–W, indicates that some conferences had failed to make anticipated contributions to the project, while all the support allocated to Dickinson by others was going into it.

115. Trustee Minutes, Jan. 23, 1954.

116. Spahr Papers 1003–83. Edel to Robert E. Woodside, June 1, 1955. Papers of Trustee Committee on College-Fraternity Relations, DCA. Faculty Minutes, April 9, 1956, p. 280.

117. Spahr to Woodside, Jan. 6, 1955. Spahr Papers 1003–83. Trustee Minutes, June 10, 1955, p. 116.

118. Spahr Papers 1003–33.

119. April 27, 1953. DCA. May 30, 1953. AAUP Chapter archives.

120. Whitfield J. Bell, Jr., to Spahr, Jan. 20, 1954. Spahr Papers 1003–B.

121. Trustee Minutes, June 10, 1955, p. 114.

122. *Ibid.*, June 11, 1954, pp. 86–88 and June 10, 1955, pp. 128–33.

123. Trustee Minutes, June 10, 1955, pp. 118–19.

124. Spahr to Chambers, Jan. 8, and reply, Jan. 24, 1958; Chambers to Spahr, April 2, 1958; and Allen to Spahr, April 11, 1958. Spahr Papers 1003–85.

125. Edel to Spahr, March 20, 1956. Spahr Papers 1003–82. Spahr to Executive Committee. *Ibid.*, 1003–15. AAUP *Bulletin*, vol. 44 (1958), pp. 137–38.

126. Faculty Minutes, March 19, 21, 1956, pp. 273–77. Edel to Spahr, May 10, 1956. Spahr Papers 1003–82.

127. Spahr to Malcolm, June 21, 1956. Spahr Papers 1003–82.

128. Spahr Papers 1003–82. Faculty Minutes, May 31, 1956, pp. 291–95. Trustee Minutes, June 1, 1956, pp. 152–55, 160–61.

129. Corson to Spahr, March 28, 1956. Spahr Papers 1003–82.

130. William Wilcox Edel, *John and Mary's College over Susquehanna* (N.Y., San Francisco & Montreal, 1956).

131. Spahr to George Henry Ketterer, April 30, 1956. Spahr Papers 1003–82.

132. Spahr to Malcolm, April 19, 1960. Spahr Papers.

133. Trustee Minutes, June 1, 1956, p. 161; Dec. 8, 1956, pp. 182–83.

134. Spahr Papers 1003–78.

135. Finck to Spahr, April 2, 1958. Spahr Papers 1003–78.

136. Edel to Spahr, Aug. 24, 1956. Spahr Papers. Faculty Minutes, Sept. 24, Oct. 1, 1956, pp. 1, 5–7.

137. Trustee Minutes, Dec. 14, 1958, "this most appropriate timing added interest to the gift."

138. Faculty Minutes, May 31, 1956, p. 296.

139. AAUP *Bulletin*, vol. 44 (1958), p. 661. The committee report appears on pp. 137–50, with reports on other cases of Communist association at New York University, University of Michigan, Reed College, University of Southern California.

140. *Dickinsonian*, May 31, 1958. Malcolm to Spahr, Sept. 23, 1958, on editor Robert Bohi; Spahr to Charles H. Nuttle, Sept. 26, 1958. Spahr Papers 1003–B.

141. Faculty Minutes, Oct. 7, 1957: Edel spoke on "Education for Change," and "The Self-educating Student." Trustee Minutes, May 30, 1957, report the Camp Shand meetings of Sept. 13–14, under the direction of the Dean's office, with 40 separate discussions leading to a report of 70 pages. Kuebler to Ness, Oct., 1957, DCA, with terse disesteem for the published conclusions.

142. Faculty Minutes, May 5, 29, 1958, pp. 182, 191.

143. Trustee Minutes, Dec. 14, 1957, pp. 220–22, 225. Executive Committee Minutes, March 27, 1958, pp. 232 A–B. DCA. Trustee Minutes, May 29, 1958 pp. 239, 249–50.

144. April 29, 1958. Spahr Papers 1003–85.

145. Trustee Minutes, June 4, 1959, p. 277. Correspondence, Spahr Papers 1003–D to G. Frank E. Masland, Jr., to Arthur D. Platt, Dec. 8, 1969. DCA.

Chapter 15. Rubendall

1. Correspondence on the nomination, Spahr Papers 1003–80A, DCA.

2. Corson to Spahr, Feb. 16, 1960, threatening withdrawal. The Church relationship, "outwardly avowed, has been allowed to inwardly slip." Spahr Papers 1003–65.

3. Faculty Minutes, March 3, April 14 and May 5, 1958, pp. 156, 162, 182. DCA.

4. Spahr to Merle W. Allen, May 14, 1959. Spahr Papers 1003–80A.

5. Information from Whitfield J. Bell, Jr.

6. Faculty Minutes, Dec. 3 and 10, 1912. Clippings and other papers on the incident, DCA.

7. Spahr to Malcolm, March 31, 1960. Spahr Papers.

8. Resolution of thanks to Meyer P. Potamkin, Trustee Minutes, Dec. 11, 1959, p. 7. DCA.

9. Spahr to Malcolm, Jan. 6, 1960. Spahr Papers 1003–82; Frank E. Masland to Spahr, March 3, 1960. *Ibid.*, 1003–78; Spahr to Masland, March 9, 1960. *Ibid.*, 1003–94.

10. Minutes, Committee on Academic Freedom and Tenure, Oct. 1, 1958. DCA. Faculty Minutes, Nov. 2, 1959, p. 290. Trustee Minutes, Dec. 18, 1958, pp. 262–63; June 4, 1959, p. 292; Dec. 12, 1959, pp. 16, 22–23.

11. Faculty Minutes, Dec. 7, 13, 1959, pp. 298 ff.

12. Trustee Minutes, June 4, 1959, pp. 277–78.

13. R. E. Nelson to Carl C. Chambers, May 7, 1960. Spahr Papers 1003–85–A.

14. Spahr memorandum, telephone conversation with Allen, June 17, 1960. Spahr Papers 1003–97.

15. *Dickinsonian*, June 6, 1959. Masland to Spahr, June 9, 1960. Spahr Papers 1003–91.

16. Co-eds to trustees, Dec. 28, 1959. Spahr Papers 1003–D to F.

17. *Campus C.R.I.E.R.*, 1960, with letter from the editor, Bruce L. Smith, '61, Dec. 30, 1969. DCA.

18. Spahr to Chambers, May 27, 1960. Spahr Papers 1003–90. Spahr to Malcolm, May 17, 1960. *Ibid* 1003–90–A.

19. Malcolm to Spahr, Oct. 4, 1960. *Ibid.* 1003–25.

20. Malcolm to Rubendall, Nov. 7, 1960. *Ibid.* 1003–94–1.

21. Trustee Minutes, June 2, 1960, p. 31.

22. Progress Report, March, 1960. Samuel W. Witwer Papers 3160–U–6, DCA. Witwer to Malcolm, Dec. 1, 1960. *Ibid.* Trustee Minutes, Jan. 5, 1961, pp. 69–70. Rubendall to Witwer, April 1, 1963. Witwer Papers 3160–U–2(a).

23. Witwer to George Shuman, Jr., April 19, 1961; Witwer to John M. Davidson, Feb. 23, 1961. Witwer Papers 3160–U–6.

24. Witwer to Spahr, Feb. 13, 1961. *Ibid.* Steering Committee Minutes, *Ibid.* Trustee Minutes, Feb. 10, 1961, p. 77.

25. R. E. Woodside to Spahr, Jan. 3, 1961. Spahr Papers 1003–83A.

26. Witwer to Sidney D. Kline, May 3, 1961. Witwer Papers 3160–U–6.

27. Rubendall to Malcolm, July 10, 1961, defining the duties of Provost. Spahr Papers 1003–91.

28. *Dickinson Alumnus,* Feb., 1933, p. 16.

29. Interview with Martha C. Slotten, Dec. 7, 1970. DCA.

30. Robert F. Rich to Spahr. Spahr Papers 1003–94–3.

31. Article by editor Ken Bowling, Dec. 15, 1961.

32. Trustee Minutes, Dec. 10, 1955, pp. 141, 145.

33. Dickinson College, Board of Trustees, "Dickinson College's Interest in the Income from the Dickinson Fund of the Education Fund of the Philadelphia Conference of the United Methodist Church," 1969. DCA. Trustee Minutes, May 31, 1963, pp. 35–40.

34. Bruce R. Andrews, papers of Academic Study, 1962–64. DCA. Trustee Minutes, June 5, 1964, pp. 119–20, 146–48.

35. Wing report, Feb. 6, 1960; Malcolm to Spahr, March 7, 1960. AAUP papers, DCA.

36. Spahr to Malcolm, March 14, 1961. Spahr Papers.

37. M. W. Allen to Spahr, May 5, 1962. Spahr Papers 1003–85.

38. Samuel W. Witwer to Spahr, Nov. 17, 1964: "We are off to a fine start," and citing the effective solicitation of Board members by Sidney Kline and Rolland Adams. Spahr Papers 1003–27–2.

39. Initials to form the word "HUB." Spahr to Masland, Dec. 23, 1964, Spahr Papers defends the use of the word "Union," some trustees having thought it inappropriate to the conservative climate of Carlisle, preferring "College Center."

40. *Dickinson Today,* Oct., 1966, p. 24.

41. Trustee Minutes, Oct. 11, 1968, p. 131.

42. *Dickinsonian,* Nov. 17, 1967.

43. Faculty Minutes, May 6, 1968, p. 63. Trustee Minutes, Jan. 25, 1969, p. 160.

44. Masland to Spahr, Dec. 14, 1959, and reply, Dec. 16. Spahr Papers 1003–33.

45. Faculty Minutes, Nov. 2, 1964, p. 55. One may trace the slow progress of academic change through Russell Thompson's assessment of the value of chapel and severe criticism of its content, 1944, to Kuebler's proposal that it be "replaced by something else," March 2, 1953, the solution finally reached twelve years later.

46. Faculty Minutes, May 4, 1959, p. 257.

47. Dickinson, Gettysburg, Hood, Western Maryland, St. Joseph, Mount St. Mary's. Faculty Minutes, Dec. 4, 1961, p. 134 and April 12, 1962, p. 166.

48. James Henry Morgan, Report to the trustees, June 2, 1917. DCA.

49. Trustee Minutes, Dec. 9, 1950, p. 518 and June 1, 1951, p. 553. Faculty Minutes, Feb. 5, p. 30, March 5, 1951, p. 35. *Ibid.,* Sept. 16, 1957, p. 89.

50. Faculty Minutes, Oct. 6, 1953, pp. 192–93.

51. "A Tri-College Project for the Greater Harrisburg Area," Feb., 1952. DCA. Faculty Minutes, May 9, 1951, p. 41 and June 2, 1952, p. 158.

52. The Consortium began as the "Six-College Faculty International Studies Program." Trustee Minutes, June 2, 1967, p. 234. Relationship with ACLCP reported by Arden K. Smith, Sept. 22, 1970. ACLCP membership had then increased to 15: Bucknell, Dickinson, Elizabethtown, Franklin and Marshall, Gettysburg, Harrisburg, Juniata, Messiah, Millersville, Pennsylvania State University, the University's Capitol Campus, Shippensburg, Susquehanna, Wilson, York. The truck service included 38 libraries.

53. James Henry Morgan, *History of Dickinson College* (Carlisle, 1933), p. 450.

54. Faculty Minutes, Nov. 4, 1946, p. 250. Trustee Minutes, Dec. 11, 1948, pp. 459–60 and June 3, 1949, p. 476.

55. Frederick Rudolph, *The American College and University: A History* (N.Y., 1962), p. 288.

56. From the Christian R. and Mary F. Lindback Foundation.

57. The Constance and Rose Ganoe Memorial Fund. Trustee Minutes, Oct. 11, 1968, p. 3.

58. Malcolm to Spahr, Aug. 22, 1958. Spahr Papers 1003–A to C.

59. Spahr to Edel, Feb. 19, 1959. *Ibid.,* 1003–73.

60. Minutes of "President's Advisory Committee," or "Cabinet," Oct. 21, 1952. DCA.

61. Edited by Hal M. Wells and Edward Rothstein.

62. *Dickinsonian,* Feb. 12, 1965.

63. Student Activity Budget, 1923–24.DCA.

64. Faculty Minutes, June 4, 1953, p. 261.

65. *Ibid.,* May 4, 1959, pp. 264–65.

66. *Ibid.,* April 18, 1966, p. 176 and Dec. 5, 1966, p. 216. *Dickinsonian,* Oct. 7, 1966. Representation began with the Committee on Student Affairs in October, followed by the Policy Committee in December.

67. Faculty Minutes, May 22, 1969, p. 225, permitting committees to give voting privileges.

68. *Dickinsonian,* Nov. 14, 1969.

69. Printed evaluations, 1966–67, DCA, are characterized by severity, and by and by, by the very small number of student respondents.

70. *Dickinsonian,* Oct. 2, 1964; April 16, 1965.

71. *Ibid.,* Dec. 11, 1964.

72. *Ibid.,* Oct. 15, 1965.

73. *Carlisle Sentinel,* April 9, 1971.

74. *Dickinsonian,* April 17, 1970.

75. Robert B. Jefferson, '69, to Rubendall May 17, 1970. DCA.

76. Trustee Minutes, Oct. 11, 1968, pp. 146–47.

77. Faculty Minutes, March 5, 1969. pp. 150–51.

78. *Haverford Horizons,* vol. 67, Dec. 1969, p. 13.

79. Trustee Minutes, June 27, 1968, p. 120.

80. Morgan, Report to trustees, June 4, 1926. DCA.

81. Thom Simpson in his column, "Very Odd Thoughts." *Dickinsonian,* April 9, 1971.

82. Catalogue, 1954–55, p. 48.

The Ceremonial Mace. By Mary O. Abbott, 1951.

Appendix A

PEOPLE

All names are in chronological order, by date of election or appointment.

PRESIDENTS OF THE BOARD OF TRUSTEES

John Dickinson. 1783–1808.
John King. 1808.
James Armstrong. 1808–1824.
John Bannister Gibson. 1824–1829.
Andrew Carothers. 1829–1833.
By charter amendment, from April 10, 1834, to February 19, 1912, the President of the College was ex officio President of the Board.
Edward William Biddle. 1912–1931.
Boyd Lee Spahr. 1931–1962.
Sidney DeLong Kline. 1962–1964.
Samuel Weller Witwer. Jr., 1964–

PRESIDENTS OF THE COLLEGE

The title of "Principal" remained in effect officially until the charter amendment of February 19, 1912, but "President" had had currency at an early date, in keeping with American usage.

Charles Nisbet. 1784–1804.
Robert Davidson. 1804–1809.
Jeremiah Atwater. 1809–1815.
John McKnight. 1815–1816.

The College was closed, 1816–1821.
John Mitchell Mason. 1821–1824.
William Neill. 1824–1829.
Samuel Blanchard How 1829–1832.
The College was closed, 1832–1834.
John Price Durbin. 1834–1845.
Robert Emory. 1845–1848.
Jesse Truesdell Peck. 1848–1852.
Charles Collins. 1852–1860.
Herman Merrills Johnson. 1860–1868.
Robert Laurenson Dashiell. 1868–1872.
James Andrew McCauley. 1872–1888.
Charles Francis Himes. *Acting,* 1888–1889.
George Edward Reed. 1889–1911.
Eugene Allen Noble. 1911–1914.
James Henry Morgan. 1914–1928; 1931–1932; 1933–1934.
Mervin Grant Filler. 1928–1931.
Karl Tinsley Waugh. 1932–1933.
Fred Pierce Corson. 1934–1944.
Cornelius William Prettyman. 1944–1946.
William Wilcox Edel. 1946–1959.
Gilbert Malcolm. 1959–1961.
Howard Lane Rubendall. 1961–

TRUSTEES

Trustees, holding ultimate responsibility for the institution's life and welfare, have a curiously insubstantial place in its history. Many of the names listed here have been difficult to identify. Some remain obscure. Some nominations were made with such easy informality that a gentleman was occasionally elected under another name than his own. The trustees of the old Carlisle Latin school were Presbyterian neighbors of property and repute. Those under the charter of 1783 were similarly men of influence, but with representatives from other denominations and a regional spread to include all Pennsylvania. It was anticipated that some would rarely, if ever, attend Board meetings, but expected that they would support appeals for state aid, recruit students and otherwise show a friendly disposition wherever able.

The College was managed at the outset, therefore, by those who lived in or near Carlisle. They conceived their duties as covering every detail of administration. The same held true elsewhere, as at Princeton and the University of Pennsylvania, sometimes to an even greater degree. Resulting confusions ended at Dickinson with the charter amendment of 1834, making the President of the College President also of the Board. There follows the gradual transformation of the President from a teacher, heading the faculty, to a purely managerial role as the trustees' man on campus.

From 1834, the individual trustees are, first of all, Methodist conference representatives friendly to higher education. Fifty years later, with the growth of invested funds independent of the church-held endowment, their responsibility and character changed proportionately, college trusteeship in the full modern sense coming in gradually after the turn of the century.

Names are followed by life dates, class (Cl.) if an alumnus, dates of trusteeship (Tr.), and professional or business identification. Principal place of residence while in office is given. Inclusion in the *Dictionary of American Biography (DAB)* or *Who's Who* and membership in the American Philosophical Society (APS) are noted.

Trustees of the Grammar School, March 3, 1773 to October 3, 1788

In 1773, the "old College Lot" had been deeded to nine trustees, for the declared purpose of building and conducting a school. They were not, however, like the trustees under the College charter, a self-perpetuating corporation. In 1788, in response to a petition from a number of townspeople, including the survivors of the older group, the property was transferred by an act of legislature to the trustees of the College, who had been administering it for five years. The Grammar School had continued without interruption as the preparatory department of the College. As will be seen below, six of the original nine served also as trustees under the charter.

Armstrong, John, 1720–1795. *(Also Tr., 1783–1794).*
Duncan, Stephen, 1729–1794. *(Also Tr., 1783–94).*
Irvine, William, 1741–1804. *(Also Tr., 1788–1803).*
Lyon, William,
Magaw, Robert, 1738–1790. *(Also Tr., 1783–90).*
Miller, Robert,
Montgomery, John, 1722–1808. *(Also Tr., 1783–1808).*
Stevenson, George, 1718–1783. (Father of George Stevenson, Tr., 1792–1827).
Wilson, James, 1742–1798. *(Also Tr., 1783–98).*

Trustees of Dickinson College from September 9, 1783

Dickinson, John, 1732–1808. Tr., 1783–1808. Lawyer; President Supreme Executive Council, Pa. Philadelphia, Pa. *DAB*. APS.

Hill, Henry, 1732–1798. Tr., 1783–98. Jurist; merchant. Philadelphia, Pa. APS.

Wilson, James, 1742–1798. Tr., 1783–98. Lawyer; Signer Declaration of Independence. Philadelphia, Pa. *DAB.* APS.

Bingham, William, 1752–1804. Tr., 1783–1803. Banker, legislator. Philadelphia, Pa. *DAB.* APS.

Rush, Benjamin, 1745–1813. Tr., 1783–1813. Physician; Signer Declaration of Independence. Philadelphia, Pa. *DAB.* APS.

Boyd, James, 1743–1814. Tr., 1783–87. Presb. clergyman. Bucks County, Pa.

McDowell, John,   –1825. Tr., 1783–1825. Physician. Chester County, Pa.

Muhlenberg, Henry Ernest, 1753–1815. Tr., 1783–1815. Botanist; Lutheran clergyman; Pres. Franklin College. Lancaster, Pa. *DAB.* APS.

Hendel, William, 1740–1798. Tr., 1783–98. Reformed Church clergyman. Lancaster, Pa. *DAB.*

McKnight, John, 1754–1823. Tr., 1783–94; 1815–20. Presb. clergyman; Pres. Dickinson College. Chambersburg, Pa.

Jacks, James   –1802. Tr., 1783–1802. Lawyer; legislator. Lancaster, County, Pa.

Black, John, 1750–1802. Tr., 1783–1802. Presb. clergyman. York County, Pa.

Dobbin, Alexander, 1742–1809. Tr., 1783–1809. Presb. clergyman; schoolmaster. Gettysburg, Pa.

Ewing, James, 1736–1806. Tr., 1783–1806. Legislator; Vice Pres., Pa. Hellam, Pa. *DAB.*

McPherson, Robert, 1730–1789. Tr., 1783–89. Lawyer; legislator. York County, Pa.

Schlegel, Henry, 1735–1811. Tr., 1783–1810. Lawyer; legislator. York County, Pa.

Hartley, Thomas, 1748–1800. Tr., 1783–1800. Lawyer. York, Pa. *DAB.*

Hahn, Michael,   –1792. Tr., 1783–92. Jurist; public official. York, Pa.

King, John, 1740–1813. Tr., 1783–1813. Presb. clergyman. Mercersburg, Pa.

Cooper, Robert, 1732–1805. Tr., 1783–1805. Presb. clergyman. Carlisle Presbytery.

Lang, James,   . Tr., 1783–98. Presb. clergyman. Greencastle, Pa.

Waugh, Samuel,   –1807. Tr., 1783–1807. Presb. clergyman. Carlisle Presbytery.

Linn, William, 1752–1808. Tr., 1783–87. Presb. clergyman; educator. Big Springs, Pa.

Linn, John, 1749–1820. Tr., 1783–1820. Presb. clergyman. Donegal (Carlisle) Presbytery.

Armstrong, John, 1720-1795. Tr., 1783-94. Soldier; politician; jurist. Carlisle, Pa.

Montgomery, John, 1722-1808. Tr., 1783-1808. Jurist; legislator. Carlisle, Pa.

Duncan, Stephen, 1729-1794. Tr., 1783-94. Physician; planter. Carlisle, Pa.

Smith, Thomas, 1745-1809. Tr., 1783-1809. Lawyer; Asst. Judge Supreme Court of U.S. Carlisle, Pa. APS.

Magaw, Robert, 1738-1790. Tr., 1783-90. Lawyer; legislator. Carlisle, Pa.

McCoskry, Samuel Allen, 1751-1818. Tr., 1783-1815. Physician. Carlisle, Pa.

Shulze, Christopher Emanuel, 1740-1809. Tr., 1783-88. Lutheran clergyman. Tulpehocken, Pa.

Spyker, Peter, -1789. Tr., 1783-94. Jurist. Tulpehocken Twp., Pa.

Arndt, John, 1748-1814. Tr., 1783-88. Public official. Northampton County, Pa.

Montgomery, William, 1736-1816. Tr., 1783-94. Jurist; legislator. Northumberland County, Pa.

Maclay, William, 1734-1804. Tr., 1783-96. Lawyer; legislator. Northumberland County, Pa. *DAB.*

Dougherty, Barnard, -1792. Tr., 1783-92. Jurist. Bedford County, Pa.

Espy, David, 1730-1795. Tr., 1783-95. Lawyer. Bedford County, Pa.

McClean, Alexander, . Tr. 1783-88. Westmoreland County, Pa.

Kurtz, Nicholas, -1794. Tr., 1784-94. Lutheran clergyman. York, Pa.

McCleary, William, . Tr. 1783-88. Washington County, Pa.

Montgomery, Joseph, 1733-1794. Tr., 1787-94. Presb. clergyman; public official. Harrisburg, Pa.

Latta, James, 1732-1801. Tr., 1787-1801. Presb. clergyman; educator. Lancaster County, Pa.

Allison, Patrick, 1740-1802. Tr., 1788. Presb. clergyman. Baltimore, Md.

Irvine, William, 1741-1804. Tr., 1788-1803. Physician; congressman. Carlisle, Pa.

Johnston, Robert, . Tr., 1788-1808. Physician; educator. Carlisle, Pa. *See faculty list.*

Snodgrass, James, 1763-1846. Tr., 1788-1833. Presb. clergyman. Carlisle Presbytery.

Creigh, John, c. 1741-1813. Tr., 1788-1813. Jurist. Carlisle, Pa.

Thornburg, Joseph, 1760-1820. Tr., 1789-99. Merchant. Carlisle, Pa.

Duncan, Thomas, 1760-1827. Tr., 1790-1816. Jurist, Supreme Court Pa. Carlisle, Pa.

Stevenson, George, 1759-1829. Tr., 1792-1827. Physician. Carlisle and Pittsburgh, Pa.

Blaine, Ephraim, 1741-1804. Tr., 1792-1804. Commissary General, Cumberland County, Pa.

Cathcart, Robert, 1759-1849. Tr., 1794-1833. Presb. clergyman. York, Pa.

Snowden, Nathaniel Randolph, 1770-1850. Tr., 1794-1827. Presb. clergyman. Williamsport, Pa.

Laird, Samuel, 1732-1806. Tr., 1794-1806. Carlisle, Pa.

McClure, Charles, 1739-1811. Tr., 1794-1811. Farmer. Carlisle, Pa.

Hamilton, James, 1752-1819. Tr., 1794-1819. Jurist. Carlisle, Pa.

Ege, Michael, Jr.,   -1815. Tr., 1794-1815. Ironmaster. Cumberland County, Pa.

Weakley, Samuel,   . Tr., 1795-1821.

Campbell, John, 1752-1819. Tr., 1796-1819. Episcopal clergyman. Carlisle, Pa.

Armstrong, James, 1749-1828. Tr., 1796-1826. Physician. Carlisle, Pa.

McPherrin, Thomas, 1751-1802. Tr., 1798-1802. Presb. clergyman. Hagerstown, Md.

Riddle, James, 1755-1837. Tr., 1798-1833. Lawyer; jurist. York, Pa.

Gurney, Francis, 1738-1815. Tr., 1798-1815. Public official; legislator. Philadelphia, Pa.

Smith, Charles, 1765-1840. Tr., 1799-1824. Jurist. Lancaster, Pa.

Denny, David, 1767-1845. Cl. 1788. Tr., 1801-33. Presb. clergyman. Chambersburg, Pa.

Watts, David, 1764-1819. Cl. 1787. Tr., 1801-19. Lawyer. Carlisle, Pa.

Williams, Joshua, 1767-1838. Cl. 1795. Tr., 1802-21. Presb. clergyman. Carlisle Presbytery.

Young, John, 1763-1803. Cl. 1788. Tr., 1802-03. Presb. clergyman. Green Castle, Pa.

Coleman, Robert, 1748-1826. Tr., 1802-26. Ironmaster; jurist. Lancaster County, Pa.

McConaughy, David, 1775-1852. Cl. 1795. Tr., 1802-34. Presb. clergyman. Carlisle Presbytery.

Brackenridge, Hugh Henry, 1748-1816. Tr., 1803-16. Author; jurist; Justice of the Pa. Supreme Court. Carlisle, Pa. *DAB.*

Herron, Francis, 1774-1860. Cl. 1794. Tr., 1803-16. Presb. clergyman; Founder, Western Theol. Sem. Carlisle Presbytery.

Walker, Jonathan Hoge, 1756-1824. Cl. 1787. Tr., 1804-24. Jurist. Northumberland County, Pa.

Grier, Nathan, 1760-1814. Tr., 1805-14. Presb. clergyman. Philadelphia Presbytery.

Helfenstein, Jonathan, 1784-1829. Tr., 1807-26. Reformed Church clergyman. Fredericktown, Md.

Duncan, James, . Tr., 1807-08. Lawyer. Carlisle, Pa.

Gustine, James, -1845. Cl. 1798. Tr., 1808-20. Physician; planter. Carlisle, Pa.

Alexander, William, -1814. Tr., 1808-14. Surveyor. Carlisle, Pa.

Hendel, Jacob, c. 1771-1836. Tr., 1808-33. Clock maker; public official. Carlisle, Pa.

Davidson, Robert, 1750-1812. Tr., 1809-12. Presb. clergyman; educator; Pres. Dickinson College. Carlisle, Pa. APS. *See faculty list.*

Brown, William Maxwell, . Tr., 1809-26. Physician.

Blaine, Robert, c. 1766-1826. Tr., 1811-26. Carlisle, Pa.

Carothers, Andrew, 1778-1836. Cl. 1800. Tr., 1814-33. Lawyer. Carlisle, Pa.

Lind, John, 1784-1824. Cl. 1802. Tr., 1814-24. Presb. clergyman. Hagerstown, Md.

Pringle, Francis, c. 1748-1833. Tr., 1814-23. Presb. clergyman. Carlisle, Pa.

Chapman, Nathaniel, 1780-1853. Tr., 1815-33. Physician. Philadelphia, Pa. *DAB.* APS.

Stiles, Edward James, 1786-1850. Tr., 1815-27. Carlisle, Pa.

Helfenstein, Albert, 1788-1869. Tr., 1815-26. Reformed Church clergyman. Carlisle, Pa.

Lyon, George Armstrong, 1784-1855. Cl. 1800. Tr., 1815-33. Lawyer; bank pres. Carlisle, Pa.

Gibson, John Bannister, 1780-1853. Cl. 1798. Tr., 1816-29. Jurist; Chief Justice, U.S. Supreme Court. Carlisle, Pa. *DAB.* APS.

Ellmaker, Amos, 1787-1851. Tr., 1816-21. Lawyer; Attorney Gen., Pa. Harrisburg, Pa.

Duffield, George, 1794-1868. Tr., 1820-33. Presb. clergyman. Carlisle, Pa. *DAB.* APS.

Wilson, Henry Rowan, 1780-1849. Cl. 1798. Tr., 1820-25. Presb. clergyman. Shippensburg, Pa. *See faculty list.*

Swartzwelder, John, . Tr., 1820-25. Clergyman.

Graham, Isaiah, -1835 Tr. 1820-34 Tanner; jurist; State Senator Cumberland County, Pa.

Moodey, John, 1776- . Tr., 1820-34. Presb. clergyman. Shippensburg, Pa.

Parker, Isaac Brown, 1783-1865. Cl. 1805. Tr., 1820-33. Lawyer. Carlisle, Pa.

Mahon, Alexander, . Cl. 1805. Tr., 1820-27. Legislator. Cumberland County, Pa.

Knox, Joseph, c. 1776-1827. Tr., 1820-27. Merchant. Carlisle, Pa.

Irvine, William Neill, 1782-1854. Cl. 1798. Tr., 1820-33. Adjutant-general, Pa. Carlisle, Pa.

Alter, Jacob, 1773-1839. Tr., 1820-33. Lawyer, legislator. Cumberland County, Pa.

Boden, Andrew,   -1835. Tr., 1820-27. Lawyer, congressman. Carlisle, Pa.

Dewitt, William Radcliffe, 1792-1867. Tr., 1821-34. Presb. clergyman. Harrisburg, Pa.

Reed, John, 1786-1850. Cl. 1806. Tr., 1821-28. Jurist. Cumberland County, Pa. APS. *See faculty list.*

Ebaugh, John S., 1795-1874. Tr., 1821-33. Reformed Church clergyman. Carlisle, Pa.

Chambers, William Chestnut, 1790-1857. Cl. 1814. Tr., 1821-33. Physician. Carlisle, Pa.

Green, Ashbel, 1762-1848. Tr., 1810-26. Presb. clergyman; legislator; Pres., College of N.J. Philadelphia, Pa. *DAB.*

Ege, Michael, Jr., 1783-1827. Tr., 1824-27. Ironmaster. Carlisle, Pa.

Keller, Benjamin,   . Tr., 1824-33. Lutheran clergyman. Carlisle, Pa.

Grier, John Ferguson, 1784-1829. Cl. 1803. Tr., 1824-29. Presb. clergyman. Reading, Pa.

Hamilton, James, Jr., 1793-1873. Cl. 1812. Tr., 1824-33. Lawyer. Carlisle, Pa.

Lochman, George, 1773-1826. Tr., 1825-26. Lutheran clergyman. Harrisburg, Pa.

Metzger, George, 1782-1879. Cl. 1798. Tr., 1825-33. Lawyer; legislator. Carlisle, Pa.

Mahon, John Duncan, 1796-1861. Cl. 1814. Tr., 1825-34. Lawyer. Carlisle, Pa.

Conyngham, Redmond, 1781-1846. Tr., 1826-27. Legislator. Lancaster, Pa. APS.

Stiles, Benjamin,   -1853. Cl. 1809. Tr., 1826-27. Lawyer. Carlisle, Pa.

Rush, Richard, 1780-1859. Tr., 1826-32. Lawyer; diplomat; statesman. Philadelphia, Pa. *DAB.* APS.

Elliott, David, 1787-1874. Cl. 1808. Tr., 1827-29. Presb. clergyman. Mercersburg, Pa.

Nevin, John,   -1829. Cl. 1795. Tr., 1827-29. Farmer. Shippensburg, Pa.

Agnew Samuel, 1777-1849. Cl. 1798. Tr., 1827-32. Physician. Harrisburg, Pa.

McClure, John, 1784-1841. Cl. 1802. Tr., 1827-33. Farmer. Cumberland County, Pa. *See faculty list.*

Creigh, John, 1773-1848. Cl. 1792. Tr., 1827-33. Physician. Carlisle, Pa.

Chambers, George, 1786-1866. Tr., 1827-34. Lawyer. Chambersburg, Pa. *DAB.*

Penrose, Charles Bingham, 1798-1857. Tr., 1827-33. Lawyer; public official. Carlisle, Pa. *DAB.*

Alexander, Samuel, 1792-1845. Cl. 1812. Tr., 1827-33. Lawyer. Carlisle, Pa.

Schmucker, Samuel Simon, 1799-1873. Tr., 1828-33. Lutheran theologian; educator. Hagerstown, Md. *DAB.*

Blythe, Calvin, 1790-1849. Cl. 1812. Tr., 1828-33. Jurist; Attorney Gen., Pa. Mifflintown, Pa.

Watts, Frederick, 1801-1889. Cl. 1819. Tr., 1828-33; 1841-44. Jurist; Commissioner of Agriculture: founder Pennsylvania State University, Carlisle, Pa. *DAB.*

Hiester, Gabriel, 1779-1834. Tr., 1828-33. Public official, Pa.; iron mfg. Harrisburg, Pa.

Coleman, James, 1784-1831. Tr., 1828-31. Ironmaster. Elizabeth Furnace, Pa.

Haldeman, Jacob Miller, 1781-1857. Tr., 1829-33. Ironmaster. Harrisburg, Pa.

Baird, Samuel, c. 1787-1833. Tr., 1829-33. Lawyer. Reading, Pa.

Paxton, John, 1796-1840. Cl. 1817. Tr., 1829-33. Physician. Carlisle, Pa.

Fridge, Alexander, 1766-1839. Tr., 1829-33. Merchant, banker. Baltimore, Md.

Thorn, John V.E., 　　　　. Tr., 1829-33. Episcopal clergyman. Carlisle, Pa.

Nisbet, Alexander, 1777-1857. Cl. 1794. Tr., 1830-33. Jurist. Baltimore, Md.

Elliott, Jesse Duncan, 1782-1845. Tr., 1831-33. Naval Officer. Carlisle, Pa. *DAB.*

Sheaffer, David F., 　　　　. Tr., 1831-33. Clergyman.

Emory, John, 1789-1835. Tr., 1833-35. Meth. Bishop. Baltimore, Md. *DAB.*

McLean, John, 1785-1861. Tr., 1833-55. Congressman; Postmaster-Gen., U.S.A.; jurist. Cincinnati, Ohio. *DAB.*

Roszel, Stephen George 1770-1841. Tr., 1833-41. Meth. clergyman. Baltimore Conference.

Lybrand, Joseph, 1793-1845. Tr., 1833-44. Meth. clergyman. Philadelphia Conference.

Griffith, Alfred, 1783-1871. Tr., 1833-69. Meth. clergyman. Baltimore Conference.

Harvey, Samuel, 1769-1848. Tr., 1833-48. Merchant; banker. Germantown, Pa.

Guest, Job, 1785-1857. Tr., 1833-36. Meth. clergyman. Baltimore Conference.

Antes, Henry, . Tr., 1833-56. Harrisburg, Pa.

Myers, Theodore, 1801-1839. Tr., 1833-39. Physician. Carlisle, Pa.

Keagy, John Miller, 1792-1837. Tr., 1833-35. Physician; educator. Philadelphia, Pa. *DAB. See faculty list.*

Baker, Samuel, 1785-1835. Tr., 1833-35. Physician. Baltimore, Md.

Davis, John, . Tr., 1833-43. Harrisburg, Pa.

Phillips, John, . Tr., 1833-60. Lawyer. Carlisle, Pa.

Anderson, Matthew, . Tr., 1833-38. Physician. Philadelphia, Pa.

Day, Ira, . Tr., 1833-66. Physician. Mechanicsburg, Pa.

Benson, Richard, . Tr., 1833-44. Philadelphia, Pa.

Sewall, Thomas, . Tr., 1833-45. Physician. Washington, D.C.

Hicks, Henry, . Tr., 1833-37. Del.

Nabb, George W., 1795-1870. Tr., 1833-40. Easton, Md.

Higgins, Samuel H., . Tr., 1833-37. Physician. Wilmington, Del.

Warfield, Charles Alexander, 1787-1868. Tr., 1833-37. Merchant. Williamsport, Md.

Roberts, James, . Tr., 1833-35. Harrisburg, Pa.

Dunlop, James, 1795-1856. Cl. 1812. Tr., 1833-39. Lawyer; legislator. Chambersburg, Pa. *DAB.*

Matthias, Benjamin, . Tr., 1833-50. Newspaper editor. Philadelphia, Pa.

McClure, Charles, 1805-1846. Cl. 1824. Tr., 1833-46. Lawyer; congressman; Sec. of State, Pa. Carlisle, Pa.

Parker, Samuel, . Tr., 1833-35. Philadelphia, Pa.

Biddle, William MacFunn, 1809-1855. Tr., 1833-55. Lawyer. Carlisle, Pa.

Budd, Thomas A., . Tr., 1833-43. Philadelphia, Pa.

Bond, Thomas Emerson, 1782-1856. Tr., 1833-35. Physician; Meth. clergyman. Baltimore, Md.

Longacre, James Barton, 1794-1869. Tr., 1833-69. Engraver. Philadelphia, Pa. *DAB.*

Holdich, Joseph, 1804-1893. Tr., 1833-35. Meth. clergyman. Philadelphia Conference.

Pitman, Charles, 1796-1854. Tr., 1833-54. Meth. clergyman. New Jersey Conference.

Hamilton, William, c. 1798-1872. Tr., 1834-38. Meth. clergyman. Baltimore Conference.

Boehm, Henry, 1775-1875. Tr., 1834-38. Meth. clergyman. Philadelphia Conference. *DAB.*

Watson, James, 1810– . Tr., 1834–39. Lawyer. Washington County, Pa.

Harper, John, . Tr., 1834–47. Carlisle, Pa.

Massey, James, . Tr., 1834–37. Queen Anne's County, Md.

Mayer, Charles F., 1795–1864. Cl. 1812. Tr., 1834–36. Lawyer; legislator. Baltimore, Md.

Thornton, Thomas C., 1790–1860. Tr., 1835–37. Meth. clergyman. Baltimore Conference.

Sorin, Matthew, 1801–1879. Tr., 1835–38. Meth. clergyman. Philadelphia Conference.

Carson, Joseph S. . Tr., 1835–64. Winchester, Va.

Higgins, Solomon, 1792–1867. Tr., 1835–38. Meth. clergyman. Philadelphia Conference.

Thompson, Thomas Jefferson, 1803–1874. Tr., 1835–1874. Meth. clergyman. Philadelphia Conference.

Weaver, Jacob, . Tr., 1835–50. Meth. clergyman. Mechanicsburg, Pa.

Andrew, James Osgood, 1794–1871. Tr., 1836–39. Meth. Bishop. Augusta, Ga. *DAB.*

Tiffany, Comfort, 1797–1879. Tr., 1836–58. Merchant. Baltimore, Md.

Martin, Samuel, . Tr., 1836–38. Physician. Baltimore, Md.

Cookman, George G., c. 1800–1841. Tr., 1836–40. Meth. clergyman. Baltimore Conference.

Ashmead, Samuel, 1771–1856. Tr., 1837–55. Manufacturer. Philadelphia, Pa.

Holden, Henry, . Tr., 1837–40. Newark, N.J.

Hayes, Alexander Laws, 1793–1875. Cl. 1812. Tr., 1837–41. Jurist. Lancaster, Pa.

Wright, James, . Tr. 1837–59. Chambersburg, Pa.

Sargent, Thomas B., 1805–1879. Tr., 1837–66. Meth. clergyman. Baltimore Conference.

Elkinton, John A., . Tr., 1837–50. Physician. Philadelphia, Pa.

Battee, Richard H., 1789–1847. Tr., 1838–47. Baltimore, Md.

Bates, Martin W., . Tr., 1838–48. Dover, Del.

Porter, John S., . Tr., 1838–57. Meth. clergyman. Burlington, N.J.

Janes, Edmund Storer, 1807–1876. Tr., 1838–39. Meth. Bishop. Philadelphia Conference.

Force, Manning, 1789– . Tr., 1838–43. Meth. clergyman. Flanders, N.J.

Davis, John, 1787–1853. Tr., 1838–53. Meth. clergyman. Baltimore Conference.

Scott, Levi, 1802-1882. Tr., 1839-41; 1858-82; Meth. Bishop. Carlisle, Pa. *See faculty list.*

Seymour, William Digley, 1805-1854. Tr., 1839-41. Carlisle, Pa.

Morris, Robert, . Tr., 1839-41. Physician. Philadelphia, Pa.

Waugh, Beverly, 1789-1858. Tr., 1839-58. Meth. Bishop. Baltimore Conference. *DAB.*

Owens, James S., 1804-1866. Tr., 1839-45. Physician. West River, Md.

Carrigan, Jacob, . Tr., 1840-57. Philadelphia, Pa.

Herr, John, . Tr., 1840-45. Baltimore, Md.

Buckman, John, . Tr., 1841-42. Burlington, N.J.

Emory, Robert, 1814-1848. Tr., 1841-45. Meth. clergyman; Pres. Dickinson College. Baltimore, Md. *See faculty list.*

Kennaday, John, 1800-1863. Tr., 1841-52. Meth. clergyman. Philadelphia, Pa.

Bishop, James, Jr., 1816-1895. Tr., 1841-61. Lawyer; congressman, N.J. New Jersey Conference.

Roberts, Charles W., . Tr., 1842-45. Salem, N.J.

Tippett, Charles B., 1801-1867. Tr., 1843-67. Meth. clergyman. Baltimore Conference.

Dodson, Richard W., 1812-1867. Tr., 1843-47. Philadelphia, Pa.

Wright, Archibald, . Tr., 1843-51. Salt merchant. Philadelphia, Pa.

Boswell, James J., . Tr., 1844-50. Merchant. Philadelphia, Pa.

Janes, Edwin L. 1807-1875. Tr., 1844-45. Meth. clergyman. Philadelphia Conference.

Myers, John J., . Tr., 1844-54. Physician. Carlisle, Pa.

Browne, Thomas, . Tr., 1845-50. Georgetown, D.C.

Creamer, David, 1812-1887. Tr., 1845-65. Meth. hymnologist. Baltimore, Md. *DAB.*

Hay, Andrew Kessler, 1809-1881. Tr., 1845-57. Winslow, N.J.

Roszel, Stephen Asbury, 1811-1852. Tr., 1845-52. Meth. clergyman. Baltimore Conference. *See faculty list.*

Durbin, John Price, 1800-1876. Tr., 1845-64. Meth. clergyman; Pres. Dickinson College, Philadelphia, Pa. *DAB.*

Bowman, Jesse, . Tr., 1846-59. Berwick, Pa.

Carter, Richard H., . Tr., 1846-48. Fauquier County, Va.

Ritchie, Albert, . Tr., 1847-56. Physician. Frederick, Md.

Smith, Abraham Herr, 1815-1894. Cl. 1840. Tr., 1847-88. Lawyer; legislator; congressman. Lancaster, Pa.

Bates, Daniel Elzey Moore, 1821-1879. Cl. 1839. Tr., 1848-65. Jurist. Dover, Del. *DAB.*

Conway, Walker Peyton, 1805-1884. Tr., 1848-64. Lawyer. Falmouth, Va.

McClintock, John, 1814-1870. Tr., 1848-59. Meth. clergyman; educator; editor. New York, N.Y. *DAB. See faculty list.*

Barton, S.A.   -1864. Tr., 1848-64. Physician. Chester, Pa.

Allen, William Henry, 1808-1882. Tr., 1850-64. Educator; Pres. Girard College; Pres. Pa. Agric. College. Philadelphia, Pa. *DAB. See faculty list.*

Whiteman, John,   . Tr., 1850-79. Merchant. Philadelphia, Pa.

Stayman, Christian,   -1881. Tr., 1850-81. Clergyman. Carlisle, Pa.

Bird, John Francis, 1816-1904. Cl. 1840. Tr., 1850-1904. Physician; legislator. Philadelphia, Pa.

Baird, Spencer Fullerton, 1823-1887. Cl. 1840. Tr., 1850-57. Naturalist; educator; Sec., Smithsonian Inst.; U.S. Commissioner of Fisheries. Washington, D.C. *DAB.* APS. *See faculty list.*

Cummings, Alexander,   . Tr., 1851-60. Newspaper publisher. Philadelphia, Pa.

Hodgson, Francis, 1804-1877. Tr., 1852-77. Meth. clergyman. Philadelphia Conference.

Peck, Jesse Truesdell, 1811-1883. Tr., 1852-56. Meth. Bishop; Pres., Dickinson College, Washington, D.C. *DAB.*

Reese, Aquila A., c. 1812-1878. Tr., 1854-69. Meth. clergyman. Baltimore Conference.

Kidder, Daniel Parish, 1815-1891. Tr., 1854-55. Meth. clergyman. Newark, N.J. *DAB.*

Tonner, James,   . Tr., 1854-64. Bellefonte, Pa.

Coombe, Pennell, 1811-1884. Tr., 1855-79. Meth. clergyman. Philadelphia Conference.

Miller, William H.   -1877. Tr., 1855-77. Lawyer. Carlisle, Pa.

Pierson, Daniel,   . Tr., 1855-57. Newark, N.J.

Baker, Charles Joseph, 1821-1894. Cl. 1841. Tr., 1855-64; 1869-94. Meth. clergyman. Baltimore, Md.

Morgan, Nicholas J.B., 1811-1872. Tr., 1856-58. Meth. clergyman. Baltimore Conference.

Hiester, Augustus Otto, 1808-1895. Cl. 1828. Tr., 1856-75. Jurist. Harrisburg, Pa.

Wright, John Armstrong, 1820-1891. Cl. 1838. Tr., 1856-91. Civil Engineer; public official. Lewistown and Philadelphia, Pa.

Tunison, W. E.,   . Tr., 1857-58. Meth. clergyman. Newark Conference.

Wilmer, Edwin, 1819-1888. Cl. 1838. Tr., 1857-70. Merchant. Elkton, Md.

Harkness, John C.,   . Tr., 1857-59. Washington, D.C.

Perry, William E.,   -1891. Tr., 1858-91. Meth. clergyman. Trenton, N.J.

Phillips, John H.,   . Tr., 1858-69. Pennington, N.J.

Fort, George Franklin, 1809-1872. Tr., 1858-67. Physician; Governor, N.J.; jurist. New Egypt, N.J.

Williams, Samuel A.,   . Tr., 1858-64. Physician. Alexandria, Va.

Nadal, Bernard Harrison, 1813-1870. Cl. 1848. Tr., 1858-69. Meth. clergyman. Washington, D.C. *See faculty list.*

Carson, John,   -1883. Cl. 1845. Tr., 1859-83. Baltimore Conference.

Woodward, William Ryland, 1819-1905. Cl. 1838. Tr., 1859-1905. Lawyer. Baltimore Conference.

Monroe, Samuel Y.,   -1867. Tr., 1859-65. Meth. clergyman. Trenton, N.J.

Rheem, Jacob, 1810-1899. Tr., 1859-78. Carlisle, Pa.

Harrington, Samuel Maxwell, 1808-1865. Tr., 1860-61. Jurist; Chief Justice, Pennsylvania Supreme Court. Dover, Del. *DAB.*

Cook, Isaac Parker, 1808-   . Tr., 1860-69. Meth. clergyman. Baltimore Conference.

Rusling, James Fowler, 1834-1918. Cl. 1854. Tr., 1861-1883; 1904-1918. Lawyer; Brigadier Gen., New Jersey District. *Who's Who.*

DeLaCour, Joseph Carl,   . Tr., 1862-63. Chemist. Camden, N.J.

Simpson, Matthew, 1811-1884. Tr., 1864-84. Meth. Bishop; Pres., Indiana Asbury Univ. (DePauw). Philadelphia, Pa. *DAB.*

Norment, Samuel,   . Tr., 1864-77. Baltimore Conference.

McCreary, John B., 1819-1879. Tr., 1864-69. Coal merchant. Philadelphia Conference.

Sewall, Thomas, Jr., 1818-1870. Tr., 1864-66. Meth. clergyman. Baltimore Conference.

Crook, Francis A., 1811-1894. Tr., 1864-91. Insurance executive. Baltimore Conference.

Patton, John, 1823-1897. Tr., 1864-67; 1882-97. Congressman, Pa. Baltimore Conference.

Edes, W.H.,   -1865. Tr., 1864-65. Baltimore Conference.

Ellis, F.A.,   . Tr., 1864-77. Philadelphia Conference.

Daniel, William, 1826-1897. Cl. 1848. Tr., 1864-76; 1894-97. Maryland legislator; Senator. Baltimore Conference.

Wright, Caleb E.,   . Tr., 1864-76. Wyoming Conference.

Milnes, William,   . Tr., 1865-67. Columbia County, Pa.

Creswell, John Andrew Jackson (later John Angel James) 1828-1891. Cl. 1848. Tr., 1865-71; 1885-91. U.S. Senator; U.S. Postmaster General. Wilmington Conference. *DAB.*

Emery, M.G.,   . Tr., 1865-78. Baltimore Conference.

Whitecar, Charles H., 1814-1892. Tr., 1865-74. Meth. clergyman. New Jersey Conference.

Chenoweth, George Davenport, 1811-1880. Tr., 1866-74. Meth. clergyman. Central Pennsylvania Conference.

Woodward, Robert C., c. 1807-1877. Tr., 1866-77. Coal dealer. Carlisle, Pa.

Lanahan, John, c. 1815-1903. Tr., 1866-69. Meth. clergyman. Baltimore Conference.

Chattle, Thomas Green, 1834-1889. Cl. 1852. Tr., 1867-89. Physician; New Jersey legislator; Senator. New Jersey Conference.

Crever, Benjamin Heck, 1817-1890. Cl. 1840. Tr., 1867-73. Meth. clergyman; Founder, Williamsport Dickinson Seminary. East Baltimore Conference, 1867-69; Central Pennsylvania Conference, 1869-73.

Hindes, Samuel, -1870. Tr., 1867-70. Baltimore Conference.

McEnally, Joseph Benson, 1825-1910. Cl. 1845. Tr., 1867-74. Lawyer. East Baltimore Conference.

McCauley, James Andrew, 1822-1896. Cl. 1847. Tr., 1869-72. Meth. clergyman; Pres., Dickinson College. Baltimore Conference.

Deale, John Summerfield, 1825-1885. Cl. 1848. Tr., 1869-85. Meth. clergyman. Baltimore Conference.

Gibson, Alexander E., c. 1825-1897. Tr., 1869-87. Meth. clergyman. Virginia Conference, 1869-75; Baltimore Conference, 1875-87.

Chaplain, John Francis, 1824-1880. Cl. 1843. Tr., 1869-80. Meth. clergyman. Philadelphia Conference.

Bodine, William H., -1908. Tr., 1869-1907. New Jersey Conference.

Lightbourne, James H., . Tr., 1869-75. Meth. clergyman. Wilmington Conference, 1869-72; Baltimore Conference, 1872-75.

Shakespeare, William H., . Tr., 1869-77. Wilmington Conference.

Thompson, Walter H., . Tr., 1870-77. Wilmington Conference.

Slape, Albert H., 1836-1898. Cl. 1858. Tr., 1870-82; 1898. Lawyer. New Jersey Conference.

Quigg, John Bolton, 1826-1898. Tr., 1872-82. Meth. clergyman. Wilmington Conference.

Eliason, Thomas W., -1893. Tr., 1872-73. Wilmington Conference.

Dunning, Thomas Stevenson, 1848-1945. Cl. 1867. Tr., 1873-74. Physician. Wilmington Conference.

Mitchell, Thompson, 1817-1897. Tr., 1873-92. Meth. clergyman; Pres., Williamsport Dickinson Seminary. Central Pennsylvania Conference.

Boynton, Jonathan, . Tr., 1874-81. Clearfield, Pa.

Wilson, John, 1823- . Tr., 1874-82. Pres., Wesleyan Female College, Wilmington, Del. Wilmington Conference.

Jackson, Clarence J., -1880. Tr., 1875-80. Central Pennsylvania Conference.

Hunter, James, . Tr., 1875-79. Philadelphia Conference.

Graw, Jacob B., 1832-1901. Tr., 1875-1901. New Jersey Conference.

Milby, Arthur Wellesley, 1818-1886. Cl. 1839. Tr., 1875-84. Meth. clergyman. Wilmington Conference.

McComas, Louis Emory, 1846-1907. Cl. 1866. Tr., 1876-1907. Jurist; congressman, senator. Baltimore Conference. *DAB. Who's Who.*

Herman, Martin Christian, 1841-1896. Cl. 1862. Tr., 1877-78. Carlisle, Pa.

Hendrix, J.W.,   -1885. Tr., 1877-85. Physician. Central Pennsylvania Conference.

Bowman, Shadrach Laycock, 1829-1906. Cl. 1855. Tr., 1877-82. Meth. clergyman; Central Pennsylvania Conference. *See faculty list.*

Sibley, William J.,   . Tr., 1877-91. Baltimore Conference.

Curtis, J.M.,   . Tr., 1877-92. Physician. Wilmington Conference.

Hopkins, Henry, P.   . Tr., 1877-79. Wilmington Conference.

Mallalieu, Thomas F.   . Tr., 1877-90. Wilmington Conference.

Sadler, Wilbur Fisk, 1840-1916. Tr., 1878-92. Lawyer. Central Pennsylvania Conference. *Who's Who.*

Mullin, Charles H.,   -1908. Tr., 1878-1908. Paper manufacturer. Central Pennsylvania Conference.

Hendrickson, Charles Elvin, 1843-1919. Tr., 1878-91; 1896-1902. Jurist. New Jersey Conference.

Mitchell, John T.,   . Tr., 1878-85. Baltimore Conference.

Albright, Charles, 1830-1880. Cl. 1852. Tr., 1879-80. Lawyer; congressman. Philadelphia Conference.

Todd, Jacob, 1838-1899. Cl. 1866. Tr., 1879-80. Meth. clergyman. Philadelphia Conference.

McKeehan, Charles Watson, 1842-1895. Cl. 1867. Tr., 1879-95. Lawyer. Philadelphia Conference.

Paxson, William J., 1826-1898. Tr., 1879-98. Meth. clergyman. Philadelphia Conference.

Groves, James H.,   . Tr., 1879-83. Wilmington Conference.

Hargis, James Hepburn, 1847-1895. Cl. 1870. Tr., 1880-83. Meth. clergyman. Carlisle, Pa.

Jackson, Mordecai W.,   -1894. Tr., 1880-94. Central Pennsylvania Conference.

Storm, John Brown, 1838-1901. Cl. 1861. Tr., 1880-1901. Congressman. Philadelphia Conference.

Boswell, William Laws, 1828-1913. Cl. 1848. Tr., 1881-1912. Meth. clergyman. Philadelphia Conference. *See faculty list.*

Pitcairn, Hugh,   . Tr., 1881-90. Physician. Central Pennsylvania Conference.

Andrews, Edward Gayer, 1825-1907. Tr., 1882-88. Meth. Bishop. Washington, D.C. *DAB. Who's Who.*

Hodson, Thomas Sherwood, 1837–1920. Tr., 1882–86. Meth. clergyman, lawyer, legislator, editor. Wilmington Conference.

Hill, Charles, c. 1822–1892. Tr., 1882–85. Meth. clergyman. Wilmington Conference.

Young, Jesse Bowman, 1844–1914. Cl. 1868. Tr., 1882–88. Meth. clergyman. Central Pennsylvania Conference. *DAB. Who's Who.*

Fisk, Clinton Bowen, 1828–1890. Tr., 1882–90. Founder, Fisk Univ. New Jersey Conference. *DAB.*

Hunt, German Horton, 1829–1907. Tr., 1883–90. Banker, foundry exec. Baltimore Conference.

Tome, Jacob, 1810–1898. Tr., 1883–98. Banker. Baltimore Conference. *DAB.*

Diverty, James,   –1890. Tr., 1883–90. Jurist. New Jersey Conference.

Long, James, 1822–   . Tr., 1883–98. Manufacturer. Philadelphia Conference.

Jackson, Job H.,   . Tr., 1884–88. Wilmington Conference.

Pattison, Robert Emory, 1850–1904. Tr., 1885–88; 1890–1904; Lawyer; Governor, Pennsylvania. *DAB. Who's Who.*

Carroll, David Henry, 1840–1912. Cl. 1868. Tr., 1885–1912. Meth. clergyman. Baltimore Conference.

Beaver, Thomas, 1814–1891. Tr., 1885–91. Central Pennsylvania Conference.

Boyle, John Richards, 1844–   . Tr., 1885–87. Meth. clergyman. Wilmington Conference.

Jones, William J., 1829–   . Tr., 1886–93. Lawyer, editor, legislator. Wilmington Conference.

Widerman, Luther Thomas, 1840–1917. Tr., 1887–1917. Meth. clergyman. Baltimore Conference.

Jones, Richard Clay, 1844–1921. Tr., 1887–91. Meth. clergyman. Wilmington Conference.

Hurst, John Fletcher, 1834–1903. Cl. 1854. Tr., 1888–91. Meth. Bishop. Washington, D.C. *DAB. Who's Who. See faculty list.*

Foss, Cyrus David, 1834–1910. Tr., 1888–99. Meth. Bishop; Pres. Wesleyan University. Philadelphia, Pa. *DAB. Who's Who.*

Allison, William Clare,   –1891. Tr., 1888–91. Car manufacturer. Philadelphia Conference.

Corner, George Washington, 1821–   . Cl. 1841. Tr., 1888–89. Baltimore Conference.

Evans, William Wilson, 1840–1916. Tr., 1888–1916. Meth. clergyman. Central Pennsylvania Conference.

Dashiell, John Hutson, 1821–1914. Cl. 1840. Tr., 1889–1901. Meth. clergyman. Baltimore Conference.

Murray, S. W.,   . Tr., 1890-1900. Central Pennsylvania Conference.

Urner, Milton George, 1839-1926. Tr., 1890-1902. Maryland Congressman. Baltimore Conference.

Mullin, James T.,   . Tr., 1890-91. Wilmington Conference.

Knight, Henry W., c. 1846-1917. Tr., 1891-92. Publisher. New York, N.Y.

Mullin, William D., c. 1826-1899. Tr., 1891-96. New Jersey Conference.

Yard, James S.,   . Tr., 1891-93. Freehold, N.J.

Shoemaker, Clement Waters, 1848-1914. Tr., 1891-1900. Glass manufacturer. Bridgeton, N.J.

McFadden, Alexander H.,   -1900. Tr., 1891-1900. Iron manufacturer. Philadelphia Conference.

Hooper, Alcaeus, c. 1859-1938. Tr., 1891-93. Manufacturer. Baltimore Conference.

Birch, W. Taylor,   . Tr., 1891-96. Baltimore Conference.

Skirm, William H.,   -1905. Tr., 1891-99. State legislator. New Jersey Conference.

Low, Myron J.,   . Tr., 1891-96. Central Pennsylvania Conference.

Jackson, William Humphreys, 1839-1915. Tr., 1891-1905. Maryland Congressman. Wilmington Conference. *Who's Who.*

Martindale, Thomas E., c. 1843-1917. Tr., 1891-1917. Meth. clergyman. Wilmington Conference.

Lippincott, Benjamin Crispin, 1827-1912. Cl. 1858. Tr., 1891-1911. Meth. clergyman. New Jersey Conference.

Pyle, Joseph,   . Tr., 1892-95. Wilmington Conference.

Cappell, George S.,   . Tr., 1892-93. Wilmington Conference.

Carnegie, Andrew, 1835-1919. Tr., 1892-94. Industrialist. Pittsburgh, Pa. *DAB. Who's Who.* APS.

Bradley, Thomas,   . Tr., 1892-1900. Philadelphia Conference.

Stephens, William Alexander, 1835-1921. Cl. 1864. Tr., 1892-1920. Central Pennsylvania Conference.

Shakespeare, Edward Oram, 1846-1900. Cl. 1867. Alumni Tr. 1892-99. Philadelphia District.

Cannon, Henry Pervis, 1847-1930. Cl. 1870. Alumni Tr., 1892-1930. Wilmington District.

Hastings, Daniel Hartman., 1849-1903. Tr., 1893-1903. Governor, Pennsylvania. Bellefont, Pa. *Who's Who.*

Bosler, John Herman, 1830-1893. Cl. 1854. Tr., 1893. Bus. Exec. Central Pennsylvania Conference.

Mullin, Alfred Foster, 1837-   . Cl. 1858. Alumni Tr., 1893-97. Principal, Dickinson Grammar School; paper manufacturer. Carlisle District.

Swindells, William M., c. 1843-1896. Tr., 1893-96. Meth. clergyman. Philadelphia Conference.

Dobbins, John Young, 1850-1917. Cl. 1875. Alumni Tr. 1893-96. Meth. clergyman. New Jersey Conference.

Allison, William Clare, Jr., . Cl. 1893. Tr., 1894-1906. Lawyer. Philadelphia, Pa.

Powell, George K., . Tr., 1894-96. Wilkes-Barre, Pa.

Barrett, Louis E., c. 1844-1922. Tr., 1894-1915. Meth. clergyman. Wilmington Conference.

Holland, Joseph E., . Tr., 1894-1919. Wilmington Conference.

Bursk, John S., -1934. Tr., 1895-1912. Merchant; Treasurer, Dickinson College. Central Pennsylvania Conference.

Wilson, Henry Merryman, 1829-1918. Cl. 1848. Tr., 1895-1914. Physician; teacher. Baltimore Conference.

Cole, Robert Clinton, 1857-1914. Cl. 1879. Alumni Tr., 1895-99. Baltimore District.

King, Horatio Collins, 1837-1918. Cl. 1858. Tr., 1896-1918, Lawyer; editor; soldier. (Congressional Medal of Honor). Brooklyn, N.Y. *Who's Who.*

Smith, Thomas C., -1913. Tr., 1896-1913. Physician. Baltimore Conference.

Lore, Charles Brown, 1831-1911. Cl. 1852. Tr., 1896-1909. Attorney Gen., Del.; Congressman; Chief Justice, Del. Wilmington Conference. *Who's Who.*

Bosler, Frank C., 1869-1919. Cl. 1890. Tr., 1897-1919. Lawyer. Carlisle, Pa.

Lippincott, Joshua Allan, 1835-1906. Cl. 1858. Tr., 1897-1906. Meth. clergyman; Pres., University of Kansas. Philadelphia Conference. *See faculty list.*

McCombs, Robert S., 1848-99. Tr., 1897-99. Physician. Philadelphia Conference.

Bosley, William Henry, 1849-1916. Cl. 1870. Tr., 1898-1906. Banker. Baltimore Conference.

Lynch, Frank Brice, 1843-1925. Tr., 1898-1925. Meth. clergyman. Philadelphia Conference.

Biddle, Edward William, 1852-1931. Cl. 1870. Tr., 1898-1931. Lawyer; Judge. Central Pennsylvania Conference. *Who's Who.*

Patton, Alexander Ennis, 1852-1904. Tr., 1898-1904. Banker, legislator. Central Pennsylvania Conference.

Woodin, William Hartman, 1868-1934. Tr., 1898-1910. U.S. Sec. Treasury. Central Pennsylvania Conference. *DAB. Who's Who.*

Connell, William 1827-1909. Tr., 1899-1904. Congressman; coal operator. Scranton, Pa. *Who's Who.*

Secor, John A., . Tr., 1899-1915. Brooklyn, N.Y.

Lloyd, John Zacharias, 1818-1903. Tr., 1899-1903. Meth. clergyman. Central Pennsylvania Conference.

Wight, George Bates, 1841 -1916. Tr., 1899-1916. Meth. clergyman. New Jersey Conference.

Shelmerdine, William H., . Tr., 1899-1901. Philadelphia Conference.

Willis, George Roberts, 1851-1919. Cl. 1872. Tr., 1899-1903; 1914-19. Lawyer, Prof. Law Balt. Univ. Baltimore.

Melick, John P., 1858-1924. Cl. 1878. Tr., 1900-13. Public official. Central Pennsylvania Conference.

Kessler, George, . Tr., 1900-06. Banker. Philadelphia Conference.

Wilson, Luther Barton, 1856-1928. Cl. 1875. Tr., 1901-28. Meth. Bishop. Baltimore Conference. *Who's Who.*

Field, John, . Tr., 1901-02. Banker. Philadelphia Conference.

Davis, William Potter, 1846-1917. Cl. 1868. Tr., 1901-17. Meth. clergyman. New Jersey Conference.

Ayres, Maurice B., . Tr., 1901-03. New Jersey Conference.

Boyer, William DeWald, 1867-1945. Cl. 1888. Tr., 1901-03; 1907-15. Coal business executive; lawyer. Scranton, Pa.

Prettyman, Cornelius Wiltbank, 1844-1928. Cl. 1872. Tr., 1901-28. Meth. clergyman. Wilmington Conference.

Appold, Lemuel Towers, 1862-1936. Cl. 1882. Tr., 1902-36. Lawyer, banker. Baltimore, Md.

Greene, Stephen W., -1908. Tr., 1902-08. Printer, engraver. Philadelphia Conference.

Heisler, William H., -1903. Tr., 1902-03. New Jersey Conference.

Zug, Charles Keller, 1860-1929. Cl. 1880. Alumni Tr., 1902-29. Lawyer, banker. Philadelphia District.

Clarke, Asbury J., 1841-1907. Cl. 1863. Alumni Tr., 1903-07. Carlisle District.

Taneyhill, George Lane, 1840-1916. Alumni Tr., 1903-15. Physician. Baltimore District.

Prettyman, Charles B., 1865-1936. Tr., 1903-15. Realtor, builder. Wilmington Conference.

Chandler, D. Harry, . Tr., 1904-11. New Jersey District.

Detrick, Reuben Baxter, 1827-1905. Cl. 1852. Tr., 1904-05. Physician; U.S. Treasury official. Baltimore District.

Paterson, Alexander, 1857-1928. Cl. 1886. Tr., 1904-11. Lawyer; ceramics engineer. Clearfield, Pa.

Speer, C. Price, -1939. Tr., 1904-39. Central Pennsylvania District.

Stokes, Edward Casper, 1860-1942. Tr., 1905-15. Gov. of N.J.; banker. New Jersey District. *Who's Who.*

Biddle, Edward MacFunn, Jr., 1865-1955. Cl. 1886. Tr., 1905-55. Lawyer; judge. Central Pennsylvania District. Carlisle, Pa.

Shepherd, James P. . Tr., 1905-11. Scranton, Pa.

McCurley, Isaac, 1840- . Cl. 1862. Tr., 1905-15. Baltimore District.

Jackson, William Purnell, 1868-1939. Tr., 1905-09. U.S. Senator; Treasurer, Md. Wilmington District. *Who's Who.*

Straw, Charles Wesley, 1863-1949. Cl. 1889. Tr., 1906-34. Meth. clergyman. Philadelphia District.

Baker, James Henry, 1872-1954. Cl. 1893. Tr., 1906-54. Lawyer. Baltimore District.

Crider, George A., . Tr., 1906-10. Clergyman. Philadelphia District. *See faculty list.*

Spahr, Boyd Lee, 1880-1970. Cl. 1900. Tr., 1908-70. Lawyer. Philadelphia District. *Who's Who. See Conway Hall List.*

Bond, Franklin Fillmore, 1854-1928. Cl. 1883. Tr., 1908-14. Meth. clergyman. Philadelphia District.

Huber, Harry I., 1873-1945. Cl. 1898. Alumni Tr., 1908-15. Lawyer. Brooklyn, N.Y.

Urner, Hammond, 1868-1942. Cl. 1890. Tr., 1908-11. Lawyer, jurist. Baltimore District. *Who's Who.*

Jones, Robley Dunglison, 1860-1917. Tr., 1909-14. Snow Hill, Md.

Woodcock, William Lee, 1844-1935. Tr., 1909-35. Altoona, Pa.

Hepburn, Charles Japy, 1872-1942. Cl. 1892. Alumni Tr., 1908-16. Lawyer. Philadelphia District.

Chenoweth, George Durbin, 1847-1930. Cl. 1868. Tr., 1909-30. Civil engineer. New Jersey District.

Baughman, Joseph J., . Tr., 1910-13. Central Pennsylvania District.

Gambrill, Melville, 1849-1925. Tr., 1910-25. Cotton mfg. Wilmington District.

Shaw, Leslie Mortier, 1848-1932. Tr., 1910-13. Governor, Iowa; U.S. Sec. of Treasury. Philadelphia District. *DAB. Who's Who.*

Davison, George Willets, 1872-1953. Tr., 1912-14. Lawyer, banker. New York, N.Y. *Who's Who.*

Irving, Robert W., -1918. Tr., 1912-18. Lawyer. Carlisle, Pa.

Simpson, Alexander, Jr., 1855-1935. Tr., 1912-23. Judge, Pennsylvania Supreme Court. Philadelphia, Pa. *Who's Who.*

Salmon, Wilmer Wesley, 1866-1936. Cl. 1886. Tr., 1913-32. Rail industry executive. Rochester, N.Y. *Who's Who.*

Bosler, Abram, 1884-1930. Cl. 1905. Tr., 1914-30. Banker. Carlisle, Pa.

Watt, Robert, c. 1856–1926. Tr., 1914–23. Meth. clergyman. Wilmington Conference.

Hoover, Thomas Leonard, 1880–1916. Cl. 1900. Tr., 1914–16. New York, N.Y.

Berry, Joseph Flintoft, 1856–1931. Tr., 1914–21. Meth. Bishop. Philadelphia, Pa. *Who's Who.*

Johnson, Lloyd Wellington, 1879–1962. Cl. 1903. Alumni Tr., 1915–62. Educator. Caldwell, N.J.

Appenzellar, Paul Peyton, 1875–1953. Cl. 1895. Tr., 1916–17; 1921–44. Instructor, Dickinson Prep. School; financier. New York, N.Y.

Burns, Charles Wesley, 1874–1938. Cl. 1896. Tr., 1916–28. Meth. Bishop. Minneapolis, Minn. *Who's Who.*

Vale, Ruby R., 1874–1961. Cl. 1896. Alumni Tr., 1917–61. Lawyer. Philadelphia, Pa.

Rich, Robert Fleming, 1883–1968. Cl. 1907. Tr., 1917–68. Congressman; wool mfg. Woolrich, Pa. *Who's Who.*

McDowell, William Fraser, 1858–1937. Tr., 1917–33. Meth. Bishop. Washington, D.C. *Who's Who.*

Baker, G. Harold, 1884–1957. Cl. 1910. Tr., 1917–57. U.S. Civil Service. Aberdeen, Md.

Randolph, Herbert F., 1872–194?. Cl. 1893. Tr., 1917–19. Meth. clergyman. Wilmington, Del.

MacAlarney, Robert Emmet, 1873–1945. Cl. 1893. Alumni Tr., 1917–21. Editor; writer. New York, N.Y. *Who's Who.*

Heisse, John Frederick, 1862–1923. Cl. 1886. Tr., 1917–23. Meth. clergyman. Baltimore, Md.

Alcock, John Leighton, c. 1868–1957. Tr., 1917–20. Lumberman. Baltimore, Md.

Haddon, Charles K., 1866–1935. Tr., 1918–28. Banker; business exec. Haddonfield, N.J.

Gravatt, Holmes Francis, 1866–1920. Tr., 1918–20. Meth. clergyman. Camden, N.J.

Steese, James Gordon, 1882–1958. Cl. 1902. Tr., 1919–55. General, U.S. Army. Washington, D.C. *Who's Who.*

Rhey, John McFeely, 1858–1950. Cl. 1883. Tr., 1920–50. Lawyer. Carlisle, Pa.

Heckman, Edgar Rohrer, 1875–1948. Cl. 1897. Tr., 1920–48. Meth. clergyman. Harrisburg, Pa.

Hays, George Metzger, 1873–1930. Cl. 1893. Tr., 1920–30. Lawyer; business exec. Carlisle, Pa.

Edwards, John Rogers, 1871–1945. Cl. 1896. Tr., 1920–45. Meth. clergyman. Washington, D.C.

Souders, Walter Grant, 1871–1934. Cl. 1898. Tr., 1921–34. Business exec. Chicago, Ill.

Stevens, Emory Miller, 1858–1927. Tr., 1923–26. Meth. clergyman. Central Pennsylvania Conference.

Phelps, Andrew Henry, 1888–1962. Tr., 1923–62. Sales economist. Mt. Lebanon, Pa. *Who's Who.*

Colona, James Wesley, 1872–1946. Cl. 1899. Tr., 1923–46. Meth. clergyman. Wilmington, Del.

Boyd, William, c. 1863–1937. Tr., 1923–37. Advertising exec. Philadelphia, Pa.

Couse, William J., c. 1873–1953. Tr., 1924–35. Banker. Asbury Park, N.J.

Hoffman, Dean Meck, 1880–1968. Cl. 1902. Tr., 1925–55. Newspaperman. Harrisburg, Pa. *Who's Who.*

Cannon, Harry Laws, 1878–1944. Cl. 1899. Tr., 1926–34. Business exec. Bridgeville, Del.

Richardson, Ernest Gladstone, 1874–1947. Cl. 1896. Tr., 1928–47. Meth. Bishop. Philadelphia. *Who's Who.*

Haldeman, Merrill James, 1882–1946. Cl. 1903. Tr., 1928–44. Banker, realtor, merchant. Detroit, Mich.

Gill, Harry, Walter, 1881–1944. Cl. 1907. Tr., 1928–44. Lawyer. Atlantic City, N.J.

Stauffer, S. Walter, 1888– . Cl. 1912. Alumni Tr., 1930–69. Congressman; business exec. York, Pa. *Who's Who.*

Landis, Merkel, 1875–1960. Cl. 1896. Alumni Tr., 1930–44; Tr. 1944–60. Lawyer; banker. Carlisle, Pa.

Bacon, Lewis Martin, Jr., 1881–1953. Cl. 1902. Alumni Tr., 1930–53. Business exec. Baltimore, Md.

Caldwell, James Hope, 1860–1941. Cl. 1880 Tr., 1930–41. Lawyer. New York, N.Y.

Ruhl, Christian H., 1853–1937. Cl. 1874. Tr., 1930–37. Lawyer. Reading, Pa.

Stuart, Robert Young, 1883–1933. Cl. 1903. Alumni Tr., 1930–33. Pennsylvania State Commissioner of Forestry. Washington, D.C.

Hays, Raphael Smead, 1875–1954. Cl. 1894. Tr., 1931–54. Business exec. Carlisle, Pa.

Morgan, James Henry, 1857–1939. Cl. 1878. Tr., 1931–39. Pres., Dickinson College. Carlisle, Pa. *Who's Who.*

McFarland, J. Horace, 1859–1948. Tr., 1932–48, Printer; horticulturist. Harrisburg, Pa.

Duke, Charles Clarke, 1882–1964. Tr., 1932–61. Banker. Baltimore, Md.

Chambers, George Gailey, 1873–1935. Cl. 1902. Tr., 1932–35. Educator. Philadelphia, Pa.

Feroe, Robert A., 1886–1950. Tr., 1932–50. Business exec. Pottstown, Pa.

Hughes, Edwin Holt, 1866–1950. Tr., 1932–49. Meth. Bishop. Washington, D.C. *Who's Who.*

Drayer, Sumner Mathias, 1872–1967. Cl. 1902. Tr., 1933–67. Business exec. Baltimore, Md.

Biddle, Edward MacFunn, 1886–1950. Cl. 1905. Tr., 1933–42. Lawyer. Philadelphia, Pa.

Kitto, Charles White, 1888–1960. Cl. 1912. Tr., 1934–56. Meth. clergyman. Philadelphia, Pa.

Price, Harry Linwood, 1873–1950. Cl. 1896. Alumni Tr., 1934–50. Lawyer. Baltimore, Md.

Heller, Eugene Foster,   –1940. Cl. 1904. Tr., 1935–40. Lawyer; judge. Wilkes-Barre, Pa.

Richards, Robert Havens, 1873–1951. Cl. 1895. Tr., 1935–51. Lawyer. Public official. Wilmington, Del. *Who's Who.*

Pettinos, Charles E., 1870–1951. Cl. 1892. Tr., 1935–1951. Manufacturer. New York, N.Y.

McConnell, Francis John, 1871–1953. Tr., 1935–44. Meth. Bishop. New York, N.Y. *Who's Who.*

Ketterer, George Henry, 1880–1958. Cl. 1908. Tr., 1937–58. Meth. clergyman. Altoona, Pa.

Goodyear, Samuel M., 1871–1955. Tr., 1937–55. Business exec. Carlisle, Pa.

Hering, George Clark, Jr., 1894–1951. Cl. 1917. Tr., 1939–50. Lawyer. Wilmington, Del.

Kremer, James Brainerd, 1876–1944. Cl. 1897. Tr., 1939–44. Insurance exec. New York, N.Y.

Leonard, Adna Wright, 1874–1943. Tr., 1941–43. Meth. Bishop. Washington, D.C. *Who's Who.*

Gay, Charles Richard, c. 1876–1946. Tr., 1942–46. Stockbroker. New York, N.Y.

Richards, Karl E., 1887–1969. Cl. 1910. Tr., 1943–62. Jurist. Harrisburg, Pa.

Buckley, James T., 1896–1971. Tr., 1943–71. Business exec. Philadelphia, Pa. *Who's Who.*

Mohler, Roy William, 1892–1964. Cl. 1917. Alumni Tr., 1944–50; Tr. 1950–64. Physician. Philadelphia, Pa.

Flint, Charles Wesley, 1878–1964. Tr., 1944–52. Chancellor, Syracuse Univ.; Pres., Cornell Coll.; Meth. Bishop. Washington, D.C. *Who's Who.*

Corson, Fred Pierce, 1896–   . Cl. 1917. Tr., 1944–67. Meth. Bishop; Pres., Dickinson College. Philadelphia, Pa. *Who's Who.*

Lloyd, George Edgar, 1878–1950. Cl. 1901. Tr., 1945–50. Lawyer; banker. Carlisle, Pa.

Kline, Sidney Delong, 1902–   . Cl. 1924. Tr., 1945–   . Banker; lawyer. Reading, Pa. *Who's Who.*

Eshelman, William L., 1891–1970. Cl. 1915. Tr., 1945–70. Manufacturer. Mohnton, Pa.

Sampson, William Croft, 1881–1958. Cl. 1902. Tr., 1946–58. Supt. of Schools, Upper Darby, Pa. Drexel Hill, Pa.

Masland, Frank Elmer, Jr., 1895–   . Cl. 1918. Tr., 1946–65. Business exec. Carlisle, Pa. *Who's Who. See faculty list.*

Edel, William Wilcox, 1894–   . Cl. 1915. Tr. 1946–59. Pres., Dickinson College. Carlisle, Pa. *Who's Who.*

Selby, Howard W., 1891–1953. Cl. 1913. Tr., 1947–53. Business exec. West Newtown, Mass.

Witwer, Samuel Weiler, 1908–   . Cl. 1930. Tr., 1948–   . Lawyer. Kenilworth, Ill. *Who's Who.*

Allen, Merle White, 1888–1961. Tr. 1948–61. Business exec. Carlisle, Pa.

Waidner, Robert A., Jr., 1910–   . Cl. 1932. Tr. 1948–   . Lawyer. Baltimore, Md.

Hutchison, Paul L., 1898–1967. Cl. 1918. Alumni Tr., 1949–67. Lawyer. Camp Hill, Pa.

Shuman, George, 1914–   . Cl. 1937. Tr., 1949–   . Financial Vice Pres. and Treas., Dickinson College. Carlisle, Pa. *Who's Who.*

Wallace, David McKee, 1892–1967. Cl. 1915. Tr., 1950–67. Lawyer. Harrisburg, Pa.

Todd, Glenn E., 1890–   . Cl. 1912. Alumni Tr., 1950–   . Manufacturer. Carlisle, Pa.

Brown, Revelle Wilson, 1883–   . Tr., 1950–57. Railroad official. Philadelphia, Pa.

Althouse, C. Scott, 1880–1970. Tr., 1950–70. Chemist; inventor; mfg. Reading, Pa.

Arnold, John Carlisle, 1887–1958. Tr., 1951–58. Lawyer, jurist. Clearfield, Pa.

Pedlow, John Watson, 1908–   . Cl. 1929. Alumni Tr., 1951–59. Chemist. Chester, Pa.

Chambers, Carl Covalt, 1907–   . Cl. 1929. Tr., 1952–   . Vice-Pres., Engineering Affairs, Univ. Pa. Philadelphia, Pa. *Who's Who.*

Woodside, Robert E., 1904–   . Cl. 1926. Tr., 1952–   . Lawyer; jurist. Millersburg, Pa. *Who's Who.*

Claster, Joel, 1891–   . Cl. 1914. Tr., 1953–69. Business exec. Philadelphia, Pa.

Du Pont, James Q., 1902–   . Tr., 1953–61. Electrical engineer. Wilmington, Del.

Hufstader, William Francis, 1895–   . Tr., 1953–57. Business exec. Detroit, Mich. *Who's Who.*

Logan, Henry, 1889–   . Cl. 1910. Tr., 1953–   . Lawyer. Brooklyn, N.Y.

Oxnam, Garfield Bromley, 1891–1963. Tr., 1953–62. Meth. Bishop. Washington, D.C. *Who's Who.*

Bell, Whitfield Jenks, Jr., 1914–   . Cl. 1935. Alumni Tr., 1954–62. Librarian, American Philosophical Society. Philadelphia, Pa. *Who's Who.* APS. *See faculty list.*

Foucht, Mary Sharp, 1896–   . Tr. 1954–   . Chicago, Ill.

Gayner, Lewis F., 1910–   . Cl. 1931. Tr., 1954–64. Mfg. Salem, N.J.

Gould, Herbert MacMillan, 1902–1968. Tr., 1954–59. Lawyer; corporation exec. Detroit, Mich.

Henninger, F. Lamont, 1900–   . Cl. 1924. Tr., 1954–71. Meth. clergyman. Harrisburg, Pa.

McKenney, Walter Gibbs, Jr., 1913–   . Cl. 1939. Tr., 1954–   . Lawyer; publisher. Riderwood, Pa.

Ness, Frederic William, 1914–   . Cl. 1933. Tr. 1955–60. Academic Vice Pres. and Dean, Dickinson College. Carlisle, Pa.

Klepser, John Mark, 1896–   . Cl. 1922. Alumni Tr., 1956–60. Lawyer; judge. Hollidaysburg, Pa.

Gallagher, Helen Douglass, 1906–1965. Cl. 1926. Alumni Tr., 1957–65. Realtor. Short Hills, N.J.

Smith, Alexander Keen, 1900–   . Cl. 1923. Tr., 1957–67. Meth. clergyman. Norristown, Pa.

Jenkins, William Sleeman, 1910–   . Cl. 1931. Tr., 1958–   . Lawyer; coal operator. Frostburg, Md.

Latch, Edward Gardiner, 1901–   . Cl. 1921. Tr., 1958–   . Meth. clergyman. Washington, D.C.

Lee, Harry W., 1894–1964. Tr., 1958–64. Lawyer. Reading, Pa.

Raffensperger, Edward Cowell, 1914–   . Cl. 1936. Tr., 1958–   . Physician. Philadelphia, Pa.

Bonisteel, Roscoe Osmond, 1888–1972. Cl. 1912. Tr., 1959–72. Lawyer. Ann Arbor, Mich. *Who's Who.*

Davidson, John Milton, 1910–   . Cl. 1933. Alumni Tr., 1959–   . Business exec. Wayne, Pa.

Holmes, Charles Wendell, 1896–   . Cl. 1921. Tr., 1959–   . School Administrator. Upper Darby, Pa.

Peters, John B., 1899–   . Cl. 1922. Tr., 1959–   . Orchardist; canner. Gardners, Pa.

Tawes, John Millard, 1894–   . Tr., 1959–67. Governor, Md. Crisfield, Md. *Who's Who.*

Welliver, Lester Allen, 1896–   . Cl. 1918. Tr., 1959–   . Meth. clergyman. Williamsport, Pa.

Baker, William Henry, 1896–1971. Tr., 1960–71. Business exec. York, Pa.

Cook, Winfield C., 1908–   . Cl. 1932. Alumni Tr., 1960–68. Sales
exec. Norristown, Pa.

Adams, Rolland Leroy, 1904–   . Cl. 1927. Tr., 1961–   . Publisher,
business exec. Bethlehem, Pa. *Who's Who.*

Bonney, Sherwood Munhall, 1909–   . Cl. 1931. Tr., 1961–   . Lawyer;
business exec. Scarsdale, N.Y. *Who's Who.*

Malcolm, Gilbert, 1892–1965. Cl. 1915. Tr., 1961–65. Pres., Dickinson
College. Carlisle, Pa. *Who's Who.*

Middleton, William Vernon, 1902–1965. Cl. 1928. Tr., 1961–65. Meth.
Bishop. Harrisburg, Pa. *Who's Who.*

Rubendall, Howard Lane, 1910–   . Cl. 1931. Tr., 1961–   . Pres., Dickinson College. Carlisle, Pa. *Who's Who.*

Kuebler, Roy Raymond, 1911–   . Cl. 1933. Alumni Tr., 1962–70.
Prof. of Biostatistics. Chapel Hill, N.C. *See faculty list.*

Spahr, Boyd Lee, Jr., 1910–   . Cl. 1932. Tr., 1962–   . Lawyer. Philadelphia, Pa.

Overholt, Weston, C., Jr., 1926–   . Cl. 1950. Alumni Tr., 1963–71
Lawyer. Philadelphia, Pa.

Stuart, John William, 1910–   . Tr., 1964–   . Business exec. New York,
N.Y. *Who's Who.*

Booth, Newell Snow, 1903–1968. Tr., 1965–68. Meth. Bishop. Harrisburg,
Pa. *Who's Who.*

Clare, Carl Peter, 1903–   . Tr., 1965–   . Electrical Eng. Arlington
Heights, Ill. *Who's Who.*

Herr, Philip C., 1906–   . Tr., 1965–66. Lawyer. Lansdowne, Pa.

Hoerner, John M., 1911–   . Cl. 1931. Tr., 1965–   . Business exec.
Winnetka, Ill. *Who's Who.*

Raffensperger, Mary Ames, 1913–   . Tr., 1965–   . Physician. Philadelphia, Pa.

Shepley, James Robinson, 1917–   . Tr., 1965–   . Publishing exec.
Port Washington, N.Y. *Who's Who.*

Carpenter, Katherine Smith, 1902–   . Cl. 1925. Alumni Tr., 1965–   .
Lawyer. Jersey Shore, Pa.

Fuoss, Robert M., 1912–   . Tr., 1966–69. Business exec. Cincinnati, O.

McCabe, Charles Law, 1922–   . Cl. 1943 Tr., 1966–   . Business exec.
Pittsburgh, Pa. *Who's Who.*

Zug, Harry Coover, 1913–   . Tr., 1966–   . C.P.A. Philadelphia, Pa.
Who's Who.

Chilton, Robert W., 1916–   . Tr., 1967–   . Business exec. Carlisle, Pa.

Lord, John Wesley, 1902–   . Cl. 1927. Tr., 1967–   . Meth. Bishop. Washington, D.C. *Who's Who.*

Wicke, Myron F., 1907–   . Tr., 1967–   . Meth. Church official. Nashville, Tenn.

McCartney, Samuel Jay, Jr., 1919–   . Cl. 1941. Alumni Tr., 1968–   . Business exec. West Orange, N.J.

Snyder, John S., 1911–   . Cl. 1933. Tr., 1968–   . Publishing exec. Scarsdale, N.Y. *Who's Who.*

McConnell, John Wilkinson, 1907–   . Cl. 1929. Tr., 1969–   . Pres., Univ. New Hampshire. Durham, N.H. *Who's Who.*

Shapiro, E. Donald, 1931–   . Cl. 1953. Tr., 1969–   . Lawyer, journalist. Harrison, N.Y. *Who's Who.*

Reynolds, Victoria Hann, 1930–   . Cl. 1950. Alumni Tr., 1969–   . Oakland, Calif.

Hopper, John D., 1923–   . Cl. 1948. Alumni Tr., 1970–   . Insurance exec. Camp Hill, Pa.

Rush, Alexander, 1910–   . Tr., 1971–   . Physician. Radnor, Pa.

Weiss, Emil R., 1932–   . Cl. 1953. Tr., 1971–   . Investment broker. Bloomfield, N.J.

Schafmeister, Vincent Joseph, Jr., 1923–   . Cl. 1949. Alumni Tr., 1971–   . Development officer. Danville, Pa.

FACULTY

Faculty of the Grammar School (to 1869) and College (to 1970)

Educators, on whom the continuance and growth of civilization so much depends, have never attracted the antiquarian interest given to artists and craftsmen—makers of more tangible objects of worth. It has been one purpose of this study, and of the archival collection underlying it, to throw some new light on the traditions and stylistic sequences of an art, or craft, whose output can only be glimpses in the impress of mind on mind and rarely, if ever, measured. At American colleges, for many years, every graduate's diploma was signed by each professor with whom he had studied—an engaging custom in which, as it were, the craftsman placed his sign manual upon the product. Today, with larger faculties, expanding curricula and specialization, the teacher's anonymity has increased—though not his importance in the shaping of our world.

Faculty membership at Dickinson has been a jealously regarded, if not always clearly defined, status. Trustee minutes are a primary source, but by no means complete. The College Catalogues include under the heading, "Faculty," some names other than those of teachers, and these are included here. Fuller information may be found in the master list and other papers at the Library.

With each name, life dates are followed by those of tenure on the College faculty (Fy.) or its grammar school (GS). For those who taught in both College and preparatory department, either consecutively or simultaneously, the dual role is indicated. The disciplines named are the principal, but not necessarily the only, ones taught. If the teacher is an alumnus, class (Cl.) is given; and if a trustee (Tr.), dates of service. Advanced and professional degrees held while at Dickinson are noted, as also listings in the *Dictionary of American Biography (DAB)* and *Who's Who,* and membership in the American Philosophical Society (APS).

Steel, John,   -1779. Pastor of the Old Side Presbyterian congregation at Carlisle, 1759-1779; founder and first teacher of the Carlisle Latin School.

(Duffield, George, 1732-1790. Pastor of the New Side Presbyterian congregation, 1759-72; teacher in his own pastorate, from which some boys and young men entered the Latin School.)

Makinly, Henry, d.c. 1784-1786. GS, 1769-76. Latin, Greek.

Creigh, John, c. 1741-1813. GS, c. 1770-76. Tr., 1788-1813.

Ross, James, 1744-1827. GS & Fy., 1780-92. Latin, Greek, Librarian. A.M. (U. of Pa.). LL.D. (Allegheny).

Nisbet, Charles, 1736-1804. Fy. & Pres., 1784-1804. Moral Philos., Belles Lettres, Theol. D.D. (Princeton). *DAB.*

Davidson, Robert, 1750-1812. Fy. & Pres., 1785-1809. History, Belles Lettres. D.D. (U. of Pa.). *DAB.* APS. Tr., 1808-12.

Johnston, Robert,   -1808. GS & Fy., 1785-87. Math., Nat. Philos. A.M., M.D. Tr., 1788-1808.

Tait, Robert,   . GS, 1785-86.

Crawford, T. James,   . GS, 1788?-   . Cl. 1789.

Grier, Isaac, 1763-1814. GS, 1788-90. Cl. 1788.

McCormick, James,   -1814. GS & Fy., 1788-1814. Math., Nat. Philos. A.M.

Scott, James,   . GS, 1788-89. Cl. 1789.

Huston, Charles,   -1849. GS 1792-93. Cl. 1789.

Davis, Henry Lyon, 1775-1837. GS & Fy., 1793-94. Latin, Greek. Cl. 1794. D.D.

Thomson, William,   - c. 1808-13. Fy., 1794-1802. Latin, Greek.

Borland, John,   . Fy., 1804-05; 1811-12. Latin, Greek, Belles Lettres, Librarian. A.M.

Hayes, John,   -1815. GS & Fy., 1805-09. Latin, Greek. Cl. 1805.

Atwater, Jeremiah, 1773-1858. Fy. & Pres., 1809-15. Logic, Metaphysics, Moral Philos. D.D. (U. of Pa.).

Wilson, Henry Rowan, 1780–1849. Fy., 1809–13. Latin, Greek. Cl. 1798. D.D. (Lafayette). Tr., 1820–25.

Aigster, Charles Frederick, . Fy., 1810–11. Nat. Philos., Chem.

Berard, Claudius, 1786–1848. Fy., 1810–15. French, Spanish, Italian. Cl. 1812. A.M.

How, Samuel Blanchard, 1790–1868. GS, 1810–11. Pres., 1830–31. D.D. (Union).

McClure, John, 1784–1841. GS & Fy., 1810–11. Tr., 1827–33.

Cooper, Thomas, 1759–1839. Fy., 1811–15. Chem., Nat. Philos. LL.D. (So. Carolina Coll.). *DAB*. APS.

Grier, Robert Cooper, 1794–1870. GS, 1812–13. Cl. 1812.

McNeily, James G., . GS, 1813–25. Cl. 1813.

Shaw, Joseph, 1778–1824. Fy., 1813–15. Latin, Greek. A.M. (U. of Edinburgh).

Nulty, Eugene, –1871. Fy., 1814–16. Math. A.M. (U. of Pa.). APS.

McKnight, John, 1754–1823. Fy. & Pres., 1815. Moral Philos. D.D. (Yale).

Trimble, , . GS, 1815– .

Kersley, , . GS, 1816– .

Stack, Gerard E., . Fy., 1816. Latin, Greek. A.M. (Aberdeen U.).

Burns, John, . Fy., 1821–22. Latin, Greek.

McClelland, Alexander, 1794–1864. Fy., 1821–29. Belles Lettres, Moral Philos., Librarian. D.D. (Princeton).

Mason, John Mitchell, 1770–1829. Fy. & Pres., 1821–24. Moral Philos. D.D. (Princeton, U. of Pa.). *DAB*.

Slack, John C., . GS, 1821–22.

Vethake, Henry, 1792–1866. Fy., 1821–29. Math., Nat. Philos. A.M. (Columbia, Princeton); LL.D. (Columbia). *DAB*. APS.

Mason, James Hall, 1803–1822. GS, 1822. Cl. 1822

Spencer, Joseph 1790–1862. Fy., 1822–30. Latin, Greek. A.M.

Agnew, John Holmes, 1804–1865. GS, 1823–24. Cl. 1823.

Scudder, William, . GS, 1823– .

Neill, William, 1778–1860. Fy. & Pres., 1824–29. Necessity and Evidences of Divine Revelation. D.D. (Union). *DAB*.

Mayer, Lewis, 1783–1849. Fy., 1825–28. History, German Lit. D.D.

Mahon, Joseph, 1805–1884. GS, 1826–28. Cl. 1827.

Vethake, John W., . Fy., 1826–27. Chem. A.M.; M.D.

Finley, John Knox, 1806–1885. Fy., 1827–29. Chem., Nat. Hist. M.D. (U. of Pa.).

Huber, Jacob Frederick, 1801–1878. Fy., 1827–28. Spanish, French, Italian.

Krebs, John Michael, 1804–1867. GS, 1828–29. Cl. 1827.

Cleveland, Charles Dexter, 1802-1869. Fy., 1830-32. Latin, Greek, Librarian. A.M. (Dartmouth); LL.D. APS.

McFarlane, Alexander W., . Fy., 1830-32. Math.

Rogers, Henry Darwin 1809-1866. Fy., 1830-31. Chem., Nat. Philos. *DAB*. APS.

Olmstead, Lemuel Gregory, 1808-1880. Fy., 1831-32. Chem. LL.D. (Hanover Coll.).

Caldwell, Merritt, 1806-1848. Fy., 1833-48. Math., Metaphysics, Pol. Econ.

Dobb, Alexander F., . GS, 1833-35.

Durbin, John Price, 1800-1876. Fy. & Pres., 1833-45. Moral Sci., Philos. *DAB*.

Emory, Robert, 1814-1848. Fy., 1834-40; Acting Pres., 1842-43; Pres., 1845-48. Latin, Greek, Librarian. Tr., 1841-45.

Hughes, Ezekiel, . GS, 1834-35. A.M.

Reed, John, 1786-1850. Fy., 1834-50. Law. Cl. 1806. LL.D. (Washington Coll.). *See Law School faculty list.*

Bunting, James, 1814-1880. GS, 1835-37.

Cary, John L., . GS, 1835-39.

Hey, John F., . GS, 1835-38.

Keagy, John Miller, 1792-1837. Fy., 1835-36. Nat. Sci. Tr. 1833-35. *DAB*.

Roszel, Stephen Asbury, 1811-1852. GS & Fy., 1835-40. Latin. A.M. Tr., 1845-52.

Allen, William Henry, 1808-1882. Fy., 1836-50; Acting Pres., 1847-48. Nat. Sci., Philos., Lit. M.D. (Bowdoin); LL.D. (Union). Tr. 1850-64. *DAB*. APS.

McClintock, John, 1814-1870. Fy., 1836-48. Math., Latin, Greek. D.D. (U. of Pa.); LL.D. (U. of Pa., Rutgers). Tr. 1848-59. *DAB*.

Thornton, Theodore, . GS, 1838?-40.

Roszel, Samuel S., . GS, 1839- .

Bowman, Thomas, 1817-1914. GS, 1840-43. Cl. 1837. A.M. *DAB*.

Scott, Levi, 1802-1882. GS, 1840-43. Cl. 1837. A.M. Tr., 1839-41; 1858-82.

Sudler, Thomas Emory, 1800-1860. Fy., 1840-51. Math. A.M.

Walker, Edward L., . Fy., 1841-47. Music.

Crooks, George Richard, 1822-1897. GS & Fy., 1841-48. Latin, Greek. Cl. 1840. D.D.; LL.D. *DAB*.

McClintock, James, . Fy., 1842-44. Anatomy, Physics. M.D.

Potts, Jonas John, 1821- . GS, 1843-45. Cl. 1843. A.M.

Baird, Spencer Fullerton, 1823-1887. Fy., 1845-50. Nat. Sci. Cl. 1840. D.P.S.; Ph.D. (Harvard); LL.D. (Harvard). Tr., 1850-57. *DAB*. APS.

Stayman, John Keagy, 1823-1882. GS, 1845; Fy., 1861-74. Latin, French, Greek, English Lit., Philos. Cl. 1841.

Blumenthal, Charles Edward,   -1883. Fy., 1846-54. German, French, Hebrew. A.M.; M.D.

Devinney, James Andrew, 1819-1851. GS, 1847-51. Cl. 1846.

McCabe, George Hawkins, 1824-1902. Fy., 1847. Math. Cl. 1844. LL.D. (Wagner Institute).

Marshall, James William, 1822-1910. Fy., 1848-62. Latin, Greek, French. Cl. 1848. LL.D.

Nadal, Bernard Harrison, 1813-1870. Fy., 1848; 1865-66. Moral Sci., Philos., English Lit. Cl. 1848. D.D.

Peck, Jesse Truesdell, 1811-1883. Fy. & Pres., 1848-52. Moral Sci. Tr., 1852-56. *DAB*.

Tiffany, Otis Henry, 1825-1891. Fy., 1848-57. Math. Cl. 1844. D.D.; LL.D.

Wilson, John, 1824-1899. GS, 1848-51. Cl. 1848. Ph.D. (Pa. Mil. Academy).

Hillman, Samuel Dickinson, 1825-c. 1911. GS & Fy., 1850-74; Acting Pres., 1868. Math., Astronomy. Cl. 1850. A.M.; Ph.D. (Lafayette).

Johnson, Herman Merrills, 1815-1868. Fy. & Pres., 1850-68. Latin, Greek, French. D.D. (Ohio Wesleyan).

Wentworth, Erastus, 1813-1886. Fy., 1850-54. Nat. Sci. D.D. (Allegheny).

Wing, Conway Phelps, 1809-1889. Fy., 1850. Nat. Sci., Philos., Lit. D.D. (Hamilton).

Musselman, Amos Forrey, 1830-1906. GS & Fy., 1851-54. Lang., Nat. Sci. Cl. 1851. A.M.

Collins, Charles, 1813-1875. Pres., 1852-60. Moral Sci. D.D.

Snively, William Andrew, 1833-   . GS, 1853-55. Cl. 1852. D.D. (Columbia).

Arbogast, Benjamin, 1825-1881. GS & Fy., 1854-56. Tutor. Cl. 1854.

Godman, William D.,   . Fy. 1854. Tutor.

Schem, Alexander Jacob, 1826-1881. Fy., 1854-60. Hebrew, French, German. A.M. (U. of Bonn). *DAB*.

Wilson, William Carlile, 1829-1865. Fy., 1854-65. Nat. Sci. Cl. 1850. A.M.

Daugherty, Thomas,   -1885. GS 1856-   . Fy., 1865-66. English Lit. A.M.; M.D. (Baltimore Med. Coll.)

Marshall, James Pede, 1833-   . GS 1856-57. Cl. 1856. A.M.

Boswell, William Laws, 1828-1913. Fy., 1857-65. Math., Greek, German. Cl. 1848. Tr. 1881-1913.

Pursell, Benjamin Franklin,   . GS, 1857-58. Cl. 1857.

John, David Clarke, 1835– . GS, 1858, Cl. 1859. A.M. (Dickinson Sem.); D.D. (Upper Iowa U.).

Stamm, John S., 1838–1871. GS, 1858–59. Cl. 1860.

Storm, John Brown, 1838–1901. GS, 1859–60. Cl. 1861. Tr., 1880–1901.

Mullin, Alfred Foster, 1837– . GS, 1860–62. Cl. 1858. A.M. Tr., 1893–97.

Coffman, Wilmer, 1840– . GS, 1861– . Cl. 1862. A.M.

Cheston, Henry Clay, 1834–1882. GS, 1862–68. Cl. 1861.

Cisna, William Reed, 1837– . GS, 1862. Cl. 1863. A.M.; M.D. (U. of Pa.).

Graham, James Hutchinson, 1807–1882. Fy., 1862–82. Law. Cl. 1827. LL.D. *See Law School faculty list.*

Hood, John, 1838– . GS, 1863–64. Cl. 1864. A.M.; M.D. (U. of Mich.).

McKeehan, Charles Watson, 1842–1895. GS, 1864. Cl. 1867. Tr., 1879–95.

Bowman, Shadrach Laycock, 1829–1906. Fy., 1865–72. Greek, Hebrew. Cl. 1855. D.D. (Rutgers); S.T.D. (DePauw).

Himes, Charles Francis, 1838–1918. Fy., 1865–96; Acting Pres., 1888–89. Nat. Sci., Physics, Chem. Cl. 1855. A.M.; Ph.D. (Indiana Asbury U.); LL.D. *DAB.* APS. *Who's Who. See Law School faculty list.*

Dashiell, Robert Laurenson, 1825–1880. Fy. & Pres., 1868–72. Moral Sci. Cl. 1846. A.M.; D.D. (Wesleyan).

Trickett, William, 1840–1928. GS & Fy., 1868–72. Philos., English Lit., Modern Lang. Cl. 1868. A.M.; LL.D. (DePauw). *See Law School faculty list.*

Harman, Henry Martyn, 1822–1897. Fy., 1870–96. Greek, Hebrew. Cl. 1848. D.D.; LL.D. (Wesleyan).

McCauley, James Andrew, 1822–1896. Fy. & Pres., 1872–88. Moral Sci. Cl. 1847. A.M.; D.D.; LL.D. (Lafayette).

Fisher, William Righter, 1849–1932. Fy., 1874–76. Modern Lang. Cl. 1870.

Lippincott, Joshua Allan, 1835–1906. Fy., 1874–83. Math., Astronomy. Cl. 1858. D.D. (Franklin & Marshall); LL.D. (U. of Mich.). Tr., 1897–1906.

Little, Charles Joseph, 1840–1911. Fy., 1874–85. Philos., English Lit., Metaphysics, Pol. Econ. Ph.D. (DePauw); LL.D; S.T.D. (Northwestern). *DAB. Who's Who.*

[*For GS Faculty 1877–1917, see Conway Hall list.*]

Richmond, Ephraim Thomas Carroll, 1843– . Fy., 1879–81. Mil. Sci.

Whiting, Henry Clay, 1845–1901. Fy., 1879–1900. Latin, German. Ph.D. (Ill. Wesleyan); L.H.D. (Rutherford).

Durell, Fletcher, 1860–1946. Fy., 1883–95. Math., Astronomy. A.M. & Ph.D. (Princeton).

Rittenhouse, Aaron, 1837–1906. Fy., 1883–90. English Lit., History. A.M. (Wesleyan); D.D.

Morgan, James Henry, 1857–1939. Fy. & Pres., 1884–1933. Dean; Greek, Pol. Econ. Cl. 1878. A.M.; Ph.D. (Bucknell); LL.D. (Gettysburg, Franklin & Marshall, U. of Pittsburgh, Wesleyan). Tr., 1931–39. *See Conway Hall list. Who's Who.*

Super, Ovando Byron, 1848–1935. Fy., 1884–1913. Modern Lang., Librarian. Cl. 1873. A.M.; Ph.D. (Boston U.). *Who's Who.*

Lindsay, William Birckhead, 1858–1922. Fy., 1885–1910. Chem. B.S. (M.I.T.); Ph.D. (Boston U.).

Muchmore, Lyman J.,   . Fy., 1887–90. Phys. Ed. A.M.

Hurst, John Fletcher, 1834–1903. Fy., 1889–91. Church History. Cl. 1854. D.D.; LL.D. *DAB. Who's Who.*

Reed, George Edward, 1846–1930. Fy. & Pres., 1889–1911. Moral Sci., Public Speaking. A.M. & S.T.D. (Wesleyan); LL.D. (Lafayette). *Who's Who.*

Lake, Willard Geoffrey, 1863–   . Fy., 1890–92. Physiology, Phys. Ed. Cl. 1887. A.M.

McIntire, Bradford Oliver, 1856–1938. Fy., 1890–1938. English Lit., History, Librarian. A.M. (Wesleyan); Ph.D. (U. of Pittsburgh).

Rogers, Robert William, 1864–1930. Fy., 1890–93. Bible, Semitic History, A.M.; Ph.D. (Haverford); D.D. (Wesleyan); Ph.D. (Leipzig). *DAB. Who's Who.*

Stephens, Henry Matthew, 1868–1921. Fy., 1892–1921. Phys. Ed., Biology. Cl. 1892, A.M.; Sc.D. (Bucknell).

Dare, William Knight, 1858–1918. Fy., 1893–99. History, Pedagogy, English, Philos. Cl. 1883. A.M. *See Conway Hall list.*

Sellers, Montgomery Porter, 1873–1942. Fy., 1893–1942. Dean; English, German, Rhetoric. Cl. 1893. A.M.; Litt.D. (Hamline). *See Conway Hall list.*

Whiting, Henry Freeman, 1870–1936. Fy., 1893–1913. Latin, Greek, Math. Cl. 1889. A.M.; Sc.D.

Barbour, Martha E.,   . Fy., 1895–96. Phys. Ed.

Landis, William Weidman, 1869–1942. Fy., 1895–1942. Math., Astronomy. Cl. 1891, A.M.; Sc.D. (Franklin & Marshall). *Who's Who.*

Mohler, John Frederick, 1864–1930. Fy., 1896–1930. Physics. Cl. 1887. A.M.; Ph.D. (Johns Hopkins). *Who's Who.*

Prince, Morris Watson, 1845–1932. Fy., 1896–1911. History, Pol. Sci. S.T.D. (Wesleyan).

Cramer, Michael John, 1835–1898. Fy., 1897–98. Philos. D.D., LL.D. *DAB.*

Harry, Emma Viola, 1875–1955. Fy., 1897–99. German, French. Cl. 1895. M.A.

Stauffer, Nathan Pennypacker, 1875– . Fy., 1897–1900. Hygiene, Phys. Culture. D.D.S. (U. of Pa.); M.D. (Hahnemann Med. Coll.).

Gooding, William Lambert, 1851–1916. Fy., 1898–1916. Philos., Educ. Cl. 1874. A.M.; Ph.D.

Wilson, George Arthur, 1864– . Fy., 1898. Philos. S.T.B. & Ph.D. (Boston U.). Who's Who.

Filler, Mervin Grant, 1873–1931. Fy. & Pres., 1899–1931. Dean; Latin Cl. 1893. A.M.; Litt. D. (Nebraska Wesleyan); LL.D. (Ohio Wesleyan, Bucknell). Who's Who. See Conway Hall list.

Hargis, Lucia Coleman, –1956. Fy., 1899–1900. French. Cl. 1899.

Pilcher, James Evelyn, 1857–1911. Fy., 1899–1903. Anatomy, Embryology, Soc., Econ. M.D. (Long Island Coll. Hosp.); A.M. & Ph.D. (Ill. Wesleyan); L.H.D. (Allegheny). See Law School Faculty list.

Craver, Forrest Eugene, 1875–1958. Fy., 1900–50. Latin, Greek, Phys. Ed., Math. Cl. 1899. A.M. See Conway Hall list.

Prettyman, Cornelius William, 1872–1946. Fy. & Pres., 1900–46. German. Cl. 1891. A.M.; Ph.D. (U. of Pa.). Who's Who.

Prince, Leon Cushing, 1875–1937. Fy., 1900–37. Librarian, History, Int'l Law, Econ. Cl. 1898. A.M.; LL.B. (Dickinson School of Law). Litt.D. (Albright). Who's Who.

Hutchinson, Ralph Fielding, 1875– . Fy., 1901–02. Phys. Ed.

McMaster, Le Roy, 1879–1946. Fy., 1901–04. Chem., Physics. Cl. 1901. A.M. Who's Who.

Hutchins, Charles Pelton, 1872–1938. Fy., 1902–04. Physiology, Phys.Ed. M.D. (Long Island Coll. Hosp.) Who's Who. See Conway Hall list.

Standing, Alfred John, 1884–1938. Fy., 1902–05. Librarian. Cl. 1905. A.M. (Lehigh).

Williams, John William, 1880–1908. Fy., 1905–07. Phys. Ed. Cl. 1904. A.M. See Conway Hall list.

Darrow, Fritz Sage, 1882– . Fy., 1906–08. Greek. A.M. & Ph.D. (Harvard).

McAnney, Lucretia Jones, 1859–1932. Fy., 1906–14. Dean of Women; Elocution.

King, John Craig, 1881–1960. Fy., 1907–08. Music. Cl. 1907.

Pipal, Joseph Amos, . Fy., 1907–09. Phys. Ed. See Conway Hall list.

Tomkinson, Paul Eldridge, 1881–1907. Fy., 1907. German, Math. Cl. 1903.

Decevee, Edwin Jacobs, 1873– . Fy., 1908–10. Music.

Rowe, Perry Belmont, 1883–1941. Fy., 1908–10. Math., Chem., Physics. Cl. 1907. A.M. *See Conway Hall list.*

Baker, Samuel, N., 1883–   . Fy., 1910–11. French. A.M. (Brown).

Crider, George A., 1845–1927. Fy., 1910–12. Social Problems and Business Institutions. A.M. Tr., 1906–10.

Jennings, Arthur Bates,   . Fy., 1910–12. Music.

Schappelle, Benjamin Franklin, 1885–   . Fy., 1910–11. German. Cl. 1908.

Shadinger, Guy Howard, 1877–   . Fy., 1910–20. Chem. Ph.D. (Johns Hopkins).

Kellogg, Edwin Henry, 1880–   . Fy., 1911–12. English Bible. B.D. (Princeton).

MacAndrews, Richard Henry, 1880–1964. Fy., 1911–49. Phys. Ed.

Noble, Eugene Allen, 1865–1948. Pres., 1911–14. Ph.D. (Wesleyan); D.D. (St. Johns); S.T.D. (Wesleyan); L.H.D.; Litt.D. *Who's Who.*

Blakey, Leonard Stott,   . Fy., 1912–15. Econ., Soc. Ph.D. (Columbia).

Cole, George Franklin,   . Fy., 1913–17. Romance Lang. A.M. (Harvard).

Learned, Henry Dexter,   . Fy., 1913. German.

Carver, David June, 1882–   . Fy., 1914–15. Philos., Educ. A.M. (Richmond College).

Cleland, John Scott, 1887–1951. Fy., 1914–15. Econ., Soc. A.M. (Princeton); Ph.D. *Who's Who. See Conway Hall list.*

Springer, Ruter William, 1863–   . Fy., 1914–19. English Bible. Greek Testament. A.M. (Northwestern), LL.B. & L.L.M. (Georgetown).

Kelly, Melvin Howard,   . Fy., 1915–20. Latin, Greek, French.

Patterson, Gaylard Hawkins, 1866–1940. Fy., 1915–40. Econ., Soc. A.M. (Harvard); Ph.D. (Yale). *Who's Who.*

Robinson, William Allen,   . Fy., 1915–17. English. A.M.; S.T.D. (Boston U.).

Wing, Herbert, Jr., 1889–1972. Fy., 1915–61. Greek, History. A.M. & Ph.D. (U. of Wisc.).

Cram, G. Lafayette,   . Fy., 1916–17. Modern Lang. A.M. (U. of Toronto).

Norcross, Sarah Helen (Burns), 1888–1953. Fy., 1916–18; 1946–49. Dean of Women, Librarian. Cl. 1912. A.M.

Norcross, Wilbur Harrington, 1882–1941. Fy., 1916–41. Philos., Educ., Psych. Cl. 1907. A.M.; Ph.D. (Johns Hopkins). *Who's Who.*

De Vilaine, Sophie Louise,   . Fy., 1918–25. Romance Lang. A.M.

Gooding, Lydia Marian,   . Fy., 1918–26. Librarian. Cl. 1910.

Warne, Walter Roy, 1883–.   . Fy., 1918–19. Math. Pd.B. (Syracuse).

Battenhouse, Henry Martin, 1885–   . Fy., 1919–20. English Bible. S.T.B. (Garrett); A.M. & Ph.D. (U. of Denver). *Who's Who.*

Bixler, Andrew Loy,   . Fy., 1919–20. Relig. Educ. Cl. 1905. A.M.

Mausert, Bernard. R.,   . Fy., 1919–20. Music. Mus.D.

Meredith, Josephine Brunyate, 1879–1965. Fy., 1919–48. Dean of Women, English. Cl. 1901. A.M.

Williams, J. Merrill,   . Fy., 1919–20. Public Speaking. Cl. 1908. A.M.; B.D.

Bullock, Hazel Jane,   . Fy., 1920–28. Romance Lang. A.M. (Columbia).

Carver, Clarence Johnson, 1884–1940. Fy., 1920–40. English Bible, Educ. Cl. 1909. A.M. & Ph.D. (N.Y.U.).

Ely, Charles Evans, 1871–   . Fy., 1920–24. Relig. Educ. Cl. 1899.

Vuilleumier, Ernest Albert, 1894–1958. Fy., 1920–58. Dean; Chem. Ph.D. (U. of Berne). *Who's Who.*

Baumgartner, William Michael, 1881–   . Fy., 1921–26. English Bible. A.M. (W.Va.U.); B.D. (Drew).

Bryan, Noah Rosenberger,   . Fy., 1921–22. Math. A.M. (U. of Pa.); Ph.D. (Columbia).

Davis, Herbert Leroy,   . Fy., 1921–25, 1927–28. Chem. Cl. 1921. Ph.D. (Cornell).

Eddy, Milton Walker, 1883–1964. Fy., 1921–55. Biology. Sc.M. (Northwestern); Ph.D. (U. of Pa.) *Who's Who.*

Shedd, Karl Eastman, 1894–   . Fy., 1921–22. Romance Lang. A.M. (Harvard).

Thomas, Charles Hastings, 1894–   . Fy., 1921–23. Math, Physics. Cl. 1921.

Brosius, Guy C.,   . Fy., 1922–23. Public Speaking.

Gates, Bertha Globisch,   . Fy., 1922–23. German. A.M.

Grimm, John Crawford Milton, 1891–1970. Fy., 1922–61. Romance Lang. Ph.D. (U. of Pa.) *Who's Who.*

Rohrbaugh, Lewis Guy, 1884–1972. Fy., 1922–53. Philos., Relig. Educ. Cl. 1907. A.M.; B.D. (Drew); Ph.D. (Iowa State). *Who's Who.*

Schecter, Ralph, 1893–   . Fy., 1922–61. English, Music.

Wass, Clifton Ennis, 1872–   . Fy., 1922–28. English, Educ. B.Ped. (U. of Maine).

Bower, Lahman Forest, 1858–1934. Fy., 1923–28. Young People's Sect'y. *See Conway Hall list.*

Murphy, B. Russel,   . Fy., 1923. Phys. Ed.

Walker, Ruth Amelia,   . Fy., 1923–26. Phys. Ed.

Bowman, Edgar Milton, . Fy., 1925–30. Romance Lang. A.M. (Haverford); Ph.D.

Rinker, B. Floyd, 1901– . Fy., 1925–28. English. Cl. 1924.

Rogers, Horace Elton, 1902– . Fy., 1925–71. Physics, Chem. Cl. 1924. M.S. (Lafayette); Ph.D. (Princeton). *Who's Who.*

Stough, Mulford, 1888–1951. Fy., 1925–50. History. A.M. (U. of Pa.).

Hammond, Dorothy M., . Fy., 1926–27. Librarian.

Packard, Jeannette R., . Fy., 1926–27. Phys. Ed.

Quimby, Chester Warren, . Fy., 1926–34. English Bible. Relig. Educ. S.T.B. (Boston U.).

Janney, Frances A., . Fy., 1927–30. Phys. Ed.

Monyer, Henry William, 1905– . Fy., 1927–30. Physics, Math. Cl. 1927.

Morris, May, 1886–1967. Fy. 1927–56. Librarian. Cl. 1909. Grad. Pratt Institute.

Ayres, Frank, Jr., 1901– . Fy., 1928–58. Math. Ph.D. (U. of Chicago).

Bishop, Arthur Vaughan, 1883–1955. Fy., 1928–54. Latin. A.M. & Ph.D. (U. of Virginia).

Bowman, Claude Charleton, 1908– . Fy., 1928–29. Chem. Cl. 1928. M.A. (U. of Kansas); M.A. (U. of Chicago); Ph.D. (U. of Pa.).

Doney, Paul Herbert, 1900–1941. Fy., 1928–41. English. S.T.B. (Boston U.); A.M. & Ph.D. (Harvard).

Folsom, Benjamin Wilbert, . Fy. 1928–30. Public Speaking.

Gerberich, Albert Horwell, 1898–1965. Fy., 1928–45. Modern Lang. Cl. 1918. A.M. (U. of Pa.); Ph.D. (Johns Hopkins).

Hardy, Jerry David, . Fy., 1928–29. Biology. S.T.B. (Westminster Theol. Sem.).

Pritchard, Paul Walburton, –1953. Fy., 1928–30. Phys. Ed. Cl. 1920.

Taintor, Mary Buckley, 1889– . Fy., 1928–59. Romance Lang. A.M. (Stanford).

Thomas, Carl Richard Walther, . Fy., 1928–35. German. A.M. & Ph.D. (U. of Pa.).

Thompson, Russell Irvin, 1898–1957. Fy., 1928–57. Dean; Educ., Psych. Cl. 1920. Ph.D. (Yale). *Who's Who.*

Chapman, Esther Winifred, . Fy., 1929–34. Phys. Ed.

Griffith, Percy Wilfred, . Fy., 1929–31. Phys. Ed.

Herber, Elmer Charles, 1900– . Fy., 1929–68. Biology. A.M. (U. of Pa.), Sc.D. (Johns Hopkins). *Who's Who.*

Stephens, George Robert, . Fy., 1929–35. English. A.M. & Ph.D. (U. of Pa.). *Who's Who.*

Fink, Cornelius Winfield, 1893–1955. Fy., 1930–55. Econ., Pol. Sci. M.A. (Ohio State).

Martindell, Marie Diane, . Fy., 1930-32. Asst. Libn. Grad. Drexel Institute.

Parlin, Wellington Amos, 1899- . Fy., 1930-55. Physics. M.S. (U. of Iowa); Ph.D. (Johns Hopkins).

Waterhouse, Francis Asbury, 1883- . Fy., 1930-35. Romance Lang. A.M. & Ph.D. (Harvard).

Barnes, Gerald, 1893- . Fy., 1931-33. Soc. A.M. (U. of Cinn.); Ph.D. (U. of Mich.).

Brunhouse, Robert Levere, 1908- . Fy., 1931-35. History, Registrar. Cl. 1930.

McCormick, Joseph H., . Fy., 1931-35. Phys. Ed.

Sinclair, Janet Kellogg, . Fy., 1931-32. Asst. Libn. A.B. in L.S. (U. of Mich.).

Waugh, Karl Tinsley, 1879-1971. Pres., 1931-33. A.M. & LL.D., (Ohio Wesleyan); A.M. & Ph.D. (Harvard). *Who's Who.*

Fisher, Amy, 1873-1938. Fy., 1932-38. Curator of Dickinsoniana. Cl. 1895. A.M. *See Conway Hall list.*

Rosa, Mary Evans, 1867-1944. Fy., 1932-39. Curator of Dickinsoniana. Cl. 1889. A.M.

Thompson, Isabella Thoburn (McMaster), 1909- . Fy., 1932-38. Ref. & Circ. Libn. B.S. in L.S. (Western Reserve).

Kuebler, Roy Raymond, 1911- . Fy., 1933-55. Math. Cl. 1933. A.M. (U. of Pa.); Ph.D. (U. of N.C.). Tr., 1962-70.

Suter, Henry Byron, 1910- . Fy., 1933-36. Asst. Libr. Cl. 1931.

Corson, Fred Pierce, 1896- . Pres., 1934-44. Cl. 1917. A.M.; D.D.; L.H.D.; B.D. (Drew); D.D. (Syracuse); Litt. D. (U. of Maryland); LL.D. (Western Maryland, Allegheny, Franklin & Marshall, Gettysburg, U. of Pa.). Tr., 1944-67. *Who's Who.*

Rehfuss, Mary Ganoe, 1897- . Fy., 1934-42. Phys. Ed.

Earp, James Pearsall, 1904- . Fy., 1935-38. Soc. A.M. (Columbia), Ph.D. (Northwestern).

Lazenby, Marion Candler, 1909- . Fy., 1935-42. German. A.M. & Ph.D. (Vanderbilt).

Swift, Charles Lowe, 1878-1956. Fy., 1935-48. English. Cl. 1904. A.M. *See Conway Hall list.*

Bell, Whitfield Jenks, Jr., 1914- . Fy., 1936-54. History. Cl. 1935. A.M. & Ph.D. (U. of Pa.). Tr., 1954-62. *Who's Who.* APS.

Mader, Frank Alfred, 1916- . Fy., 1936-37. English. Cl. 1936.

Straka, Mildred Caroline, 1912- . Fy., 1936-47. Cat. Libn. Cl. 1938. B.S. (Columbia).

Gould, William Drum, 1897- . Fy., 1937-63. History, Pol. Sci., Philos., Relig. B.D. (Garrett); Ph.D. (Boston U.). *Who's Who.*

Hartman, William Emory, . Fy., 1938–39. Bible. S.T.B. & Ph.D. (Boston U.).

Nicholson, John Burton, Jr., 1912– . Fy., 1938–43. Asst. Libn. A.M. (Washington & Lee); B.S.L.S. (Columbia). *Who's Who.*

Novack, John Arnold, 1913– . Fy., 1938–42. German. Cl. 1936.

Trayer, John K., . Fy., 1938–39; 1940. Psych. A.M. (Columbia).

Warner, Wellman Joel, 1897– . Fy., 1938–46. Soc. B.D. (Yale); Ph.D. (London Sch. of Econ.).

Kahler, Arthur Daniel, 1898– . Fy., 1939–42. Phys. Ed. D.Sc. (Southwestern).

Detweiler, Philip 1915– . Fy., 1940–41. Libr. Asst. Cl. 1936. LL.B. (Dickinson School of Law).

Morrison, Donald Ray, 1917– . Fy., 1940–52. Psych. Cl. 1940. A.M. (Temple).

Pedrick, Walter Roberts, 1919– . Fy., 1940–41. Biology. Cl. 1940.

Bowman, Raymond Palmer Garber, 1899– . Fy., 1941–51. Psych. M.S. & Ph.D. (U. of Virginia).

James, Benjamin David, 1912– . Fy., 1941– . Dean of Students; Educ., Psych., Admissions. Cl. 1934. A.M. (Bucknell); Ph.D. (U. of Pa.). *Who's Who.*

Kistler, Mark Oliver, 1918– . Fy., 1941–46. German. Cl. 1938. A.M. (Columbia).

Llewellyn, Robert H., 1917– . Fy., 1941–42. English. Cl. 1939. A.M.

Mathews, Philip, 1885–1958. Fy., 1941–42. Dir. pre-induction educ.

Norcross, Isabel M., 1920–1969. Fy., 1941–42. Psych. Cl. 1941.

Peacock, Leishman Arnold, . Fy., 1941–42. English. A.M. (Wake Forest).

Sanborn, William L.C., 1919–1969. Fy., 1941–42. Modern Lang. Cl. 1941.

Snyder, E. Bayne, Jr., 1919– . Fy., 1941–42. Chem., Physics. Cl. 1941.

Barkman, Marjorie Ann, 1919– . Fy., 1942–44. Phys. Ed.

Broverman, Dorothy, 1921– . Fy., 1942–44. Chem., Physics. Cl. 1942.

Evans, Jane Lee, 1913– . Fy., 1942–44. Math. A.M.

Hepler, John C., 1913– . Fy., 1942–46. English. A.M. & Ph.D. (Peabody Coll.). *Who's Who.*

Kennedy, Charles Henry Bellows, 1910–1951. Fy., 1942–51. Phys. Ed. Cl. 1911. M.Ed. (Pa. State U.).

Rich, Catherine, . Fy., 1942–43. Ref. Libn.

Shultz, Jacob Resler, 1905– . Fy., 1942–43. Philos. Cl. 1926. B.D. & S.T.B. (Boston U.).

Smith, Henry Elmore, 1891-1955. Fy., 1942-55. Math., Physics. Cl. 1911. A.M. (Columbia).

Zissa, Bernice K. (Grubb), 1917-   . Fy., 1942-45; 1946-47. Romance Lang. A.M. & Ph.D. (U. of Rochester).

Bragg, Clara,   . Fy., 1943-44. Libr. Asst.

Bowman, Annie Louise, 1906-   . Fy., 1944-52. Libr. Asst.

Doney, Lucy Holt, 1900-1958. Fy., 1944-58. Cat. Libn. M.L.S. (Carnegie Tech.).

Smith, Frances S. (Fackler), 1920-   . Fy., 1944-50. Phys. Ed.

White, Fred Carlton,   . Fy., 1944-46. History. A.M.

Butler, Charles Chauncey,   . Fy., 1945-46. Math. A.M. (Columbia).

Klaus, Germaine L., 1909-   . Fy., 1945-46. Romance Lang. Cl. 1932. A.M.

Avery, William Turner, 1912-   . Fy., 1946-48. Classical and Mod. Lang. M.A. & Ph.D. (Western Reserve).

Barnes, Eric Wollencott, 1907-1962. Fy., 1946-53. English. *Diplome d'Etudes Supérieures*; D.Litt. (U. of Paris). *Who's Who.*

Bigelow, Richard Lynn, Jr., 1915-   . Fy., 1946-47. Pol. Sci. M.S. (Pa. State U.); LL.B. (Dickinson School of Law).

Bowman, James Donald, Jr., 1920-   . Fy., 1946-48. Econ.

Cooper, Anna Jarman, 1908-   . Fy., 1946-50. Ref. Libn. M.A. (N.Y.U.).

Dorey, J. Milnor,   . Fy., 1946. English. Cl. 1900.

Eaton, Stacey Elliott, 1900-1953. Fy., 1946-52. Romance Lang. A.M. (Bates); Ed.M. (Harvard).

Edel, William Wilcox, 1894-   . Pres., 1946-59. Cl. 1915. A.M.; D.D.; S.T.B. (Boston U.); L.H.D. (Keuka); D.D. (Hobart); LL.D. (Gettysburg, U. of Pa.), D.Hum. (Boston U.), J.U.D. (Lebanon Valley). *Who's Who.*

Embick, John Reigle, 1897-   . Fy., 1946-54. Geology, Chem. M.A. (Columbia).

Englemann, Hans Bernhard, 1915-   . Fy., 1946-47. German. M.A. (Columbia).

Gleim, David Ivan, 1896-   . Fy., 1946-65. Chem. M.A. (Columbia).

Horn, Robert A.,   . Fy., 1946. Soc. Sci. Ph.D.

Hudson, Richard Carroll, 1922-   . Fy., 1946-47. English. M.A. (U. of Pa.).

James, Walter Thomas, 1919-   , Fy., 1946-54. Philos., Religion. Cl. 1941. B.D. (Drew); M.A. & Ph.D. (Columbia).

Jarvis, Chester Edward, 1910-   . Fy., 1946-50. Pol. Sci. M.A. (U. of Calif.).

Karns, Charles W., 1920– . Fy., 1946. Math. Cl. 1941.

Kellogg, Charles Flint, 1909– . Fy., 1946– . History. M.A. (Harvard); Ph.D. (Johns Hopkins); L.H.D. (Bard).

Kepner, Charles David, 1893–1971. Fy., 1946–63. Soc. A.M. (Harvard); S.T.B. (Andover Theol. Sem.); Ph.D. (Columbia).

Ketterer, John J., 1921– . Fy., 1946. Biology. Cl. 1943.

King, Weir L., 1920– . Fy., 1946. Biology. Cl. 1946.

Kirk, William Wright, 1908– . Fy., 1946– . Mod. Lang. A.M. (Middlebury); Ph.D. (U. of Illinois).

Knapp, Ronald Ernest, 1910– . Fy., 1946–47. Phys. Ed. M.A. (Columbia).

Malcolm, Gilbert, 1892–1965. Vice-Pres., Pres., Provost, 1946–63. Cl. 1915. A.M.; LL.B. & LL.D. (Dickinson School of Law); LL.D. (Western Maryland). *Who's Who.*

Meals, Donald Weigel, 1922– . Fy., 1946. Soc. Sci. Cl. 1944.

Niehoff, Walter Hugo, 1910– . Fy., 1946–51. Pol. Sci. M.A. (Pa. State U.).

Orth, Andrew Park, 1894– . Fy., 1946–48. Econ. B.S.C. (Drexel); A.M. (U. of Pa.).

Pflaum, John Christian, 1903– . Fy., 1946–72. History. M.A. (U. of Pa.).

Phillips, James W., 1916– . Fy., 1946–47. Asst. Libn. B.S. in L.S. (Columbia).

Ricker, Ralph Ross, 1908– . Fy., 1946–50. Pol. Sci. M.A. (Pa. State U.).

Sandels, Friedrich, 1889– . Fy., 1946–59; 1960–62. German. Ph.D. (U. of Giessen).

Sloane, Margaret Mater (Martin), 1913– . Fy., 1946–49. French. Cl. 1935.

Sloane, William, 1910– . Fy., 1946– . English. M.A. & Ph.D. (Columbia). *Who's Who.*

Smith, Joseph Burkholder, 1921– . Fy., 1946–51. History. A.M. (U. of Pa.).

Spong, Richard Miller, 1916– . Fy., 1946–47. English. M.S. (Columbia).

Steckbeck, John Stohler, 1914– . Fy., 1946–55. Phys. Ed., Choir. M.Sc. (U. of Pa.).

Tayler, William Lonsdale, 1899– . Fy., 1946–61. Pol. Sci. M.A. (American U.); M.A. & Ph.D. (Columbia). *Who's Who.*

Taylor, Constance Hazelwood, 1922– . Fy., 1946–48. Biology.

Wanner, Richard Henry, 1917– . Fy., 1946–54, 1961– . Dean; Educ., Psych. Ed.M. & Ed.D. (Harvard).

Weigel, Harold Wildie, 1909–   . Fy., 1946–63. German. Cl. 1930. M.A.
& Ph.D. (Pa. State U.).

Crocetti, Guido, 1920–   . Fy., 1947–49. Sociology.

Dobson, Elinor Mae, 1924–   . Fy., 1947–49. Asst. Cat. Libn.

Fitzpatrick, Lucie 1903–   . Fy., 1947–49. Modern Lang. M.A. (Middlebury).

Flower, Milton Embick, 1910–   . Fy., 1947–   . Fine Arts, Pol. Sci.
A.M. & Ph.D. (Columbia).

Graf, Christian Victor, 1917–   . Fy., 1947–48. German. Cl. 1939.

Griswold, Robert Ralph, 1917–   . Fy., 1947–48. Curator Dickinsoniana. M.A. (Columbia).

Hess, Kenneth Widner,   . Fy., 1947–48. Math. M.Ed. (Pa. State
U.); LL.B. (Dickinson School of Law).

Horlacher, Amos Benjamin, 1902–   . Fy., 1947–70. Dean of Men; English. S.T.B. (Union); M.A. & Ed.D. (Columbia); D.D. (Wesleyan).

Kepner, Dorothy Warren, 1902–   . Fy., 1947–48; 1950–51. English.

Kirk, David Harvey, 1918–   . Fy., 1947–50. Phys. Ed.

McCullough, James Clair, 1885–1971. Fy., 1947–55. Educ. Cl. 1909.
A.M.; Ph.D. (N.Y.U.).

Mowery, Bob Lee, 1920–   . Fy., 1947–1951. Cat. Libn. B.L.S. (U. of
Chicago). *Who's Who.*

Price, Robert Vincent, 1920–   . Fy., 1947–49. Math. M.A. (Columbia).

Ricker, Virginia Dale,   . Fy., 1947–48. English. M.Ed. (Pa. State
U.).

Sowers, Doris Hamilton,   . Fy., 1947–48. Phys. Ed.

Swartz, Morris Emory, 1901–   . Fy., 1947–48. English. Cl. 1923.

Warlow, Francis Wayland, 1909–   . Fy., 1947–   . English. M.A. &
Ph.D. (U. of Pa.).

Wise, Robert Morrow, 1905–   . Fy., 1947–49. German. B.D. (Gettysburg).

Zaret, Daniel A., 1895–   . Fy., 1947–51. Modern Lang. M.A. (Moscow
U.).

Bowden, William Robert, 1914–   . Fy., 1948–   . English. A.M.
(Duke); Ph.D. (Yale).

Coren, Benedict Emanuel, 1924–   . Fy., 1948–52. Phys. Ed.

Davis, Bertram Hylton, 1918–   . Fy., 1948–57. English. A.M. & Ph.D.
(Columbia). *Who's Who.*

Gardner, George Redman, 1878–1966. Fy., 1948–53. Accounting. A.M.
(Columbia).

Hinkel, Jeannette Bastress, 1912–   . Fy., 1948–51. Phys. Ed. Cl. 1934.

Kennedy, Caroline Heath, 1906–   . Fy., 1948–71. Modern Lang. A.M.
(U. of Alabama); *Docteur d'Université* (U. of Laval).

McGee, William Harry, 1919– . Fy., 1948–50. Biology. M.S. (Kansas State Coll.).

Maurino, Ferdinando Dante, 1915– . Fy., 1948–61. Romance and Classical Lang. A.M. & Ph.D. (Columbia).

Miner, Thelma May (Smith), 1915– . Fy., 1948–51. English. Cl. 1935. A.M. & Ph.D. (U. of Pa.).

Nestor, Oscar Weamer, 1924– . Fy., 1948–49. Econ. M.B.A. (U. of Pa.).

Prinz, Arthur Max, 1898– . Fy., 1948–66. Econ. Ph.D. (U. of Berlin).

Robb, John Wesley, 1919– . Fy., 1948–54. Philos., Religion. Th.M. (U. of So. Calif.).

Bacon, Phoebe G. (Follmer), 1923– . Fy., 1949–51. Dean of Women. M.A. (Columbia).

Climenhaga, Asa W., 1889– . Fy., 1949–59. Registrar, Educ. M.A. (Wittenberg); Ed.D. (Syracuse).

Corcoran, Paul Aubrey, 1923– . Fy., 1949–51. Econ. M.A. (U. of Pittsburgh).

Horlacher, Thelma Race, 1905– . Fy., 1949–52. Psych. M.A. (N.Y.U.).

Josephson, Eric Jonathan, 1924– . Fy., 1949–51. Soc. M.A. (Columbia).

Nelson, Roger Eastman, 1902– . Fy., 1949–71. Dean; Math. M.A. (Dartmouth).

Sellers, Charles Coleman, 1903– . Fy., 1949– . Librarian, Curator of Dickinsoniana. A.M. (Harvard); Litt.D. (Temple). *Who's Who.*

Yates, Dorothy Custer, 1927– . Fy., 1949–51. Circ. Libn. M.S.L.S. (Western Reserve).

Bridgham, Philip Low, 1921– . Fy., 1950–52. Pol. Sci. M.A. & Ph.D. (Fletcher School of Law and Diplomacy).

Eimer, Jane Thatcher, 1925– . Fy., 1950–52. Cat. Libn.

Groom, John Louis, 1922– . Fy., 1950–52. Pol. Sci. B.D. (Northern Baptist Sem.).

Kellogg, Mary Margaret, 1917– . Fy., 1950–54. Dean of Women.

Maze, Frank Richard, 1919–1971. Fy., 1950–52. Phys. Ed. M.S. (Syracuse).

Miller, Sarah Louise, 1928– . Fy., 1950–51. Biology. Cl. 1950.

Montgomery, Robert Elsworth, 1926– . Fy., 1950–51. Math. M.S. (U. of Illinois).

Olewine, Donald Austin, 1926– . Fy., 1950–51. Biology. Cl. 1950.

Ramos, Margaret McAlpin, 1898– . Fy., 1950–66. Mod. Lang. M.A. (U. of Tenn.).

Remsberg, Henry Calvin, 1916– . Fy., 1950–57. Music, Band. Cl. 1938.

Stevenson, Gerald McMonies, Jr., 1923– . Fy., 1950–55. Ref. Libr. M.A. (Kent State).

Uhland, Jean Harper, 1926– . Fy., 1950–51. Economics. M.A. (Ohio State).

Alexander, Galen Stiteler, . Fy., 1951–52. Asst. Libn. M.S.L.S. (Columbia).

Bartsch, Rose, 1896– . Fy., 1951–52. Modern Lang. Ph.D. (U. of Hamburg).

Foose, Jean B., . Fy., 1951–52. Library Asst.

Gates, Warren James, 1920– . Fy., 1951– . History. A.M. & Ph.D. (U. of Pa.).

Hays, Edward Gardner, . Fy., 1951–56. Phys. Ed.

Hopper, John De Wolf, 1923– . Fy., 1951–52. Phys. Ed. LL.B. (Dickinson School of Law). Tr., 1970– .

Hursky, Jacob, 1923– . Fy., 1951–52. Modern Lang. Ph.M. (Ukrainian Free U., Munich).

McGill, Robert Alan, 1924– . Fy., 1951–59. English. Cl. 1949. M.A. & Ph.D. (U. of Pa.).

Memory, Marian Randolph, 1926– . Fy., 1951–52. Phys. Ed.

Mercer, Hugh Hathaway, 1927– . Fy., 1951–53. Econ. A.M. (Cornell).

Westlake, Thayer Addison, 1915– . Fy., 1951–52. English. Th.B. (Westminster Theol. Sem.). M.A. (U. of Pa.).

Bush, Charles Harry, 1925– . Fy., 1952–54. Phys. Ed.

Carpenter, Charles Albert, 1929– . Fy., 1952–54. Circ. Libn. M.A. (Kent State).

Davis, Hamilton Chace, 1927– . Fy., 1952–55. History, Admissions. Cl. 1950.

Dietze, Gottfried, 1922– . Fy., 1952–54. Pol. Sci. Dr.Jur. (Heidelberg); A.M. & Ph.D. (Princeton).

Donofrio, Harold Charles, 1928– . Fy., 1952–53. Mil. Sci.

Finck, Edgar Moore, 1888–1966. Fy., 1952–58. Education. M.A. (Princeton); Ph.D. (N.Y.U.).

Flaherty, Donald William, 1921– . Fy., 1952– . Pol. Sci. Ph.D. (Syracuse).

Glendening, William Aloysius, . Fy., 1952. ROTC.

Graffam, Donald Turner, 1905– .Fy., 1952–71. Psych., Educ. A.M. & Ed.D. (U. of So. Calif.).

Hinkle, James Currey, 1923– . Fy., 1952–54. English. M.A. (Harvard).

Iorio, John Joseph, 1925– . Fy., 1952–53. English. M.A. (Columbia).

Kolodinsky, Joseph Elias, . Fy., 1952. ROTC.

Lauro, Lindy Lindoro, 1921– . Fy., 1952–55. Phys. Ed.

Ness, Frederic William, 1914– . Fy., 1952–60. Dean; English. Cl. 1933. M.A. (U. of Cinn.); Ph.D. (Yale). *Who's Who.*

Rachal, Daniel William, 1914–   . Fy., 1952–54. Mil. Sci.

Ransom, Alured Chaffee, 1908–   . Fy., 1952–55. Phys. Ed. M. Ed. (U. of Pittsburgh).

Rath, Arthur, 1919–   . Fy., 1952–53. French, Spanish. Teacher's diploma. (State Board, Basel, Switzerland).

Roper, James Edgar, 1918–   . Fy., 1952–54. English. M.A. (Yale).

Smith, Irvine Noble, 1923–   . Fy., 1952–56. Drama & Speech. M.A. (U. of N.C.).

Tharp, Charles Conway, 1921–   . Fy., 1952–53; 1961–63. Cat. Libr. M.S.L.S. (U. of Illinois).

Tucker, Walter Ferson,   . Fy., 1952–53. Mil. Sci.

Wagner, Lee Ann Bonne, 1926–   . Fy., 1952–61; 1966–   . Phys. Ed.

Wildman, Clyde Everett, 1889–1955. Fy., 1952–55. English Bible. S.T.B. & Ph.D. (Boston U.); D.D. (Cornell Coll.); LL.D. (Northeastern, Wabash); S.T.D. (Northwestern); D.Sc. Ed. (Boston U.); Litt.D. (Rose Poly. Inst.). *Who's Who.*

Zuber, Stephanie Primevere,   . Fy., 1952–53. Modern Lang.

Baynes, William Fraser,   . Fy., 1953–57. ROTC.

Bloodgood, Willard Gordon, 1924–   . Fy., 1953–56. Econ. M.S. (U. of Mass.).

Cahn, Harold Archambo, 1922–   . Fy., 1953–56. Biology. M.A. (U. of Wyoming).

Eurich, James Charles,   . Fy., 1953–56. ROTC.

Hammatt, Hallett Barker, 1902–   . Fy., 1953–57. Math. M.A. (Harvard).

Jordan, Harvie Brannon,   . Fy., 1953–54. ROTC.

Karp, Stephen Arnold,   . Fy., 1953–54. Psych. M.A. (New School for Soc. Res.).

Kenagy, Herbert Glenn, 1892–   . Fy., 1953–55. Econ., Asst. to Pres. A.M. (U. of Minn.).

Kennedy, William Cosgrove,   . Fy., 1953–56. Mil. Sci.

Nevensel, Harverd L., 1917–   . Fy., 1953–56. Mil. Sci.

Shoaf, Frank Robert, 1926–   . Fy., 1953–54. Psych. Cl. 1952.

Street, John Edward,   . Fy., 1953–58. ROTC.

Taylor, Jed Harbottle, 1902–   . Fy., 1953–58. Cat. Libn. M.A. (Boston U.).

Trease, B. David, 1916–   . Fy., 1953–57. Modern Lang. A.M. & Ph.D. (U. of Mich.).

Burkle, Howard Russell, 1925–   . Fy., 1954–58. Philos., Religion. S.T.D. & Ph.D. (Yale Divinity School); Ph.D. (Yale U.).

Creech, Leo E.,   . Fy., 1954–55. ROTC.

Dentler, Robert Arnold, 1928–   . Fy., 1954–57. Soc. M.A. (Northwestern, American U.); Ph.D. (U. of Chicago.).

Difford, Winthrop Cecil, 1921–   Fy., 1954–66. Geology. M.S.
  (W.Va.U.); Ph.D. (Syracuse).

Eason, George Winifred, 1916–   . Fy., 1954–57. Mil. Sci.

Frogen, George H., 1910–70. Fy., 1954–60. Classical Lang. M.A. & Ph.D.
  (U. of Minn.).

Harper, Heber Reece, 1920–   . Fy., 1954–   . Pol. Sci. M.A. (U. of
  Mich.).

Jantzen, Robert Manny,   . Fy., 1954–56. ROTC.

Kaiser, Richard Lamont, 1923–   . Fy., 1954–55. Psych. M.A. & Ph.D.
  (U. of Texas).

Livermore, Bettie Yvonne, 1924–   . Fy., 1954–57. Soc. M.So.W. (Carnegie Inst.).

Long, Albert Webster,   . Fy., 1954–55. ROTC.

Mayfield, Clifton Elvans, 1918–   . Fy., 1954–61. Psych. Ph.D. (U. of
  Pa.).

Mayfield, Jane Farr,   . Fy., 1954–60. Psych. M.A. (U. of Pa.).

Moore, Frank McCaughey, 1919–   . Fy., 1954–57. Mil. Sci.

Pattinson, John Patrick, 1920–   . Fy., 1954–59. English. M.A. (Cambridge U.).

Peterkin, Lionel Denis, 1888–1957. Fy., 1954–57. Humanities. M.A. (Durham U.).

Reynolds, Victoria Kathryn (Hann), 1930–   . Fy., 1954–59. Dean of
  Women. Cl. 1950. M.A. (Columbia). Tr., 1969–   .

Ripley, Julien Ashton, Jr., 1908–   . Fy., 1954–57. Physics. M.A. (Harvard). Ph.D. (U. of Virginia).

Sia, Richard Mae, 1906–   . Fy., 1954–   . Physics. M.S. (U. of Chicago).

Skinner, Carl Frederick, 1929–   . Fy., 1954–55. Debate. Cl. 1953.

Stone, Raymond Pitman, 1928–   . Fy., 1954–57. Pol. Sci. M.A. (Princeton).

Taylor, Charles Alton, Jr.,   . Fy., 1954–55. ROTC.

Yaverbaum, Irving, 1906–   . Fy., 1954–59. Taxation, Accounting.

Benson, William Howard, 1902–   . Fy., 1955–70. Math.

Coleman, Harold James, 1921–   . Fy., 1955–56.

Conte, Angelo James,   . Fy., 1955–58. ROTC.

Davis, Walter Richardson, 1928–   . Fy., 1955–56. English. M.A. (Yale).

Del Rio Setien, German, 1925–   . Fy., 1955–56. Modern Lang.

Du Charme, Joseph Gordon, 1923–   . Fy., 1955–   . Phys. Ed. M.A.
  (N.Y.U.).

Eavenson, David Balbach, 1917–   . Fy., 1955–   . Phys. Ed.

Flandreau, Arthur Conover, Jr., 1927–   . Fy., 1955–61. Ref. Libr.
  M.A. (U. of Chicago).

Folden, Dewey Bray, Jr., 1923–   . Fy., 1955–57. Biology. M.S.
  (W.Va.U.).

Gallub, Arnold M., 1913–   . Fy., 1955–56. Physics. M.S. (N.Y.U.).

La Vallee, Laurent Raymond, 1913–   . Fy., 1955–56. Economics. M.A. (Indiana U.); Ph.D. (Syracuse).

Maguire, John Anderson, 1906–   . Fy., 1955–60. Romance Lang. M.A. (Catholic U.); Ph.D. (Johns Hopkins).

Piez, Brinton Carl, 1923–   . Fy., 1955–57. Phys. Ed. M.A. (Ohio State).

Royer, Ruth Christine, 1927–   . Fy., 1955–59. English. M.A. (U. of Pa.).

Sheppard, Joseph Sherly, 1930–   . Fy., 1955–57. Fine Arts.

Shuman, George, Jr., 1914–   . Fy., 1955–67. Financial Vice-Pres. and Treasurer. Cl. 1937. LL.D. (Lycoming). Trustee 1949–   .

Smith, Nancy Page, 1920–   . Fy., 1955–56. Music. M.A. (U. of N.C.).

Smith, Paul Alan Lawrence, 1928–   . Fy., 1955–58. Pol. Sci. Ph.D. (Princeton).

Walker, Albert, 1920–   . Fy., 1955–60. Asst. to Pres. Journalism. M.S. (Northwestern).

Wells, Raymond James, 1925–   . Fy., 1955–57. Philos., Relig. Ph.D. (U. of Edinburgh).

Ziegler, George William, Jr., 1916–   . Fy., 1955–57. Chem. Ph.D. (Ohio State U.).

Andrew, Kenneth L., 1919–   . Fy., 1956–57. Physics. M.A. (Johns Hopkins); Ph.D. (Purdue).

Arnold, Arthur Edward, II, 1920–   . Fy., 1956–58. Modern Lang. Cl. 1950.

Brubaker, David Frantz, 1924–   . Fy., 1956–   . Dramatic Arts.

Bruchey, Stuart Weems, 1917–   . Fy., 1956–57. History. M.A. & Ph.D. (Johns Hopkins). *Who's Who.*

Carson, James William, 1925–   . Fy., 1956–   . History. M.A. (Miami U.).

Gavrilovic, Stoyan, 1894–1965. Fy., 1956–63. Pol. Sci. Dr. Jur. Int'l. Law (U. of Geneva).

Haller, William, Jr., 1914–   . Fy., 1956–58. Economics. M.A. & Ph.D. (Columbia).

Havens, Mary Hamilton,   . Fy., 1956–57. Phys. Ed.

Herrick, Mildred,   . Fy., 1956–57. Visiting Libn. A.M.L.S. (U. of Mich.).

Houston, Andrew Craig, 1929–   . Fy., 1956–   . Econ. Ph.D. (Pa. State U.).

Kent, Thaddeus Francis,   . Fy., 1956–59. ROTC.

McDonald, Barbara Brown, 1924–   . Fy., 1956–   . Biology. M.A. & Ph.D. (Columbia).

McDonald, Daniel James, 1925– . Fy., 1956– . Biology. M.A. & Ph.D. (Columbia).

McLennand, William John, 1906– . Fy., 1956–57. Educ., Psych. M.A. (U. of Toledo).

Peterson, Charles Edwin, Jr., 1927– . Fy., 1956–58. Educ., Asst. Dean Admissions. M.A. (Bucknell).

Prentice, James Stuart, 1889– . Fy., 1956–59. Econ. M.A. (Queens U., Canada).

Reagan, Mike Charles . Fy., 1956–57. ROTC.

Scandling, John D., 1925– . Fy., 1956–59. Mil. Sci.

Ultan, Lloyd, 1929– . Fy., 1956–62. Music. M.A. (Columbia); Ph.D. (State U. of Iowa).

Allen, John William, . Fy., 1957–64. Physics.

Beierschmitt, Robert John, . Fy., 1957–62. ROTC.

Casper, Elizabeth Warren, 1934– . Fy., 1957–59. Soc.

Coutts, Alan, 1907–1963. Fy., 1957–63. Dean of Men; Speech. M.A. (Northwestern).

Deshon, George Ellis, 1915– . Fy., 1957–59. Mil. Sci. M.B.A. (U. of Texas).

Dixon, John Wesley, Jr., 1919– . Fy., 1957–58. Fine Arts. Ph.D. (Chicago).

Henschen, Homer Ernst, . Fy., 1957–64. Physics, Chem.

Israel, Thomas Andrew 1917– . Fy., 1957–59. Pol. Sci. M.A. (U. of Chicago).

Kiser, Howard Francis, . Fy., 1957–63. ROTC.

Kuhinka, Ernest, 1922– . Fy., 1957–62. Soc. M.A. & Ph.D. (U. of Utrecht).

Leatherman, Jay Artley, 1918– . Fy., 1957–63. Practical Theol. S.T.B. (Boston U. School of Theol.).

Lerch, Donald Paul, . Fy., 1957–59. Physics.

Leslie, James Stewart, 1925– . Fy., 1957–60. Dir. of Religious Life. S.T.B. (Boston U. School of Theol.); Ph.D. (Boston U.).

Miller, Walter McKinley, 1896–1966. Fy., 1957–64. Math. M.A. (Pa. State U.); Ph.D. (U. of Illinois).

Modder, Montagu Frank, 1891–1958. Fy., 1957–58. English. A.M. (Clark U.); Ph.D. (U. of Mich.).

Moser, Donald Carl, 1929–1961. Fy., 1957–61. Psych. A.M. & Ph.D. (Columbia).

Ogren, Robert Edward, 1922– . Fy., 1957–63. Biology. M.S. (Northwestern), Ph.D. (U. of Illinois).

Oldenburg, Edgar Bradley, . Fy., 1957–65. Chem. M.S. (Wayne U.).

Patton, James H., Jr., . Fy., 1957–63. ROTC.

Pusey, John Drake, 1905–1966. Fy., 1957–65. Fine Arts.

Ream, Charles Robert, 1928–   . Fy., 1957–60. Phys. Ed. M.Ed. (U. of Pittsburgh).

Richter, Horst Paul, 1922–   . Fy., 1957–58. Physics. *Staatsexamen* Goethe U.).

Rinker, Jacob Aaron, 1886–   . Fy., 1957–58. Physics. M.S. (U. of Chicago).

Rothstein, Edward, 1916–   . Fy., 1957–61. Soc. M.Ed. (U. of N.H.).

Russell, Albert Lawrence, Jr., 1923–   . Fy., 1957–60. Mil. Sci.

Seibert, Donald Reck, 1922–   . Fy., 1957–   . Phys. Ed. M.A. (Columbia).

Stewart, John A.,   . Fy., 1957–60. ROTC.

Strayer, Daisy Wilson, 1918–   . Fy., 1957–60. Phys. Ed.

Thomson, Herbert Fergus, Jr., 1917–   . Fy., 1957–61. Econ. S.T.M. (Union Theol. Sem.); M.A. (U. of Colorado); Ph.D. (Columbia).

Vernon, William W., 1925–   . Fy., 1957–   . Geology. M.S. & Ph.D. (Lehigh).

Wells, Hal Marion, 1920–   . Fy., 1957–60. Psych., M.A. (Columbia).

Wishmeyer, William Hood, 1918–   . Fy., 1957–   . English. M.A. & Ph.D. (U. of Pa.).

Young, Henry James, 1908–   . Fy., 1957–   . Curator of Dickinsoniana, History. Ph.D. (Johns Hopkins).

Andrews, Robert Nathan Hale, 1926–   . Fy., 1958–63. English. M.A. (Columbia).

Baranger, Claude Marie Louise, 1933–   . Fy., 1958–59. French. *Lic. d'Anglais* (U. of Paris).

Beaty, Nancy Lee, 1923–   . Fy., 1958–63. English. Ph.D. (Yale).

Bonney, Katharine A., 1910–   . Fy., 1958–64. Philos., Relig. M.A. (Teachers Coll., Columbia); Ph.D. (Boston Univ. Sch. of Theol.).

Hartshorn, Alfred Newlon, 1909–   . Fy., 1958–   . English. A.M. (U. of Rochester).

Jarrett, Jack Marius, 1934–   . Fy., 1958–61. Music. M.A. (Eastman School of Music, U. of Rochester).

Kahler, Conrad Andrew, 1927–1961. Fy., 1958–61. Asst. Cat. Libn. M.S. (Kansas State Coll.); M.L.S. (Rutgers).

Kaufman, Belle S., 1919–   . Fy., 1958–59. Math.

Long, Howard Charles, 1918–   . Fy., 1959–   . Physics, Astronomy. Ph.D. (Ohio State U.).

Miller, Frank Arnold, 1924–   . Fy., 1958–62. History.

Naff, Anna S., 1920–   . Fy., 1958–59; 1963–64. Chem., Sci. Libn. M.S. (U. of Kentucky); M.A. (U. of Mich.).

Naff, M. Benton, 1918–   . Fy., 1958–66. Chemistry. M.S. (U. of Kentucky); Ph.D. (Oregon State Coll.).

Newman, Herbert Ellis, 1914–   . Fy., 1958–66. Economics. A.M. & Ph.D. (U. of Virginia).

Olin, Jacqueline Smith, 1932–   . Fy., 1958–60. Chem. Cl. 1954. M.A. (Harvard).

Schiffman, Joseph, 1914–   . Fy., 1958–   . English. M.A. (Columbia); Ph.D. (N.Y.U.). *Who's Who.*

Scott, Samuel Gray, 1930–   . Fy., 1958–61. Psych. Ph.D. (Cornell).

Seabury, Claire Clifford, 1902–   . Fy., 1958–59. Math. M.C.E. (Rensselaer Poly. Inst.).

Stark, Anna Magdalena, 1912–   . Fy., 1958–59. German. Ph.D. (U. of Munich).

Stone, Alexander P., 1928–   . Fy., 1958–60. Physics. M.S.E.E. (Newark Coll. of Eng'r.)

Swaim, Kathleen Mackenzie, 1936–   . Fy., 1958–60. English. M.A. (Pa. State U.).

Wiley, Robert Burbank, 1926–   . Fy., 1958–62. Philos. M.A. (U. of Toronto).

Yeagley, Henry Lincoln, 1899–   . Fy., 1958–69. Physics, Astronomy. M.S. & Ph.D. (Pa. State U.).

Bodkin, John P.,   . Fy., 1959–61. ROTC.

Brougher, John F., 1903–   . Fy., 1959–62. Educ. M.A. (Columbia); Ed.D. (Geo. Washington U.).

Dewis, Diane Isabel, 1927–   . Fy., 1959–64. French. A.M. (U. of Kansas).

Erickson, Luther Eugene, 1933–   . Fy., 1959–62. Chem. Ph.D. (U. of Wisconsin).

Flandreau, Janet Elder, 1929–   . Fy., 1959–61. Classical Lang. Cl. 1950.

Harrison, Bradford, III, 1931–   . Fy., 1959–60. Asst. Ref. Libn. M.S. (Drexel).

Jeffries, William Bowman, 1926–   . Fy., 1959–   . Biology. M.A. & Ph.D. (U. of N.C.).

Kerr, Carl Elwood, 1926–   . Fy., 1959–69. Math. M.A. (U. of Del.)., Ph.D. (Lehigh).

King, John Lloyd, 1921–   . Fy., 1959–   . Accounting. M.A. (U. of Denver).

Light, John Henry, 1924–   . Fy., 1959–   . Math., Registrar. M.S. in Physics & M.S. in Eng'r Mechs. (Pa. State U.).

Masland, Frank Elmer, Jr., 1895–   . Fy., 1959–65. Nat. History. Cl. 1918. H.H.D. (Lycoming); LL.D. (Lebanon Valley). Tr., 1946–65. *Who's Who.*

Moyle, William Henry, 1922–   . Fy., 1959–61. Sociology. Cl. 1946. M.S. (Columbia).

Peer, Nancy Edwards, 1937–   . Fy., 1959–60. Biology. Cl. 1959.

Pinson, William Calvin, 1921–   Fy., 1959–62. Mil. Sci.

Rittgers, Forest Sheldon, Jr., 1931–   . Fy., 1959–62. Mil. Sci.

Royce, Herbert, 1900–   . Fy., 1959–67. Modern Lang. Dr. Rel. Pol. (U. of Koenigsberg).

Secor, Philip B., 1931–   . Fy., 1959–63. Pol. Sci. A.M. & Ph.D. (Duke).

Smead, Jane Van Ness, 1888–   . Fy., 1959–61. Modern Lang. M.A. & Ph.D. (Johns Hopkins).

Trépanier, Estelle, 1918–   . Fy., 1959–60. French, Spanish. *Doctorat* (U. of Paris).

Wang, Yi Chu, 1916–   . Fy., 1959–60. Soc. Ph.D. (U. of Chicago).

Wishmeyer, Barbara Townsend (Stevens), 1933–   . Fy., 1959–67 Dean of Women. M.S. (Indiana U.).

Andrews, Bruce Rawnsley, 1926–   . Fy., 1960–   . Pol. Sci. Ph.D. (Syracuse).

Barber, Kathleen White, 1925–   . Fy., 1960–   . Phys. Ed.

Broughton Suzanne Myers, 1936–   . Fy., 1960–62. Physics. M.A. (Brandeis).

Coslett, Stephen B., 1931–   . Fy., 1960–   . Psych., Counselling. M.A. & Ph.D. (U. of Denver).

Davis, Jean White, 1932–   . Fy., 1960–61. English. A.M. (Temple).

Frey, John William, 1916–   . Fy., 1960–66. Russian. A.M. & Ph.D. (U. of Illinois).

Gillespie, Harold Reese, Jr., 1929–   . Fy., 1960–   . English, Dean of Students. M.A. (U. of Texas).

Gobrecht, Wilbur Jacob, 1930–   . Fy., 1960–   . Phys. Ed. Cl. 1952. A.M. (Duke).

Gordon, Donald E., 1931–   . Fy., 1960–69. Fine Arts. A.M. & Ph.D. (Harvard).

Hartman, Frank Rittenhouse, 1931–   . Fy., 1960–   . Psych. M.S. & Ph.D. (Pa. State U.).

Jacobs, Rene Curtiss, 1922–   . Fy., 1960–63. Mil. Sci.

Kneen, Judith Folger, 1936–   . Fy., 1960–67. Math. A.M. (Radcliffe).

Loughridge, Nancy Joanne, 1930–   . Fy., 1960–68. Ref. Libn. M.A.L.S. (U. of Mich.).

Means, Thomas, 1889–1961. Fy., 1960–61. Classical Lang. M.A. (Yale, Harvard).

Ricois, Micheline Marie, 1930–   . Fy., 1960–61. French. *Licence d'Anglais, Dipl. d'Études Sup., C.A.P.E.S., l'Agrégation* (Sorbonne).

Simpson, William Stanley, Jr., 1925–   . Fy., 1960–61. Mil. Sci.

Smith, Robert Ernest, III, 1931–   . Fy., 1960. English. M.A. (Johns Hopkins).

Webb, William H., 1893–   . Fy., 1960–61. Chem. Ed.M. (Harvard).

Zeladonis, Vincent M.,   . Fy., 1960–61. ROTC.

Beekey, Lois Elva, 1933–   . Fy., 1961–63. Russian.

Carson, Martha Church, 1924–1967. Fy., 1961–65. Ref. & Doc. Libn. M.A. (Miami U.); M.S.L.S. (Syracuse).

Clipper, Lawrence Jon, 1930–   . Fy., 1961–63. English. M.A. (Geo. Washington U.).

Doebler, Bettie Anne, 1931–   . Fy., 1961–70. English. M.A. (Duke); Ph.D. (U. of Wisc.).

Doebler, John Willard, 1932–   . Fy., 1961–70. English. M.A. & Ph.D. (U. of Wisc.).

Edberg, George John, 1924–   . Fy., 1961–65. Romance Lang. A.M. (U. of Havana); Ph.D. (U. of Kansas).

Gray, William L., 1933–   . Fy., 1961–64. Modern Lang. A.M. (Middlebury).

Gulledge, William Dixon, 1915–   . Fy., 1961–64. ROTC.

Hays, Raphael Smead, 1934–   . Fy., 1961–64. Phys. Ed. Cl. 1956

Kally, Konstantin M., 1914–   . Fy., 1961–62. Russian. M.A. (Indiana U.).

Kendall, Ann Reiter, 1924–   . Fy., 1961–65. Physics. M.A. (Wellesley).

Lezzer, Dolores June (Bracken), 1937–   . Fy., 1961–67. Phys. Ed.

Morrison, Gerald K.,   . Fy., 1961–63. Math.

Mueller, Frank Frederick, Jr., 1937–   . Fy., 1961–65. Music. M.Mus. (U. of Mich.).

Nodder, Stanley, Jr., 1931–   . Fy., 1961–71. Classical Lang. A.M. & Ph.D. (U. of Pa.).

Rubendall, Howard Lane, 1910–   . Pres., 1961–   . Cl. 1931. D.D. (Union Theol. Sem.); L.H.D. (Trinity Coll.); LL.D. (U. of Pa.); LL.D. (Dickinson School of Law). *Who's Who.*

Ruiz, Roberto, 1925–   . Fy., 1961–63. Romance Lang. M.A. (National U. of Mexico).

Seaford, Henry Wade, 1922–   . Fy., 1961–   . Sociology, Anthropology. A.M. & Ph.D. (Harvard).

Wiley, Marion Elizabeth, 1928–   . Fy., 1961–63. German. M.A. (Pa. State U.).

Williams, Clarence Oscar, 1895–   . Fy., 1961–66. Educ., Asst. Admissions. M.A. (Teacher's Coll., Columbia), Ed.D. (N.Y.U.).

Wood, George Frederick, 1917–   . Fy., 1961–63. ROTC.

Angiolillo, Paul Francis Mathew, 1917–   . Fy., 1962–   . Modern Lang. A.M. & Ph.D. (Columbia); *Officier des Palmes Académiques.*

Dengler, George Henry, 1936–   . Fy., 1962–63. History. M.A. (U. of Rhode Island). M.A. (U. of Rhode Island).

Enders, Donald E.,   . Fy., 1962–64. Educ. M.A. (N.Y.U.); Ed.D. (Pa. State U.).

Ferré, Frederick Pond, 1933–   . Fy., 1962–   . Philos. M.A. (Vanderbilt); Ph.D. (U. of St. Andrew).

Fischer, David, 1929–   . Fy., 1962–65. History. A.M. (Columbia).

Furman, Marian Schwalm,   . Fy., 1962–63. Soc. LL.B. (Dickinson School of Law).

Greenwalt, Robert L.,   . Fy., 1962–63. ROTC.

Hastings, Thomas Hubert,   . Fy., 1962–65. Mil. Sci.

Heddendorf, Russell Howard, 1930–   . Fy., 1962–64. Soc. M.A. (Columbia).

Hurst, Cam Jennings, Jr., 1925–   . Fy., 1962–65. Mil. Sci.

Laws, Kenneth L., 1935–   . Fy., 1962–   . Physics. M.S. (U. of Pa.); Ph.D. (Bryn Mawr).

Magill, Samuel Hays, 1928–   . Fy., 1962–68. Chaplain, Dean; Relig. B.D. (Yale), Ph.D. (Duke).

Markley, Kenneth Alan,   . Fy., 1962–63. Psych. Cl. 1955. M.A. (N.Y.U.).

Maurer, Warren Melvin, 1927–   . Fy., 1962–69. Educ., Psych. M.S. (Stout State Coll., Wisc.).

Nilsson, Karl Robert, 1927–   . Fy., 1962–   . Pol. Sci. M.A. (Johns Hopkins); Ph.D. (Columbia).

Perry, Donald Munson, 1938–   . Fy., 1962–65. Soc. M.A. (U. of Conn.).

Posey, J. Forrest, Jr., 1930–   . Fy., 1962–   . Music. M.Mus. (U. of Texas); M.A. (Harvard).

Roper, Gerald Chester, 1933–   . Fy., 1962–   . Chem. Ph.D. (Boston U.).

Sabin, Hilbert S., 1935–   . Fy., 1962–71. Fine Arts. M.F.A. (U. of Pittsburgh).

Tenelly, Cosmo Paul,   . Fy., 1962–63. ROTC.

Young, Patricia Bradley, 1931–   . Fy., 1962–64. English. Cl. 1953.

Alexander, Herbert S., 1939–   . Fy., 1963–   . Psych. M.A. & Ph.D. (Columbia).

Allan, George James, 1935–   . Fy., 1963–   . Philos. Ph.D. (Yale).

Allshouse, Merle Frederick, 1935–   . Fy., 1963–70. Philos. M.A. & Ph.D. (Yale).

Beougher, Howard T.,   . Fy., 1963–64. ROTC.

Biebel, Paul Joseph, 1928–   . Fy., 1963–   . Biology. M.S. (St. Louis U.); Ph.D. (Indiana U.).

Bloom, Joseph, . Fy., 1963–64. ROTC.

Bogojavlensky, Marianna, 1915– . Fy., 1963– . German, Russian. M.A. (U. of Helsinki); Ph.D. (Yale).

Broujos, Louise, 1927– . Fy., 1963– . English, Public Speaking. M.L. (U. of Pittsburgh).

Campbell, W. Donald, 1939– . Fy., 1963–64. Asst. Chaplain.

Crist, Ray Henry, 1900– . Fy., 1963–71. Chem. Cl. 1920. A.M. & Ph.D. (Columbia); Sc.D. (Dickinson).

De Borde, John, Jr., . Fy., 1963–66. ROTC.

Giglio, Ernest David, 1931– . Fy., 1963–65. Pol. Sci. M.A. (Albany State Coll.).

Giglio, Karin Kluge, 1940– . Fy., 1963–64. German.

Jefferson, David Rowe, 1931– . Fy., 1963–69. Dean, Admissions. B.D. (Yale).

Kogut, Walter J., . Fy., 1963–64. ROTC.

Learned, Mary R., 1895– . Fy., 1963–66. Romance Lang. Cl. 1921. M.A. (U. of N.C.); Ph.D. (Radcliffe).

Light, Ellen Susan, 1940– . Fy., 1963–64. Romance Lang. M.A. (Yale).

Lockhart, Philip North, 1928– . Fy., 1963– . Classical Lang. M.A. (U. of N.C.); Ph.D. (Yale).

McBride, Eugene Ronald, . Fy., 1963–66. Mil. Sci.

McElhaney, Harold N., 1935– . Fy., 1963–64. Phys. Ed.

Morrissey, Leroy John, 1935– . Fy., 1963–65. English. M.A. (U. of Chicago); Ph.D. (U. of Pa.).

Neitz, Cordelia Miller, 1911– . Fy., 1963– . Cat. Libn. B.S. in L.S. (Syracuse), M.S.Ed. (Temple).

Pease, N. Ronald, 1933– . Fy., 1963–68. Dean of Men. M.A. (Colgate).

Swinton, Cordelia Westervelt, . Fy., 1963–66. Cat. Libn. M.L.S. (U. of Pittsburgh).

Tomko, George Peter, 1933– . Fy., 1963–64. Fine Arts.

Washington, Joseph Reed, Jr., 1930– . Fy., 1963–66. Religion, Chaplain. Th.D. (Boston U.).

Whitehouse, Robert Stanley, 1893– . Fy., 1963–66. Modern Lang. M.A. (U. of Rochester).

Ashnault, Edward Joseph, 1934– . Fy., 1964–67. Phys. Ed. M.Ed. (Fairfield U.).

Baric, Lee Wilmer, 1932– . Fy., 1964– . Math. Cl. 1956. M.Sc. & Ph.D. (Lehigh).

Barrick, Mac Eugene, 1933– . Fy., 1964–68. Spanish Cl. 1955. M.A. (U. of Illinois).

Bechtel, Daniel Rodney, 1932–   . Fy., 1964–   . Religion. B.D. (Yale), Ph.D. (Drew).

Benson, John Edward, 1924–   . Fy., 1964–   . Chem. M.A. & Ph.D. (Princeton).

Berczeller, Eva Borsodi-Berkovitz, 1926–   . Fy., 1964–65. Philos. Ph.D. (U. of Debrecen, Hungary).

Biel, Bruce Edward, 1926–   . Fy., 1964–65. English. Cl. 1951. M.A. (U. of Pa.).

Booth, Harry Fehr, 1927–   . Fy., 1964–   . Religion. S.T.B. & Ph.D. (Boston U.).

Broujos, John Horace, 1929–   . Fy., 1964–66. Public Speaking. LL.B. (Dickinson School of Law).

Conner, Marcia Bacon, 1925–   . Fy., 1964–   . English. M.A. (Columbia).

Diehl, John Edwin, 1929–   . Fy., 1964–65. Chem. M.S. & Ph.D. (Pa. State U.).

Kavolis, Vytautas Martynas, 1930–   . Fy., 1964–   . Soc. M.A. & Ph.D. (Harvard).

Kehoe, Anthony Francis,   . Fy., 1964–66. ROTC.

Lange, Liliane Emilie Marie-Jeanne, 1922–   . Fy., 1964–66. French. 2nd degree (U. of Law Aix-en-Provence).

Lin, Linda Pin-Cheau, 1934–   . Fy., 1964–65. Asst. Cat. Libn. M.A.L.S. (George Peabody Coll.).

Ludwig, Allan Ira, 1933–   . Fy., 1964–68. Fine Arts. M.A. & Ph.D. (Yale).

McDermott, John J.,   . Fy., 1964–65. Biology. M.S. (U. of Del.).

Marshall, Robert E., 1939–   . Fy., 1964–71. Phys. Ed. M.S. (W. Va. U.).

Page, Lois Anne (Mecum), 1939–   . Fy., 1964–66. English. M.A. (W.Va.U.).

Rhoads, Charley Ann (Perkins), 1938–   . Fy., 1964–66. French. M.A. (Middlebury).

Rollfinke, Dieter Juergen, 1942–   . Fy., 1964–   . German. M.A. (Columbia).

Ruff, Joseph Russell, 1931–   . Fy., 1964–66. English. M.A. (Temple).

Schmidt, Marilyn Low 1939–   . Fy., 1964–66. Fine Arts. M.A. (U. of Calif., Berkeley).

Skok, Joseph Aloysius, 1933–   . Fy., 1964–67. Educ. M. Ed. (Pa. State U.).

Smoller, Sanford Jerome, 1937–   . Fy., 1964–67. English. M.A. (Columbia).

Spain, William Herbert, Jr., 1938–   . Fy., 1964–67. Mil. Sci.

Taylor, Jeff J.,   . Fy., 1964–67. ROTC.

Tuttle, Carolyn May, 1941–   . Fy., 1964–65. Spanish. M.A. (Middlebury).

Vukcevich, Ivo, 1934–   . Fy., 1964–69. Pol. Sci. M.A. (N.Y.U.).

Yuan, Dan Da-Yuan, 1932–   . Fy., 1964–65. Soc. M.A. (C.C.N.Y.); Ph.D. (Brown).

Andrews, Patricia Baldwin, 1928–   . Fy., 1965–67. Asst. Ref. Libn. M.S.L.S. (Drexel).

Belcher, Gerald Lee, 1941–   . Fy., 1965–66. History. M.A. (U. of Mich.).

Billings, Elizabeth Jean, 1923–   . Fy., 1965–   . French, German. M.A. (Western Reserve); M.A. (Middlebury).

Bullard, Truman Campbell, 1938–   . Fy., 1965–   . Music. M.A. (Harvard); Ph.D. (U. of Rochester).

Datta, Arun Kumar, 1927–   . Fy., 1965–66. Econ. M.A. & Ph.D. (S.U.N.Y., Buffalo).

De Repentigny, Michel Laurier, 1941–   . Fy., 1965–68. French. M.A. (Laval U.).

Eshelman, Larry Le Roy, 1938–   . Fy., 1965–66. Ref. Libn. M.L.S. (Rutgers).

Forbis, Yates McDonald, 1929–   . Fy., 1965–   . Librarian. M.A. & M.S.L.S. (Columbia).

Fox, Johnnie L.,   . Fy., 1965–68. ROTC.

Garrett, Clarke William, 1935–   . Fy., 1965–   . History. M.S. & Ph.D. (U. of Wisc.).

Jones, Kenneth N.,   . Fy., 1965–   . ROTC.

Kudlawiec, Dennis Paul, 1934–   . Fy., 1965–69. Music. M.S. (U. of Illinois).

Lardner, Peter James, 1938–   . Fy., 1965–69. Biology. Ph.D. (U. of Arizona).

Laws, Priscilla Watson, 1940–   . Fy., 1965–   . Physics. M.A. & Ph.D. (Bryn Mawr).

Marleski, Donald Theodore, 1941–   . Fy., 1965–68. English. M.A. (Northwestern).

Martin, Peter Evans, 1927–   . Fy., 1965–   . Math. M.A. & Ph.D. (Harvard).

Martinez-Vidal, Enrique José, 1932–   . Fy., 1965–   . Romance Lang. *Licenciatura, Filosofia y Letras* (U. of Barcelona); B.D. & Th.M. (Eastern Baptist Theol. Sem); M.A. (Temple); Ph.D. (U. of Pa.).

Mentzer, Thomas Cartwright, 1934–   . Fy., 1965–69. Geology. M.S. & Ph.D. (Lehigh).

Munch, John Howard, 1938–   . Fy., 1965–69. Chem. Ph.D. (U. of Wisc.).

Ormsby, Robert John, 1936–   . Fy., 1965–66. Classics. M.A. (U. of Washington).

Peacock, D. Grant, 1935–   . Fy., 1965–66. Accounting.

Platt, Charles Edward, 1920– . Fy., 1965–66. Psych. M.A. & Ph.D. (Ohio State).

Rhyne, George Nelson, 1938– . Fy., 1965– . History. M.A. & Ph.D. (U. of N.C.).

Richard, Michel Paul, 1933– . Fy., 1965–68. Soc. M.A. (U. of Chicago).

Rosi, Eugene Joseph, 1931– . Fy., 1965– . Pol. Sci. M.A. (Syracuse); Dipl. (Johns Hopkins Sch. of Advanced Int'l Studies); Ph.D. (Columbia).

Schwartz, Paul M., 1937– . Fy., 1965–66. Math. M.S. (U. of Illinois).

Selander, Stanley Waldemar, 1920– . Fy., 1965–68, Mil. Sci.

Soyer, Avron Joel, 1939– . Fy., 1965–68. Soc. M.A. (Cornell).

Stegink, Gordon Albert, 1939– . Fy., 1965–70. Math., Dir. Computer Center. A.M. (Washington U.).

Warner, Larry John, 1940– . Fy., 1965–69. Pol. Sci. M.A. (Princeton).

Bitton, Janine, 1932– . Fy., 1966–67. French. M.A. (Middlebury).

Buck, Keith Taylor, 1940– . Fy., 1966–68. Chem. Ph.D. (Ohio State).

Buzzell, Philip Roger, 1937– . Fy., 1966–69. Mil. Sci.

Cage, William Edwin, 1940– . Fy., 1966–67. Econ. Ph.D. (U. of Virginia).

Cutler, John Baker, 1938– . Fy., 1966–69. Fine Arts. M.A. (Yale).

Dembinski, Mark Louis, 1934– . Fy., 1966–68. Mil. Sci.

Eaton, Richard D., . Fy., 1966–69. ROTC.

Fox, Arturo A., 1935– . Fy., 1966– . Spanish. *Doctor en Derecho* (U. of Havana); Ph.D. (U. of Minn.).

Giegengack, Jane Marie, 1942– . Fy., 1966–68. Classics. M.A. (Yale).

Greene, Peter Clune, 1939– . Fy., 1966–69. Psych.

Hanson, Henry William Andrew III, 1932– . Fy., 1966– . Geology. M.S. & Ph.D. (Pa. State U.).

Henderson, John Stanton, 1939– . Fy., 1966– . French. M.A. & Ph.D. (Brown).

Nickey, William James, 1932– . Fy., 1966– . Phys. Ed. M.Ed. (West Chester State Coll.).

Parker, Elizabeth, 1938– . Fy., 1966–69. Fine Arts. M.A. (U. of Toronto); Ph.D. (Courtauld Inst. of Art, U. of London).

Parsly, Nancy Layton, 1938– . Fy., 1966–67. Cat. Libn. M.S.L.S. (Drexel).

Slotten, Ralph L., 1926– . Fy., 1966– . Religion. B.D. (Drake Div. Sch.) M.A. & Ph.D. (U. of Chicago).

Smith, Okey L., . Fy., 1966–68. ROTC.

Sokolowski, Richard, 1933– . Fy., 1966–67. French. Certif. (U. of Paris).

Steinberg, Adrian L., 1941– . Fy., 1966–68. Spanish. M.A. (Temple).

Williams, Glenn E., . Fy., 1966–68. ROTC.

Zobel, Klaus, 1930– . Fy., 1966–67. German. Ph.D. (U. of Göttingen).

Bowers, Dorothy Wingerd, 1916– . Fy., 1967– . Ref. Libn. M.S.L.S. (Drexel).

Chase, William Clark, Jr., 1937– . Fy., 1967–69. Mil. Sci.

Cieslicki, Dorothy Huffman, 1925– . Fy., 1967– . Serials Libn. M.S.L.S. (Columbia).

Doran, Michael John Arthur, 1940– . Fy., 1967–68. Music. M.A. (U. of Chicago).

Dornemann, William Eugene, 1936– . Fy., 1967– . German. M.A. (U. of Conn.).

Forbis, Ida Cock, 1935– . Fy., 1967–68. English.

Gahn, Joseph Anthony, 1933– . Fy., 1967–70. History. M.A. (S.U.N.Y.); Ph.D. (Syracuse).

Garrett, Margaret Davenport, 1935– . Fy., 1967–69. English.

Hecker, Andrew Carlyle, Jr., 1943– . Fy., 1967–68. Classical Lang. Cl. 1965.

Joyce, Anne-Marie, 1939– . Fy., 1967– . French. M.A. (Johns Hopkins).

Kaylor, Paul Evans, 1930– . Fy., 1967– . Religion, Chaplain. M.Div. (Yale).

Kress, Frank, 1928– . Fy., 1967–69. German. Ph.D. (U. of Conn.).

Lane, Richard Michael, 1937– . Fy., 1967– . Biology. M.S. & Ph.D. (U. of Maryland).

Long, Barbara Messner, 1943– . Fy., 1967–69. English. M.A. (U. of Pa.).

Mach, Anthony, 1930– . Fy., 1967– . Econ. M.B.A. (U. of Pa.); Ph.D. (Boston Coll.).

Mandowsky, Erna Minna, 1906– . Fy., 1967–68. Fine Arts. Ph.D. (U. of Hamburg).

Meyer, Marvin William, 1939– . Fy., 1967– . Biology. M.S. & Ph.D. (Northwestern).

Sandler, Ralph Erling, 1939– . Fy., 1967–69. English. M.A. & Ph.D. (U. of Wisc.).

Saputelli, Gregory Dante, 1943– . Fy., 1967–68. Russian. Certif. Russian Studies (Moscow U.).

Smillie, James Benjamin, 1939– . Fy., 1967–70. Asst. Cat. Libn. M.L.S. (Rutgers).

Stodghill, Jack Richard, 1935– . Fy., 1967– . Math. M.S. (Purdue).

Takeuchi, Kenji, 1932– . Fy., 1967–68. Econ. Ph.D. (Duke).

Tirumalai, Candadai Krishnadesikan, 1937– . Fy., 1967– . English. M.A. & Ph.D. (U. of Pa.).

Watkins, David Lamberson, 1935– . Fy., 1967– . Phys. Ed. M.A. (State U. of Iowa).

Wolf, Neil Stephan, 1937– . Fy., 1967– . Physics. M.S. & Ph.D. (Stevens Inst. of Tech.).

Ayre, Pamela Jean, 1945– . Fy., 1968–69. Chem. Cl. 1967.

Bond, Gene T., 1929– . Fy., 1968– . Mil. Sci.

Bullard, Beth Alice, . Fy., 1968–69. Music. M.A. (Harvard).

Crofts, Daniel Wallace, 1941– . Fy., 1968–69. History. M.A. & Ph.D. (Yale).

Draper, John William, 1943– . Fy., 1968– . Spanish. M.A. (Middlebury).

Erskine, Stephen Curtis, 1940– . Fy., 1968–70. Asst. Ref. Libn. M.S.L.S. (Simmons Coll.).

Harms, Joan Parker, 1939– . Fy., 1968–70; 1971– . Soc. M.A. (Mich. State U.).

Harms, William Albert, 1939– . Fy., 1968– . English. M.A. (Mich. State U.); Ph.D. (Indiana U.).

Israel, Marvin, 1938– . Fy., 1968– . Soc.

Kilgore, Arthur, . Fy., 1968–69. ROTC.

Kline, Michael B., 1939– . Fy., 1968– . French. M.A. & Ph.D. (Brown).

Kolb, Carolyn Jo, 1940– . Fy., 1968–69. Fine Arts. M.A. (Harvard).

Luetzelschwab, John William, 1940– . Fy., 1968– . Physics. M.A. & Ph.D. (Washington U.).

Murray, Michael Edward, 1941– . Fy , 1968–70. Philos. M.A. (U. of Texas); Ph.D. (Yale).

Noyes, Garrett Raymond, 1936– . Fy., 1968–71. Mil. Sci.

Podol, Peter Lauren, 1942– . Fy., 1968– . Spanish, Italian. M.A. (Columbia); Ph.D. (U. of Pa.).

Schearer, William R., 1935– . Fy., 1968– . Chem. M.A. & Ph.D. (Princeton).

Sham, Deborah Yee-Shing, 1936– . Fy., 1968–70; 1971–72. Asst. Cat. Libn. M.L.S. (Texas Women's U.).

Sider, Robert Dick, 1932– . Fy., 1968– . Classical Lang. M.A. (U. of Saskatchewan); M.A. & D. Phil. (Oxford).

Stone, Thomas Arthur, 1938– . Fy., 1968– . Econ.

Swoyer, Leroy E., 1926– . Fy., 1968–69. Educ. M.A. (Lehigh).

Woodworth, Lewis Crandall, 1926– . Fy., 1968– . Russian, German, Linguistics. M.A. (U. of Calif., Berkeley).

Wrecsis, Gerald, . Fy., 1968–69. ROTC.

Akin, Dennis Peter, 1930– ,. Fy., 1969– . Fine Arts. M.F.A. (U. of Colorado).

Annis, Norman L., 1931– . Fy., 1969. Fine Arts. M.F.A. (U. of Iowa).

Ayre, James T., 1913– . Fy., 1969–71. Educ. M.S. (Bucknell).

Barber, John William, 1941– . Fy., 1969– . Mil. Sci.

Boris, Richard Joseph, 1942– . Fy., 1969– . Pol. Sci. M.A. (Indiana U.).

Bowie, Donald Vincent, 1945– . Fy., 1969– . English. M.A. (Johns Hopkins).

Butler, Sara, 1938– . M.S.B.T. 1969–70. Religion. M.A. (Catholic U.).

Clarke, Robert Ebersole, 1945– . Fy., 1969–71. Soc. M.A. (U. of Pittsburgh).

Davis, Cecilia Jean, 1945– . Fy., 1969–70. Fine Arts.

Dondero, Russell Allan, 1942– . Fy., 1969– . Pol. Sci. M.A. (U. of Minn.).

Engberg, Larry A., 1946– . Fy., 1969–70. Psych.

Fréval, Daniel Joel, 1938– . Fy., 1969– . Modern Lang., Audio-Visual Media. *Certif. d'Etudes Litt. Gen.* (U. of Caen).

Goldstein, Malcolm 1936– . Fy., 1969–71. Music. M.A. (Columbia).

Gustafson, Sandra Louise, 1941– . Fy., 1969–70. English. M.A. (U. of Kansas); M.A. (U. of Pa.).

Hawkins, Gerald Stanley, 1928– . Fy., 1969–71. Dean, Astronomy. Ph.D. & D. Sc. (U. of Manchester).

Jackson, Robert Everett, 1943– . Fy., 1969– . Math. M.A. & Ph.D. (U. of Texas).

Jarvis, Charles Austin, 1941– . Fy., 1969– . History. M.A. & Ph.D. (U. of Missouri).

Katz, Jean Braley, 1938– . Fy., 1969– . Modern Lang. M.A.T. (Johns Hopkins); M.A. (U. of Calif.); Ph.D. (Vanderbilt).

Leyon, Robert Edward, 1936– . Fy., 1969– . Chem. M.A. & Ph.D. (Princeton).

Meil, David Balfour, 1940– . Fy., 1969–71. Philos. M.A. (U. of Pittsburgh).

Mester, Richard Arnold, 1939– . Fy., 1969–70. Philos. M.A. & Ph.L. (Aquinas Inst. School of Philos.).

Morsell, Frederick Albert, 1940– . Fy., 1969. Drama. Cl. 1962.

Pence, Clifford Arthur, Jr., 1943– . Fy., 1969– . Math. A.M. (U. of Illinois).

Phillips, Edward Albert, Jr., 1945– . Fy., 1969–70. Classical Lang. Cl. 1967. M.A. (U. of Chicago).

Potter, Noel, Jr., 1940– . Fy., 1969– . Geology. M.A. (Dartmouth); Ph.D. (U. of Minn.).

Reeves, Kenneth Earl, 1942– . Fy., 1969– . Mil. Sci.

Robinson, Johnny Sumner, 1939– . Fy., 1969– . Mil. Sci.

Rosen, Kenneth Mark, 1938– . Fy., 1969– . English. M.A. (San Francisco State); Ph.D. (U. of New Mexico).

Sheeley, Richard Moats, 1934– . Fy., 1969– . Chem. M.S. (Pa. State U.); Ph.D. (Brigham Young U.).

Smith, Thomas Scott, 1941– . Fy., 1969– . Physics. Ph.D. (U. of Maryland).

Staggers, Harry Joseph, 1943– . Fy., 1969–70. History. M.A. (William & Mary).

Steiner, Peter Leonard, 1940– . Fy., 1969– . Modern Lang. M.A. & Ph.D. (U. of Pittsburgh).

Van Buren, Anne Hagopian, 1927– . Fy., 1969–70. Fine Arts. M.A. (U. of Texas).

Voris, Harold Knight, 1940– . Fy., 1969– . Biology. Ph.D. (U. of Chicago).

Wachter, David Alan, 1937– . Fy., 1969–70. Phys. Ed. M.A. (Columbia).

Weinberger, Stephen, 1942– . Fy., 1969– . History. M.A. & Ph.D. (U. of Wisc.).

Woodworth, Isingard Moller, 1921– . Fy., 1969– . German, Asst. Cat. Libn. M.L.S. (U. of Calif., Berkeley).

Arnold, Edward James, 1943– . Fy., 1970– . Philosophy. M.A. (U. of Chicago).

Cheung, Wai Ling, 1936– . Fy., 1970– . Asst. Cat. Libn. M.L.S. (S.U.N.Y., Geneseo).

Clarke, Helen Jenks, . Fy., 1970–71. Soc.

Connor, John Martin, 1934– . Fy., 1970–71. Phys. Ed. M.Ed. (Shippensburg State).

Culp, Dorothy Woodward, 1930– . Fy., 1970– . English. M.A. (U. of Pa.); Ph.D. (Columbia).

Danoff, Ira Michael, 1940– . Fy., 1970– . Fine Arts. M.A. (U. of N.C.); Ph.D. (Syracuse).

Dwiggins, Cyril William, 1933– . Fy., 1970– . Philos. M.A. (Aquinas Inst. School of Philos.).

Hoffman, Joseph Robert, 1943– . Fy., 1970– . Fine Arts. Cl. 1965; M.A. (U. of Wisc).

Kiselev, Alexey A., 1935– . Fy., 1970– . Russian. M.A. (U. of Pa.).

McDade, Madelyn Carole, 1947– . Fy., 1970– . Asst. Ref. Libn. Cl. 1969; M.L.S. (Drexel).

Murphy, Madeline Wheeler, 1922– . Fy., 1970–71. Soc. Certif. (Temple U. School of Commerce).

Nicoll, Philip Dennis, 1941– . Fy., 1970– . Pol. Sci. M.A. (Southern Ill. U.).

Ramsey, Stanley David, 1942– . Fy., 1970– . English. M.A. (Lehigh).

Reid, Robert Kuntz, 1943– . Fy., 1970– . Biology. Cl. 1965. M.A. (Oberlin).

Rosen, Rosalind Domnitz, 1941– . Fy., 1970– . Classical Studies. M.A. (U. of Calif., Berkeley).

Rosenbaum, Stanley Ned, 1939– . Fy., 1970– . Religion. M.A. (Brandeis).

Steiner, Ethel Miriam, 1943– . Fy., 1970–71. Pol. Sci. M.P.I.A. & M. A. (U. of Pittsburgh).

Voris, Helen Louise Hahn, 1944– . Fy., 1970–71. Biology.

Weller, Eric Corville, 1941– . Fy., 1970– . Fine Arts. (U. of Colorado).

Bechtel, Joan Margaret, 1933– . Fy., 1971– . Asst. Cat. Libn. M.S. (Drexel).

De Grys, Mary Schweitzer, 1936– . Fy., 1971– . Soc. & Anthropology.

Fossett, Charles Kenneth, Jr., 1942– . Fy., 1971– . Psych. M.A. (Kent State).

Houghton, Gareth Charles, 1935– . Fy., 1971– . R.O.T.C.

Kempf, Wilhelm Ulrich, 1941– . Fy., 1971– . Dir., Computer Center. M.S. & Ph.D. (U. of Munich).

Kohn, Harold William, 1920– . Fy., 1971– . Chem. Ph.D. (Syracuse).

Petty, Fred Curtis, 1939– . Fy., 1971– . Music. M.A. (Cornell U.).

Rossi, Dean Michael, 1936– . Fy., 1971– . Phys. Ed. M.S. (W. Va. U.).

Rubin, Lawrence H., 1946– . Fy., 1971– . Physics. Ph.D. (U. of Rochester).

Schrock, John William, 1942– . Fy., 1971– . Phys. Ed. M. Ed. (Indiana U. of Pa).

Faculty of Conway Hall Preparatory School, 1877–1917

The old Grammar School of Colonial days was closed in 1869, after a life of more than a hundred years. The acceptance of scholarship certificates to cover its tuition as well as that of the College had made it a financial burden. It was revived by President McCauley in 1877. President Reed, coming into office in 1889, made it a part of his expansionist program. He would raise the College to university status, and make the School, as one of its components, the peer of the best preparatory institutions in the country, with a wide curriculum, ample faculty and a fully developed life of its own.

The building of Conway Hall, projected in 1902, completed in 1904, made this possible. The name "Conway Hall" was first applied to the

School as a whole in the College Catalogue of 1905. Conway Hall, growing into a life and traditions of its own such as the old Grammar School had never had, came to a sudden end, again for financial reasons, in 1917, its passing deeply mourned by alumni and faculty, its memories long preserved.

Elden, James, 1847–   . Headmaster, 1878–82. A.M. (Allegheny).

Morgan, James Henry, 1857–1939. Fy. & Headmaster, 1882–84. Cl. 1878. *See College faculty list.*

Dare, William Knight, 1858–1918. Fy & Headmaster, 1883–97. Cl. 1883. *See College faculty list.*

Bower, Lahman Forest, 1858–1934. Headmaster, 1884–87. *See College faculty list.*

Baker, Franklin Thomas, 1864–1949. Fy., 1885–92. Cl. 1885. A.M.

Bikle, Charles Earl, 1867–1949. Fy., 1891–92. Cl. 1886. A.M.

Norton, Lyon L.,   . Fy., 1892–94. A.M.

Prettyman, Vergil, 1874–1957. Fy., 1892–94. Cl. 1892. A.M.

Shaeffer, William Jefferson,   . Fy., 1892–93. Cl. 1891. A.M.; LL.B. (Dickinson School of Law).

Filler, Mervin Grant, 1873–1931. Fy., 1893–99. *See College faculty list.*

Downes, Fred Elliott, 1871–1937. Fy. & Headmaster, 1894–1904. Cl. 1893. A.M.; D. Ped.

Sellers, Montgomery Porter, 1873–1942. Fy., 1894–95. Cl. 1893. *See College faculty list.*

Appenzellar, Paul Peyton, 1875–1953. Fy., 1895–97. Cl. 1895. Tr., 1916–17; 1921–44.

Fisher, Amy, 1873–1938. Fy., 1895–97. Cl. 1895. *See College faculty list.*

Heckman, Edgar Rohrer, 1875–1948. Fy., 1897–1900. Cl. 1897. A.M. Tr., 1920–48.

McKeehan, Joseph Parker, 1876–1950. Fy., 1897–1900. Cl. 1897. A.M.; LL.B. (Dickinson School of Law). *See Law School faculty list.*

Sigmund, John Luther, 1874–1949. Fy., 1898–1907. Cl. 1898. A.M.

Craver, Forrest Eugene, 1875–1958. Fy., 1905; 1909–11. Cl. 1899. *See College faculty list.*

Van Burkalow, James Turley, 1870–   . Fy., 1899–1901. Cl. 1893. A.M.; Ph.D. (U. of Pa.).

Gilbert, George Clayton, 1880–1908. Fy., 1900–01. Cl. 1900.

Hoover, Thomas Leonard, 1880–1915. Fy., 1900–06. Cl. 1900. A.M. Tr., 1914–15.

Spahr, Boyd Lee, 1880–1970. Fy., 1901. Cl. 1900. LL.B. (U. of Pa.). Tr., 1908–70.

Hutchins, Charles Pelton, 1872–1938. Fy., 1902–04. *See College faculty list.*

Kline, Irvin Eugene, 1874–1936. Fy., 1902–03. Cl. 1901. A.M.

Lamberton, Clark Diven, 1881–   . Fy., 1902–03. Cl. 1902.

Presby, Edmund Janes, 1878–   . Fy., 1902–08. Cl. 1901.

Johnson, Lloyd Wellington, 1879–   . Fy., 1903–06. Cl. 1903.

Killen, Arthur Houghton,   . Fy., 1903–04.

Tomkinson, Paul Eldridge, 1881–   . Fy., 1903–05. Cl. 1903.

Hutchison, William Albert, 1864–1923. Headmaster, 1904–17. Cl. 1892.
    A.M.; D.Ped.

Weatherby, Milton,   . Fy., 1904–05.

Rogers, William Harlow,   . Fy., 1905–06. Cl. 1905.

Smith, Harry Walter,   . Fy., 1905–06.

Stevens, Roland Drew,   . Fy., 1905–06.

Williams, John William, 1880–1908. Fy., 1905–07. Cl. 1904. A.M. *See*
    College faculty list.

Chadwick, George Irvin, 1881–1964. Fy., 1906–10. A.M. (Yale).

Goodrich, Henry Wilson,   . Fy., 1906–07.

Hadden, Charles Wesley, 1883–   . Fy., 1906–09. A.M. (Colgate).

Mason, Marvin Garfield, 1881–   . Fy., 1906–10. Cl. 1906.

Salter, Charles Morgan,   . Fy., 1906–07. Cl. 1906.

Kline, George Alfred, 1880–   . Fy., 1907–10. Cl. 1907. A.M.

Pipal, Joseph Amos,   . Fy., 1907–09. *See College faculty list.*

Rowe, Perry Belmont, 1883–1941. Fy., 1907–08. Cl. 1907. *See College*
    faculty list.

Swift, Charles Lowe, 1878–1956. Fy., 1907–11. Cl. 1904. *See College*
    faculty list.

Hunt, Clayton Edward, 1885–   . Fy., 1908–09.

Ohl, Frederick William, 1883–   . Fy., 1908–09. A.M. (Harvard).

Wilder, Harry L.,   . Fy., 1908–09.

Lammert, Lloyd Leslie, 1884–   . Fy., 1909–11.

McKee, James Hugh, 1887–   . Fy., 1909–13. Cl. 1909.

Super, John Henry, Jr., 1887–   . Fy., 1909–12. Cl. 1909.

Arnold, Thomas Ellison, 1886–   . Fy., 1910–12.

Bashore, Luther E.,   . Fy., 1910–11. Cl. 1910.

Blades, Webster Strayer, 1888–   . Fy., 1910–12.

Cleland, John Scott, 1887–   . Fy., 1910–12. *See College faculty list.*

Shenton, Clarence Strayer, 1887–   . Fy., 1910–14. Cl. 1910.

Pifer, Henry Weber, 1886–   . Fy., 1911–14.

Weber, Hans Karl, 1889–   . Fy., 1911–14.

Andrus, Fred L., 1876–1944. Fy., 1912–13. Cl. 1912.

Collord, James Harold,   . Fy., 1912–13. A.M. (Princeton).

Little, Wilson Vaughan, 1887–   . Fy., 1912–14. A.M. (U. of Pa.).

Van Auken, Charles Simeon,   . Fy., 1912–13. Cl. 1912.

Cook, Jay D.,   . Fy., 1913–15. Cl. 1914.

Garton, Robert R.,   . Fy., 1913. Cl. 1913.
Maurer, Charles Lewis,   . Fy., 1913-15. Ped. M.; A.M.
Whitmoyer, Raymond B.,   . Fy., 1913. Cl. 1913.
Brenneman, Foster E.,   . Fy., 1914-17. Cl. 1914.
Burriss, Eli Edward, Jr.,   . Fy., 1914-15.
Schimmler, Ernest A.,   . Fy., 1914-15.
Steckel, Harvey H.,   . Fy., 1914-15. Cl. 1912. A.M.; LL.B.
    (Dickinson School of Law).
Adams, Frank R.,   . Fy., 1915-16. Cl. 1918.
Park, Luther Augustine,   . Fy., 1915-17. M.A. (U. of Pa.).
Hart, Frank Leslie,   . Fy., 1916-17. Cl. 1916. A.M.
Laverty, Lawson Schwarz, 1891-   . Fy., 1916-17. Cl. 1915. A.M.
McCraven, Bonner N.,   . Fy., 1916-17.
Reitz, Charles Herbert,   . Fy., 1916-17. Cl. 1916.

Law School Faculty, 1834-1911

With the retirement of President Reed in 1911 the College Catalogue ceased to list faculty and curriculum of the Dickinson School of Law. This marks the end of Reed's dream of a university but not of the association between the two institutions.

Reed, John. Fy., 1834-50. LL.D. D.C., Cl. 1806.

Graham, James Hutchison. Fy., 1863-82. LL.D. D.C., Cl. 1827.

Trickett, William. Dean, 1890-1928. LL.D. D.C., Cl. 1868. *Who's Who.*

Jacobs, Michael William. Fy., 1890-1901. Professor of Equity, International and Patent Law. *Who's Who.*

Sadler, Wilbur Fisk. Fy., 1890-1919. Professor of Practice, Constitutional Law.

Thorpe, E.L. Fy., 1890-1902. Professor of Criminal Law, Civil and Internal Law. LL.B.; Ph.D.; D.C.L.

Weakley, James Marion. Fy., 1890-1907. Professor of law of Torts, Law of Pleading.

Beltzhoover, F.E. Fy., 1892-1901. Special Lecturer on Processes of Federal Legislation.

Biddle, Edward William. Fy., 1892-1901. Special Lecturer on Practice in Orphans' Court. D.C., Cl. 1870. *Who's Who.*

Brewster, F. Carroll. Fy., 1892-1900. Lecturer on Law of Contracts and Torts. LL.D.

Endlich, Gustav Adolf. Fy., 1892-1901. Lecturer on Law of Domestic Relations. *Who's Who.*

Furst, Austin O. Fy., 1892-1901. Special Lecturer on Origin of Land Titles in Pennsylvania and Methods of the Study of the Law.

Hays, John. Fy., 1892-1901. Lecturer on Commercial Law and Banking D.C., Cl. 1857. *Who's Who.*

Henderson, Robert Miller. Fy., 1892–1901. Special Lecturer on the Action of Assumpsit. D.C., Cl. 1845. *Who's Who.*

Herman, Martin Christian. Fy., 1892–96. Special Lecturer on Ejectment. D.C., Cl. 1862.

Mills, George Edward. Fy., 1892–1901. Professor of Law of Torts. LL.B. D.C., Cl. 1891.

Neely, Thomas Benjamin. Fy., 1892–1901. Lecturer on Parliamentary Law. Ph.D. *Who's Who.*

Rhone, D.L. Fy., 1892–1901. Lecturer on Law of Decedents' Estates.

Sharpe, A.B. Fy., 1892. Special Lecturer on Legal Ethics.

Simonton, John Wiggins. Fy., 1892–1901. Lecturer on Law of Corporations. *Who's Who.*

Smead, Alexander Dallas Bache. Fy., 1892–1901. Special Lecturer on Nuisances on Highways. D.C., Cl. 1868.

Stewart, John. Fy., 1892–1901. Lecturer on Law of Evidence. *Who's Who.*

Stuart, Hugh Silas. Fy., 1892–1908. Lecturer on Law of Partnership and on Partition in Orphans' Court.

Wetzel, John Wise. Fy., 1892–1901. Special Lecturer on Jury Trial. D.C., Cl. 1874.

Bolles, Albert H. Fy., 1893–1901. Professor of Law of Contracts. Ph.D.

Himes, Charles Francis. Fy., 1895–1901. Lecturer on Scientific Expert Testimony. Ph.D. LL.D. D.C., Cl. 1855. DAB.

Hoober, John A. Fy., 1895–1901. Lecturer on Patents. D.C.L.

Sadler, Sylvester Baker. Fy., 1898–1919. Professor of Criminal Law, Practice, Constitutional Law. D.C., Cl. 1895. *Who's Who.*

Snodgrass, Robert. Fy., 1898–1901. Lecturer on Development of Equity Jurisprudence. *Who's Who.*

Woodward, Frederic Campbell. Fy., 1898–1901. Professor of Law of Agency and Negotiable Instruments. LL.M. *Who's Who.*

Brown, William Hardcastle. Fy., 1899–1901. Lecturer on Divorce.

McClure, Howard M. Fy., 1899–1901. Lecturer on Bills and Notes.

Pilcher, James Evelyn. Fy., 1899–1907. Professor of Medical Jurisprudence. Ph.D.; M.D. *Who's Who.*

Swartz, George Wilson. Fy., 1901–07. Professor of Practice.

Hutton, A. J. White. Fy., 1902–19. Professor of Decedents' Estates and Partnership. LL.B.

McKeehan, Joseph Parker, Fy., 1902– . Professor of Law of Contracts and Torts. D.C., Cl. 1897. *Who's Who.*

Hitchler, Walter Harrison. Fy., 1906–30; Dean, 1930–54. Professor of Equity and Criminal Law. *Who's Who.*

Sellers, Francis Benjamin. Fy., 1906–11. Professor of Practice. LL.B. D.C., Cl. 1861.

OFFICERS OF ADMINISTRATION, 1900-1972

Provosts
Thompson, Russell Irvin, 1952-54. Fy., 1928-57.
Malcolm, Gilbert, 1961-63. Fy., 1946-63.

Deans of The College
Morgan, James Henry, 1903-14. Fy. & Pres., 1884-1933.
Filler, Mervin Grant, 1914-28. Fy. & Pres., 1899-1931.
Sellers, Montogomery Porter, 1928-34. Fy., 1893-1942.
Vuilleumier, Ernest Albert, Acting Dean, 1933-35. Dean, 1935-47. Fy., 1920-58.
Thompson, Russell Irvin, 1947-51. Fy., 1928-57.
McCullough, James Clair, Acting Dean, 1950-52. Fy., 1947-55.
Ness, Frederic William, 1952-60. Fy., 1952-60.
Nelson, Roger Eastman, 1960-63. Fy., 1949-71.
Magill, Samuel Hays, 1963-68. Fy., 1962-68.
Wanner, Richard Henry, Acting Dean, 1968-69. Fy., 1946-54; 1961- .
Hawkins, Gerald Stanley, 1969-71. Fy., 1969-71.
Wanner, Richard Henry, 1971- . Fy., 1946-54; 1961- .

Associate Deans
Kuebler, Roy Raymond, Assistant to the Dean, 1950. Fy., 1933-55.
Wanner, Richard Henry, Assistant Dean, 1965-67; Associate Dean, 1966-68. Fy., 1946-54; 1961- .
Allshouse, Merle Frederick, Associate Dean, 1968-70. Fy., 1963-70.
Nodder, Stanley, Jr., Associate Dean, 1970, 1971. Fy., 1961-71.
Laws, Kenneth L., Assistant Dean, 1971- . Fy., 1962- .

Registrars
Ames, Chester, 1900-01.
Black, Sara Martha, 1909-11.
Brunhouse, Robert Levere, 1930-35. Fy., 1931-35.
Thompson, Russell Irvin, 1935-44. Fy., 1928-57.
Ayres, Frank, Jr., 1944-45. Fy., 1928-58.
Bowman, Raymond Palmer Garber, 1945-49. Fy., 1941-52.
Climenhaga, Asa W., 1949-58. Fy., 1949-59.
Benson, William Howard, 1958-66. Fy., 1955-70.
Light, John Henry, 1966-69. Fy., 1959- .
Anderson, Paul Henry, 1969- .

Directors of Admission
Rohrbaugh, Lewis Guy, 1942-47. Fy., 1922-53.

James, Benjamin David, 1948-62. Fy., 1941-   .
Williams, C. O., Acting Director, 1962-63.
Jefferson, David Rowe, 1963-69. Fy., 1963-69.
Howard, Robert Allan, 1969-   .

Deans of Students
McAnney, Lucretia Jones, Dean of Women, 1906-12. Fy., 1906-14.
Meredith, Josephine Brunyate, Dean of Women, 1919-46. Fy., 1919-48.
Norcross, Sarah Helen Burns, Dean of Women, 1946-49. Fy., 1916-18;
    1946-49.
Horlacher, Amos Benjamin, Dean of Men, 1947-57. Fy., 1947-   .
Bacon, Phoebe G. (Follmer), Dean of Women, 1949-51. Fy., 1949-51.
Kellogg, Mary Margaret, Acting Dean of Women, 1950-52; Dean of Wo-
    men, 1952-54. Fy., 1950-54.
Warlow, Francis Wayland, Acting Dean of Men, 1953-54. Fy., 1947-   .
Reynolds, Victoria Kathryn (Hann), Dean of Women, 1954-59. Fy.,
    1954-59.
Coutts, Alan, Dean of Men, 1957-63. Fy., 1957-63.
Wishmeyer, Barbara Townsend (Stevens), Dean of Women, 1959-67. Fy.,
    1959-66.
James, Benjamin David, Dean of Students, 1962-67. Fy., 1941-   .
Pease, N. Ronald, Dean of Men, 1963-68. Fy., 1963-66.
Gillespie, Harold Reese, Jr., Dean of Students, 1967-   . Fy., 1960-67.
Rhude, Beth E., Dean of Women, 1967-68.
Carson, Mary Frances (Watson), Associate Dean of Students & Dean of
    Women, 1968-   .
Carver, Thomas William, Assistant Dean of Students & Dean of Men,
    1968-70.
Markwood, Stephen E., Dean of Men, 1970-   .

Chaplains
Bixler, Andrew Loy, Christian Associations Secretary, 1919-20.
Bower, Lahman Forest, Young People's Secretary, 1923-28.
Magill, Samuel Hays, Chaplain, 1962-63. Fy. & Dean, 1962-68.
Washington, Joseph Reed, Chaplain, 1963-66. Fy., 1963-68.
Yeo, Lawrence Thomas, Acting Chaplain, 1966-67.
Kaylor, Paul Evans, Chaplain, 1967-   . Fy., 1967-   .

Assistants to the President
Hunsberger, Wesley A., 1906-11.
Wing, Herbert, Jr., 1942-44. Fy., 1915-61.
Lehman, Rowland R., 1950-52.

Kenagy, Herbert G., 1953-55.
Walker, Albert, 1955-60. Fy., 1955-60.
Wing, Herbert, Jr., 1960-61. Fy., 1915-61.
Platt, Arthur Dwight, 1961- .

Directors of Development
Bacon, John F., 1949-50.
Shuman, George, Jr., 1954-62.
Cheshire, Richard D., 1962-65.
Kuch, George Richard, Campaign Director, 1965-67.
Lumb, Fred A., 1967-71.
Frey, Evan C., Acting Director, 1971-
Green, Asa N., 1971- .

Treasurers
Evans, Frysinger, 1900-07.
White, J. Irvin, 1907-10.
Bursk, John S., 1910-25.
Malcolm, Gilbert, 1925-58. Fy. & Pres., 1946-63.
Shuman, George Jr., 1948- .
Rowe, Allen I., Comptroller, 1964-66.
Bloodgood, Willard Gordon, Business Manager and Comptroller, 1967-70.
Woltjen, John Wallace, Business Manager, 1970- .
Belyea, Robert W., Comptroller, 1970- .

Appendix B

BRANCHES OF LEARNING

The origins and growth of Dickinson's curriculum are indicated here in an outline compiled largely from the College Catalogues (a source which, admittedly, sometimes presents ideal rather than fact) and from trustee and faculty minutes. "Departments" emerge gradually, the term having little significance when applied to one professor, or in a period when an ability to meet any class was rated as high professional competence. They become clearly defined with the increase in faculty and student body after World War II. Department chairmen, though recognized earlier, are first so designated in the Catalogue of 1949. Departmental growth in personnel or as a result of new buildings may be followed in Appendices A and D.

American Studies
1965   Interdisciplinary program, approved as a major.

Biology
1834   First taught as Natural Science by Merritt Caldwell. Offered in Senior year as Geology, Botany, and Animal and Vegetable Physiology.
1845   Spencer Fullerton Baird introduced field trips.
1893   William Birckhead Lindsay taught first course in Biology, a Senior elective.
1896   Biology Department created, with Henry Matthew Stephens appointed the first Professor of Biological Sciences, 1897.
1938   Department increased to two; 1940, three; 1971, nine.

Chemistry

1798 Robert Davidson's Natural Philosophy included lectures on gases, acids and different theories of electricity "such as those of Dr. Franklin and Dr. Priestley."

1810 Frederick Aigster, first Professor of Chemistry, dismissed as insane.

1811 Thomas Cooper, Professor of Chemistry; acquisition of Joseph Priestley laboratory equipment.

1865 Scientific Course instituted by Charles F. Himes; laboratory work added, 1866.

1885 Chemistry and Physics divided, following completion of Tome Scientific Building; William B. Lindsay, Professor of Chemistry.

1901 Department increased to two.

1929 First course in Physical Chemistry initiated by Horace E. Rogers.

1955 Staff of five, three with doctorate; accreditation by the American Chemical Society.

1956 Gift of C. Scott Althouse, $300,000 for a chemistry building.

Classical Studies

1769 Pastor John Steel succeeded as teacher by Henry Makinly, "who professes to teach the Latin and Greek Languages in the most concise and perfect Manner."

1784 James Ross, first Professor of Greek and Latin.

1825 First non-classical program, leading to a certificate rather than degree.

1879 Separate departments of Latin and Greek.

1893 Faculty of five teaching Classics, including Hebrew.

1920 Greek and Latin each taught by one professor.

1940 Both merged into Department of Classical Languages and Literature.

1947 Ancient languages eliminated as a degree requirement.

1965 Became Department of Classical Studies, with addition of courses in Hellenic and Roman History.

1970 Summer Classical Institute added, for study abroad.

Dramatic Arts

1785 Student production, Dec. 29, of John Home's tragedy, "The Fatal Discovery," followed by James Townley's enormously popular farce, "High Life Below Stairs." This and later productions encouraged and coached by certain trustees, the proceeds going to town charities.

1797 "The Fair Penitent" by Nicholas Rowe, described in a letter from George Ridgely to his mother: "It was performed as well as any I ever saw done in Philadelphia . . . . I had on a white satin petticoat and jacket with a long mussilin train . . . extreamly like a bride in the first four acts & in the last I was dressed in black . . . . There was more money cleared with it than any other play that has been acted here this great while, which went to the Poor about town- . . . . You said you thought Edward the Black Prince would have been a better play to act but nothing but the most tragical thing could move the People about this town." This appears to have been the last student production before clerical opposition was fully asserted.

1853   Shakespeare Club meeting at Mrs. Hall's boarding house; 1857, "Romeo and Juliet," with Tom Conrad as Lady Capulet. Later in the century student productions, mostly skits, mock trials, light comedy, became more frequent.

1890   A Dramatic Club organized and continuing with some hiatus until 1944 under the guidance of Lucretia McAnney, Wilbur Norcross and others.

1944   Dickinson Little Theater organized by John C. Hepler.

1948   Eric W. Barnes' Dramaturgy, "a laboratory course in the arts of the theater . . . . The year's work will include two major productions." From this class came The Mermaid Players, producing "Ladies of the Jury," 1949, and "The Tempest," 1950.

1952   Irvine N. Smith, first Professor of Drama and Speech.

1956   Department of Dramatic Arts, offering three courses. David F. Brubaker came as Instructor in Drama.

1970   With Brubaker as coordinator, Studies in Theater and Dramatic Literature approved as a major.

Economics

1784   "Oeconomics" and Political Economy included in Charles Nisbet's lectures.

1888   Political Economy listed under Political Science.

1900   James E. Pilcher, first Professor of Economics (and Sociology).

1915   Economics listed under Social Sciences.

1947   First listed as a separate department, and with three members.

1960   Department increased to six; in 1971, four.

Education

1893   William Knight Dare, Professor of History and Pedagogy, offered a "history of education and a study of the science and art of education."

1900   William Lambert Gooding taught courses in Psychology and Education.

1920   Offerings in Education doubled, with more emphasis on Psychology and vocational training.

1922   Practice teaching first offered in the local schools.

1944   Education and Psychology merged again into one department, with emphasis on Psychology as a major. Majors for teachers in training were in subject fields and with less emphasis given to pre-professional training.

1947   With the coming of J. Clair McCullough, the time of one man in the department was given to Education alone.

1963   The number of Education courses was reduced markedly, and the professional semester was initiated, giving students a semester of intensive training in Education instead of many courses throughout the four years.

1971   Six members in Department of Psychology and Education.

English

1785   Belles Lettres first taught by Robert Davidson and then by others into mid-nineteenth century, included English Grammar, Rhetoric and Criticism.

1848   William Henry Allen, first Professor of English Literature.

1900   Six courses offered by Bradford O. McIntire and Montgomery P. Sellers.

1940   World Literature taught by Charles Lowe Swift, with lectures by other faculty, required of all Juniors.

1970   Freshman Composition requirement for graduation dropped.

1971   Fourteen members in the department.

Fine Arts

1916   William W. Landis, Professor of Mathematics, taught the first Art History course, "from the time of Giotto to the present"; offered annually until his death in 1942.

1947   Milton E. Flower, first Professor of Fine Arts, organized the first department.

1955   Third member, Joseph S. Sheppard, added for first studio course.

1957   John Drake Pusey, artist-in-residence.

1960   Fine Arts approved as a major under the chairmanship of Donald E. Gordon.

1969   Revised curriculum balancing Art History and Studio; increase in majors from seventeen in 1960 to sixty by 1971.

Geology

1811   Thomas Cooper included Geology and Mineralogy in his lectures.

1830   Henry Darwin Rogers briefly on the faculty, at the beginning of his internationally distinguished career as a geologist.

1840   Geology offered to both Freshmen and Seniors. Smellie's *Philosophy of Natural History* was the Freshman text.

1846   A valuable mineralogical collection reported, in addition to Baird's collections of fossils, shells, reptiles, birds, rocks, etc.

1930   Geology apparently not taught following the death of Dr. John Frederick Mohler.

1946   John Reigle Embick became first Professor of Geology (and Chemistry), offering seven courses by 1947.

1957   Approval of a Geology major; second member added to the department.

1971   A three-man department, with emphasis on extended field trips.

History

1785   History and Chronology taught by Robert Davidson, first Professor of History.

1889   History, previously listed under English, included with Political Science as a separate department.

1902   Morris W. Prince and his son, Leon C., supported the Department until 1910, when the former retired.

1913   First listed as a department apart from Political Science, with six courses offered by one man.

1925   Department increased to three.

1935   Mulford Stough's Seminar on the Problems of the Far East, first course in non-western civilization.

1940   Staff and course offerings doubled in the decade 1940–50.

International Studies

1969   An interdisciplinary major adopted, with Departments of Economics, History, Modern Languages and Political Science.

Law

1814   Thomas Cooper established a "Dickinson College Law Course," including Elements of Moral Science, Elements of the Law of Nature and Nations, History and Elements of Civil Law, Feudal Law, Common Law of England, History of English Jurisprudence, History of Maritime Law, Chancery Jurisdiction, Medical and Chemical Jurisprudence.

1833   Law Department established under Judge John Reed, continuing until his death in 1850.

1862   J. H. Graham Professor of Law, but remained inactive.

1890   Dickinson School of Law established under Dean William Trickett, as a department of the College but with separate board of trustees. (Curriculum development may be followed in Law School Faculty List, Appendix A.)

1891　Pre-law undergraduate program established. Open only to upper-classmen, the number of law electives was gradually increased from two hours in each year to six and twelve. By 1900 it was recognized that the student could thus earn his LL.B. in two years of graduate work rather than three. The program was ended in 1968 on the initiative of the Law School.

Mathematics

1786　Robert Johnston, first Professor of Mathematics.

1790　Euclid, Trigonometry, Surveying, Navigation, Spherica, Conic Sections, Algebra, Mensuration, Gauging and Astronomy among the "branches" taught.

1870　Trustees approved a plan for ten "Departments of Study," to include "Pure Mathematics," "Physics and mixed Mathematics, and the application of Calculus to Natural Philosophy, Astronomy and Mechanics" and "Civil and Mining Engineering and Metalurgy."

1890　Mathematics and Astronomy a separate department.

1895　Department increased to two with the coming of William W. Landis.

1939　Last catalogue listing of Astronomy until 1950, when it reappears in the Physics curriculum.

1971　Faculty of eight in the Department.

Military Science

1857　"Carlisle Junior Cadets" organized by J. D. Stevenson, '61; continued until 1859.

1879　Dickinson College Cadet Corps. a government-supported program under Lt. E. T. C. Richmond, U.S.A., as Professor of Military Science. "An agency of physical culture . . . conducing . . . to manly development, and to ease and grace in attitude and movement." The corps numbered sixty-seven in its first year. Refusal of the faculty to make it a requirement for credit brought its withdrawal in 1881.

1942　Col. Philip Mathews, Director of Pre-induction Training.

1952　Establishment of ROTC unit with Lt. Col. Daniel W. Rachal heading a six-man Department of Military Science and Tactics.

1956　Faculty of nine, reduced to six by 1964.

1970　Academic credit withdrawn, beginning with the Class of 1974.

Modern Languages and Literature

1810　Claudius Berard appointed "Teacher of the French, Spanish & Italian languages in the College." Elected Professor of the Modern

Languages, 1814. Modern Languages were offered as an elective requiring an additional fee until 1860–61, when German was added to the professorship of Greek, and French to that of Latin.

1825   German first taught by Lewis Mayer, President of the German Reformed Seminary at the College.

1846   Charles E. Blumenthal appointed Professor of Hebrew and Modern Languages. The Catalogue noted that "French or German may be substituted, in the Junior year, for Greek, and in the Senior for Mathematics," an early extension of the elective principle. Only French and German taught.

1849   French and German required for all Juniors and Seniors.

1853   Instruction declared too little "for proficient scholarship." In 1854, extended to all classes, under Alexander J. Schem, Professor of Modern Languages.

1884   Establishment of "A course of four years with Modern Languages in place of Latin and Greek."

1897   Emma V. Harry, first woman faculty member, teaching French and German.

1900   Separate departments of Germanic Languages and Literature under C. W. Prettyman and Romance Languages and Literature under Ovando Byron Super.

1914   Romance Languages and Literature offered Spanish and Italian for the first time since mid-nineteenth century.

1917   Romance Languages faculty increased to two; 1921, to three; 1930, to four.

1928   German Department faculty increased from one to three; 1938, to four; in 1943, one member.

1945   The two departments merged into the Department of Modern Languages and Literatures, with four members.

1946   Russian first offered. Discontinued, 1951–60.

1947   Ten members in the Department.

1954   Language laboratory established.

1959   Italian, not offered since 1952, restored to the curriculum.

1967   Chinese first offered.

1971   Faculty of eighteen teaching six languages. Language requirements for graduation reduced from four semesters to three, with an increase in class hours for the lower level courses.

Music

1841   Edward L. Walker, Professor of Music until 1847. No successor until 1907.

1880   A nine-piece college band from the corps of student cadets gave concerts in town, at the Indian School, at Commencement and they also marched in President Garfield's inaugural parade.

1897   President Reed's "general musical organization" included the Glee Club and Orchestra, then making annual tours.

1907   Reed secured outside financial support for a Department of Music taught first by John Craig King, Class of 1907, and director of the earlier Lyric Club, a town-and-gown chorus. The Department flourished until soon after President Reed's departure.

1922   With the coming of Ralph Schecter, who taught both English and Music, the Department has had a continuous academic history, supported by him alone until 1950.

1956   Lloyd Ultan the first Ph.D. member of the Department; course offerings increased from four to eleven by 1962, with a choir, a concert and marching band, the concert chorale, orchestra, instrumental ensembles and an opera workshop as extra-curricular offerings. The faculty approved a Music major in this year.

1970   Faculty of three offer twenty courses on the premise "that musical styles and forms are neither accidents or processes divorced from other aspects of man's evolution, but are reflections of his best thought throughout the ages, and therefore constitute a history of ideas."

Philosophy

1784   Charles Nisbet's Moral Philosophy taught by Presidents of the College through Reed with variations in title and content.

1848   William Henry Allen, the first listed Professor of Philosophy.

1888   Philosophy, formerly listed under English or Ethics, now under Christian Evidences and Ethics.

1891   Philosophy first listed as a separate "Method of Instruction," offering Psychology, Philosophy and Logic, with Dewey's *Psychology* and Stuckenberg's *Introduction to the Study of Philosophy* as texts. By 1894, three members, McIntire, Morgan and Dare.

1896   Offerings included Psychology, Philosophy, Logic, Pedagogy, Ethics and Evidences, all taught by William K. Dare.

1900   Philosophy and Education combined under William L. Gooding with the same course offerings.

1929   Listed as Philosophy and Religion, under L. G. Rohrbaugh until 1944 when he was joined by William Drum Gould.

1946   Department increased to three, and by 1964 had eight members.

1966   Philosophy a separate department with four members.

Physical Education

1783   Benjamin Rush, *Plan of Education:* "Whereas the health & figure of the body contribute much to display ye endowments & accomplishments of the mind, the youth in Dickinson College shall be permitted to learn the exercises of swimming, skating, and such other exercises as are innocent, conducive to health & external elegance." This section "expunged" by the trustees.

1884   First gymnasium, furnished with bowling alleys. Prof. Fletcher Durrell drilled students with Indian clubs and calisthenics.

1887   Rev. Lyman J. Muchmore, Adjunct Professor of Hygiene and Physical Culture. New equipment the highest product "of invention and mechanical skill, for giving effect to the suggestions of medical science for securing harmonious physical development."

1891   Two years of Physical Culture required for degree. The requirement has remained unchanged.

1895   Martha Barbour, instructor in Physical Culture for Young Ladies.

1897   Committee on Athletics one of first two faculty committees.

1922   A "For Women" section added to the course description, with use of a separate gymnasium and the campus of Metzger College.

1928   Department first listed as Physical Education. Women's Athletic Association organized.

1930   Swimming first offered, on completion of Alumni Gymnasium.

1941   First Aid and Civilian Defense included "to advance the ends of the physical fitness program sponsored by the government"

1954   Credit in Physical Education given for military science courses.

1965   Ten members in the Department.

Physics and Astronomy

1785   Both subjects first taught by the Professor of Mathematics and Natural Philosophy.

1808   Purchase by Benjamin Rush of new apparatus, including static electricity machine, air pump and hydro-pneumatic blow pipe.

1811   Purchase of Joseph Priestley laboratory apparatus.

1857   New telescope, with observatory on South College.

1865   New emphases with appointment of Charles F. Himes as Professor of Natural Science.

1869   Samuel Dickinson Hillman first Professor of Mathematics and Astronomy, Astronomy continuing with Mathematics until 1939

1876   "Experiments in Physics" and "Experimental Lectures by the Students" in the curriculum for Seniors under Himes, with new apparatus imported from Germany. Each spark from the Holtz electrical machine "is from eight to ten inches long and is blinding in its vividness, and accompanied with a deafening report. It is an instrument capable of the most magnificent effects." (*Dickinsonian*, Dec., 1876.)

1885   Following the completion of Tome Scientific Building, Himes appointed Professor of Physics and William B. Lindsay Professor of Chemistry.

1896   John Frederick Mohler succeeded Himes, carrying the Department alone until the appointment of Horace E. Rogers, 1925.

1950   Astronomy added to the Physics curriculum. First course in Atomic Physics given.

1957   Department increased from four to nine.

1960   Department became Physics and Astronomy.

1971   Seven members.

Political Science

1785   Dr. Nisbet's lectures frequently expounded the science of government.

1822   Following the revival of classes under Dr. Mason, Political Economy was included in the curriculum, but the public assured that "PARTY POLITICS" will be excluded. (*American Volunteer,* Jan. 17, 1822.)

1888   "Constitution of the United States, with History of American Politics" taught by James Henry Morgan. Political Science first listed as a "Method of Instruction," but thereafter, until 1913, in conjunction with History of Political Economy.

1896   Morris Watson Prince, first Professor of Political Science.

1913   Political Science courses listed under Law or Social Science until:

1947   First listed as an independent department, under the chairmanship of William Lonsdale Tayler, with four other members.

1960   Increase in the preceding decade from five to seven members and from eighteen to twenty-seven courses.

1971   Nine members.

Psychology

1891   A Psychology course listed under Philosophy, using Dewey's *Psychology* as a text. Both Psychology and Education courses in Philosophy Department until 1921.

1921   Psychology and Philosophy Department, with three courses in Psychology and five in Psychology and Education.

1922   A separate Psychology Department, taught by Wilbur Norcross, who was joined in 1928 by Russell Thompson.

1929   A course in Anthropology listed under Psychology and continued until 1937.

1946   Became Department of Education and Psychology, with five members offering fourteen courses. Legal Psychology introduced this year and continued until 1953.

1957   Department of nine members dominated by Psychology courses, since Education was not a major.

1970   Three-track offering initiated: Experimental, Clinical and Applied Psychology. Creation of an Educational Diagnostic Clinic.

Public Speaking

Public speaking was from the first a major emphasis in an institution preparing for citizenship in a democracy, fostered in literary society debates, "oratorical exhibitions," class recitations, oral examinations, with the commencement oration as final proof of the earned degree.

1821   New curriculum under Dr. Mason, with courses in English Composition, Declamation and Elocution.

1856   John Grigg Medal for Oratory awarded annually; replaced in 1862 by the gold and silver medals of the Pierson Prize.

1879   The literary societies initiated Sophomore prizes and gold medals for Composition and Declamation.

1888   Oratory, or "all matters pertaining to the Art of Public Discourse," to be taught by the President.

1889   President Reed chaired this department, offering "Practical drill in Voice building, Declamation and kindred matters."

1906   Lucretia J. McAnney, first Professor of Elocution (and Dean of Women), joined Reed in Department of Oratory.

1914   First listed as Department of Public Speaking, with Debating included. In 1917, required of all Freshmen.

1928   Until 1956, generally included in English Department offerings.

1938   Until 1947, taught as Oral English, by Ralph Schecter.

1956   Separate Department of Public Speaking, with Schecter and Brubaker.

1967   Dramatic Arts and Public Speaking in one department.

Religion

In eighteenth and early nineteenth centuries religion pervaded all teaching, and was offered separately under such headings as Moral Philosophy. Truth and Evidences of Divine Revelation, or Christian Ethics. The culminating Senior course was usually taught by the President.

1834   Until 1840, Religion was listed with English Department offerings. Butler's *Analogy* was the Senior text from 1834 until 1889, when it was last used in the Christian Ethics course. Paley's *Evidences* and *Natural Theology*, usually Junior texts, were in use from 1836 to 1868.

1840   Religion a separate department with offerings for each class.

1860   A two-year "Biblical Course" introduced for "young men preparing for the ministry who cannot take a full course." In 1867, incorporated into the last two years of the B.A. program. Discontinued, 1888.

1870   Henry Martyn Harman, Professor of Ancient Languages, bringing a new emphasis on Hebrew. From 1872–1890 the Catalogue listed his Sabbath afternoon Bible class, "for critical examination of the most noted and valuable of the ancient manuscripts."

1920   Until 1924, a Department of Religious Education and Rural Leadership offered four courses, including the first given in History of Religions.

1922   Department of Philosophy and Religious Education; changed, 1929, to Philosophy and Religion.

1962   Major reorganization of the department by Dean Magill, former Chaplain, with Frederick P. Ferré, as Chairman.

1966   Religion and Philosophy Departments separated. New emphasis on History of Religions. Catholic and Jewish scholars given term appointments beginning 1969.

Russian and Soviet Area Studies

1964   Major and minor approved as an interdisciplinary program involving the Departments of Economics, History, Modern Languages, Political Science and Sociology-Anthropology.

Sociology-Anthropology

1896   Sociology, taught under History and Economics by Morris W. Prince, included "a discussion of some of the important social problems such as Socialistic Schemes and Social Reform, Communism, Individualism, Immigration, and the Defective and Dependent Classes." Social Science a Senior elective, with "monographs and Lectures."

1898   "Recitations and discussions" in Sociology based upon Henderson's *Social Elements* and Gidding's *Elements of Sociology.*

1900   Sociology and Economics a separate department under Dr. James Evelyn Pilcher (formerly taught Anatomy and Physiology). Still a Senior elective on "the Tariff, Monetary Standards, Labor Problems and other living questions."

1902   Anthropology added as a Senior elective, "as a practical application of sociology."

1903   Department of Sociology and Economics until 1906, when only a course in Social Institutions remained in the History and Political Science Department.

1910   Establishment of the Department of Peace and Public Service, with courses in Social Problems and Business Institutions taught by George A. Crider through 1912.

1915   Changed to Department of Social Science.

1929   A course in Anthropology listed under Psychology and continued until 1937.

1932   Sociology major established.

1936   First course in The Modern City.

1938   First course in Cultural Anthropology.

1946   Course in Racial and Cultural Minorities (Retitled, 1953, The American Negro) taught by Charles D. Kepner until 1963.

1963   Became Department of Sociology and Anthropology.

South Asian Area Studies

1969   An interdisciplinary program drawing upon Anthropology, Economics, History, Philosophy, Political Science, Religion, Sociology and Fine Arts. Includes a summer and a final year's study at the University of Pennsylvania.

1970   Study offered at Mysore, India, in cooperation with four other area colleges.

Appendix C

BROTHERHOOD

Some of the more durable core groups of college life are listed here. A complete roster of every club and coterie through two hundred years would fill a lively volume. The procession begins with the literary societies of 1786 and 1789, dedicated to debating issues of the day, to oratory and literature, and to maintaining each its library. Enjoying at the first almost complete freedom under student management, they inspired loyalties more intense than any other. From 1822 on, however, trustees and faculty asserted increasing control, and successive efforts to obtain independence under acts of incorporation failed. The secret social fraternities, meanwhile, had raised a stouter bastion against college regulation. By 1853, the societies were imitating fraternity ritual, and by 1874 we find them debating such frivolous issues as, "Which is most serviceable to a man, a house or a woman?" The fraternities were then becoming an integral part of college life with their sponsorship of living and dining arrangements, and themselves subject to regulation. This is the period in which the class emerges as a coherent organization unencumbered by any function other than that of defeating and dismaying all rivals. The societies, with every student a member of one or the other, continued to fade before the selective elitism of the fraternities. Elitism was enlisted in support of scholarship and character with the revival of Phi Beta Kappa and the founding of new recognition and honorary groups. Now the old ideals of brotherhood and selectivity remain, both challenged and enlarged, within a new and more democratic sense of community.

LITERARY

Belles Lettres Literary Society

Founded, Feb. 22, 1786. As the second oldest student literary society in Pennsylvania, Belles Lettres was to some extent a model for the others which became a characteristic feature of college life throughout the country. Its library was founded in 1791. Its badge was then a blue ribbon. It had taken Washington's birthday as its official founding date, and someone may have recollected that a blue ribbon had been the insignia of the Commander-in-Chief in the late war. By 1837, this had given way to the red rose, and in 1852 this was supplanted by a fraternity-type gold badge. When some wag compared this to a policeman's badge, another was chosen, 1855, of four Greek columns with the motto, "To Καλον." In 1934, "due to the lack of interest and appreciation of many students," Belles Lettres united with its rival (see below) in forming the Union Literary Society, for "fostering of interest in culture." Two years later, on the initiative of Belles Lettres, whose sesquicentennial was at hand, the two were reestablished, and Belles Lettres continues to foster creative work in literature and the arts. Its minutes, library circulation records and other papers have been preserved almost wholly intact.

Union Philosophical Literary Society

Founded, Aug. 31, 1789, "for mutual improvement in science and literature." The Unions followed the lead of Belles Lettres in establishing a library, 1791. The white rose insignia of earlier days was supplanted in the 1850's by a gold cross supporting a disk with a circle of white roses and the letters "UPS." In 1844, the General Union Philosophical Society organized its alumni behind Society and College, a step not followed by Belles Lettres until 1856. In late years the Society has tended to stay with its traditional role of political discussion and debate. Its records were almost wholly destroyed in the Denny Hall fire, 1904.

Neo-Cosmean Society

Organized in Jan., 1856, to bring, as its name implies, a fresh, New-World spirit into play, it had a short life. Constitution and bylaws were written, a library planned, but the first debates led on to in-fighting and disintegration.

Scientific Society of Dickinson College

Founded in 1867 as part of Professor Himes' energetic new program. With its provision for student lectures, its seal showing the light from a star passing through a prism with the motto, *"Nunc ad Sidera,"* it seems to have aimed at a place in College life equal to that of Belles Lettres and

Union. Actually, it stands midway between the literary society and the departmental clubs of a later day. It became inactive at the time of the building of Tome, and was succeeded, 1911, by the Mohler Scientific Club.

Harman Literary Society

Founded in 1896 "to create an organized center of thought and action among the women of Dickinson College," the Society was named, with wry and affectionate humor, in honor of the faculty's most inveterate foe of coeducation, retiring that year. It published a small literary magazine, *Salmagundi*, 1904–08. Its members are featured for the last time in the *Microcosm* of 1935, after an active year under the presidency of Eleanor Betts.

McIntire Literary Society

For women. Founded in 1921 and named in honor of Bradford O. McIntire, then retiring after thirty-nine years of service, the group seems to have been active only in its first year.

W. A. Hutchinson Literary Society

Named in honor of Headmaster William Albert Hutchinson. Active, 1913.

In the Dickinson School of Law William Trickett, formerly a teacher in both College and Grammar School, was familiar with literary society procedures, and aware of how well they could be adapted to his purpose. On a more mature level, the societies took other forms sooner than at the College:

Reed Society

Founded in 1890, "for the purpose of advancing themselves in the knowledge of the Law, and in the acquisition of the arts of debate and public speech . . . . This society, it is believed, is one of the most important educational instrumentalities of the school." Named in honor of Judge John Reed, founder of the School. Active until 1895.

Dickinson Law Society

Active, 1894–1903.

Allison Society

Active, 1895–1903.

Dickinson-Allison Law Society

A merger lasting one year only, 1903–04.

The old Grammar School had also its literary societies, increasing in coherence and importance when the School, as Conway Hall, became a peer of the best preparatory institutions:

Oratorical Society

Founded, 1836. To be remembered chiefly for the ardor with which it assembled a library. In particular the appeals of teachers Levi Scott and Thomas Bowman, 1840–43, brought in rare volumes more appreciated in later generations than theirs.

Young Men's Debating Society

Founded, 1841.

Reed Literary Society

Named in honor of President George Edward Reed, and active from 1891 until the closing of Conway Hall, 1917.

Gamma Epsilon Literary Society

Active, 1896–1917.

Sigma Epsilon Literary Society

Founded, 1897.

SOCIAL

Phi Nu Theta, known as the Eclectic Fraternity, 1852

Founded 1837, at Wesleyan. Short-lived chapter at Dickinson was suppressed by the faculty in July, 1852. The history of the fraternity does not list the Dickinson chapter; indeed categorizes ΦΝΘ as a local fraternity at Wesleyan, still in existence.

Zeta Psi; Alpha Chapter, 1852–1856

Founded 1847, at New York University. By 1853, the trustees had required the members to sign written pledges to disband, and the record book, initiation ritual, roll book, by-laws and constitution were burned. It seems that the brothers were able to meet secretly after proscription, but disbanded in 1856 when the last members graduated.

Phi Kappa Sigma; Epsilon Chapter, 1854–1876; 1895–

Founded 1850, at the University of Pennsylvania. Having entered the campus sub rosa, ΦΚΣ flourished until 1876 and was then inactive until

1895, when it took over the local fraternity Alpha Zeta Phi. In 1906 it built a house on South College Street, next to the Sigma Chi house, and in 1923 purchased the former Lindner property on North College Street. This house was razed in 1963 to make room for the Holland Union Building, and the chapter moved to the Fraternity Quadrangle in 1964.

Phi Kappa Psi; Pa. Zeta Chapter, 1859–
Founded 1852 at Jefferson College. Kept alive "in devious ways" in its early years on campus, ΦΚΨ vies with Sigma Chi for the title of oldest fraternity in continuous existence. Purchased the Abram Bosler residence next to the President's House in 1904, and remained there until 1963, when it was sold to the College and razed. Moved to Fraternity Quadrangle in 1964.

Sigma Chi; Omicron Chapter, 1859–
Founded 1855 at Miami University. Entered the campus the same year as Phi Kappa Psi. In 1900 the Chapter bought a lot on Main Street (now High Street) next to old South College, and on it built a "neat little fraternity house" designed by Ray Zug, Class of 1896, dedicated in 1905. In 1925, the property was sold to the College and rented to Tau Epsilon Phi, a Law School fraternity, until 1927, when it was razed. ΣX bought the former Charles Berg property on South College Street in 1924, and members lived there until 1964, when the Fraternity Quadrangle was opened, and the house became Todd House, a dormitory.

Theta Delta Chi; Sigma Chapter, 1861– 1875; 1880– 1895
Founded 1847 at Union College. ΘΔX had a fairly vigorous life on campus until 1875, when the active chapter lapsed. Reestablished in 1880 by the graduate members, it again ceased to function in 1895.

Chi Phi; Omega Chapter, 1869– 1893
Founded 1824 at the College of New Jersey (later Princeton).

"Independents"; local fraternity, 1871– 1874
Originally founded by students with an anti-fraternity bias, this group became the Alpha Sigma Chapter of Beta Theta Pi in 1874.

Beta Theta Pi; Alpha Sigma Chapter, 1874–
Founded 1839 at Miami University. The Chapter's nucleus was the "Independents" (above). In 1906 BΘΠ built a house at 402 West High Street, and occupied it until it was sold to the College in 1964 and demolished to make room for Malcolm Hall. Moved to Fraternity Quadrangle in 1964.

Phi Delta Theta; Pennsylvania Epsilon Chapter, 1880–

Founded 1848 at Miami University. ΘΔΧ in 1899 was permitted to build a stone lodge on the northwest corner of the campus. Finding this house to be too small by 1931, the Chapter built a stone house on West Street, occupying it until it was bought by the College in 1964 and remodeled for the Office of Communication and Development. Moved to the Fraternity Quadrangle in 1964.

Theta Nu Epsilon, 1888–1905

Founded 1870 at Wesleyan University, ΦΝΕ was a loosely-governed social fraternity for sophomores, accepting members of other brotherhoods. The campus chapter is not mentioned in the fraternity history, and may not have been authorized by "National."

Sigma Alpha Epsilon; Sigma Phi Chapter, 1890–

Founded 1856 at the University of Alabama. ΣΑΕ bought the W. F. Sadler house at College and Louther Streets in 1922, remodeling it in 1928. After a period of inactivity during World War II, the Chapter bought a house at 200 South College Street and occupied it until the Quadrangle house was ready in 1964. The South College Street house was sold to the Law School and later demolished.

Alpha Zeta Phi; local fraternity, 1891–1895

ΑΖΦ was a successful local venture, the owner of a house on West Pomfret Street. This group was the nucleus of the revival of Phi Kappa Sigma in 1895.

A H L; local sorority, 1893–1894

A H L appears in the *Microcosm* dated 1894, with no explanation or description, other than a list of members and a statement of its "colors," lavender and gold.

Delta Chi; Dickinson Chapter, 1893–1933

Founded 1890 at Cornell. In its early days, the fraternity was for law students only, but was soon extended to include other collegiate departments. At Dickinson, however, it seems to have been substantially a Law School fraternity.

K K K; local fraternity, 1893–1897

Very little is known about this small brotherhood which seems not to have been connected with either of two national groups bearing these initials.

Kappa Gamma; Delta Charge, 1894–1902
Founded at Wesleyan. An inter-fraternity Greek letter society whose "yell" was first heard on campus at Commencement, 1894.

Gamma Zeta; local sorority, 1896–1897
ΓZ appears only once in the College records, with a charming photograph of its members and a list of their names.

Phi Alpha Pi; local sorority, 1898–1903
It is said that an earlier ΦΑΠ had been inaugurated but "died a natural death from want of support." This group was stronger, and was absorbed by the national sorority, Pi Beta Phi, in 1903.

Omega Psi; local sorority, 1899–1907
ΩΨ was adopted by the national sorority, Chi Omega, in 1907.

Kappa Sigma; Beta Pi Chapter, 1902–
Founded in 1869 at the University of Virginia. After over twenty years' residence in East College, KΣ bought the Irving house at College and Louther Streets, where the members lived until it was destroyed by fire in late 1963. In 1964 they moved to the Fraternity Quadrangle. A "pagoda" occupied the back yard of the house on Louther Street, closely resembling the one which once stood in the middle of the John Dickinson campus. It is now pleasantly situated on the grounds of a house occupied by Mr. and Mrs. Richard Wagner on North Hanover Street.

Pi Beta Phi; Pennsylvania Gamma Chapter, 1903–
Founded 1867 at Monmouth College. The campus chapter of Pi Phi was formed out of the local sorority, Phi Alpha Pi.

Theta Lambda Phi; local fraternity, 1903–1913
Merged in 1913 with Delta Phi Delta and Alpha Kappa Phi to become Delta Theta Phi. The fraternity drew its members from the Law School.

Alpha Chi Rho; Beta Chapter, 1905–
Founded 1895 at Trinity College. Beta Chapter bought a house at 36 North College Street in 1919 and sold it in 1946 to Phi Epsilon Pi. This same year "Crow" moved into its new house at High and College Streets, the former residence of Mrs. Abram Bosler. Purchased by the College in 1965, this building now houses the Admissions Office, the fraternity having moved to the Quadrangle.

Chi Omega; Delta Chapter, 1907–
Founded 1895 at the University of Arkansas. ΧΩ was organized on the campus from a local sorority, Omega Psi.

Contemporary Club; local fraternity, 1907–1916
"The Contemporary Club was formed with the object of keeping its members up to the 'times' in college life for mutual help and advancement", says the *D-Book* for 1908–09. It was the nucleus out of which Theta Chi formed its Pi Chapter in 1916.

Corpus Juris (Skorms); local fraternity, 1912–
Corpus Juris draws its membership from the Law School, and is the only surviving social fraternity there.

Delta Theta Phi; Holmes Senate, [1903] 1913–1932
Founded 1913 at the Cleveland Law School of Baldwin University, out of a union of Delta Phi Delta (whose founding date of 1900 it officially uses), Alpha Kappa Phi and Theta Lambda Phi (founded at Dickinson School of Law in 1903). The Chapter in 1923 bought a house at 47 South College Street which had been occupied by Phi Kappa Sigma.

Phi Kappa Delta; local fraternity, 1913–1914
Little is known about this fraternity, but it appears to have drawn its members from both Law School and College. Some of them are listed later as members of Phi Epsilon Pi.

Torah Society; local fraternity, c. 1914
This Law School society was the forerunner of Phi Epsilon Pi.

Phi Epsilon Pi; Iota Chapter, 1914–[1970]
Founded 1902 at the City College of New York. Iota Chapter was originally considered a Law School fraternity, but was added to the Dickinson College Senate in 1931. The next year it took over the section of East College just vacated by Kappa Sigma, and in 1946 bought the former Alpha Chi Rho house at 36 North College Street, members living there until 1963. After a short stay at Mathews House, the Chapter moved to the Quad in 1964. In 1970 the national fraternity merged with Zeta Beta Tau, and took that name.

Old grads will fondly remember the annual spring water fight initiated by the Phi Eps at number 36 North College Street and the Phi Kaps next door at number 28. A relatively tame exchange of ammunition grew stronger and wilder as other fraternities joined in the fray with buckets, pitchers, hoses, and baskets of eggs and rotten vegetables. There came a time when the town fathers decided that the hilarious battle was too disruptive of traffic and destructive of property, and the custom died out under the dampening and stern chaperonage of firemen and policemen.

Theta Chi; Pi Chapter, 1916–

Founded 1916 at Norwich University. The Chapter grew out of the Contemporary Club. It occupied a section of East College until 1925, when it purchased a house on West High Street which it occupied until it went into the Quad in 1964.

Alpha Gamma Psi; local sorority, 1917–1919

The forerunner of Gamma Chapter of Phi Mu.

Phi Mu; Beta Delta Chapter, 1919–1967

Founded 1852 at Wesleyan Female College. Beta Delta Chapter was formed out of the local sorority, Alpha Gamma Psi. In 1968, the Chapter members reorganized into a local sorority, Alpha Delta Epsilon, having voted unanimously to withdraw from Phi Mu Fraternity following disagreement with the National Office over interracial pledging regulations.

Sigma Alpha Mu; Chapter designation unknown, 1919–1921

Founded 1909 at City College of New York. The fraternity's founders were of Jewish faith with a strong Zionist bent, although its constitution has been amended to allow membership of anyone of "good moral character."

Zeta Eta Phi; local sorority, 1921–1924

The forerunner of Zeta Tau Alpha on the campus.

Tau Epsilon Phi; Tau Chapter, 1922–1930

Founded 1910 at Columbia. The Chapter drew its members from the Law School; at one time rented the former Sigma Chi house on West High Street from the College (1925–1927).

Phi Delta Delta; Omicron Chapter, 1923–

Founded 1911 at the University of Southern California. This Chapter of the international women's legal fraternity draws its membership from the Law School.

Commons Club; local fraternity, 1924–1959

Organized on the campus in 1924, the Club's primary purpose was to afford to men who did not belong to fraternities social privileges and contacts which they otherwise would not enjoy. By 1959, the need for such a group had lessened considerably, and the club was disbanded officially.

D A L; local sorority; 1924–1925

Formed as a society for independent women, D A L was followed (with approximately the same membership) by Wilohea and Delta Sigma.

Zeta Tau Alpha; Beta Beta Chapter, 1924–1969

Founded 1898 at Longwood College. The sorority was formed from a local group, Zeta Eta Phi. In 1969, the Chapter was disaffiliated from the National fraternity, and the members disbanded.

Wilohea; local sorority, 1925–1926

The successor of D A L, the predecessor of Delta Sigma, a society for independent women.

Delta Sigma; local sorority, 1926–1927

The successor of Wilohea, a society for independent women.

Sigma Tau Phi; Epsilon Chapter, 1926–c. 1933

Founded 1918 at the University of Pennsylvania. The Chapter was admitted to the Dickinson College Senate in 1931, along with Phi Epsilon Pi, and for a short time occupied the third section of East College. The national fraternity merged with Alpha Epsilon Pi in 1947, taking the latter name.

Buchanan Club; local fraternity, 1927–1931

Founded on the campus in 1927, the Club adopted a Greek letter designation in 1929, to become Beta Psi.

Independent Women; local organization, 1946–1955

Sometimes called the "Indevians," this group drew its membership from those women on campus who wished to remain unaffiliated with Greek-letter sororities. Becoming less active in the early Fifties, the organization was disbanded in 1955 only to reactivate the next year as Sui Generis.

Sui Generis; local organization, 1956–1961

A society for independent women.

Alpha Delta Epsilon; local sorority, 1968–
Founded on Dickinson campus with Gamma Chapter of Phi Mu as its nucleus.

Gamma Phi Epsilon; independent local fraternity, 1968–
The first coeducational fraternity on campus.

Zeta Beta Tau; Dickinson Chapter, 1970–
Founded 1898 in New York City by a group of undergraduates from several colleges. ZBT was the pioneer social fraternity of Jewish men, but has been non-sectarian since 1954. Following ZBT's merger with Phi Epsilon Pi, Iota Chapter of that fraternity took the new name of Zeta Beta Tau.

Conway Hall Fraternities

Upsilon Gamma Sigma, Pennsylvania Alpha Chapter. Established 1904.
Kappa Delta Pi, Pennsylvania Mu Chapter. Established 1906.
Omega Chi, Pennsylvania Alpha Chapter. Established 1906.

RECOGNITION and HONORARY

Phi Beta Kappa; Alpha Chapter of Pennsylvania, April 13, 1887
Election to Phi Beta Kappa is the highest academic honor attainable by a Dickinson College student.

Raven's Claw, 1896
Local honorary society of seven Senior men, the "White Hats," tapped at the Old Stone Steps during commencement weekend. A group reminiscent of Yale's Skull and Bones, Scroll and Key, or Wolf's Head, promoting loyalty and that "sense of sodality that helps to make the world a pleasant place." Meeting fortnightly at midnight, Raven's Claw developed a rhythmic tapping of canes on the pavements in an eerie, complicated beat as the brothers went by.

Skitch-A-Genee, 1908
Local Sophomore honorary for men. Last noted in *Microcosm*, 1924.

Skull and Key, 1909
Local Junior honorary for men. Since 1935 the "Black Hats" have presented a silver loving cup annually to a Freshman man judged the outstanding member of his class.

Tau Kappa Alpha, 1915
National forensic fraternity for men and women. Merged in 1963 with Delta Sigma Rho.

Woolsack, 1920
Senior law honorary.

Tau Delta Pi, 1922
Local Drama fraternity. Revived after a lapse in 1938 and continuing until 1949 when it was superceded by the national Alpha Psi Omega.

Wheel and Chain, 1924
Local honorary leadership fraternity for Senior women, limited to nine members. The "Blue Hats" once sternly enforced Freshman rules, and help sponsor the orientation program for Freshman women, present an annual award to the outstanding girl in the entering class and help to coordinate various events.

Omicron Delta Kappa, 1927
National honorary fraternity for Senior men recognized for leadership.

Alpha Gamma, 1928
Local recognition fraternity promoting cooperation among journalistic organizations. Superceded, 1948, by Pi Delta Epsilon.

Alpha Sigma Gamma, 1932
Local honorary recognizing outstanding work in publications and journalism. Superceded, 1948, by Pi Delta Epsilon.

Lambda Sigma Pi, 1938
Local honorary science fraternity. Women were admitted, 1940.

Delta Phi Alpha, 1948
National honorary fraternity for students in advanced German courses.

Pi Delta Epsilon, 1948
National honorary society to coordinate campus publications and recognize meritorious work in campus journalism. Limited to Juniors and Seniors.

Alpha Psi Omega, 1949

National honorary for men and women, recognizing talent and ability in Drama.

Pi Gamma Mu, 1959

National honorary recognizing superior scholarship in Social Studies. Membership of Juniors and Seniors, elected by the faculty.

Phi Mu Alpha (SINFONIA), 1960

National fraternity recognizing talent and ability in Music.

Pi Delta Phi, 1962

National honorary of Juniors and Seniors who have earned scholastic honors in French.

Sigma Delta Pi, 1962

National honorary recognizing scholarship in Spanish language and culture.

Eta Sigma Phi, 1964

National honorary fostering scholarship in the Classics.

Tau Pi Chi, 1965

Local honorary for women, recognizing their contributions to the campus in Music.

Alpha Nu, 1969

Local honorary stimulating interest in Astronomy.

RELIGION AND SOCIAL SERVICE

In all, more than fifty organizations are recorded, ranging from the eagerly spontaneous to a perfunctory and callous piety. Only the few most enduring are noted here. The earliest student religious activity had been within the Presbyterian church organization to 1832, and then the Methodist. This led to increased emphasis upon College chapel, and supported the formation of the separate College church, for which Emory Chapel was built in 1858. It is in this second half of the century that separate student groups multiply, indicating a wider variety of religious background, and, following World War II, an ever clearer identification of religious and social idealism.

Society For Religious Inquiry, 1857–1886

Founded as an aid to preparation for the Christian ministry, it gradually declined and disappeared, its only service at the last apparently being the sermon preached before its members during commencement week.

Young Men's Christian Association, 1880–1934

Stimulating speakers and conferences enlivened its meetings, first in the College Chapel, now Memorial Hall, and later in the Y.M.C.A. Room on the basement level directly below. An avenue for student contact with the larger world of Christian service, it sponsored the Dickinson-in-China movement (1925), and its Deputation Commission sent students out to conduct services in the local jail, county home and nearby churches. In 1893, the Y.M.C.A. began publication of the *"D Book,"* the student handbook, to be followed after more than fifty years by the *Mermaid's Tale*. The Y.W.C.A. (1896), at first an adjunct of the men's group, served similar national and regional goals.

Dickinson College Religious Association, 1934–1950

With fresher viewpoints and a broader purpose, DCRA superceded Y.M.C.A. and Y.W.C.A. as the dominant religious force on campus, representing a new awareness of the wide range of religious beliefs and idealism. Student-faculty committees were set up heading and coordinating the activities of diverse Protestant, Catholic and Jewish groups.

Dickinson College Interfaith Council, 1950–1959

Successor to the DCRA under a title more indicative of its ecumenical aim, it carried on as best it could against the prevalent apathy of these years in American student life.

Student Christian Association, 1950–1959

With functions similar to those of the Y.M.C.A., this group had an only slightly less lacklustre existence than that of the Interfaith Council.

Dickinson College Religious Affairs Council, 1958–1967

A new agency to "coordinate the religious affairs of the College" came in response to the rise of new groups and revived interest in older ones—the Christian Association, Methodist Student Movement (since 1956), Jewish Affairs Council, Canterbury Club, Catholic Club, Intervarsity Christian Fellowship (launched in 1960 by the militant fundamentalists), Concern (1961, peace and disarmament) and others.

Faith and Society, 1964–

Heralded a series of religious organizations which implemented the aims of a newly created chaplaincy under an administration determined to bring "faith" and "society" closer together on a strong intellectual and service-oriented basis. Renamed *Action-In-Society*, this group now co-ordinates voluntary student action projects both in the College and the community.

The College Church, 1965–

Abolition of compulsory chapel and student estrangement from de-nominational church attendance were followed in 1965 by the establish-ment of an interfaith campus congregation. Initially attempting to be all-inclusive, it finally defined itself as ecumenical and Christian. In 1967, a decision was made to provide occasions for authentic Christian and Jewish worship services on campus. Thus the College Church became the Christian congregation, and a Synagogue service was formally established by the Hillel Council and the Office of the Chaplain, with Sabbath evening ser-vices and observances of the Jewish Holy Days. The first Jewish High Holy Days services in the history of Carlisle were held in the fall of 1967. Provision was also made for the celebration of the Roman Catholic Mass each week. The Chaplain of the College serves as pastor of the ecumenical College Church, and the other worship services are coordinated through his office.

As the culmination of a long development from strict demoni-nationalism followed by many years of dubious compromise, College Church and the two smaller congregations answer the community's desire to be authentic and at the same time responsive to innovation and open-ness, offering individual and group enrichment within the broad traditions of western religion.

Appendix D

BUILDINGS AND GROUNDS

Entries are chronological, showing the growth of campus and plant. Some buildings held for short terms or otherwise of no significant importance in the life of the College are omitted. Fraternity-owned houses are noted in Appendix C, and are included here only as acquired by the College. The material given is condensed from the DCA file on College Properties.

"Old College"
Built 1781–82 on town lot no. 219, acquired on March 30, 1773 to house the Latin school. Sponsored by the Presbyterian congregation of Carlisle. This acquisition marks the accepted founding date of Dickinson College. John Creigh's bill for construction, DCA, itemizes costs of £42/3/5½. The two-storey brick building faced on Liberty Alley with a frontage of 60 feet and a length of 240 feet south to Pomfret Street. This was the hall and campus of Dickinson College where Charles Nisbet assumed the office of Principal, July 5, 1785. An addition in stone, doubling its size, was authorized on October 20 and completed by December, 1786, at a cost of $583.62. Legal transfer of the property to the College trustees was enacted, October 3, 1788. As "New College" neared completion in 1802, the property was sold to Charles McClure for £200 ($533.33), but continued in use after the burning of the new building until West College could be occupied. "Old College" became the home of private schools under John B. Murray, Gad Day and other masters until it burned, April 28, 1860. The brick building erected on its site reproduced, somewhat enlarged, the original (illustrated, J. H. Morgan, *Dickinson College* [Carlisle, 1933], opp. p. 41).

"New College"

Authorized, September 26, 1798. Cornerstone laid, June 20, 1799. John Keen, of the Carpenters' Company, Philadelphia, architect. Cost, about $12,000. This brick building, standing on the site of the present West College, and nearly as large, was destroyed by fire, February 3, 1803, when still unfinished and only partly occupied.

West College

Authorized, March 14, 1803. Cornerstone laid, August 8, 1803. First use, November 1805. Architect, Benjamin Henry Latrobe. Cost, about $20,000. Four storeys in height, 150 by 45 feet, of the native limestone with brownstone trim, it was a larger and more impressive edifice than its predecessor. West College was also known as "New College" until the completion of "Old East" in 1836, and still later, gained the affectionate title, "Old West." Years went by before the building was functionally complete. John Montgomery wrote to John Dickinson, November 20, 1805, that it could soon lodge and board forty students. In 1809, $12,000 was spent on additional work toward this goal, central chapel, dining hall directly below, with kitchen and oven adjoining. In 1821, upper rooms were finished for the first time, with other extensive improvements. On November 26, 1844, a fire in the east end, "especially in the Museum," threatened the whole—Professor Sudler "the generalissimo of that occasion" as a bucket brigade of citizens and students "fought the angry flames," and Durbin's high clear voice was heard above the uproar. No faculty resided in the building after 1890, and as the fraternity houses absorbed student population, offices and classrooms took over. Denny Hall was for a while the campus administrative center, the change symbolized by the removal of the College bell to its tower, but this distinction returned to Old West with later renovations. The gifts of Lemuel T. Appold, '82, were a major factor in this, notably, in 1919, "Memorial Hall" in the old chapel area, honoring the Dickinsonians who died in World War I. The John Dickinson portrait was added in the next year; then the McCauley Room, below, for faculty and other meetings; and the entrances with stone steps at either end of the central corridor in which, 1929, the "Presidents Gallery" was created. Later, the "Trustees Gallery" was commenced on the level above. The "Durbin Oratory" was added in 1949, dedicated under that name, February 23, 1954, and completely renovated as an interfaith chapel in 1969. In 1954, perhaps with the crisis of 1844 in mind, a sprinkler system was ordered installed throughout the building. The historic Mermaid, battered and imperilled by pranksters through the years, was replaced by a sheet metal surrogate and in 1970 the original was mounted in Spahr Library's Morris Room on a pedestal de-

Dickinson College Campus. Watercolor by Daniel Dinkle, *c.* 1845.

Engraving by Richard Rummell, 1910.

Jacob Tome Scientific Building, built in 1885; rebuilt in 1958.

C. Scott Althouse Science Hall, built in 1957.

signed by Richard C. Reed. "Old West" has been a Registered National Historic Landmark since 1963.

North College

In 1822 a "Wood House," built of stone, 80 by 22 feet, costing $265, and an icehouse sunk 15 feet into the ground, were added to the campus just north of West College and therefore accessible to the basement kitchens. On July 12, 1847, the trustees authorized a remodeling by contractor William H. Horn at a cost of $300, and with the dignity of a new name, "North College." Three large dormitory rooms with six closets for tools and a basement with both living quarters and space in which students could carry on familiar trades were provided. It was intended to meet the need of young tradesmen earning a college education. Apparently the trades were practiced with success, for a year later Carlisle residents were petitioning the College for the prohibition of "the sale of merchandise or the establishment of any manufactory within the limits of the college grounds." Mary Johnson Dillon remembered a schoolroom for faculty children in North College. The building was destroyed by fire on the night of James Buchanan's election to the presidency, 1856. Some material was salvaged for the building of Emory Chapel, 1858.

South College I and II

Purchase of the former German Reformed Church facing West College from across High Street was authorized on January 7, 1835, at a price of $2,050. It had been occupied by schoolmaster Henry Duffield's "Dickinson Institute," and was renovated as a new home for the old College Grammar School. Burned down on December 23, 1836, it was replaced by a "larger and more noble edifice," completed January 1, 1838. Architect, Peter B. Smith. Cost, $5,825. An enlargement, authorized in 1886, was reported by President Reed, June 28, 1887: "Casing the front and sides of the building externally with new brick, adding a story thereto and remodelling internally so as to furnish a residence for the Principal and lecture rooms and dormitory accommodations for as many students as the space at command would serve." Contractor, Samuel Wetzel. Cost, $5,215. Besides Grammar School the building housed at various times the College Library, the science department and Museum, an observatory in its cupola, and, in the twentieth century, dormitory rooms, offices and College commons. In 1927, after nearly ninety years of service, it was razed to make room for the Alumni Gymnasium.

East College

Completed, November 5, 1836. Architect and builder, Henry Myers. Cost, $9,588. Typical of college buildings of its period, "Old East" was divided into four sections with fireproof dividing walls. It included both dormitory and classrooms, while the eastern section served as President's House, later dignified by a handsome front porch. In 1890, the President moved to the residence his successors have occupied ever since (see below). In 1924 an extensive renovation was made under architect William W. Emmart. The old entrance stairways were removed at this time and the former basement area incorporated into the whole. From 1946 to 1952, returning old grads were shocked to find co-eds nesting in "Old East." The building has also housed the Commons Club and other fraternities, Deans of Men and Women, College Chaplain, faculty lounge, Chaplains's office, Development Office and an art studio, and was headquarters for the army training program in World War II. In 1968-70 it was completely rebuilt as The Bernard Center for the Humanities (see below).

"The Pagoda"

A pentagonal wooden gazebo or bandstand in front of Old West was a campus landmark from 1871 to 1887, painted, according to a treasurer's voucher of June 5, 1871, "white and chrome yellow, touched up with Indian red and ultramarine blue." It was the sole acomplishment in President Dashiell's ambitious building program. *"Mons ruit, mus fuit,"* they said.

Emory Chapel

Built in 1858 at the northeast corner of West and Pomfret Streets as a Methodist church for the College community apart from that of the town. The cost of over $10,000 came from College funds, secured by a mortgage. Architect, Thomas Balbirnie, using the Victorian Gothic style he had brought to the Franklin and Marshall campus. His working drawings have been preserved. Emory Female College used the building, 1863-66. In 1877 the College assumed the debts of the church, using the building for its Grammar School until 1886. It was leased to the revived Dickinson School of Law, 1890-1917. In 1919 it was sold to the United Brethren Church and torn down.

Old Gymnasium

Made possible by the gift of Clemuel Ricketts Woodin, and completed in 1885 at a cost of $7,513.28. Architect, Charles L. Carson. Equipped through the gift of William Clare Allison, and dedicated, Jan. 6, 1888. In 1931, after the completion of the Alumni Gymnasium, it was converted into a social, recreational and banquet hall; and in 1946 to a College Commons. On May 17, 1953, the western wall collapsed during a storm, and the building was razed, leaving only the central heating plant (see below).

Tome Scientific Building

Made possible by Jacob Tome's gift of $25,000 and completed June 24, 1885. Architect, Charles L. Carson. A final realization of the dream of Charles Francis Himes, the design is a much reduced version of the grandiose plans prepared for him by Montgomery Cunningham Meigs five years before: classroom and office wings flanking a central museum area. In 1947 the chemical laboratories were enlarged at a cost of $35,000, necessitating the dispersal of the old Museum. Priestley apparatus was moved to the Dickinsoniana Room in Bosler Hall, and the stuffed birds harking back to Spencer Fullerton Baird's day to Baird Hall, where they molted drearily until Baird was razed in 1966. In 1958 Tome's interior was completely rebuilt at a cost of about $165,000, with much new equipment, including the planetarium given by Roscoe O. Bonisteel in memory of Henry E. Smith, Professor of Astronomy.

James Williamson Bosler Memorial Library Hall

Completed on June 23, 1886, at a cost of $68,000, the gift of Mrs. Bosler in memory of her husband. The architect, Charles L. Carson, had been a student of Henry Hobson Richardson, and the original design echoed the Richardson library style. Alterations planned by William W. Emmart and completed in 1941 enlarged and transformed the building, refacing it with limestone in Georgian style. In 1965, the large upper level hall, used from the first chapel and assemblies, was finally readapted for library use. In 1968, after the completion of the Spahr Library, major alterations were authorized to adapt the building to use by Fine Arts, Modern Languages, Music and others, with language laboratory, electronic learning center, classrooms and offices.

Heating Plants

As a major first reform of President Reed, 1889, a central heating plant was built into the basement of the Old Gymnasium, and by 1890 all dormitory and classroom stoves were discarded. In 1954–55, another plant was added to the rear of the Alumni Gymnasium, at a cost of nearly $70,000, to serve the south side of the campus. By 1965–66, this was put on a standby basis, and a complete replacement of the original plant effected at a cost of about $150,000. So passed, as the Treasurer reported, June, 1966, "the last remnants of the old gym," including "the old Keeler boiler," after thirty-eight years of unfailing service.

The President's House

Built in 1833, this house at the corner of High and West Streets was the home of the Hon. John Reed, who conducted his law classes in its basement. It was purchased by George Edward Reed at his first coming to

Carlisle, and sold to the College, January 9, 1890 at a price of $8,000, with enlargement from one storey to two and a half, made possible by the $7,000 gift of William Clare Allison. It had formerly been called "the villa" because of its Italianate architecture. Further changes in the twentieth century, some through the gifts of Mrs. Paul Appenzellar, have made it an attractive home of indeterminate style and period, further enhanced by the addition of a pleasant garden on the site of the old Allison Methodist Church.

Athletic Field, 1890–1909

With the formation of the Dickinson College Athletic Association, March, 1884, team sports moved from the campus to the old County Fair Ground, later occupied by the C. H. Masland and Sons plant. Its constitution was amended, March, 1889, to permit purchase of a field. Land between West Louther and West North Streets, later the site of the Reeves-Hoffman plant, was rented with option, and its purchase announced, June 6, 1892. A grandstand seating 250 was burned after a few years' use and never rebuilt.

Lloyd Hall

The former home of Samuel M. Hepburn on Pomfret Street was acquired, May 16, 1893, on a $5,000 mortgage by President Reed and Professors Whiting and McIntire. It was occupied by a local fraternity, Alpha Zeta Phi, until taken over by the College as a residence for co-eds, 1895. It basked in the title "Ladies' Hall" until renamed, February 7, 1905, in recognition of the $10,000 gift of the Rev. J. Z. Lloyd. It was sold in 1919, and torn down fifty years later.

Denny Memorial Hall I and II

Classroom and office building, completed June 8, 1896. Architect, Thomas P. Lonsdale. Cost, $40,000. The Denny family property on the northeast corner of High and West Streets had been purchased for $100 on the condition that the building become a Denny Memorial. A major gift of Eliza E. Smith, honoring her brother, Abraham Herr Smith, '40, was applied to large top-storey meeting halls for the two literary societies. The building burned to the ground on March 3, 1904.

After a concentrated drive for subscriptions, Denny Hall was rebuilt in grander style, June 6, 1905. Architect, Miller I. Kast. Cost, $62,964.84. Many individual memorials were included, the most conspicuous being the "Lenore Allison Tower," recognizing William Clare Allison's gift of $2,500. Vaults in the tower adjoined the principal College administrative offices.

Metzger Institute, built in 1881. Photograph, *c.* 1890.

Conway Hall, built in 1902; razed in 1966.

Baird Hall, *c.* 1950.

Montgomery Hall, built in 1837; acquired in 1950.

"Fink Hall"

This building at 333 West High Street was purchased by the College for $7,000, December 26, 1900, as a residence for the Headmaster of Conway Hall. It was made into a double house about 1930, to serve as a faculty residence and College Health Center. It had use also as a women's dormitory until razed in 1966 to make way for the Spahr Library. The name "Fink Hall" was first applied by the students during infirmary use and gained wide acceptance without official endorsement. It commemorates the long regime and kind heart of Oneta M. Fink, R.N., Director of Health Services. Similarly, in student parlance the phrase "to fink out," already in general currency, took on a new meaning at Dickinson—"to escape duty on a plea of illness," or, more specifically, "to enter the infirmary."

Conway Hall

Completed in the spring of 1902, Conway Hall provided the Dickinson Preparatory School with classrooms, offices, dormitory and a name. Architect, Miller I. Kast. Cost, $63,480. The property included grounds, and a Headmaster's residence (see above). Andrew Carnegie financed the "Mount Holly brick" edifice, honoring his friend, Moncure D. Conway, '49. After the closing of the School in 1917, it was used as a men's dormitory until razed in the summer of 1966.

Herman Bosler Biddle Memorial Athletic Field

Edward William Biddle's gift of June 8, 1909, is a memorial to his son, an alumnus of 1903. It provided a field of over six acres, "with brick and stone entrance and iron gates," and a permanent grandstand. The Dickinson College Athletic Association has enlarged the field with purchases from its own funds. The Training and Locker Building was authorized on December 15, 1962, financed by contributions from the Washington Redskins professional football team made in return for use of the field in pre-season practice. The stands were substantially rebuilt in 1967.

Metzger Hall

George Metzger, Class of 1798, bequeathed $25,000 and his land in Carlisle to found the Metzger Institute, a college for young ladies. A building was erected, and opened September 28, 1881. Funds proving inadequate, however, in 1913 it was leased, rent-free, to Dickinson College, the College also to receive the income as long as it was maintained "for the education of women." For many years Metzger Hall was the home of Dickinson co-eds, providing dormitory rooms, dining hall and reception rooms, a small gymnasium and little theater, not to mention the presumably therapeutic aspects of the long walk to and from the main campus. In 1963, the key was returned to the Metzger trustees in a symbolic ceremony, the property sold and the building razed soon after.

Trickett Hall

Built by the Dickinson School of Law in 1917. The building is 132 by 62 feet, with a tower 112 feet high. A semi-detached library building designed by Richard C. Reed was added in 1963.

Alumni Gymnasium

Built on the site of old South College, the new gymnasium was opened, January 9, 1929, with a basketball game (University of Pennsylvania 37–Dickinson 28, unhappily breaking a seven-year winning streak). The building itself, however, was a triumph, reflecting the revival and effectiveness of the General Alumni Association, which had here accomplished what the church-oriented financial campaign of 1922 had failed to achieve as one of its major objectives.

Music Building

The limestone house on the northwest corner of the John Dickinson Campus was built in 1899 by the Phi Delta Theta Fraternity. Its purchase by the College at a price of $8,300 was authorized, June 5, 1931. It was first remodeled as classroom and office space for the Department of Education and Psychology. In 1958, when that department moved to Reed Hall, the building was assigned to the Music Department.

Rush Campus and Baird Hall

"Mooreland," the former home and deer park of sportsman Johnston Moore, Class of 1829, was purchased by the College after the death of the last of his daughters. The long-hoped-for acquisition was announced on October 20, 1932. One of its earlier owners had been President John Mitchell Mason, whose ghost has been seen, generally on dark nights in early spring, driving his buggy at a rapid pace between house and campus. The old three-storey mansion became the home of the Biology Department, dedicated to the memory of Spencer Fullerton Baird, '40, faculty member 1845–50 and afterward Secretary of the Smithsonian Institution. It was demolished in 1966 to make room for Witwer Hall. The twelve-acre tract was later denominated the "Benjamin Rush Campus," distinguishing it from the "John Dickinson Campus," where West College stands.

Parker House

Known also as "Junior House," the former residence of William H. Parker on North Hanover Street across from Metzger Hall was leased in September, 1938, and used intermittently thereafter as a women's dormitory until the opening of Drayer Hall in 1952.

Gibbs House

The former home and carriage house of John Hays, across Hanover Street from Metzger Hall, was acquired in June, 1939 by an endowment from Rebecca McClure Gibbs. Cost, $23,000, including alterations. It was the first senior dormitory, and has served as a residence both for women and for men. It was sold in 1964 to Roy E. Hoffman.

Sellers House

Known to older alumni as the Leidigh House, the former residence of Dean Montgomery P. Sellers was purchased, June 28, 1943, for $15,000. It has served as a dormitory for men, 1943-44, as the College Health Center, 1944-52, as the Dean's residence, 1952-60, and from 1960 as a women's residence.

Biddle House

Purchased on December 14, 1946, for $25,000, the former home of trustee Edward M. Biddle, Jr., has been a dormitory for men and for women, while its large basement area has served as rooms for Independent Women, Superintendent of Buildings and Grounds, Alumni Office and Faculty Club.

South College III

After World War II a frame government surplus building was placed south of the Alumni Gymnasium, faced with limestone and later enhanced by a cupola donated by Boyd Lee Spahr. The building was opened, June, 1948. Architect, John K. Bixler. Cost, $46,943. South College provided a common room for students and faculty, with classrooms and offices above. Dr. and Mrs. Spahr and Mrs. C. A. Fife made possible the addition of a squash court, 1955. A snack bar was later added to the common room. With the building of the Holland Union, this area was converted to classrooms and offices. In 1967, an IBM 1130 computer and related equipment were installed with the aid of a grant from the National Science Foundation.

McIntire House

The residence of Professor Bradford O. McIntire on South College Street was purchased from his estate, June 5, 1948, for use as a men's dormitory. Cost, $15,000; alterations, $6,000. The Commons Club occupied the house, 1950–52, and in 1953 it was again renovated for use as a women's residence.

Four Church Avenue Houses

This row of brick cottages was purchased from an absentee landlord, December 27, 1948, for $13,200. It had been deemed inappropriate that rumored houses of ill fame should stand directly behind the official residence of the President. Respectability, as well as the convenience of having the College plumber and others available on a twenty-four-hour basis, were assured by rental to employees of the maintenance staff. Later tenants, including students, sensed and respected (within due bounds) the earlier tradition of nightly revelry.

Montgomery Hall

This residence, a rare example in this area of a pure Greek Revival facade, was built in 1837 by President Robert Emory, who lived here until 1842. It was owned by Professors William H. Allen, 1847–49, and John McClintock, 1853–70. Long the residence of the Rev. Harry B. Stock, it was acquired by the College, March 27, 1950, at a cost of $25,000; and $96,500 was spent for remodeling and enlargement, with seven apartments for faculty use. In 1968 it became a women's dormitory. The name honors Col. John Montgomery, who, with Benjamin Rush, had been so closely concerned in the founding of the College, and makes belated amends for the razing of his home, "Happy Retreat," near Biddle Field.

Drayer Hall

The first residence hall for women built by the College for that purpose, and the first new building on the Rush Campus since that land had been acquired twenty years before, was completed May 1, 1952. Architect, Sydney E. Martin. Cost, $775,000. It had been financed by a capital campaign, and honors in its name two major donors, Sumner M. Drayer, '02, and Agnes Pettigrew Drayer. Trustee Mary Sharp Foucht contributed the Sharp Memorial Lounge, honoring her father, Dr. Alexander A. Sharp, '83. In 1965, a recreation area and its dining and kitchen space were converted, respectively, into dormitory rooms and the College Health Center.

Chapel in West College. Photograph by Charles F. Himes, 1890, before removal of the gallery.

Chapel in Bosler Hall. Photograph, c. 1950, with the oft-parodied quotation from Henry Newbolt's "Clifton Chapel."

Trickett Hall of the Dickinson School of Law.

Sadler Curtilage

The second building erected by the Dickinson School of Law is its attractive residential group around an open courtyard, dedicated on June 7, 1952. The plans had been drawn in 1946 by architects Walter Karchar and Livingston Smith. Cost, $550,000.

Reed Hall

The former Allison Memorial Church House was acquired on June 11, 1854, as part of the property exchange with the Church. It was remodeled at a cost of $25,589, named in honor of President George Edward Reed, and assigned to use by the Department of Psychology and Education.

Morgan Hall

The first residence hall for men built solely for that purpose was dedicated on November 12, 1955, and named in honor of President James Henry Morgan. It was financed by a federal loan of $570,000. Total cost, $660,000. Architect, Martin, Stewart and Noble. In 1965, dining hall and kitchens were converted into dormitory rooms.

Mathews House

Col. Philip Mathews and his sister, Ann, deeded their home on Mooreland Avenue to the College under a life annuity contract, January 7, 1957. The large brick house, valued at $32,500, was remodeled for use as a women's dormitory at a cost of $39,218. It has been used also as a men's residence and housed the Phi Epsilon Pi Fraternity, 1963-64.

"Potato Chip Factory"

Built in 1949 by Edison S. Nickel for the production of potato chips, the cement block building adjacent to South College was purchased in 1957 for conversion into a rifle range. Cost, $16,000. Instead, it has been leased to agencies of the federal government and renovated to their specifications from time to time. Students have twice raised serious questions as to whether the government's carefully guarded use of the building has been appropriate to an academic setting, possibly confusing the initials of the International Cooperation Administration (ICA) with those of the Central Intelligence Agency (CIA).

Art Studio

The Fine Arts studio program began in Bosler, found "make-do" quarters in East, and then, 1958-66, occupied the premises of the former Carlisle Commercial College at the corner of High and Pitt Streets, leased for that period. John Drake Pusey, artist-in-residence, praised the high-ceilinged rooms as "better than the studios at Yale when I was a student there."

William Clare Allison Memorial Methodist Church

Following the fire which destroyed the first Allison Church, January 20, 1954, the College deeded a large segment of the Benjamin Rush Campus to the Church, in exchange for its property at West and High Streets. The College also contributed $200,000 toward construction of the "Church-Chapel." The building was completed, April 20, 1958, at a cost of $850,000. Architect, Hensel Fink.

Althouse Science Hall

A major objective of the Ten Year Development Program launched in 1948, the building was made possible by the $300,000 gift of Dr. C. Scott Althouse, and completed on November 7, 1958. Architect, Elmer H. Adams. Cost, $618,029. A gift of $35,000 from Irénée du Pont provided the library facilities, a memorial to Alfred Victor du Pont of the Class of 1818. In 1964 the seven-telescope observatory was added at a cost of $50,000, the gift of Roscoe O. Bonisteel, '12.

Filler Hall

The former residence of R. P. Masland, 14 North College Street, was purchased in March, 1959, for $32,000, and served briefly as a memorial to the life of President Mervin Grant Filler. A gift of $50,000 from Irénée du Pont made possible the installation of a thirty-booth electronic language laboratory, with necessary remodeling. Architect, Richard C. Reed. The building was razed in the summer of 1963 to make way for the Holland Union.

Indian School Farm

By an agreement authorized on January 5, 1961, 65.1 acres of surplus land were deeded to the College at no charge by the federal government, to be used continuously for educational purposes for twenty years, after which the land will become unconditionally the property of the College. The farmhouse has been remodeled into faculty apartments, a large barn is a storage area, the acreage has been graded for recreation and sports, and the swamp land along Letort Creek is used by botany and zoology classes for field study.

Jackson House

The large brick residence of W. L. Jackson, College and Louther Streets, was purchased, July 14, 1961 for $37,500 as part of land acquisition for the Holland Union site. It served as a men's honors dormitory until razed in 1963.

"Honors Dorm"

Purchased on July 28, 1962 at a cost of $10,500, the brick house at 127 North College Street, formerly the home of Mrs. Norman Minnick, housed male honors students until 1971-72.

Adams Hall

Authorized on December 10, 1960, and completed, October 5, 1963, the building was made possible by the $250,000 gift of Dr. and Mrs. Rolland L. Adams. Architect, Elmer H. Adams. Cost, $1,031,000. Adams Hall, housing 165 women students also contains the College Guest Suite, furnished and decorated by the Mary Dickinson Club.

Admissions Building

Purchased on June 6, 1964. Cost, $55,000. The former "Crow House" of Alpha Chi Rho at the corner of High and College Streets had been the home of Abram Bosler. Mr. Bosler, having had a family experience with fire, built his house of reinforced concrete, the first Carlisle residence so constructed.

Office of Communication and Development

Purchased on June 13, 1964. Cost, $57,000. Built as a fraternity house by Phi Delta Theta in 1931, the building was remodeled by the College at a cost of $24,000 to house the offices of Alumni Affairs, Development, News Bureau and Public Relations.

Todd House

The purchase, June 23, 1964, of the former Sigma Chi fraternity house for use as a dormitory was made possible by the gift of Mr. and Mrs. Glenn E. Todd under a $100,000 life annuity agreement.

Fraternity Quadrangle

Authorized on December 10, 1960, and occupied in September, 1964. Architect, Howell Lewis Shay and Associates. Cost, $2,124,000. Financed by a federal loan and a bond issue, the ten living units are located at Cherry and High Streets on land formerly owned by the Pennsylvania Railroad. Each fraternity unit houses forty-four students, including independent men. Of the former fraternity houses (see Appendix C), only two of which had been built for that purpose, seven were demolished and three adapted to College use. An essential element of the new plan was the Holland Union Building, with its dining and recreational facilities.

Holland Union Building

Designed by the same architectural firm and opened at the same time as the Fraternity Quadrangle, HUB was made possible by the $200,000 subscription of Homer C. Holland, '13, a government bond issue and private bank loans. Cost, $2,230,000. It houses food service and commons, snack bar, recreation and social hall, game rooms, meeting and seminar rooms, the College radio station, College store and a fully-equipped little theater, a memorial to James M. Mathers, '31, supported by a gift of $100,000 from his widow.

"HUB" became the first and essential step in the development of the new area representing a revolutionary break with the past and a more coherent student life in the future—the development initiated by Samuel W. Witwer, and dedicated at completion as the "Charles Nisbet Campus."

Art Studio

Its purchase authorized April 7, 1966, at a price of $200,000, the former home of Dr. Frederick M. Lawrence provides space for studio art, while the land is maintained for future expansion.

Malcolm Hall

Completed in September, 1966, this dormitory for men on the site of the Beta Theta Pi fraternity house was named in honor of President Gilbert Malcolm. Architect, Elmer H. Adams. Cost, $475,000.

Witwer Hall

Completed September 9, 1966, this dormitory for women was named in honor of the Witwer family. Architect, Elmer H. Adams. Cost, $500,000.

Charles A. Dana Biology Building

Made possible by grants of $300,000 from the Charles A. Dana Foundation and $480,000 from the Longwood Foundation, Dana Hall was built to the specifications of the Biology faculty, and completed, October 8, 1966. Architect, Elmer H. Adams. Cost, $1,300,000.

Florence Jones Reineman Wildlife Sanctuary

A 3,000-acre sanctuary in Perry County was established, October 7, 1966, through a trust under the will of Mrs. Florence W. Erdman, in

Fraternity Quadrangle, completed in 1964.

Malcolm Hall, built in 1966.

Boyd Lee Spahr Library, completed in 1967.

Holland Union Building, from the roof of Spahr Library.

memory of her mother. In exchange for general supervision and educational use by the College, the trustees of the estate will underwrite all capital costs and program funding. The wilderness land, approached through historic Waggoner's Gap and lying in Green Valley, is to be used solely for field study in botany, biology and geology, and for conservation and preservation of wildlife. Hunting, fishing, trapping and other types of recreation are prohibited.

Otto Farm

On January 3, 1967, a farm of 180 acres, valued at $109,000, in South Middleton Township between Mount Holly Springs and Boiling Springs was given to the College by Ivo V. Otto, '04, to be used for educational purposes and future development.

Boyd Lee Spahr Library

Authorized on December 12, 1964, with ground-breaking on May 7, 1966, the new structure climaxes Boyd Lee Spahr's long interest in advancing the collections and services of the College Library. It was made possible by his gift of $250,000, with further financing by federal grant and loan. Architect, Howell Lewis Shay and Associates. Cost, $2,250,000. The building contains three levels: main floor (reference and operational), with stacks above and below. The Alexander A. Sharp Room for recreational reading near the main entrance continues the memorial to her father established in Bosler Library by trustee Mary Sharp Foucht. The May Morris Room on the upper level brings together in a complex of reading room, workroom, and vault and closed stacks housing the Dickinsoniana Collection, rare books and manuscripts. The Library has a gross floor area of 72,463 square feet, a book capacity of approximately 315,000 volumes, and 800 reader stations, including 21 closed carrels for faculty research and 88 open "honors carrels" for student use.

Landis House

Acquired on January 25, 1968, at a cost of $26,000, the former home of Merkel and Mary Lamberton Landis on South College Street contains faculty meeting rooms, offices and the Faculty Club.

Kisner-Woodward Hall

Made possible by their large bequest, the College's first co-ed dormitory was named for Hugh B. Woodward and Helen Kisner Woodward, both of the Class of 1908. It consists of two living areas connected by a common lounge, each unit housing forty-six students, and was first occupied, April, 1969. Architect, Howell Lewis Shay and Associates. Cost, $820,000.

Kisner-Woodward Hall, built in 1969.

Anita Tuvin Schlecter Auditorium, built in 1971.

Bernard Center For The Humanities

The complete rebuilding of "Old East" as the new Humanities Center, 1968–71, was accomplished through a gift of $334,000 from the B. A. and Reba Bernard Foundation, reinforced by alumni gifts and a federal loan and grant. Architect, Howell Lewis Shay and Associates. Cost, $1,171,432. An entirely new building repeats the exterior design of the old, using the original stone. It houses the Departments of Classics, English, Philosophy and Religion. The entrance lobby is a memorial to Charles Keller Zug, '80, a prominent trustee. On the upper level, the Moncure Daniel Conway Library stands as a memorial to one of Dickinson's most eminent humanists.

Anita Tuvin Schlecter Auditorium

Authorized January 25, 1969 and dedicated on May 22, 1971, this complex cultural center was made possible by the $500,000 gift of Louis Alfred Tuvin, '10, in memory of his daughter. Designed by Architects Collaborative, Inc. Cost, $2,000,000. The auditorium, seating nine hundred, can be divided into three soundproofed sections, and is equipped for the performing arts in every aspect and for any variation of classroom use.

INDEX